Leisure and Life Satisfaction

Foundational Perspectives

Leisure and Life Satisfaction

Foundational Perspectives

FOURTH EDITION

Christopher R. Edginton

UNIVERSITY OF NORTHERN IOWA

Donald G. DeGraaf

CALVIN COLLEGE

Rodney B. Dieser

UNIVERSITY OF NORTHERN IOWA

Susan R. Edginton

UNIVERSITY OF NORTHERN IOWA

McGraw Hill

Boston   Burr Ridge, IL   Dubuque, IA   Madison, WI   New York   San Francisco   St. Louis
Bangkok   Bogotá   Caracas   Kuala Lumpur   Lisbon   London   Madrid   Mexico City
Milan   Montreal   New Delhi   Santiago   Seoul   Singapore   Sydney   Taipei   Toronto

Higher Education

LEISURE AND LIFE SATISFACTION: FOUNDATIONAL PERSPECTIVES
FOURTH EDITION

Published by McGraw-Hill, a business unit of The McGraw-Hill Companies, Inc., 1221 Avenue of the Americas, New York, NY 10020. Copyright © 2006, 2002, 1998, 1995 by The McGraw-Hill Companies, Inc. All rights reserved. No part of this publication may be reproduced or distributed in any form or by any means, or stored in a database or retrieval system, without the prior written consent of The McGraw-Hill Companies, Inc., including, but not limited to, in any network or other electronic storage or transmission, or broadcast for distance learning.

Some ancillaries, including electronic and print components, may not be available to customers outside the United States.

This book is printed on acid-free paper.

1 2 3 4 5 6 7 8 9 0 QPF/QPF 0 9 8 7 6 5

ISBN 0-07-288507-6

Editor-in-chief: *Emily J. Barrosse*
Sponsoring editor: *Christopher Johnson*
Developmental editor: *Lynda Huenefeld*
Senior marketing manager: *Pamela S. Cooper*
Project manager: *Carlisle Publishing Services*
Senior production supervisor: *Rich DeVitto*
Design manager: *Preston Thomas III*
Cover image: *Royalty-Free/CORBIS*

The text was set in 10/12 Times Roman by Carlisle Communications, Ltd. and printed on 45# New Era Matte by Quebecor World Fairfield, PA.

The text and illustration credits are found on page 519 and constitute an extension of the copyright page

Library of Congress Cataloging-in-Publication Data

Leisure and life satisfaction : foundational perspectives / Christopher R. Edginton . . . [et al.] — 4th ed.
　　p.　cm.
　　Includes bibliographical references and index.
　　ISBN 0-07-288507-6
　　1. Leisure—United States.　3. Leisure industry—United States.　5. Quality of life—United States.
　I. Edginton, Christopher R.

GV14 .L394 2002
790'.01'3097—dc21
2001034513

The Internet addresses listed in the text were accurate at the time of publication. The inclusion of a website does not indicate an endorsement by the authors or McGraw-Hill, and McGraw-Hill does not guarantee the accuracy of the information presented at these sites.

www.mhhe.com

DEDICATION

DEDICATION

The fourth edition of *Leisure and Life Satisfaction* is dedicated to Hanna, Jacob, Joseph, Lily, Isaac, Rochelle, Chayce, Jonas and Zachary. For the Edginton grandchildren and the DeGraaf and Dieser children, we promise greater life satisfaction through leisure.

—The Authors

CONTENTS

CHAPTER 4
PHILOSOPHICAL AND CONCEPTUAL THEMES 112

CHAPTER 5
MASS LEISURE 140

CHAPTER 6
LEISURE AND THE LIFE CYCLE 172

CHAPTER 16
FUTURE TRENDS 478

PREFACE

It has been a decade since the initial edition of *Leisure and Life Satisfaction: Foundational Perspectives* was published. A great deal has happened in the United States during this period of time. Most pronounced has been the impact that the events of September 11, 2001 have brought to our lives. We directly see in our profession and everyday lives the impact that this devastating event has had. We have seen our psychological well being challenged, political freedoms abridged, and a downturn in the economy. We are at war. Our very freedoms and way of life have been placed in jeopardy. How does this event and its subsequent effects influence the ability of Americans to find satisfaction in their lives through leisure?

Our profession has been called in many ways to assist and support the transition of America during these difficult times. Although it may not be readily apparent, our leisure has become more important as a way to support us in our everyday lives. We seek the comfort that comes from being with family, friends, and others involved in leisure experiences that bind us together in meaningful, relevant, and positive ways. Leisure participation serves as a way for us to rediscover and reaffirm our basic values, beliefs, and commitment to our ideals. Today we find our travel experiences are likely to be more within the continental United States than to other countries. We tend to stay closer to our home and seek leisure in our local communities. We find, through leisure, a greater sense of community belonging and a renewed spirit in living our lives within our communities.

A decade ago we defined leisure as ". . . one of life's greatest gifts—an important dimension influencing the quality of individual's lives." In subsequent additions, we have suggested that leisure is a "power medium—a perfect gift" providing individuals with the opportunity for reflection, relaxation, the acquisition and enhancement of knowledge and skill, and the expression of one's creative interests. We have noted that leisure is freedom and contributes greatly to one's satisfaction in life. Our theme, *Leisure and Life Satisfaction,* as reflected in the title of the book, calls for seeing leisure ". . . as a way of uplifting the spirit, improving our well being, and enhancing our relationships with others." Leisure ". . . helps us shape our sense of self-worth, assist in the formulation and communication of values and norms, and aids us in improving the livability in our lives and our communities." Leisure is a way of energizing individuals to pursue those individual interests they value. While liberating individuals, leisure time affords opportunities to celebrate community living. It is a powerful medium that provides opportunities for us to enhance our social, cultural, and economic development.

As professionals we are involved in assisting individuals in seeking happiness and satisfaction in their lives through the provision of leisure experiences and environments. Our work focuses on enhancing the human condition, creating a sense of hope for individuals and communities, underscoring the promise of greater life satisfaction. As we have stated in previous editions, our work involves ". . . crafting leisure environments to assist individuals, groups of people, and whole communities in achieving a higher quality of life and a greater level of happiness and satisfaction." Our work as professionals has become increasingly valued, respected, and sought in American communities. The management of leisure resources and amenities has become a central factor in promoting a greater quality of life and in improving the well being, happiness, and satisfaction of individuals.

Our Focus

This book was written to assist entry-level professionals gain a greater knowledge of the phenomenon of leisure in American society, as well as an understanding of the ways in which leisure services are organized and delivered. In addition, the book presents information regarding issues influencing professional practice. The 4th edition of *Leisure and Life Satisfaction* has been updated with new information, statistics, and insights into the phenomenon of leisure and its provision. We have focused this edition exclusively with a focus on the United States of America. Like previous editions, the book provides the reader with a complete overview of many of the aspects of leisure, including: basic concepts, definitions, fundamentals and terms, the organization and delivery of leisure services, and critical professional trends, issues, and future perspectives.

The current issue of *Leisure and Life Satisfaction* maintains three parts as in previous publications. Part 1 provides an overview of basic terms, concepts, and ideas related to leisure, recreation, and play. In addition, historical, philosophical, and ethical elements are presented. Part 1 also presents an overview of leisure and the life cycle and mass leisure. Part 2 offers a basic overview of organizations involved in the delivery of leisure services from a public, commercial, or nonprofit perspective. Part 3 focuses on providing information dealing with issues, trends, and elements affecting future professional practice.

New to This Edition

The 4th edition of *Leisure and Life Satisfaction* has been substantially revised with additional content, illustrations, and examples from professional practice. Approximately every 3 years we have updated the book in an incremental fashion. The authors have often traded chapters to provide additional insights and perspectives on a given topic. In this edition of *Leisure and Life Satisfaction,* the authors have, in the main, returned to their original chapters. This has provided a new perspective for each of us in terms of the process of revision. We all feel a great sense of responsibility to ensure that the material presented in *Leisure and Life Satisfaction* is contemporary and up to date. Returning to our original chapters has reminded us how rapidly information becomes obsolete and reinforced the importance of the need to stay current with emerging theoretical knowledge and with "best" professional practice.

Chapter 1: Leisure and Life Satisfaction

- Expanded discussion on leisure and the pursuit of happiness
- Integration of new research and concepts on happiness
- Cross national comparison of elements of life satisfaction
- Enhanced work leisure discussion
- Linkage of leisure to the rise of the creative class
- New *Leisure Lines* focusing on contemporary leisure concerns

Chapter 2: The World of Leisure, Recreation, and Play

- New definitions of leisure
- Updated and improved information on constructs of leisure
- New information on theories of leisure
- Leisure theories classified according to work related, psychological, sociological, feminist, anthropological, and philosophical orientations
- New tables representing leisure theory typologies
- Revision of discussion questions

Chapter 3: A Historical Perspective

- Expansion of the discussion of 20th Century conditions and today
- Clarification of timing and conditions of the Industrial Revolution
- Greater connection made between allied social reform movements and parks and recreation
- Additional information on the establishment of the National Park Service
- New information on Joseph Lee
- New section on recreation centers and settlement houses
- Trends from the information era
- New *Leisure Line* on freeriding

Chapter 4: Philosophical and Conceptual Themes

- Professional and personal philosophy of leisure expanded

- Physiological perspectives and ethical doctrines discussed
- New examples from professional practice
- A model to guide professional practice
- New *Leisure Lines* providing additional insights in professional practice

Chapter 5: Mass Leisure

- New information on the "Take Back Your Time Movement"
- Updated info on where and how people recreate
- New information on creating cool cities
- Clarified several definitions (e.g., outdoor recreation)
- Additional information on social capital and its relationship to leisure
- Updated tourism statistics in light of the September 11, 2001 tragedy
- New section on computer usage and leisure time
- New *Leisure Lines*
  - *I could do that: The best sports lure the fan*
  - *Leisure for pets: An untamed market*
  - *Teaching Kindness: A lesson for parents*

Chapter 6: Leisure and the Life Cycle

- Expanded definition of psychographics included
- Updated discussion regarding how leisure experiences are related to human development
- New section focusing on obesity
- Expansion of a framework for youth programming
- Revised discussion on youth development competency frameworks
- Inclusion of theories of aging
- Updated references and statistics

Chapter 7: Delivery of Leisure Services: Local Government

- Updated information on expenditures for leisure services
- Many new examples from professional practice
- Updated information on the public benefits of leisure
- Revised statistics on individuals employed in the field

- New *Leisure Lines* highlighting contemporary issues

Chapter 8: Delivery of Leisure Services: State Government

- New statistics for state government expenditures
- Updated information on individuals employed by state governments
- Revised state park facts and statistics
- Expanded discussion on travel and tourism
- New *Leisure Lines*

Chapter 9: Delivery of Leisure Services: Federal Government

- Review of current practices of the Federal Government
- Updated information on tourism
- New statistics on expenditures at the federal level
- Revised and updated information on federal agencies
- New *Leisure Lines* drawing contemporary issues and elements from professional practice

Chapter 10: Delivery of Leisure Services: Non-profit

- New examples drawn from professional practice
- Revised statistics on expenditures in the nonprofit sector
- Additional information on charitable giving in the United States
- Extensive rewrite of programs and services provided by youth and other nonprofit organizations
- New *Leisure Lines* focusing on growth of the nonprofit sector

Chapter 11: Delivery of Leisure Services: Commercial

- Revised statistics on business ownership in America
- Updated information on commercial leisure services
- Latest facts and figures regarding personal consumption of recreation

- An analysis of profits in the leisure service industry
- New *Leisure Lines* emphasizing developments in the commercial sector

Chapter 12: Delivery of Leisure Services: Therapeutic Recreation

- All new statistical information
- Additional models of therapeutic program delivery
- Updated information on jobs for CTRS
- Inclusion of the mission statement of NCTRC
- New section on documentation of outcomes

Chapter 13: Leisure Programming: Promoting Quality Services

- New information regarding the movement of marketing from goods to experiences
- Expanded information on ways on which services can be distinguished from goods
- New *Leisure Lines* that can be useful in marketing leisure services

Chapter 14: Professional Career Development

- New information added on a public service ethic
- Updated and expanded information on professional organizations
- New info on locating internships
- New *Leisure Lines*
  - *Park and recreation growing body of knowledge*
  - *Ten questions that can transform your life*
  - *Career growth timeline*

Chapter 15: Leisure and Cultural Diversity

- New introduction sharpening the focus of the chapter as related to professional issues and concerns
- Inclusion of Wheeler's four-stage diversity education and training model
- Addition of Dahl's five administrative strategies that can be used to develop a leisure organization that promotes diversity

- An Explanation of the "I" Triad model, which is a programming structure for the development of diversity in leisure organizations
- A new case study of the Arizona branch of the Bureau of Land Management regarding administrative strategies to develop a diversity workforce

Chapter 16: Future Trends

- A new section regarding future trends in leisure services post September 11, 2001 (9/11, Federal Tax Cuts, and No Child Left Behind)
- Updated information regarding family composition/family concerns
- New *Leisure Line*
- Updated information regarding latch-key children and youth at risk
- Revised section on cardiovascular fitness and obesity
- New section on recreational user conflict
- Expanded section on environmental concerns and global issues
- Revised statistical information on a variety of topics

Successful Features

The following successful features are being continued in this new edition:

- *Introductions*—These opening paragraphs spark the reader's interest in the chapter topic and outline how the material will be presented.
- *Leisure Line boxes*—These boxes highlight timely topics of interest, such as creating balance in your life, the right to take risks, virtual leisure, and the fast-food lifestyle.
- *Tables, figures, and photographs*—The tables provide statistics and facts to complement the text. A variety of figures and photographs highlight leisure themes and activities.
- *Summaries*—The summary at the end of each chapter offers a capsule view of the content, reinforcing learning and providing an effective tool for review.
- *Discussion Questions*—These end-of-chapter questions provide a valuable way to review the content and a starting point for further learning and individual activities.

Ancillaries

Instructor's Manual and Test Bank

The Instructor's Manual and Test Bank to accompany *Leisure and Life Satisfaction* features learning objectives, key terms and concepts, chapter outlines, and teaching hints. The Test Bank portion consists of true/false, multiple-choice, and short essay questions.

Brownstone's Diploma/Exam IV Computerized Testing

A Computerized Test Bank us available for use with this edition of *Leisure and Life Satisfaction*. Brownstone's Diploma Computerized Testing is the most flexible, powerful, easy-to-use electronic testing program available in higher education. The Diploma system allows the test maker to create a print version, an online version (to be delivered to a computer lab), or an internet version of each test. Diploma includes a built-in instructor gradebook, into which student rosters and files can generally be imported. Diploma is for Windows users, and the CD-ROM includes a separate testing program, Exam IV, for Macintosh users.

PowerWeb

This edition of *Leisure and Life Satisfaction* has been packaged with PowerWeb, a valuable learning tool. Power Web is an easy-to-use online resource from McGraw-Hill that provides current articles, curriculum-based materials, weekly updates with assessment, informative and timely world news, related web links, research tools, student study tools, interactive tools, and more.

Access to PowerWeb also offers these resources:

- Study tips with self-quizzes
- Links to related sites
- Weekly updates
- Current news
- Daily newsfeed of related topics
- Web research guide

PowerWeb is a password-protected website. Your McGraw-Hill Sales Representative can guide you in creating a student package with PowerWeb. Preview this website at: www.dushkin.com/powerweb.

Acknowledgments

We have been fortunate to have the opportunity to work with our colleagues at McGraw-Hill Publishing. The editorial staff at McGraw-Hill has provided continuous encouragement and support for this project for over a decade. We appreciate their faith in our efforts and we value the relationship that we have developed with McGraw-Hill. In particular, we would like to acknowledge the efforts of Nick Barrett and Christopher Johnson, Sponsoring Editors, for their continued support of our efforts. Lynda Huenefeld served as Developmental Editor for the project. Lynda is a great person with whom to work. She was very professional in her interactions with us, providing encouragement to our writing efforts. She was persistent in her pursuit of our written word. Easy to communicate with and supportive, Linda provided a steady hand in the management of this edition. The production staff at McGraw-Hill also provided excellent support for the project. We would like to thank Melissa Williams, who served as production editor, and Becky Barnhart at Carlisle Communications, for moving the project to its completion. All of the individuals who we work with at McGraw-Hill operated in a exceedingly professional manner, bringing the project to a satisfactory conclusion. Last, we would like to acknowledge the work of Pam Cooper in marketing. Editors seem to come and go but Pam has been with us during the entire history of this writing effort. We appreciate Pam greatly! As one who is engaged in marketing should be, Pam is always enthusiastic, positive, and upbeat about our writing endeavors.

We would like to extend our appreciation to a number of individuals who served as reviewers for this edition of *Leisure and Life Satisfaction*. The comments they provided were extremely insightful, enabling us to view the effort not only from their perspective, but also through the eyes of their students. The reviewers of this edition of the book included:

Jane Broida, Metropolitan State College of Denver;

Roger Coles, Central Michigan University;

Charles Hammersley, Northern Arizona University;

Sherri Hildebrand, Black Hawk College; and

Dean A. Zoerink, Western Illinois University.

At the University of Northern Iowa, we are extremely fortunate to have an outstanding support staff. A number of individuals contributed to the development of this project, including Carol Bean, Karen Peterson, and Mary Franco. A word about each of these individuals is not only appropriate, but also necessary. Carol Bean is an extremely dedicated, loyal, and committed staff member of the School of Health, Physical Education, and Leisure Services at the University of Northern Iowa. She approaches her work in a diligent, organized, and thoroughly professional manner. Carol is a delight to work with on a day-to-day basis and has made this project possible because of her efforts. Likewise, Karen Peterson has contributed greatly to the effort. Karen has the ability to develop outstanding interpersonal relationships while applying her clerical skills to any project of this magnitude. We thank Karen for her effort. Mary Franco was responsible for searching information so that we were able to update statistical information for many of the chapters of the book. Mary is an excellent researcher and also a dedicated and loyal staff member.

We would also like to thank our colleagues at the University of Northern Iowa and Calvin College. Larry Hensley, Iradge Ahrabi-Fard, Susan Hudson, Sam Lankford, Joe Wilson, Kathy Scholl, Deepak Chhabra, Chris Kowalski, Betty van der Smissen, Stacy Van Gorp, Juli Gassman, Jason Lau, Diane Engbertson, Angie Noll, Glen Van Andel, Kim Gall, Ellen Van't Hoof, Jong-II Kim, Nancy Meyer, Jeff Pettinga, Jim Timmer, Kevin VandeStreek, Julie Walton, Deb Bakker, and Amber Warners have all provided great encouragement and support for our efforts in general. We greatly appreciate their continued support for our intellectual endeavors. They often provide positive, constructive criticism and critique for our writing efforts. They are also equally adept at lending a book, helping us further develop an idea or concept, or even sharing a new idea or perspective that they believe would enhance our writing efforts. We have great work environments and it is that environment that makes such endeavors possible.

Without question, family members, friends, and parents have assisted us in our professional journey. We would like to thank them for their support to this and other endeavors. In particular, we would like to thank our daughter Carole and our son David. Carole is currently pursuing a Master's Degree at Iowa State University. She is intellectually astute, creative, and driven in her academic interests. Currently, David serves as a Foreign Service Officer with the US Department of State. Both Carole and David have been great supporters of our academic work, vesting their time, intellectual prowess, and interests in our efforts. They have also provided us with four wonderful grandchildren: Hanna, Jacob (Jakie), Joey, and Lily.

My family, Kathy, Isaac, and Rochelle DeGraaf, have long provided a loving supportive environment for me to pursue my dreams. Without their understanding and encouragement as well as their creativity and inspiration, this project would not have happened. So . . ., for all those times when you allowed me to check out one more resource or let me write one more paragraph before . . . I say thank you.

My wife, Ricki Dieser, as in my first days as a university student, continues to hold my hand, providing continuous encouragement, love, and support. The Dieser boys, Chayce, Jonas, and Zachary, have supported their father while pursuing this project. Without their collective help in creating a nurturing family environment, completion of this project would not have been possible in a timely manner. The Dieser family picked up additional responsibilities, enabling their father to devote intensive time and energy in a short period of time to this project.

Christopher R. Edginton
Donald G. DeGraaf
Rodney B. Dieser
Susan R. Edginton

Leisure in Today's Society

Leisure provides opportunities for dynamic, challenging, and fulfilling life experiences.

CHAPTER 1

Leisure and Life Satisfaction

Leisure experiences promote greater life satisfaction. There are many benefits to be derived from leisure. Some experiences offer great challenges, others provide opportunities for reflection, introspection, and/or relaxation.

Introduction

Leisure is an important social, cultural, and economic force that has great influence on the happiness, well-being, and life satisfaction of all individuals. The idea that leisure promotes great life satisfaction, however, is not a new one. A number of ancient civilizations, including the Greeks, realized the importance and value of leisure and its role in life satisfaction. The Greek historian Herodotus notes, ". . . man [sic] is most nearly himself when he achieves the seriousness of a child at play." In the last 150 years, the growth of leisure in the public, private nonprofit, and commercial sectors reflects the ever increasing value that both Americans and Canadians place upon leisure.

This book, with leisure and its relationship to life satisfaction as its theme, presents historical and contemporary concepts of leisure, recreation, and play. It describes what people in the United States do in terms of their leisure pursuits, what motivates them, and what they value. The types of agencies and institutions providing leisure services are also discussed. This book has been written to assist students preparing for professional careers in the leisure service industry.

As leisure professionals, we are in the *life satisfaction* business. Our role in society helps to improve the quality of life of individuals through the provision of quality leisure opportunities, thus enhancing intellectual, social, physical, spiritual, and psychological well-being. This chapter focuses on defining and understanding the terms "leisure" and "life satisfaction." In addition, the chapter discusses why leisure is important in people's lives and presents the benefits derived from participation in leisure. Further, a discussion of constraints to participation in leisure and strategies to enhance life satisfaction are included.

Leisure and the Pursuit of Happiness: Affirming Our Basic Rights

The political, economic, social, and cultural organization of societies has provided for a focus on enhancing human rights, encouraging greater freedom, and promoting higher standards of the quality of one's life. A common framework for such basic concepts is found in the foundational documents underlying the structure of our society and culture. In the United States, the Declaration of Independence provides the foundational underpinning that sets forth the basic concepts upon which our society has been built. In a more global sense, the United Nations (U.N.) Declaration of Human Rights provides a standard of achievement and a framework outlining the basic inalienable rights of all members of the human family.

As a people, we Americans have framed our society on certain inalienable rights. These rights were reflected in the Declaration of Independence of July 4, 1776. In declaring our independence, the framers of our American society focused the attention of our culture on the rights of each individual to pursue life, liberty, and happiness. As our forefathers stated, "We hold the inalienable rights to every man to be life, liberty and the pursuit of happiness" (Declaration of Independence, July 4, 1776). This declaration sets forth our society's basic commitment toward assisting individuals in achieving happiness as well as pursuing their being or living in a state of freedom. This grand vision provides the foundational underpinning for American society.

Burns (2003, p. 1) has written that:

> . . . the pursuit of happiness was not trivial pleasure seeking. It was fundamental to the conditions of peoples' lives and their efforts to change and improve them. It was one of the great public values that took new form and urgency from the creative thinkers of the Enlightenment. Along with life, liberty, equality, justice, community—and intertwined with them—the pursuit of happiness was grounded in the most basic wants of human beings.

The U.N. Declaration of Human Rights establishes a common standard for people throughout the world. It, like our Declaration of Independence, sets forth inalienable rights for all members of the human family. Article 3 emphasizes that "everyone has the right to life, liberty and the security of the person." Further, the U.N. Declaration of Human Rights specifically mandates "the right to rest and leisure including reasonable limitation of work hours and periodic holidays with pay" (Article 24). In addition, the U.N. Declaration of Human Rights encourages individuals to freely participate in the cultural life of the community and to enjoy the arts.

Thus, these two foundational documents are the keystones for the commitment of our society to ensuring the happiness of individuals as well as guaranteeing that one has access to leisure. Both of these elements are linked to one's life satisfaction. Often, it is through one's leisure that one finds happiness and some sense of satisfaction in their life's quest. Undoubtedly, leisure is a powerful medium that assists individuals to find greater life satisfaction. Leisure experiences can be a conduit to greater happiness, joy, and fulfillment in one's life.

World Leisure's Charter for Leisure

In support of the United Nations Universal Declaration of Human Rights, World Leisure has developed a charter for leisure that supports and further emphasizes the right to rest and leisure, as well as the nature of freedom and choice as central elements of leisure. World Leisure's Charter for Leisure is found in figure 1.1.

Figure 1.1

World Leisure's statement about individual's rights for leisure.

Source: World Leisure (2000) Charter for Leisure.

CHARTER FOR LEISURE

Introduction

Consistent with the Universal Declaration of Human Rights (Article 27), all cultures and societies recognise to some extent the right to rest and leisure. Here, because personal freedom and choice are central elements of leisure, individuals can freely choose their activities and experiences, many of them leading to substantial benefits for person and community.

Articles

1. All people have a basic human right to leisure activities that are in harmony with the norms and social values of their compatriots. All governments are obliged to recognise and protect this right of its citizens.

2. Provisions for leisure for the quality of life are as important as those for health and education. Governments should ensure their citizens a variety of accessible leisure and recreational opportunities of the highest quality.

3. The individual is his/her best leisure and recreational resource. Thus, governments should ensure the means for acquiring those skills and understandings necessary to optimize leisure experiences.

4. Individuals can use leisure opportunities for self-fulfilment, developing personal relationships, improving social integration, developing communities and cultural identity as well as promoting international understanding and co-operation and enhancing quality of life.

5. Governments should ensure the future availability of fulfilling leisure experiences by maintaining the quality of their country's physical, social and cultural environment.

6. Governments should ensure the training of professionals to help individuals acquire personal skills, discover and develop their talents and to broaden their range of leisure and recreational opportunities.

7. Citizens must have access to all forms of leisure information about the nature of leisure and its opportunities, using it to enhance their knowledge and inform decisions on local and national policy.

8. Educational institutions must make every effort to teach the nature and importance of leisure and how to integrate this knowledge into personal lifestyle.

Approved by the World Leisure Board of Directors July 2000. The original version was adopted by the International Recreation Association in 1970, and subsequently revised by its successor, the World Leisure and Recreation Association in 1979.

The Onset of the Leisure Era

By 2015, technological and social changes will reduce both time at work and in the household. Increased life expectancy and earlier retirement, fewer years devoted to rearing fewer children, and so on, are opening up opportunities for over 50 percent of a lifetime to be spent, one way or another, pursuing leisure interests. Shortly beyond that point, providing goods and services to satisfy leisure time undertakings will become the "economic mainspring" of U.S. business.

Sizing up the Leisure Era depends upon what is counted. Specific activities within this massive wave of economic activity include, but are not limited to: recreation, hospitality, entertainment, travel and tourism, pleasure cruises, adventure seeking, hotel and motel lodgings and services, dude ranches, ecotourism, spas, reading, hobbies, sports, games, computer games (hardware, software), gambling and wagering (legal and illegal), outdoor activities, cultural interests (theater, drama, arts, poetry, opera, symphony, disco), night clubs, bars and taverns, country clubs, retreats, moving pictures and theaters, broadcast media (television, radio, citizens band transmitter/receivers, shortwave, etc.), exercise services and equipment, visiting and socializing, clubs and volunteer activities, audio and video recordings (including production, distribution, retailing, sales, rentals, etc.), Internet and on-line activities, sailing and yachting, skiing and skating. In short, you name it. Calculations, it becomes glaringly evident, depend upon how one tallies up the activities.

Leisure time dominance ushers in new attitudes, outlooks, and activity preferences. Lifestyles, near term, will concentrate on instant gratification, hedonism, self-indulgence, living for the moment, narcissism, and self-centeredness. Materialism, fixated on an endless quest for more of everything, may be waning. Work and spending behavior will be undercut as consumers finally sate their desire for "things."

The new paradigm will emphasize experiences, instead of things. Leisure time dominance will usher in a host of new attitudes, outlooks, and activity preferences. As materialism wanes and experiences and self-development ascend, new business opportunities will grow by leaps and bounds.

Source: Abstracted from Molitor, G.T.T. 2000. Here Comes 2015. *City News Publishing Co., Inc.*

Leisure: Toward the Twenty-First Century

In the twenty-first century, there will be tremendous changes in the way people live, the material bounty available, and the opportunities for leisure pursuits. In a 150-year period in Canada and the United States, society has been transformed from rural, agrarian cultures to urban, highly technical societies. Millions of inventions have dramatically changed the way we live our lives. One of the greatest gifts we have been given as a culture has been the gift of increased leisure for many.

Changes will impact work, play, family structures, and mental and physical well-being. We have witnessed in the past century dramatic increases in the amount of leisure available to U.S. citizens, resulting in changed attitudes toward seeking leisure experiences. We have moved from a society harnessed by a work ethic that demanded toil fourteen to sixteen hours per day, six days a week, to one in which the average industrial worker works a five-day, less-than-forty-hour workweek. Meanwhile, attitudes toward play and leisure— once seen as frivolous, nonessential activities or, at best, amusements or diversions—have changed so that leisure is viewed as a central focus in life that helps individuals define their self-concept.

Godbey writes that although we think of society ". . . as being composed of individuals who have shared common experiences, in reality our society is made up of . . . distinct generational groupings" (Godbey, 1986, p. 1). Each of these generational groupings has been influenced by a host of historical and cultural values that have shaped and molded their perspective of leisure. This, in turn, has greatly influenced the extent to which these groupings have derived satisfaction from their leisure experiences. From a personal family perspective, we all have seen dramatic changes in terms of the way various family members perceived work and leisure. One of the authors reflects on leisure in the lives of his family members.

My Grandparents' View of Leisure. My grandparents viewed leisure and play *as being frivolous.* As gender roles of the era dictated, my grandfather worked hard to survive in order to achieve the "American Dream" for his family. He worked as a coal miner and for the railroads, and often toiled sixty to seventy hours per week to clothe, feed, and shelter the family. My grandmother fulfilled her expected roles as well. She worked in the home, cooking, cleaning, raising the family, and serving as a helpmate for my grandfather. All of these tasks were accomplished, of course, without the modern conveniences of today. My grandfather loved the out-of-doors and enjoyed tent camping with friends when he could pursue it—which was not very often. My grandmother engaged in quilting and canning. Leisure activities during my grandparents' era often were justified as being in *support of subsistence* or were *utilitarian in nature.* When my grandfather died at age ninety-seven, he had been retired for more than thirty years.

My Parents' View of Leisure. My parents were born in the early 1900s and were raised during the Great Depression. That event shaped their entire lives. Always concerned about pursuing financial security, they often would forgo the pleasures of everyday leisure opportunities to ensure their financial well-being. Interestingly, during his leisure time, my father enjoyed playing the stock market and engaging in real estate investments—both activities related to acquiring financial security. My mother primarily worked in the home, focusing on raising the family. My father served in World War II and subsequently worked as an engineer for an electronics firm in the Silicon Valley, California. Like my grandparents, both my mother and father worked extremely hard, but they placed emphasis on using their leisure time *to restore or refresh themselves to work* harder on the job. Every summer, my father initiated family vacations to Oregon. We camped and fished and toured, enjoying the scenery. On these trips, my parents engaged in activities sufficiently different from daily tasks so as to be restorative.

My Generation's View of Leisure. I graduated from high school four decades ago, about the time of the United States' heightened involvement in Vietnam. My generation's values differed vastly from those of my parents and grandparents. We did not pursue financial security or stability; we had it. I grew up, when compared with my parents, in an affluent era. It was also an era of immediacy—instant leisure entertainment in the form of television and electronic home entertainment. Educational opportunity and the pursuit of college degrees were readily available. I rode the crest of the baby boom generation. During this period of time, work was not necessarily the focus of life or one's time—leisure became a predominant shaper of culture. Many of my generation *"worked to play."* We did not seek financial security; we sought greater enjoyment in life via leisure pursuits. As Kelly and Godbey (1992) note, the emphasis of this generation changed from "we" to "me."

My Children's View of Leisure. My son and daughter recently graduated from college. One has begun his professional work life, and the other continues in graduate school. They are both married, and their family life is an important determiner of their leisure. They have a different set of values toward their work and leisure than my grandparents, my parents, and I have had. They appear to view leisure as a right rather than a luxury, although they are not currently as economically affluent as the previous generation. They appear to be more status oriented. They are a part of today's *"just do it"* society, the *"work hard, play hard"* group (Patterson, 2000). Leisure in many respects is a commodity to them to consume; they have many leisure experiences, but I'm not sure they experience leisure (Harper and Hultsman, 1994). The outward symbols of their leisure participation are often used as measures of personal success and achievements. Individuals in this age group desire to have meaningful, creative, fulfilling lifestyles both on and off the job. This generation seeks opportunities for continuous growth, personal and physical development, and increased spiritual awareness.

My Grandchild's Play. Nearly four years ago, my granddaughter was born two and a half months premature. Although her early life was in question, she has grown into a robust child full of the exuberance that comes from one's young age. She is vibrant and curious to learn, to discover new and exciting elements of our world. I am constantly amazed at her intellectual curiosity and ability to seek meaning in the world she encounters. Her world is one of play. From her early life she has learned about the importance of leisure in promoting greater quality of life. She is playful and joyful and expresses great enthusiasm in the pursuit of her play activities. At times she lives in a fantasy world, as all children do. Her play objects give meaning to her life, symbolically and realistically. For her, her play is her work. It is serious business that she pursues. There is no question in my mind that her life is being shaped by her world of play. It is interesting to observe how culturally her play activities are defining her role in future society. She has begun to assimilate into her role as a female through her play activities. She likes to dress up, build, read (or be read to), sing, pretend, and be with other children. She is gregarious and outgoing, yet shy and reserved at the same time. Her play is central to her well-being. Her leisure life will be vastly different from the generations that have preceded her. I believe that her quality of life and the livability of the community setting in which she lives will be important features in her future.

In review, each of these generations has different expectations, values, and attitudes that shape and mold its leisure interests and pursuits (see figure 1.2). One generation more strongly values economic stability, whereas another views leisure as a status symbol. Current status symbols associated with leisure include involvement in fitness, the ownership of clothing endorsed by professional sports teams, and participation in activities such as skydiving. Each of these generations approaches leisure in different ways in order to enhance its life satisfaction. For one generation, actual participation in leisure serves as an important yardstick in measuring life satisfaction and well-being; for another generation, leisure is an ideal that is to be pursued.

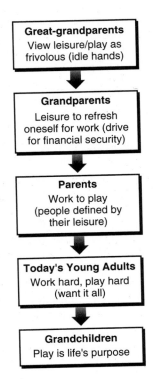

Figure 1.2

Generational views of leisure.

Although in the last 100 years society has developed in a way that contributes to individual material and spiritual well-being, we have also witnessed tragic wars and tumultuous devastation. In that time, more people have been killed in wars than in the entire history of humankind. On the other hand, conditions have given rise to opportunities for creative endeavors, intellectual developments, and opportunities for greater self-actualization. Today, people can use leisure to build life satisfaction and to enhance the well-being of individuals; it can serve as a positive force to enhance society and culture as a whole.

Life Satisfaction

A discussion of leisure and life satisfaction requires a working definition of terms. The next chapter presents a thorough discussion of the meanings and definitions of leisure, but for now we will define leisure as a *multidimensional construct in which one feels relatively free from constraints, has a feeling of positive affect, is motivated by internal forces, and allows the exercise of perceived competence.*

What is meant by life satisfaction? People often think of life satisfaction as *a sense of well-being, happiness, or quality of life* that is available to an individual (Shichman and Cooper, 1984). Happiness, morale, psychological well-being, and life adjustment are all indicators of the overall quality of our inner experience; ". . . happiness is often considered the extent to which we have positive attitudes and feelings about various aspects of our lives" (Russell, 1996, p. 38). To more precisely define life satisfaction or well-being is a complex and difficult task, as there are no universally accepted definitions. In fact, the question of life satisfaction or well-being is often a subjective, philosophical one, rather than one that can be stated in objective terms. Surveys can objectively measure the economic well-being of individuals, their mental and physical health, and other factors, but subjective measures are required to evaluate quantitative and qualitative factors that contribute to life satisfaction, such as one's spiritual well-being.

Seligman (2002) notes that the terms *happiness* and *well being* are interchangeable. He suggests that happiness and well being are desired outcomes of what he defines as a "positive psychology." Positive psychology refers to positive past, present, and future emotions. "Satisfaction, contentment, and serenity are past-oriented emotions; optimism, hope, trust, faith, and confidence are future-oriented emotions" (p. 261). He further subdivides position emotions into two categories: pleasures and gratifications. Pleasures are those that can be derived immediately through the bodily senses and ones that are higher in nature. Bodily pleasures are ". . . delicious tastes and smells, sexual feelings, moving your body well, delightful sights and sounds" (p. 262). Higher pleasures are reflected in feelings that produce ". . . ecstasy, rapture, thrill, bliss, gladness, mirth, glee, fun, ebullience, comfort, amusement, relaxation, and the like" (p. 262). Gratifications according to Seligman are not feelings but activities that we like doing.

The literature concerning life satisfaction and well-being, while diverse, is primarily concerned with how and why people experience their lives in positive ways, including both intellectual factors and emotional reactions (Diener, 1984). Most of the literature has focused on terms such as happiness, satisfaction, morale, life satisfaction, well-being, and quality of life. In 1967, a review of the area of life satisfaction by Wilson suggests that the ". . . happy person emerges as a young, healthy, well-educated, well-paid, extroverted, optimistic, worry-free, religious, married person with high self-esteem, high job morale, [modest aspirations, of either sex], and of a wide range of intelligence" (p. 294). Seligman (2002, p. 51) confirms Wilson's perspective that an indication that people are happy is when they are well-paid, married, young, healthy, well-educated, and religious. Myers (2000) reports that happy people are less self-focused, less hostile and abusive, and less vulnerable to disease. They also are more loving, for-

Clarifying Happiness

The popular connotation of happiness is equivalent to contentment; a psychological state that exists when current needs and desires are satisfied. Happiness, therefore, strengthens and weakens on the basis of how content one feels from one moment to the next. In order to measure happiness, or contentedness, one would employ a psychological calculus of duration and intensity rather than normatively assess the way in which one lived.

Conversely, the ethical term happiness means well-being or the totality of moral goods harmoniously arranged for a fulfilling life. Aristotle defined happiness as self-fulfillment, praising it as the ultimate good. Thus, happiness includes all of the best pleasures and excellences befitting a human being freely chosen and carved out over a lifetime. It is the "well-traveled road," a life of dynamic growth and self-fulfillment, appraised according to where it has led and what had adorned it.

Source: From Sylvester, C. *Therapeutic Recreation and the End of Leisure*. In Sylvester, C., Hemingway, J.L., Howe-Murphy, R., Mobily, K., and Shank, P. A. 1987. *Philosophy of Therapeutic Recreation: Ideas and Issues*. Alexandria, VA: National Recreation & Park Association, p. 80.

giving, trusting, energetic, decisive, creative, sociable, and helpful. Positive emotions are conducive to sociability, optimistic goal-striving, even healthy immune systems (Weisse, 1992). It is interesting to note that an electronic search of *Psychological Abstracts* since 1887 turned up 8,072 articles on anger, 57,800 on anxiety, and 70,856 on depression, while only 851 abstracts mentioned joy, 2,958 happiness, and 5,701 life satisfaction (Myers, 2000).

Positive emotions are conducive to sociability, optimistic goal-striving, even healthy immune systems (Weisse, 1992). It is interesting to note that an electronic search of *Psychological Abstracts* since 1887 turned up 8,072 articles on anger, 57,800 on anxiety, and 70,856 on depression, while only 851 abstracts mentioned joy, 2,958 happiness, and 5,701 life satisfaction (Myers, 2000). Seligman (2002, p. 50) suggests that Americans underestimate how happy people actually are. His studies have suggested that Americans, on average, believe that the lifetime prevalence of clinical depression is 49 percent. He reports that it is actually between 8 and 18 percent. Further, he goes on to note that Americans report 49 percent of us achieve positive life satisfaction. The actual number of individuals perceiving that they have positive life satisfaction is 83 percent.

Diener has suggested that definitions of happiness or well-being can be broken into three categories (1984, p. 543). These are as follows:

1. *External/Normative Criteria*. The value framework of one's culture or society will influence one's perception of life satisfaction or well-being. Normative definitions outline what is desirable in the ideal state. For example, the Constitution of the United States defines many expectations related to life satisfaction, such as "life, liberty and the pursuit of happiness."
2. *Internal/Subjective Criteria*. One's personal assessment regarding what constitutes quality of life based upon one's own chosen criteria, and the degree to which these criteria are achieved, is a determinant of life satisfaction and well-being. For example, some individuals may desire to pursue leisure activities that enhance their social status or sense of self-esteem. Others may desire to pursue leisure activities that promote family togetherness or physical well-being.

3. *Internal/Emotional State.* Simply put, the degree to which one experiences pleasant emotions during life's activities can be used as a measure of life satisfaction. This is determined by the individual him/herself. During certain life activities, the individual may feel happy, content, creative, uplifted, socially rewarded, or spiritually moved, and these emotions may contribute to life satisfaction.

Diener goes on to suggest that all three of these measures should be combined for a total global assessment of life satisfaction. In other words, we should not only consider the external factors that influence a person's life satisfaction or well-being but also the internal ones. These measures help in identifying what constitutes quality of life for an individual and provide measures for determining quality of life.

More specifically, Csikszentmihalyi (1990) has focused on life satisfaction as related to involvement in specific life experiences, including those that can be defined as leisure. His paradigm is known as the concept of "flow." Flow is the experience that

> . . . lifts the course of life to a different level. Alienation gives way to involvement, enjoyment replaces boredom, helplessness turns into a feeling of control, and psychic energy works to reinforce the sense of self, instead of being lost in the service of external goals. When experience is intrinsically rewarding life is justified in the present, instead of being held hostage to a hypothetical future gain. (Csikszentmihalyi, 1990, p. 69)

Flow can be viewed as that state of being between "boredom and anxiety," where the challenge of the activity matches the skills of the participant. If you were a soccer star playing with a group of novices, you would likely be bored. On the other hand, if you were a novice playing with a group of highly skilled players, you would be agitated and anxious. Flow is that experience where it all seems to come together; skills correspond to the level of play.

Csikszentmihalyi (1990) presents several elements of enjoyment or flow directly related to satisfaction. The elements of enjoyment are as follows:

1. *A Challenging Activity that Requires Skills.* As reported by participants, most optimal experiences occur within activity that is goal-directed, bounded by rules and requiring a certain level of skill. Csikszentmihalyi (1990) notes that skills and activity need not imply physical skill and activity alone. Reading requires skill and has a goal of completion; it could very well provide the stage for flow to occur.
2. *The Merging of Action and Awareness.* When all of a person's skills are necessary to deal with the activity at hand, that person becomes totally immersed in the activity. Distractions seem to fade away and the participant becomes one with the event. For example, a gymnast becomes so absorbed in the event that she is unaware of the noise of the crowd. People who experience this merging of action and awareness speak of being one with everything, losing touch with the world, and a feeling of being relaxed and energetic at the same time.
3. *Clear Goals and Feedback.* Optimal experiences result from clearly directed goals. The participant knows what to do, where to aim. In addition, constant feedback relates to those goals. In playing cards as one hand is lost and another dealt, players know the score. In playing a musical instrument a composer hears the tones and melodies and knows how the music relates to the goal of composing a new song.
4. *Concentration on the Task at Hand.* One aspect of the merging of action and awareness involves tremendous concentration on the task at hand. Those who experience flow often talk about such total immersion as to be able to forget the unpleasant tasks awaiting them. Omitting worries from conscious thought allows complete concentration on the activity. For example, you have been worrying about an uncompleted assignment, yet engage a friend in a

game of tennis. During the tennis match you forget about the assignment as you concentrate on winning each point. You must concentrate to succeed in reaching your goals.

5. *The Paradox of Control.* Flow experiences involve a sense of personal control over one's destiny with regard to the activity of choice. Enjoyment comes from the sense of being skilled enough to eliminate or minimize risk of failure or injury; one exercises control by matching one's skill with the appropriate level of challenge. Competition related to martial arts always holds the risk of physical injury; however, competitors placed in classes with appropriate skill levels face little danger of injury.

6. *The Loss of Self-Consciousness.* Csikszentmihalyi (1990) talks about losing awareness of self in the flow experience. Being totally immersed in an activity, when concentration levels are high and action and awareness have merged, a person temporarily forgets about self as a being. This loss of self frequently accompanies a feeling of oneness with something else—the environment, the ball, other participants.

7. *The Transformation of Time.* The most commonly reported characteristic of flow or optimal experience is the change in perception of the passage of time. During the experience, people speak of time standing still, yet after the experience is over, time seems to have sped by. For example, all of us can remember at least one conversation we have had with another person when we had no idea how much time had passed—the conversation absorbed us, engaged our concentration, and gave us clear and continuous feedback.

Csikszentmihalyi (1990) suggests that all of these elements are present in a truly engrossing, enjoyable, and satisfying experience. Taken together, these factors help in identifying what constitutes quality-of-life experiences and provide measures for evaluating quality-of-life factors.

Hill (2002, p. 125) has noted that the theory of flow has been initially applied within the area of leisure; however, it may be applied and more readily experienced in the context of work. Thus, the theory of flow speaks to the proposition that we are, in fact, in a life satisfaction business and it may be important to look at individuals in a holistic sense applying theories derived from leisure to one's entire life experience. Bryce and Haworth (2002, p. 249) confirmed this perspective, suggesting the flow is experienced more in work than in leisure.

Leisure participation can affect and be affected by life satisfaction or well-being variables. Leisure, in fact, can be an important component contributing to the daily well-being of an individual. For example, on a day-to-day basis we all engage in mundane events and activities such as sleeping, eating, housework, and, for some, a monotonous work environment. These activities do not necessarily increase our pleasure, happiness, or well-being. As Reich and Zautra note, "if we do not do them, we do not necessarily feel worse, we simply do not increase our pleasure" (1983, p. 43). On the other hand, *leisure activities*—usually intrinsically motivated and often freely chosen—may provide more opportunities for pleasure, hence increased life satisfaction.

Are North Americans happy? Periodic studies by the National Opinion Research Center (Myers, 2000) report that nine out of ten individuals surveyed report that they are very happy, or pretty happy. Only one in ten indicate that they are not too happy. Further, individuals express great satisfaction with their life in general. Myers reports that eight of ten individuals in selected studies rate themselves more satisfied with life than dissatisfied. Likewise, some three-fourths of people say that they have felt excited, proud, or pleased at some point during the last few weeks; only a third indicate that they are lonely, bored, or depressed (Myers, 2000).

What do North Americans believe contributes to life satisfaction? Does money buy happiness? Does material gain influence life satisfaction, happiness, or well-being? Happiness tends to be lower among the very poor (Myers, 2000). Earning more money, however, does not necessarily improve one's happiness. Although, as Diener (2000) reports, individuals living in wealthy nations tend to be more satisfied with their lifestyles, in wealthy nations (United States, Canada, and Europe) the correlation between income and personal happiness is surprisingly weak (Inglehart, 1989). Interestingly, the more people strive for extrinsic goals such as monetary gain, the less robust is their well-being (Myers, 2000). What does produce happiness, life satisfaction, or well-being? The need to belong, close relationships, and friendships are all elements that contribute to greater happiness, life satisfaction, and well-being. Further, religiously active people also report higher levels of happiness (Inglehart, 1989).

When Americans are compared to others throughout the world, how do we compare with them? In a cross-national study comparing the average level of satisfaction as well as purchasing power, Seligman (2002) reports some interesting findings. Americans, along with individuals from the Netherlands, Ireland, Canada, Denmark, and Switzerland, have the highest levels of satisfaction. Interestingly, not all of the countries ranked high in life satisfaction have high levels of purchasing power, although most are high when compared with the United States. The lowest levels of life satisfaction are Bulgaria, Russia, Belarus, Latvia, Romania, Estonia, Lithuania, and Hungary. See table 1.1.

If one views the benefits that may motivate individuals to participate in leisure found in table 1.1 (see p. 19), it is evident that many of the potential elements are focused on factors that influence happiness, life satisfaction, and well-being. For example, learning, exploration, being with friends, slowing down mentally, spiritual introspection, meeting people, and being with individuals with similar values are all factors that can promote greater life satisfaction. Leisure provides opportunities for individuals to find all of these ends.

A large number of identified variables contribute to life satisfaction or well-being. Some of the *subjective variables* include life satisfaction and its relationship to self-esteem, satisfaction with self, standard of living, family life, work, mental and physical health, community, mood, place of residence, physical attractiveness, and leisure. *Demographic variables* often studied and linked to life satisfaction and well-being include income, age, gender, race/ethnicity, employment, education, marriage, and family. When discussing *psychological dimensions* and life satisfaction, variables often include social contact, personality, creativity, and involvement in activities. All of these variables can be studied within the leisure experience itself. For example, one could view the relationship between life satisfaction, income, and leisure pursuits. The study of activities, for example, suggests that participation in leisure events, including hobbies and formal organizations, increases social contact, which, in turn, increases life satisfaction.

Leisure and Its Relationship to Life Satisfaction

A number of studies have focused on the topic of leisure and life satisfaction. Iso-Ahola (1980) reported that all of the studies he had reviewed showed a positive relationship between leisure and life satisfaction. Kelly and Godbey (1992) reported similar findings twelve years later. Leisure and life satisfaction consist of many elements. According to Kelly (1996), life satisfaction includes self-expression, companionship, integration, health, rest and relaxation, meeting new people, experiencing nature, and family relationships. Hull, Stewart, and Yi (1992) found that satisfaction is dynamic and that it fluctuates along experience patterns. People experience peaks in satisfaction, lulls in boredom, peaks in excitement, and peaks in relaxation. Leitner and Leitner (1996, p. 26) report ". . . that leisure behavior is the most important or one of the most important determinants of life satisfaction and psychological well-being. . . ." They note

TABLE 1.1

CROSS-NATIONAL STUDY OF LIFE SATISFACTION AND PURCHASING POWER

Nation	Life Satisfaction	Purchasing Power
Bulgaria	5.03	22
Russia	5.37	27
Belarus	5.52	30
Latvia	5.70	20
Romania	5.88	12
Estonia	6.00	27
Lithuania	6.01	16
Hungary	6.03	25
Turkey	6.41	22
Japan	6.53	87
Nigeria	6.59	6
South Korea	6.69	39
India	6.70	5
Portugal	7.07	44
Spain	7.15	57
Germany	7.22	89
Argentina	7.25	25
People's Republic of China	7.29	9
Italy	7.30	77
Brazil	7.38	23
Chile	7.55	35
Norway	7.68	78
Finland	7.68	69
USA	**7.73**	**100**
Netherlands	7.77	76
Ireland	7.88	52
Canada	7.89	85
Denmark	8.16	81
Switzerland	8.36	96

Source: Seligman, M.E.P. 2002. *Authentic Happiness.* New York: Free Press. p. 52

that "... many studies support the assertion that leisure participation and life satisfaction are positively related to psychological well-being and life satisfaction" (Leitner and Leitner, 1996, p. 26).

For example, Kim (2000, p. 28) found that there is a direct relationship between leisure participation and life satisfaction and that participation in leisure activities explains a significant portion of the variance in life satisfaction measures.

Many studies conducted in the area of leisure and life satisfaction have focused primarily on the variable of age, with a special focus on older men and women. Studies also have explored the relationship between leisure activities and life satisfaction, and leisure and community well-being.

Leisure and Life Satisfaction as Related to Age

The relationship of life satisfaction, leisure, and age has been examined in a number of studies. Kelly, Steinkamp, and Kelly (1987) have suggested that in their later years men demonstrate a greater desire for companionship in their leisure than do women. The study also found that those kinds of leisure that provide satisfying interaction with other persons and those that require skill acquisition over a long period of time produced higher levels of life satisfaction than those that did not. When viewing leisure activities and their relationship to life satisfaction by age, the researchers found that (1) travel and cultural activities were most important to those forty-five to fifty-four years old; (2) social, cultural, and travel activities were most important to those fifty-five to sixty-four years old; (3) social and travel activities were most important to those sixty-five to seventy-four years old; and (4) home-based and family activities were most important to life satisfaction for those individuals seventy-five and older.

Kelly, Steinkamp, and Kelly (1987) also studied the relationship of social activity and leisure involvement to life satisfaction. They found a reduction in the level of leisure activity with age, although they noted that social activities and leisure activities related to family show the least decline. Leisure activities related to primary relationships with family and friends are usually maintained throughout later life. The findings are consistent with those of Gordon, Gaitz, and Scott (1976), who suggest that participation in seven leisure categories, many related to social entertaining and activities, is consistent throughout the life span. Sneegas (1986), studying life satisfaction of middle-aged and older adults and its relationship to perceived social competence, found that age was not related to social competence. She found one's perception of social competence affects the degree of leisure participation and leisure satisfaction, thereby influencing life satisfaction.

Riddick (1985) has also studied the relationship of life satisfaction to age. She found, in a national sample of men and women age sixty-five and over, that the strongest predictor of life satisfaction was involvement in leisure activities. For both males and females, she found that income and health problems impact participation in leisure activities and, hence, life satisfaction. As Bammel and Burris-Bammel (1996, p. 342) write, ". . . social participation has long been considered an important factor in determining the happiness, morale, well-being, and life satisfaction of elderly individuals." In 1990, Cutler and Hendricks reported similar results whereby engagement in activity was the determinant of life satisfaction.

Riddick (1986) also has studied leisure satisfaction among ten age groups, ranging from eighteen to sixty-five years old. She found that two factors—knowledge of leisure resources and leisure values—have significant influence on leisure satisfaction. Mobily, Lemke, Ostiguy, Woodard, Griffee, and Pickens (1993) found successful adaptation to the aging process depended largely on maintaining or enhancing one's competence and retaining a sense of self-determination. People with a large leisure repertoire were happiest. Kelly and Godbey (1992) agreed, indicating that a sense of worth, even productivity, and sharing oneself with others led to the greatest level of life satisfaction.

Work, Leisure, and Life Satisfaction

Are work and leisure linked to one another in such a way as to contribute to life satisfaction? Bergermaier, Borg, and Champoux (1984) tested three theories related to work, leisure, and life satisfaction. They postulated the following: (1) one's work might spill over into leisure and influence life satisfaction; (2) one might use leisure to compensate for a dissatisfying work experience or vice versa; or (3) there would be no relationship between work and leisure, and life

U.S. Workers Feel Burn of Long Hours, Less Leisure: Employees Pay Cost of Rising Productivity

A backlash is building against America's work epidemic.

More employees are resisting companies' demands for longer hours on the job, the 24/7 pace of business that means operations never cease, and the surrender of leisure time to work because of new technology such as cell phones and e-mail.

"People are putting in 40 and 50 hours a week, and there's not enough time for anything," says Gretchen Burger, in Seattle, an organizer with Take Back Your Time, a grass-roots movement focusing attention on the issue of overwork. "There is an alternative."

Some workers, unwilling to clock extra hours without extra pay, are suing their companies over alleged overtime violations. In fiscal 2003, the Labor Department collected $212 million in back wages, which included overtime violations. That's a 21% increase over the record-setting amount collected in 2002.

Some economists also believe that many productivity gains of the `90s can be attributed to longer work hours rather than the efficiency of new technology.

For the first time, industries that have been notorious for their taxing schedules are scaling back. New guidelines now limit the number of hours that medical residents can work. And starting Jan. 4, federal regulations will require many truck drivers to set aside more time for breaks.

Some beleaguered workers are also taking action, changing to less-demanding occupations or leaving corporations to start their own businesses, where they can feel more in control of their work lives. Others are scaling back to spend more time with families.

U.S. workers put in an average of 1,815 hours in 2002. In Major European economies, hours worked ranged from about 1,300 to 1,800, according to the International Labor Organization (ILO). Hours were about the same in the USA and Japan.

Combined weekly work hours for dual-earning couples with children rose 10 hours per week, from 81 hours in 1977 to 91 hours in 2002, according to a new study by the New York-based Families and Work Institute.

Employees feel the strain. Mounting research shows there's a tangible downside to overwork, from mental-health problems to physical ailments and job injuries caused by fatigue and stress. It's also a bottom-line issue: A study by the Economic Policy Institute found that mandatory overtime costs industry as much as $300 billion a year in stress- and fatigue-related problems.

Some doubt the effort to curb hours will cause the USA to adopt the more leisurely approach of Europe, where women in Sweden get 96 weeks of maternity leave and workers in France enjoy about five weeks of vacation a year.

An ILO report in September found that U.S. productivity grew in 2002, surpassing Europe and Japan in annual output per worker for the first substantial period since World War II. The report found that the difference was due to the longer hours worked by Americans.

But the data showed a recent uptick in the average workweek for production and non-supervisory workers as the economic recovery picked up steam.

Hours are rising in part because of new technology, which makes it easier to work outside the office, and a sluggish economy, which has led companies to lay off workers, leaving fewer workers shouldering the same (or more) work.

Even vacations are going by the wayside: Employees are handing companies more than $21 billion in unused vacation days each year, according to a study by Expedia.com.

Source: Armour, S. 2003. U.S. Workers Feel Burn of Long Hours, Less Leisure. *USA Today:* 1B, 2B.

satisfaction. Their research supports a "spillover" theory and "no-relationship" model in terms of the connection between work and non-work and life satisfaction. They suggest that there is little relationship between work and leisure, although work and leisure may spill over into one another, and this may affect life satisfaction. Controversy still exists as to the relationship of work, leisure, and life satisfaction, although many now view these aspects of life as multidimensional and extremely complex (Kelly and Godbey, 1992). For example, Siegenthaler and O'Dell (1997) report that individuals with greater knowledge about leisure and its benefits feel more positively about their leisure than those with less knowledge.

Lobo (2001) has written that the work leisure paradigm has changed over the past four decades. Reflecting the controversy regarding the relationship of work and leisure, Lobo has stated the following:

> In the 1960s and 1970s anticipation of long-term declines in working hours were expected to result in increased leisure time. Researchers of that period examined theories on conditions when work values spilled over into leisure, and when leisure activities compensated for stresses of work. Contrary to expectations, the 1980s and 1990s provided strong evidence that people worked longer hours; nonstandard work hours were normalized; substantial underemployment and unemployment prevailed; and occupational restructuring resulted in workforces divided in the professional core, contractual fringe, and flexibility labor forces, resulting in development of three societies—consumers, leisure industry workers, and marginalized impoverished groups. (2001, p. 36)

Several years ago Pierce (1980) suggested that certain dimensions provide satisfaction in both leisure and work environments, either separately or simultaneously. Four "satisfaction dimensions" were particularly significant—intimacy, relaxation, achievement, and power. In support of this multidimensionality, Kelly and Godbey (1992) indicated that people find both meaning and satisfaction in family, work, and leisure. They conclude that ". . . both work and leisure are too complex in motivations, styles, associations, and other factors to fit neatly into any circumscribed approach" (p. 133). Brown and Cashel (1995) have studied the relationship of job satisfaction and perceived amount of leisure and leisure satisfaction. They found that individuals participating in leisure activities that provided psychological rewards, social interaction, and/or were considered to be relaxing perceive themselves to have more leisure. In turn, they found that individuals with greater amounts of leisure have greater amounts of job satisfaction.

Leisure, Satisfaction, and Community Well-Being

Leisure also influences satisfaction in community life. Allen and Beattie (1984), seeking to understand what factors contribute to one's sense of community satisfaction, studied seven dimensions, including leisure. These researchers found that the economic dimension (how affluent the community was) was the most influential. The leisure dimension ranked fifth in importance; however, it was the best predictor of overall satisfaction with community life. Thus, participation in fulfilling leisure experiences appears to strongly influence individuals' perceptions of community well-being. In addition, the existence of leisure services aids in the economic development of a community.

In examining functions of leisure within a community, Kraus (1990) maintains that a primary function of leisure is to enrich the quality of life. The reduction of stress, emotional satisfaction, enjoyable social contacts, and feelings of achievement correspond closely to life satisfaction and directly relate to community well-being (Kraus, 1990). Leisure also contributes to personal development and makes a community a more attractive place to live. Each year popular periodicals publish a "best place to live" list, where the extent of leisure services available to community members is a primary consideration.

Life satisfaction and community well-being also increase as neighborhood ties are strengthened and intergroup and intergenerational relations improve (Kraus, 1990). When citizens share tasks, such as building a playground or a city beautification project, they enhance the quality of life for the entire community. Through leisure we can often move past the biases and prejudices—based on age, sex, mental or physical abilities, race/ethnicity, sexual orientation, or economic status—that we allow to interfere with relationships. The free flow of ideas and sharing through the medium of leisure benefits us all. Kelly and Godbey (1992) found that the most significant aspect of leisure is its ability to promote social bonding. Anything that supports a sense of family (loosely defined as close ties achieved through intense and ongoing relationships) will benefit the community.

Leisure, Life Satisfaction, and the Rise of the Creative Class

The transformation of the social organization of work at the end of the twentieth century has given rise to service and knowledge-based workers. Such occupations can be contrasted with industrial-based work, such as manufacturing, factory employment, and assembly line production. Florida (2002) postulates that knowledge-based workers can be further subdivided into what he defines as the *creative class.* This group of employed individuals represents some 38 million Americans or 30 percent of the workforce. It includes individuals employed in such occupations as science and engineering, architecture and design, education, arts, music, and entertainment. In addition, Florida suggests that this creative class ". . . also includes a broader group of creative professionals in business and finance, law, health care, and related fields (p. 8)."

What distinguishes the work of individuals of the creative class? The creative class is differentiated by the type of work with which they are involved. "These people engage in complex problem-solving that involves a great deal of independent judgment and requires higher levels of education or human capital." Such individuals ". . . share a common creative ethos that values creativity, individuality, difference, and merit . . . every aspect and every manifestation of creativity . . . technological, cultural and economic . . . is interlinked and inseparable" (Florida, 2002, p. 8). Such individuals are creating new perspectives on work, leisure, and community life. They are often shaping their ". . . identities along the very dimensions of . . . creativity . . . what we consume, new forms of leisure and recreation . . [and] . . . efforts at community building" (p. 7).

As Florida noted, we are witnessing the rise of human creativity, and it is transforming the social, cultural, political, and economic fabric of our lives. The ongoing transformation process has resulted ". . . in the emergence of a new society and new culture—indeed a whole new way of life" (2002, p. 12). In particular, four significant dimensions of our lives have been transformed. Florida identifies these basic categories of human existence as work, lifestyle, time, and community (2002, p. 12). He suggests that work environment is being transformed into one which evidences greater degrees of self-management, peer recognition and pressure, and intrinsic forms of motivation. He refers to these as soft control and suggests that people seek greater autonomy and control of their work schedule, the ability to learn and grow on the job, and the desire to express their individual identities through work. Further, he notes that the creative class is building its lifestyle around creative experiences. Identities are being shaped and expressed through multiple venues, which may include not only one's occupation but also their leisure pursuits. In a holistic sense, people are living a lifestyle that is reflected and expressed through multiple experiences. People no longer have their work life expressed exclusively from their leisure lives. They are intertwined through their creative activities, and the distinctions between work and leisure are increasingly blurred. Thus, the use of time also has become blurred and intensified. There are no boundaries for the expression creativity, and as Florida indicates, a whole new construction of time is emerging. Last, individuals seek to express their creative ideas not only in work and leisure settings, but also in ways they live in any community setting. This new class seeks to have their communities reflect their expressions of creativity as well as serving as a stimulus to enhance, expand, and enrich their creative expressions.

Lifestyle and Leisure

One's lifestyle can greatly influence life satisfaction or well-being. *An optimal lifestyle is the integration and balance of the physical, mental, emotional, intellectual, social, and spiritual aspects of a person.* Each person strives to attain—and is capable of achieving—an optimal level of life satisfaction or well-being. Although levels of life satisfaction are often measured against external standards of appraisal, comparisons between individuals are usually not reliable. People have unique needs and pursue different levels of life satisfaction according to these needs.

While leisure influences lifestyle, it may not be the dominant factor in many people's lives; the focal point can be work, family, religion, social roles, societal commitments, or other factors. One's lifestyle is the sum total of all of these factors, some of which contribute greatly to life satisfaction and well-being, whereas others can detract. This is true for leisure as well. Leisure can contribute in a positive way to the maintenance of a healthy, vigorous lifestyle; on the other hand, it can detract from one's well-being in a significant manner.

Leisure services professionals have often failed to examine how leisure activities integrate with other factors that influence the lifestyles of individuals. The work of a leisure services professional, along with encouraging life satisfaction, should focus on facilitating both social (behavioral) and environmental (physical) conditions that help people achieve optimal lifestyles. This might involve the creation of activities or the development of areas and facilities. Further, it could also involve building a greater public awareness of the need for healthier, more satisfying lifestyles.

Lifestyle Management

How do the benefits sought in leisure experiences relate to the various programs that are directed toward enhancing optimal lifestyle behaviors? Figure 1.3 presents a model of lifestyle management developed by Ellis, Edginton, and Howard (1985). This model demonstrates some of the potential leisure activities in which people voluntarily engage. Some of these activities help to increase life satisfaction, whereas other activities have a negative impact. For example, eating for pleasure is one of the most popular leisure activities in many countries and cultures. This can be a positive use of leisure that optimizes life satisfaction by encouraging positive social relations in a relaxing atmosphere. On the other hand, eating to excess or eating the wrong kinds of foods can be detrimental to long-term life satisfaction.

It is interesting to note, and the model illustrates, that nearly all potential leisure experiences can have a great deal of impact—both positively and negatively—on the well-being of an individual. In addition, most of these experiences are directly tied to the work of leisure service organizations. Further, many of these activities can be initiated by an individual or carried out together with a leisure service organization, agency, or business.

Hull (1990) presents a three-dimensional representation of mood—a factor often considered to be integral to experiences of satisfaction. The two primary dimensions include pleasure and arousal. The third dimension, dominance, relates to feelings (e.g., anger, fear) one might

Lifestyle

Figure 1.3

Lifestyle management.

Source: After M. J. Ellis, C. R. Edginton, and D. R. Howard, Lifestyle and Health Promotion, *1985. Academy of Leisure Sciences, Dallas, TX.*

Fitness management

Hypokinetic lifestyle

Exercising

Health enhancement

Other personal health behaviors

Wellness

Leisure counseling

Communication disorders

Belonging

Leisure

Relaxing

Stress-inducing lifestyle

Stress management

Substance abuse management

Tobacco, alcohol and substance abuse

Drinking

Eating

Poor dietary habits

Nutrition management

Risk behaviors

Risk inductor

Safety/risk management

Management

experience when engaged in certain activities such as competitive sports or mountain climbing. As illustrated in figure 1.4, something that is sleepy and unpleasant would be boring; an experience that is arousing and unpleasant would result in stress; an arousing yet pleasant experience would be exciting, and a pleasant but sleepy experience would be relaxing. Obviously, moods, leisure, and life satisfaction are interrelated. Quality of life is generally measured and intuitively felt on a subjective scale; we base our decisions about our own quality of life on primarily intangible and highly personal factors.

Leisure serves as a central life force that the individual can shape to have either positive or negative consequences. Leisure joins work, family, religion, and other social contacts as another of the important variables that shape life. Leisure professionals should recognize the whole person and deal with individuals in a complete or holistic manner. Leisure services professionals in Hong Kong, for example, take a holistic approach to providing leisure services for

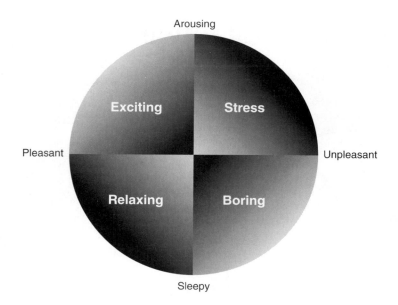

Figure 1.4

Factors that influence mood.

Arousing

Exciting

Stress

Pleasant

Unpleasant

Relaxing

Boring

Sleepy

young people. At their recreation centers, they not only provide leisure programs and activities but also offer support for studying and homework, as well as opportunities for personal counseling. Leisure influences the behavior of people during much of their life, not only during their free time. Almost all of the behaviors represented in the model figure 1.3 require personal choice and are engaged in voluntarily. These are hallmarks of the leisure experience.

Leisure, Organizations, and Life Satisfaction

Why do leisure service organizations exist? What is their role in society? What is the relationship of these organizations to life satisfaction? From an ideal perspective, any organization exists to meet the needs of those it serves. Organizations, like individuals, however, also have needs—to be of service, to make a profit, or to shape or mold the character of individuals and/or society. Some leisure service organizations pursue a combination of all three of these ends.

In formulating a service strategy, a leisure service organization should work to develop mutually beneficial relationships where both the needs of the individuals it serves and its organizational needs are met. The organization must clearly focus upon its goals and simultaneously acknowledge the needs of individuals. A mutually beneficial relationship results when an organization commits itself to the needs of the individuals it serves and consciously pursues its goals. Focusing on individual needs and organizational goals at the same time serves as the most effective way of planning, organizing, and implementing services.

In promoting life satisfaction, via leisure experiences, leisure service organizations can engage in a number of roles. Some of these include the following:

1. *Awareness Building.* Leisure service organizations can help build awareness of different leisure opportunities. Awareness building can be as simple as providing interpretive information, or as complex as assisting individuals in understanding their attitudes, value states, and other factors influencing leisure participation. Awareness building helps people discover external resources that can assist them in achieving their full potential, and it can also help them learn more about themselves.

2. *Transmission of Cultural Heritage.* Leisure service organizations play an important role in transmitting a society's culture. Games often serve to help children and youth prepare for their adult roles. Leisure activities also reinforce customs and rituals. For example, in the United States, the celebration of Kwanzaa (an African American celebration of community and life) as a ritual is done in connection with leisure events and activities. People often associate involvement in such activities with leisure pursuits.

3. *Knowledge and Skill Acquisition.* Leisure service organizations play an important role in helping individuals acquire knowledge and skills to participate in leisure; for many organizations it serves as a prime focus. Tennis classes, swim lessons, craft instruction, dance lessons, and gymnastics are just a few of the literally thousands of instructional programs that can be offered by leisure service organizations.

4. *Attitude and Character Formation.* A primary thrust of many leisure service organizations, especially those in the nonprofit private sector, is attitude and character formation. Leisure offers opportunities to teach sporting behaviors, fair play, teamwork, citizenship, social skills, and conflict resolution. Further, for the many organizations concerned with the spiritual and moral development of individuals, leisure becomes an important vehicle in which values can be shaped, molded, and influenced. It also provides opportunities for the creation of situations that foster discussion and formulation of beliefs.

5. *Fun.* Paul Haun once noted that ". . . fun is the steadfast goal of recreation, yet not its purpose" (1965, p. 18). Leisure provides a medium where people can pursue happiness and be playful, merry, joyful.

6. *Sensory Stimulation/Reduction.* Leisure also provides an opportunity for sensory stimulation or reduction. Leisure environments provide opportunities for our senses to be stimulated in terms of seeing, hearing, touching, tasting, and smelling. For example, walking on a nature trail can provide an individual with an opportunity to come into contact with new shapes, textures, sights, and smells. We can also choose to participate in leisure settings that reduce sensory stimulation and, in effect, relax us.

7. *Promotion of Social Skills/Interaction.* Many leisure activities occur in social occasions. They involve interaction among people, who often form groups. These types of leisure opportunities provide individuals with a chance to learn and practice their social skills. In addition, leisure provides opportunities for people to be with one another—to have contact with others. Perhaps it is this dimension of leisure that makes it such a powerful

component in society. People want to be with other people, and leisure provides such opportunities.

8. *Promotion of Joy in Life.* Leisure activities and opportunities are often joyful experiences. Joy is pleasure, happiness, delight, rapture, and bliss. Leisure events or celebrations create opportunities for individuals who are brought closer together to share a common time of joy.

9. *Promotion of Psychological Well-Being.* Leisure service organizations also provide and promote activities that contribute to the psychological well-being of individuals and nurture the human spirit by enhancing stability, growth, health, self-esteem, self-confidence, and feelings of competence. Leisure leaders can build the self-confidence of individuals by encouraging them, equipping them with skills they need to successfully pursue activities, and rewarding their successes. Such action can contribute strongly to the psychological well-being of participants.

10. *Promotion of Creativity.* Leisure service organizations often provide opportunities that enable individuals to express or expand their creative abilities. These organizations provide opportunities for people to test their abilities, to extend their horizons, and to make new and original contributions. To be creative means to be imaginative and inventive, and leisure is an excellent medium within which to explore one's creative potential.

11. *Providing Space for Enjoyment of Leisure.* Leisure services organizations often provide open spaces for play, reflection, contemplation, and communion and interaction with nature. Space to move openly and freely contributes to a variety of the previously mentioned factors such as psychological well-being, sensory stimulation/reduction, awareness building, and so forth. Parks, wilderness areas, and other leisure areas provide opportunities to get in touch not only with the natural environment but with ourselves.

12. *Providing Structures and Facilities for Enjoyment of Leisure.* Leisure service organizations construct and manage structures and facilities that enable the leisure experience. Theme parks, recreation centers, swimming pools, gymnasiums and fitness centers, ice rinks, bowling centers, theaters, and tennis and racquetball courts are examples of leisure structures and facilities.

Many types of leisure service organizations exist, including public agencies at the local, state, and federal levels, private nonprofit organizations, and commercial leisure service organizations. Each of these different types of organizations has unique goals, strategies for garnering resources, and different approaches to relating to their customer groupings. Some organizations emphasize more strongly one or more of the above roles, depending upon their organizational goals and values.

Edginton (2000) offers a useful framework to understand the importance of the work of leisure service organizations, as they relate to individual and community satisfaction. Using Frederick Hertzberg's "Theory of Motivation," which suggests that individual human needs can be placed on a continuum and divided into two types of needs—hygiene factors and motivators—Edginton writes:

> Hygiene factors refer to elements within the environment related to an individual's security, safety, and status. According to Hertzberg, hygiene factors do not motivate individuals. However, when they are not provided an individual becomes dissatisfied. On the other hand, motivators are factors that promote life satisfaction. The opportunity for people to achieve, have recognition, and be engaged in activities considered to be worthwhile to oneself and to society are all considered to be motivators. (p. 33)

Edginton suggests that these concepts can be applied to the opportunities that are made available by businesses, government agencies, and nonprofit organizations. Specifically, as noted in figure 1.5, Hertzberg's motivation/hygiene theory can be applied to government ser-

Parks, Recreation, Cultural Attractions, Museums, Festivals, Events, Heritage Sites, and Others

Fire, Police, Utilities, Sewage Treatment, Transportation, and Others

Hygiene Factors

Figure 1.5

Life satisfaction: What factors move people?

Data from Edginton, C. R. Community Livability: A Model for Iowa. In Edginton, C. R. (Ed.) (2000). Enhancing the Livability of Iowa Communities: The Role of Recreation, Natural Resource Development and Tourism. *Cedar Falls, IA: The University of Northern Iowa, 29–41.*

vices. As one can see, viewing the model, government services such as fire, police, utilities, sewage treatments, and transportation systems are not motivators for people. On the other hand, recreation parks, cultural attractions, museums, festivals, events, heritage sites, and others give meaning to people, promote happiness, and hence contribute to greater life satisfaction.

What Motivates People to Pursue Leisure?

Why do people pursue leisure and leisure opportunities? The answer to this inquiry may produce as many different responses as there are individuals. People pursue leisure opportunities for different reasons and with different levels of intensity, depending upon the nature of their needs, values, and attitudes at any given time. Leisure can be pursued very intensely, as an end in itself, perhaps compensating for dissatisfaction in other areas of life, such as work. On the other hand, leisure may be pursued as an expression of status in society.

Schreyer (1986), in discussing motivation for participation in outdoor recreation, says that *individuals participate in leisure because it is a desirable, inherent value.* He notes, ". . . recreation is desirable: We all do it. Its value is inherent: Try to live without it" (p. 1). Schreyer suggests that all human behavior is goal-oriented and focused on trying to meet a need or needs. Leisure behavior is merely a subcomponent of human behavior. Just as we have needs that are fulfilled in other areas of our lives, leisure fulfills a need in a particular niche of our lives.

To maintain one's existence and subsistence, a person works, sleeps, or eats. These are necessary to maintain life. During one's leisure, goal-directed activity is not necessarily focused toward life maintenance activities. Leisure provides opportunities for expanding one's physical, social, intellectual, and spiritual needs. As Schreyer notes, leisure can be ". . . a nice, superficial and irrelevant way to pass the time . . . [or, leisure] . . . can be considered as playing an instrumental role in helping individuals fully complement the quality of their existence" (1986, p. 2).

Leisure Motives

Many factors motivate individuals to pursue leisure. These factors vary from person to person, depending upon their unique personalities, lifestyles, goals, and needs. Kraus (1994) indicates that many participants pursue leisure primarily for "fun" and "enjoyment." In reporting research conducted by Angier, Kraus notes the positive relationship of fun and enjoyment to quality of life. Driver and Brown (1986) have identified numerous factors that contribute to the motivation of individuals for leisure. Table 1.2 presents a composite list of factors, grouped

TABLE

1.2 FACTORS THAT MAY MOTIVATE INDIVIDUALS TO PURSUE LEISURE

1. Enjoy Nature
   A. Scenery
   B. General Nature Experience
   C. Undeveloped Natural Area
2. Physical Fitness
3. Reduce Tension
   A. Tension Release
   B. Slow Down Mentally
   C. Escape Role Overloads
   D. Escape Daily Routine
4. Escape Noise and Crowds
   A. Tranquillity/Solitude
   B. Privacy
   C. Escape Crowds
   D. Escape Noise
   E. Isolation
5. Outdoor Learning
   A. General Learning
   B. Exploration
   C. Learn Geography of Area
   D. Learn About Nature
6. Share Similar Values
   A. Be With Friends
   B. Be With People Having Similar Values
7. Independence
   A. Independence
   B. Autonomy
   C. Being in Control
8. Family Kinship
9. Introspection
   A. Spiritual
   B. Personal Values
10. Be With Considerate People
11. Achievement Stimulation
    A. Reinforcing Self-Confidence/Self-Image
    B. Social Recognition
    C. Skill Development
    D. Competence Testing
    E. Seeking Excitement/Stimulation
    F. Self-Reliance
12. Physical Rest
13. Teach/Lead Others
    A. Teaching/Sharing Skills
    B. Leading Others
14. Risk Taking
15. Risk Reduction
    A. Risk Moderation
    B. Risk Prevention
16. Meet New People
    A. Meet New People
    B. Observe New People
17. Nostalgia

Source: Data from B. Driver and P. Brown, "Probable Personal Benefits of Outdoor Recreation" in *A Literature Review of the President's Commission on Americans Outdoors,* GPO, (1986) Washington, DC.

into seventeen leisure experience preference domains, that might motivate individuals to pursue leisure. They are focused primarily toward outdoor recreation activities.

Tinsley, Teaff, and Colb (n.d.) present eight motivations identified as important to elderly individuals in pursuing leisure: (1) self-expression, (2) companionship, (3) sense of power/control, (4) security, (5) compensation, (6) service to others, (7) stimulation, and (8) solitude. This information reveals a vast number of factors that can potentially motivate individuals to participate in leisure. Some individuals seek risk-taking opportunities, whereas others seek risk reduction. Some individuals seek tranquillity and solitude; some desire interaction with people. Still further, some individuals seek stimulation where others seek to reduce the overloads that come as a result of work or family demands. Ibrahim and Cordes (1993) suggest that experiences that are intrinsically motivating can lead to happiness.

Driver and Brown (1986) also present a taxonomy of probable personal benefits that can be gained from leisure experiences in the out-of-doors, and Ibrahim and Cordes (1993) reported similar benefits. The results also apply to indoor leisure pursuits. The following factors may be strong motivators for pursuit of leisure opportunities:

1. *Personal Development.* The nature of the leisure experience is such that much of what motivates individuals to pursue leisure is personal. Leisure experiences can contribute to building self-concept, self-actualization, self-reliance, humility, and spiritual growth. They can also provide opportunities for values clarification and introspection, leadership opportunities, aesthetic enhancement, and learning. These all may be strong motivators influencing a person to participate in a given leisure activity or program.

2. *Social Bonding.* Leisure provides opportunities to have interactional needs met. As Driver and Brown (1986) indicate, social bonding increases the social cohesiveness of personal relationships and can take place in various forms. It can occur in primary groups such as the family or in groups that have been constructed to facilitate leisure experiences, such as teams, clubs, or instructional classes.

3. *Therapeutic Healing.* We live in a world of great stress, complexity, and demands. Many individuals need to escape or recover from the pressures or problems that arise in day-to-day living. Leisure provides opportunities for temporary escape from stress of work, family, interpersonal relationships, and others. Participation in positive, constructive forms of leisure provides an excellent alternative to negative forms of escape such as substance abuse.

4. *Physical Well-Being.* Human beings have a basic need for physical activity—to engage in fine and gross motor movement—so they often seek such activity during leisure participation. In fact, most scales of leisure pursuits show that among the highest rated are those associated with fitness or physical movement. For many people, active leisure pursuits provide the only alternative to the sedentary, work-oriented behaviors of a technological/information-based society.

5. *Stimulation.* Human beings are curious by nature. They constantly seek stimulation to satisfy their desire for newness or novelty, desire for exploration, and their need to relieve boredom and anxiety. Leisure pursuits provide an excellent medium within which new forms of stimulation can be introduced and experienced—observe the variety of stimulation provided by electronic home entertainment equipment, computers, and other technological developments that are available to people during their leisure.

6. *Freedom and Independence.* Some philosophers have argued that freedom and independence are necessary to nurture the human spirit. Because most leisure activities are noncompulsory, pursued on a voluntary basis, or freely chosen, a strong element of independence and freedom exists in such pursuits. Thus, the need to be free and independent can be nurtured, encouraged, and pursued through leisure. Leisure and freedom are often thought of in synonymous terms. There are few definitions that do not include "freedom" as a component of leisure.

7. *Nostalgia.* The need for reflection or for reflecting upon one's heritage or roots appears to be basic among all humans. Leisure often provides opportunities to learn about one's historical, cultural, and family heritage. As the philosopher Eric Hoffer once noted, when humankind was first freed from toiling in the soil and had the opportunity to think and explore, the first questions asked were "Where did we come from?" and "Why are we here?"

Although Driver and Brown (1986) framed their taxonomy in terms of probable personal benefits from leisure, such benefits only hold value for the individual in direct relationship to

Under Pressure

The number of hours worked by couples has increased by more than 10% in 25 years. Combined work hours of all couples (dual and single earner).

1977	70
2002	82

Combined work hours of dual-earner couples with children:

1977	81
2002	91

Source: Families and Work Institute 2002 National Study of the Changing Workforce

Source: from Gonzalez, A. 2003. Under Pressure. *USA Today*.

Increased hours could be contributing to unhappiness on the job.

Not satisfied with their job

83%

Not happy with their work/life balance

80%

Consider themselves overworked

57%

Source: Monster's 2003 Work/Life Balance Survey of between 36,128 and 61,346 users.

---

meeting needs. Thus, one could infer that the preceding benefits listed are, in fact, elements that motivate individuals to pursue leisure.

Other motives can be categorized differently. Rolston (1986), Cheek and Burch (1976), and others have suggested additional ways of defining needs that can be met as a result of participation in leisure experiences including psychological (self-concept, confidence, self-sufficiency, sensation-seeking, actualization, well-being, personal testing), sociological (comparison, group cooperation, respect for others, communication, behavior feedback, friendship, belonging), and physical needs (fitness, skills, strength, coordination, catharsis, exercise, and balance).

Cheek and Burch (1976) have suggested that numerous social benefits, including family cohesion and social interaction, are motivators. Allen (1990) has discussed the benefits of leisure to one's satisfaction with community life. Interestingly, he suggests that the relationship between leisure and community satisfaction is unclear and that there is a need for stronger theoretical and methodological procedures to help accurately reflect this dimension.

In discussing motives for participation in the natural environment, Rolston (1986) believes that outdoor recreational activities provide an extra dimension that indoor leisure activities do not. He notes, "one touched base with something greater . . ." (p. 9). He suggests that life support, aesthetics, natural history, philosophical, religious, scientific, and other topics can all be pursued in leisure experiences in the out-of-doors, a location that also enhances participation. Discussing philosophical and religious benefits in outdoor recreation experiences, he notes the following:

> Nature generates poetry, philosophy and religion and at its deepest educational capacity, Americans are awed and humbled by staring into the stormy surf or the midnight sky, by overlooking the canyon lands or by an overflight of migrating geese. If we must put it so, nature is a philosophical resource, as well as a scientific, recreational, aesthetic or economic one. Encounter with nature is the cradle of spirituality. The significance of nature is one of the richest assignments of the mind, and this requires

The Right to Risk

If we are to have any chance at happiness in this uncertain world, we must learn to embrace its insecurities, to give in to change, to celebrate the present moment. To do otherwise is to do battle with ourselves. We are as a wave moving forward to a distant shore. No matter how turbulent the sea, no matter how strong the urge to return to port, there is no turning back. Our happiness rests in our recognition of this fact of life and in our subsequent determination to enjoy the ride.

The notion, then, that we human beings have "a right to risk" is misleading. We have no choice in the matter. There is nothing but risk. What we do have a choice in, however, is the way we deal with risks. We can delude ourselves, hide behind our fears, and pretend it just isn't so. Or we can confront the risks, announce our fears, and give it a go.

Source: Dustin, *The Wilderness Within*, p. 5, 1993.

detection, imagination, participation and decision. The great outdoors works on . . . [the] soul as well as the muscles and the body. (Rolston, 1986, p.109)

Rolston's point is important in terms of understanding those factors that motivate individuals to participate in leisure. The wellspring of motivation occurs not only as a result of physical needs or even social needs, but also *spiritual needs*.

One's desire to participate in leisure may be either intrinsically or extrinsically driven, although most definitions of leisure suggest that leisure is pursued for its intrinsic rather than extrinsic value. Proposing a model to measure the individual differences in intrinsic motivation, Weissinger and Bandalos (1995) have identified the following components that contribute to an individual's motivation disposition:

- **Self determination.** Self determination is characterized by awareness of internal needs, a strong desire to make free choices based on these needs. Persons high in this intrinsic motivation component usually want to feel in control of their leisure behavior and display a high degree of willfulness.
- **Competence.** Competence is characterized by attention to feedback that provides information about effectiveness, ability, and skill. Persons high in this intrinsic motivation component tend to seek out leisure behaviors that convey feedback about competence.
- **Commitment.** Commitment is characterized by a tendency toward deep involvement in, rather than detachment from, leisure behaviors. Persons high in this intrinsic motivation component tend to value leisure behaviors and feel dedicated to leisure in their lives.
- **Challenge.** Challenge is characterized by a tendency toward seeking leisure experiences that stretch one's limits and provide novel stimuli. Persons high in this intrinsic motivation component tend to select leisure behaviors that slightly exceed their skills and should perceive this state as challenging rather than adverse or threatening.

It is evident, in reviewing the literature, that a variety of factors can and do influence an individual's motivation to participate in a given leisure experience. For example, according to Ewert (1993) the outcomes of a leisure experience—that is, perception of success or failure—may impact on the individual's perception of underlying motives of participation in retrospect. He reports that climbers who failed to reach the goal of their climb placed higher levels of importance on disengagement, photography, wilderness, and scenery, whereas climbers who did reach the goal of their climb reported higher levels of importance for exhilaration, risk, and recognition.

Bergin (1992) studied the relationship between leisure activity, motivation, and academic achievement in high school students. This researcher found that leisure activity is a predictor of high school achievement and further notes that an in-school experience can be a motivating factor for continuing leisure interests outside of the school environment. Clough, Shepherd, and Maughan (1990) studied motives for participation in recreational running. Using six motivational categories—well-being, social, challenge, status, fitness/health, and addiction—they found that the prime motivations for running were challenge, health/fitness, and well-being.

Constraints to Leisure

If a major goal of leisure service professionals is to provide opportunities for satisfying life experiences, then it is necessary to recognize the constraints that prevent individuals from attaining satisfaction from and through their leisure. Constraints, those factors that intervene between the preference for an activity and participation in it (Henderson, Bialeschki, Shaw, and Freysinger, 1989, 1996), can come from many sources. Some constraints exist as a result of perceptions that individuals hold. For example, a perceived lack of the skill necessary to engage in a particular leisure activity may result in a constraint. Constraints may also be organizational in nature; programs and services provided by an agency may not be offered at a convenient time or location. As Kay and Jackson (1991, p. 32) write, ". . . for many providers, low participation levels among certain population subgroupings have long been regarded as self-evident proof of the existence of constraints which their organization should try to reduce." Environmental constraints relate to structural constraints within areas and facilities or the inaccessibility of natural areas.

Ellis and Rademacher define a constraint to leisure as ". . . *any factor which precludes or limits an individual's frequency, intensity, duration or quality of participation in recreation activities*" (1986, p. 33). The term "constraint" has been defined by Jackson (1988, p. 69) as ". . . a subset of reasons for not engaging in a particular behavior." He maintains that the term "constraint" is more appropriately used than that of "barrier." Edginton, Hudson, Dieser, and Edginton (2004) have discussed the difference between constraints and barriers. They point out that individuals often see these terms as being synonymous. They write, "Whereas a leisure barrier presupposes that people have an interest in participating in a leisure activity but are blocked by doing so, a leisure constraint acts to limit interest in a leisure activity itself." (2004 p. 477) Jackson (1988, p. 203) notes that "the commonly-used word 'barriers' fails to capture the entire range of reasons for behaviors such as leisure nonparticipation, ceasing participation, etc." These factors can prevent individuals from successfully engaging in leisure experiences. Constraints include obstacles, limitations, impediments, restrictions, and other factors placed in front of individuals either by themselves or by the culture, society, or environment. These constraints prevent people from engaging in satisfying leisure experiences.

Constraints are not to be confused with limits that ensure order, safety, and stability, although some view many of society's rules and regulations as constraints to their freedom in leisure. For example, regulations limiting where people can use skateboards or in-line skates in public areas were likely developed for safety of pedestrians; to some avid in-line skaters, however, the restrictions appear to have been written simply to ruin their fun.

Freedom is usually considered a necessary part of the leisure experience. To facilitate freedom of thought, choice, and participation, it becomes necessary to understand the constraints that prevent people from successfully participating in leisure. Some of these constraints can be minimized or eliminated by the leisure professional; those constraints related to an individual participant's frame of reference are more difficult to influence or remove.

Jackson (1990) suggests two categories of constraints that can influence one's leisure participation. *Antecedent constraints* interfere or impact upon one's preferences for certain leisure activities. For instance, Kelly and Godbey (1992) interviewed older African Americans whose engagement in water-based activities (swimming and boating) was limited. Analysis indicated that during their childhood, neighborhood pools had been closed to children of color, resulting in an avoidance of water-based recreation for those interviewed and their children. Antecedent constraints might include incomplete knowledge of recreation and leisure opportunities, personal beliefs about entitlement to leisure, and "buying into" socially imposed gender roles.

Intervening constraints come between a preference for an activity and actual participation in it. Intervening constraints might include availability of recreation facilities, hours of operation, the ability to afford entrance and user fees, and safety of facilities. A number of authors have identified commonalties represented in a variety of studies conducted to identify constraints to leisure. Crawford, Jackson, and Godbey (1991) also have proposed categories of constraints. They have identified three types including intrapersonal, interpersonal, and structural. According to these authors, *intrapersonal constraints* represent psychological factors that arise internally in an individual (e.g., attitude, personality, moods). *Interpersonal constraints* arise out of interactions with other people or circumstances (e.g., family members, friends, community members). *Structural constraints* are external factors in the environment (e.g., inaccessible buildings, cost of activities, lack of community infrastructure). In particular, Jackson (1993) and Hultsman (1995) identify six commonalties often associated with constraints to leisure participation as noted in various research studies. These include accessibility, social isolation, personal reasons, costs, time commitments, and facilities. Table 1.3 presents each of the six dimensions with descriptors to help define each of these terms.

According to Jackson (2000), the study of leisure constraints is important for a number of reasons. These are as follows:

- Barriers or obstacles exist to achieving a meaningful quality of life on both an individual and a societal basis.
- Access to and enjoyment of leisure are central to a high quality of life for individuals, and indirectly related to the quality of the society as a whole; therefore, leisure can play an important part in removing or alleviating these barriers.
- A wide range of barriers also may preclude people from achieving their leisure goals and realizing the full benefits of a high quality of leisure.
- Understanding the distribution of constraints in society, how they affect people's lives and leisure, and how people adapt to these constraints is a crucial task for leisure researchers.

Numerous studies have focused on leisure constraints. A number of these, according to Jackson, have offered theoretical propositions and provided information regarding their practical implications (Goodale and Witt, 1989; Jackson, 1988, 1991; Jackson and Scott, 1999; McGuire and O'Leary, 1992; Searle and Jackson, 1985). Others have discussed the impact of constraints on individuals' lives (Crawford, Jackson, and Godbey, 1991; Henderson and Bialeschki, 1993; Jackson, Crawford, and Godbey, 1993). Sylvester, Voelkl, and Ellis (2002, p. 227–231), using the term *barriers,* have discussed implications with persons with disabilities. Building on the work of Scleien, Ray, and Green (1997, p. 52), they note that there are two

TABLE

1.3   CONSTRAINTS COMPRISING SIX IDENTIFIABLE DIMENSIONS

Dimension	Constraints
Accessibility	Cost of transportation
	Lack of transportation
	No opportunity to participate near home
Social Isolation	Lack of knowledge about where to participate
	Difficulty in finding others with whom to participate
Personal Reasons	Lack of necessary skills
	Physically unable to participate
	Requires too much self-discipline
	Low energy level
	Lost interest in participating
Costs	Cost of equipment, materials, supplies
	Admission, rental fees, other charges for facilities or programs
Time Commitments	Work commitments
	Family commitments
	Lack of time due to other leisure activities
Facilities	Overcrowded recreation facilities or areas
	Recreation facilities/areas poorly maintained

From W. Hultsman, "Recognizing Patterns of Leisure Constraints: An Extension of the Exploration of Dimensionality" in *Journal of Leisure Research, 27*(3), p. 229, 1995. Reprinted by permission of National Park and Recreation Association, Alexandria, VA.

classes of barriers: external and internal. External barriers include financial constraints, lack of qualified staff, lack of transportation, inaccessible facilities, poor communication, ineffective service systems, and negative attitudes. Internal barriers include skill limitations, dependence, health and fitness, and lack of knowledge.

Jackson (2000) effectively summarizes the following patterns regarding leisure constraints that have emerged over the past two decades from the studies just mentioned:

- Allowing for variations in the number, range, and content of the items included in a given study, a reasonably stable and replicable set of constraints "dimensions" has consistently emerged from a variety of studies. These dimensions typically include constraints related to the costs of participating, time commitments, the availability and quality of facilities, isolation (sometimes subdivided into social isolation and geographical isolation), and personal skills and abilities.
- No constraint is experienced with equal intensity by everyone, although time- and cost-related constraints rank among the most widely and intensely experienced inhibitors of the achievement of leisure goals and a balanced lifestyle.
- The experience of constraints varies among individuals and groups: no subgroup of the population is entirely free from constraints, and each group is characterized not only by varying intensities of the experience of each type of constraint, but also by a unique combination of constraints. Thus, young people, relatively less constrained by time, are typically affected in their leisure by a lack of partners, opportunities, and costs. The

transition to middle adulthood sees a decline in these types of constraints but a marked increase in time commitments, largely due to family and employment circumstances. Time- and cost-related constraints may decline in older adulthood, but problems of skills and isolation may become increasingly important.

- In addition to age, the effects of constraints are modified by other personal and social factors, such as family size and structure, gender, income, ethnicity, and race (Jackson and Rucks, 1995; Phillips, 1995; Scott and Munson, 1994; Stodolska, 1998).

Recently there has been a criticism of the leisure constraint research. Samdahl and Jekubovich (1997) have suggested that although this area of study was originally conceptualized as a way of understanding barriers to activity participation as well as helping professionals to understand the broader factors and influences that shape people's everyday leisure behaviors, research activities have stopped painfully short of a full explanation. As these authors explain, ". . . there is nothing in the constraints' theory to explain *why* some situations were viewed as constraints, or *why* some people were motivated to negotiate those constraints" (p. 49).

Summary

Leisure has been a means to promote greater life satisfaction throughout the history of humankind. In the last 100 years, leisure has increased in importance and value to society. Not only have we seen a rise in the amount of free time available to people, but we have also witnessed a qualitative and a quantitative growth of leisure programs and services. Leisure has become an important force, shaping not only individual values, but also collectively the values of U.S. and Canadian societies as a whole.

Life satisfaction and well-being are often linked to happiness and quality of life. Leisure and the presence of leisure opportunities have also been linked to life satisfaction and often identified as *flow*. Flow is the experience of matching skill with the challenges of the activity; it is reported as a natural "high." Nearly all studies report a positive relationship between leisure and life satisfaction. Life satisfaction and leisure are also related to community well-being, with leisure being an important factor when predicting community satisfaction.

Organizations providing leisure services play an important role in contributing to the life satisfaction of individuals. Not only do they serve those individuals toward whom their services are directed, but they often work actively to shape or mold the character of individuals and/or society. Leisure service organizations can be involved in a number of roles, including awareness building, transmission of cultural heritage, knowledge and skill acquisition, attitude and character formulation, fun, sensory stimulation/reduction, promotion of social skills/interaction, promotion of joy, promotion of psychological well-being, promotion of creativity, and provision of space as well as provision of structures and facilities for leisure.

A myriad of factors motivates individuals to participate in leisure. Leisure appears to be a desirable and inherent value. Reasons people pursue leisure, however, vary from individual to individual, community to community, and region to region. Some of the probable personal benefits from leisure include personal development, social bonding, therapeutic healing, mental and physical well-being, stimulation, freedom and independence, and nostalgia.

One of the major functions of any leisure service organization is to remove constraints to leisure—factors that preclude or limit an individual from participating satisfactorily in a leisure activity, event, program, or service. Constraints may be individual, cultural, or environmental. Some common constraints include lack of knowledge, previous negative experiences, work commitments, and socially imposed roles. Constraints often are greatly affected by demographic variables. For example, working married women with families may experience greater constraints to leisure than other groupings do within the population.

Discussion Questions

1. How does leisure relate to life satisfaction and well-being?
2. What does it mean to be in the life satisfaction business?
3. How do generational differences impact upon leisure value states, attitudes, and behaviors?
4. What is your generation's view of leisure versus that of your parents, grandparents, or great grandparents?
5. What does life satisfaction mean?
6. What motivates people to participate in leisure activities?
7. What benefits can result from leisure experience?
8. What roles do leisure service organizations play in the delivery of leisure services?
9. How do these organizational roles contribute to the life satisfaction and well-being of individuals?
10. Identify and provide examples of several constraints to leisure.

References

Allen, L. R. 1990. Benefits of leisure attributes to community satisfaction. *Journal of Leisure Research 22*(2), 183–196.

Allen, L. R., and R. Beattie. 1984. The role of leisure as an indicator of overall satisfaction with community life. *Journal of Leisure Research 16*(2), 99–109.

Bammell, G., and L. Burris-Bammel. 1996. *Leisure and Human Behavior.* Madison, WI: Brown & Benchmark.

Bergermaier, R., I. Borg, and J. Champoux. 1984. Structural relationships among facets of work, nonwork, and general well-being. *Work and Occupations 11*(2), 163–181.

Bergin, D. A. 1992. Leisure activity, motivation, and academic achievement in high school students. *Journal of Leisure Research 24*(3), 225–239.

Brown, K. A., and C. Cashel. 1995. Female elementary school teachers' job satisfaction, perceived amount of leisure, and leisure satisfaction. *Abstracts from the 1995 Symposium on Research Leisure 104.*

Bryce, J., and Haworth, J. 2002. Wellbeing and flow in sample of male and female office workers. *Leisure studies 21*(3/4), 201–220.

Burns, J. M. 2003. *Transforming Leadership: A New Pursuit of Happiness.* New York: Grove Press.

Cheek, N. H., and W. R. Burch. 1976. *The Social Organization of Leisure in Human Society.* New York: Harper and Row.

Clough, P., J. Shepherd, and R. Maughan. 1990. Motives for participation in recreational running. *Journal of Leisure Research 21*(4), 297–309.

Crawford, D. W., E. L. Jackson, and G. Godbey. 1991. A hierarchical model of leisure constraints. *Leisure Sciences 13*, 309–320.

Csikszentmihalyi, M. 1990. *Flow: The Psychology of Optimal Experience.* New York: HarperCollins.

Cutler, S., and J. Hendricks. 1990. Leisure and time use across the life course. Edited by R. Binstock and L. George, in *Handbook of Aging and the Social Sciences.* New York: Academic Press.

Davidson, J. "Overworked Americans or Overwhelmed Americans?" *Public Management,* May, 1993.

Diener, E. 1984. Subjective well-being. *Psychological Bulletin 95*(3), 543.

Diener, E. 2000. Subjective well-being: The science of happiness and a proposal for a national index. *American Psychologist 55*(1), 34–43.

Driver, B., and P. Brown. 1986. Probable personal benefits of outdoor recreation. In *A Literature Review of the President's Commission on Americans Outdoors,* Values, 63–70. Washington, DC: U.S. Government Printing Office.

Dustin, *The Wilderness Within,* Champaign, IL. Sagamore. p. 5, 1993.

Edginton C. R., Hudson, S. D., Dieser, R. B., & Edginton S. 2004. *Leisure Programming.* Boston: McGraw-Hill.

Edginton, C. R. 2000. Community livability: A model for Iowa. Edited by C. R. Edginton, in *Enhancing the Livability of Iowa Communities: The Role of Recreation, Natural Resource Development and Tourism,* 29–41. Cedar Falls, IA: The University of Northern Iowa.

Ellis, G., and C. Rademacher. 1986. Barriers to recreation participation. In *A Literature Review of the President's Commission on Americans Outdoors,* Motivations, 33–50. Washington, DC: U.S. Government Printing Office.

Ellis, M. J., C. R. Edginton, and D. R. Howard. 1985. *Lifestyle and Health Promotion.* Academy of Leisure Sciences, Dallas, TX.

Ewert, A. 1993. Differences in the level of motivation based on trip outcome, experience level and group type. *Journal of Leisure Research 25*(4), 335–349.

Florida, R. 2002. *The Rise of the Creative Class.* New York: Basic Books.

Godbey, G. 1986. Societal trends and the impact on recreation and leisure. In *A Literature Review of the President's Commission on Americans Outdoors,* Demand, 1–8. Washington, DC: U.S. Government Printing Office.

Goodale, T. L., and P. A. Witt. 1989. Recreation non-participation and barriers to leisure. Edited by E. L. Jackson and T. L. Burton, in *Understanding Leisure and Recreation: Mapping the Past, Charting the Future* (421–449). State College, PA: Venture Publishing.

Gordon, C., C. Gaitz, and J. Scott. 1976. Leisure and lives: Personal expressivity across the life span. Edited by R. Binstock and E. Shanas, in *Handbook of Aging and the Social Sciences,* 310–341. New York: Van Nostrand-Reinhold Co.

Harper, W., and J. Hultsman. 1994. Whaling away at leisure. *Schole 9,* 41–52.

Haun, P. 1965. *Recreation: A Medical Viewpoint.* New York: Teacher's College Press.

Henderson, K. A., and M. D. Bialeschki. 1993. Exploring an expanded model of women's leisure constraints. *Journal of Applied Recreation Research 18,* 229–252.

Henderson, K., D. Bialeschki, S. Shaw, and V. Freysinger. 1989. *A Leisure of One's Own: A Feminist Perspective on Women's Leisure.* State College, PA: Venture Publishing.

Henderson, K., D. Bialeschki, S. Shaw, and V. Freysinger. 1996. *Both Gains and Gaps: Feminist Perspectives on Women's Leisure.* State College, PA: Venture Publishing.

Hill, J. M. 2002. Finding flow in postsecondary teaching. *Schole: a journal of leisure studies and recreation education,* 125–143.

Hull, R. B. 1990. Mood as a product of leisure: Causes and consequences. *Journal of Leisure Research 22*(2), 99–111.

Hull, R. B., W. P. Stewart, and Y. K. Yi. 1992. Experience patterns: Capturing the dynamic nature of a recreation experience. *Journal of Leisure Research 24*(3), 240–252.

Hultsman, W. 1995. Recognizing patterns of leisure constraints: An extension of the exploration of dimensionality. *Journal of Leisure Research 27*(3), 228–244.

Ibrahim, H., and K. Cordes. 1993. *Outdoor Recreation.* Dubuque, IA: Brown & Benchmark.

Inglehart, R. 1989. *Culture Shift in Advanced Industrial Society.* Princeton, NJ: Princeton University Press.

Iso-Ahola, S. 1980. *The Social Psychology of Leisure and Recreation.* Dubuque, IA: Wm. C. Brown.

Jackson, E. L. 1988. Leisure constraints: A survey of past research. *Leisure Sciences 10,* 203–215.

Jackson, E. L. 1990. Variations in the desire to begin a leisure activity: Evidence of antecedent constraints? *Journal of Leisure Research 22,* 55–70.

Jackson, E. L. 1991. Leisure constraints/constrained leisure: Special issue introduction. *Journal of Leisure Research 23,* 279–285, and *Leisure Sciences 13,* 273–278.

Jackson, E. L. 1993. Recognizing patterns of leisure constraints: Results from alternative analyses. *Journal of Leisure Research 25,* 129–149.

Jackson, E. L. 2000. Will research on leisure constraints still be relevant in the twenty-first century? *Journal of Leisure Research 32*(1), 62–68.

Jackson, E. L., D. W. Crawford, and G. Godbey. 1993. Negotiation of leisure constraints. *Leisure Sciences 15,* 1–11.

Jackson, E. L., and V. C. Rucks. 1995. Negotiation and leisure constraints by junior high and high school students: An exploratory study. *Journal of Leisure Research 27*(1), 85–105.

Jackson, E. L., and Scott, D. (1999). Constraints to leisure. Edited by E. L. Jackson and T. L. Burton, in *Leisure Studies: Prospects for the Twenty-First Century,* 299–321. State College, PA: Venture Publishing.

Kay, T., and G. Jackson. 1991. Leisure despite constraint: The impact of leisure constraints on leisure participation. *Journal of Leisure Research 23*(4), 301–313.

Kelly, J. R. 1996. *Leisure.* 3rd ed. Boston: Allyn and Bacon.

Kelly, J. R., and G. Godbey. 1992. *Sociology of Leisure.* State College, PA: Venture.

Kelly, J. R., M. Steinkamp, and J. Kelly. 1987. Later life satisfaction: Does leisure contribute? *Leisure Sciences 9,* 187–200.

Kim, M. S. 2000. Life satisfaction, acculturation, and leisure participation among older urban Korean immigrants. *World leisure journal, 42*(2), 28.

Kraus, R. 1990. *Recreation and Leisure in Modern Society.* 4th ed. New York: HarperCollins.

Kraus, R. 1994. *Leisure in a Changing America.* New York: Macmillan.

Leitner, M. J., and S. F. Leitner. 1996. *Leisure Enhancement.* 2nd ed. New York: Haworth.

Lobo, F. 2001. The work-leisure paradigm: changing relationships and challenges for service delivery. *Journal of the International Council for Health, Physical Education, Recreation, Sport, and Dance 37*(1), 36–41.

McGuire, F. A., and J. T. O'Leary. 1992. The implications of leisure constraint research for the delivery of leisure services. *Journal of Park and Recreation Administration 10,* 31–40.

Mobily K., J. Lemke, L. Ostiguy, R. Woodard, T. Griffee, and C. Pickens. 1993. Leisure repertoire in a sample of midwestern elderly: The case for exercise. *Journal of Leisure Research 25*(1), 84–99.

Myers, D. G. 2000. The funds, friends, and faith of happy people. *American Psychologist 55*(1), 56–67.

Patterson, M. E. 2000. Philosophy of science and leisure research. *Journal of Leisure Research 32*(1), 106–110.

Phillips, S. F. 1995. Race and leisure constraints. *Leisure Sciences 17,* 109–120.

Pierce, R. 1980. Dimensions of leisure I: Satisfactions. *Journal of Leisure Research 12*(1), 5–19.

Reich, J., and A. Zautra. 1983. Demands and desires in daily life: Some influences on well-being. *American Journal of Community Psychology 11*(1), 43.

Riddick, C. 1985. Life satisfaction determinants of older males and females. *Leisure Sciences 7*(1), 47–63.

Riddick, C. 1986. Leisure satisfaction precursors. *Journal of Leisure Research 18*(4), 259–265.

Rolston, H. 1986. Beyond recreational value: The greater outdoors preservation related and environmental benefits. In *A Literature Review of the President's Commission on Americans Outdoors,* Values, 103–113. Washington, DC: U.S. Government Printing Office.

Russell, R. V. 1996. Pastimes: *The Context of Contemporary Leisure.* Madison, WI: Brown & Benchmark.

Samdahl, D. M., and N. J. Jekubovich. 1997. A critique of leisure constraints: Comparative analyses and understandings. *Journal of Leisure Research 29*(4), 430–452.

Schleien, S., Ray, M., and Green, F. 1997. *Community recreation and people with disabilities: Strategies for inclusion.* 2nd ed. Baltimore, MD: Paul H. Brookes.

Schreyer, R. 1986. Motivation for participation in outdoor recreation and barriers to that participation. In *A Literature Review of the President's Commission on Americans Outdoors,* Motivation, 1–8. Washington, DC: U.S. Government Printing Office.

Scott, D., and W. Munson. 1994. Perceived constraints to park usage among individuals with low incomes. *Journal of Park and Recreation Administration 12*(4), 79–96.

Searle, M. S., and E. L. Jackson. 1985. Recreation non-participation and barriers to participation: Considerations for the management of recreation delivery systems. *Journal of Park and Recreation Administration 3,* 23–26.

Seligman, M. E. P. (2002). Authentic happiness. New York: Free Press.

Shichman, S., and E. Cooper. 1984. Life satisfaction and sex role concept. *Sex Roles 11*(3/4), 227–240.

Siegenthaler, K. L., and O'Dell, I. 1997. Comparison of leisure attitude, leisure satisfaction and perceived freedom in leisure over the lifespan. *Abstracts from the 1997 Symposium on Leisure Research.*

Sneegas, J. 1986. Components of life satisfaction in middle and later life adults: Perceived social competence, leisure participation and leisure satisfaction. *Journal of Leisure Research 18*(4), 248–258.

Stodolska, M. 1998. Assimilation and leisure constraints: Dynamics of constraints in leisure immigrant populations. *Journal of Leisure Research, 30* (4), 521–555.

Sylvester, C., Voelkl, J., and Ellis G. 2001. *Therapeutic Recreation Programming: Theory and Practice.* State College, PA: Venture.

Tinsley, H., J. Teaff, and S. Colb. n.d. *The Need Satisfying Properties of Leisure Activities for the Elderly.* Southern Illinois University and Andrus Foundation.

United Way of America. 1992. *What Lies Ahead: A Decade of Decision.* Alexandria, VA: United Way Strategic Institute.

Weisse, C. S. 1992. Depression and immunocompetence: A review of the literature. *Psychological Bulletin 111,* 475–489.

Weissinger, E., and D. L. Bandalos. 1995. Development, reliability and validity of a scale to measure intrinsic motivation in leisure. *Journal of Leisure Research 27*(4), 379–400.

Wilson, W. 1967. Correlates of avowed happiness. *Psychological Bulletin 67,* 294–306.

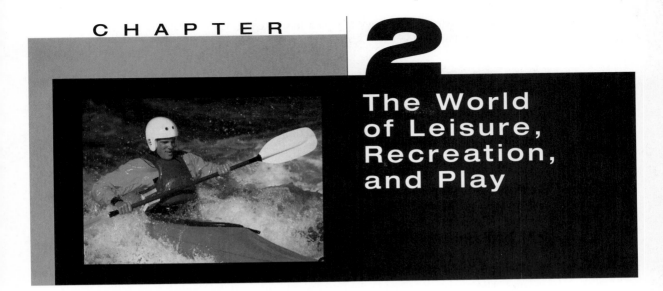

C H A P T E R 2

The World of Leisure, Recreation, and Play

Introduction

Leisure and life satisfaction are inextricably linked, yet their terminology is often difficult to define. Leisure, recreation, and play are difficult to define and measure because their meanings vary from individual to individual, community to community, and culture to culture. What constitutes leisure to one individual may not be the same to another. Furthermore, different communities perceive leisure in different ways, and terms may be culturally defined. For example, in the United States, leisure is usually associated with free time and often may be viewed as a commodity that is consumed. In India, adult leisure is reserved for special occasions such as birth, marriage, and religious festivals, while in old communist Soviet Union, leisure was heavily controlled and viewed as ". . . time in which one regenerates for the real purpose of life—work" (Ibrahim, 1991, p. 111). In other countries, the language often offers no equivalent word for leisure. Rather, terms such as sport and culture, and recreation and sport are used to describe much of what North Americans view as leisure.

Why is it necessary to define these terms? Developing definitions and ways of measuring leisure, recreation, and play helps both the practicing leisure professional and those who study the leisure phenomenon. By defining and measuring these terms, we can more accurately predict the consequences and actions of our work as leisure professionals. As Edginton and Rossman (1988, p. viii) state, terms, definitions, and theories help leisure professionals ". . . understand our roles and responsibilities in providing service . . . [and] . . . help us define, explain, control, and ultimately predict the consequences of our intervention as professionals." The leisure professional can more accurately predict specific leisure benefits and deploy resources more effectively when terms are understood.

This chapter offers several definitions of leisure, recreation, and play. In addition, some of the more contemporary theories of leisure, recreation, and play will be presented. A discussion of how people make leisure choices and what people do in their leisure time will be included.

Finally, a discussion of the ways in which leisure contributes to various factors in our culture and society will be explored.

What Is Leisure?

Leisure is an elusive term—the meaning of which has been pursued by individuals for centuries. In ancient cultures, leisure was often viewed as the opposite of physical labor. Leisure provided the opportunity for individuals to think, to develop their spirituality, and to improve their physical culture. It was subject to the work rhythm of the seasons and was a way of freeing oneself from the toil of physical labor. It was viewed as a desired state of being and as a way of advancing civilization through intellectual, contemplative, and aesthetic activities. We now know leisure to be a component of lifestyle, another elusive concept in our search for life quality (Russell 2005).

In Chapter 1, we have defined leisure as a multidimensional construct in which one feels relatively free from constraints, has a feeling of positive effect, is motivated by internal forces, and allows the exercise of perceived competence. The term *leisure* is derived from the Latin word *licere,* to be free. The Greeks used the terms *scol, schole,* or *skole* to define leisure. These terms resulted in the Latin word *scola* and the English term *school. Schole,* according to Dare, Welton, and Coe (1998), can be thought of as a state or condition of being free from work. Barker (1946) has noted that the Greeks identified *schole* as an activity and differentiated the concept from work (occupation), recreation, and amusement. Barker wrote that *schole*

> is, therefore, contrasted not with activity, but with "occupation" (*ascholia*)—in other words with the sort of activity which is pursued not for its own sake (as the activity of leisure is), but for the sake of something else . . . it is also contrasted with, or distinguished from, "recreation" (*anapausis*) and "amusement" (*paidia*—"the sort of thing children do"). Amusement and recreation mean rest after occupation, and preparation for new occupation: they are thus both essentially connected with the idea of occupation. Leisure stands by itself, in its own independent right. Aristotle thus operates with three different notions; the notion of leisure; the notion of occupation; and the notion (in one sense intermediate between the two, but in another sense closer to the latter) of amusement and recreation. (pp. 323–324)

It wasn't until the 1940s that we began to see the term leisure used in American Society (Cordes and Ibrahim, 2003). The evolution of this term has led us to view leisure as a way of bringing balance into one's life. Leisure is sought not only for the opportunity for relaxation, self-improvement, and cultural and family stability and interaction, but also for escape, novelty, complexity, adventure, excitement, and fantasy. In many societies, people use leisure as a way of counterbalancing stresses that result from living and working in a technologically oriented, competitive, rapidly changing society that requires attention to a high degree of stimulation in the form of information, media communications, and human interaction. Leisure has become many different things to different individuals. A definition of leisure often eludes agreement among leisure professionals and researchers even today.

Factors Related to a Satisfying Leisure Experience

In the past several decades, researchers studying leisure, such as Ellis (1973), Neulinger (1974, 1981), Csikszentmihalyi (1975), Iso-Ahola (1999), Kelly (1982), Unger (1984), Shaw (1985), Kleiber, Larson, and Csikszentmihalyi (1986), Gunter (1987), Samdahl (1988, 1991), Lee and Shafer (2002), and Pavelka (2002) have identified a number of factors that help to identify and

Leisure and Culture

Benjamin Franklin (1784) once related an experience he had concerning how different cultures value different behaviors as follows:

At the treaty of Lancaster in Pennsylvania, anno 1744, between the Government of Virginia and the Six Nations, the commissioners from Virginia acquainted the Indians by a speech, that there was at Williamsburg a college with a fund for the education of Indian youth and that if the chiefs of the Six Nations would send down half a dozen of their sons to that college, the government would take care that they be well provided for, and instructed in all the learning of the white people.

The Indians' spokesperson replied thus:

. . . We are convinced . . . that you mean to do us good by your proposal and we thank you heartily. But you, who are wise, must know that different nations have different conceptions of things; and you will not therefore take it amiss, if our ideas of this kind of education happens not to be the same with yours. We have had some experience of it; several of our young people were formerly brought up at the colleges of northern provinces; they were instructed in all your sciences; but, when they came back to us, they were bad runners, ignorant of every means of living in the woods, unable to bear either cold or hunger, knew neither how to build a cabin, take a deer, nor kill an enemy, spoke our language imperfectly, were therefore neither fit for hunters, warriors, nor counselors; they were totally good for nothing.

We are however not the less obligated by your offer, though we decline accepting it; and, to show our grateful sense of it, if the gentlemen of Virginia will send us a dozen of their sons, we will take care of their education, instruct them in all we know, and make men of them.

define the leisure experience. Some of these were touched upon in Chapter 1. A brief discussion of the four prevailing factors used to define the leisure experience—freedom, perceived competence, intrinsic motivation, and positive affect—follows:

Freedom. The term *freedom,* or *perceived freedom,* is often used synonymously with the term *leisure.* Freedom implies that individuals have choice or perceive they have choice in the pursuit of a leisure experience. Freedom also suggests that an individual is free of the obligations that might arise from family, work, or home activities or of the constraints that may inhibit participation or involvement. Freedom is an abstraction that has been pursued by humankind consistently throughout history. To be free means to be able to act without the interference or control of another, to choose or to act in accordance with one's own will. Freedom also often implies the absence of external constraints or compulsions on an individual to act in a prescribed manner.

Perceived Competence. Perceived competence refers to the skills an individual believes he or she possesses that, in turn, relate to satisfying participation in leisure experiences. In other words, the perception of having skills and abilities necessary to successful participation leads to a satisfying leisure experience. It can be frustrating, anxiety-producing, or discouraging not to possess the required skills and abilities necessary to participate successfully in a leisure experience. Lack of skills, or lack of confidence in one's skills, can serve as a major constraint to participation or to fulfilling participation. For a successful leisure experience to occur, individuals must perceive themselves to have a degree of competence commensurate with the challenges of the intended leisure experience. This matching of skills and challenges is necessary for satisfying experiences. Whether or not this perception of competence is accurate or reality-based is irrelevant; the person's perception of competence while engaged in the experience is essential.

Intrinsic Motivation. A number of researchers have postulated that the leisure experience must be intrinsically satisfying and/or participation in leisure experiences must be intrinsically motivating. In other words, involvement in leisure pursuits often occurs because participants are moved from within and not because they are influenced by external factors. Lee and Shafer (2002) note that intrinsic motivation is a major dimension of leisure. This motivation from within results in personal feelings of satisfaction, enjoyment, and gratification. In addition, intrinsic motivation is directly related to perceived competence. Iso-Ahola (1999) has noted, "People seek out activities that are likely to provide intrinsic rewards, of which a sense of competence is the most important" (p. 39).

Often, motivation by external factors reduces perceived freedom and, as a result, affects leisure participation. The engrossment or commitment that comes from being internally motivated and/or deriving internal satisfaction from a leisure experience is far more powerful than participation that results from external factors. Csikszentmihalyi (1975, 1990) refers to the concept of being totally engrossed in a leisure experience—where one's actions and intellect are completely synchronized—as "flow," or the "autotelic" experience. This level of engrossment, according to Csikszentmihalyi, produces its own reward and reinforcement.

Positive Affect. The fourth leisure-defining factor, the concept of positive affect, refers to the feelings individuals experience when they have some control or influence within the leisure process. This is sometimes referred to as a sense of choice, or self-determination (Iso-Ahola, 1999). This does not mean that individuals must be actively involved in planning or organizing the experience, but they must feel some degree of control as the experience unfolds.

Leisure professionals, when organizing programs and services, often plan for this type of input to occur by allowing freedom within structure. Programmers provide the participant with an opportunity to make decisions about some aspects of the experience by providing alternatives and choices. The leisure experience is dynamic; it is not static. Individuals play an important role in shaping the experience as they interact within an event, facility, or natural setting. Positive affect is produced by enhancing an individual's opportunity to ". . . play an active role in organizing their leisure experiences" (Rossman, 1988, p. 5).

All of the preceding variables are interrelated; they have in common an element of control. The greater the degree to which an individual perceives personal control in terms of feeling confident, shaping the leisure experience, feeling free from constraints and obligations, and feeling that the experience has personal relevance and meaning, the more satisfying and fulfilling the leisure experience. If an individual is not constrained and can participate in an activity, yet the activity does not provide opportunities for the individual to shape the experience, the leisure experience may be diminished. Thus, various factors are linked and related to one another and, in fact, may be mutually dependent on each other to produce the leisure experience.

Underlying Constructs of Leisure

As indicated, leisure means different things to different people, resulting in a number of ways of viewing the concept of leisure. These approaches often depend on the perception of leisure

Cruise Lines: Adventure Recreation?

Cruise lines are seeing a huge increase in younger vacationers. According to the Cruise Lines International Association, 72 percent of cruise goers are between the ages of twenty-five and fifty-nine. In addition, the adventure component of cruise ship vacations has increased tremendously. For example, Royal Caribbean International launched two new ships in 2000—they accommodate 3,100 passengers and are the length of three football fields. On board vacationers find rock-climbing walls, eighteen-hole computer golf courses, in-line skating, and ice rinks. Other cruise lines keep passenger numbers small as they turn to eco-conscious outdoor adventures. Temptress Adventure Cruises take 100 passengers at a time and involve them in eco-tourism trips to Costa Rica, Panama, and other Central American jungles.

Source: *USA Weekend*, January 12–14, 2001.

in the minds of individuals, professionals, researchers, or, in an even broader perspective, society as a whole. Leisure does shape culture (and culture shapes leisure), and collective perceptions vary in terms of the value and importance of leisure, as well as the way it is ultimately defined. Today there are at least eight ways of looking at or defining leisure: leisure as time, as an activity, as a state of mind, as a quality of action, as a social construction, as a social instrument, as an anti-utilitarian concept, and as a part of a holistic process (see figure 2.1).

Leisure as Time   Over the past century, one of the chief ways of viewing leisure was to perceive it as time—similar to work time, free time, and time to maintain bodily needs (i.e., sleep, eating, personal hygiene). Time, according to those advocating this approach of viewing life, can be divided into three segments—existence (work), subsistence (addressing physical needs), and discretionary (free or unobligated) time. Free or discretionary time is that time focus on the benefits or outcomes of the activities. For example, MacKay and Crompton (1988) propose that leisure activities should be clustered in terms of such outcomes as relaxation, achievement, intimacy, power, or socialization. Caldwell, Baldwin, et al, (2004) believe that leisure is the constructive use of free times. Nearly all forms of leisure which is not obligated in terms of subsistence and existence activities; it is free for rest or a choice of activity. In this approach to defining leisure, Iso-Ahola (1999) notes, "In everyday usage of the language, people refer to all nonworking hours as free time. But as we know only a small portion of this time may indeed be free, free from obligations and free to do what one wants to do." The idea of viewing leisure as time occurred primarily as a result of the Industrial Revolution. During this period, lives were fragmented or segmented into work time and free time, where one's free time was used to rest and recuperate in order to go back to work (Juniu, 2000).

Several authors maintain that leisure time can be viewed from two perspectives. The first views leisure as a product of residual time—time left over from other obligations. Such leisure time could occur as unplanned, unchosen leisure time. This type of time often produces casual, unstructured opportunities for leisure (Cordes and Ibrahim, 2003; Pavelleg, 2003). The second perspective views leisure as discretionary time (Russell, 2005), free from work and life-maintenance activities. Discretionary time implies that individuals have choice, autonomy, and freedom to exercise their will to experience leisure (Russell, 2005).

Figure 2.1

Definitions
of leisure.

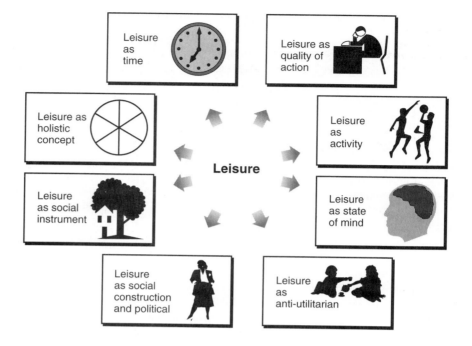

Leisure as a State of Mind This approach to defining leisure suggests that the leisure experience is a function of one's state of mind. In other words, leisure is a subjective attitude, an experience that is based on an individual's own perspective, feelings, values, and past life experiences. As Lee and Shafer (2002) note, leisure is associated with the challenges of the leisure environment, satisfaction, mood, and emotions. It is a highly personal experience. This approach emphasizes what happens in a person's mind as he or she is engaged in an experience.

Leisure has been referred to as not only a mental, but a spiritual attitude, ". . . a condition of the soul" (Pieper, 1963, p. 40). Authors subscribing to this perspective maintain that one can participate in activities that for all appearance seem to be leisure, but if the individual's attitude or mind-set is not positively open to the potential fullness of the experience, it may not result in leisure. While going on a vacation or holiday can provide the opportunity for leisure, many work roles are fulfilled while vacationing. A vacation can be full of stress, anxiety, and frustration if it holds too many of the negative aspects of work, or if one's mental mind-set is essentially negative. One family might go to Disneyland on vacation and have a wonderful leisure experience, virtually unaffected by minor inconveniences such as long lines. Another family may go to the same Disneyland theme park and on the same rides but be unable to attain a true leisure experience due to their tendency to focus on the negative aspects of the endeavor. Or the children may enjoy the experience, but the adults may not, having seen the attractions before. Different members of the family could experience the event differently in terms of the quality of the leisure experience depending upon their state of mind.

Russell (1996, p. 35) provides perspective to the discussion of leisure as a subjective attitude, and has suggested the following:

> Although the psychological condition of leisure suggests it is a matter of "feeling good," the connotation goes beyond this. Leisure is an entire way of being—an opportunity for building purpose into life—capable of providing opportunities for self-expression, self-achievement and self-actualization.

Leisure is engaging in flights of imagination, developing talents, looking at things in new ways, and being ourselves.

Leisure as an Activity   Another definition views leisure as a discrete set of activities. In this framework, leisure activities can be differentiated from other life activities, such as those that are work-oriented or involve life maintenance. This approach to defining leisure suggests that leisure and work/life-maintenance activities are not interrelated, but rather are each a unique and distinct set of functions. Dumazedier (1967) states that leisure can be viewed as an activity ". . . apart from obligations of work, family, and society—to which the individual turns at will for either relaxation, diversion, or broadening his [or her] knowledge and his [or her] spontaneous social participation, the free exercise of his [or her] creative capacity" (pp. 16–17).

This definition pays no attention to the concept of leisure as related to what happens within an individual's mind; rather, leisure is simply defined by categories of activity. This can be problematic because many activities serve dual purposes (e.g., cooking, walking) (Raymore, 2002). As Kelly (1996, p.19) writes, ". . . defining leisure simply as specified activities presents a strange paradox; almost no one actually defines leisure in that way in theory. There are no lists of activities that are said to encompass leisure." Kraus (2000) suggests that this view of leisure is closely aligned with that of recreation in that it involves the way free time is used. It is difficult, if not impossible, to list the myriad of activities in which one could participate during leisure. In addition, activities that some individuals consider to be leisure-oriented might be considered work-oriented by others (Pavelka 2002). Thus, the line between leisure and work is not clear-cut but is subjective. Nonetheless, researchers and leisure professionals continue to use this definition of leisure as one of the bases for contemporary discussion of definitions of leisure.

Kelly (1996) suggests that leisure as activity can be viewed from two unique perspectives. The first of these views the forms that leisure activities take, and numerous classification systems cluster leisure activities by their common components. Edginton, Hudson, Dieser, and Edginton (2004) suggest, for example, that areas of programming can be classified in the following ways: the arts; literary activities; self-improvement/education; sports, games, and athletics; aquatics; outdoor recreation; wellness; hobbies; social recreation; volunteer services; and travel and tourism. As DeGraaf, Jordan, and DeGraaf (1999) have written, "Classifying experiences that offer satisfying leisure and recreation experiences can be a difficult task. The possible categories are limitless and the means of classification often arbitrary" (p.121). The second perspective views leisure activities in terms of their meaning. Such typologies appear to be a part of a conscious effort to align the leisure goods and services chosen with the status or image the consumer wishes to project. Leisure apparel provides a visible, external symbol of perceived status and values. Individuals consciously seek to present an image during their leisure that reflects their image of themselves and, often, what they desire to reflect to others. This is a form of social exhibition manifested by those in the higher social strata. The symbolic nature of leisure is one of "ostentation, luxury, pleasures, and squander" (Juniu, 2000, p. 70).

The downside of this phenomenon results when individuals make inordinate, inappropriate sacrifices in the quality of their daily lives in order to possess certain leisure status symbols. In addition, many leisure products and services can only reasonably be purchased by a certain segment of society, excluding others from participation. This raises issues of equity in the delivery of services and also promotes concern for the values that may be associated with some leisure purchases.

Another perspective of leisure as a symbol of social status is the value that is attached to having leisure. Today, many individuals seek more freedom, autonomy, and flexibility in both their leisure and their work. In addition, people desire meaningful and satisfying experiences in all aspects of life. In the information era, many professional workers have the opportunity for more flexible work hours, more concentrated, focused leisure experiences (referred to as time deepening) and, in general, more control over their creative potential and ability. Socioeconomic status influences this phenomenon; greater resources result in greater work flexibility. Great status is attached to individuals who work/play on their own terms and at their discretion; there is an understanding of associated social class. Such individuals often fuse their work and leisure lives in such a way as to take advantage of their creative potential. Our society is moving from a work-hard-play-hard orientation to attaching great status to an integrative, creative, flexible, and discretionary work-play lifestyle.

Leisure as a Social Instrument   Leisure can also be viewed as a social instrument (Murphy, 1974). From this perspective, leisure can be viewed as a way of enhancing individual or community life in ways that promote instrumental (useful) ends. One view of therapeutic recreation meets this criteria. TR is often viewed as a way to promote health and wellness for people who are recovering from an illness or injury (Sylvester, 2000; Wise, 2002). More and Averill (2003) note that leisure serves various functions: biological, social, psychological, and cultural. Further, viewing leisure from this perspective also contains elements that see "free time" as having potentially negative or undesirable consequences. With this orientation, leisure would be controlled in order to promote social order and harmony within a given economic, political, or social framework or ideology. For example, the misuse of leisure time at the turn of the century was viewed as being detrimental to effectiveness at work. As Murphy (1974, p. 12) writes,

> In industrial society, leisure is separate from the rest of man's [sic] life. It has become, not a part of life, but a means to life—a thing of extrinsic value, useful only because it relaxes and restores the individual for work.

Today, misuse of leisure time has been linked to social disruption, poor health practices, and other issues. This approach to defining leisure has been criticized in that it has the potential to rob leisure of its spontaneity and freedom. As Leitner and Leitner (1996, p.10) write, ". . . a drawback to this concept is that it can lead to a stressful attitude toward leisure, in which achievement during leisure activity is overemphasized. Leisure can become work-like in nature, approached with an emphasis on end results rather than as an experience in itself." Thus, as one can see, the idea that leisure is a social instrument has some drawbacks. However, in recent years, with a great emphasis on defining the social, economic, and other benefits of leisure, renewed emphasis on this approach of viewing leisure has gained value. The platitudes of leisure as promoting stress reduction, health, psychological well-being, human happiness, enhanced community life, and others are a part of the professional jargon of leisure. (Sylvester, 2002).

Leisure as an Anti-Utilitarian Concept   The anti-utilitarian concept of leisure is not new. In *The Normal Course of Play* (1925), Lee suggests that the value of play is not tied to instrumental ends. He notes that ". . . the joy of play for its own sake is universally recognized. Play is above a mere instrument or means and, as a phase of life, it has its own justification" (p. 86). In a more contemporary context, Murphy (1974) has advanced the concept that leisure can be viewed from an anti-utilitarian perspective. That is, leisure need not serve any purpose and needs no justification. As Murphy (1974, p.10) explains, "The social structure of the industrial society, governed by an economic principle of rationality, clashes with the emerging values of the culture, and anti-utilitarian, hedonistic, pleasure-seeking rationale based on openness, choice, flexibility, change and spontaneity." Quoting Charles Reich, Murphy (1974) further notes, that ". . . the anti-utilitarian philosophy, believing and doing what one wants to do rather than responding passively to outside pressures . . . provides an arena for fellowship, spontaneity, authenticity, and creativity" (p.10).

The anti-utilitarian concept of leisure gained some interest among leisure theorists in the early 1970s as a way of explaining the emergence of a new leisure ethic evidenced in postindustrial society. This new leisure ethic was best reflected in the lifestyle of the countercultural movement of that period of time that rejected prevailing cultural norms and customs calling for a more open, spontaneous, and free society. Leitner and Leitner (1996, p.10) suggest that this concept has several drawbacks. First, they note that ". . . anti-utilitarian view . . . is difficult to utilize in objectively quantifying leisure for research purposes." Another drawback, according to these authors, is that ". . . it can be used to justify leisure activities that are detrimental to health self-development" (p.10).

Leisure as a Holistic Concept   The holistic concept of leisure, championed by Murphy (1981) and presented by other authors such as Neulinger (1974), Godbey (1981), Kraus (1984), and Kelly (1996), broadly suggests that all parts of a person's life have the potential for leisure. It integrates and combines many features of the preceding definitions with particular emphasis on individuals' ability to shape and control their own leisure destiny. As Murphy (1981) writes:

> The holistic concept of leisure is seen as a potentially synthesizing theoretical perspective in which elements of leisure are to be expressed in all aspects of human behavior—in work, play, education, and other social spheres. There is much debate as to whether the unique character of leisure, particularly as influenced by social organization of work can be effectively analyzed and operationalized because such a conceptual approach has not lent itself to either empirical testing or accurate prediction. (p. 34)

The holistic perspective is now being viewed as a way to characterize the dynamic and multi-phasic nature of leisure (Lee and Shafer, 2002; Pavelka 2002). From this perspective, an individual might find the opportunity for leisure in work, church, school, or other settings that heretofore may have only focused on the potential for more specific, narrow outcomes. The holistic perspective forces examination of our work and other endeavors to determine whether they contain elements of leisure. It also raises the possibility that one's life cannot be fragmented into neatly organized and structured components.

Kelly (1990) offers a perspective on the holistic orientation, suggesting that leisure may be a realized action. He suggests the following:

> Leisure takes place in time. It is not defined by time or place, but it does not float off into an unrelated attitude or feeling. It is connected to the realities of identifiable spatial and temporal dimensions. Further, leisure has form. The forms are almost infinite in their variety, but it is possible to identify activity, be it contemplation or competition, in which leisure occurs. It is legitimate to study these forms, not as leisure, but as the events in which leisure happens. Finally, leisure is experience. It involves perceptions of the actor—going into the experience, during it and coming out of it. Such perceptions are essential dimensions of the action. (pp. 22–23)

According to the holistic perspective, leisure addresses dimensions of time, activity, and experience. Lee and Shafer (2002) note that leisure is often operationalized with mood, emotions, and the passing of time. To be considered leisure, an activity must have an outcome; something must have occurred to indicate that leisure has taken place—it is not solely a thought or attitude, but involves experience. Even during contemplation, the formation of thoughts and ideas hold value for the individual.

Kraus (1990) also promotes the holistic view of leisure. He suggests that this perspective ". . . implies a lifestyle which is holistic, in the sense that one's view of life is not sharply fragmented into a number of spheres, such as family activities, religion, work, and free time. Instead, all such involvements are seen as part of a whole . . ." (p. 53). The holistic perspective of leisure, according to Kraus, finds the individual developing a lifestyle of enriching life experiences that promote a ". . . sense of being creative, involved, expressive and fully alive" (1984, p. 46). Linked to Murphy's definition stated earlier, this interpretation of the holistic concept emphasizes an integrated lifestyle in which opportunities to operate creatively, expressively, physically, and intellectually are found in all spheres of one's life and are not fragmented into subcategories such as sports and games, arts, work, leisure, and family life.

The holistic perspective to understanding leisure provides a broad basis for interpreting leisure. This integrative concept helps one to understand leisure in light of the nature of work and the contemporary technology of today's society. The information era has provided a different set of assumptions about the way people think and organize social institutions. The holistic perspective provides a fluid, organic approach to defining leisure that may be suited to the lifestyles emerging during this decade.

Leisure as Quality of Action   Simply stated, leisure is the self-taking action, or doing something, that is rooted in real choice and meaningfulness. For example, someone can visualize hiking, spend time in planning how to build a dollhouse, or become actively involved in collecting stamps. As Freysinger and Kelly (2004) underscore:

> This approach [leisure as quality of action] begins by asserting that leisure is more than a state of mind; it is doing something. That something may be mental and imaginative as well as physical. It may be solitary or socially involved. But it involves doing something in a real time and place. . . . The quality of the action—its "playfulness"—makes it leisure. It can take place anywhere and any time, but it has a quality of self-containing meaning. (p. 19)

Leisure as Social Construction and Political   Leisure is learned and has a political identity that is also learned or socially constructed (Freysinger and Kelly, 2004). Leisure is shaped by the culture and context (Rojek, 1985, 1995, 2000; Wearing, 1998) and the context is shaped by the politics of gender, race, social class, age, able-bodiedness, and other markers of social stratification. As such, leisure is a political act where the privileges that accompany dominant culture (e.g., White males over Black females) are challenged and negotiated. As such:

> . . . in leisure those with more power and privilege seek to maintain power and privilege and control those with less power and privilege. At the same time for those without (or with less) power and privilege, leisure is a context within which to challenge or resist those with power and privilege and transform the existing social order. (Freysinger and Kelly, 2004, p. 20)

Contemporary Theories of Leisure

As Caldwell (2001) has noted, "The word 'theory' usually makes people shudder. To many theories seem grand and esoteric and certainly not very practical . . . The truth is, however, that theories are very useful and practical" (p. 349). Theory is important because it attempts to explain a phenomenon (e.g., leisure) and highlight its practical relevance. For example, if a leisure professional understands the conditions that develop leisure experiences, they are in a better position to provide leisure service delivery (Edginton, Hudson, Dieser, and Edginton, 2004). This section of the chapter will explain various contemporary theories of leisure that have developed within different academic frameworks (see table 2.1).

TABLE

2.1   CONTEMPORARY THEORIES OF LEISURE

Theory Typology	Leisure Theories	Explanation
Work-Related Theories (Leisure is related to work)	Spillover Theory	Workers participate in leisure activities that have similar characteristics (spillover) to their work-related tasks.
	Compensation Theory	Deprivations experienced at work are made up for (compensated) during leisure.
Psychological Theories (The study of leisure behaviors and experiences of the individual)	Neulinger's Leisure Paradigm	Perceived freedom and intrinsic motivation are the two core elements of leisure.
	Flow Theory	A state of being, based upon skill and challenge level, in which a person becomes so involved in an activity or experience that nothing else seems to matter.
	Self-as-Entertainment Theory	The ability to fill free time or entertain oneself. It is based on the three modes of self, environment, and mind-play.
Sociological Theories (The study of leisure within its broader social context [e.g., family, community, age, life course, gender, cultures])	Veblen's Theory of the Leisure Class	Leisure is a symbol of social class.
	Kelly's Sociological Theory of Leisure	Freedom and meaning are the two core elements of leisure.
	Serious and Casual Leisure	Serious leisure: The systematic pursuit of an amateur, hobbyist, or volunteer activity that is so interesting that people launch themselves on a career centered on acquiring special skills, knowledge, and experience. Casual Leisure: Pleasurable activity that requires no special skills or knowledge.
	Postmodern Leisure	Skilled and pleasurable activity that can be a method of social control.
Feminist Theories (A set of beliefs and theoretical constructs regarding the nature of women's oppression and the constraints imposed by the sociopolitical status to which women have been regulated)	Kelly's Sociological Theory of Leisure	Freedom and meaning are the two core elements of leisure (social meaning has greater relevance to women's issues, such as relationships and family).
	Wearing's Feminist Theory of Leisure	Heterotopias: Freedom or personal space for both men and women to be or become (e.g., challenge dominant gender norms, develop identities).
Anthropological Theories (The study of people and culture, which paints a holistic picture of the human condition)	The Theory of Anti-Structure	Leisure includes the rituals that set people outside their norms or the anti-structure parts of life.
Philosophical Theories (The inner search for understanding that is connected to daily life)	Classic Leisure	Leisure is contemplation of the good life.
	Nash's Pyramid of Leisure	Reflective understanding of leisure based upon values.

Work-Related Theories of Leisure

The early theories of leisure explained leisure as relating to work. As both Mannell and Kleiber (1997) and Rojek (1995) underscore, leisure was valued in capitalistic America in an effort to improve worker productivity. For example, Henry Ford's production system envisaged the work and leisure of the worker to be part of a comprehensive system of management control—he even employed social workers in the homes of workers to ensure that their leisure was morally sound and consistent with corporate expectations (Rojek, 1995). As such, two theories of leisure developed in the 1960s and 1970s—spillover and compensation theory suggested that the nature of people's work directly influenced their choice of leisure (Wilensky, 1960; Kando and Summers, 1971; Parker, 1971). Whereas spillover theory posits that workers participate in leisure activities that have similar characteristics (spillover) to their work-related tasks, compensation theory posited that deprivations experienced at work are made up for (compensated) during leisure (Mannell and Reid, 1999). For example, a person may become involved in risk recreation (e.g., ice climbing) to compensate for a job that is boring, allows little risk taking, and has little recognition. On the other hand, a person who has mastered carpentry skills for employment may experience leisure by volunteering at Habitat for Humanity and using his/her skills in building homes for people who are struggling economically. Although there has been some research support for spillover theory, research testing regarding both of these leisure theories has provided findings that are contradictory (Mannell and Reid, 1999). Furthermore, Russell (2005) reminds us that spillover and compensation theory can contribute to stereotypes about social status and leisure choices. Not all construction workers like bowling and not all corporate executives play golf at the country club.

Beyond spillover and compensation theory other leisure theories underscore the work and leisure relationship. Recently Stebbins (2004) has underscored that serious leisure and devotee work are much alike (the theory of serious leisure is explained as a sociological discipline). For example, a coin collector (serious leisure hobbyist) can create a small business related to coin collecting, and a person who is an expert in fly fishing can conduct fly fishing workshops for a local fish and bait store. Likewise, Csikszentmihalyi (1997) reported that flow occurs more often on the job than in leisure time (the theory of flow is explained as a psychological discipline).

Psychological and Social Psychological Theories of Leisure

Psychology is the study of human behavior, experience, and development of the individual and the psychology of leisure is the study of leisure behaviors and experiences of the individual (Mannell and Kleiber, 1997). A sub-discipline of the psychology of leisure is the social psychology of leisure defined as the study of the leisure behavior and experience of individuals in social situations (Mannell and Kleiber, 1997). The following section will explain psychological and social psychological theories of leisure.

Neulinger's Leisure Paradigm   A dominant psychological theory of leisure is Neulinger's leisure paradigm. Neulinger (1981) identified perceived freedom and intrinsic motivation as the two core elements of leisure (with perceived freedom serving as the primary element and intrinsic motivation serving as a secondary element). Intrinsic motivation occurs when the rewards to participation are seen as coming from engaging in the activity itself (opposed to external pressure), and perceived freedom refers to a state in which a person feels that what he/she is doing is done by choice (Neulinger, 1981). Neulinger (1976) divided these two elements across a "state of mind" continuum to explain six types of psychological states of leisure (see figure 2.2):

Figure 2.2
A paradigm of leisure: A psychological definition.

Source: After J. Neulinger, "The Need for and the implications of a Psychological Conception of Leisure" in The Ontario Psychologist, 8, 1976.

Perceived Freedom

Freedom			Constraint		
Motivation			Motivation		
Intrinsic	Intrinsic and Extrinsic	Extrinsic	Intrinsic	Intrinsic and Extrinsic	Extrinsic
(1) Pure Leisure	(2) Leisure-Work	(3) Leisure-Job	(4) Pure Work	(5) Work Job	(6) Pure Job

◄——————————— State of Mind ———————————►

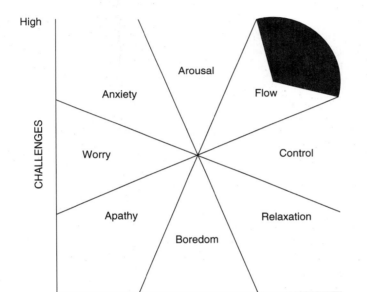

Figure 2.3
Flow theory.

Source: Csikszentmihalyi, M. (1997). Finding flow: The psychology of engagement with everyday life. *New York: Basic Books.*

- Pure leisure: Perceived freedom and intrinsic motivation
- Leisure-Work: Perceived freedom and extrinsic and intrinsic motivation
- Leisure-Job: Perceived freedom and extrinsic motivation
- Pure Work: Perceived constraint and intrinsic motivation
- Work-Job: Perceived constraint and extrinsic and intrinsic motivation
- Pure Job: Perceived constraint and extrinsic motivation

Flow Theory   Another dominant psychological theory of leisure is Csikszentmihalyi's (1990, 1997) theory of flow. Flow describes a state of being in which a person becomes so involved in an activity or experience that nothing else seems to matter. As Gardner, Csikszentmihalyi, and Damon (2001) remarked, "In flow we feel totally involved, lost in a seemingly effortless performance. Paradoxically, we feel 100 percent alive when we are so committed to the task at hand that we lose track of time, our interests—even of our own existence. Intense flow can happen anywhere: in making love, in listening to music, in playing a good game of squash or chess" (p. 5). Flow is often referred to as "being in the zone" by athletes and is presented in figure 2.3.

There are eight characteristic dimensions to the flow experiences (Csikszentmihalyi, 1993, 1997). First, the activity is challenging and requires skills. Intense flow occurs when a person's skills are fully involved in overcoming a challenge that is just about manageable. If the challenge level is too high, a person may experience anxiety; if the challenge level is too low, a person may experience boredom. Second, there must be clear goals—an objective is distinctly defined with immediate feedback regarding performance. Csikszentmihalyi (1997) noted:

> Flow tends to occur when a person faces a clear set of goals that require appropriate responses. It is easier to enter flow in games such as chess, tennis, or poker, because they have goals and rules for action that make it possible for the player to act without questioning what should be done, and how. (p. 29)

Third, action and awareness merge. During flow, a person's attention is completely absorbed by the activity so intensely that there is no extra mental energy to consider anything other than the activity. Fourth, and related to the previous characteristic of flow, there is intense concentration on the task at hand. People in flow temporarily suspend their worries and concerns. That is, people in flow are able to forget negative aspects of their lives and remain completely focused on doing the activity. Fifth, there is a loss of self-consciousness. When in flow, there is no opportunity to think about oneself or to engage in self-scrutiny. Sixth, during flow, there is a sense of control. Although it is possible to lose control during a flow experience (e.g., a horseback rider can fall and break an arm), there is a perception of being in control. A research participant who Csikszentmihalyi (1993) interviewed explained the following regarding chess: "The best things about chess are being in control of a situation and having all the evidence right there . . . In chess everything is in front of you to see. No other variables . . . you can control it" (p. 182). Seventh, during flow, there is an altered sense of time, which usually seems to pass faster. People in flow will lose track of time and are often surprised that so much time has passed. Eighth, flow is an autotelic experience. The activity is worth doing, or done, for its own sake instead of for some external benefit or reward.

Self-as-Entertainment Theory Another psychological theory of leisure is the self-as-entertainment (S-A-E) theory. S-A-E theory attempts to characterize the way people differ in their ability to fill free time or entertain themselves. People that are high in entertaining themselves are less likely to be bored during leisure and tend to have leisure that is more fulfilling. Mannell and Kleiber (1997) underscored that S-A-E theory is based upon three modes: self, environmental, and mind-play. The self-mode is the extent to which people perceived they could successfully structure their own free time instead of relying on others. That is, their self is the primary means of fulfilling free time. For example, someone who is high on self-entertainment will use daydreams and inner thoughts to structure free time instead of external venues such as watching television. The environmental mode reflects the extent to which people fill their free time by going places or by seeking out other people. For example, a person who is bored would take the initiative to visit historical sites or call people to set up a leisure activity (e.g., playing a game of baseball). The mind-play mode refers to the extent to which people are able to use fantasy and imagination to fill their time. Mannell and Kleiber highlighted that there is some consistency between S-A-E theory and flow theory with the autotelic personality orientation—daydreaming, experiencing healthy mind-play (fantasy), and directing inner thoughts are done for its own sake. Furthermore, Mannell and

Klieber also outlined the importance of learning healthy mind play in early childhood through play and the influence of family.

Sociological Theories of Leisure

Sociology attempts to understand human behavior by placing it within its broader social context (Henslin, 2001). To this end, Kelly (1999) underscored that leisure should be located within a sociological framework that explores leisure in relation to family, community, age, life course, gender, cultures, and so forth. Likewise, Rojek (1995, 2000) has rejected the psychological theories of leisure that associate leisure with freedom and has argued that leisure must be contextualized within culture and society. Recently, Rojek (2005) posited:

> Most [psychologically-oriented] leisure researchers would accept that the individual's definition of leisure choice [freedom] is pivotal in interpreting leisure . . . However, this is very different from maintaining that individual choice is freely selected . . . location and context . . . [are] indispensable elements in leisure theory because they correlate individual choice with situated dimensions that influence action. (p. 14)

Likewise, Coalter (1999) has suggested that psychological theories of leisure study leisure without society and that sociological theories of leisure study leisure in society.

As Burton and Jackson (1999) noted, the modern era in the study of leisure began with Veblen's (1899) sociological study of leisure. This section will begin by explaining Veblen's theory of leisure and the leisure class, followed by other sociological theories of leisure.

Veblen's Theory of Leisure and the Leisure Class

From a historical perspective, leisure as a symbol of social status has existed since the beginning of agricultural civilizations. The evolution of the "leisure classes" emerged as a result of increased social organization, complexity, and functional differentiation of agricultural societies. Leisure as a symbol of social class was reflected in the writings of Thorsten Veblen in 1899 in his work, *Theory of the Leisure Class*. Veblen coined the term "conspicuous consumption" in his classic work of economic and sociological literature. He noted that ". . . as wealth accumulates, the leisure class develops further in function and structure and there arises a differentiation within the class[es]" (1899, p. 76). He suggests that the evolution of conspicuous expenditures, whether of goods, services, or human life, runs the obvious implication that in order "to effectively [maintain] . . . the consumer's good fame, it must be . . . wasteful" (Veblen, 1899, p. 96).

Today, people still use leisure as a way of claiming or demonstrating social status in society by virtue of the products and services that people consume or purchase. The brand name of an athletic shoe confers a certain social status on the owner of the shoe. Vacationing at Club Med provides a greater social status than camping at a state park.

Kelly's Sociological Theory of Leisure   Kelly's work on developing a sociological leisure theory began in the early 1970s (e.g., Kelly, 1972) and developed throughout the 1980s (Kelly, 1982). A core element of leisure for Kelly was the concept of meaning, which, he argued, could not be separated from context (Kelly, 1999). To this end, Kelly, (1978, 1983) developed a theory of leisure that is based upon the core elements of freedom and meaning. Freedom was considered from a high or low continuum, and meaning was considered from an intrinsic and social continuum. That is, the development of meaningfulness

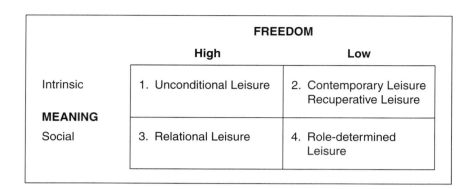

Figure 2.4

Kelly's Sociological Theory of Leisure.

Source: Kelly, J. R. (1982). Leisure. Englewood Cliffs, NJ: Prentice-Hall.

	FREEDOM	
	High	**Low**
Intrinsic	1. Unconditional Leisure	2. Contemporary Leisure Recuperative Leisure
MEANING Social	3. Relational Leisure	4. Role-determined Leisure

is contextualized within social frameworks such as family, community, relationships, and so forth. Kelly (1978, 1982) divided these two elements to explain four types of sociological states of leisure (see figure 2.4):

- Unconditional leisure: High intrinsic meaning and high freedom
- Recuperative (compensatory) leisure: High intrinsic meaning and low freedom
- Relational leisure: High social meaning and high freedom
- Role-determined leisure: High social meaning and low freedom

Recently, Dieser (2004) posited that Kelly's sociological theory of leisure has relevance to how people from different cultures experience leisure:

> Kelly's model extends the meaning of leisure beyond intrinsic motivation—social meaning of leisure may be relevant to people from collectivistic cultures where priority is given to group membership (e.g., family, ethnic group) . . . For example, a person from a collectivistic culture (Asian-American) may experience relational leisure from participating in an ethnic-oriented parade (e.g., Chinese New Year celebration). In this example a person may attain a high degree of freedom and experience social meaning . . . Further, a parent from a collectivistic culture may experience role-determined leisure via watching a son or daughter participate in swimming lessons. In this experience, the parent may experience a low degree of freedom (the activity is an obligation) but find social meaning from following an important family role (e.g., father or mother). (pp. 16–17)

A study of three American communities suggested that a slight majority of adults experience unconditional leisure (31%), followed by recuperative leisure (30%), relational leisure (22%) and role-determined leisure (17%) (Kelly, 1978).

Serious Leisure/Casual Leisure Stebbins (2004) has also highlighted that serious leisure must be viewed within a sociological framework, which explores leisure in relation to family, gender, social class, and so forth. Stebbins (1992) has offered an alternative view to leisure, which seems to fit between how we understand leisure and how we understand work. He indicates that *serious leisure* is the "systematic pursuit of an amateur, hobbyist, or volunteer activity that participants find so substantial and interesting that, in the typical case, they launch themselves on a career centered on acquiring and expressing its special skills, knowledge, and experience" (1992, p. 3). This is commonly contrasted with *casual leisure,* which is leisure that is intrinsically rewarding and pleasurable, and requires no special training to enjoy it. According to Stebbins (1999), activities such as play, relaxation, passive and active entertainment, sociable conversation, and sensory pleasures are considered casual leisure.

Serious leisureists are defined by six distinctive qualities:

1. the need to persevere (often in the face of danger or fear);
2. finding a career in the endeavor;
3. a significant personal effort based on special knowledge, training, or skill;
4. durable benefits (self-actualization, self-enrichment, self-expression, renewal, social interaction, lasting physical products);
5. strong identification with their chosen pursuits; and
6. a unique ethos, or special social world, which arises when enthusiasts pursue their leisure experiences over the years (Stebbins, 1999).

As one might imagine, there are many examples of people engaged in serious leisure pursuits. They might include amateur photographers or astronomers, members of HOGs (Harley Davidson motorcycle Owner Groups), career volunteers, and members of community bands and community garden clubs. Yoder (1997) notes that events such as tournament bass fishing are examples of how individuals can become involved in serious leisure pursuits.

Postmodern Leisure Rojek's (1985, 1995, 2000) academic work in understanding leisure has developed a sociological theory of leisure that has been dubbed a sociological imagination of leisure (Bramham, 2002) and postmodern leisure (Rojek, 1995). Rojek believes that the psychological theories of leisure that stress that the essence of leisure is freedom (e.g., Neulinger's leisure paradigm) are illusory and, instead of developing freedom, leisure can actually be used as a mechanism for social control and order (Rojek, 1985, 1995). Drawing upon the proposition from Karl Marx that the dream of economic man was an illusion so that the wealthy could dominate the working class, Rojek (1985, 1995) argued that leisure as freedom is an illusion so that the prevailing class (e.g., wealthy capitalists) can dominate people via leisure. The crux of his position is expressed in the following quotation:

> Leisure is the "reward" of the many who toil in domestic labour and paid employment for the profit of the few. The pleasure which derives from "free" time activity is rule bound and conforms to an historically specific economy of political and cultural regulation. (Rojek, 1989, p. 9)

Rojek posited that leisure is skilled and pleasurable (Rojek, 1985) and must be contextualized and related to social formations and norms (Rojek, 1995, 2000). That is, there is no such thing or space as essentially leisure; rather, leisure is always embedded in social and cultural norms. Because the postmodern era in contemporary societies is oriented toward flexibility, fragmentation, acceleration, diversity, challenging authority, irrationality, restlessness, and disengagement, postmodern leisure remains a site for transgression, societal change, diversity, and challenging dominant social norms (Rojek, 1995). Hence, leisure becomes fast, accelerated, and fragmented:

> Fast leisure simply refers to an acceleration in the velocity and density of leisure relations with other leisure actors. For example . . . the phenomenal growth of computer games, gameboys and playstations over the last decade is built on the hunger of constant novelty. It is an industry requirement for games to be replaced rapidly so that the market continuously expands. Computerized games typically involve attention spans to be concentrated in short bursts rather than continuously developed. They encourage the development of fragmentary consciousness since they permit the individual to concentrate on one part of the game instead of the unfolding whole. (Rojek, 2000, pp. 22–23)

Recently, Rojek (2005) suggested that because leisure is related to social formations and norms, it can enhance social capital and should be repositioned in relation to social norms oriented toward the "care of the self" and the "care for the other" (p. 20).

Furthermore, under the framework of postmodern leisure, deviant leisure should be re-examined and certain aspects of deviant leisure should be valued (e.g., challenging authority through political dissent). Rojek (1999) suggests four types of deviant leisure categories. First, revolutionaries use leisure to attempt to transform societal norms. For example, meetings, processions, rallies, and radical discussion groups use leisure to strengthen revolutionary movements (e.g., Civic Rights Movement in the United States). Second, political dissenters attempt to modify social conditions through criticism, propaganda, agitation, and dissent. For example, contemporary animal rights campaigners or environmental protesters use leisure to organize and implement change to social conditions (e.g., protest against oil development in the Arctic National Wildlife Refuge). Third, retreatist lifestylers disengage from dominant society through fantasy, dress, linguistic codes, and religious beliefs. For example, someone can use drugs as an unhealthy method to disengage or can volunteer through the Peace Corps or religious service as a healthy way to disengage from mainstream society. Fourth, criminals use leisure as a method to achieve goals (e.g., wealth). For example, the countless images of wealth in magazines, movies, and television contribute to a fantasy world in which people think about becoming wealthy through breaking the law.

Feminist Theories of Leisure

Feminism is a set of beliefs and theoretical constructs regarding the nature of women's oppression and the constraints imposed by the sociopolitical status to which women have been relegated (Corey, 2005). To this end, a major goal of feminism is to remove oppression practiced against all people and to further develop the right of every woman to equity, dignity, and freedom of choice (Henderson, Bialeschki, Shaw, and Freysinger, 1996).

Although feminist research in the field of leisure has provided important contributions, such as developing leisure service delivery relevant to women and girls (see Bialeschki and Henderson, 2000; James, 2000) and understanding leisure constraints of women and girls (Jackson and Henderson, 1995), the development of feminist theories of leisure needs greater attention.

Henderson and colleagues (1996) suggest that Kelly's sociological theory of leisure is particularly relevant to understanding women's leisure because, by distinguishing intrinsic from social meaning, Kelly directed attention to how leisure revolves around family and relationships. In particular, relational leisure is relevant in the lives of many women.

Wearing's Feminist Theory of Leisure   Drawing upon postmodern thinking (and Rojek's sociological theory of leisure), Wearing (1998) suggested that leisure should be heterotopias, which is defined as ". . . real existing places of difference which act as counter-sites or compensatory sites to those everyday activities . . . for struggle against and resistance to the domination . . . a space for reconstituting the self and rewriting the script of identity" (p. 146). Simply stated, leisure is freedom or personal space for both men and women to be or become. Similar to the womb in which a baby is safe and developing, leisure should be a safe place where people can develop and become. For example, if interested, girls and women can participate in what has traditionally been masculine leisure activities (e.g., rugged sports), and boys and men can participate in traditional feminine leisure activities (e.g., scrapbooking).

Similar to Rojek (1995, 2000), Wearing also suggests that leisure theory must be contextualized and related to social formations and norms. In particular, she suggests that leisure spaces need to provide resistance to rigid gender stereotypes, which include women being viewed as sexual objects (e.g., Barbie doll image) for the male gaze and men being viewed as rugged and muscular warriors/heroes (e.g., G.I. Joe image). Furthermore, because women spend so much time and energy on child care and household duties, Wearing suggests that women need to have periods of freedom to escape the ethic of care so that they have time for themselves and develop their identities beyond being a caregiver. For example, a theater group can help women develop drama skills and self-confidence, and involvement in a sport can help women get in touch with and enjoy control of their own bodies.

Anthropological Theories of Leisure

According to Crapo (2001), anthropology is the scientific study of people and culture, which paints a holistic picture of the human condition. Although there are (1) anthropological writings on play as a basis of culture (Huizinga, 1950), (2) a call for the need of an anthropological emphasis in understanding leisure (Chick, 1998; Hemingway, 1998; Kelly, 1998), and (3) some research in understanding leisure of people and cultures (e.g., Fox, 2000), to date there are few anthropological theories of leisure.

The Theory of Anti-Structure The theory of anti-structure, proposed and developed by Victor Turner (1969, 1982), posits that there are formal rituals that govern people's behaviors both inside and outside of everyday life. The rituals that are outside daily life are "anti" the norm or opposed to everyday structure. Leisure are the rituals that set people outside their norms or the anti-structure parts of life. For example, in everyday life, it is socially unacceptable to yell, "Let's kill them"; however, at football games, it is common practice to yell such things.

To this end, Turner suggested that anti-structure events develop intense comradeship and smaller structured communities of equal individuals. For example, Gore and Gore (2002) highlight how a group of strangers in a run-down neighborhood in North Philadelphia initially developed a community garden so that strangers could move outside the norm of being unaware and unfriendly to their neighbors. This small community garden mushroomed into a large Village of the Arts, which has sculptures, murals, vegetable gardens, drama theater, dance programs, a community newspaper, and a working tree farm. The Village ". . . gathers people that nobody wants . . . [and] somehow in all this dysfunctional scenario, we come together; we hold each other dear; we remake it. We transform places and people become transformed" (p. 291). As Deegan (1989) noted: "The ability to have something in common with strangers, to sing and yell and cry in public, to root for one's team, and to publicly participate reaffirms one's values, are strong bonds that help us tolerate and give meaning to life" (p. 87). Leisure as anti-structure is the medium to develop comradeship, friendships, build communities, and find meaning in one's life.

Philosophical Theories of Leisure: Classic Leisure

According to Dare, Welton, and Coe (1998), philosophy is the inner search for understanding that is connected to daily life. Leisure in ancient Greek was called *skole,* which referred to quiet or peace and to rest and to think without distraction (Dare, Welton, and Coe, 1998). It was a life space for contemplation or freedom from the necessity of work. The life space to contemplate in ancient Greece has been called classic leisure and is defined as an activity that involves the pursuit of truth and self-understanding (Gray, 1973).

Classic Leisure According to Pieper (1952), to contemplate ". . . means to open one's eyes receptively to whatever offers itself to one's vision and the things seen enter into us, so to speak, without calling for any effort or strain on our part to possess them" (p. 9). Contemplation can occur alone or in a group setting. As such, most students of leisure learn about Aristotle's theory of leisure and leisure in Ancient Greek life (see Chapter 3), which posits that leisure is contemplation toward truth, virtue, and good or the good life (Dare, Welton, and Coe, 1998). However, the classic theory of leisure did not die with Aristotle's death or the demise of Ancient Greek society; rather, Kingwell (1998, 2002) has attempted to develop classic leisure in the contemporary period.

Kingwell (1998) suggested that people need to find a life space to contemplate regarding the good life (classic leisure) and that such reflection leads to eudaimonsitic happiness. Whereas hedonistic happiness refers to pleasures of the bodily kind, eudaimonsitic happiness is:

- A life of ethical action manifested in virtuous character associated with community, friends, and family
- Virtue or conformity to a standard of right
- Rational satisfaction with one's character via reflection on whether behaviors align to virtue or the good life

To this end, Kingwell (1998) has highlighted that the recent growth of philosophical cafes in Canada and Europe:

> . . . quickly spread as part of an "applied philosophy" movement that captured the imaginations of ordinary people who wanted philosophical discussions (and even enlightenment) but weren't interested in the scholasticism and elitism of traditional universities. In some way, this was a rather self-conscious attempt to re-create the kind of public forums that used to be more common: the coffee houses and salons of the eighteenth century, the clubs and self-improvement groups of the nineteenth and the sort of café society enjoyed by Proust, Wilde, de Maupassant, and Sarte. Like 1990s book circles, the "café-philo" idea speaks to a need to have intellectual discussion as a regular, and social, part of modern life. (p. 239)

In many ways, debate forums and chat rooms that can be accessed through the Internet (e.g., www.debateforums.net) can act in the same manner—a life space for people to have dialogue and reflection so that they can search for inner understanding that is connected to daily life.

Nash's Leisure Pyramid   Another theory of leisure that is based on the inner search for understanding that is connected to daily life is Nash's (1953) Leisure Pyramid. Nash has suggested that there is a scale of values that can be applied to one's leisure. He writes ". . . there is a wide scale of values to be applied to the activities chosen for one's leisure" (p. 93). As indicated in figure 2.5, the use of one's leisure can have both positive and negative effects. The

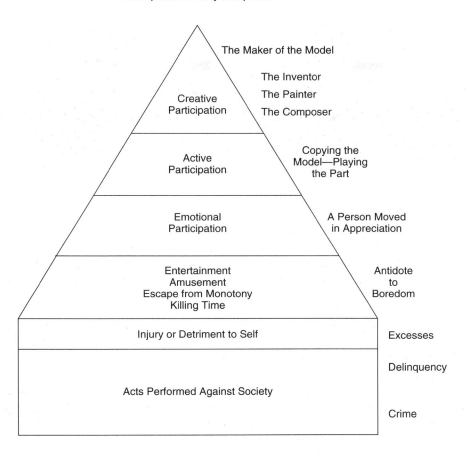

Man's Use of Leisure Time
Participation Broadly Interpreted

The Maker of the Model

The Inventor
The Painter
The Composer

Creative
Participation

Active
Participation

Copying the
Model—Playing
the Part

Emotional
Participation

A Person Moved
in Appreciation

Entertainment
Amusement
Escape from Monotony
Killing Time

Antidote
to
Boredom

Injury or Detriment to Self

Excesses

Delinquency

Acts Performed Against Society

Crime

How Do You Rate?

Figure 2.

Nash's leisure pyramid.

Source: Nash, J. B. (1953). Philosophy of Recreation and Leisure. Dubuque, IA: C. V. Mosby.

negative effects Nash describes as antisocial types of behaviors. For example, using one's leisure to perform acts against society are forms of crime and delinquency. They have no redeeming value socially. At the top of the pyramid, Nash refers to leisure experiences that lead to opportunities for creative participation. These can include inventing, painting, or composing. In between are various types of participation that, according to Nash, have increasing value to the individual and society.

Nash's leisure pyramid provides a framework for reflective understanding of leisure. It is useful because it provides the individual with opportunity for ethical reflection in terms of their leisure. It has been stated elsewhere that leisure is like the "force" in the movie Star Wars. It can be used for good or for evil. Nash's framework provides a way of determining what constitutes good or bad use of one's leisure. His philosophical ideas provide moral and ethical clarity regarding leisure. The pyramid can serve as a social compass guiding individuals and society as a whole as they experience leisure.

Nash's pyramid runs contrary to the notion that leisure in an absolute sense should enable individuals to do whatever they desire. Such a philosophical framework can root an individual to the broader societal norms, customs, and values that bind people to one another and allow them to live harmoniously together. In addition, it prescribes acceptable forms of leisure and underscores how leisure can have undesirable benefits to individuals and society.

What Is Recreation?

The term *recreation* is not as challenging to define as the term *leisure*. Professionals and researchers have used far more consistency in defining recreation. Recreation is often seen as *an activity that is engaged in during one's free time, is pleasurable, and which has socially redeeming qualities* (Cordes and Ibrahim, 2003; Kraus, 2002; More and Averill, 2003; Russell, 2005). Recreation involves an individual's participation in specific, wholesome, and voluntary activities. This is contrasted with leisure, which has no value orientation. By this we mean that participation in leisure or the leisure experience is neither good nor bad; the only value it holds is that which the individual places on it. Recreation participation, however, usually must result in constructive, positive, socially acceptable behaviors (Caldwell and Baldwin, 2004). This does not discount the often unhealthy and antisocial activities that some people undertake during their leisure. Recreation is intended to be good for the people of a society in specific ways and is organized and supported to produce such results.

Two Latin terms provide the root for the word *recreation*. The first, *recreatio,* means "to refresh." The second, *recreare,* means "to restore." Thus, most dictionary definitions suggest that the term derives from concepts related to restoring or refreshing oneself. Synonyms for the term *recreation* include "relaxation," "amusement," "pleasure," "diversion," "pleasant," "create anew," "recreated," "refreshing," "reinvigorating," "refreshment," and "comfort." Other terms associated with recreation include *recreate, recreational,* and *recreative.*

Kraus (1990, 2000) provides one of the most complete analyses of the term *recreation* found in literature. He notes that over the past several decades most definitions of recreation include similar terms, and he suggests that there is a logical consistency between and among most definitions. Kraus' (1990, 2000) analysis includes the following elements as consistent terms found in most definitions of recreation:

1. Recreation is widely regarded as an activity in contrast to sheer idleness or complete rest.
2. Recreation may include an extremely wide range of activities. Activities may be engaged in briefly or in a sustained way, for single episodes or throughout one's lifetime.
3. Recreation is voluntary and does not occur because of outside pressures, compulsory or obligatory.
4. Recreation activities are socially redeeming, wholesome, and contribute to the development of society.
5. Recreation has the potential for many desirable outcomes—fun is the steadfast goal of recreation, yet not its purpose (Haun, 1965).
6. Recreation takes place during one's free time, although it is not so much the activity that one pursues, but rather the reason for engaging in it.

These elements suggest a vast range of activities and that recreation involves activity as contrasted to idleness. Furthermore, recreational activities may be pursued in short periods or may consume an individual's interest over an extended period of time. An important aspect of Kraus' analysis is that recreation activities are participated in on a voluntary basis; the individual must feel free to participate. Also, Kraus' analysis provides for a wide range of ben-

Balancing Work and Leisure

If I don't do something like play music or work out or fly my airplane or ride a bike every day, I can't survive. . . . I can be creative and excited at work only if I have a chance to think about something else.

Source: Philippe Kahn, CEO, Borland, *Computer World,* June 22, 1992.

efits or outcomes. One might engage in a variety of recreation behaviors including socializing behaviors, associative behaviors, competitive behaviors, risk-taking behaviors, exploratory behaviors, vicarious experiences, sensory stimulation, and physical expression (Kraus, 1990, 2000).

Recreation as a Social Instrument

From a recent historical perspective, recreation programs and services have been used as ways of promoting desirable social ends. During the Industrial Revolution, individuals had work time and free time. The misuse of free time was viewed as a social problem, and wholesome recreation activities became a tool to help alleviate or overcome concerns related to this problem. A host of social institutions were created to provide programs and services that were socially redeeming. In a sense, recreation was used to control certain classes of people (typically the working class), to support their productivity, and to keep them prepared for work. Laws outlawed unhealthy forms of recreation (gambling, drinking) and hours of operation for businesses were curtailed to encourage workers to get enough sleep to be ready for work the next day (Kelly and Godbey, 1992).

In discussing recreation as a social institution, Ibrahim (1991) suggests that mass leisure activities occur in industrial-urbanized societies. Such leisure includes what Ibrahim defines as recreative leisure; that is, purposeful leisure, distinguished from either contemplative activities or amusement. Kelly postulates that mass recreation occurred in Roman society as a way of diverting attention from problems of unemployment and social inequities (1996). It is interesting to note in reviewing historical literature from the leisure services field, one of the first textbooks written to provide professional training for individuals, *The Normal Course in Play,* states the following:

> Recreation, someone has said, is no longer merely desirable for our pleasure; it is physiologically necessary in order to retain normal equilibrium in the midst of the deadening monotony and the excess strain of the common life today, both in the city and country. (Lee, 1925, p. 15)

In 1917, Henry Curtis, writing in the book *The Play Movement and Its Significance,* discussed the need for institutionalized, wholesome recreation environments. He justified the sources of the need for such types of environments by stating the following:

> Nearly every parent and observer of children has seen that there has been little for children to do in the cities, and that in this time of idleness, the devil has found much for idle hands to do; that the children are an annoyance to their parents and the neighborhood and that they acquire many vicious habits during this unused time. . . . There has come a general, though dim, realization that if we would stem this tide, we must surround children with a different environment. (p. 8)

Curtis went on to suggest that there was a need to create institutionalized forms of play (recreation) to deal with this problem. It could be argued that this need still exists in contemporary society.

Over the past century in the United States, there has been an increased investment in recreation and park systems at the local, state, and federal levels of government. In addition, voluntary and/or youth-serving organizations, as well as nonprofit private and commercial leisure service organizations, have seen tremendous growth. No doubt this growth has occurred because of the importance of the use of recreation as an instrument of social reform or change.

Today, numerous institutions focus on providing recreation environments and/or using recreation activities or services as a way of promoting, teaching, and reinforcing organizational values. In fact, many recreation-oriented organizations have greatly influenced the shape and character of culture and values in the United States. For example, it is likely that three-fourths of the people who read this book will have been a member of a youth-serving organization such as the Boy Scouts, Girl Scouts, YMCA, YWCA, YMHA, YWHA, Boys and Girls Clubs, and Camp Fire, Inc. These types of organizations provide a fundamental foundation of values that influence individuals throughout their lives. Such organizations have become important social institutions, using recreation activities, facilities, and other services to shape and guide the character of literally millions of young people.

What Is Play?

Like *leisure* and *recreation,* the term *play* is also complex and difficult to define. Like other human endeavors, it has great potential to nourish, enrich, and enhance life. Play has shaped the values, norms, and customs of all cultures; it is a major force in which all cultures participate. Play, like music, is universal. All animals engage in play behaviors. In every culture one can see people playing. In nearly every culture, some attention has been given to providing special environments in which to promote playful behavior. The universality of play links humankind in the same way that other shared experiences bind us to one another. Kraus (1990, 2004) suggests that play is essentially purposeless in the view of the participant. People who study play have discovered that it is a way to express surplus energy, to restore oneself after work, to prepare for adult roles and tasks, and to help maintain emotional balance.

Mannell and Klieber (1997) suggest that play is nonliteral behavior and a transformation of reality—it is imaginative. In addition, it is intrinsically motivated, freely chosen, and actively engaging. It is a way for children to learn about the world around them and their place in it. Play is a mechanism for self-expression and enjoyment and shares many elements of leisure and recreation.

Throughout the history of humanity, play has served as a socializing force for its youth, as play transmits values, customs, traditions, and societal norms. Gender and other roles are often acted out in play environments and, as a result, our earliest notions of self-identity are formed in play environments. In preliterate societies, play rituals provided the major mechanisms used to pass information from one generation to the next. In more contemporary times, play activities are used for the same purpose of transmitting cultural values. Competition, cooperation, winning versus losing, preparation for adult roles, along with pursuit of happiness, pleasure, and joy and all cultural values are transmitted in play environments. As Winston Churchill noted, "The wars of England were won and lost on the playing fields of Eton."

Play is often viewed as frivolous rather than as a serious, important activity and is often considered acceptable only for children. Because many consider play to be the exclusive domain of children, an adult's ability to play is questioned. In reality, however, children and adults do play, although it is a complex, structured play and often laden with rules and regulations. Children often engage in spontaneous, uninhibited, joyful, and free play activity; however, adults seem more constrained. As a result, adults play but tend to identify play as recreation or leisure activity. Such activity is usually instrumental in nature (purposeful) and has benefits other than simply free play expression.

Theories of Play

According to the *Oxford English Dictionary,* the word *play* is derived from the Old English term *plegan,* meaning "to dance, to leap for joy, to rejoice and to be glad," as well as the term *plega,* which means "to exercise or occupy oneself, to busy oneself." Play often occurs in association with games, amusement, fun, freedom, diversion, sport, frolic, pleasure, joy, and delight.

Although many definitions of play have been offered during the last century, no real definitive or universally accepted theories have emerged. A number of empirically based theories, such as those advanced by Ellis (1973), Csikszentmihalyi (1975), and Levy (1978), have provided a basic foundation for the study of play. Theorists over the years have structured a number of theories to explain play behavior. For example, one of the earliest explanations of play during the industrial period was presented by the German poet Schiller in 1875. Schiller believed that people were only truly human when they were at play—when they engaged in creative activity for its own sake.

Today, nearly twenty theories of play can be identified. Because of the complexity of human behavior, however, it is difficult to develop a precise definition or theory of play. In the past several decades, renewed interest in the study of play has been evidenced by an increasing number of empirical or scientific investigations. Examination and acknowledgment of one or more theories of play can provide the leisure service professional with a foundation for practice. Professional practice must be guided by some theoretical underpinning; acknowledgment of a theory provides for direction, consistency, coordination of efforts, and, ultimately, evaluation of one's efforts. Some of the theories explaining play that have emerged over the past century include the following (see figure 2.6):

Surplus Energy Theory. The surplus energy theory of play (Schiller, 1875; Spencer, 1873) suggests that play occurs as a result of the excess energy available to people after their basic needs for survival are met. Spontaneous games of tag and running about with no apparent purpose meet this definition.

Recreation Theory. The recreation theory of play proposed by Lazarus in 1883 suggests that the need for play is created when fatigue occurs, as a result of misuse or overuse of one's body energy. Play acts in a restorative capacity, rejuvenating the fatigued individual. Thus, going jogging to restore oneself when fatigued serves as an example of this theory.

Contemplating values related to discretionary time.

FRANK AND ERNEST reprinted by permission of Newspaper Enterprise Association, Inc.

Figure 2.6

Fifteen theories
of play.

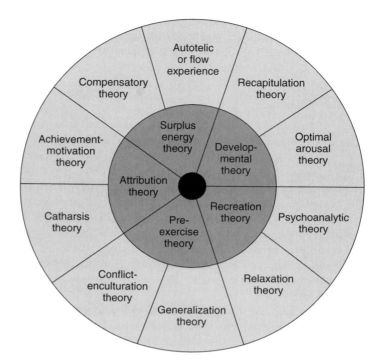

Preexercise Theory. The preexercise theory of play, proposed by Karl Groos in 1898, suggests that play is an instinct which is practiced as a result of inherited factors. This theory derived its conceptual base from and was strongly influenced by Charles Darwin. An example of this theory would be children playing family roles (pretending to be parents complete with teddy-bear children); it is believed this type of play is instinctual and prepares children for adult roles.

Recapitulation Theory. In the early 1900s, Hall proposed the recapitulation theory of play. He suggested that play essentially involves a recapturing or reenactment of the elements inherent in the development of humankind. Through play, children are thought to be enacting the lives of their ancestors (an evolutionary approach to understanding play).

Relaxation Theory. Patrick proposed an extension of the recreation theory of play, the relaxation theory, in 1916. This theory suggests that the need to play results from the need for relaxation. It is the opposite of the surplus energy theory.

Catharsis Theory. The catharsis theory of Carr and Claparede in the early 1900s suggests that play results from an individual's pent-up energies. Play, viewed as a release or safety valve, vents excess energies and emotions. The catharsis theory has an element of purging antisocial tendencies or urges.

Compensatory Theory. The compensatory theory of play, proposed by Reaney (1916) and Robinson (1920), suggests that play becomes a substitute outlet for desires and goals when other avenues to accomplish such goals are blocked. Play allows an individual to make up for unpleasant or unavailable experiences.

Psychoanalytic Theory. Proponents of the application of the psychoanalytic theory to play behavior include Waelder (1933), Peller (1952), and Erikson (1973). At the core of the psychoanalytic theory, memories, needs, and wishes can be deleted from an individual's *conscious* awareness; however, they will continue to be involved in the individual's behavioral repertoire. The relationship of this theory to play, therefore, involves the individual's use of play to react and respond to personal needs, desires, and wishes.

Developmental Theory. The developmental theory of play, advocated by Swiss child psychologist Piaget (1952, 1961), suggests that reality and play behavior are molded by the child to fit each stage of cognitive development. Toddlers play within their physical and intellectual abilities, five- to six-year-olds are more advanced in their play, and nine- to ten-year-olds even more advanced.

Generalization Theory. The generalization theory of play assumes that any learned play behavior will be generalized to other settings and behaviors by the participant (Witt and Bishop, 1970). This resembles the spillover effect (Kando and Summers, 1971), where enjoyable tasks at work spill over into one's play environment.

Attribution Theory. The attribution theory of play suggests that an individual's locus of control is a major determinant affecting the forms of play in which one is engaged. This theoretical proposition maintains that an individual exercising an internal locus of control will participate in forms of play behavior over which there is control and which has measurable outcomes of performance. On the other hand, individuals who are disposed to an external locus of control will select activities over which they have no control and for which they are not directly responsible.

Achievement-Motivation Theory. This theory of play was proposed by Levy (1978) building on the work of Atkinson (1964). The achievement-motivation theory suggests that play, like other life endeavors, involves the desire to strive, excel, master, and succeed. The theory incorporates risk-taking as an element in producing play-related outcomes in competitive situations. We tend to engage others who are more highly skilled than ourselves to increase our mastery and to continue to excel.

Optimal Arousal Theory. Ellis (1973) proposed the optimal arousal theory of play. He suggests that play elements include a combination of complexity, novelty, and dissonance. When individuals become bored, they seek stimulation in their environment. Thus, play occurs as an individual seeks stimulation from the surrounding environment.

The Autotelic or Flow Experience. Csikszentmihalyi (1975, 1990) offers an additional perspective on play by introducing the concept of the flow or autotelic experience. As discussed in Chapter 1, the individual who has entered into flow experiences a loss of ego and self-consciousness, engages in self-forgetfulness, is engaged in the transcendence of individuality, and loses an awareness of self. In this state, the individual is in control of his or her actions and of the environment. A person has no active awareness of control but is simply not worried by the possibility of the lack of control or failure. In this situation, one feels a sense of personal control or power. When one reaches this state, it is known as flow, and it occurs when the skill or mastery of the individual is equal to the challenge presented in the environment. Play is one environment in which flow can occur.

Conflict-Enculturation Theory. The conflict-enculturation theory of play suggests that play offers the participant an opportunity to experience and learn new behaviors in a safe environment (Sutton-Smith and Roberts, 1982). The individual can become involved in play situations and learn social and other skills with a minimum of emotional risk. This theory proposes that through play experiences the child is prepared for adult roles and trained to assume such abilities—cooperation, competition, ideals of fair play, and handling of intense feelings.

Kraus (1984) notes that play is ". . . a positive form of human experience or behavior . . . [although] . . . play may also have some less desirable connotations" (p. 34). In other words, if play is powerful enough to positively influence the individual, it also has the potential to affect people negatively from a physical or psychological standpoint. Kraus' (1984) comprehensive definition includes the following adapted elements:

1. Play is a form of behavior that is generally regarded as not being instrumental in purpose.
2. Play is often carried out in the spirit of pleasure and creative expression.
3. Play can be aimless, disorganized, and casual or highly structured or complex.
4. Play is commonly thought of as activity engaged in by children, but adults also play.
5. Play stems from an instinctive drive, although much play behavior is culturally learned.
6. Play is regarded as voluntary, pleasurable, and nonserious, although it may involve risk and intense commitment.
7. Play appears to be found in all cultures.
8. Play is linked to important social functions such as law, religion, warfare, art, and commerce.

Kraus' presentation of the elements of play points out the important social function of play in society. Play is simple, yet it is complex. It is pleasurable, nondirective, yet can be structured and highly organized. In most cultures, play is joyful, delightful, and pleasurable, although it can also be demanding, intense, and competitive. Play occurs instinctively, yet much of our play behavior is derived from cultural and societal norms, customs, and values. Without question, play has been used as a major vehicle to transmit cultural and societal values as reflected in activities that emphasize competition, cooperation, spontaneity, problem solving, and other outcomes.

Summary

Understanding the concepts of leisure, recreation, and play is fundamental to professional success and to life satisfaction. Leisure, recreation, and play are interwoven concepts, yet they also have their own unique definitional properties. Collectively, leisure, recreation, and play, all elements of human culture, meet many basic human needs and have served to shape, define, and provide meaning to human civilization.

In recent years, our understanding of leisure has been greatly advanced by the work of scientists and scholars studying this area. They have suggested that to experience leisure, certain properties must be in evidence. Four prevailing factors in the literature characterize the leisure experience—freedom, perceived competence, intrinsic motivation, and positive affect. Freedom implies choice, spontaneity, and being free from constraints that inhibit participation. Perceived competence refers to the skills that an individual believes he or she possesses that will contribute to successful participation. Intrinsic motivation refers to an individual's desire to participate in leisure experiences based on personal needs and desires, rather than external motivation. Positive affect refers to the need of an individual to control elements of the leisure experience once he or she is engaged in the process.

Leisure can be viewed from a number of different perspectives, theories, and constructs. Some theorists suggest that leisure is an element of time, whereas others have perceived it as a set of unique or discrete activities in which individuals participate. Still further, leisure has been defined as a state of mind—a subjective attitude—and as a symbol of social status. Likewise, there are numerous theories of leisure that have been developed from different areas and backgrounds.

Recreation can be thought of as a wholesome activity in which individuals participate in their leisure time. Current definitions of recreation are fairly discrete; most definitions are set in the context of such factors as time, activity, and the social implications of such experiences. Recreation is a more commonly used and understood term among the general public than either leisure or play, although in business and commercial sectors the terms *leisure* or *entertainment* are often used to describe that segment of the field.

Play is an exceedingly interesting, yet diverse and difficult topic to identify. Although many think of play as the exclusive domain of children, it is not. Many theories have emerged to explain play, yet today it has no generally accepted explanation or definition. Play is universal; it occurs in all cultures and is often associated with pleasure, delight, and joy. It plays a major role in transmitting the values, culture, and traditions of a society. Leisure, recreation, work, and play all contribute to one's quality of life.

Discussion Questions

1. Why is it necessary to define leisure, recreation, and play?
2. Define five underlying constructs of leisure.
3. Define six different theories of leisure.
4. How are sociological theories of leisure different from psychological theories of leisure?
5. Define recreation. What are its defining elements?
6. Select three theories of play and compare and contrast them.
7. Create a collage on how the media views leisure, recreation, and play. How does this differ from the definitions and theories presented in this chapter?
8. How do leisure, recreation, and play interact in your life?
9. Locate a professional in your community and learn about his or her definition of leisure, recreation, and play.
10. Provide examples of play environments in your home, school, and community.

References

Atkinson, J. W. 1964. *An Introduction to Motivation*. Princeton, NJ: Van Nostrand.

Barker, E., trans. 1946. *The Politics of Aristotle*. London: Oxford University Press.

Bialeschki, D., and Henderson, K. 2000. Gender issues and recreation management. In M. T. Allison and I. E. Schneider (Eds.), *Diversity and the recreation profession: Organizational perspectives* (pp. 73–97). State College, PA: Venture.

Bramham, P. 2002. Rojek, the sociological imagination and leisure. *Leisure Studies, 21*(3/4), 221–234.

Burton, T. L., and Jackson, E. L. 1999. Reviewing leisure studies: An organizing framework. In E. L. Jackson and T. L. Burton (Eds.), *Leisure studies: Prospects for the twenty-first century* (pp. xvii–xxiii). State College, PA: Venture.

Caldwell, L. 2001. The role of theory in therapeutic recreation: A practical approach. In N. J. Stumno (Ed.), *Professional issues in therapeutic recreation: On competence and outcomes* (pp. 349–364). Champaign, IL: Sagamore.

Carr, H. H. 1934. The survival value of play. *Investigation of Department of Psychology and Education*. The University of Colorado, 1902, as cited in Elmer D. Mitchell and Bernard S. Mason, *The Theory of Play*, p. 77. New York: Barnes.

Chick, S. 1998. Leisure and culture: Issues for an anthropology of leisure. *Leisure Science, 20*(2), 111–133.

Claparede, E. 1911. *Psychologie de l'Enfant et Pedagogie Experimentale*, translated by M. Louch and H. Holman. New York: Longmans, Green.

Coalter, F. 1999. Leisure science and leisure studies: The challenge of meaning. In E. L. Jackson and T. L. Burton (Eds.), *Leisure studies: Prospects for the twenty-first century* (pp. 507–519). State College, PA: Venture.

Cordes, K., 2000. and Ibrahim, H. 2003. *Applications in recreation and leisure*. Boston: McGraw-Hill.

Corey, G. 2005. *Theory and practice of counseling and psychotherapy*. 7th ed. New York: Wadsworth.

Crapo, R. H. 2001. *Cultural anthropology: Understanding ourselves and others*. 5th ed. New York: McGraw-Hill.

Csikszentmihalyi, M. 1975. *Beyond Boredom and Anxiety*. San Francisco: Jossey-Bass.

Csikszentmihalyi, M. 1990. *Flow: The Psychology of Optimal Experience*. San Francisco: Jossey-Bass.

Csikszentmihalyi, M. 1993. *The evolving self: A psychology for the third millennium*. New York: Harper Collins.

Csikszentmihalyi, M. 1997. *Finding flow: The psychology of engagement with everyday life*. New York: Basic Books.

Curtis, H. 1917. *The Play Movement and Its Significance*. New York: Macmillan.

Dare, B., G. Welton, and W. Coe. 1998. *Concepts of leisure and western thought*. (2nd. ed). Dubuque, IA: Kendall Hunt.

Dare, B., Welton, G., and Coe, W. 1998. *Concepts of leisure in western thought: A critical and historical analysis* 2nd ed. Dubuque, IA: Kendall/Hunt.

Deegan, J. J. (1989). *American ritual dramas: Social rules and cultural meaning.* New York: Greenwood.

DeGraaf, D., D. Jordan, and K. DeGraaf. 1999. *Programming for Parks, Recreation, and Leisure Services: A Servant Leadership Approach.* State College, PA: Venture.

Dieser, R. B. 2004. Leisure education: Breaking free from individualistic notions. In M. A. Devine (Ed.), *Trends in Therapeutic Recreation: Ideas, concepts, and applications* (pp. 1–25). Ashburn, VA: National Park and Recreation Association.

Dumazedier, J. 1967. *Toward a Society of Leisure.* New York: Free Press.

Edginton, C. R., and J. R. Rossman. 1988. Leisure programming: Building a theoretical base. *Journal of Park and Recreation Administration 6*(4), viii.

Edginton, C. R., Hudson, S. Dieser, R. and Edginton, S., 2004. *Leisure programming: A service-centered and benefits approach.* 4th edition. WCBS/McGraw-Hill: St. Louis.

Edginton, C. R., Hudson, S. R., Dieser, R. B., and Edginton, S. R. 2004. *Leisure programming: A service-centered and benefits approach* 4th ed. Boston, MA: WCB McGraw-Hill.

Ellis, M. 1973. *Why People Play.* Englewood Cliffs, NJ: Prentice-Hall.

Erikson, E. H. 1973. Thought on the city for human development. *Ekistics 35* (29), 216–220.

Fox, K. 2000, October. *Manawa Nanea: Native Hawaiian leisure.* Paper presented at the National Recreation and Park Association Leisure Research Symposium, Phoenix, AZ.

Freysinger, V. J., and Kelly, J. R. 2004. *21st century leisure: Current issues.* State College, PA: Venture.

Gardner, H., Csikszentmihalyi, M., and Damon, W. 2001. *Good work: When excellence and ethics meet.* New York: Basic Books.

Godbey, G. 1981. *Leisure in Your Life.* Philadelphia: Saunders.

Gore, A., and Gore, T. 2002. *Joined at the heart: The transformation of the American family.* New York: Henry Holt and Company.

Gray, D. 1973. This alien thing called leisure. In D. Gray (Ed.), *Reflections on the park and recreation movement* (pp. 1–10). Dubuque, IA: Wm. C. Brown.

Groos, K. 1901. *The Play of Man.* New York: Appleton.

Gunter, B. G. 1987. The leisure experience: Selected properties. *Journal of Leisure Research 19* (2), 115–130.

Hall, G. S. 1906. *Youth.* New York: Appleton.

Haun, P. 1965. *Recreation: A Medical Viewpoint.* New York: Teachers College Press.

Hemmingway, J. L. 1998. Culture, the basis of leisure? Commentary on Chick leisure and culture. *Leisure Science, 20*(2), 153–156.

Henderson, K. A., Bialeschki, M. D., Shaw, S. M., and Freysinger, V. J. 1996. *Both gains and gaps: Feminist perspectives on women's leisure.* State College, PA: Venture.

Henslin, J. M. 2001. *Essentials of sociology: A down-to-earth approach.* 4th ed. Scarborough, ON: Allyn & Bacon Canada.

Huizinga, J. 1950. *Homo ludens: A study of the play elements in culture.* Boston, MA: Beacon.

Ibrahim, H. 1991. *Leisure and Society.* Dubuque, IA: Wm. C. Brown.

Iso-Ahola, S. 1999. Motivational foundations of leisure. Edited by E. Jackson and T. Burton, in *Leisure Studies: Prospects for the 21st Century.* State College, PA: Venture.

Jackson, E. L., and Henderson, K. A. 1995. Gender-based analysis of leisure constraints. *Leisure Science, 17,* 31–51.

James, K. 2000. You can feel them looking at you: The experiences of adolescent girls at swimming pools. *Journal of Leisure Research, 32*(2), 262–280.

Juniu, S. 2000. Downshifting: Regaining the essence of leisure. *Journal of Leisure Research, 32*(1), 69–73.

Kando, T. M., and W. C. Summers. 1971. The impact of work on leisure: Toward a paradigm and research strategy. *Pacific Sociological Review 14,* 310–327.

Kelly, J. R. 1972. Work and leisure: A simplified paradigm. *Journal of Leisure Research, 4,* 50–62.

Kelly, J. R. 1978. Leisure styles and choices in three environments. *Pacific Sociological Review, 21,* 187–207.

Kelly, J. R. 1982. *Leisure.* Englewood Cliffs, NJ: Prentice-Hall.

Kelly, J. R. 1983. *Leisure identities and interactions.* New York: Unwin and Hyman.

Kelly, J. R. 1990. *Leisure.* 2d ed. Englewood Cliffs, NJ: Prentice-Hall.

Kelly, J. R. 1996. *Leisure.* 3d ed. Boston: Allyn & Bacon.

Kelly, J. R. 1998. Greater possibility for leisure anthropology. *Leisure Science, 20*(2), 157–158.

Kelly, J. R. 1999. Leisure and society: A dialectical analysis. In E. L. Jackson and T. L. Burton (Eds.), *Leisure studies: Prospects for the twenty-first century* (pp. 81–95). State College, PA: Venture.

Kelly, J. R., and G. Godbey. 1992. *Sociology of Leisure.* State College, PA: Venture.

Kelly, J. R., and V. Freysinger. 2000. *21st Century Leisure: Current Issues.* Boston: Allyn & Bacon.

Kingwell, M. 1998. *Better living: In pursuit of happiness from Plato to prozac.* Toronto, ON: Penguin Books.

Kingwell, M. 2002, May. *Keynote address.* Canadian Congress of Leisure Research, Edmonton, AB, Canada

Kleiber, D., R. Larson, and M. Csikszentmihalyi. 1986. The experiences of leisure in adolescence. *Journal of Leisure Research 18,* 169–176.

Kraus, R. 1990. *Recreation and Leisure in Modern Society.* 4th ed. New York: HarperCollins.

Kraus, R. 2000. *Leisure in a changing America: Trends and issues for the 21st Century.* Boston: Allyn & Bacon.

Kyle, G., and Chick, G. 2002. The social nature of leisure involvement. *Journal of Leisure Research 34*(4), 426–448.

Lazarus, M. 1883. *About the Attractions of Play.* Berlin: Dummler.

Lee, B. and Shafer, C. 2002. The dynamic nature of leisure experience: An application of affect control theory. *Journal of Leisure Research, 34* (3), 290–310.

Lee, J. 1925. *The Normal Course in Play.* New York: Barnes.

Leitner, M. J., and S. F. Leitner. 1996. *Leisure Enhancement.* 2d ed. New York: Haworth.

Levy, J. 1978. *Play Behavior.* New York: John Wiley.

MacKay, K. J., and J. L. Crompton. 1988. Alternative typologies for leisure programs. *Journal of Park and Recreation Administration 6*(4), 52–64.

Mannell, R., and D. Klieber. 1997. *A Social Psychology of Leisure.* State College, PA: Venture.

Mannell, R., and D. Reid. 1999. Work and leisure. Edited by E. Jackson and T. Burton, in *Leisure Studies: Prospects for the 21st Century.* State College, PA: Venture.

More, T., and Avevill, J. 2003. The structure of recreation behavior. *Journal of Leisure Research, 35*(4), 372–395.

Murphy, J. F. 1974. *Concepts of Leisure.* Englewood Cliffs, NJ: Prentice-Hall.

Murphy, J. F. 1981. *Concepts of Leisure.* 2d ed. Englewood Cliffs, NJ: Prentice-Hall.

Nash, J. B. 1953. *Philosophy of Recreation and Leisure.* Dubuque, IA: C.V. Mosby.

Neulinger, J. 1974. *The Psychology of Leisure.* Springfield, IL: Charles C. Thomas.

Neulinger, J. 1981. *To Leisure: An Introduction.* Boston: Allyn & Bacon.

Parker, S. 1971. *The future of work and leisure.* New York: Praeger.

Patrick, G. T. W. 1916. *The Psychology of Relaxation.* Boston: Houghton Mifflin.

Pavelka, J. 2002. *It's not about time!* Carp, Ontario: Creative Bound, Inc.

Peller, L. E. 1952. Models of children's play. *Mental Hygiene 36,* 66–83.

Piaget, J. 1952, 1961. *The Origins of Intelligence in Children.* New York: International University Press.

Piaget, J. 1952. *Play, Dreams and Imitation in Childhood,* translated by G. Cattegno and F. Hodgson. New York: W. W. Norton.

Pieper, J. 1963. *Leisure: The Basis of Culture.* New York: Random House.

Raymore, L. 2002. Facilitators to Leisure. *Journal of Leisure Research, 34*(1), 37–51.

Reaney, M. J. 1916. The psychology of the organized group game. *Psychological Review,* Mong., Sup. 4, 76.

Reich, C. 1970. *The Greening of America.* New York: Random House.

Robinson, E. S. 1920. The compensatory function of make-believe play. *Psychological Review, 27,* 429–439.

Rojek, C. 1985. *Capitalism and leisure theory.* Tavisock, London.

Rojek, C. 1989. *Leisure for leisure: Critical essays.* Macmillan, London.

Rojek, C. 1995. *Decentering leisure: Rethinking leisure theory.* Thousand Oak, CA: Sage.

Rojek, C. 1999. Deviant leisure: The dark side of free-time activity. In E. L. Jackson and T. L. Burton (Eds.), *Leisure studies: Prospects for the twenty-first century* (pp. 81–95). State College, PA: Venture.

Rojek, C. 2000. *Leisure and culture.* Palgrave, Basingstoke.

Rojek, C. 2005. An outline of the action approach to leisure studies. *Leisure Studies, 24*(1), 13–25.

Rossman, J. R. 1988. Development of leisure programming theory. *Journal of Park and Recreation Administration 6*(4), 1–13.

Russell, R. 2005. *Pastimes: The context of contemporary leisure.* 2nd ed. Champaign, IL: Sagamore.

Russell, R. V. 1996. *Pastimes: The context of contemporary leisure.* Madison, WI: Brown and Benchmark.

Russell, R. V. 2005. *Pastimes: The context of contemporary leisure* 3rd ed. Champaign, IL: Sagamore.

Samdahl, D. M. 1988. A symbolic interactionist model of leisure: Theory and empirical support. *Leisure Sciences 10*(1), 27–29.

Samdahl, D. M. 1991. Measuring leisure: Categorical or interval? *Journal of Leisure Research, 23*(1), 87–94.

Schiller, F. V. 1875. *Essays Esthetical and Philosophical.* London: George Bell.

Shaw, S. M. 1985. The meaning of leisure in everyday life. *Leisure Sciences 7*(1), 1–24.

Spencer, H. 1873. *Principles of Psychology.* New York: Appleton.

Stebbins, R. 1992. *Amateurs, Professionals, and Serious Leisure.* Montreal, Quebec: McGill-Queen's University Press.

Stebbins, R. 1999. Serious leisure. Edited by E. Jackson and T. Burton, in *Leisure Studies: Prospects for the 21st Century.* State College, PA: Venture.

Stebbins, R. A. 2004. *Between work and leisure: The common ground of two separate worlds.* New Brunswick, NJ: Transaction Publications.

Sutton-Smith, B., and J. Roberts. 1982. Play, games, sports. Edited by H. Triandis and A. Heron, in *Handbook of Cross-Cultural Psychology: Developmental Psychology,* 425–443. Boston: Allyn & Bacon.

Sylvester, C. 2002. Ethics and the quest for professionalism. *Therapeutic Recreation Journal, 36*(4), 314–334.

Turner, V. 1969. *The ritual process: Structure and anti-structure.* Chicago: Aldine.

Turner, V. 1982. *From ritual to theatre: The human seriousness of play.* New York: Performing Arts Journal Publication.

Unger, L. S. 1984. The effect of situational variables on the subjective leisure experience. *Leisure Sciences 6*(3), 291–312.

Veblen, T. B. 1899. *The Theory of the Leisure Class.* New York: Macmillan.

Waelder, R. 1933. The psychoanalytic theory of play. *Psychoanalytic Quarterly 2,* 208–224.

Wearing, B. 1998. *Leisure and feminist theory.* Thousand Oak, CA: Sage.

Wilensky, H. 1960. Work, careers and social integration. *International Social Science Journal, 12,* 4.

Wise, J. 2002. Social cognitive-theory: A framework for therapeutic recreation service. *Therapeutic Recreation Journal, 36*(4), 335–351.

Witt, P. A., and D. W. Bishop. 1970. Situational antecedents to leisure behavior. *Journal of Leisure Research,* Winter, 2, 64–77.

Yoder, D. 1997. A model for commodity intensive serious leisure. *Journal of Leisure Research 29*(4), 407–429.

Leisure: A Historical Perspective

State parks are part of our early heritage. Here, a state park ranger in Iowa casually guides the observations of two young children.

Source: Department of Natural Resources, State of Iowa. Used by permission.

Introduction

Humankind has a natural curiosity as to why events occurred, how people became prominent and influential, how they lived, how they worked, and how they played. The study of history fosters understanding about what has occurred in the past and the factors that shaped the evolution of events, people, and activities. This is true for leisure just as it is for other areas of human history.

Studying history provides a view of the evolving concepts of leisure, what people have done during their leisure, and what institutions have emerged in order to meet people's leisure needs. Further, these can be tied to broader societal trends and events to show the relationships among them. Last, and perhaps even more fascinating, is to study about the individuals whose visionary leadership propelled the park and recreation movement forward.

What is history? It is *the record of important activities that have occurred in relation to an individual concept, person, institution, or geographical location* (such as a nation). Historians seek to describe what has happened—and try to determine the causes and effects of certain events and changes in people's behavior or thinking.

When historians engage in a review of past events or people, they are involved in historical research. *Historical research can be thought of as an orderly and systematic reconstruction of the past.* Such research is done rigorously, objectively, and often in relationship to the tenability of a set of research questions or a hypothesis statement. Historians use many resources to investigate the leisure area. Some of these historical sources include written laws, official records, diaries, letters, oral traditions (including eyewitness accounts of events), pictorial records, photographs, newspapers, physical remains, printed materials, and records from institutions and agencies. Even a review of textbooks can provide an understanding into the thinking taking place during a given period of time.

This chapter presents a short discussion of reasons to study history. It provides the reader with an understanding of the importance of a solid historical foundation in relation to leisure and the organized recreation movement in the United States. Next, it presents the history of leisure, from preliterate society to the information era. It also includes a discussion of the history of several of the early activities of the organized park and recreation movement and vignettes of early leaders of the movement.

Why Do We Study History?

Present understanding often stems from knowledge of the past. Some have said that those who ignore the lessons of history may be doomed to repeat its [history's] failures. Chief Justice Oliver Wendell Holmes noted, "to understand the todays, to talk about the tomorrows, I spent time in the yesterdays." A knowledge of history provides reference points from the past, which can be used to trace events and to make comparisons with other eras and cultures. It facilitates a sense of appreciation for those factors that have contributed to the present-day status of events and institutions. More specifically, a study of the history of leisure and of the organized park and recreation movement provides a knowledge of leisure concepts by which to develop an appreciation for the foundations of the profession, to understand the roles of people in history, to gain knowledge of historical events and places, and to understand our place in history. A discussion of these points follows (see figure 3.1, a creative approach to studying history).

Knowledge of Leisure Concepts

Perhaps the first and most important reason to study history is to understand the *evolution of concepts of leisure.* As forces in society have changed, influencing work, religion, and politics, so have leisure concepts evolved. In the industrial era, for example, clearly defined work time and free time occurred at regularly scheduled times. People were tied to a machine, a schedule, and a manager, and their life activities were regulated accordingly. Children and adults worked long hours established by company owners. Shopping, playing, and socializing were held to certain time periods as hours of operation for stores, taverns, and other establishments were heavily regulated by law. Today's information era offers more flexible work times, and attitudes toward work and leisure are more fluid. This has resulted in a blurring of the distinction between work and leisure; for some, work has become so interesting and rewarding that it could be considered a form of leisure activity. For many, however, work and leisure are still well segregated. Most of those who work have firmly established hours of work; leisure tends to be found only after work hours.

Figure 3.1

Multiple choice.

PEANUTS reprinted by permission of United Feature Syndicate, Inc.

Appreciation for the Foundations of the Profession

The study of history also imparts knowledge regarding the *foundations of the leisure service profession,* its emergence, and the evolution of the provision of park and recreation services in the United States and Canada. It reveals social conditions that led to the establishment of agencies and institutions providing leisure services. Every organization has evolved because it met some societal need at some time and place in history, and it survives because it continues to change to meet present needs. These founding conditions are instrumental in the way a movement shapes itself and finds its place in history.

The modern park and recreation movement grew out of the need for social reforms that occurred during the Industrial Revolution in the mid-1800s in the United States. Urbanization, immigration, industrialization, child labor, poor sanitation, lack of open spaces, and other social and human conditions created a need for social reform. Early efforts aimed at providing proper play spaces for children, public baths, parks and other open spaces, and settlement houses were directed toward improving the human condition. The study of history provides an appreciation for the driving forces behind the creation of such areas, facilities, and other services.

Understanding People in History

History is a story about people and their actions and behaviors. Some of humankind's accomplishments have been noble, and some have not. A study of what people thought and did during various historical periods, however, can provide real understanding of how events were shaped. Many of the early leaders of the organized park and recreation movement had a deep commitment to social reform and to enhancing the dignity and welfare of people in the United States. This commitment extended to the notion that people should have access to natural environments to enable them to stay in touch with their rural pastoral roots.

Many of the early leaders of the park and recreation movement were leading thinkers whose concepts influenced a variety of fields. They gave birth not only to the park and recreation movement, but also to social welfare, city planning, landscape architecture, and youth serving organizations. As the radicals of their generation, they encouraged people to change and urged governments and businesses to become more responsive to human needs. Studying such individuals—their thoughts and actions—provides an appreciation and understanding of the development of the park and recreation movement and its relationship to and influence upon society.

Knowledge of Significant Historical Events and Places

Studying history enables people to gain knowledge about historical events and places. In addition, the study of history provides cause-and-effect information in order to trace the impact of events. Conversely, we can determine the factors that caused specific events to occur. We can examine historical events from economic, social, political, cultural, and other perspectives. Knowledge of events, coupled with the reasons they have occurred and their impact, provides critical insight into the historical evolution of the profession.

For example, the Playground Association of America, founded in 1906, held its first Play Congress in Chicago in 1907. Why Chicago? One of the reasons for selecting Chicago as the meeting site may have been the fact that between 1901 and 1903 the Chicago South Park District passed a $4 million bond issue to build field houses (gymnasiums and meeting rooms) and public baths (swimming pools). Four million dollars, when factored for inflation, is an enormous sum of money—more than $40 million today. In planning a conference for a newly emerging national organization, a likely location would be one that was on the cutting edge of the profession.

Knowledge That Can Be Useful—Present and Future

A study of history helps in decision making, both in the present and for the future. The history of the park and recreation profession, like the history of other professions, provides relevant information for the present and the future. Strategies used in the past to provide areas, facilities, and services have been both successful and unsuccessful. Studying these attempts can help in current planning efforts.

Tom Peters, writing in his book *Thriving on Chaos* (1987), notes that leaders of organizations must respect and acknowledge their heritage in designing visions for the future. Organizations have identifiable traditions, rituals, customs, and norms. These factors have historical bases that provide substance and meaning to the work of an organization or agency. To ignore these historically important factors actually denies or minimizes their contribution to the development of an organization or agency.

As a specific example within the context of parks and recreation, consider that many of the institutions we know today emerged during the late 1800s as a part of the broader social reform movement to address the tremendous social, psychological, and general welfare needs that grew out of the Industrial Revolution and waves of European immigration. Social reformers saw the potential of using play and recreation to improve people's quality of life. For instance, the Boston Sand Gardens (the first playground) were established to meet the play needs of disadvantaged children and give them a safe place to play. Also, many of the first organized camps were designed for and targeted at "sickly boys." Large city parks (e.g., Central Park in New York) were designed in an attempt to regain the rural countryside in the middle of the city and thus give people who lived in crowded slum tenements a place to relax and get away from it all. Further, the settlement house movement used recreation as a means to ease the transition of immigrants to living in large urban American cities.

Today, we are seeing another wave of immigrants entering America as the total number of immigrants per year (including illegal and refugees) is only somewhat less than it was in the peak years at the start of the twentieth century (United States Citizenship and Immigration Services, 2004). Many of the same urban problems still plague us today. By studying the beginnings of the recreation movement, we may gain insight into delivering services today. As Putnam, (2000) states:

> We desperately need an era of civic inventiveness to create a renewed set of institutions and channels for reinvigorating our civic life that fits the way we have come to live. Our challenge now is to reinvent the twenty-first century equivalent of the Boy Scouts or the Settlement House or the playground . . . What we create may well look nothing like the institutions Progressives invented a century ago, just as their inventions were not carbon copies of the earlier small town folkways whose passing they mourned. We need to be as ready to experiment as the Progressives were. Willingness to err—and then correct our aim—is the price of success in social reform. (pg. 401)

Understanding Our Place in History

It is vital that individuals, organizations, cities, and nations have an appreciation for their place in history. An understanding of how one's actions contribute in making history is to understand one's destiny and direction. This sense of history applies in terms of the world stage, on a national basis, or, perhaps more importantly, at the local community level where most leisure service professionals will operate.

When viewed in a global sense, history also grants a view of the differences and similarities among individuals, organizations, and movements in various cultures. People in different parts of the world have participated in similar movements that have occurred in response to social needs. For example, some developing nations, such as South Korea, are currently experiencing social movements that stress the need for increased leisure and social services similar to the movement in the United States in the mid- and late 1800s. Perhaps the social reform movements in these countries have been stimulated by many of the same forces of industrialization (urbanization and lack of open space) that stimulated the social reform movements (including park and recreation services) in the United States. By studying history and by making cross-cultural comparisons, one can detect patterns in the development of people, institutions, and nations.

The History of Leisure

In the broadest sense, the history of leisure should be viewed in the context of the history of humankind. Futurist Alvin Toffler (1982), writing in the book *The Third Wave,* suggests that recorded history emerged approximately 10,000 years ago. In general, historians have divided the history of humankind into four distinct periods. Thus, for the purposes of analyzing concepts of leisure, there are four distinct eras—precivilized or preliterate society, the agricultural era, the industrial era, and the technological era. John Naisbitt (1982), in his book *Megatrends,* refers to the technological era as the information era. Bell (1968), in the book *Toward the Year 2000,* refers to this period of time as the postindustrial era. Figure 3.2 portrays these four eras. A brief description of each of the time periods is offered, followed by a more comprehensive discussion of each one.

1. *Preliterate society* existed prior to written history. As MacLean, Peterson, and Martin (1985) note, "We can only surmise which types of activities occupied humans before recorded history" (p. 30). They further note the struggle of preliterate times: Life in prehistoric times was a struggle for mere physical existence. In fact, the problems of daily survival are still a major concern in many parts of the world today. Yet, examples of the continuing search for a more enjoyable life through forms of recreation are evident. Wherever and whenever humans have existed, they have found some time for recreation.

2. The *agricultural era* began approximately 8,000 years ago, with the domestication of animals and crops and the establishment of civilization in Mesopotamia. Approximately 6,000 years ago, agricultural activity was initiated in Central America. Both of these events gave birth to the beginning of today's civilization.

3. The *industrial era* began in Europe, more specifically in Great Britain, in the 1700s and the early 1800s; it spread to the United States by the mid-1800s. The industrial era had both positive and negative consequences. First and foremost, it greatly improved the quality of life available to individuals. Inventions during this period led to newer and more efficient means of production that resulted in greater access to material goods and better transportation and communication systems. As previously mentioned, negative consequences of the industrial era—crowded conditions, child labor, poor sanitation, and other factors—resulted in the need for social reform.

4. The *technological or information era* began in the mid-1950s. The advent of computers and the changing nature of work in developed countries contributed to the evolution of this newer era. As a hallmark of this era, many more people work in service- and information-based

Figure 3.2

Four eras
of history.

industries in the United States and Canada today than in either manufacturing or agricultural occupations (Kelly and Godbey, 1992). The technological era has resulted in greater access to information and increased speed of transportation and communication.

Life in the information age has accelerated the rate of change in our world, thereby creating a common need to understand change. Godbey (1997) notes that while "technological change always runs ahead of the ability of the human race to understand or evaluate it prior to its introduction, today such change defies both our understanding and even our imagination" (p. 3). This environment has created unique opportunities for leisure service organizations that are able to understand the past as well as the changes that are taking place in our society and transform this knowledge to visualizing the future.

In each of these eras, people have conceptualized and engaged in leisure in different ways. The same has been the case with work and time. The ways in which people have enjoyed their leisure and/or the ways in which leisure has emerged as a social institution have varied during each of these historical periods.

Leisure in Preliterate Societies

In preliterate societies, survival was the main concern of life. Life was short and opportunistic. Much of what we know or understand about humankind before recorded history comes from one of two sources. The first source is the work of physical anthropologists, who have studied humankind in all periods of history. Anthropologists not only attempt to reconstruct the daily life and customs of prehistoric groups and populations but study their evolution and current practices as well.

The second source of anthropological information about preliterate people results from the study of primitive groups of people in the world today, such as the Tsaddi, discovered in a remote area of the Philippines more than a decade ago. These people apparently had never come into contact with modern civilization. By analyzing their environment, family life, religion, style of art, and dress, some broad assumptions made concerning their play and work behavior could indicate patterns of other preliterate groups. Discussing play in primitive cultures, MacLean, Peterson, and Martin (1985) write the following:

> . . . we strongly assume that children's play was essentially what it has always been. Children frolicked in streams and lakes; climbed trees; played with pets; planned mock battles against the enemy—both human and animal; and learned the art of survival. Times of rest for pre-historic peoples were filled with sewing, stringing beads, partaking in songs, chants, and dances; and telling stories and myths around the home fire. (p. 30)

The sharp distinction between work time and leisure time that emerged during the industrial era did not exist in preliterate days. In a sense, work and leisure activities were fused together. As Kraus (1990) writes, "Primitive people do not make a clear distinction between work and leisure that we tend to do in more technologically advanced societies . . .

Figure 3.3

Ancient Egyptians singing and playing musical instruments.

Painted relief from the tomb of Nenkheftikai at Sakkarah, Fifth Dynasty. Photo by Tor Eigeland/Black Star.

a primitive society has no precise separations; instead, work is customarily done when it is available or necessary and it is often fused with rites and customs that lend it variety and pleasure" (p. 114).

Clearly, it becomes difficult to distinguish between the work and play of primitive peoples. Play was often infused with ritual, transmitting the culture of preliterate societies from generation to generation. Numerous examples of activities now associated with leisure pastimes were a part of everyday life in preliterate society. Most of the leisure and play activities that existed during preliterate society related to the acquisition of survival skills, and included fishing, hunting, skiing, boating, swimming, horseback riding, combative activities, and arts and crafts (such as pottery, weaving, and leather work) (Kraus, 1990). Many of these activities served as the basis for the development of later civilizations. Today, for example, we do our hunting and gathering by proxy in that someone else grows, kills, cleans, packages, and sells meat and food goods to us. In our memories, however, we preserve ". . . the chase lingering in our joyful pursuit of anything weak or fugitive, and in the games of our children—even in the word *game*" (Durant, 1963, p. 7).

Interestingly, people in preliterate societies lived their lives primarily by life rhythms. When they were hungry, they hunted, fished, or gathered food; when they were joyful, they celebrated; and when they were tired, they slept. People moved at a natural pace depending upon their current state of need and natural conditions of the environment.

Much current knowledge about early historical cultures, such as the Egyptian culture, comes from the remains of their tombs or inscriptions. They had a well-developed class system with the lower classes engaging in athletics and physical sport while the upper classes were more sedentary and enjoyed being entertained (Kraus, 1984). Egyptian games included checkers and dice; children played with toys such as marbles, bouncing balls, ten pins and tops; they enjoyed wrestling contests, boxing matches, and bullfights (Kraus, 1984). At feasts and recreation functions, participants were anointed by attendants and were wreathed with flowers, feted with wines, and presented with gifts (Kraus, 1984). Figure 3.3 depicts ancient Egyptians engaging in leisure activity.

The Egyptians also enhanced outdoor spaces. Tomb paintings often depicted garden areas surrounding developments. Plantings provided an environment that protected individuals from the harshness of the climate. In preliterate times, gardens were established in and around the palaces and ziggurats of Mesopotamia. Among these, the Hanging Gardens of Babylon, referred to by Herodotus, were considered one of the seven wonders of the ancient world. The gardens, planted at a height of seventy-five feet, consisted of a variety of flowers and plants, including large and deep-rooted trees.

Leisure in the Agricultural Era

"The first form of culture was agriculture" (Durant, 1966, p. 2). Agriculture provided a stable supply of food, and when humankind began to labor in the soil, provided an opportunity for a long-term perspective on life. The development of agriculture enabled people to develop a sense of security resulting from a dependable food supply. With their energies no longer solely devoted to hunting or gathering enough food to survive, they could participate in other activities—activities that resulted in the advancement of civilization.

During the agricultural era, society established property rights for cultivation and farming. Prior to this no one person owned property; hunting or gathering occurred wherever food was found. As agriculture developed, so did the need for private property on which to produce crops. In order to protect and manage this property, a division of labor occurred. A ruling elite formed; government officials owned and managed the land; a military protected the land; and a peasant class farmed the land. A more complex form of social organization evolved than had been in place during preliterate society. For the first time in history, humankind produced a surplus of commodities, thus forming classes of people who were not involved directly in their production. Landowners, governmental officials, scribes, and artists were all supported by the efforts of others. These individuals became the *leisure class,* as contrasted with individuals in the *working class.*

For the people living during the agricultural era, the concept of time changed. Time became a regulatory dimension of life, and people tied their lives more closely to changes in the seasons. When it was time to plant, people planted; when it was time to harvest a crop, the harvest occurred. Leisure time and leisure activities became attached to these events, such as autumn harvest celebrations. When the harvest was in, the great celebrations included games, food, dancing, socializing, and rituals. Furthermore, strong evidence indicates that people had a great deal of leisure time during certain seasons of the year when field work was slow.

In many cultures, the new class of individuals not directly associated with the production of commodities met their responsibility to society in the development of civilization. They used their time and intellectual capabilities to enhance the economic well-being of their culture, to establish political organizations, to develop religions, and to pursue intellectual and artistic activities. The Greeks, in particular, used leisure to advance civilization. According to the Greeks, ". . . without a leisure class, there can be no standards of taste, no encouragement of the arts, no civilization. No man [*sic*] in a hurry is quite civilized" (Durant, 1966, p. 277).

Leisure in Ancient Greece The Greeks believed that civilization advanced through the cultivation of the mind, body, and spirit. As a result, the Greeks, especially the Athenians, took great interest in a variety of activities linked to the development of civilization. These activities included writing, artistic endeavors, and athletics (Kraus, 1984). Children living in ancient Greek society participated in a variety of play pursuits.

> Babies have Terra Cotta rattles containing pebbles; girls keep house with their dolls; boys fight campaigns with toy soldiers and generals; nurses push children on swings or balance them on seesaws; boys and girls roll hoops, fly kites, spin tops, play hide and seek or blind man's bluff, or tug of war, and wage a hundred meter contest with pebbles, nuts, coins and balls. (Durant, 1966, p. 288)

School activities also prepared children for future leisure pursuits. Writing, reading, arithmetic, music, gymnastics, drawing, and painting were all part of the curriculum. Sports activities of youth served as a form of military preparation for males; they ran, hunted, wrestled, drove chariots, and hurled javelins (Kraus, 1984).

Perhaps the most influential Athenian philosopher recognizing the need for leisure was Aristotle, who believed that the end of labor was to gain leisure. More importantly, Aristotle believed that

TABLE

3.1 THE LEISURE LEGACY OF ANCIENT GREECE

Parks in Greece	• To the ancient Greek, trees—primarily olive trees—were a very sacred symbol. From the trees flowed the very lifeblood of the civilization. It is not surprising, then, that when the ancient Greeks were searching for a way of honoring fallen heroes, they would decorate tombs with trees, the very symbol of life. As time progressed, groves of trees dotted the landscape.
Olympic Games	• National festivals were conducted every four years at Olympia to honor Zeus. Commenced in 776 B.C. and continued until the fifth century A.D., the games lasted five days.
	• All warring tribes were expected to observe a truce while the games were in progress—the truce of the gods.
	• Although women were not allowed in, in other respects the games were very democratic—noble and peasant competed on equal terms.
Greek Theater	• Began with elegy—poems reflecting on the disillusionment of life. Gradually replaced by the lyric, which was sung to music.
	• Tragic drama was the supreme literary achievement of the Greeks. Greek tragedy had as its theme the conflict between human and the universe. The purpose of Greek tragedies was not merely to depict suffering and interpret human actions but to purify the emotions of the audience by representing the triumphs of justice.
Greek Theater—Structure	• As impressive as the plays were the physical structures developed to house the dramas. Ancient Greek theaters were acoustically sound. Generally the stage was either built against a cliff or strategically placed in a round. Little modification of the basic structure has occurred today.
Greek Art	• The art of the Greeks also reflected their character and their view of the world. Architecture and sculpture embodied the idea of harmony, order, balance, and moderation.

Note: Beyond philosophy, the Greek legacy extends into recreation from both programmatic and facility standpoint. Although Aristotle would not consider these items leisure, they have contributed to our "leisure legacy" in the modern sense.

leisure was not "freedom from" but rather "freedom to" pursue the good life, which is a state of being well and doing well. Leisure, according to Aristotle, provides the opportunity for intellectual development, provides a way of relaxing the soul, and enhances enjoyment of life. Table 3.1 presents several practical aspects of the Greeks' leisure legacy that have stretched into today.

Leisure in Ancient Rome Ancient Roman society was fascinating in terms of the leisure lifestyles of its citizens. Leisure pursuits and activities tended to be much more utilitarian than in Greek society. Although activities for the leisure or privileged classes provided entertainment, they were primarily directed toward maintaining the rigor of the young men of this militaristic society. As Rome adopted a more luxurious standard of living, leisure and spare time became a serious problem. A few members of the senatorial aristocracy exerted efforts to check the pleasure tendencies. One such leader was Cato the elder, who said "that a great man was accountable for every moment of his spare time as much as for every moment of his working day." According to Cato there were two charges that a man in prominent society must be careful to avoid. The first was self-indulgence and the second was idleness.

Wealthy Romans surrounded themselves with sculpture, painting, and other objects of art. By the fourth century A.D., Rome had more than 1,300 public swimming pools or baths

(Durant, 1944). Baths became the social and athletic clubs of Roman citizens and for the leisure class, the daily routine of exercise, bathing, and eating was the usual order of the day. The baths were elaborate structures with pillars and walls of granite, and marble floors of mosaic and tile. Privately owned, the baths were erected by wealthy men as gifts to the city or were constructed from public funds. They were managed by people who leased them and charged fees for use.

Some of the larger bath houses became immense cultural centers that included libraries, lounges, art galleries, and dining rooms. The leisure activities in which wealthy male Roman citizens participated varied, as evidenced by the following:

> Baths were usually preceded by a vigorous workout, where individuals would run, jump, or play a ball game, using an object like a medicine ball. Following this, individuals were provided rooms for games like dice, chess, galleries of paintings and statues and areas where friends might sit and converse, libraries with reading rooms, and halls where a musician, poet might give a recital. (Durant, 1944, p. 375)

Entertainment in Rome was plentiful and inexpensive. Rome exhibited forms of leisure found in previous civilizations—gambling, reading, dancing, drinking, sports, and games were all part of the Roman way of life. In figure 3.4 young Roman women enjoy a gambling game. Recitations, lectures, concerts, mimes, plays, athletic contests, prize fights, chariot races, mortal combats of men with men or men with beasts, not-quite-sham naval battles on artificial lakes— never was a city so bountifully amused. Sports were popular. In Roman culture, sports were divided into three areas: hunting, riding, and competition of arms; boxing, wrestling, running, throwing the discus and javelin; weight lifting, trundling a hoop, and a great variety of ball games. In the fourth century A.D. there were twenty-nine libraries in Rome. These libraries seemed generally to have been in the vicinity of temples. They served the upper classes by lending books and scrolls for reading.

One of the most popular activities was the *circus maximus*. These chariot races were the center of attention of the community, and men gambled heavily on each of the five-mile chariot races that took place. The games concluded with the contests of animals and gladiators in the

Figure 3.4

Young Roman women playing a gambling game.

Museo Archeologico Nazionale, Naples, Italy, Scala/Art Resource, NY.

amphitheater-coliseum. The *circus maximus* also featured exhibitions of exotic animals from throughout the world. Approximately 2,000 feet long and 600 feet wide, the *circus maximus* accommodated about 385,000 people. Races were financed by the state or private individuals. Syndicates were identified by the colors the drivers wore. In the early days of the Republic, anyone could race, but in the later times "respectable" citizens did not participate. The race drivers were slaves.

The Roman Coliseum was the facility in which gladiators fought. The arena covered six acres and had walls 160 feet high; it could accommodate 90,000 spectators. Subterranean areas contained chambers for gladiators, dens for animals, and a maze of pipes to flood and drain the area for sea battles. Gladiators were mostly slaves, criminals, or captives. Originally the fights were small privately sponsored affairs. During the third century A.D. a mass of 500 pairs of men contested in a huge spectacle. Usually fighting continued until death was decided by the victor—"Thumbs up or thumbs down." The Nauchmacha was an amphitheater constructed to hold sea battles. In one event, four naval vessels fought a minibattle until all eventually were lost. One battle had 19,000 men fighting at once.

As in Greece the games began mainly as religious festivals to which were added festivals in honor of heroes, victories, and so on. At the time of the first emperor, ninety days were devoted to the games. Three hundred years later, there were twice as many days devoted to the games, plus special celebrations. At one time, seventeen of twenty-nine days in April were spent at the circus, amphitheater, or coliseum. The Greeks and Romans had differing views of leisure as related to the games. To the Greeks, the games were great events in which every person aspired to compete. The Romans, on the other hand, regarded the games as spectator entertainment.

Historians often depict the leisure pursuits of Romans as being hedonistic, vulgar, and corrupt. The maiming and butchering of individuals and animals have been viewed historically as obscene. The downfall of Rome has been linked with the inability of that culture to use its leisure in a positive and productive manner. When faced by the challenges of excesses of wealth, luxury, and time, the Romans responded by yielding to corruption and losing the simple virtues that had made them strong as a nation (Kraus, 1984).

Leisure and Christianity The Christian faith has had a strong impact on attitudes and values toward work and leisure of U.S. citizens. Early Christians believed that work was good for humankind and that idleness was not good. Work, framed in the context of being productive, provided a surplus of commodities to share with others. Thus, early Christians focused their activities on producing more in order to help those who had less and who needed charity.

This philosophy contrasted with that of early Catholic philosophers who had begun to distinguish between physical and intellectual labors. They perceived that they should engage in intellectual and spiritual activities while others engaged in physical labor. They believed that because a leisurely lifestyle allowed for prayer and contemplation, it was best for a priest. Early Catholic philosophers felt that work need not necessarily be emphasized when one's reward was realized in the life to come.

The Protestant Reformation, spearheaded by Martin Luther, changed the way Christians viewed work and, hence, play. Luther viewed work as being good and that God *calls* his people to their work or their vocation. His views reflected his belief that all callings are equally worthwhile in the eyes of God and individuals are not to seek material gains but to develop their own abilities to seek perfection. He maintained that religious work was not superior to other types of work. Work of any type was valued, whereas idleness was viewed as a sin. Luther's views supported a value system that promoted the desirability of work and thrift.

Whereas Luther fostered the Protestant Reformation, another reformer named John Calvin fostered the Protestant work ethic. Calvin built on Luther's sense of calling and further articulated that the purpose of work was to glorify God, not to accumulate wealth. "We are created for the express purpose of being in labor of various kinds, and that no sacrifice is more pleasing to God than when we apply ourselves diligently to our own callings, and endeavor to live in such a way as to contribute to the common good" (Calvin, as quoted in *An Engagement with God's World,* 1999, p. 7). Today many theologians have noted that proponents of capitalism used both Luther's and Calvin's idea of *calling,* and used it unjustly, to create a Protestant work ethic to supply the labor it needed to grow. This new Protestant work ethic not only encouraged hard work but also connected material blessings as a sign of God's approval. This Protestant work ethic is deeply embedded into North American culture today and in some ways has countered the development of a leisure ethic and influences the leisure-work guilt phenomenon experienced by many in society today.

Not all Christian philosophy suggests hard work, however. Numerous writings refer to the enjoyment of life and celebration of the harvest. As the church increasingly gained control over the affairs of the state with a corresponding merger of social, political, and religious beliefs, Sunday became an institutionalized day of prayer and leisure. Kraus (1984, 1990) notes that during the Middle Ages individuals may have had as many as 170 days off work per year, counting religious holidays and Sundays.

Leisure in the Middle Ages   The Middle Ages in Western Europe linked ancient civilization with modern times; it spanned the years from A.D. 400 to A.D. 1500. The major civilizing force during the Middle Ages was the Christian Church. During this period of time,

Figure 3.5

A band of performers during the Middle Ages.

Detail from the Canterbury Psalter. Illuminated manuscript. 12c, Trinity College Cambridge, England.

Figure 3.6

Card playing in the late Middle Ages.

THE CARD PLAYERS by Lucas van Leyden, Samuel B. Kress Collection, © 1994 National Gallery of Art, Washington, D.C.

most areas of Western Europe were divided into feudal states. These feudal states saw a continued social and political hierarchy where large feudal states were managed by lords, and peasants worked the land in support of these individuals.

Spectacles in the form of religious pageants, political processions, tournaments, and festivals all formed a part of the revelry during the Middle Ages. In fact, during the Christmas season many towns appointed a "Lord of Misrule" to organize events. (Could this have been the first recreation leader?) Travel was possible, not only for merchants, but also for tourists who lodged at wayside inns. Minstrels, jugglers, exhibitions of exotic animals, and acrobats entertained as a part of circuses traveling among the villages. Figure 3.5 portrays a band of performers in the Middle Ages.

Class distinctions were evident during the Middle Ages, in terms of leisure pursuits as well as other activities. The male nobility engaged in such activities as hunting, jousting, falconry, skating, horse racing, archery, fishing, bowling, hockey, quoits, wrestling, boxing, tennis, and football. For example, hunting was regulated by strict game laws and was usually conducted in preserves set aside for the nobility. Sporting activities, often conducted in front of large crowds, became a leisure pursuit for spectators. Historical record of women's leisure is extremely limited. We do know that women were viewed as property of their fathers and, when they were married, their husbands. We can only speculate that the mores of the times dictated work and leisure in the home focusing on servitude to one's husband and family. Figure 3.6 shows a group of individuals engaged in leisure activities in the late Middle Ages.

While many perceived the Middle Ages to be a harsh period because of the rigors of Christian morality, individuals did indeed enjoy themselves in their leisure. It was a period of merriment, marked by celebration—not a period, as historians have often described it, where rigorous codes of behavior squelched satisfying life experiences.

Leisure and the Renaissance The Renaissance began in Italy about A.D. 1300 and lasted for approximately 300 years. The Renaissance, particularly notable because of advancements in the sciences and the arts, was a period of great intellectual activity and of great

Figure 3.7

Young people
enjoying a game
of chess.

*The Metropolitan
Museum of Art,
Bequest of
Maitland Griggs,
1943. Maitland
F. Griggs Collection
(43.98.8).*

creative force. During the Renaissance, many changes in style in painting, sculpture, and architecture emerged.

The Renaissance saw the strict moral codes of the time held in contempt. Amusements such as dancing, conversation, and dramatic plays were often of a coarse nature and deliberately defied moral codes of the day. Records of the many leisure activities in which men participated during this period mention fencing, gambling, chess, bullfighting, horse racing, hunting, falconry, boxing, tennis, boating, and foot racing. People often walked or rode into the countryside to visit others and to view the scenery, and they enjoyed carnivals, processions, and festivals as in the Middle Ages. Women were sometimes allowed to accompany their husbands and fathers to these events. Figures 3.7 and 3.8 depict individuals of this period engaged in chess and a primitive form of tennis.

During the Renaissance period the arts flourished, with a revitalization of literature, architecture, sculpture, painting, music, and drama. Music concerts became an important leisure pastime available to women and all social classes. Artistic activities resulted in a creative frenzy that spawned such artists as Michelangelo, Raphael, Leonardo da Vinci, Titian, Bellini, and others. The Renaissance also saw the development of the first printing press in the mid-1400s in Germany, set up by Guttenberg.

Leisure in Colonial America   As Europe went through a great period of change in the 1500s and 1600s, it produced religious reformation and economic development. This reformation gave rise to the development of the theology of Martin Luther and economic expansion into what has become known as the United States and Canada. Protestant leaders in England emphasized family life, industriousness, participation in community activities, and education. These reformers fell into two categories: the Puritans, who sought to change the Church of England from within; and the Separatists, who wanted to separate from the Church of England.

In 1607, the Virginia Company of London received the charter for the establishment of an economically based settlement in what was then called the New World (present-day

Figure 3.8

Young woman of
the Renaissance
period playing an
early form of
tennis.

*Anonymous, LADY
PLAYING BALL.
Palazzo Borromeo.
Milan, Italy. Scala/
Art Resource, NY.*

Canada and the United States). This economically based community established at Jamestown nearly met with collapse during its first decade of existence. Only 1,200 of the 8,000 people who immigrated to the Virginia-based colony between 1607 and 1625 remained alive after those ten years.

In 1608, a group of separatists left England for Holland. Displeased because their children were adopting the culture of Holland, they negotiated for passage on the Mayflower. In 1620, these Separatists, or Pilgrims, arrived at Plymouth Rock. In 1629, a group of Puritans in England organized the Massachusetts Bay Company. Moved by both economic and religious motives, they undertook a massive expedition in 1630. Between 1629 and 1640, a great exodus of Puritans left England; 25,000 individuals landed in New England. The Massachusetts Bay Colony, a religious colony, set the tone for leisure in the United States for years to come.

The original immigrants to the lands of Canada and the United States had little time to engage in leisure. The harshness of the environment and the need to survive placed great demands on them. To ensure that work was encouraged and idleness diminished, early Puritan leaders established strict regulations. "Religion provided the strongest moral sanction for every law suppressing amusements" (Dulles, 1965, p. 5).

One view of the Puritans was that they were legalistic and did not permit leisure. They valued frugality, hard work, self-discipline, and strict observance of civil and religious codes. They viewed play as the devil's handiwork and tried to legislate morality. For example, consider the following law from the colony of Massachusetts (presented in old English): "all men are ordered to work the whole day allowing convenient time for food and rest and that no person householder or other, shall spend his time idly or unprofitably under pain of such punishment as the Court shall think meet to inflict" (Records of the Court of Assistants of the Colony of the Massachusetts Bay 1633–1644, as quoted by Swanson and Spears, 1995, p. 46).

Although this view of the Puritans is widely held, Ryken (1994) presents an alternative view. According to Ryken, the original Puritan work ethic included in its basic principles that God calls people to work, that all legitimate work has dignity, that work can be stewardship to God and a service to self and humanity, and that work should be pursued in moderation and in deference to spiritual concerns. These ideas do not exclude leisure; they advocate balance in living a life to glorify God. Work and leisure give meaning to each other. Ryken goes on to verify that the Puritans were opposed to some types of recreation as well as keeping the Sabbath holy apart from pastimes. However, Puritans enjoyed such varied sports as fishing, hunting, bowling, reading, music, swimming, skating, and archery. Regarding recreation, a Puritan preacher said that Christians should "enjoy recreation as liberties, with thankfulness to God that allows these liberties to refresh themselves" (p. 41).

Virginia also enacted laws that restricted idleness. For example, in 1619 the Virginia Assembly decreed that any individual who was found idle could be made to work. It also prohibited gambling and regulated drinking and other amusements. Similar legal codes were established throughout the colonies.

Despite the harshness of the life of early colonists, leisure pursuits did emerge. Drinking, in particular, and meeting friends at the local tavern became commonplace for men. Women met in town centers while shopping or tending to other family needs. After the initial decades of Puritan influence, colonists generally sought to develop broader leisure pursuits. Such activities as animal baiting, country dances, music, sports, hunting, fishing, husking bees, skittles, horseback riding, tennis, cockfighting, dice, cards, and shuffleboard became popular. On the frontier, hunting, shooting matches, racing, pitching horseshoes, footraces, wrestling, card playing, horse racing, log rolling, and dancing all became important leisure pursuits. Traveling performers featured animal acts, acrobats, and dramatic readings. In addition, spiritual revivals on the frontier became important leisure events.

Although few specific organized activities related to the development of park and recreation services, several significant events occurred. The early colonists recognized the need for common open areas and subsequently established commons in Boston. Initially, the commons primarily served as an area for common use by individuals in the community; use for leisure was incidental. In 1641, the Massachusetts Great Ponds Act was passed. This legislation decreed that all bodies of water over ten acres were open to the public for fishing and hunting. Further concern for environmental issues was seen in the establishment of squares and plazas by communities in Spanish colonies. Founders of Saint Augustine, Santa Fe, and San Diego brought with them the concept of open spaces as an integral part of town planning (Frye, 1980). In addition, in Savannah, Georgia, James Oglethorpe included open spaces as a part of his grand design for that community.

Leisure in the Industrial Era

The industrial revolution started in Britain and then moved to the rest of Europe throughout the eighteenth century. In the United States, industrialization did not begin until the early to mid 1800s. There were many factors that entered into how and why countries began the industrialization process. Dare, Welton, and Coe (1987) identified many of the following factors as contributing to the development of the industrial revolution in Europe and the United States:

- Population began building up in and around cities, furnishing the human capital needed to operate labor-intensive factories.
- Limited land supply began to run out (especially in places like Britain). This created a climate of innovation as individuals looked for other ways to move up in society.

- Wilderness became more accessible, making vast amounts of natural resources available for development.
- Competition between nations in the market place and on the battlefield encouraged innovations in weapons, which eventually trickled down to other society uses. Likewise, governments encouraged innovations as they began seeing the benefits of performing well in the global marketplace.
- Advancements in transportation and communication increased humankind's ability to move goods to centralized and specialized production.
- Advancements in manufacturing techniques allowed for more mass production.

The industrial era brought about sweeping changes, not only in Europe, but also in the United States. The new conditions brought about by industrialization changed the basic assumptions about the way people lived their lives. New conditions created new needs for political, economic, and social systems. The industrial era greatly improved the standard of living for many individuals, but, at the same time, greatly disrupted the social order for a period of time. During the agricultural era, less than 5 percent of the population lived in cities and towns. During the industrial era, that statistic changed dramatically.

Many historians point out that the transition from an agricultural-based society to an industrial-based society was not a smooth one. In fact, many scholars point out that the American Civil War was, in part, a product of the changing power structure from a feudal to an industrial-based society. The American Civil War was a time of economic conflict, social disorder, and racial concern.

The industrial era produced boom-and-bust economic cycles in the United States; it also produced mass waves of immigration and urbanization. Concentration of populations around economic concerns in urban areas created the need for social reform. Initially, social reform was undertaken by private philanthropists. Later, however, it required the support of government. Governmental intervention resulted in a social welfare philosophy. Through taxation, government redistributed income to help solve social problems in a variety of areas, including education, health, and leisure.

Class distinctions between men and women sharpened. Men went into the world of work (and worth) while women, essentially homebound, worked without pay. Middle-class women benefited from their husband's or father's financial success. They engaged in social activities, went to theaters and shows, and were entertained by diverse amusements. On the other hand, women from lower socioeconomic classes were forced to work in poor conditions and difficult circumstances out of economic necessity. This work, in addition to the housework and child care expected in the household, placed a double burden on women (Henderson et al., 1989, 1996).

During the Industrial Revolution, life became clock-driven; the clock regulated both work and play. Children and adults adjusted their work efforts to a schedule—not to personal desires, needs, and abilities. Thus, time was viewed differently than it had been viewed in the agricultural era. There was work time and there was free time. The misuse of free time came to be viewed as a social problem and the provision of wholesome productive leisure activities became an instrument of social reform.

The way in which work was organized also impacted general life satisfaction. Perhaps the great contribution of the Industrial Revolution involved the ability for mass production via the establishment of the division of labor and the creation of assembly lines. As work became more and more specialized, however, it robbed individuals of their sense of purpose. Not seeing a product to completion, people often found work to be tedious, boring, and monotonous. People began to look outside of their work environments for satisfaction. Leisure became a method for compensating for dissatisfying work experiences.

It was also during the industrial revolution that we began to see more and more Americans become self-made millionaires, thus giving new meaning to the term *leisure class.* It was during this time period that Thorsten Veblen (1899) wrote *Theory of the Leisure Class,* which identified the ethic of economic accumulation for leisure. For the first time in America, the wealthy had plenty of money and free time but little experience on how to use either. This led to conspicuous consumption being seen as leisure, and people used leisure as a way to demonstrate their social status.

The commercialization of leisure made leisure more accessible to the general public, but it also brought bad influences for youth that many reformers thought needed to be addressed. Edwards writes in his book *Popular Amusements* (1915), ". . . the professional entertainer holds sway in every field from which he is not rigidly excluded, every field in which the rights of the amateur are not vigorously asserted.. . . A social disease has been spreading broadcast among us.. . . The disease of spectatoritis abounds in the land."

Excursion boats on Lake Michigan left Chicago with as many as 5,000 on board at a time. These boats carried unsupervised teenagers, and although they were billed as daytime outings, they often did not return until the early hours of the morning. "The Juvenile Protection Association . . . discovered that these boats were violating many laws. Gambling machines and devices of every sort were run openly upon the boats, liquor was sold to minors, while staterooms were rented over and over again throughout the night. These boats were largely patronized by young people who . . . became drunk and engaged in orgies" (Bowen, 1914).

In response to these conditions, several social movements were initiated by reformers. Many early movements and later institutions saw the use of recreation as a tool for furthering social, intellectual, and moral development.

Out of these conditions emerged women and men of great vision, energy, and drive. Such individuals as Jane Addams, Luther Gulick, Joseph Lee, John Muir, Henry Curtis, Stephen Mather, Gifford Pinchot, Frederick Law Olmstead, Theodore Roosevelt, Mabel Peters, Ernest Atwell, Jacob Riis, Juliette Lowe, and William D. Boyce made contributions to the development of new and innovative agencies and institutions to solve the emerging social problems of the industrial era (see table 3.2). This section of the text focuses on the development of some of the major movements that emerged and became institutionalized during this era.

Movements to Institutions   What is a movement? What is an institution? When does a movement become institutionalized? Many, if not all, of the strategies used to provide park and recreation services that emerged in the industrial era started out as the dream, idea, or vision of one or more people. The vision held by early leaders in the United States, in terms of providing meaningful leisure services, often met with public apathy, lack of financial support, and political opposition. Early leaders were often crusaders, zealots, or missionaries who championed their cause. Thus, the work of early leaders focused on the spearheading of a movement related to leisure.

A *movement* may be thought of as a crusade—a cause to which people become highly committed emotionally. A movement usually has a clear sense of direction that is well articulated by its leader or leaders and tied to a specific set of values and/or goals. Those involved in movements direct their energies toward attacking real problems—social, political, or otherwise. Movements often spawn more than political rhetoric and result in the actual creation and delivery of innovative services. For instance, the play movement resulted in the development and implementation of model playground programs.

As a movement becomes more and more accepted by the public, it becomes *institutionalized.* Its aims and objectives become widely supported by the public and its programs may

TABLE

3.2   PIONEERS IN LEISURE SERVICES

Jane Addams (1860–1935)	Social reformer, founder of Hull House (1889), viewed as the creator of social welfare in America
Ernest T. Atwell (1842–1949)	Staff member National Recreation Association, pioneered programs for African Americans
Lord Robert Baden-Powell (1857–1941)	Founder of Boy Scouts (1909)
W. P. Bowen (1864–1928)	Educator, author of *Theory of Organized Play Its Nature and Significance*
Samuel Bowles (1826–1878)	Advocate for the preservation of Niagara Falls, Adirondocks Forest, and Yosemite Valley
William D. Boyce (1858–1929)	Founder of Boy Scouts of America (1910)
Neva L. Boyd (1876–1963)	Established training school for playground workers, Chicago, IL
Howard S. Braucher (1881–1949)	Executive Director of the National Recreation Association
Charles K. Brightbill (1910–1966)	Educator, author of *The Challenge of Leisure, Man and Leisure* (1960)
Virgil K. Brown (1883–1974)	Professional leader, Chicago, IL; first president, American Recreation Society
William Cullen Bryant (1794–1878)	Advocate for public parks in New York
George D. Butler (1894–1985)	Author, director of research National Recreation Association
Reynold Carlson (1901–1997)	Educator, author, leader in nature recreation, camping
Rachel Carson (1907–1964)	Author of *Silent Spring* (1962); raised environmental consciousness
George Catlin (1796–1872)	Author, painter, advocate for establishing national parks
Anna Botsford Comstock (1854–1930)	Environmentalist, author, *Handbook of Nature Study*
Abbie H. Condit (1883–1948)	Managing editor of *The Playground, Playground and Recreation, & Recreation*
Calvin Coolidge (1872–1933)	Established Presidents' Conference on Outdoor Recreation
E. Coulter (1871–1952)	Founder of the Big Brothers/Big Sisters of America in 1904
Robert Crawford (1906–1995)	Professional leader, Philadelphia, PA
Henry S. Curtis (1870–1954)	Author of *Education Through Play,* and *The Play Movement and Its Significance,* playground administrator; early leader Playground Association of America
John Dewey (1859–1952)	Educator advocating community use of schools
Walt Disney (1901–1966)	Innovator in theme parks, motion pictures
Gustavus C. Doane (1840–1892)	Spearheaded the movement to establish Yellowstone National Park
Charles E. Doell (1894–1983)	Park Administrator, Minneapolis, MN; author
Andrew Jackson Downing (1815–1852)	Early advocate of horticulture, editor of the *Horticulturist*
Summer F. Dudley (1854–1897)	Founder of Camp Dudley, the first YMCA camp in Newbugh, NY, in 1885
Foster Ray Dulles (1900–1970)	Author of *America Learns to Play: A History of Recreation* (1940)
Charles Eliot (1859–1897)	Metropolitan regional parks system, Boston, MA
Lottie (Charlotte) Gulick (1865–1928)	Cofounder of Camp Fire Girls
Luther H. Gulick (1865–1919)	First President Playground Association of America; co-founder of Camp Fire Girls
Frederick William Gunn (1816–1881)	Operated first camp, Gunnery Camp, NH
Kurt Hahn (1886–1974)	Founder of Outward Bound
Lee F. Hanmer (1871–1961)	Professional leader, Playground Association of America
Ferdinand V. Hayden (1829–1887)	Led scientific expedition in Yellowstone National Park
Cornelius Hedges (1831–1907)	Spearheaded the movement to establish Yellowstone National Park
C. Hanford Henderson (1861–1941)	Author, educator, proposed different patterns of camp activities
Ernst Hermann (1869–1943)	Pioneer in industrial recreation
Clark W. Hetherington (1870–1942)	Educator, prepared the normal course in play
Rev. George Hinckley (1853–1950)	Founder of first church camp
George Hjelte (1893–1979)	Professional leader Los Angeles, CA
Johan Huizinga (1872–1945)	Author of *Homo Ludens: A Study of the Play Element in Culture*

—continued

TABLE

3.2   CONTINUED

L. P. Jacks (1860–1955)	Advocated education through recreation
Jens Jensen (1860–1951)	Promoted forest preserves in Chicago, IL
George E. Johnson (1862–1931)	Philosopher, educator, play leader; author of *Education by Plays and Games*
Robert Underwood Johnson (1853–1937)	Early wilderness enthusiast
Pierre L'Enfant (1754–1825)	Planner of Washington, DC, a vision of parks and pleasure grounds
Nathaniel P. Langford (1832–1911)	Spearheaded the movement to establish Yellowstone National Park
Joseph E. Lee (1862–1937)	Founder of recreation, philanthropist, author of *Play in Education* (1915)
Aldo Leopold (1886–1948)	Educator, conservationist, author of *Sand County Almanac* (1949)
Eugene T. Lies (1876–1954)	Early leader in recreation in the public schools
Juliette Gordon Low (1860–1927)	Founder of Girl Scouts in 1912
Otto T. Mallery (1880–1956)	Recreation Administrator, Philadelphia, PA
Robert Marshall (1901–1939)	Promoted wilderness preservation
Stephen T. Mather (1867–1930)	Founder of the National Park Service
Laura Mattoon (1873–1946)	Professional Association leader, advocate for camping for women and girls
John McLaren (1847–1943)	Landscape planner Golden Gate Park, San Francisco, CA
Herald D. Meyer (1842–1974)	Professional leader, educator, author
George L. Meylan (1873–1960)	Early YMCA camping leader
Horace Moses (1862–1947)	Founder of Junior Achievement in 1919
Robert Moses (1888–1981)	Park advocate, New York, NY
William Penn Mott, Jr. (1909–1992)	Park Administrator, Director of National Park Service
John Muir (1838–1914)	Conservationist, founder Sierra Club
J. B. Nash (1886–1965)	Author of *Philosophy of Recreation and Leisure* (1960), educator, philosopher
Esther Neumeyer (1893–1975)	*Aspects* (1958)
Martin Neumeyer (1892–1978)	Authors of *Leisure and Recreation: A Study of Leisure and Recreation in Their Sociological*
Eugene Odum (1913–)	Founder and Pioneer of Ecosystem and Ecology—Father of Modern Ecology
James Oglethorpe (1696–1785)	Established plan with open spaces in Savannah, GA
Frederick Law Olmsted (1822–1903)	Founder of landscape architecture, Creator Central Park, NY
Sigurd Olson (1899–1982)	Philosopher, promoted wilderness preservation, author of numerous texts
Harry A. Overstreet (1875–1970)	Philosopher, author of *A Guide to Civilized Loafing* (1934), educator
George Amos Parker (1853–1926)	Founder, New England Association of Park Superintendents
Mabel Peters (1861–1914)	Early leader of playground movement in Canada
John A. Pettigrew (1844–1912)	First president, New England Association of Park Superintendents
Paul Petzoldt (1908–1999)	Founded the first Outward Bound school in the U.S., founded the National Outdoor Leadership school, cofounded the Wilderness Education Association
Gifford Pinchot (1865–1946)	Conservationist, leader of the U.S. Forest Service
Janet Pomeroy (1915–1988)	Professional leader, founder of Recreational Center for the Handicapped, Inc., San Francisco, CA, author
Clarence Rainwater (1884–1925)	Author of *The Play Movement in the United States: A Study in Community Recreation* (1922)
Jacob Riis (1849–1914)	Author of *Battle With the Slum,* first vice president Playground Association of America
Thomas E. Rivers (1892–1977)	International recreation leader
Theodore Roosevelt (1858–1919)	President advocating conservation
Charles R. Scott (1874–1954)	First president of the Camp Directors Association of America
Ernest Thompson Seton (1860–1946)	Founder of Woodcraft Indians
L. B. Sharp (1895–1963)	Educator, leader in outdoor education

TABLE 3.2 CONCLUDED

Julian Smith (1900–1975)	Outdoor education leader
Ellen Gates Starr (1860–1940)	Co-founder of Hull House, Chicago, IL
Thomas Sullivan (1800–1859)	Founder of the Young Men's Christian Association in the United States (Boston) in 1851
Henry David Thoreau (1817–1862)	Nature advocate, author of *Walden* (1854), called for wilderness preservation
Ellen M. Tower (1848–1938)	Chaired committee that established sand gardens, Boston, MA
Pearl H. Vaughn (1914–1986)	African American recreation educator
Calvert Vaux (1824–1895)	Co-creator of Central Park plan *Greensward*
Thorstein B. Veblen (1857–1929)	Educator, author of *Theory of the Leisure Class*
William G. Vinal (1881–1976)	Early leader in nature recreation, naturalist, educator
Henry D. Washburn (1832–1871)	Spearheaded the movement to establish Yellowstone National Park
Lebert H. Weir (1878–1949)	Early author and park leader
George Williams (1821–1905)	Founder of the YMCA movement
Theodore Wirth (1863–1949)	Dean of park administrators in America
Marie E. Zakazewska (1829–1902)	Established sand gardens, Boston, MA

be subsidized through tax dollars. Bureaucratic structures emerge and managers handle the functions of the movement. Often, the focus veers more toward the establishment of codified rules and procedures than toward the ideals of the movement. Further, as the workers within the institutions become more entrenched, they begin to think of themselves as belonging to a *profession.*

Recreation organizations emerged during the late 1800s as a part of the larger social reform movements taking place at that time. The movement began with the idea that human intelligence was an instrument that could be used to shape the human condition and to shape social and collective life. Man could intervene on his own behalf and channel the evolution of community and social life. The reformers were deeply concerned about welfare, especially that of children, and they were deeply troubled by the conditions of an urban life bereft of opportunities for healthy exercise and play. Reformers sincerely believed that the United States could become a model nation and that every facet of life could be improved. Reform movements included such areas as adult education, recreation, health, and social work, as Sessoms and Stevenson (1981) have noted:

> Adult education, recreation, and social group work all have a common heritage. Each is a product of the social welfare reforms that occurred in our cities and industries at the turn of the nineteenth century. Their founders shared a belief—they were concerned with the quality of life and believed that through the "proper" use of leisure it could be achieved. (p. 2)

The creation of early institutions in the park and recreation movement is often referred to as the *Golden Era of the Parks and Recreation Movement* (1880–1920). One view of leaders during this time was that they were social reformers concerned with the plight of the urban poor, children, and immigrants. Financial support came mostly from philanthropists who felt a moral responsibility to help those less fortunate than themselves. These individuals were moved by ". . . an altruistic mission to create the civic ideal—to move urban populations toward a finer, purer, collective life" (Williams, Lankford, and DeGraaf, 1996, p.1).

Another perspective of the development of the park and recreation movement suggests that it was a product of a class conflict. The movement, from this perspective, may be seen as a process of ". . . social control, often masquerading as social reform" (Williams, Lankford, and DeGraaf, 1996, p. 2). From this orientation, the park and recreation movement can be viewed as a way of promoting ". . . moral control . . . a more subtle and complex process that influenced behavior and molded character by consciously planning and transforming the urban environment . . . reforms were instituted by elites, generally local government leaders and business owners to inculcate values necessary for the growing commercial economy" (Williams, Lankford, and DeGraaf, 1996, p. 2).

During the 1920s more Americans were living in cities than in rural areas. Labor reform created more free time for workers as the five-day work week was created. New inventions, like the automobile, gave people increased mobility and made life easier. Women's roles changed dramatically as they were given the vote and new careers were opened up to them. Faith in government was high and all levels of government became increasingly involved in recreation opportunities. The federal government became more involved in outdoor recreation and resource management, state governments opened more state parks, and local governments saw more government support for parks and programs than in earlier years. Institutions moved from serving only children to serving people of all ages, from the provision of facilities to the definition of standards for the use of leisure time, and from the satisfaction of individual interests to the meeting of group and community needs. The 1920s also brought about the beginnings of mass culture through the radio.

In the 1930s, the Depression brought unemployment and caused public funding for recreation programs to be cut just when the need for recreation was greatest, as people had an abundance of free time. Many new jobs were created in large federal work projects such as the Work Project Administration (WPA), which constructed recreation centers and parks in cities. At the same time the Civilian Conservation Corps (CCC) constructed recreation facilities on publicly owned lands such as state and federal parks.

Following War World II (1945–1959) there was an explosion of the middle class as an increased number of people were prosperous, and war goods production was switched to consumer goods. Opportunities for education became more abundant. Many educators began to be viewed as leaders in the parks and recreation field. Local public recreation and parks departments thrived. In addition, commercial recreation began to take off as Americans gained increasingly more disposable income.

A healthy economy and technological innovations continued to fuel growth in commercial recreation after World War II. The advancement of the car and the interstate highway system greatly expanded the areas accessible to American tourists. Electronic innovations generated a huge home entertainment industry of television, stereo, video recorders, and computers. Synthetic materials greatly improved sports and recreation equipment performance and durability (e.g., ski equipment, golf clubs, skateboards, windsurfing, and outdoor clothing).

For public recreation the period of 1960 to 1975 has been referred to as the *Zenith Era* of recreation. This was a time of great social change—civil and women's rights, the war in Vietnam, lifestyle changes, environmental movements, and economic inflation were contemporary issues. It was a time when Americans established the Great Society to address the social ills of the day. This time period was characterized by the rise of popular culture, as visual images through television opened the world to all U.S. and Canadian citizens. Increased government spending enabled the park and recreation profession to expand greatly.

Chubb and Chubb (1981), writing in the book *One Third of Our Time,* classify the 1960s as a time period of the second recreation revolution. Americans had high disposable incomes, high employment, and great aspirations. One reason that this time period has been

Did You Know that the Civilian Conservation Corps . . .

- Restored 3,980 historical structures
- Spent 2,094,713 participant days razing undesirable structures and obliterations
- Spent 6,111,258.2 participant days in the operation of nurseries
- Built 63,246 buildings
- Built 800 state parks
- Built 7,622 impounding and large diversion dams
- Erected 405,037 signs, markers, and monuments
- Collected 13,634,415 pounds of hardwood seeds and 875,970 bushels of cones
- Developed 6,966.7 miles of wildlife streams
- Built 46,854 bridges
- Built 28,087.8 miles of foot and horse trails

- Spent 1,067,800 participant days on archaeological investigation
- Covered 13,099,701 acres in tree insect pest control
- Built 46,000 campground facilities
- Involved 225,000 World War I veterans
- Transplanted 44,927,339 trees and shrubs
- Built 32,148 wildlife shelters
- Spent 1,301,945 participant days on wildlife activities
- Built 395 bathhouses
- Built 38,550 vehicle bridges
- Spent 4,827,421 participant days surveying and mapping
- Built 204 lodges and museums
- Planted over 3 billion trees

Source: Data from the National Association of Civilian Conservation Corps, St. Louis, MO.

called the Zenith Era of the recreation movement is the fact that immediately following it, funding for public programs dropped substantially as a result of property tax limitations. The events of the 1960s were a reaffirmation that the public valued the park and recreation movement. Great environmental gains were made in these years and in following years. America set aside vast amounts of land for wilderness and recreation during this time period and into the 1970s. Table 3.3 compares the Golden Era of recreation to the Zenith Era. As is evident from table 3.3 both periods were times of great social change, and change promotes opportunity.

Since the mid-1970s the park and recreation movement has been trying to deal with the shift society is experiencing from an industrial society to a postindustrial one. This uncertainty, although unsettling, presents the movement with great opportunities to urge the profession into a time of innovation. This window of opportunity or innovation may not be open long, however, so the time to act is now.

In current times, many of the same problems of poverty and the need for social reform still exist while additional problems (drugs, AIDS, homelessness, underemployment) are also being identified. Professionals must look to the underlying concepts that will govern postindustrial society and develop programs and institutions that can deal with the recreational needs of a changing society while still maintaining the proud history of the movement's past. Inherent in this process must be the reemergence of the passion that gripped early leaders in the Golden Era. As a movement becomes a profession, it becomes more institutionalized and it often loses some of its early passion. Rekindling this passion is a major challenge of the profession today.

A brief description of the early history of some of the major movements that emerged and became institutionalized during the industrial era follows, including movements to establish municipal, state, and national parks and to establish play areas for children.

TABLE 3.3   COMPARING THE GOLDEN AND ZENITH ERAS OF RECREATION IN THE UNITED STATES

Golden Era	Zenith Era
Background	
Seeing the needs of rapidly changing society and working to create social reform	The Great Society, national campaign against poverty, enjoying a high standard of living—Americans thought they could do it all. Rapid and radical change in recreation legislation, attitudes, and behavior
Great social change: immigration, social reform, urbanization, economic cycle of boom and bust, WWI, and Americans struggling with their role in the world	Period of great social change: civil and women's rights, the war in Vietnam, environmental movement, and economic inflation. America's role was to make the world safe for democracy; we were the "good guys"
Immigration saw the beginning of a pluralistic society	Great emphasis on civil rights and equality
Clash between agricultural wave and industrial wave was just finishing; Americans just beginning to deal with these changes	Start of the clash between industrial and postindustrial society; Americans just realizing these changes would take place
Concentration of people	
Urbanization in cities	Decay of many inner cities; new park districts developed as families moved from cities to suburbs
City slums were horrible places to live	
Suburbanization: concentration of people in suburbs	
Makeup of park and recreation departments	
Federal and local agency formation	Agencies became big bureaucratic organizations
Initially few public facilities were available; many large cities developed recreation facilities during this time	City parks and recreation centers become overused, under-maintained, and vandalized. Some federal money made available for renovations; often not used. States make use of federal funds
Great leaders dedicated to improving recreation opportunities that could be considered beneficial to the character and physical health of participants	Profession was institutionalized. Creation of National Recreation and Parks Association (NRPA)
Funding	
The idea of using substantial amounts of tax funds for the development of recreation was introduced. Philanthropic money was still relied upon to a great extent	Federal, state, and local governments were expected to fund all major projects—the Great Society. We could provide facilities and provision of recreation opportunities for all
Thrusts of the movement	
Concentrated on helping the urban disadvantaged	Recreation for all
Preservation and conservation of national resources began	In 1965 Congress, known as the Conservation Congress, passed 51 conservation bills

Municipal Parks   The creation of Central Park in New York City in the 1850s is generally acknowledged as the first public landscaped park established solely for leisure purposes. Major advocates of the park concept, William Cullen Bryant, editor of New York's *The Evening Post,* and Andrew Downing, editor of *The Horticulturist,* recommended strongly the establishment of public open areas in urban settings. In 1853, the city of New York passed legislation for what is now known as Central Park. In 1858, Frederick Law Olmsted and Calvert Vaux submitted the design of Central Park, entitled *Greensward.* Figure 3.9 depicts a map of Central Park in New York City as designed in the 1850s, and one as it appears today.

a

b

Figure 3.9

(a) A map that depicts the original 1858 plan for New York City's Central Park, and (b) as it is today.

Central Park Conservancy.

The work of Olmsted became instrumental in the development of parks, park systems, and city planning across the United States and in Canada. Central Park was developed to provide a pleasant contrast to the surrounding chaotic conditions of the city of New York. Although many attempts were made to amend the park plan, Olmsted sought to ensure the design's integrity and resigned from the project a number of times. Olmsted's principles of park design greatly influenced the park movement throughout the United States and Canada. He designed parks in New York, California, Connecticut, New Jersey, Massachusetts, Illinois, Pennsylvania, Michigan, Washington, DC, Rhode Island, Kentucky, Missouri, Wisconsin, and Quebec (Canada). The municipal park movement in the United States grew from one park in 1853 to a system in 1882, to 100 systems in 1889, and to 800 systems in 1902. By comparison there are more than 3,000 park systems today.

The first park system in America was the establishment of a Metropolitan Park Commission in Boston, Massachusetts, in the 1890s. This park system was established under the leadership of a protégé of Olmsted, Charles Eliot. Eliot thought in broad terms. He felt that a park system for Boston should encompass the entire urban region, linking beaches, rivers, and other open spaces. The park system, developed as a result of Eliot's vision, brought thirty-six cities and communities together under a metropolitan district.

The establishment of the Cook County Forest Preserve District in Illinois paralleled the development of Boston's park system. This development, established under the visionary leadership of Jans Jensen, became a special district by popular vote in 1914. The Forest Preserve District emphasizes the preservation of natural forested areas and has created a green belt surrounding the city of Chicago.

Enabling legislation for the park function occurred first in the state of New Jersey in 1885. This legislation allowed for the establishment of individual municipal park systems, organized into one unified, countywide system. In the state of Illinois, in 1893, the Pleasure Driveway and Park District Act gave communities in unincorporated areas the opportunity to establish park systems. The importance of these two forms of legislation was that they encouraged the development

Yellowstone Park Legacy

The diary of Nathaniel P. Langford relates the specific origins of Yellowstone Park:

One member of our party suggested that if there could be secured by preemption a good title to two or three quarter sections of land opposite the lower fall of Yellowstone and extending down the river toward the canyon, they would eventually become a source of great profit to the owners. Another member of the party thought it would be more desirable to take up a quarter section of the land at the great Upper Geyser Basin, for the reason that the locality could be more easily reached by tourists and pleasure seekers. A third suggestion was that each member of the party preempt a claim, and in order that no one should have an advantage over the other, the whole should be thrown into a common pool for benefit of the entire party.

Mr. Hedges then said that he did not approve of any of these plans—that there ought to be no private ownership of any portion of that region, but that the whole of it ought to be set aside as a great national park and that each one of us ought to make an effort to make this accomplished.

Source: Lee, 1972, pp.11–12.

Figure 3.10

Major people and events influencing the municipal park movement in Canada and the United States.

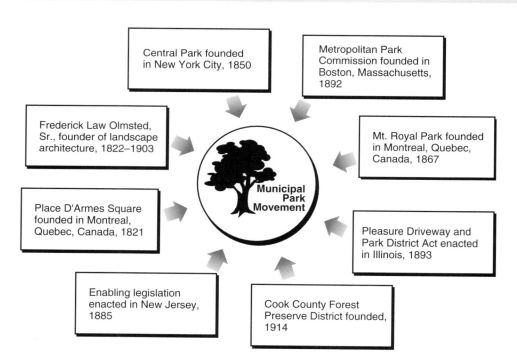

of local park systems. Figure 3.10 outlines some of the important developments of the municipal park movement in the United States and Canada.

Frederick Law Olmsted, Sr. (1822–1903). Frederick Law Olmsted, Sr., known as the founder of landscape architecture in America, was a visionary leader with extraordinary personal accomplishments. He was a noted author, an adept administrator, an excellent engineer, and a man of political and social conviction. "Olmsted believed implicitly that a close association with natural beauty was

TABLE 3.4 THE CREATION OF NATIONAL PARKS, 1872–1916

1872	(March 1)	Yellowstone, Montana-Wyoming-Idaho
1875	(March 3)	Mackinac Island, Michigan (ceded to Michigan, 1895)
1890	(September 25)	Sequoia, California
	(October 1)	Yosemite, California
	(October 1)	General Grant, California
1899	(March 22)	Mount Rainier, Washington
1902	(May 22)	Crater Lake, Oregon
1903	(January 9)	Wind Cave, South Dakota
1904	(April 27)	Sullys Hill, North Dakota (converted to Game Preserve, 1931)
1906	(June 29)	Platt, Oklahoma
1906	(June 29)	Mesa Verde, Colorado
1910	(May 11)	Glacier, Montana
1915	(January 26)	Rocky Mountain, Colorado
1916	(August 1)	Hawaii, Hawaii
1916	(August 9)	Lassen Volcanic, California
1916	(August 25)	Enabling Act to create a National Park Service

one of the most necessary elements of human life" (Fabos, Milde, and Weinmayr, 1968, p. 12). The scope and range of his projects were a testament to his genius. They include the design of urban parks, state and national parks, community design, regional planning, campus design, estate design, and urban design.

National Parks National parks are a unique contribution of the United States to the world. The first national park, Yellowstone National Park, was established on March 1, 1872, by the U.S. Congress. It was the first large-scale preservation of a land area as a park or wilderness concern. The establishment of Yellowstone, a social invention created to stem the exploitation of wilderness areas, acknowledged that natural resources were limited and that they needed to be preserved for future generations.

The national park concept sought to create permanent reserves of land for U.S. citizens. Although eighteen years passed between the creation of the first national park and the subsequent establishment of others, the national park concept became firmly entrenched as a U.S. institution. Table 3.4 presents a list of the early parks in the United States. The Antiquities Act of 1906 provided presidential power to claim and thus protect areas of scenic wonder and natural beauty. Many national monuments, established in this manner, later became a part of the National Park System. Figure 3.11 presents some key historical events in the development of national parks in the United States.

In 1916, the National Park Service was established. Prior to this time, parks were administered by a variety of federal areas, such as the U.S. Forest Service. The enabling legislation establishing the National Park Service stated its fundamental purpose "to conserve the scenery and the natural and historic objects and the wildlife therein and to provide for the enjoyment of the same in such manner and by such means as will leave them unimpaired for the enjoyment of future generations." Inherent in this legislation is a conflict between preservation and use (provide enjoyment) that is still present today. Finding the right balance is a constant juggling

Figure 3.11

Major people and events influencing the national park movement in Canada and the United States.

Stephen Mather becomes director of National Park Service, 1915

Rocky Mountain Park Act to establish Banff National Park in Canada, 1887

Antiquities Act enacted, 1906

National Park Movement

President Theodore Roosevelt supports conservation, 1901–1909

Yellowstone Park founded, 1871

act for the National Park Service, yet the national park movement has been called one of the greatest ideas America has ever had, and the national park concept rapidly transferred to countries around the world.

Stephen T. Mather (1867–1930). Stephen T. Mather was the first director of the National Park Service. A self-made millionaire with a deep love for the protection of natural resources, Mather became involved in the directorship when he wrote then Secretary of the Interior, Franklin Lane, to complain about the way in which the national parks were being managed. Lane wrote to Mather, "If you don't like the way the national parks are being run, come down to Washington and run them yourself" (Runte, 1979, p.101). Mather accepted the challenge and performed admirably. He secured legal authorization to manage the parks, established policies to manage the park service, worked to promote tourist activities to national parks, secured financial resources to manage the park systems, and, in general, helped to secure a much broader base of support for the work of the national park system.

State Parks   The romantic and artistic efforts of poets, writers, artists, and explorers helped to plant the seeds of the state park movement, as well as the national park movement. Individuals such as George Catlin, James Fenimore Cooper, Ralph Waldo Emerson, and Henry David Thoreau all provided a philosophy of nature that awakened the consciousness of the public. The state park movement in the United States began in 1864, when Yosemite Valley and the Mariposa Big Tree Grove were ceded to the State of California to become state parks. Frederick Law Olmsted was involved in the development of a management plan for this program. Olmsted emphasized that the effort to secure Yosemite as a resort and recreation area was a testament to the advancement of civilization (Sax, 1987). Two decades passed, however, before additional developments at the state level occurred, when the State of New York set aside land in the Adirondacks as a forest preserve and set aside Niagara Falls as a state park in 1885.

Little happened with the state parks in the United States between 1885 and the 1920s. A few states—New York, Indiana, Wisconsin, California, and Connecticut—established what could be

America's Public Lands: Continuing the Legacy

Pioneers such as John Muir, Stephen Mather, Bob Marshal, and Aldo Leopold have given us a great legacy of wilderness on public lands in America. Legislation in America protecting our natural resources is an example that has inspired countries around the world to follow the lead of America and establish national parks and wilderness areas. Yet managing our public lands is a constant juggling act, as there are and always will be multiple values connected to public lands. Preservation versus conservation, tourism versus scientific importance, habitat versus resource extraction—multiple values means constant juggling. Read the following summary of Mark Vanderhoff's article in the *Lewiston* (Idaho) *Morning Tribune* on July, 2004, and consider the questions within the Points to Ponder Section.

Freeriding, the latest new form of mountain biking, has public land managers worried about the effects. When freeriding, any challenge is fair game—from bombing down steep mountain inclines to dropping off ten-foot cliffs. The allure of freeriding is catching on, and the International Mountain Bicycling Association recently devoted a full newsletter to the sport, while ski resorts in the west develop new trails for enthusiasts.

Homemade freeriding trails are being made on public lands in a variety of locations in the west, and with this growth has come controversy. "Public land managers across the United States worry that risky structures pose great risks and illegally built trails damage the environment and other resources. While freeriding has invigorated the sport of mountain biking, it might be sowing a new crop of problems on public lands" (Vanderhoff, 2004).

Sometimes, mountain bikers don't realize the impacts they are having; they are just focused on the activity. Another concern for large federal agencies like the U.S. Forest Service is that with limited dollars they have to focus on trails that will serve the greatest number of people. The trails freeriders need are not easily utilized by any other group of outdoor enthusiasts.

As freeriders become more vocal, the U.S. Forest Service is starting to work with mountain biking groups to find compromises. Towns like Breckinridge, Colorado, have allowed groups to construct freeride areas in some parks, and the International Bicycling Association has published extensive literature to teach freeriders how to work with public agencies and how to construct safe, environmentally friendly, and long-lasting freeride trails and features. Yet the question remains: how can public land managers juggle all the various needs and wants from our public land?

Points to Ponder:

- This case study is not fictional. It is a problem affecting a wide variety of public land agencies (especially in the west). Do some library research for a more thorough briefing of the dilemma. What has happened since 2004? How are land managers and the mountain biking public working together to address the issues brought up in this scenario?
- What are the main issues in this case? Is it a matter of whose rights should prevail? Which side do you favor?
- How is this issue related to the enabling legislation of the National Park Service in 1916? What other types of conflict of uses or values exist on public land today?
- How do you think early pioneers in the preservation and conservation movement might have dealt with this issue?

Source: Vanderhoff, M. 2004. Freeriding blasts off: New form of mountain biking has public land managers worried about the effects. *Lewiston Morning Tribue* (July 29). Lewiston, ID.

identified as state park systems. Newton (1971) reports that two significant factors influenced the development of state parks in the United States after this period of time. The first was the automobile. The automobile gave impetus to travel (as the precursor to what is now known as tourism) and provided people an opportunity to enjoy outdoor recreation resources. The second resulted from the work of Stephen T. Mather. Mather organized a general park conference. He encouraged

Figure 3.12
The Civilian
Conservation
Corps in Iowa.

The
Civilian
Conservation
Corps
In Iowa

The Iowa
Civilian Conservation Corps
Museum

Backbone State Park
Dundee, Iowa 52038
(563)924-2527

the governors of each of the states to send representatives to this conference. Twenty-five states responded, with 200 representatives participating. The group was organized as the National Conference on State Parks.

Impetus for the development of state parks came in the 1930s from the federal government when it launched the submarginal land program and purchased many areas as "recreation demonstration areas." These areas were ultimately leased back to states and became part of their park systems. In addition, the newly organized Civilian Conservation Corps aided in the development of state park programs (see figures 3.12 and 3.13). The CCC helped expand the

Iowa received many benefits from the conservation efforts of Franklin Roosevelt. Backbone Park, as it stands today, is a result of the hard work put forth by the Civilian Conservation Corps (CCC).

While Company 1756 was busy building the dam to create the lake, Company 781 worked hard to prevent erosion. Trees were planted, and retaining walls were erected to hold the soil on the hills. In addition to work that conserved and preserved the natural beauty of the park, the corps installed telephone lines, firebreaks and sewage and irrigation systems.

Natural materials from the park were used in most projects. Limestone, timber and boulders can still be seen today in the bathhouse, boathouse, sundial, water fountains, bridges, trails, retaining walls and latrines that dot the park's landscape. In addition, the State Forest located near the north entrance to the park is a living reminder of the thousands of trees that were planted.

The CCC provided many intangible benefits, as well. Many of the camp members were young and away from home for the first time. Living, working and playing together instilled values that spurred many of them on to successful, productive lives. Many of the CCC members continued on as employees of the U.S. Forest Service or National Park Service.

Economically, times were hard, but the CCC camps provided a job, a chance for an education, an opportunity to learn a skill and time to have fun. Boxing and wrestling matches, ping-pong tournaments, orchestras, glee clubs, theatrical groups, science clubs and camp newspapers are some of the many activities that were enjoyed.

Designed By
Leslie E. Smith

Printed on Recycled Paper

IOWA DEPARTMENT OF NATURAL RESOURCES
Wallace State Office Building
Des Moines, Iowa 50319

Figure 3.13

A Civilian Conservation Corps historical document.

Camp SP-2
Company 1756
Dundee, Iowa

Camp SP-17
Company 781
Lamont, Iowa

Backbone State Park
Dundee, Iowa 52038
Telephone 563-924-2527

1. Barrack
2. Barrack
3. Latrine and Bath
4. Mess Hall and Kitchen
5. Barrack
6. Barrack
7. Barrack
8. Barrack
9. Barrack
10. Education Building
11. School
12. Hospital
13. Officers' Quarters
14. Headquarters Rec Hall
15. Telephone Office
16. Tools
17. Storage
18. Foreman's Quarters
19. Oil House
20. Blacksmith Shop
21. Army Repair Garage
22. Garage

state parks systems from a handful of parks to a total of 1,346 in 1950 (Newton, 1971). Figure 3.14 portrays important historical events in the state park movement.

John Muir (1838–1914). John Muir was a naturalist and one of the most eloquent authors advocating for the preservation of natural resources. His efforts led to the preservation of the Yosemite Valley area. Muir dedicated his life to the preservation of wildland and wilderness areas. His advocacy

Figure 3.14

Major people and events influencing the state park movement in the United States.

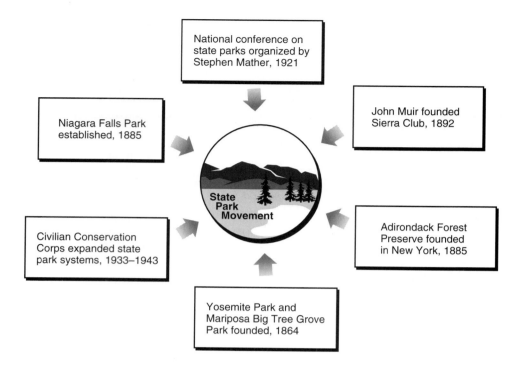

National conference on state parks organized by Stephen Mather, 1921

John Muir founded Sierra Club, 1892

Niagara Falls Park established, 1885

State Park Movement

Adirondack Forest Preserve founded in New York, 1885

Civilian Conservation Corps expanded state park systems, 1933–1943

Yosemite Park and Mariposa Big Tree Grove Park founded, 1864

for preservation of natural resources often brought him into direct confrontation with both conservationists and developers.

The Play Movement   The play movement in the United States began in response to child labor and crowded urban conditions. Figure 3.15 portrays important events and people that influenced the play movement in the United States. Early efforts at providing play environments for children drew inspiration from examples in Germany. Germans valued play and had systematized it as a part of their approach to education. Henry Curtis, writing in *The Play Movement and Its Significance,* in 1917, outlined five distinct and independent play movements in the United States.

1. *Play Spaces.* The first of these is what is ordinarily known as the play movement. It seeks to provide a place for play where children can go in their leisure time and be off the street and away from the evil influences they might encounter. Play spaces offer constructive leadership of trained directors as well.
2. *Play and Child Development.* The second play movement ". . . is built on the assumption that play is essential to the development of children and it must be furnished to every child every day" (p. 19). The focus of this type of play program is in the schools.
3. *Outdoor Play for Young Children.* This phase of the play movement ". . . consists of furnishing an adequate opportunity for outdoor life and play to children below school age. This must come through the facilities and yards of houses, in the interior courts of tenements, and by leaving an open park and playground in the center of all congested blocks" (p. 20).
4. *Public Recreation.* The movement for public recreation asserts that the ". . . development of recreation would mean the providing of social centers in the schools with public gymnasiums, dance halls, and swimming pools, either there or elsewhere, the

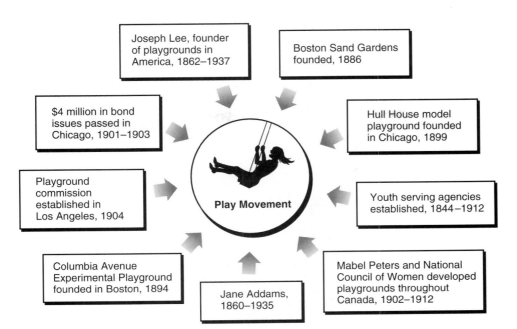

Figure 3.15

Major people and events influencing the play movement in Canada and the United States.

Joseph Lee, founder of playgrounds in America, 1862–1937

Boston Sand Gardens founded, 1886

$4 million in bond issues passed in Chicago, 1901–1903

Hull House model playground founded in Chicago, 1899

Playground commission established in Los Angeles, 1904

Play Movement

Youth serving agencies established, 1844–1912

Columbia Avenue Experimental Playground founded in Boston, 1894

Jane Addams, 1860–1935

Mabel Peters and National Council of Women developed playgrounds throughout Canada, 1902–1912

municipalizing of the moving picture and the subsidizing of drama and the opera . . . the organization of pageants and community celebrations, choral music . . . and the development of parks and amusement resorts" (p. 20).

5. *Spirit of Play.* The fifth movement is not a movement for the rebirth of play, but the spirit of play. For example, in the United States, we have become overmaterialized with our energies directed toward consumption of material goods—and have forgotten how to live. We must come to see the essential values in life, to work more moderately, to find more joy in our work.

What causes have contributed to the growth of the play movement in the United States and Canada? Joseph Lee (1925) has written in *The Normal Course in Play* that a number of causes contributed to the development of the play movement, including an appreciation of the value of play in the life of a child, prevailing social conditions (urbanization of population, child labor, juvenile delinquency, monotonous work), and commercial recreation. Most commercial recreation opportunities were viewed as passive. Figure 3.16 depicts Joseph Lee, founder of the playground movement in the United States.

In 1868, the city of Boston established an organized playground program as a part of one of its school yards. In 1886, Dr. Maria Zacharuski, following a visit to Germany, established a sand garden in Boston, sponsored by the Massachusetts Emergency and Hygiene Association. This is usually identified as the first supervised playground in the United States. By 1889, more than twenty-one playgrounds of this type had sprung up in Boston. Also, in 1886, the Charles Bank Outdoor Gymnasium opened. This park setting emphasized physical recreation facilities.

Initially, the playground movement was focused on providing *places* for play. As the movement progressed, the importance of organized programs was acknowledged. Curtis (1915) wrote "the playground that has no program achieves little" (p. 163). Boden and Mitchell (1923) suggested that "programs are necessary to make playgrounds more interesting and efficient" (p. 264).

Figure 3.16

Joseph Lee,
founder of
playgrounds.

*Courtesy of the
National Recreation
and Park
Association.*

Joseph Lee (1862–1937). Joseph Lee was born into a wealthy family in Boston, Massachusetts. As a young man he attended Harvard Law School and started working as a lawyer in 1889. However, practicing law did not appeal to Lee, so he resigned and became more involved in Boston's social reform movement. In 1889, he began his famous ten-year study of child delinquency in Boston. By 1900, Lee had become a nationally known social worker, devoting his life and financial resources to the solution of social problems in Boston. Initially, Lee was very involved in setting up playgrounds throughout Boston, but soon he realized that playgrounds were not enough and programs were needed to meet the needs of children. From his experiences working with playground programs, he wrote *Play in Education,* which became a major resource for other cities in developing playground programs. He later became a national leader in the play movement. Saporo (1989) states that Lee's contributions can be explained in three general phases: "(1) His leadership in recreation in New England after 1907 and his early work with the Playground Association of America (PAA); (2) His outstanding leadership as president of the National Recreation Association (NRA) and his promotion and broad development of its program for 27 years; (3) The effect of his financial contributions to promote the movement; and his accomplishments as the leading philosopher of the early movement" (p. 73).

Recreation Centers and Settlement Houses Recreation centers also emerged around the turn of the century, growing out of the settlement house movement at the end of the eighteenth century. Settlement houses were first established in England with the desire of the more privileged to share the lives of those less favored. Settlement houses offered something new in place of old-fashioned modes of relief to the poor; they provided mutual engagement across class lines and a broad education for working men and women. In America, settlement houses offered a means by which to ease the transition of immigrants living in large, urban American cities.

One of the most famous settlement houses in America was the Hull House in Chicago, established by Jane Addams, Ellen Gates Starr, and Mary Keyser in 1889. Hull House quickly became a center of community life, attracting both people from the neighborhood as well as staff (called residents). Residents were often idealistic young middle-class men and women who committed to live for an extended period of time in urban slums seeking to bring education and other programs to the immigrant poor. What made Hull House unique was that Addams thought of those who came and went as citizens, or citizens in the making, not as clients or receivers of services (Eishtain, 2002). In the process, the residents of Hull House combined with their working-class poor neighbors to create the following firsts (Eishtain, 2002):

- first social settlement in Chicago
- first social settlement in the United States with men and women residents
- first public paths in Chicago
- first public playground in Chicago
- first gymnasium for the public in Chicago
- first little theater in the United States
- first citizenship preparation classes in the United States
- first public kitchen in Chicago
- first college extension courses in Chicago
- first group work school in Chicago
- first painting loan program in Chicago
- first fresh air camps (school) in Chicago
- first public swimming pool in Chicago
- first Boy Scout troop in Chicago

Underlying all of Addam's efforts at Hull House was the drive to build citizens and equip them with the skills they needed to succeed in a new world. In this endeavor, everyone contributed and became partners in working for the common good. "Addams was adamant throughout her life that Hull House should offer shelter from the storm and a new way of being in this world. It was a place of civic education, a spirited enterprise that served as a vehicle for the creation of community and the sustaining of identities" (Eishtain, 2002, pp. 153–155). Addams and the others at Hull House saw the potential of recreation to promote fellowship and friendship and through relationships were able work together with others to improve the quality of life for so many.

As municipal parks, playgrounds, and settlement houses grew and developed, a new model for public parks and recreation began to emerge. In the early 1900s, the Chicago South Park District initiated an innovative model program for the development of small neighborhood parks that included playgrounds and field houses as well as public baths. Between 1901 and 1903, this district passed two bond issues totaling $4 million. With these funds, the district constructed field houses or neighborhood center buildings with indoor gymnasiums, swimming pools, assembly halls, libraries, medical services, playgrounds, day care centers, and small meeting rooms. The success of these new parks brought together municipal parks, playgrounds, and recreation centers, and they have been linked historically ever since.

Jane Addams (1860–1935). Jane Addams was a humanitarian who was closely associated with social work and made significant contributions to the play movement. She served as the first vice-president of the Playground Association of America and presented at the association's first Congress in 1907. Addams (see figure 3.17) developed a model playground at Hull House and strongly advocated for the rights of youth, particularly in poor, urban areas. She advocated for the eight-hour workday, child labor laws, and dignity for all.

Youth Serving and Voluntary Organizations Strongly aligned to the play movement, many youth serving organizations were established during the period of 1880 to 1920 to respond to such problems as unhealthy social conditions arising in big cities, decline in

Figure 3.17

Jane Addams,
founder of Hull
House in
Chicago.

Bettmann Archive.

fitness in youth, and the need for moral education. Early goals of youth serving organizations included personality development, character development, social integration, development of new skills and interests, constructive use of leisure time, as well as physical health and spiritual growth. For example, consider the following excerpt from the Federal Charter of the Boy Scouts of America on June 15, 1916, by the U.S. Congress: "the purpose of the corporation shall be to promote, through organization and cooperation with other agencies, the ability of boys to do things for themselves and others, to train them in Scoutcraft, and to teach them patriotism, courage, self-reliance, and kindred virtues, using the methods which are now in common use by Boy Scouts.

Throughout their history, youth serving organizations have had an important impact on the development of youth and children. These organizations were often based on religious or educational goals as well as leisure ones. For example, the Young Men's Christian Association (YMCA) was founded by George Williams in 1844 in Great Britain. The first YMCA in the United States was established in Boston in 1851. The Young Women's Christian Association (YWCA) was established shortly after this, also in Great Britain in 1855. The first YWCA in the United States was established in Boston in 1866. The YWCA organization, operating throughout the United States today, was founded in 1906.

The Young Men's Hebrew Association was first established in New York City in 1874, and another group was established in Philadelphia in 1875. The first Young Women's Hebrew Association was established in New York in 1902.

The Boys Club was established in 1860 in Hartford, Connecticut, but not until several decades later was a national organization combining Boys Clubs in several communities established. This occurred in 1906, when a national Boys Club organization was created. The first Girls Club was established in 1864 in Waterbury, Connecticut. These clubs currently exist as one national organization, the Boys and Girls Clubs of America.

A number of organizations have primary themes built on outdoor recreation activities. The Boy Scouts were founded in England in 1909 by Lord Robert Baden-Powell and brought to the

First Recreation Center in the United States

Jane Addams and Ellen Gates Starr started Hull House in 1889 in an old mansion on Chicago's South Halsted Street. By 1910 Hull House had grown into an imposing complex of thirteen buildings that covered nearly a city block. Within this complex Addams and her staff offered programs in sports, crafts, cooking, citizenship training, dancing, theater, music, and photography. Hull House also served as a center for studying the urban experience and much public policy was created and advocated through the staff at Hull House. At its height of influence more than 9,000 people came weekly to Hull House to participate in its many activities. In many ways Hull House served as the first American community and recreation center.

Hull House established the first public gymnasium in 1893, and, a short time later, the first women's basketball team in the city was established. By the mid-1920s the Hull House gymnasium had been enlarged to include bathing facilities for the neighborhood. In 1925, it was reported that over 6,000 paid showers and 12,000 baths were taken in the gymnasium building.

Hull House also ran an after-school program in which numerous clubs and classes were offered each day after school. In the mid-1920s the average weekly attendance was about one thousand, with sixty-four clubs and classes in existence. A Boys Band was created and was one of the most prestigious activities of the Boy's Club within Hull House. It is reported that Benny Goodman was a member of this band in 1912.

The Hull House program also included a summer camp near Waukegan, Illinois, that looked over Lake Michigan. This camp became an increasingly popular place for activities and programs, and by the 1920s had become a second location for many Hull House activities.

Hull House programs were always responsive to the needs of nearby residents. As Jane Addams wrote: "The one thing to be dreaded in the settlement is that it lose its flexibility, its power of quick adaption, its readiness to change its methods as its environment may demand."

Source: From *The Many Faces of Hull House: The Photographs of Wallace Kirkland,* edited by Mary Ann Johnson, Urbana: University of Illinois Press, 1989.

United States by William D. Boyce in 1910. The forerunner of the Boy Scouts of America, the Woodcraft Indians, was established in 1902 by Ernest Thompson Seton. The Girl Scout program, preceded by the Girl Guides, was also initiated in England; it was brought to the United States in 1912 by Juliette Lowe. The Camp Fire organization was founded in 1910 by Dr. Luther H. Gulick and his wife, Charlotte Gulick, and incorporated in 1912.

One specific type of youth serving organization related to outdoor recreation was organized camping. The pioneers of organized camping were men and women with a vision of the impact of outdoor living experiences on the lives of girls and boys. Many of these pioneers saw camping as a healthy and educational antidote to the effects of urban life and industrialization as well as a "fun alternative" to a summer of idleness in the city. These early programs were geared to affluent families, were activity based, and were designed to help participants develop wholesome habits for life (Eells, 1986).

Whereas private independent camps developed around the strength and personality of individuals, agencies' camps developed as a part of the overall programs of larger church denominations and social service agencies. Church camps can be traced back to the early 1800s as believers gathered in outdoor frontier meetings for days at a time. Slowly, the needs of young people began to be addressed, and eventually the youth camp came into being (Mattson, 1983).

In addition to church camps, many national youth serving organizations (e.g., YMCAs, Boy Scouts, Girl Scouts, Camp Fire, 4-H, and the Boys and Girls Clubs) developed camping programs to complement the programs they offered in urban areas. Proponents of organized camping within large youth serving organizations saw the opportunity camps provided for children and youth to learn and practice the skills needed to sustain democracy. As one early camp director wrote, "in camp, poor and rich lads stripped to their swimming trunks as on an absolute equality; the best man wins. Courage, generosity, goodwill, honesty are the touchstones to success in camp" (Talbot, 1905). The YMCA was the first to integrate camping into its national program when Sumner Dudley began YMCA camping in 1885.

A third type of camp also developed in the late 1800s. These camps were related to the Fresh Air movement that started in the late 1800s out of a deep concern for the needs and conditions of the poor in inner-city slums and ghettos. The movement created vacation places in the country for needy children and families. The goal of the new program was to place city mothers and children with farm families or in small towns for ten days of good food and healthful outdoor living. Since willing farm families were hard to find, alternative plans were made to create Fresh Air camps. Many Fresh Air camps are still in existence today along with more than 8,500 other resident and day camp programs. These programs continue to be both agency and private and together serve more than 6 million children annually (American Camping Association, 1998).

> **Luther H. Gulick** (1865–1918). Luther Halsey Gulick was an individual of multiple skills and talents. He was the first president of the Playground Association of America. Gulick was a physical education instructor, founder and president of Camp Fire Girls, and a noted writer and speaker for the play movement. He performed a leading role in founding the American Social Hygiene Association, the Boy Scouts of America, and the American Folk Dance Society. A highly energetic, enthusiastic and dynamic individual, his talent lay in the conceptualization of ideas that he would develop and institutionalize.

Although studying history cannot help recreational professionals predict the future, it can provide insights that help them make informed decisions in building their programs and organizations into the next century. The industrial era fostered many accomplishments. Leisure and work were clearly delineated, and the modern parks and recreation movement began. In reviewing the early history of this movement, several insights need to be highlighted as park and recreation professionals look to build programs in the future. These insights include the power of passion, the evolving nature of programs, and the benefits of inclusivity.

The Power of Passion Individuals who are passionate about their work with children and youth can make a difference in people's lives. Wilson (1981), in her book *Survival Skills for Managers,* states that the world has plenty of talent (creativity) but lacks passion. She further quotes James Austin: "the best creative work represents passion fulfilled, whereas a neurosis may be thought of as passion thwarted. Enthusiasm is the elixir that pervades creativity, inspires it, frees it so that anything seems possible, and enlists others in the cause." This fact is reiterated in the words of Dr. Seuss (1971, p. 58) "Unless someone like you cares a whole awful lot, nothing is going to get better, it's not."

This fact has been modeled throughout the history of the parks and recreation movement. People who have been passionate about what they do have given us a legacy of institutions and programs that have made a difference in this world. Thus the greatest resource inherent to all organizations is the creativity and passion of its staff. While creativity and passion take many different forms and vary from individual to individual, key elements include open-mindedness, perseverance, collaboration, resourcefulness, and commitment.

The Evolving Nature of Programs   In examining the wide range of leisure service organizations that have developed over the last twenty-five years, Godbey (1997) notes that all successful leisure service organizations share three common characteristics. These characteristics include the desire to help people, an entrepreneurial spirit, and the ability to respond to the social needs of the times. Programs should be dynamic rather than static; they must grow and evolve. The evolving nature of recreation programs is a constant reminder of the need to understand local needs and the willingness to adapt to meet these needs. As the early social reformer Jane Addams wrote in 1893, "the one thing to be dreaded in the settlement (house movement) is that it lose its flexibility, its power of quick adaption, its readiness to change its methods as its environment may demand" (Addams, 1893, p. 22).

Inclusivity   In addition to evolving programs, the history of the recreation movement is a constant reminder to reach out to new groups of people in need of services. For example, organized camps started with serving just boys and later incorporated programs for girls, as well as people with disabilities and those who are economically disadvantaged. Today camp programs are still reaching out and trying to create more inclusive environments where children and youth can be integrated with others of different abilities and backgrounds. Likewise, other parks and recreation organizations have expanded programs to meet the new needs of emerging groups (i.e., younger children and older youth, single-parent families, nontraditional families, etc.). This drive to expand to include the needs of emerging groups is imperative as programs look to survive and thrive in the years ahead.

The Technological or Information Era

The technological, or information, era began in the mid-1950s in the United States and continues to the present. Enormous changes have occurred as industrialized society has given way to a new socioeconomic structure that emphasizes the creation and distribution of information and services. Two factors are usually attributed to the development of the technological or information era—the advent of the computer and a shift in the workforce. Computers have had a dramatic impact on the way people live. The growth of an electronic culture has created a dramatic transformation affecting the ability of people and organizations to process and use information (Bullaro and Edginton, 1986). Simply put, humankind is taking a quantum leap in the volume, speed, and versatility of the average person's use of information. In 1956, for the first time in United States, white-collar workers—technical, managerial, and clerical—outnumbered blue-collar workers. Thus, the industrialized state gave way to a new society in which most individuals work with information rather than with the production of goods.

The information era is built on a different set of assumptions than the industrial era. As a result, it requires new ideas, new concepts, and new strategies to respond to the values that exist and that continue to emerge. Most of our existing leisure service delivery systems are based on "Industrial Revolution" assumptions; and these assumptions may no longer be relevant.

As we shift from the industrial era to the information era and beyond, several factors have a direct impact on leisure. A few selected factors include:

- Changing Demographics—The United States is continuing to experience a changing demographic landscape. These changes include:
- American metropolitan areas are attracting new waves of immigrants. Cities like New York, Houston, Los Angeles, and Chicago are watching the Anglo percentage of the

population drop dramatically (Tilove, 2004b). Consider that, in 1960, more than half of Californians were born in other states, and fewer than one in ten were born abroad. By 2000, more Californians were foreign born (26 percent) than were born elsewhere in America (Tilove, 2004a). As a result, cultural infusion and a growing awareness of the recreation and leisure practices of Asians, Native peoples, those of African descent, Hispanics, and others will strongly influence the nature of leisure and recreation. Celebrations such as Cinco de Mayo, Kwanzaa, and other culturally relevant services will be found throughout our communities.

- The Midwest continues to lose its youth, who leave after college to other parts of the country. Between 1980 and 2000, the population of states such as New York, California, Texas, and Florida grew by a third and the states in the New Sun Belt (Virginia, Carolinas, Georgia, Tennessee, Arizona, Nevada, Colorado) increased by 43 percent. But the heartland grew barely 10 percent. The states of the Midwest were struggling to hold their own, losing many of their most talented and ambitious young people to other areas of the country (Tilove, 2004b).

- The graying of America is continuing. Hanson (2003) writes about California that "we are sitting on a demographic time bomb in which a shrinking, mainly white elite is nearing retirement and ready to be subsidized by more numerous, poorly compensated, and younger Mexicans."

- People are continually moving out into the suburbs. Population densities have increased near timberlands, parks, and wilderness areas. For example, the Yellowstone ecosystem, if combined, would represent the fastest growing state in the country (Machlis, 2003, p. 65).

    The implications of these changes are significant. Increased population levels and densities will lead to higher demand for open space and parks, while growing ecological impacts from development will further threaten natural areas. The age shift will be reflected in the kinds of activities that people will seek during their leisure, and ethnic changes also will impact the kinds of recreation opportunities that the profession needs to provide (Machlis, 2003). Leisure service providers will need to be increasingly cognizant of the diverse markets to meet the needs of their constituents.

- Shifting public values, along with a wider diversity in what is important for people will make it more difficult to come to consensus on issues. Americans will demand more involvement in public decisions regarding parks and recreation, but there will be more conflict about the type of values we need to emphasize. For example, everyone seems to be concerned for our environment but how to deal with specific environmental issues is open to debate. We continue to see the increase of special interest groups advocating for their positions.

- New technology continually changes the way we relate to one another as well as how we engage in leisure. Cell phones, computers, and e-mail all help us stay connected to friends and family while new toys are constantly being developed to help us fill our "free" time. New technology brings both opportunities and challenges. For example, Americans are becoming more sedentary as a result of passive recreation of watching television, playing computer games, etc. The many health problems connected to inactivity present both an opportunity and a challenge to improve the overall health of Americans today.

- The most marked change in the structure of developed economies in the last half of the twentieth century has been the societal transformation from a manufacturing to a service economy. In the United States alone, the percentage of workers employed in the service sector has risen from a mere 30 percent in 1900 to an estimated 80 percent in 1995 (Rust,

Zahorik, and Keiningham, 1996). As we move into the twenty-first century, this trend will continue, as the service-producing sector of the economy is projected to grow by 19.1 million wage and salary jobs between 1998 and 2008. This represents nearly 95 percent of the total employment growth in the American economy over this period (Monthly Labor Review, 1999).

The service economy is also changing as Pine and Gilmore (1999) note that we are now moving beyond a service economy to an economy based on experiences. "Experiences have always been around, but consumers, businesses and economists lumped them together with such uneventful activities as dry cleaning, auto repair, wholesale distribution, and telephone access. When a person buys a service, he purchases a set of intangible activities carried out on his behalf. But when he buys an experience, he pays to spend time enjoying a series of memorable events that a company stages to engage him in a personal way . . . companies stage an experience when they engage customers in a memorable way" (p. 3). In this way consumers can be compared to tourists; they are "sensation seekers and collectors of experience; their relationship with this world is primarily aesthetic; they perceive the world as a food for sensibility—a matrix of possible experiences" (Bauman, 1998, p. 94).

For those providing leisure services, seeking to improve people's quality of life, there will be a constant need to monitor societal trends to provide appropriate programs and services. There are a variety of resources that monitor and project such trends. One such resource is the Popcorn Report, published by Faith Popcorn on a regular basis. Consider two such trends, which connect with leisure presented by Popcorn for 2003 and beyond:

- Food coaches. Obesity is becoming an increasingly bigger problem for Americans. Sedentary living habits have increased in the last twenty years with the increase in desk jobs and the lack of exercise in people's day-to-day lives. The increasing use of automobiles has decreased physical activity. Sedentary living contributes to poor health and the rising level of obesity in the United States. It is estimated that physical inactivity and obesity are contributing factors in 300,000 to 500,000 deaths each year in the United States. There has been an increase in the prevalence of obesity among adults in the United States over the last twenty years, adding over $100 billion/year to our national health care costs. Nationwide, the proportion of children ages six to eighteen that were overweight increased from 6 percent in 1976–1980 to 15 percent in 1999–2000. Alarmingly, one in every seven kids is overweight in the United States (Jackson and Kochtitzky, 2001). As Americans grapple with their eating habits, there will be many opportunities for park and recreation to be part of the solution. Popcorn (2002) predicts that a new vocation will emerge—food coaches. Part psychologist, part sociologist, part family therapist, and part nutritionist, these individuals will emerge as part of the solution in the struggle to control obesity.
- Family First. There will an increasing pressure to re-order our priorities in order to increase time spent with family rather than time spent working and making money. Instead of living to work, people will once again be working to live (Popcorn, 2002). Consider the following program developed by one community, Ridgewood, New Jersey, to bring families together. The program, Ready, Set, Relax, is a community initiative designed to raise awareness about the impact of overscheduling on families and children. It is a one night community event designed with the support of school administrators, sports officials, and religious leaders. All homework, sports practices, and religious classes were cancelled for the evening. Hundreds of families spent time together playing board games, making special meals, watching home videos, and just relaxing together (Ready, Set, Relax, 2004).

Changes in Perceptions of Leisure   Dramatic changes have occurred in perceptions of leisure during the technological or information era, with leisure increasingly viewed as an end in itself. Previous eras (especially the industrial era) viewed leisure instrumentally; that is, individual leisure was thought to be socially valuable. During the industrial era it was held that work time and leisure time were discrete. In the information era every life experience presents opportunities for leisure.

Environmental Services   One of the areas of greatest growth during the information era has been the increase in legislation and services related to the environment. Perhaps the most important factor influencing the growth of outdoor recreation services in the United States was the establishment of the Outdoor Recreation Resources Review Commission (ORRRC) in 1958. This commission made multiple recommendations leading to the expansion of outdoor recreation services at the federal, state, and local levels. A similar study—Canadian Outdoor Recreation Demands Study (CORDS), completed in the early 1970s—provided similar information for decision making in Canada.

In the 1960s, a federal Bureau of Outdoor Recreation was established in the United States to coordinate the work of various agencies. One of the most significant pieces of legislation passed was the Land and Water Conservation Fund Act in 1964. In the same year, the Wilderness Preservation Act was passed, and in 1968 the Wild and Scenic Rivers and National Trail System Act was established. Furthermore, the National Park System expanded dramatically through the acquisition of large tracts of land in Alaska in 1980. President Jimmy Carter authorized the Alaska National Interest Lands Conservation Act, tripling the size of the national preservation system. In 1986, President Ronald Reagan established a Commission on Americans Outdoors to encourage support for environmental issues. The report produced by this commission will be discussed in detail in a later chapter.

The increasing demand for outdoor recreation opportunities will create challenges for recreation professionals, but it also will create opportunities. People are interested in making a difference in the quality of our environment today. As a result, the parks and recreation profession has a wonderful opportunity. To make the most of this responsibility, Dustin, McAvoy, Schultz (1995) advocate that parks and recreation professionals should serve as this society's environmental conscience and through the personal example of our lives demonstrate environmental wisdom in the conduct of our own lives.

Services for People with Disabilities   Leisure services for people with disabilities also have expanded tremendously during the information era. Prior to the early 1950s, the historical development of services for the disabled could be traced to work of the American Red Cross in military hospitals and the development of recreation services in state hospitals and institutions. In the mid-1960s, the war in Vietnam and the human rights movement created new opportunities to fulfill the needs of persons with disabilities in a positive fashion.

Federal legislation has played an important role in expanding the public's awareness of the need for special services. Public Law 94–142, Education for All Handicapped Children Act, mandated equal rights for persons with disabilities and included therapeutic recreation services. In 1973, Section 504 of the Rehabilitation Services Act mandated that no discrimination could occur because of a disabling condition. Furthermore, a basic philosophical change occurred in the 1970s—services were deinstitutionalized and individuals were mainstreamed into community services. This resulted in an increased awareness of the need for local services for the disabled as a part of a community's offerings.

In the 1980s the influence of government in relation to services for those with disabilities lessened. Basically, this resulted in a number of strategies to finance the delivery of health-care services, including therapeutic recreation services for the disabled. Third-party (insurance) reimbursement systems have emerged and these, in turn, have created entrepreneurial opportunities for therapeutic recreation-service providers.

The 1990s saw a recommitment by the government to ensure that people with disabilities were treated fairly in all aspects of their lives. The Americans with Disabilities Act (ADA) of 1990 mandated fuller opportunities for persons with disabilities in community and educational services. The ADA is discussed more fully in other chapters of this book.

Travel and Tourism   Tremendous changes have taken place since the early 1950s in the travel and tourism industry. Today, more people are mobile, and travel opportunities are available to wider segments of the population than in past years. Tourism is now the world's largest composite industry with continued growth forecasted as we embarked in the twenty-first century. Tourism in the twenty-first century will likely continue to change; this is already evident as we see the number of options for tourists expanding. For example, eco-tourism options are increasing, according to the Stanford Research Institute; eco-tourism experienced 30 percent annual increases between 1990 and 1995 (Godbey, 1997). Furthermore, individuals continue to have more options in booking their own flights and setting up their own itineraries using the World Wide Web. These changes also are creating opportunities for many public parks and recreation departments as well as many private, nonprofit organizations (e.g., museums, nature centers, symphony orchestras) as they begin to recognize their role in tourism and seek to reposition themselves as sustainers and promoters of tourism.

Commercial Leisure Services   The past several decades have seen tremendous growth in the area of commercial leisure services. One segment of the industry has provided a model for family leisure entertainment—family theme parks. The modern theme park can trace its origin to 1955 when Disneyland opened in Anaheim, California. Today, nearly every standard metropolitan area has a theme park. In four decades of operation, Disneyland increased its attendance from 3.8 million to 10 million visitors per year.

Leisure industries have become major contributors to the U. S. economy. Estimates reveal that in 1965, $58 billion was expended for leisure products; funds for leisure expenditures in the 1990s exceeded $430 billion. Televisions, radios, records, musical instruments, wheeled goods, toys, sports equipment, boats, and pleasure craft accounted for the majority of these sales. *Business Week* magazine ranked a composite of leisure-time industries seventeenth out of forty industries in the United States. Entrepreneurial activities in the commercial leisure field have resulted in a host of innovations from video home entertainment to leisure-related eating establishments featuring animatronics.

Summary

History may be thought of as the orderly and systematic reconstruction of the past. An analysis of the historical development of leisure can be useful for a number of reasons. By studying history, one gains knowledge of leisure concepts, an appreciation for the foundations of the profession, an understanding of the role of individuals in history, and knowledge of historical events and places. For professionals, the study of history fosters an understanding of the nature of life satisfaction and the impact of decision making, both in the present and for the future.

For the purposes of studying history and analyzing concepts of leisure, there are four distinct eras—preliterate society, the agricultural era, the industrial era, and the information era. During preliterate society, survival was the main concern, with few boundaries between work and leisure. During the agricultural era, division of labor created a leisure class.

The industrial era dramatically changed society's view of time, with a strong distinction between work time and leisure time. Many institutions were created during the Industrial Revolution, including parks, playgrounds, settlement houses, national parks, and youth serving organizations (e.g., Girl Scouts, Camp Fire, Inc., YMCA). The current information era, built on a different set of assumptions than the industrial era, requires a new set of strategies to meet people's needs.

Discussion Questions

1. What is history? What is historical research?
2. Why is the study of history useful to us as professionals?
3. The history of humankind can be divided into four distinct eras; what are they? How do the concepts of leisure vary within each era?
4. Compare and contrast leisure during the Middle Ages with leisure during the Renaissance.
5. Discuss how the concept of industriousness influenced early American colonials' perception of leisure.
6. Define a movement. Define an institution. When does a movement become institutionalized?
7. Identify four social reform movements leading to institutions during the industrial era.
8. Identify ten key leaders in the early organized park and recreation movement in Canada and the United States.
9. How does the information era differ from the industrial era?
10. List and discuss four new trends that have occurred in response to the information era.

References

Addams, J. 1893. The subjective necessity for social settlements: A new impulse to an old gospel. Edited by T. Y. Croswell, in *Philanthropy and Social Progress.* New York: Crowell.

American Camping Association. 1998. *ACA Fact Sheet.* Available at www.aca-camps.org/factsheet.htm.

Bauman, Z. (1998). *Globalization: The human consequences.* Cambridge, England: Polity.

Berstein, C. 1990. The leisure empire. *Time.* 136, 27.

Boden, W.P., and Mitchell, E.D. 1923. *The theory of organized play.* New York: Barnes.

Bowen, L. K. 1914. *Safeguards for City Youth at Work and at Play.* New York: Macmillan.

Bullaro, J., and C. Edginton. 1986. *Commercial Recreation: Managing for Profit, Service and Personal Satisfaction.* New York: Macmillan.

Chubb, M., and H. Chubb. 1981. *One Third of Our Time.* New York: John Wiley & Sons.

Curtis, H. 1915. *The practical conduct of play.* New York: Macmillan.

Curtis, H. 1917. *The Play Movement and Its Significance.* New York: Macmillan.

Dare, B., Welton, G., and Coe, W. 1987. *Leisure in western thought: A critical and historical analysis.*

Dryfoos, J. 1998. School-based health centers in the context of education reform. *Journal of School Health,* 68(10), 404–405.

Dulles, F. 1965. *A History of Recreation: America Learns to Play.* New York: Simon & Schuster.

Durant, W. 1944. *The Story of Civilization: Part III Caesar and Christ.* New York: Simon & Schuster.

Durant, W. 1963. *The Story of Civilization: Part I Our Oriental Heritage.* New York: Simon & Schuster.

Durant, W. 1966. *The Story of Civilization: Part II The Life of Greece.* New York: Simon & Schuster.

Dustin, D., McAvoy, L., and Schultz, J. 1995. *Stewards of access, custodians of choice: A philosophical foundation for the park and recreation profession.* Champaign, IL: Sagamore.

Edwards, R. H. 1915. *Popular Amusements.* New York: Association Press.

Eells, E. 1986. *History of Organized Camping: The First 100 Years.* Martinsville, IN: American Camping Association.

Elshtain, J. B. 2002. *Jane Addams and the dream of American democracy.* New York: Basic Books.

Fabos, J., G. Milde, and V. Weinmayr. 1968. *Frederick Law Olmsted, Sr.* Amherst, MA: The University of Massachusetts Press.

Frye, V. 1980. Development of municipal parks and recreation. Edited by S. G. Lutzin, in *Managing Municipal Leisure Services*. International City Management Association.

Godbey, G. 1997. *Leisure and Leisure Services in the 21st Century*. State College, PA: Venture.

Hanson, J. 2003. *Mexifornia*. San Francisco: Encounter Books.

Henderson, K., D. Bialeschki, S. Shaw, and V. Freysinger. 1989. *A Leisure of One's Own: A Feminist Perspective on Women's Leisure*. State College, PA: Venture.

Henderson, K., D. Bialeschki, S. Shaw, and V. Freysinger. 1996. *Both Gains and Gaps: Feminist Perspectives on Women's Leisure*. State College, PA: Venture.

Jackson, R., and C. Kochtitzky. 2001. *Creating a healthy environment: The impact of the built environment on public health*. Center for Disease Control and Prevention.

Johnson, M., ed. 1989. *The Many Faces of Hull House*. Chicago, IL: University of Illinois Press.

Kelly, J., and G. Godbey. 1992. *Sociology of Leisure*. State College, PA: Venture.

Kraus, R. 1984. *Recreation and Leisure in Modern Society*. 3d ed. Glenview, IL: Scott, Foresman.

Kraus, R. 1990. *Recreation and Leisure in Modern Society*. 4th ed. New York: HarperCollins.

Lee, J. 1925. *The Normal Course in Play*. New York: Barnes.

Lee, R. 1972. *Family Tree of the National Park System*. Philadelphia: Eastern National Park and Monument Association.

Lothian, W. 1977. *Extract from a history of Canada's national parks*. Parks Canada.

Machlis, G. 2003. *Five Trends that will shape our Future*. Parks and Recreation (February), 65–70.

MacLean, J., J. Peterson, and D. Martin. 1985. *Recreation and Leisure: The Changing Scene*. 4th ed. New York: John Wiley and Sons.

Mattson, L. 1983. *The Camp Counselor: A Guidepost to Better Christian Camping*. Duluth, MN: Camping Guideposts.

Monthly Labor Review. 1999, December. *Service Sector dominant source of new jobs*. U.S. Department of Labor and Bureau of Labor Statistics. Retrieved from http://stat.bis.gov/opub/ted/1999/Nov/wk5/art05.htm.

Naisbitt, J. 1982. *Megatrends*. New York: Warner Books.

Newton, N. 1971. *Design of the Land*. Cambridge, MA: The Belknap Press of Harvard University Press.

Olmsted, F. 1865. *The Yosemite Valley and the Mariposa Big Trees*.

Peters, T. 1987. *Thriving on Chaos*. New York: Alfred A. Knopf.

Pine J., and Gilmore, J. 1998. Welcome to the experience economy. *Harvard Business Review* (July/August), 97–105.

Pine, J., and Gilmore, J. 1999. *The experience economy: Work is theatre and every business a stage*. Boston: Harvard Business School Press.

Popcorn, F. 2002, December. *Trends for 2003: The Popcorn Report*. New York: Brain Reserve.

Putnam, R. (2000). *Bowling alone: The collapse and renewal of American community*. New York: Simon & Schuster.

Ready, Set, Relax. 2004. Informational packet. Ridgewood, NJ.

Runte, A. 1979. *National Parks: The American Experience*. Lincoln, NE: University of Nebraska Press.

Rust, R., Zahorik, A., and Keiningham, T. 1996. *Service marketing*. New York: HarperCollins.

Ryken, L. 1994. The Puritan ethic and Christian leisure for today. Edited by P. Heintzman, G. Van Andel, and T. Visker, in *Christianity and Leisure: Issues in a Pluralistic Society*. Sioux Center, IA: Dordt Press.

Saporo, A. 1989. Joseph Lee. In H. Ibrahim (ed), *Pioneers in Leisure and Recreation*. Reston, VA: American Alliance for Health, Physical Education, Recreation, and Dance.

Sax, J. 1987. *Mountains without Handrails: Reflections on the National Parks*. Ann Arbor: University of Michigan Press.

Sessoms, D., and Stevenson, J. 1981. *Leadership and group dynamics in recreation services*. Boston: Allyn & Bacon.

Seuss, Dr. 1971. *The Lorax*. New York: Random House.

Staff. 1999. *An Engagement with God's World*. Grand Rapids, MI: Calvin College.

Swanson, R., and B. Spears. 1995. *History of Sports and Physical Education in the United States*. Boston, MA: WCB McGraw-Hill.

Talbot, W. T. 1905, May. Summer camp for boys. *The World's Work 6,* 174.

Tilove, J. 2004a. Half full, or half empty? *USA Today* (February 29).

Tilove, J. 2004b. The Dream Lives: America's major metropolitan areas attract wave of immigrants. *USA Today* (February 15).

United States Citizenship and Immigration Services. 2004. *US Immigration Facts*. Retrieved from http://www.rapidimmigration.com/usa/1_eng_immigration_facts.html

Veblen, T. (1899). *Theory of the Leisure Class*. New York: Macmillan.

Williams, A., S. Lankford, and D. DeGraaf. 1996. A Presentation at the Leisure Research Symposium, Congress for Parks and Recreation, National Recreation and Park Association, Kansas City, MO.

Wilson, M. 1981. *Survival Skills for Managers*. Boulder, CO: Volunteer Management Associates.

Philosophical and Conceptual Themes

Here, a woman painting in a garden is provided opportunites for creativity, self-expression, quiet thought, and reflection.

Introduction

A philosophy of leisure, so essential in guiding the work of a professional, provides understanding of direction, goals, and purpose. It provides a framework for action. Both individual and organizational philosophies reflect values, beliefs, priorities, and ideas about what is considered worth pursuing. In this light, philosophy has a direct relationship to perceived quality of life.

A philosophy, a highly practical tool in the hands of a leisure service professional, provides enduring stability and changes only marginally as the years pass. On the other hand, management techniques, types of programs, and types of areas and facilities change continuously. A philosophy provides vision and a core set of values that offer a long-term perspective. In addition, it provides a rationale for professional action, in contrast to the professional who operates without an underlying philosophy, in a vague, nondirected fashion.

A philosophy of leisure allows professionals to understand the "why" of their actions. To be successful as a professional, it is important not only to be a good technician but also to understand how one's professional actions have been influenced by underlying philosophical beliefs. Philosophy deals with the whys of our own beliefs as well as those of the organizations within which we work. For example, the Boys and Girls Club of America believes, philosophically, that their program shapes the character of young people in the United States by providing them with wholesome alternatives to life on the streets. This organization is built upon certain specific values, beliefs, and priorities. Its philosophy is directed toward providing educational, social, and recreational programs for children and young adults to build character, to train in responsibilities of community life, and to develop positive social skills. The Boys and Girls Club of America also cooperates and collaborates with various community groups with philosophies compatible with its own. Thus, Boys and Girls Club of America is often aligned philosophically with various religious, educational, civic, fraternal, business, and labor organizations, as well as corporations and professional associations.

This chapter has five major sections. The first section answers the question "What does the term philosophy mean?" The next section discusses the relationship of values and ethics. This is followed by a section examining why it is important to build a philosophy of leisure. The fourth section sets forth a process for developing a philosophy, and the last section discusses the role of philosophy in the work of an organization.

What Is Philosophy?

A *philosophy* may be thought of as a collection of *systematically defined values, beliefs, and preferences; its primary tool is reason.* A philosophy serves as a system that clarifies the values and principles used to guide and conduct one's professional life. It defines a set of beliefs that can be acted upon and which give meaning and direction to one's efforts.

Searle and Brayley (2000) help us to understand the importance of one's philosophy. They have written that one's philosophical approach ". . . influences how he or she conceptualizes leisure, recreation, play and so forth" (p. 49). And they note, ". . . we think of philosophy as denoting a set of basic values and attitudes toward life, the environment and society. It is a set of beliefs that guide our behavior" (p. 49).

A philosophy helps to determine priorities. It serves as a guide in dealing with the difficult questions that arise in everyday professional activities. It helps sort out what is important and what is not. Today, leisure service professionals face many problems and issues: overuse of resources, lack of funding, leisure awareness, and hedonism. These problems and issues, as well as others, require that the professional make decisions based on a set of core values. A philosophy can help to guide the professional in the assessment of these problems.

A philosophy is usually expressed as an abstract idea or set of constructs. These ideas or constructs, organized into a coherent framework, are called a philosophy of leisure or a philosophy of the management of leisure service organizations. While a professional's personal philosophy of leisure may not always be written, the philosophy used to manage leisure service organizations is imbedded in the vision or mission statement of the agency. The value of documenting an agency's philosophy lies in effective communication of its intentions to other individuals, groups, and organizations.

Philosophy and Circumstances

From where do philosophical ideas come? Philosophical beliefs derive from our society as well as from individual belief structures. Individual beliefs and cultural expectations constantly interact with one another to produce philosophical positions. As each life event occurs, philosophical ideas are engaged, challenged, affirmed, or in some way acted upon. In these interactions philosophy influences behavior and actions; life events have an influence upon our philosophical thought. Goodale and Godbey (1988) note ". . . there are numerous examples in history which provide clear indication of the interaction of philosophy and circumstances, some of which have and continue to have a direct bearing on our understanding of leisure" (p. 2).

Building a Philosophical Attitude

The park, recreation, and play movement was strongly motivated by a set of discrete values and principles at the turn of the century. In a study of the ethics of play, leisure, and recreation between 1900 and 1983, however, Sylvester (1987) observed that little research had been conducted on this subject. His research provides a descriptive map of the ethics of play, leisure, and recreation in the twentieth century. Sylvester analyzed more than eighty books, reports, articles, and monographs published between 1900 and 1983. Paraphrasing Sylvester, the following categories may be used to distinguish among philosophical approaches reported in these sources:

1. *Divine ends.* This philosophical approach suggests that play, leisure, or recreation is a part of God or a means of spiritual values of a religious, contemplative life.
2. *Happiness.* This approach includes creative work, personal happiness, spiritual balance, intellectual activity, spiritual freedom, harmonious living, and cultivation of the mind as ends of leisure, recreation, and play.
3. *Combination of work, play, love, and worship.* This philosophical approach finds a union of work, play, love, and worship. Basically, it perceives recreation as a means of revitalizing the individual.
4. *Self-actualization.* The self-actualization approach implies fulfillment or self-fulfillment through leisure.
5. *Play.* Play relates to play instincts or becomes a component of the ideal.
6. *Utopia.* Leisure play activities are an ends and a means leading to a utopian life according to this approach. Play and happiness are interrelated.
7. *No final end.* This approach views no grand end to play, leisure, or recreation, only personal ends or goals.
8. *Others.* Other philosophical approaches include life or knowledge, balance, character development, aesthetic appreciation, abundant living, joy, growth, personal freedom, well-being, and purposelessness.

As Sylvester (1987) notes, the most common end addressed by writers he studied in the twentieth century associated play, leisure, and recreation with divine ends. One quarter of the writers focusing on philosophical concerns of the leisure field associated values relating to play, leisure, and recreation to God, Christ, divine contemplation, and spiritual themes. The second most common end views play, leisure, and recreation in relationship to human happiness. These two categories account for 50 percent of the philosophical writings in the leisure service field from 1900 to 1983 (Sylvester, 1987).

Cooper (1999) has suggested that many questions can be probed from a philosophical perspective that are central to the question of understanding leisure. He writes: ". . . Most of us share a concept of leisure as free time, but there is considerable disagreement about which conception of this concept is best suited to guide theory" (Cooper, 1999, p. 3). He offers the following probing philosophical questions regarding leisure theory:

- Does unemployment count as free time, and hence leisure?
- How constraining can one's choice situation be to leisure?
- Can one be at leisure while at work?
- Is the freedom of leisure the absence of causal determination, as an indeterminist philosopher might suggest?
- Is the freedom of leisure the freedom to exercise one's faculties as one wants, without care for the instrumental value of doing so?
- Does our clock-bound modern existence count as free time, or was true leisure available only in a past Golden Era, prior to the Industrial Revolution, when time for us was cyclical rather than linear, thanks to our being closer to the seasons and other aspects of nature (de Grazia, 1962)?
- Is the freedom of leisure more a reality for men than for women?
- Is our leisure distorted by class conflict? (p. 3)

Examination of these and other philosophical questions can help professionals discern their philosophy of leisure. To develop a philosophy of leisure one must probe such questions as an important first step in the process of clarifying one's ideas regarding leisure. Fundamentally, it is important to seek an understanding of the meaning of leisure for one's self in not only a personal context, but also a professional one. Still other important philosophical considerations can influence one's development. These may include framing a discussion regarding leisure by including such concepts as social justice, democracy, freedom, aesthetic appreciation, and others that give greater clarity and meaning to understanding one's concept of leisure.

Discussing the emergence of philosophical perspectives in the leisure service field, Murphy (1981, p. 2) suggests that the field ". . . has largely failed to provide the prospective educator and practitioner the opportunity to develop a meaningful, comprehensive interpretation of leisure because of a lack of significant guidelines". Ten years later, Fain (1991) suggests that "inquiry concerning the relationship between leisure and philosophy remains largely unconnected in both philosophy and leisure studies" (p. 16). In light of changes in social, cultural, and economic structures in the United States in recent years, one would expect changes in the philosophical approaches as well. As Fain (1991) notes, in recent years social circumstances have heavily influenced orientations to philosophies of leisure. Society tends to view leisure as an end in itself, as conceptually amoral, and as focusing on the value of exercising self-expression and satisfying individually determined needs.

It is interesting to note that the philosophical directions of the early play movement in America followed a reform pattern (Hunnicutt, 2000). Hunnicutt writes that a group of activists in the mainstream of America's Progressive movement provided powerful critiques of industrialization, urban society, and the excesses of capitalism. Their philosophical critiques suggested that modern life was alienating individuals and, with respect to leisure, Americans "were becoming passive in their free time, consuming rather than creating their amusements. 'Spectatoritis' was sweeping the land, alienating more and more people as fat, lazy, and quarrelsome bench-warmers" (p. 59). Hunnicutt (2000, p. 59) contends, "the best hope for men and women alienated at work was increasing leisure, leaders of our field were animated by inspiring vision of the mass, abundant leisure . . . leisure was opening astonishing new democratic vistas . . . [and] . . . with increasing leisure humans would be able to progress". These basic values or philosophical positions held by the early leaders of the movement strongly influenced their work in building the profession. Today, there is much debate about the availability of free time. Juliet Schor (1992), writing in *The Overworked American,* suggests that men and women who are employed full time are working longer hours. This is juxtaposed against the work of John Robinson and Geof Godbey (1997), writing in *Time for Life: The Surprising Ways Americans Use Their Time,* and Jeremy Rifkin's (1995) book *The End of Work,* which suggest increased free time, perhaps even enforced leisure.

The establishment and use of philosophical positions in the planning, organizing, and delivery of leisure services has been ambiguous in the United States in the past quarter of a century, with a few exceptions. For example, at the federal level of government in the United States, a strong commitment to preservation of natural resources guides the work of the National Park Service, and a strong orientation toward multiple use guides the work of the Forest Service. From a philosophical perspective, the work of local park and recreation agencies tends to be diffused, using varied means and seeking varied ends, depending upon local conditions. Far too often philosophical orientations at the local level of government are not articulated clearly, however, resulting in a lack of support, commitment, and direction for the work of these types of organizations. The work of youth serving agencies directed toward character development, citizenship, and other values (physical fitness, spiritual development) has provided a variety of philosophical orientations that meet this age group's needs. Today, some of these agencies are prospering, whereas others are seeking not only program redirection, but also philosophical reorientation.

The development of a clear and consistent philosophy regarding the purpose of work in the leisure services field is a demanding task. It requires considerable commitment to viewing alternatives and to debating the potential merits and outcomes of various philosophical approaches. All organizations are created for specific purposes. Like other organizations, leisure service organizations have goals; their goals are their reason for existence. Leisure service professionals must ask, "What goals are to be pursued?" "What human values within the leisure milieu are desirable and should be promoted?" and "What human experiences should be encouraged?" These questions require deliberation, analysis, and interaction with others. The development of an individual philosophy of leisure or a philosophy to manage a leisure service organization is the starting point for the work of a professional.

As one begins to examine her or his philosophical position, it becomes necessary to first review and articulate personal values as they interrelate with stated philosophies. Morality and ethics influence the world's systems—social, educational, leisure, work, religion, the military, the family, the environment, and others. In determining one's professional philosophical position and in articulating values, leisure service professionals question themselves: Do we promote competition over cooperation? Do we facilitate leisure experiences that might harm the environment? Are we passive about others' rights?

> A century ago, those interested in health, physical education, and recreation were among the nation's leaders—advocates, activists, and reformers campaigning for opportunities for children and youth and for a safe and healthy environment for us all. They cared about those to follow. We are their legatees, their beneficiaries. Unlike them, however, despite exceptions in some quarters and protestations from all, we no longer care about those to follow. Harsh words, but the evidence is persuasive. (Goodale, 1990, p. 27)

This reflection on the state of affairs in contemporary society challenges leisure service professionals to live responsibly in caring for future generations. All actions affect others, both today and tomorrow; no one lives in isolation. Making a choice today, no matter how minuscule, affects many others in future years.

Values and Philosophy

Most definitions of philosophy suggest that a philosophy reflects the values of the individual and/or organization. Just what are values? Edginton and Ford (1985) write that ". . . values are principles or guidelines that individuals regard as being important in life" (p. 178). As an ideal, a value has great usefulness or importance and affects all aspects of a person's life. Individuals and organizations operate based on an established set of ideals that govern their actions.

From a historical perspective, the park, recreation, and leisure service movement has pursued a number of specific values and principles. Some of these include the following:

1. *Preservation of natural resources.* To preserve natural resources suggests that land and water areas be maintained in a pristine or natural state for future generations.
2. *Conservation of natural resources.* Conservation of natural resources concerns the wise use of resources for multiple and compatible purposes. To conserve means to protect land and water resources while allowing compatible use of them for leisure and other activities.
3. *Wise use of leisure.* Much of the philosophical writing of the profession in the last decades focuses on using leisure for creative and spiritual development. Aristotle believed that wise

Enough Things

In an excerpt from her book *Finding Joy: 101 Ways to Free Your Spirit and Dance with Life,* Charlotte Davis Kasl writes the following:

There was a cartoon in the *New Yorker* portraying a man running toward the end of the rainbow only to see a pot of baked beans there. Whenever I think of striving for something I think of that image and realize it's time to stop, breathe, and remember there's beauty in the ordinary.

Recently I visited a dear old friend. His sense of graciousness and ritual was as I remembered. . . . I sat at the table with the same green table cloth I had sat at 25 years before. I also saw the same bookshelves, the same tables, the same dishes, and the same couch as before. In a passing moment, a painful image flashed through my mind of the thousands of dollars I had spent on such items over the years and how little it mattered. How peaceful it was to be with him in this uncluttered home. I hold that image as I struggle to detach from wanting more things.

I went through a period of buying lots of pretty things in a compulsive way. I would buy something, and then after I had enjoyed it for a little while, I would start thinking about the next thing I would buy. One day a catalogue came in the mail with pictures of beautiful quilt covers and I started to fill out the order

form. Then a part of me said, "No, stop." And as if I were led, I walked upstairs to my bedroom and sat down on my plain, natural cotton comforter and rubbed my hand over it. I said to myself, "Isn't this beautiful. It's mine, it's paid for, and it's restful. It is enough." Again and again I need to quell my restless mind and remind myself, *this is enough.*

So next time you sit down to a simple supper, crawl into a cozy bed, have a warm chat with a friend—imagine that you are at the end of the rainbow. This is it. This is life, and it's wonderful just in this moment.

Points to Ponder

- What ramifications does this quotation have for leisure experiences? Do you agree or disagree with the quotation? Explain your answer.
- How does this quotation support the theory that leisure is a state of mind? How can leisure professionals encourage this state of mind—encouraging people to enjoy the little things in life, to live in the present and make the most of their leisure time?
- Identify the philosophical orientation found within this quotation.

use of leisure was necessary in order to exercise the mind to promote intellectual thinking and advancement of civilization. This is known as the Aristotelian notion of leisure.

4. *Democracy, citizenship, and freedom of choice.* The assumption that freedom is essential to the leisure experience is fundamental to many concepts of play, leisure, and recreation (Sylvester, 1987). Organizations pursue this value in the creation of leisure services. The practice of democracy and promotion of patriotic values have been historically a function of institutions, particularly public institutions, in promoting leisure.

5. *Human happiness.* Human happiness, joy, fun, relaxation, pleasure, self-gratification, inner satisfaction, personal worth, and self-fulfillment are all values pursued within the leisure experience. Happiness and joy in life often occur through the act of engaging in freely chosen, meaningful leisure pursuits.

6. *Protection and promotion of human dignity.* Using leisure mediums to interact with people in a positive, constructive way—a value cherished by many leisure service organizations—promotes cooperation, respect for others, integrity, accessibility, and similar values.

7. *Personal growth.* One of the underlying values of leisure service organizations has involved promoting human growth and development. Organizations are often structured to encourage physical, intellectual, spiritual, social, and educational development.

The Wisdom of Paul Haun

A career in professional recreation calls for exceptional people—alert, understanding, mature, willing to give of themselves, eager to share their enthusiasms, patient, unafraid of rebuffs, able to try the hundredth time when they have failed for ninety-nine.

Source: From Haun, p. 1965. *Recreation: A Medical Viewpoint.* New York: Teachers College Press.

8. *Leisure awareness.* Another value subscribed to by individuals and organizations has been the education of individuals to the availability of leisure opportunities. These values often provide the foundation for development of lifelong leisure skills.
9. *Leadership and moral character development.* Leisure professionals and organizations have long cultivated leadership skills and techniques and moral character development as important values. This is especially true in the creation of volunteer opportunities and in athletic clubs.
10. *Quality of life.* The creation of support networks to promote a hospitable living environment for individuals has constituted a major value. Professionals in the leisure field promote aesthetic opportunities (physical environment, beauty in community life), social opportunities (contact with others), psychological well-being (safety), and economic (tourism) components that, when present, assure a higher quality of life.

By no means are these the only values that are pursued by individuals or agencies providing leisure services. They do represent many of the major values, however, that have been pursued by the movement as a whole.

Values and Ethics

Whether a part of the major value movements identified above or personally desired, values are the underlying structures that shape and influence each person's ethics. Philosophies help to define values, and ethics are the exercise of those values. Values are not facts. They are principles and belief systems and tend to be enduring; that is, once they are learned, values tend to persist (Hitt, 1990). They serve as a foundation for a particular philosophical position one takes. This section deals with the role of values in defining self.

A values-free environment? Contrary to a belief held by many, a values-free or totally objective environment does not exist. People continually impart values, whether intentionally or unintentionally (Edginton and Edginton, 1993). What is or is not said, attitudes, and actions taken or left undone—these factors all communicate values. Values provide guidance to people's lives in two particular areas: (1) modes of conduct (behaviors), and (2) desired end-states (goals). Societies in the United States and Canada tend to attribute more worth to things that require the exercise of an ethical position—wrestling with the pros and cons of an issue.

Values shape individual lives. Hitt (1990) suggests that values shape personal lives, contribute to beliefs about the good life, provide direction, and give meaning to lives. Values determine what actions, thoughts, and attitudes constitute acceptable behavior for individuals and society. For instance, if a person values the rights of all living beings, environmental preservation and conservation might take precedence in that person's life with behaviors that could include recycling, planting only native plants in the backyard, watching nature shows, and becoming involved in local environmental groups. Seeing these behaviors, others might identify that individual as an environmentalist.

The need for value clarity. Individuals are bombarded with many different types of values every day—at school, on television, in church, at home, and in other activities. Certainly, MTV (Music Television) may impart different values than PBS (the Public Broadcasting System). Young people, as well as older people, can become confused by the avalanche of conflicting information regarding values. The following quotation from Raths, Harmon, and Simon, cited as a foundational concept in Purpel and Ryan (1976), serves as a base for discussion of moral education in the schools. It addresses the need for individuals to attain value clarity in order to function in a positive, productive manner.

Persons experiencing values confusion ". . . are often identifiable by idiosyncratic behavior patterns—apathy, flightiness, extreme uncertainty, and inconsistency; drift, overconformity, overdissension, and chronic posing, and frequently underachievement." On the other hand, those who have attained value clarity do not manifest these characteristics, but are "positive, purposeful, enthusiastic and proud." With this in mind, it is of paramount importance that each individual consider and clarify his/her values. (p. 153)

The good life. Values contribute to basic beliefs about the good life and what constitutes life satisfaction. They serve as markers by which people measure levels of satisfaction. If a person believes that "the one who dies with the most toys wins," then accumulating material goods would be top priority. The need for more things would drive that person's decisions, actions, and search for fulfillment. If, on the other hand, an individual believes that life satisfaction comes from making others happy, then behaviors would be so directed. Volunteerism and an altruistic mind-set, giving to others, donating one's time and creativity, and being empathetic are manifestations of this values-based orientation.

Values as underlying structures. Underlying values guide individuals in making choices. They affect a person's choice of food, friends, activities, language or dialect, clothing, and responses to others. A belief or values system influences whether hair is worn long or short, braided or loose. Values make the person, help to provide self-definition, and determine when one will stand or yield. Values also give meaning to life—people feel good about themselves when their thoughts, attitudes, and actions agree with their values.

Figure 4.1 shows a cartoon character who appears to be questioning his values. He appears to have highly valued winning, but after achieving his goal, he is disappointed and is now reconsidering that value.

The Value in an Ethic of Care

The value exhibited in the comic strip is unsatisfactory in and of itself; people will want to examine the topic from alternative paradigms or worldviews. One paradigm views values and ethics issues from a rights and justice approach, which assumes one right answer that is fair and just for everyone. In leisure service organizations, this manifests in fairly cut-and-dried pronouncements through policies, regulations, and rules.

Calvin and Hobbes

by Bill Watterson

An ethic of care, on the other hand, considers values and ethics from a different view. It involves seeing and responding to needs, includes a sense of relationship, and takes care of issues while maintaining connections. A leisure services professional who follows the ethic of care would respond to moral and ethical issues and develop a personal philosophy out of caring and concern for others, and might not follow rules and policies exactly. As an example consider the following ethical dilemma:

> A leisure service employee consistently arrives late to work. As the assistant director, the employee is scheduled to arrive at 8:00 A.M. each morning to open the recreation facility. Every day, however, he arrives between 8:15 and 8:30 A.M. Upon being questioned by the executive director about the consistent tardiness, the employee indicates that the responsibility for seeing off his young child for school each day rests with him; he cannot arrive at the center any earlier.
>
> If one were to apply an ethic of rights and justice in dealing with this individual, the executive director might indicate that while she understood the dilemma, no one else received special consideration for family obligations, and if he could not arrive at work on time, perhaps he should rethink his position with the department. After all, it would not be fair to others.
>
> Applying the ethic of care, the executive director and the assistant director would attempt to make arrangements to accommodate the employee's obligations at home. In an ethic of care, what is right is what maintains connections and relationships. An arrangement to open later or have someone else be responsible for opening the center would allow the assistant director to meet both his family and work obligations without compromising either. The relationship to family and work were both considered in the decision-making process.

Increasingly, an ethic of care orientation has entered the workplace. Shared management styles and tools such as Total Quality Management (TQM) use aspects of an ethic of care and have become established in business practices in manufacturing, technology, and human services. Treating employees like family members, sharing in the decision-making responsibilities, promoting a concern for others, and cooperative work teams all help to establish an ethic of care within an organizational structure. Understanding personal values and ethics aids in the development of a philosophy; now is the time to examine why it is important to build a personal philosophy of leisure.

Why Build a Philosophy of Leisure?

A number of important reasons exist to establish a personal philosophy of leisure as well as to understand the philosophies of leisure service organizations. From an individual perspective, having a personal philosophy of leisure provides a value structure upon which one might act. A personal philosophy presents a source of beliefs that guide an individual's behavior and professional actions.

What's the World Coming To?

To the editor:
Although I am only 12 years old I can tell poor sportsmanship when I see it. Not among young people like myself but among adults.

On June 16 our team was playing the Rockway team. With four minutes left to play and the score 1–0 in our favor a Rockway boy kicked the ball down the sideline. I and most people thought it went out, and the ref called it that way. Suddenly a Rockway father jumped out on the pitch and started hassling the ref. After a great deal of arguing the man hit the ref. When the ref walked away the man spit on him. After the game the man punched the ref again. He hassled the ref all the way to his car.

We have had many similar experiences and it ruins the game. It must be very frustrating for the referees who are only trying to do their best.

My friends and I play soccer for the fun of it, and we wonder, what is the world coming to?

Letter to the editor that appeared in the *Kitchener-Waterloo Record,* June 19, 1976.

A personal philosophy can serve as a strong sense of inspiration and encouragement to an individual. If one believes in an ideal strongly enough, it can encourage enthusiastic and committed behavior. When channeled toward an ideal, these types of behaviors can result in the creation of programs, services, organizations, and institutions that influence individuals, communities, and perhaps an entire society.

A philosophy of leisure can be useful not only for students seeking a professional career in the leisure services area, but also for students who will be challenged with leisure opportunities in their personal lives. Developing a personal philosophy will enable an individual to address this important element in living their lives on a personal, individual level. Every individual has choices that they will make in their lives that will influence the quality of their life experiences and, hence, their well-being. Knowledge of the importance of making appropriate choices during one's leisure can lead to improving one's well-being from many perspectives, including their physical, social, mental, and spiritual development. Certainly having balance in one's life is a sought-after goal. Individuals seek satisfaction from all components of their lives—their work, leisure, and other elements that contribute to their essence.

By knowing the philosophy of a leisure service organization, one can align his or her energies in a harmonious fashion with the work of that agency. When one's personal philosophy is consistent with the philosophy of the organization, harmony and congruence will likely exist. This can result in increased productivity and greater work satisfaction. On the other hand, if an individual's personal philosophy does not align with that of the organization, that individual might seek to influence the philosophy of the organization. Interestingly, ". . . one sign of a healthy organizational culture is congruence between the organization's statement of values and the daily behavior of its members" (Hitt, 1988, p. 86). Four major reasons for building a philosophy follow (see figure 4.2).

To Know Yourself as Well as Your Organization

A personal philosophy of leisure helps to clarify important personal values regarding leisure. As Goodale and Godbey (1988, p. 2) write, "One of the uses of philosophy may be to help us understand ourselves and our circumstances and thereby reduce or at least better cope with our

The Foundation of a Profession

The foundation of a profession consists of the principles and values a field stands for and stands on. What a field stands *for* refers to its purpose, mission, or "calling." What a field stands *on* refers to the fundamental beliefs and values that explain and justify the field's existence in relation to its purpose, which gives guidance to theory and practice. A foundation states to the world, "This is *who* we are and *why* we are here." A foundation, therefore, is the single most important structural dimension of a profession, providing a rational basis for its existence as a legitimate social institution. Without it, a field literally has nothing to support its existence.

Source: From Sylvester, C., Voelkl, J.E., and Ellis, G.D. 2001. *Therapeutic Recreation Programming: Theory and Practice.* State College, PA: Venture p. 4.

uncertainty and anxiety". The search for values forms a central theme throughout people's lives; individuals are confronted with major decisions about how they live. The way in which people have been socialized to certain values throughout their lives has a great impact on their responses to events and experiences. For example, if we have been socialized in our youth to value cooperation as contrasted with competition, this value will affect our personal philosophy and our leisure choices. If we value individual behavior versus teamwork, this, too, will have an impact.

One can examine personal beliefs by developing a personal philosophy of leisure. By focusing on what they consider important and articulating it, professionals begin to know themselves, their values, and what they believe. These values and beliefs, in turn, influence one's actions. If a person believes that the leisure experience is a spiritual or emotional one, that person will act differently than one who believes that the leisure experience is a frivolous expression of status in society. Perhaps the greatest challenge an individual has is to truly understand personal beliefs and values.

As mentioned, it is imperative to determine the value system of the organizations with which one interacts. All organizations have a set of guiding beliefs that influence their work.

Figure 4.2

Reasons for building an organizational philosophy.

Know yourself and your organization

Clarify relationships with consumers and clients

Clarify organizational relationships

Clarify relationships with other institutions

Figure 4.3

Mission and
Vision Statement.

*Parks and
Recreation, City
of San Diego,
California.*

Our Mission

To acquire, develop, operate, and maintain a park and recreation system which enriches the quality of life for residents and visitors alike, and preserves it for future generations.

Our Vision

"We Enrich Lives Through Quality Parks and Programs"

Come out today and play!

- be happier
- feel great
- lose weight
- reduce stress
- increase community pride
- provide safe places to play
- diminish gang violence
- protect the environment
- increase tourism
- create memories

- build family unity
- reduce unemployment
- build self esteem
- eliminate loneliness
- reduce crime
- lower health care costs
- boost employee productivity
- live longer
- boost economy & attract business

Figure 4.4

Mission
Statement.

*South Suburban
Special Recreation
Association,
Frankfort, Illinois.*

MISSION STATEMENT
Our Mission: To promote the power of choice and to enhance the quality of life of individuals of all abilities, by providing accessible recreation in an environment that promotes dignity, success, and fun.

These guiding beliefs represent their philosophical underpinnings and as fundamental foundational statements, they rarely change. They are usually written broadly enough to incorporate a diverse number of situations that arise. Such beliefs, usually viewed as universal enduring truths, have broad appeal to both the individuals working within the organization and to the constituency served by the organization and society as a whole.

The vision statement of the Park and Recreation Department of the city of San Diego, California, provides an example of a set of forthright guiding beliefs for a leisure service organization. Their vision, "we enrich lives through quality parks and programs," is direct, establishing a powerful focus for the work of the organization. It is written in a fashion not only to provide inspiration and direction to the individuals working within the organization but to their stakeholders as well. Their foundational beliefs of enriching lives, as well as providing quality in their program offerings and facilities, sets forth a clear focus for this department (see figure 4.3). Their mission statement links their vision of enriching the quality of life for those they serve. In addition, it provides more specific detail in terms of its mission in acquiring, developing, operating, and maintaining park and recreation services. Further, it provides an inspirational message of preserving resources for future generations. This mission is found in figure 4.3.

Figure 4.4 is a mission statement for the South Suburban Special Recreation Association. This organization is an extension of seven park districts and three recreation and parks departments. It is organized to provide year round recreational opportunities for individuals with disabilities and/or special needs. Its mission statement provides clear intention to the work of the organization by emphasizing the power of choice, enhancement of quality of life, and the provision of accessible recreation services that promote dignity, success, and fun.

Daily actions within an organization partly depend upon personal beliefs and values and partly upon understanding, knowledge, and acceptance of the guiding beliefs or values of the agency. As previously mentioned, a higher correlation between one's personal beliefs and the organization's beliefs contributes to higher productivity. Conversely, a low relationship between one's personal beliefs and the organization's goals results in poor organizational performance. This is referred to in the management literature as *goal interdependence* or *work alignment* (Jordan and Mertesdorf, 1994; Naisbitt and Aburdene, 1985).

To Clarify Relationships with Consumers/Clients

Understanding one's own value system and that of the organization provides a basis for interaction with consumers or clients. From a broad perspective, the leisure professional who operates from a particular value structure is in a position to influence the interaction that occurs with a client or consumer. A positive relationship of influence is mutually beneficial and satisfies the needs of the consumer in a manner consistent with the value structure of the organization. On the other hand, the professional can use influence in inappropriate ways that are detrimental to consumers and the organization.

Organizational values help the consumer or client understand what services the organization will provide and from what perspective. Therefore, establishment of organizational values makes the work of the professional easier because it specifies the spheres of activity. Also, foundational statements or beliefs can provide information concerning specific consumer/client relations and deal with topics such as confidentiality, autonomy, degree of independence, service orientation, and openness to new ideas. The professional gains an advantage in knowing these values because they establish a code of ethics or behavior to guide professional practice.

To Clarify Relationships within the Organization

Knowledge of the guiding beliefs of an organization also can contribute to harmonious working relationships within the organization as a whole. Every organization has various components or units. Some of these components engage in work that could be defined as central to the mission of the organization, while others serve in a support capacity. Various units use various approaches to solving problems, managing resources, and conducting business. As long as all of the units pull toward the overriding, guiding beliefs and values of the organization, harmony will exist.

Often, leisure service organizations establish a set of policies and procedures based on guiding values and beliefs. These policies and beliefs usually translate values into practice. They help in making the daily decisions that guide organizational work. Shared values within an organization provide for a degree of internal consistency and allow for the work of an organization to become directed toward a common end.

To Clarify Relationships with Other Institutions

Knowledge of the guiding beliefs of an organization helps clarify interactions with other agencies and institutions. External relationships affect the success of an organization as much as internal ones. Externally communicated values and beliefs create a mental image of the quality, value, and caliber of professional efforts. For example, if a leisure service organization promotes such values as innovation, integrity, quality, service, teamwork, and community involvement, these will, in turn, influence others' perception of that organization.

Nash's Hierarchy of Leisure Pursuits

In his book, *Philosophy of Recreation and Leisure* (1960), J. B. Nash has suggested that leisure is an age-old dream of humankind. He placed different kinds of recreation into a hierarchy on the basis of their potential value to the individual and society. Nash suggests that to use leisure intelligently and profitably is the most important test of a civilization. As he indicates, "the machine liberates, but for what? Does real happiness lie in achievement and the anticipation of the adventure or in rest and security?" Nash has suggested that people can use leisure in many different ways. Some contribute to society's well-being, whereas others do not. A little of each above zero, depending on work patterns, may be good, but too many activities low on the scale are dulling, and in the end progress and development of the individual and the group are slowed.

Some value statements directly relate to relationships with other agencies and emphasize values such as cooperation, communication, and coordination of services. Interestingly, organizations that are perceived to be successful and of great benefit to society often attract individuals and agencies who want to be aligned with them. A positive set of values or philosophy, backed by action, can result in the cultivation of highly positive attitudes toward the organization. For example, corporations that recognize their citizenship responsibilities and contribute to the development of the communities within which they operate tend to be more successful over the long term than those corporations that ignore broader societal values.

Building a Philosophy

As indicated in Chapter 1, leisure involves the pursuit of happiness, joy, and the satisfaction in one's life. Thus, it may be implied that leisure is pleasing to individuals. As Russell (2002, p. 40) has written, ". . . almost all characterizations of leisure, pleasure is included." Russell states very clearly "leisure is pleasing" (p. 40). The physiological basis for connecting leisure to pleasure comes from the ancient Greek philosophical perspectives or ethical doctrines of cynicism, skepticism, stoicism, Epicureanism, and hedonism. She has suggested that these ancient physiological views have influenced modern thinking regarding leisure (2002, p. 40)

A brief review of these physiological perspectives or ethical doctrines can provide insight into their modern day application to understanding leisure. The Cynics were a sect of ancient Greek philosophers who believed that virtue is the only good. They believed that self-control was the only way to achieve virtue. Thus, cynicism held that one would seek virtue before one seeks pleasure. Skepticism is a physiological doctrine that suggests that absolute knowledge is impossible. Skeptics engage in a process of doubting enquiry. Again, as Russell states, ". . . skeptics doubt everything." A skeptic would habitually doubt, question, or disagree, rejecting the absolute possibility of experiencing pleasure. Stoicism holds that an individual is different and/or unaffected by joy or pleasure as well as grief or pain. It is a middle ground. Epicureanism seeks freedom from pain and is devoted to the pursuit of pleasure. Hedonism is an ethical doctrine in which pleasure and pleasurable consequences are the only intrinsic good.

Much has been written regarding hedonism and its applications to contemporary society. Many have suggested that Americans seek pleasure above all. It is as if the pursuit of pleasure is the chief end or goal or even virtue sought by our society. Smith (1991) has suggested that

Figure 4.5

Seven major
philosophical
contructs.

the types of pleasure can be categorized from leisure pursuits include the following: 1) sensory, 2) expressive, and 3) intellectual. Sensory pleasures refer to those pleasures that are derived through our basic functions of hearing, seeing, touching, smelling, and tasting. Sensations derived from these means can provide gratification and pleasure. The pleasures derived from the act of expressing are conveyed through literary expression, art, music, or physical movement such as dance. Intellectual pleasures can be derived from one's cognitive abilities. All of these types of pleasures evoke emotions within individuals. For example, after reading an intellectually stimulating book, a person may feel great delight and elation from mastery of the subject matter and the challenge.

Major Philosophies

In building a philosophy of leisure, one will draw upon these perspectives or ethical dimensions to formulate their beliefs. It is evident that a number of philosophical constructs may be applied to leisure and may assist in the development of leisure. One can review the previously mentioned ancient Greek concepts, or one may use philosophical constructs that reflect more contemporary thinking. Seven such philosophical constructs have general application to this discussion—perennialism, idealism, realism, experimentalism, pragmatism, existentalism, and humanism (see figure 4.5).

These philosophies represent a broad spectrum of thinking that applies to understanding leisure as well as to the management of leisure service organizations. They present particular explanations as to the nature of truth and provide principles that can serve to guide the conduct of a professional. Individuals holding these various philosophical positions may have different views regarding the leisure experience and, as a result, create different approaches or methods for organizing services.

NTRS Philosophical Position Statement

The purpose of the National Therapeutic Recreation Society's (NTRS) Philosophical Position Statement is to articulate the values of therapeutic recreation for persons with disabilities and other special populations. Professional responsibilities, skills, techniques, and service delivery models have been intentionally omitted. The purpose of this document is not to suggest how to practice therapeutic recreation, but rather to articulate a value structure for a variety of practice models to operate within.

Accordingly, the NTRS Philosophical Position Statement encompasses three broad values.

1. *Right to leisure*—this value includes related concepts, such as leisure as part of a healthy lifestyle, the importance of leisure for everyone, and other dialogues that articulate and explain the role of leisure as part of a healthy and productive life. The right to leisure is grounded in the notion that the individual is entitled to the opportunity to express unique interests and pursue, develop, and improve talents and abilities because of his/her potential. The right to leisure is a condition necessary for human dignity and well-being.

2. *Self-determination*—this value holds that leisure is an arena of action wherein the individual can express unique abilities, predilections, and preferences that are encompassed within leisure experiences. "Action" includes cognitive, communicative, psychological activities, and behaviors that facilitate a quality recreation experience for the person with a disability or other special condition. This meaning of action clearly steps beyond the limitations imposed if action is taken to mean only observable behavior. Self-determination embodies two sub-concepts.

   a. The first relates to freedom as a matter of self-determination. The value of self-determination represents a bias toward choice, self-regulation, and individual preference on the part of the participant ("freedom to" choose and act) and away from unnecessary impediments ("freedom from" constraints and barriers).

   b. The second meaning of freedom entails living a life according to higher ideals. The "freeing" qualities are acquired through learning and development of a better person. This type of self-determination is commonly referred to as wisdom or virtue.

3. *Quality of life*—the leisure of persons with disabilities and other special populations contributes to quality of life. Leisure should be "fun," enjoyable, or satisfying, regardless of the participant's abilities.

In addition, quality of life extends beyond the idea of fun. Leisure activities may help prevent illness and secondary disabilities. However, the circumstances under which leisure may prove to prevent further deterioration of the individual or promote the health of the participant occur within a context, which is unmistakably leisure in its orientation. Quality of life also includes prevention of illness (e.g., chronic conditions, mental illness, etc.) within the context of pre-existing impairments and promotion of health and functional abilities through leisure.

Source: Abridged from NTRS Philosophical Position Statement, National Therapeutic Recreation Society, Approved by the NTRS Board of Directors, October 23, 1996.

What a person believes affects that person's behavior. In the context of organizing leisure services, if one believes, for example, that a leisure service organization is focused on helping individuals develop their potential as human beings, one acts upon the philosophy of humanism. On the other hand, when a leisure service organization, such as the YMCA, uses its progress to promote spiritual values, it acts upon the philosophy of perennialism. A discussion of each of these seven philosophical constructs follows.

Perennialism and Leisure   As Sylvester (1987) reports, much of the philosophical literature written over the last eighty years presumes that play, leisure, or recreation is linked to spiritual values. Perennialism builds on the belief that life is constant and unchanging, and that eternal truths exist. Perennialists believe that the distinguishing characteristic of human beings is the ability to reason; therefore, life events should focus on developing rationality and discovering truth through study and divine inspiration.

A perennialist views leisure as an opportunity to bring individuals closer to God and to promote spiritual values. Play, leisure, and recreation are seen in the context of eternal truths presented in documents such as the Bible, the Koran, or the teachings of Buddha or Confucius. Reviewing the writings within such documents, leisure becomes a means or opportunity for celebration, harmony, union with God, joy, peace, revitalization, and contemplation. Many youth serving organizations are built upon philosophies emphasizing the philosophical position of perennialism. For example, in 1844, the Young Men's Christian Association (YMCA) was established for the purpose of ". . . influencing young men to spread the Redeemer's kingdom amongst those by whom they are surrounded" (Hopkins, 1951, p. 5).

Idealism and Leisure   The philosophical construct of idealism builds upon the notion that some individuals act according to what they believe in, regardless of what people think or the consequences of their actions. Idealists value and attempt to adhere to fine ideals. They formulate and define their own individual ideals, which may or may not be reality based. Reality emerges from within the person's own mind. Zigler (1964) writes,

> Idealists believe, generally, that the mind (or spirit) as experienced by all men [*sic*] is basic and real. . . . One's own self is the immediate reality in his conscious experience; man is more than just a body; he possesses a soul. . . . Idealism holds that the world's order is due to a spiritual reality . . . man [should be] able to interpret his world accurately and as a part of the whole." (p. 196)

Idealists value consistency of ideas. To the idealist, values remain constant and unchanging and must be preserved. How would one use idealism to develop a philosophy of leisure? Idealists pursue specific values that they perceive to be reality itself, regardless of most practical limitations. The extent to which these values could be attained through leisure would depend upon the individual's ability to choose appropriate leisure experiences that promote or protect cherished values. From an idealist's perspective, many values are promoted through leisure services (e.g., preservation, conservation, quality of life). These ideals remain constant, represent the wisdom of the ages, and are worthy of pursuit. Leisure services supporting the idealistic philosophy might pursue activities such as promoting understanding and harmony among people of the world, promoting the ideal in nature, and other similar global themes.

Realism and Leisure   Realism as a philosophy builds on works drawn from Aristotle. A realist is concerned with revealing the natural order of the world and of the universe. Realists hold that objects have an existence independent of human consciousness of them. A realist would be interested in what is real and practical rather than what is ideal or theoretical. Realists hold a different perception toward change than do either perennialists or idealists. They view change as a natural evolution that results in a perfection of order.

The realist sees the world as it is materially. As a result, the individual using realism as a philosophy in the context of a leisure service organization would use the leisure experience to learn about and define reality—to help people get in touch with the world. For the realist, goodness lies in the laws of nature and the natural order of the world and the universe.

According to Zigler (1964), the realist sees play and work as distinct and sharply defined separate parts of life. These two elements may or may not be connected. For example, the realist may view leisure as a means to rejuvenate individuals to work more effectively. This may imply that there is, in fact, a direct relationship between the two. However, the point to be made is that they are distinctly separate life elements, and although in certain circumstances one may influence the other, they are not fused.

Pragmatism and Leisure Pragmatism tests the value and truth of ideas by their practical consequences. Several American philosophers in the 1800s formulated this philosophy. Such individuals as William James, Charles Pierce, and John Dewey were proponents of this philosophy. They claimed that an idea only worked when actions based upon it produced results. Pragmatists view the world as constantly changing. Ideas must be tested through experience and are practical in nature.

Pragmatists believe that leisure should promote specific ends or specific observable, measurable results. Pragmatists maintain that if leisure services have true value they should produce practical, measurable results. For example, using a pragmatic approach, if a day camp staff surveyed its campers to determine the effects of the day camp experience on self-concept and the program intervention produced an increased level of positive self-concept in the campers, then this type of leisure experience promoted specific, measurable ends, supporting the pragmatist ideal.

Experimentalism and Leisure Experimentalism is a philosophy that suggests the world is ever changing. Like the pragmatist, the experimentalist is concerned with what works and what does not. Experimentalists seek to discover and expand the society and culture in which they live and to share these experiences with others. Leisure used as a medium by the experimentalist would help people explore different life experiences. Experimentalists encourage decisions to be made about the outcomes of leisure experiences in light of the consequences to the individual and to society as a whole.

Experimentalists see the role of leisure service organizations as emphasizing experiences. The leisure service leader would aid or consult with participants to help them discover and experience their world. They would be encouraged to test reality to determine what works in light of societal norms, customs, and values. Experimentalists openly accept change and shape the leisure experience in such a way as to improve upon the conditions of society and culture. Leisure programs would have a strong value component and would rely upon group cohesion, group problem solving, and group norms to shape individual behavior.

Existentialism and Leisure Existential philosophy developed in the 1800s from the works of Kierkegaard and Nietzche. Existentialism suggests that reality consists of living. Furthermore, existentialist philosophy suggests that individuals develop themselves and are responsible *only* to themselves for their behavior. For the existentialist, life is a world of existing, of personal choice, subjective choice, and freedom.

"Existentialists at play want no prescribed formations, no coach calling plays and destroying the players' 'authenticity,' and no crowd exhorting them to win at any cost" (Zigler, 1977, p. 200). Through leisure, participants guided by existentialism pursue unregimented experiences. The individual leisure experience focuses on developing or creating one's own rules. For the existentialist, change is constant and viewed as a natural and necessary phenomenon.

Leisure service organizations based on existentialist philosophy would view themselves as existing to enable participants to define and pursue their own leisure means and ends. No attempt would be made to impose organizational values upon participants; rather, an attempt would be made to help individuals know themselves.

Humanism and Leisure   Humanism, as a philosophy, deals with the actions or thought processes that focus on human interests and values. More specifically, humanists suggest that humans are ". . . the supreme value in the universe and that human beings should, therefore, be concerned with human interests rather than . . . [with those of spiritual or divine beings, such as God]" (Murphy, 1981, p. 18). Humanism is concerned with the development of the potential of the individual. It focuses upon the promotion and protection of human dignity as well as cultivating the capabilities of the individual. Humanistic philosophy is contrary to perennialism. It does not espouse an eternal or universal set of means or ends. In addition, whereas perennialism speaks to the existence of a divine being, humanism does not.

Humanism has been actively applied to the leisure services field. In particular, Grey and Greben (1974) suggest that the park and recreation field ". . . adopt a humanistic ethic as the central value system of the movement" (p. 53). Murphy (1981) suggests that ". . . leisure provides each person with an opportunity to realize his or her full potential" (p. 19). He further indicates that through leisure individuals will have the opportunity to achieve joy, mastery, uniqueness, self-realization, and shared experience. Leisure serves as a wellspring for personal liberation and in this way can enable individuals to be personally autonomous, not only in their intellectual beliefs but in their aesthetic experiences, their romantic preferences, their moral tastes and values, and, ultimately, their development as human beings.

Steps to Building a Philosophy

The construction of a philosophy of leisure is no easy task. It involves examining information from a variety of sources and carefully analyzing this information with the knowledge gained about approaches to studying philosophy (see figure 4.6). A number of specific activities can be used to collect information for examination. Some of these involve reading, interviewing others, or studying the ideas found in existing leisure organizations. Still others involve taking a critical view of one's own ideas and values as well as identifying some of the major values that influence society as a whole. Specific steps that can be taken in the development of a philosophy of leisure include the following:

1. *Examine the historical philosophical foundations of the profession.* An important step in the process of developing a philosophy of leisure involves examining the historical foundations of the profession. A wide array of books, articles, and monographs written in the past century espouse various philosophies and serve as the foundation of current thinking today.
2. *Examine one's own personal values.* Development of a philosophy requires consideration of one's own personal values. For example, what do you value as a result of your own thinking, as well as the influence of your family, peers, education, religion, and community? What specifically about the field of leisure do you value or consider worthwhile? What events have shaped your values and philosophy? What has frustrated you or disillusioned you regarding leisure values? What has excited you about the field of leisure? What contributions do you think you can make to others and the leisure field based on your values and philosophy of leisure?
3. *Discuss with professionals their philosophy and values.* Professionals working in the field provide an excellent source of information concerning the philosophy and values of the

Figure 4.6

Building a leisure philosophy.

How to Build a Philosophy

Examine

Values of your community

Values of your society

Historical philosophical foundations

Personal values

Other professionals' values

Leisure organizations' values

field. Often, they have developed well-articulated values or philosophies that guide their professional actions. Discussions with professionals from various subfields within the profession (i.e., youth serving agencies, federal agencies, commercial organizations, and community park and recreation centers) can provide valuable insight into the differences in philosophical orientation between agencies. Often asking professionals the question, "Why did you decide to become a part of this field?" opens communication and begins instructional dialogue.

4. *Examine the values of organizations delivering leisure services.* Organizations delivering leisure services often have explicit or expressed and implicit or implied values. The explicit, expressed values appear in mission statements, vision statements, goals and objectives, and policy and procedure documents. A review of these documents can provide valuable insight into the values of the leisure service organization. One agency promotes social interaction within a community, whereas another emphasizes the acquisition of land and water resources for preservation or conservation purposes. Implicit, implied values, often difficult to grasp, form the unwritten values of an organization. These can be learned by discussing values with several members of an organization to determine whether consistency exists between expressed and implied values and if there is consistency among several staff members, even if the values are only implied.

5. *Examine the values of the local community.* A person's local community consists of individuals, groups, and institutions, all of whom have values. Some communities are far more homogeneous than are others in the pursuit of a common set of values. However, every community holds a set of common values, norms, and customs that bind people together to produce community life. These values can have a great impact on how people live their lives and upon each person's values. Every community also has agencies within it, including leisure service agencies, that actively work to promote and cultivate certain values. Think of the influence upon the development of public character and morals by organizations and agencies such as senior centers, Girl Scouts, Camp Fire Boys and Girls, city parks and recreation departments, special park and recreation districts, Special Olympics, 4–H, YMCA, or military recreation departments.

Selected Philosophical Books and Articles That Matter

Anderson, N. 1985. *Work and Leisure.* New York: Glencoe Press.

Brightbill, C. K. 1960. *The Challenge of Leisure.* Englewood Cliffs, NJ: Prentice-Hall.

Brightbill, C. K. 1961. *Man and Leisure: A Philosophy of Recreation.* Englewood Cliffs, NJ: Prentice-Hall.

Dare, B., G. Welton, and W. Coe. 1987. *Concepts of Leisure in Western Thought: A Critical and Historical Analysis.* Dubuque, IA: KendallHunt Publishing Co.

de Grazia, S. 1962. *Of Time, Work and Leisure.* Garden City, NY: Doubleday.

Driver, B. L., T. Dustin, T. Baltic, G. Elsner, and G. Peterson. 1996. *Nature and the Human Spirit.* State College, PA: Venture.

Dustin, D. L., L. H. McAvoy, and J. H. Schultz. 1995. *Stewards of Access, Custodians of Choice.* 2d ed. Champaign, IL: Sagamore.

Dumazedier, J. 1974. *Sociology of Leisure.* New York: Elsevier.

Fain, G., ed. 1991. *Leisure and Ethics: Reflections on the Philosophy of Leisure.* Reston, VA: American Alliance of Health, Physical Education, Recreation and Dance.

Godbey, G. 1990. *Leisure in Your Life.* 3d ed. State College, PA: Venture.

Goodale, T. L., and G. C. Godbey. 1988. *The Evolution of Leisure: Historical and Philosophical Perspectives.* State College, PA: Venture.

Goodale, T. L., and P. A. Witt, 1990. *Recreation and Leisure: Issues in an Era of Change.* 3d ed. State College, PA: Venture.

Grey, D., and S. Greben. 1974. Future perspectives. *Parks and Recreation Magazine 9* (7), 26–33, 47–56.

Henderson, K., M. D. Bialeschki, S. Shaw, and V. Freysinger. 1996. *Both Gains and Gaps: Feminist Perspectives on Women's Leisure.* State College, PA: Venture.

Henderson, K., M. D. Bileschki, S. M. Shaw, and V. Freysinger, 1989. *A Leisure of One's Own.* State College, PA: Venture.

Huizinga, J. 1955. *Homo Ludens: A Study of the Play Element in Culture.* Boston, MA: Beacon Press.

Kaplan, M. 1975. *Leisure: Theory and Policy.* New York: Wiley.

Kelly, J. 1987. *Freedom to Be.* New York: Macmillan.

Kimeldorf, M. 1994. *Serious Play.* Berkeley, CA: Ten Speed.

Lee, J. 1916. *Play in Education.* New York: Macmillan.

Lee, R. 1964. *Religion and Leisure in America.* Nashville, TN: Abingdon Press.

Leitner, M. J., and S. F. Leitner. 1996. *Leisure Enhancement.* New York: Haworth Press.

Levy, J. 1978. *Play Behavior.* New York: Wiley.

Lindner, S. B. 1970. *The Harried Leisure Class.* New York: Columbia University Press.

Murphy, J. 1981. *Concepts of Leisure.* Englewood Cliffs, NJ: Prentice-Hall.

Nash, J. B. 1965. *Recreation: Pertinent Readings.* Dubuque, IA: Wm. C. Brown.

Nash, J. B. 1981. *Philosophy of Recreation and Leisure.* Dubuque, IA: Wm. C. Brown.

Peiper, J. 1963. *Leisure: The Basis of Culture.* New York: Mentor-Omega Books.

Roberts, K. 1970. *Leisure.* London: Longman Group.

Rojek, C. 1985. *Capitalism and Leisure Theory.* New York: Travistock.

Russell, R. 1996. *Pastimes: The Context of Contemporary Leisure.* Madison, WI: Brown & Benchmark.

Shivers, J. S. 1981. *Leisure and Recreation Concepts: A Critical Analysis.* Boston, MA: Allyn & Bacon.

Staley, E. J., and N. P. Miller, eds. 1972. *Leisure and the Quality of Life.* Washington, DC: AAHPER.

Sutton-Smith, B., and D. Kelly-Byrne, eds. 1984. *The Masks of Play.* New York: Leisure Press.

Sylvester, C. 1987. The ethics of play, leisure and recreation in the twentieth century, 1900–1983. *Leisure Sciences 9,* 173–188.

Thoreau, H. D. 1910. *Walden.* Boston, MA: Houghton Mifflin.

Veblen, T. 1963. *The Theory of the Leisure Class. An Economic Study of Institutions.* New York: New American Library.

Wade, M., ed. 1985. *Constraints on Leisure.* Springfield, IL: Charles C. Thomas.

6. *Examine the values of society as a whole as they relate to leisure.* The United States and Canada are greatly influenced by the Judeo-Christian ethic, which permeates and influences our basic value structure. The Judeo-Christian ethic aligns hard work with righteousness, integrity, and morality. It also emphasizes other values such as love of fellow human beings and faith. Democratic institutions also provide a set of societal values; democracy implies freedom of choice. Other institutions that greatly influence values include work, school, the family, the national media, and the military.

A periodic review of one's philosophy can be beneficial, especially in light of the emergence of new knowledge and changing conditions within the environment. Professionals find it useful to write down ideas concerning values and philosophy throughout their careers. Often, a review of personal and professional philosophies and values serves to reinforce and recommit individuals to their original beliefs. Having a written philosophical statement and referring to it frequently provides a convenient guide and reference point for decision making. It enables the individual to stay focused on important values and not become sidetracked by peripheral or temporary issues.

The Meaning of a Philosophy in a Leisure Service Organization

The foundation of any leisure service organization is its philosophy. From an organizational perspective, a philosophy refers to the guiding concepts or premises upon which the organization builds. Organizational philosophies, also referred to as overarching or superordinate goals, provide significant meaning that the leisure service organization attempts to impart to its employees.

A philosophy is useful to a leisure service agency for a number of reasons. As mentioned, it provides an opportunity for decisions to be made on a consistent basis, with a set of values and ideals that remain relevant over a long period of time. In addition, a philosophy helps an organization define itself and its uniqueness. A leisure service organization cannot be all things to all people. It must identify its direction and its scope. Direction and scope mean defining what benefits the organization wants to address, what populations it seeks to serve, and what services it intends to provide. A carefully thought-out philosophy helps build consensus, coordination, and cooperation among individuals working within the organization.

Over a period of time, an organization develops a unique personality, based on the values and beliefs that have emerged within the organization. In general, the philosophy of a leisure service organization addresses three primary areas: (1) the goals and objectives of the organization; (2) the methods and procedures used within the organization to produce leisure services; and (3) the relationship that the organization develops with its constituents, the physical environment, and the community within which it operates.

As indicated, a philosophy provides direction to the organization and helps define its values and beliefs. Hitt (1988, p. 86) writes ". . . whether the values are explicit or implicit, they constitute the essence of the organization's management philosophy. Values are the soul of the organization." Leisure service organizations often develop management philosophies to guide the distribution of resources. The management philosophy found in figure 4.7 from the Willamalane Recreation and Park District illustrates the application of this concept.

What types of values do leisure service organizations pursue as a part of their management philosophy? Deppe (1986), examining trends and forces in the administrative environment affecting future managers, suggests that values have changed regarding the management of leisure service organizations. For example, he notes that ". . . privatization of local park and

Figure 4.7

Example of a
management
philosophy
statement.

Philosophy Statements:

Service to district residents: Willamalane has a responsibility to promote superior quality park and recreation facilities and services to the residents of our District, services which promote personal and community growth, programs which recognize and preserve personal and community integrity and positive self and community image. We recognize that a superior product is the result of the effort of professionally trained people united to meet our purpose who are sensitive to the unique needs and hopes of our residents and who are aware of the ability of the community to economically support our plans.

Place in the community: Willamalane consists of individual staff and residents who have pride in our collective place in the community. We recognize the obligation to be a good citizen in Springfield which means that our efforts will complement and supplement already existing services. We will promote the responsibility of other individuals and organizations to maximize their potential and acknowledge that our efforts will not unnecessarily compete or duplicate the services of others.

Individual commitment: Willamalane is a team of individuals. We recognize and encourage the diversity of our talents but understand that real strength and effectiveness come from unity. True unity is much more than a blending of self-interests; it results when values, ideals, and goals are shared. We recognize that we share pride in our work, pride in our organization, knowledge that loyalty flows in many directions and a belief that our power is strongest when shared. These beliefs provide a basis for the future of Willamalane and all who depend on it.

recreation departments calls for a new mission statement" (pp. 46–47). Deppe (1986) also points out that administrators strongly disagree with the idea that the social welfare philosophy is no longer fundamental to public parks and recreation. These two orientations are value-based and provide direction to the work of agencies. While a need exists for local park and recreation departments to continue to try to serve all of their clients, privatization places a much stronger emphasis on assessing fees and charges in support of programs and services.

Edginton (1987), discussing the creation of organizational cultures in the leisure service field, writes ". . . the culture of any leisure service organization is reflected in the norms, customs and values to which it is committed" (p. 7). He further notes that core organizational values can be tied to ethical concerns, relationship to customers and employees, and relationship to the community. Core values, according to Edginton, can focus on quality, consistency, dependability, integrity, safety, and value.

The following statement helps us understand why one's philosophical position is important as a tool to guide one's professional efforts:

The philosophical position adopted by any particular leisure service professional or scholar will influence his or her conceptualization of leisure and leisure services. There have been a number of views expressed over time and, more recently, there has been growing interest in studying philosophy and leisure contextually. It is important for leisure service professionals and scholars to consider their philosophy because it contributes to the perspective they adopt and guides much of their behavior. For professionals, it is essential that they articulate their philosophy so employees and employers may better understand the goals they seek to achieve. (Searle and Brayley, 2000, p. 54)

We Are Creators of Hope

We are a profession of developers, builders, and creators of hope. Our professional work emerged from the social transformation as we moved from the agricultural era to the industrial era. We have transformed society in the last 150 years with a minimum of attention, friction, or even public acknowledgement for our efforts. We have created andor applied from others a host of innovative social institutions including parks, open spaces, and other amenities, such as recreation centers, public baths, settlement houses, playgrounds, child care programs, and services for older persons in response to the conditions of a new social era. We have breathed life into individuals and into the communities in which they live by providing meaningful opportunities for individuals to interact with one another and learn new skills. We have promoted finding human happiness and joy in life. We have promoted greater well being. We have helped to break down barriers of racism and discrimination between people through the leveling experiences that come from playing together. These types of experiences promote positive forms of competition and cooperation and build respect and understanding. We have created a degree of social equity by offering programs and services for the masses that were formerly available only to a few. We have encouraged a conservation and preservation ethic that has increased the likelihood that tomorrow's children will have access to our precious environmental resources.

Source: From Edginton, C. R. 1998, April. *The Art & Science of Managing Leisure Services: Reflecting, Rethinking and Repositioning for the 21st Century* J. B. Nash Scholar Lecture. Invited paper presented at the American Association for Leisure and Recreation, American Alliance for Health, Physical Education, Recreation and Dance National Convention, Reno, NV.

A Model to Guide Professional Practice

Developing a philosophy to guide one's effort requires one to think about and reflect on one's actions in the context of their endeavor as a professional. As Palmer (2000) has suggested ". . . true vocation joins self and service." It is as Buechner (1993) has written ". . . the place where your deep gladness meets the world's deep needs." Putting one's philosophy into action is important. It has been said "to know is to do, to do is to know, and to know and not to do is really not to know." Therefore, putting what we know into action is important, and by doing we also are reflecting the applied or engineered skills found in the practice of our profession. But to know, and not to do or act on what you know, is to fall short as a professional.

Edginton (2001) has suggested a template that can be employed for our work as professionals. His model consists of three interrelated elements—*being, doing,* and *becoming* a professional.

Being a Professional   One essence as humans is in our "being." It is a state or fact of existence or living. It is our fundamental or essential nature and reflects all of the physical and mental qualities that make us who we are as humans. To seek one's being is to seek the fulfillment of the possibilities that exist in one's life. Some of the guidelines we seek in being a professional include:

- **Living Up to the Calling.** We are called to serve others by promoting joy and happiness through leisure.
- **Forming versus Training.** We are involved in the formulation of the character values and approaches that individuals take in living their lives. We don't train people but provide them with the ability to acquire lifelong skills of learning, thinking, reflecting, and problem solving.

- **Acquisition of Presence versus the Acquisition of Skills/Competencies.** Your presence has the possibility of influencing others. We have all been influenced by those qualities of genuiness, loyalty, sincerity, caring, love, etc.
- **Commitment to the Values of the Profession.** Our professional work involves wise use of leisure time, conservation and preservation of the environment, and promotion and protection of human dignity.
- **Promoting Critical Inquiry.** Our job is to improve the quality of life for all human beings. It involves our critical inquiry as to the conditions of human kind and the ability to frame new solutions and social innovations.
- **Facilitating the Construction of Experiences versus Imposing Activities.** Our work as professionals involves promoting within structure. Facilitating rather than imposing.
- **Role Modeling.** We serve as role models for others. Living up to and modeling high standards is important.

Doing the Work of a Professional   What is the work of a professional? Our work is people-focused, knowledge-based, and customer-service oriented. To be successful, one must consider the following elements:

- **Knowledge of What We Do.** There is no substitute for competence; you must have knowledge of what you do.
- **Organizing.** Successful professionals are well organized and focused.
- **Listening and Communicating.** Listening is an important part of the communication process. We show empathy by listening.
- **Reading the World and Reading People in Context.** It is important to understand the context of the lives of the individuals that you serve. To develop true empathy, one must walk in the shoes of another.
- **Promoting Discipline without Authoritarianism.** Professional autonomy must parallel with professional discipline and be acted out in a way that does not enforce one's viewpoint on others. Self-control and discipline are critical keys here.
- **Promoting Appreciation for Diversity.** We live in a diverse world. One's ability to understand diversity and difference may be the key to creating harmonious leisure environments.
- **Learning to Anticipate Needs.** It is not enough to simply meet the needs of others; one must learn to anticipate needs before they occur.

Becoming a Professional   To be a professional requires a continuous process of search. In a sense, we as professionals are in a constant state of becoming. We need to recognize that we are on a journey; a journey that requires a continuous search for our being as professionals, an ongoing review of our values, and our ways of relating to and interacting with those that we serve. Some of the elements central to the process of becoming a professional involve the following:

- **Caring.** Our profession is committed to crafting "caring environments." Caring people are individuals who show concern or interest in others, reaching out in a non-judgmental way and providing social and emotional support.
- **Believing in People's Abilities and Possibilities.** Our profession must be dream makers, not dream breakers. To do so, we must believe in the inherent abilities and possibilities of others.

Americans and Leisure Philosophy

In America there has been no leisure time philosophy for the simple reason that up to this generation there has been no leisure. Our [ancestors] found the conquering of the wilderness a difficult task. There have been only three generations since the ox team was used.

Civilizations, in other days, paid dearly for the privilege of leisure. The great philosophers of Greece even went to the limit of justifying slavery because it gave leisure to the citizens. Greece had a philosophy for leisure; [but] America has despised it.

America has confused leisure with idleness . . . the reason for this has been quite simple. America's philosophy of success too often has been centered around quantitative things. One must make money—get on in the world. To get on in the world meant to be continuously at one's vocation. . . . Leisure has never been considered quite respectable.

Source: J. B. Nash, *The Philosophy of Recreation and Leisure*, 1960.

- **Growing With.** As we interact with those with whom we serve, they present us with new circumstances that require us to reflect, rethink, reevaluate, and reexamine our own behaviors.
- **Aspiring.** To aspire means to be ambitious or to rise to high expectations. Aspire to a higher calling in your life.
- **Learning to Learn.** Learning how to learn is fundamental to one's success in a knowledge-based society where the half-life of knowledge is increasingly being reduced.
- **Teaching to Learn.** Teaching to learn involves creating authentic dialogue between the participant and the professional. Learning occurs not where individuals are taught, but where the learner is an active participant in the process.

The guidelines can be useful in framing one's professional philosophy upon which they act. Serious consideration must be given to how one frames one's actions and efforts by being, doing, and becoming a professional. Our work in the leisure service field is special and unique. We have the opportunity to influence others in a positive, uplifting fashion. We have the opportunity to enhance, nourish, and enrich the lives of others, bringing joy and happiness and enabling them to reach their potential as human beings.

Summary

The development of a philosophy of leisure in order to guide the work of the professional is essential. Likewise, the philosophy of a leisure service organization guides the work of the people within that agency. Philosophies, whether individual or organizational, provide a framework for action and an understanding of the purpose and reasons governing behavior and actions.

What is philosophy? Philosophy, in its original meaning, suggests the search for the wisdom and meaning of life. A philosophy may be thought of as a systematically defined set of values, beliefs, and preferences. A philosophy is usually expressed as an abstract idea or set of ideas.

There are numerous reasons to build a philosophy of leisure. First and foremost, a philosophy provides a value structure to guide action. A philosophy can also be a strong source of inspiration and encouragement. Knowledge of an organization's philosophy can help clarify the relationships one encounters working within an agency. More specifically, a philosophy can help individuals know themselves, know their organization and its expectations regarding relationships with customers, colleagues, and external institutions.

How do we build a philosophy? Those wishing to build a philosophy may pursue it from several different standpoints. Three basic approaches can be used—speculative, normative, and analytical. Furthermore, a number of different philosophical constructs can be applied to leisure, such as perennialism, idealism, realism, experimentalism, existentialism, pragmatism, and humanism.

The actual construction of a philosophy requires a number of steps. It involves examination, not only of one's personal values but also of the philosophy and values that have emerged within the leisure service profession itself. The development of a personal philosophy of leisure as well as acknowledgment of an organizational philosophy is an important step for the professional. By clarifying what one believes, one can better focus on certain goals and direct his or her behavior toward the achievement of those goals. A philosophy provides a reasoned framework within which to view leisure and the work of leisure service organizations.

Discussion Questions

1. What is meant by the term *philosophy?* What is meant when it is suggested that philosophy is a practical tool for the professional?
2. Why is the development of a personal philosophy important to the development of a professional?
3. Why is it important to understand the philosophy underlying leisure service organizations?
4. How do values, ethics, and philosophy relate with one another?
5. What discrete values and principles have philosophers pursued that offer insight into the leisure phenomenon during the twentieth century?
6. What foundational values of the leisure service movement exist in society today? List ten from the chapter, citing examples of how various leisure service organizations pursue them.
7. List the major reasons for building a philosophy. What process would you use to develop your own personal philosophy?
8. Briefly describe seven major philosophies.
9. Locate five different types of leisure service organizations in your community and categorize their philosophies, values, and beliefs.
10. Write down your personal philosophy of leisure so it is understandable to others.

References

Brightbill, C. 1961. *Man and Leisure: A Philosophy of Recreation.* Englewood Cliffs, NJ: Prentice-Hall.

Cooper, W. 1999. Some philosophical aspects of leisure theory. Edited by E. L. Jackson and T. L. Burton, in *Leisure Studies: Prospects for the 21st Century.* State College, PA: Venture.

de Grazia, S. 1962. *Of Time, Work and Leisure.* Garden City: Doubleday.

Deppe, T. 1986. New Federalism: The great federal switch and its impact upon municipal parks and recreation. *Journal of Parks and Recreation Administration 4*(1), 46–47.

Driver, B. L., D. Dustin, T. Baltic, G. Elsner, and G. Peterson. 1996. *Nature and the Human Spirit.* State College, PA: Venture.

Dustin, D., L. McAvoy, and J. Schultz. 1982. *Stewards of Access, Custodians of Choice: A Philosophical Foundation for the Park and Recreation Profession.* Minneapolis: Burgess.

Edginton, C. 1987. Creating an organizational structure. *Management Strategy 11*(1), 1.

Edginton, C., and P. Ford. 1985. *Leadership in Recreation and Leisure Service Organizations.* New York: Macmillan.

Edginton, C. R. 2001. A Profession as One's Calling: A Personal Reflection. *Revista do Instituto Politecnico de Macau 4*(1), 131–153.

Edginton, S. R., and C. R. Edginton. 1993. *Youth Programs.* Champaign, IL: Sagamore.

Fain, G., ed. 1991. *Leisure and Ethics: Reflections on the Philosophy of Leisure.* Reston, VA: American Alliance of Health, Physical Education, Recreation and Dance.

Godbey, G. 1990. *Leisure in Your Life.* 3d ed. State College, PA: Venture.

Goodale, T. 1990. Intergenerational inequities: The abuse and neglect of those to follow. *Leisure Today* 3–7 (October), in *Journal of Physical Education, Recreation, and Dance,* 27–31.

Goodale, T., and G. Godbey. 1988. *The Evolution of Leisure: Historical and Philosophical Perspectives.* State College, PA: Venture.

Goodale, T., and P. Witt. 1990. *Recreation and Leisure: Issues in an Era of Change.* 3d ed. State College, PA: Venture.

Grey, D., and S. Greben. 1974. Future perspectives. *Parks and Recreation Magazine* 9(7), 26–33, 47–56.

Henderson, K., D. Bialeschki, S. Shaw, and V. Freysinger. 1996. *Both Gains and Gaps: Feminist Perspectives on Women's Leisure.* State College, PA: Venture.

Hitt, W. 1988. *The Leader Manager.* Columbus: Battelle Press.

Hitt, W. 1990. *Ethics and Leadership.* Columbus: Battelle Press.

Hopkins, H. 1951. *History of the YMCA in North America.* New York: Association Press.

Huizinga, J. 1955. *Homo Ludens: A Study of the Play Element in Culture.* Boston: Beacon Press.

Hunnicutt, B. K. 2000. Our reform heritage: Recovering the vision of community leisure service. *Journal of Leisure Research* 32(1), 58–61.

Jordan, D., and J. Mertesdorf. 1994. The effects of goal interdependence between leisure service supervisors and employees. *Journal of Applied Recreation Research* 19(2), 101–116.

Kelly, J. 1987. *Freedom to Be.* New York: Macmillan.

Kimeldorf, M. 1994. *Serious Play.* Berkeley, CA: Ten Speed.

Leitner, M. J., and S. F. Leitner. 1996. *Leisure Enhancement.* New York: Haworth Press.

Murphy, J. F. 1981. *Concepts of Leisure.* 2d ed. Englewood Cliffs, NJ: Prentice-Hall.

Naisbitt, J., and P. Aburdene. 1985. *Reinventing the Corporation.* New York: Warner Books.

Nash, J. 1981. *Philosophy of Recreation and Leisure.* Dubuque, IA: Wm. C. Brown.

Pieper, J. 1963. *Leisure: The Basis of Culture.* New York: Random House.

Purpel, D., and F. Ryan. 1976. *Moral Education: It Comes with the Territory.* Berkeley, CA: McCutcheon.

Rifkin, J. 1995. *The End of Work.* New York: Putnam.

Robinson, J., and G. Godbey. 1997. *Time for Life: The Surprising Ways Americans Use Their Time.* University Park, PA: The Pennsylvania University Press.

Russell, R. 1996. *Pastimes: The Context of Contemporary Leisure.* Madison, WI: Brown & Benchmark.

Russell, R. V. 2002. *Pastimes: The Context of Contemporary Leisure.* Champaign, IL: Sagamore Publishing

Schor, J. 1992. *The Overworked American.* New York: Basic Books.

Searle, M. S., and R. E. Brayley. 2000. *Leisure Services in Canada: An Introduction.* 2d ed. State College, PA: Venture.

Sylvester, C. 1987. The ethics of play, leisure and recreation in the twentieth century, 1900–1983. *Leisure Sciences 9,* 173–188.

Zigler, E. 1964. *Philosophical Foundations for Physical, Health, and Recreation Education.* Englewood Cliffs, NJ: Prentice Hall.

Zigler, E. 1977. *Physical Education and Sport Philosophy.* Englewood Cliffs, NJ: Prentice Hall.

Mass Leisure

Many leisure activities occur in group settings that produce opportunities for connecting with others and joyful social interaction.

Introduction

The Industrial Revolution, which began in the 1800s in the United States and Canada, increased the amount of leisure available to most individuals, giving them the opportunity to use it as an expression of their needs and lifestyles. Transformation of an industrial-based economy to one focused on the creation and dissemination of information has produced further opportunities for leisure. The pursuit of quality leisure experiences will continue to influence the culture and society of the United States and Canada.

Leisure both shapes and reflects culture. Although leisure involves personal time, society influences leisure behavior through its norms, values, and customs. As a result of this influence, various patterns of leisure behavior, referred to as *mass leisure,* have developed and evolved. Mass leisure is both fluid and dynamic and reflects the popular fads, trends, and interests of individuals in a culture. Similar to popular or mass culture, mass leisure consists largely of everyday activities, habits, beliefs, and tastes often shared by many people (Kando, 1980). Within popular culture, *mass leisure reflects the everyday, recreational activities of the majority of the population.* Godbey (2002), suggests that the United States is moving toward becoming a leisure democracy where more types of leisure activities are available to more people.

This chapter examines the phenomenon of mass leisure. It focuses on the concept of time and mass leisure, explaining what has led to the proliferation of mass leisure in this century and identifying some of the many forms that mass leisure can take.

Mass Leisure: Is There Time?

Historically, leisure has been tied to discretionary time, left over "after the practical necessities of life have been attended to" (May and Petgin, 1928, p. 3). Throughout the twentieth century people have sought to increase discretionary time for leisure. The number of work hours decreased greatly from the turn of the century until the mid-1960s. For example, it took approximately forty years, from 1919 to the 1960s, to reduce the workweek from forty-eight to forty hours. During this same time frame, numerous technological advances in the workplace, as well as appliances, such as dishwashers, microwaves, and washing machines, were developed. These trends led many sociologists in the early 1960s to predict the creation of a thirty-hour workweek, with a society based more on leisure and recreation than on work.

Yet, something happened along the way—a leisure society hasn't developed. In fact, the reverse seems to have occurred! A headline in a cover story from *Time* in the late 1980s read "How America Has Run Out of Time: Workers are weary, parents are frantic, and even children haven't a moment to spare: Leisure could be to the 1990s what money was to the 1980s." The article states that ". . . according to a Harris survey, the amount of leisure time enjoyed by the average American has shrunk 37 percent since 1973. Over the same period the average workweek, including commuting, has jumped from under forty-one hours to nearly forty-seven hours. . . . Vacations have shortened to the point where they are frequently no more than weekends. And the Sabbath is for—what else?—shopping" (Gibbs, 1989, p. 58).

This trend has continued in the 1990s and into the twenty-first century. According to the Bureau of Labor Statistics, Americans have by far the shortest vacations in the industrialized world—see table 5.1 (Robinson, 2003).

The most systematic approach to studying time use in the United States has been undertaken at the University of Maryland in the Americans' Use of Time Project. The findings of these studies contradict the Harris survey. Findings concerning the time use of individuals living in the United States came from a series of subjective questions taken over a period of time from 1965 to 1985. In these studies, participants responded to subjective questions about time use. In addition to recording all their activities on a single day, respondents were asked whether they "always," "sometimes," or "almost never" felt rushed to do things they have to do (Robinson, 1990a). From these studies, Robinson determined a number of interesting factors:

- Americans have more free time today than ever before. Men have forty hours of free time a week, and women have thirty-nine hours (Robinson, 1989; Spring, 1993).
- Increases in free time for women can be attributed to less household work, less time involved in child care, and a shorter workweek (Robinson, 1989).
- Unmarried people have more free time than married couples (Robinson, 1989).

TABLE

5.1 VACATIONS ARE OPTIONAL

Country	Vacation Days Required by Law	Average Number of Vacation Days Taken
China	15 days	15 days
France	25 days	32–42 days
Italy	20 days	30 days
Japan	10 days	17.5 days
Spain	25 days	30 days
U.K.	20 days	25 days
United States	0 days	10.2 days

- Most free time gains have occurred between 1965 and 1975 (Robinson, 1989). Between 1982 and 1988, the average workweek of an employed American increased by 1 hour to 43.8 hours (Cutler, 1990).
- People aged fifty-one to sixty-four have gained the most free time since 1965 (Robinson, 1989).
- For every extra hour of increased leisure time Americans have gained since 1965, they spend an extra hour watching television. Television takes up 38 percent of Americans' free time (Robinson, 1990b).
- Although Americans have more free time now than in the 1960s or 1970s, they report feeling frantic and rushed, especially those aged thirty-five to fifty-four (Robinson, 1990a). Individuals feel that they are in a "time crunch" (Robinson, 1991).
- Four out of ten Americans report cutting back on sleep to gain time. Nearly one-third of adults feel that they haven't accomplished what they set out to do in a typical day. More than one in four adults describe themselves as workaholics (Robinson, 1991).
- Americans value leisure time as highly as they value money (Robinson, 1991).
- A gap exists between the amount of free time that individuals have and the amount they desire (Robinson, 1991; Spring, 1993).

Robinson and Godbey (1997) note that since 1985 the workweek has shown virtually no change in the estimated hours worked per week, that television continues to play a large role in how we use our free time, and that the amount of free time has stayed close to the 1985 figures presented in the original Use of Time project. This information suggests that the amount of time available to Americans has increased. Yet Americans still feel rushed, frantic, and crunched in the use of time.

In contrast to the findings from time use diary studies, Schor (2003) has used data from Current Population Survey, a household survey of the Economic Policy Institute, to demonstrate that the annual work hours in the United States continued to rise from 1973 to 2000. The survey indicates that the average American worker added 199 hours to his or her annual schedule, or nearly five additional weeks of work per year (assuming a forty hour workweek) (Schor, 2003).

In explaining this phenomenon, Schor (1991) has identified several possible reasons for people overworking. First, she reports that in 1990 the average American owned and consumed more than twice as much as he or she did in 1948, and that people need to be working more hours or taking a second job to support their families at the level to which they have become accustomed. As one twenty-eight-year-old factory worker stated, "Either I can spend time with my family, or support them—not both" (Schor, 1991, p. 21).

The second situation finds that the desire for more leisure is distinctly secondary to the desire for more material goods. As de Grazia (1962) observed, what we want today are things; things cost money; money costs time. The increasing accumulation of goods also means spending more time in the consumption and maintenance of them. Consumption will become more commodity intensive, and people will attempt to speed up consumption since time is both limited and expensive in relation to things. International comparisons found that Americans spend more time shopping than any other group of people in the world.

The third situation can be attributed to downsizing, in that downsizing-fueled job insecurity has led some Americans to work through their vacations in a practice known as "defensive overworking," a futile attempt to insulate themselves from future layoffs. On average, Americans gave back 175 million days of paid vacation to employers in 2002, time they already had coming. It was a $20 billion gift to business (Robinson, 2003).

Several other studies seem to support the conclusions of Schor. One study conducted for Hilton hotels found that two-thirds of respondents were stressed out and that seven out of ten

I Could Do That: The Best Sports Lure The Fan

Poker, on TV and on-line, is dealing itself as the next hot thing in entertainment/sports. Competitive bass fishing is ESPN's latest bid for the male viewer. And their role model, stock car racing, which four years ago was still regarded as a poor rural cousin of Indy-style racing, is now being criticized for becoming too popular too fast and deserting its grass roots for urban fans and Hollywood tie-ins.

The emergence of cars, cards, and fishing is the freshest thing that has happened to sports since the nineteenth century, when James Naismith invented basketball. It brings sports back to the fans, even if only in fantasy for a while.

I'm saying this at the peak of the traditional sports season. Baseball is hurtling toward the World Series, college and pro football are raging, and basketball is right around the corner. If you haven't noticed, maybe it is because you, too, are growing weary of games played by oversized brats whose style, ethics, and chemical balances make them hard for most of us to identify with.

The popularity of these non-traditional sports can be found in the fact that they are played by people that seem just like us. Players are not particularly large, cool, or well dressed; in essence, they are just like us. This leads us to believe that if only we had more free time or a more understanding spouse or a larger bank account, we could be beating them at their own game.

This is being bore out in the wave of new TV poker shows as well as the fact that participation in these events is surging. In 2003, the World Series of Poker drew 839 competitors willing to pay the $10,000 entry fee. In 2004, this tournament drew more than 2,500 competitors. As one participant states, "it's a chance to be 18 years old again, to stay up all night, to be served free drinks . . . to walk around with rolls of bills held together by rubber bands in your front pocket. Only now your mother isn't around to yell you that you have to go to bed."

Points to Ponder

- Do you think that the sports of poker, car racing, and fishing will ever become more popular than the sports baseball, football, and basketball, or are they just fads that will decline in popularity in the near future?

What sports do you see emerging in the future?

Source: Adapted from Lipsyte, R. 2004. I could do that: The best sports lure the fans. *USA Today* (October 12). p. 23A.

respondents said they needed more fun in their lives, and as a result nearly half believe time is more important than money with a third of respondents saying they would trade a day's pay for a day off (Hilton Generational Time Study, 2001). The results of yet another study supporting Schor's conclusions are presented in table 5.2.

In understanding the differing opinions of such scholars as Schor and Robinson and Godbey, a third alternative is emerging. In his recent book, *The Rise of the Creative Class,* Florida (2002) contends that human creativity is the new driving force in our economy and society, and it is changing how we live, work, play, and build community. Creativity—"the ability to create meaningful new forms"—is now the decisive source of competitive advantage. Within this new environment, the fundamental source of creativity is people, and thus people are the critical resource of the new age. Using this creativity is allowing people to integrate their work and leisure in ways never before thought possible. As a result, working longer hours is to be expected but only in relation to exciting and interesting projects.

TABLE 5.2   KEY FINDINGS OF HARRIS'S WORK AND LEISURE STUDY (2003) (N = 1,559)

- Only 14 percent of respondents think we have our priorities correct as a culture; one-third of respondents believe we have our priorities decidedly in the wrong place.
- Three-fourths of respondents think that, as a culture (American), we place a higher value on our success in the workplace than at home.
- Respondents were split as to whether the American work ethic of hard work and long hours has a positive or negative effect on our culture.
- If given the chance to live their lives over, 40 percent of respondents would spend more time enjoying leisure activities, and 15 percent would spend more time working.
- Eighty percent of respondents experience medium to high stress at work, 60 percent experience the same level of stress at home.
- Nearly 50 percent of respondents said their stress level is higher today than it was five years ago.
- Four out of ten respondents report that they are already in a negative state at the beginning of their work week—either already tired, stressed or apprehensive. Another quarter of respondents say they are on autopilot, while only 23 percent say they are energized and ready for the week ahead.
- Nearly half of respondents think they have less leisure time now than five years ago, while one third of respondents expect to have more leisure time in the next five years than now.
- Ironically, respondents perceive that they have less than half the leisure hours each week than reality—on average Americans enjoy 33.2 leisure hours per week, but we think that the average American has only 14.8.
- Respondents spent as much time each day with the television as they did with their families and admit that watching TV is their biggest time waster each week.
- One-quarter of respondents pursued absolutely no hobbies in their free time.
- On average, respondents spend less than 3 percent of their waking hours simply thinking, meditating, or daydreaming.
- At the end of a typical weekend, one-quarter of respondents said they have often or always done everything they wanted to do.

Source: Harris Interactive Study, 2003 as reported by Walker, K. (2004, June 11). *Redefining Leisure.* Presented at the Take Back Your Time Day Conference, Chicago, IL.

The question of time and work and leisure will continue to be an important one in the years ahead. An important component of this issue will be technology. With the increased use of computers and technology, where time is marked by the nanosecond, people's concept of time will likely change. In the future, will time be defined in human terms or in terms that machines have created? What does progress mean and how does it relate to the amount of things produced, distributed, and consumed or discarded? Is good health, which is almost assuredly related to happiness, related to the production of things, and, if so, how? Will people's lives slow down or speed up? While people may be happier if their pace of life slows down, is it possible for them to slow down?

How technology will change the work/leisure relationship was examined in an article entitled "The End of Leisure," which documents that today's average married couple labors a staggering 717 hours more each year than a working duo in 1969. Computers, cellular phones, palm pilots, and so on, that were to "free us from our desks have bound us to our jobs in ways unimaginable just a decade ago. They are electronic umbilical cords to the workplace" (Stein Wellner, 2000, p. 52). Does this all mean the end of leisure? Stein Wellner (2000) answers no, but it does signal a change in the way we view work and leisure. Today the lines between work and leisure are blurring. Today, Americans are taking work on vacation and surfing the Internet at work. "Rather than trying to isolate hours of the day that are completely free of work or slog through hours totally devoid of leisure, we're melding the two together" (Stein Wellner, 2000, p. 52).

Beyond society's view of time is its view of leisure. Perhaps people's definition of leisure will change from that of free time to that of leisure as a state of mind where satisfaction with time becomes a key component, and work and leisure can be fused. Thus, the issue becomes not one of satisfaction with work or leisure but with life's endeavors. Perhaps people will continue to combine activities as Robinson and Godbey (1997) explain in the concept of time deepening, which can occur in one of four ways. *Time deepening* involves "attempting to speed up a given activity, substituting a leisure activity that can be done more quickly for one that takes longer, doing more than one activity at once, or undertaking a leisure activity with more precise regard to time" (p. 39).

In this process of truly claiming free time as leisure, it will be increasingly important to understand how leisure experiences are consumed, in that despite the perception or reality of decreasing amounts of leisure time in society, the consumption of leisure experiences continues to grow. The idea of consuming leisure experiences may be an important idea to grasp in understanding the concept of mass leisure. Individuals appear more concerned with the quality and quantity of their leisure experiences and tend to view their well-being from the standpoint of the experiences they have collected or consumed rather than the material possessions they may own. As Molitor (2000) states, "The new paradigm will emphasize experiences, instead of things. Leisure time dominance will usher in a host of new attitudes, outlooks, and activity preferences. As materialism wanes and experiences and self-development ascend, new business opportunities will grow by leaps and bounds. Responding to the dreams and hopes will evoke a dazzling profusion of new opportunities and entrepreneurial undertaking catering to every imaginable whim and fancy. Experiences, not things, are slated to become the focus of consumer interest. A dizzying array of incomparable choices will provide a dazzling array of pursuits suited to individual desires and needs of a growing leisure class. The new will replace the old" (pp.15–16).

For leisure service organizations seeking to improve people's quality of life, this could mean taking a multi-dimensional approach to helping people experience the promise of leisure. One approach might be to follow Florida's (2002) advice in creating cool cities, making sure leisure service organizations are a part of creating communities where creative people can integrate their work and leisure. According to Florida, the characteristics of creative communities are:

- Creative centers encourage the development of "third places"—venues like coffee shops, bookstores, and cafés in which we find less formal acquaintances. These third places comprise the heart of a community's social vitality where people hang out simply for the pleasures of good company and lively conversation.
- Creative centers provide recreation on a just-in-time basis by offering lifestyle amenities close at hand; such amenities include urban parks, bike lanes, and off-road trails for running, cycling, rollerblading, or just walking the dog. In addition, creative centers encourage people to seek out leisure experiences that involve them, support their search for an active and fitness conscious lifestyle, as well as foster their desire for an energetic, organic, and indigenous street level culture.
- Creative centers celebrate diversity. A diverse community is the sign of a place open to outsiders. Diversity also means excitement and energy. An attractive place doesn't have to be a big city, but it has to be cosmopolitan—a place where anyone can find a peer group to

TABLE

5.3   TAKE BACK YOUR FAMILY TIME

Time Changes for Young Children and Their Families Since the Early 1980s

- Children ages 3–12 have lost 12 hours per week of free time between 1981 and 1997. They play less and their unstructured time has declined significantly (Hofferth, 1999).
- Children's structured sports time has doubled from 2 hours, 20 minutes per week to 5 hours, 17 minutes per week from 1981–1997. Boys and girls increased equally in structured sports time, but boys still spent twice as much time as girls in sports. (U.S. Department of Health and Human Services, 1999). Their time spent "on the sidelines" watching siblings and others play has increased fivefold.
- Young children, on average, spend 50 percent more time studying than they did twenty years ago, with little to show in overall academic gains (U.S. Department of Health and Human Services, 1999).
- Religious participation has declined 40 percent for children (ages 3–12) (U.S. Department of Health and Human Services, 1999).
- Families' household conversation (talking together as a family, with no other activity going on) has declined from infrequent to non-existent on average. Overall, children in 1997 averaged about 45 minutes per week in conversation with anyone in the family, when the conversation was the primary activity. Family meal time declined by nearly an hour per week from 1981–1997, from about 9 hours per week to about 8 hours a week (Putnam, 2000).
- There has been a 28 percent decrease over two decades in the number of families taking a family vacation each year (Putnam and Goss, 2000).
- Although TV watching has increased in American homes, watching TV as a family has declined by nearly 25 percent. TV has become a more solitary activity.

(Continues)

be comfortable with and also find other groups to be stimulated by; a place seething with the interplay of cultures and ideas, a place where outsiders can quickly become insiders.
- Creative centers are authentic. Authenticity comes from several aspects of a community: historic buildings, established neighborhoods, a unique music scene, or specific cultural attributes.
- Creative centers offer a vibrancy of street life, café culture, arts, music, and people engaging in outdoor activities—altogether a lot of active, exciting, creative endeavors.

The bottom line, according to Florida, "is that cities need a people climate even more than they need a business climate. This means supporting creativity across the board and building a community that is attractive to creative people, not just to high tech companies . . . instead of subsidizing companies, stadiums and retail centers, communities need to be open to diversity and invest in the kinds of lifestyle options and amenities people really want" (p. 283).

A second approach to helping people experience the promise of leisure would be to help people slow down and take back their time. In the last five years, a grass roots movement has begun to emerge entitled Take Back Your Time; this national movement tries to educate individuals, organizations, and communities on the problems of overwork, over-scheduling, and time urgency. People involved in the Take Back Your Time movement come from "varied walks of life—business, academia, family organizations, social justice campaigns, environmental groups, unions, faith communities, youth serving organizations, and many others to seek common answers to time poverty in a spirit of mutual respect for the diversity of our viewpoints" (DeGraaf, 2004). Some of the work being done by organizations and individuals connected with the *Take Back Your Time Movement* (www.timeday.org) is presented in tables 5.3 and 5.4.

TABLE

5.3 CONTINUED

How Some Families Have Taken Back Their Time

- Examining Priorities: It all begins here. What kind of family do you want, how much family time do you need to have that kind of family, and how much time do your children need to just hang out? Pay the family first with time, then add outside activities.

- Reducing outside activities: Pick one that consumes a lot of time or interferes with an important family activity such as dinner, bedtime, or weekends at the lake. In one family, the parents decided that one sport had to go and let their son decide which one. Another family told their twelve-year-old daughter that she could stay in dance, but not on the traveling dance team, because of the toll on the family and her own schedule.

- Adding family activities: Family meals are a good place to start, if you are not having many of them. You might add just one dinner a week, say, on Sunday night when there are usually no outside activities. Be sure to make it special. You might also add to two or more areas of family time simultaneously, say regular bed time rituals and a weekly game night. You could put a family vacation on your calandar and inform the world that nothing will keep you from it, even if your kid reaches the Little League World Series.

- Eliminating television and other media from activities where you want family conversation: You might move the television from the area where you eat, or at least make sure it is turned offer before you eat. You might move a television and computer out of a child's bedroom in order to promote more family interaction.

- No weak links: In two-parent families, the parents have to be together. Both have to agree on the values at stake and on how to implement these values. If this is not the case, then spend your energy talking with your co-parent before trying to steer the family in a different direction.

- Persevering: You have to be committed to change. If your children let you know they think having regular dinners is inconvenient and boring, resist the temptation to cave in before the payoff. Just as with good bedtime rituals that children will love once they adjust to having a bedtime, many other changes require perseverance in the parents.

- Emphasizing your values: Enduring changes have to be based on your values about family life, so when you discuss changes with a child make sure you stress the family reasons as well as any benefits the child will gain. Stress that this is not a punishment, but a re-balancing, and acknowledge the child's feeling of loss or anger, if these are present. Be a leader with a vision.

Source: Reported by Doherty, W. 2004. University of Minnesota's College of Human Ecology Marriage and Family Therapy Program. http://www.puttingfamilyfirst.org/html/research.html

Source: Doughty W., and Carlson B., 2002. *Putting Family First.* Henry Holt Publishers.

Regardless of where one stands on the question of "Mass Leisure: Is there time," there is much to be done in helping people experience the promise of leisure. All leisure service organizations and professionals have a role to play in providing experiences that promote life satisfaction.

Mass Leisure: Common Elements

Throughout history, activities have emerged that could be classified as mass leisure. Examples of early forms of mass leisure include the circuses of the Roman empire and the playhouses of London in the thirteenth and fourteenth centuries. Not until the twentieth century, however, did mass leisure grow to epic proportions. This proliferation of mass leisure has resulted from a number of unique factors.

The daily use of leisure has been radically reshaped since the Second World War. Not only has technological change played a major role in this reshaping, so too have changing economic and social conditions as well as our value systems. The mass media, pleasure travel, outdoor recreation, and local institutions such as museums, botanical gardens, parks, and libraries all

5.4   SELECTED ORGANIZATIONS CONNECTED WITH THE TAKE BACK YOUR TIME MOVEMENT

The Center for a New American Dream—www.newdream.org
> The Center for a New American Dream helps Americans consume responsibly to protect the environment, enhance quality of life, and promote social justice.

Ackerman Center for Time, Work, and the Family—www.ackerman.org
> The Center for Time, Work, and the Family is dedicated to maximizing family and individual well-being along with satisfaction and productivity in work. Using high-quality research-based programs in the community and collaborating with those it serves in designing and refining the programs, the Center assists families at all socioeconomic levels with the challenges of integrating work and family life.

The Living Simply Network—www.simpleliving.net
> Our goal is to share with you the many paths of simple living. Our goal is to help you find meaning and purpose in all that you do. We are encouraging conscientious consumerism through making informed lifestyle choices.

The Hilton Family Leisure Time Advocacy (LTA)—www.myleisuretrip.com/en/mlt/lta/
> Our present-day, "hard-working" culture has created a leisure time deficit. Increased workloads, workweeks that extend into weekends, long commutes, and crunched family schedules have left little time for leisure activities, including vacations. The time-starved everywhere need a new "leisure ethic" to balance this strong "work ethic." That is why the Hilton Family of Hotels has formed the Leisure Time Advocacy™ (LTA). Through LTA, the Hilton Family hopes to encourage, persuade, and excite people to embrace more leisure activities, enjoy some hard-earned time off, and reflect on all that life has to offer.

became an expected part of the leisure experience of millions of Americans. The post—World War II era was characterized by optimism, materialism, the emergence of a mass society, concern about quality of life and a variety of environmental and social issues, and a heightened belief in science and technology (Kelly and Godbey, 1992).

An increase in discretionary income, a change in values regarding mass leisure, improved infrastructure and technology, and an explosion of the amount of mass media to which people are exposed on a daily basis—these factors have all shaped the proliferation of mass leisure.

Increase in Discretionary Income

The period following World War II was an era of affluence in the United States. The United States was in an enviable position compared with many other countries. A period of rising income during the fifties and sixties produced a large middle class, unprecedented in the history of the world. As incomes expanded so did the opportunity for leisure, along with a great array of leisure choices. This relationship between income and leisure opportunity still exists today. To participate in most mass leisure activities requires some discretionary income that can be used for admissions, equipment, and travel.

Change in Values

To participate in mass leisure, individuals must value the experiences that exist within its realm. Traditionally, culture has been divided into popular, or mass culture, and high culture. For many years, the activities categorized as mass culture were considered inferior to the activities that constitute high culture. According to Kando (1980), this elitist position was based on the assumption that a necessary inverse relationship exists between the quantity and the quality of leisure. The question for such purists becomes as follows:

> Is it possible to extend a higher civilization to the lower classes without debasing its standard and diluting its quality to the vanishing point? Is not every civilization bound to decay as soon as it begins to penetrate the masses . . . [the author answers] . . . the mass of men [*sic*] dislikes and always has disliked learning and art. It wishes to be distracted from life rather than to have it revealed; to be comforted by traditional truths, rather than to be upset by new ones. (Van den Haag, 1964, p. 55)

More writers have responded in recent years to this argument by highlighting the growth in the arts as well as the demonstrated ability of all people to enjoy all types of recreation. An increasingly educated populace has produced a greater number of people who enjoy cultural events and other traditional forms of high culture. At the same time, the popularity and participation in mass leisure activities continues to rise. This increase in participation accompanies increased acceptance, for the most part, of the leisure activities that are a part of mass culture.

The increased popularity of mass leisure also results from an important realization: popular culture reflects the society and the freedoms individuals enjoy—it is a rich expression of democracy (Brown, 1978). Thus, while popular culture has become legitimized and more accepted in this century, it carries with it great responsibility. "The study of popular culture [mass leisure], like that of other areas of human behavior, goes hand in hand with a search for solutions to human problems and a concern for the quality of human life" (Kando, 1980, p. 60).

Improved Infrastructure Related to Physical and Natural Resources

Federal, state, and local governments have encouraged mass leisure by helping to establish accessible environments for leisure activities. An improved highway system has greatly enabled access to mass leisure activities in the past three decades, as have improved technology and other factors. Continued efforts will ensure availability of leisure activities.

In addition, more natural areas are being opened to a wide variety of leisure pursuits. For example, the U.S. Forest Service (USFS) has committed itself to dedicating more of its budget to providing outdoor recreation experiences. The USFS now has more than 35,000 employees and a budget of more than 3 billion dollars. It provides a vast landscape for camping, fishing, hunting, boating, hiking, backpacking, and so on, especially in the western half of the United States. As the organization moves away from emphasizing timber production to maximizing the outdoor recreation opportunities within its borders it will continue to open up large natural areas for the enjoyment of a wide range of Americans (Robinson and Godbey, 1997).

Improved Technology

Technology impacts all aspects of leisure behavior. For example, consider how transportation has affected mobility and travel, mass media has influenced communication and information, credit cards have revolutionized shopping, and contraceptives have radically altered sexual behavior. In the coming decades the speed of innovation and new technologies will accelerate change. For example, the ongoing electronics revolution promises to continue to change our patterns of everyday life as the home becomes a multimedia center.

The continued infusion of new technology will greatly influence the nature of mass leisure activities of the future. Such technology will help meet the needs of people to seek novelty and new experiences in their lives and will assist many people in their quest for new adventures.

Leisure For Pets: An Untapped Market

Dogs have long been thought of as human's best friend. Public parks and recreation departments across the country are recognizing this bond and the need for creating areas where dogs and their owners can interact in a less-structured environment (e.g., no leashes). However, in recent years parks and recreation have gone beyond providing simple areas for dog parks. The new parks have new amenities and programs, like ponds for dogs to swim in, vibrantly painted fake fire hydrants, walking trails, doggie showers, an agility course, sandboxes, drinking stations, educational clinics, grooming sessions, dog walks, picture days, and dog festivals.

Based on the success of early dog parks, cities are looking at other locations to create more dog parks. Animal wellness now ranks Fort Lauderdale, with its Bark Park, as the second ranked city in dog wellness. The top ten United States animal friendly cities are:

1. Boulder, CO
2. Fort Lauderdale, FL
3. Seattle, WA
4. San Diego, CA
5. Portland, OR
6. Denver, CO
7. Sacramento, CA
8. Atlanta, GA
9. Greensboro, NC
10. Eugene, OR

A recent Gallup poll stated that 42 percent of households in the United States have dogs and that there are now over 700 dog parks nationwide, with more being constructed on a daily basis. There is no doubt that dogs and their dog owners represent a major market for recreation-based organizations.

Points to Ponder

- How do you see Americans pampering their pets? Do you think this is a form of mass leisure? Why or why not?

Source: Avrasin, M. 2004. Playgrounds for pups. *Parks and Recreation* (July), 44–48.

For example, television will continue as a major vehicle for transmitting mass leisure activities and values. New technologies will use television as a medium to expand the individual viewing choices as well as to create new entertainment possibilities. This is particularly true as cable networks and direct TV increase individual choice in watching television.

Mass Leisure: What Do People Do?

What do people do in their leisure time? Numerous studies have examined this question and have found that Americans engage in a wide variety of leisure activities. These activities include television watching, social visits, reading, arts, crafts, dancing, sports and exercise, indoor games, relaxing (doing nothing), movies, music, computer games, surfing the Internet, hunting, fishing, attending sport events and cultural activities, and traveling. To understand the various types of mass leisure (figure 5.1), this chapter examines the following broad categories of mass leisure behavior:

Social activities. These leisure experiences are carried out in a social context, often with other people.

Sports. This type of activity can be divided into two areas—active participation in any sport (either physically or mentally challenging) and spectator sports such as football, basketball, auto racing, and baseball.

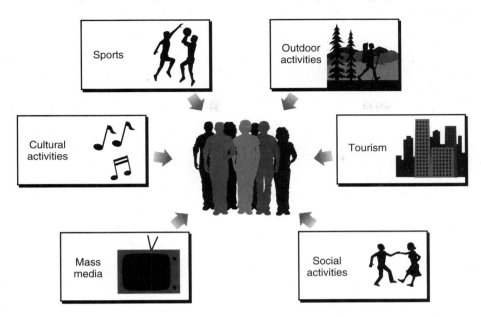

Figure 5.1

Types of mass leisure.

Cultural activities. The diverse cultural area includes such activities and events as ballet, opera, classical music, art galleries, museums, and theater.

Outdoor activities (environmental). More broadly defined as outdoor recreation, these experiences involve any enjoyable leisure time activity pursued outdoors involving knowledge, use, or appreciation of natural resources.

Tourism activities. While not synonymous with recreation, tourism often includes recreation and leisure activity. "Tourism definitions usually include these components: travel from home; personal and business motivations; the expenditure of money; and many service businesses related to travel" (Gunn, 1986, p. 2).

Mass media and other technology-related activities. This realm of leisure activities includes time spent by people in front of the television as well as attending movies, listening to radio, or utilizing electronic equipment for entertainment, learning, and other forms of leisure. (e.g., computers)

Social Activities as Mass Leisure

Leisure can and usually is viewed within a social context. That is, most leisure activities involve some form of human interaction. Beyond the specific social interaction that can and does take place during leisure, the social fabric of our society helps to define our leisure behavior. Our society's norms, customs, and rituals greatly shape the very leisure activities in which we participate as well as how these activities are perceived and valued. Within this context, this section of the book examines how social capital is being lost in America, as well as how we can build social capital through leisure; the types of social activities in which Americans participate; and how values impact our view of social leisure.

Building the Social Capital Needed for Leisure and Life   Robert Putnam (2000), in his recent review of the "state of community" in America, writes about improving a sense of community by thinking in terms of developing the physical, human, and social capital of an area. Just as a new recreation center (physical capital) or an opportunity to gain new knowledge (human capital) can increase the livability of a community, so too do social contacts affect the livability of individuals and communities. Whereas *physical capital* refers to physical objects and *human capital* is linked to the properties of individuals, *social capital* refers to connections between individuals, networks, norms, and trust that enable participants to act together more effectively to pursue shared objectives. As a result of his work Putnam declares we are losing community and that our collective civic life is weakening. This loss of a sense of community is in part due to a decline in social capital.

This decline in social capital is documented by the downward trend of Americans participating in politics, civic organizations, religious organizations, and volunteer opportunities. According to Putnam (2000, p.183), "during the first two-thirds of this century Americans took a more and more active role in the social and political life of their communities—in churches and union halls, in bowling alleys and clubrooms, around committee tables and card tables and dinner tables. Year by year we gave more generously to charity, we pitched in more often in community projects, and we behaved in an increasingly trustworthy way toward one another. Then, mysteriously and more or less simultaneously, we began to do all those things less often."

Putnam (2000) attributes our loss of social capital to a variety of factors such as changing work patterns, urban sprawl, generational change, television, and other changes in technology. Regardless of the cause, the issue of social capital is an important issue for leisure service professionals, because one of the benefits of our programs and services is building social capital within communities. Leisure not only builds social capital but, as we have seen in Chapter 1, also contributes to one's sense of community satisfaction.

The connection between leisure and social capital can be seen from the early beginnings of the idea of social capital. The first official use of the term *social capital* was by L. Judson Hanifan in 1916. Hanifan noted the need for and importance of renewed community involvement to sustain democracy and development. He was reporting on the demise of neighborliness and civic engagement, which was a result of the decline of such events as debating societies, barn raisings, and apple cuttings. As these customs became wholly abandoned, people became less neighborly and the community's social life gave way to family isolation and community stagnation. Once he had identified the problem, Hanifan went on to outline how social capital could be fostered (note the importance he places on recreation):

> When the people of a given community have become acquainted with one another and have formed a habit of coming together occasionally for entertainment, social discourse, and personal enjoyment, then by skillful leadership this social capital will be directed toward the general improvement of community well-being. (Hanifan, 1916, as cited by Putnam & Goss, 2002, p. 4)

Since 1916, the term *social capital* has been used in a variety of ways. Jane Jacobs used the term in her book *Death and Life of Great American Cities* to emphasize the collective value of informal neighborhood ties in modern cities. Coleman (1990) distinguished social capital from natural, physical, human, or economic capital. From this distinction, in the last ten years, researchers have identified the following benefits and drawbacks from social capital (DeGraaf and Jordan, 2003).

Benefits of Social Capital

- Social connectedness is a stronger predictor of perceived quality of life in a community than community income or educational level.
- Personal happiness is more closely tied to the level of community social connectedness and trust than to income or educational levels.
- Bridging social capital is important in producing community solidarity.
- Higher social capital and social cohesion leads to improvements in health conditions.
- The lower the trust among citizens, the higher the mortality rate in a community.
- Communities with higher levels of social capital are likely to have higher educational achievement, better performing governmental institutions, faster economic growth, and less crime and violence.
- Joining one group cuts your odds of dying over the next year in half. Joining two groups cuts it in quarter.
- Each ten minutes of additional commuting time cuts all forms of social capital by 10 percent—there is 10 percent less church-going, 10 percent fewer club meetings, 10 percent fewer evenings with friends, etc.
- Television is the only leisure activity where doing more of it is associated with less social capital.

Drawbacks of Social Capital

Research also has reported that, taken to an extreme, social capital may be detrimental to a community's health:

- Like all types of capital, research reports unequal access to social capital among the differing social strata.
- Those with less financial and human capital also have less social capital.
- High levels of within-group trust may generate distrust of out-group members.
- Social capital develops social ties, which enable community members to work together and can exclude outsiders. Exclusionary cliques can form, which may be detrimental to the overall health of a community.
- Community pressure to conform to group norms can result in the development of unhealthy traditions; taken to an extreme, social capital can rally people around unhealthy causes—particularly if the group is strong in bonding social capital and short in bridging social capital.
- There is a risk of decreased autonomy—individuals may not be able to break out of a group to which they have belonged (i.e., gang members who try to break away).
- There is a need to understand what kind of support individuals and families will need in the future. We can not be bound by the past, and we must be willing to consider that "the life we think about as uniquely American—close families and friends, tight neighborhoods, civic clubs, vibrant electoral politics, strong faith based institutions and a reliance on civic leadership—is giving way to something new" (Florida, 2002, p. 269).

Today, scholars in many fields are studying the many dimensions of social capital, and there is still debate on whether social capital is really declining or just changing into new ways for people to connect. As this debate plays out, there is consensus that social capital is an important concept that requires continued study, especially in relationship to leisure. Leisure managers with great experience will attest that common benefits of a good leisure program could include such items as social capital, community identity, and a sense of cohesiveness. As a result, as we move into the twenty-first century, leisure service managers must continue to look for ways to promote concepts like social capital in their programs.

Social Activities   It is difficult to isolate specific social leisure, as almost all forms of leisure and recreation have a social dimension, which strongly affects the quality of the overall experience. For example, what we decide to do on a given night may be a function of schedules, finances, or location. First and foremost, however, is usually who we want to be with for the evening. Kelly and Godbey (1992) note the importance of leisure in the building of friendships and relationships: "In a social world in which workers seldom live in ethnic neighborhoods around the workplace with a thick network of interrelationships, many friendships are developed around leisure. Friends entertain and go out to eat together. They share cabins on vacations. Men fish together, teens water-ski together. Grandmothers share pictures together. Neighbors exchange tools and talk. What is surprising is that increasingly friendships are inaugurated and developed in leisure" (p. 215).

In researching the social psychology of leisure, Samdahl (1992) suggests that most leisure experiences occur in casual, social settings. In other words, as people walk side by side, sit informally, "hang out" with friends who they trust and feel comfortable with, or interact quietly with their environment, opportunities for leisure emerge. It may be that although leisure is pervasive throughout our society, leisure experiences may well in fact find us, rather than the reverse. This implies that leisure, for most of us, "just occurs" and is not often characterized by special activities or events.

Leisure occurs in the minute-to-minute interactions of our daily living. An implication of this finding suggests that although leisure service programmers give great attention to planning, organizing, and implementing formal leisure activities, this type of leisure is relatively rare. Therefore, the challenge in programming is "to focus not only on the creation of the rare and exotic, but also facilitating and influencing the casual and 'just occurring' life events that have potential for leisure. This can be done by recognizing that the conditions of the leisure experience—perceived freedom, intrinsic motivation, and perceived competence—can be facilitated by programmers in a variety of life spaces" (Edginton, Hudson, Dieser, and Edginton, 2003).

Social leisure activities have been identified as important categories of leisure interests by a number of authors in the literature (Ragheb and Beard, 1992). Yet it is hard to identify specific social activities beyond visiting with friends or talking on the telephone. The reason for this is clear: Social interaction is a component of almost all types of leisure, but it generally is associated with another activity such as playing cards, going to church, belonging to a fraternal organization, attending a sport or cultural event, going out for dinner, and so on.

Social Leisure: Value Laden or Value Free?

Viewing mass leisure in a social context allows the examination of widespread activities that are not embraced as part of socially or legally acceptable behaviors. Within these types of activities, sometimes referred to as purple recreation, values have been made about what is socially acceptable or not acceptable. Despite socially looking down on these activities (especially if they are done in excess), such behaviors pervade society and compose a significant use of leisure in a social context by subcultures within society. A number of these behaviors are related to some kind of negative addiction on the part of the participant and can include drug use, abuse of alcohol, gambling, and sexual deviance.

Teaching Kindness: A Lesson For Parents

Youth Sports have exploded over the last ten years and with that explosion has come a variety of new problems. Many of these problems are associated with parental behavior. We have all read the headlines of fighting, violence, and bad sportsmanship by parents. In an effort to be proactive in dealing with these types of problems, the city of Grand Rapids, Michigan has initiated a mandatory. Kindness Clinic for parents. At least one parent is required to attend a meeting if their child signs up to play for one of the teams in the city's youth soccer program.

The meetings stress good sportsmanship and parental conduct at games. The centerpiece of the clinic is a fifteen-minute video created by the National Alliance for Youth Sports. The clinic is meant to help parents with expectations. It de-emphasizes the ideas of always having to win as well as shares the philosophy of the city's youth sports program, which is to be fun and educational, focusing on skill development. Parents are encouraged to foster these goals rather than worrying so much about scores and yelling at coaches. The program has had a favorable response from parents, and other youth sport programs throughout the area are considering replicating the program.

Points to Ponder

- To what extent should public recreation organizations impose mandatory requirements on participants?
- How can youth serving organizations involve parents of participants as partners in the experience?

Source: Harger, J. 2002. Kindness clinic: Soccer Parents in Grand Rapids required to attend sportsmanship course. *The Grand Rapids Press* (August, 21), A21.

Use of alcohol has long been a part of human history. It costs little to produce and has almost always been available to the masses. Within many traditional cultures its consumption served many purposes. Wine was used as a substitute for impure water while both beer and ale in medieval Europe served as a readily available source of nutrition. "In modern societies, however, the purposes of wine, beer and spirits have less to do with sanitation or nutrition than with socialization or intoxication" (Kelly and Godbey, 1992, p. 470).

Antisocial use of alcohol often centers around the binge drinker and those who drink with the sole intention of getting drunk. With such binge drinkers or drug users there is a process of socialization that takes place in a subculture that values such activities. Kelly and Godbey (1992) have noted that such socialization "teaches the novice to experience the activity as pleasurable. The use of alcohol, tobacco, LSD, and a variety of other drugs is not inherently pleasurable to the beginner, who without the positive reinforcement of the social group as well as instruction, would often find the experience negative" (p. 472).

The growth of gambling is also a concern for many people. Twenty years ago gambling was a contained activity in such places as Las Vegas, Nevada, or more recently Atlantic City, but in the last ten years, opportunities to gamble have grown tremendously. According to Molitor (2000), gambling is one of the fastest-growing segments of the entertainment industry. Legal revenues from gambling totaled more than $394 billion in 1993 and $650 billion in 1999, and they are projected to reach as high as $1.5 trillion in 2005. According to Platz and Millar (2001), more money was spent on gambling than on tickets to sports events, movies, theme parks, video games, and recorded music combined. Today casinos are appearing on riverboats, Indian reservations, cruise ships, and even the Internet. Gambling in some form is allowed in forty-seven states, with Utah, Tennessee, and Hawaii being the only states where all types of gambling are illegal. Surveys reveal that 63 percent of all Americans engaged in some sort of gambling in 1998 (Molitor, 2000). As with alcohol use, the antisocial use of gambling often centers around the compulsive gambler, and as opportunities expand, so does the risk of financial devastation for the compulsive gambler.

Another dimension within the social context is sexual behavior. People's sexual behavior has changed greatly in the last several decades, and men and women stand on more equal ground when it comes to the consequences of being sexually active. Yet some sexual behavior is viewed as antisocial even though it prevails in pockets of the population. As Kelly (1996) observes, "despite ideologies of mutual decision, enjoyment and self determination, sexual intercourse is still defined as conquest by some. It becomes something less than leisure when the aims are winning a score, and the social prestige of success. Sexual activity is hardly relational leisure when one person becomes a trophy" (p. 391). This behavior was exposed in a group of high school athletes in California that nicknamed itself "the posse," which developed an elaborate scoring system for rating their various "conquests" with girls and women. Even after the group was exposed, many of the members of this group did not express remorse but in fact described their group with great pride.

When antisocial behavior emerges in leisure pursuits, it brings out many fundamental questions. These questions revolve around the values and morals we think should be espoused in leisure activities. Is there a universal set of values related to leisure? Should society try to identify those leisure activities it finds offensive and channel that energy into other "more acceptable" forms of leisure? Who should be making these decisions? By what process should these decisions be made? What should be the role of the leisure programmer in this process? Does the leisure programmer have a responsibility to serve the popular tastes for recreation or should leisure service programmers have allegiance to other personal or professional values?

Sport as Mass Leisure

Sports can mean different things to different people. Therefore, it is important to place some parameters on what is meant by sport and sports activities. Kelly (1996, p. 214) defines sport as an "... organized activity in which physical effort is related to that of others in some relative measurement of outcomes with accepted regularities and forms."

He further notes that

> ... sport has a major place in modern society as an element of the economy, a spectacle with symbolic meanings, an arena of the development for the young and in the leisure lives of many individuals. Within these parameters sports can be active or passive, individual or team-oriented, as well as done for a variety of motives from fun to fitness. Thus, for some individuals sport is leisure (both passive and active); for others it is work, education or development. (p. 241)

This section of the chapter examines several selected spectator sports as well as favorite active sporting events of Americans.

The desire to be spectators, to watch others involved in sporting contests, is evident all through human history. From the gladiators of the Roman Empire to the jousting of the Middle Ages to the popularity of boxing in the early part of the eighteenth century, people have enjoyed being spectators. The foundation of today's teams sports, however, can be traced to baseball, the American pastime. In 1876, the National League of Professional Baseball Clubs was formed. The American League was founded in 1899, the first World Series was held in 1903—and an American tradition was born.

During the twentieth century, spectator sports have grown into a national obsession, with a tremendous growth of spectator sports at all levels of competition (professional and amateurs—

5.5	ATTENDANCE FIGURES FOR SELECTED SPECTATOR SPORTS (1985–2000) (IN THOUSANDS)	

Sport	1985	2000
Baseball (professional)	47,742	74,316
Basketball		
Men's (college)	26,584	29,025
Women's (college)	2,072	8,698
Men's (professional)	11,534	21,503
Football		
College	34,952	39,059
Professional	14,058	20,954
Greyhound racing	23,858	14,306
Hockey	11,621	18,831

Source: U.S. Census Bureau, 2002.

college, high school, and even youth leagues), see table 5.5. For example, the big three professional sports—football, baseball, and basketball—all have increased their yearly attendance by at least 4 percent a year since 1970—football 6.1 percent, basketball 6.35 percent, and baseball 4.2 percent (Rockerbie, 2004). Another spectator sport that has experienced a great deal of growth recently is auto racing. While automobile racing in Europe tends to remain an elite affair (formula one racing), the United States Auto Club and National Association for Stock Car Racing events have become true forms of mass leisure. On any given weekend in the summer, hundreds of thousands of fans jam racetracks around the country. Large tracks such as those found in Indianapolis or Daytona can attract 400,000 fans in a weekend, while small town tracks attract fewer numbers but can be found throughout the states. Beyond these major sports, several other spectator sports have flourished, at least for a time, in this century and include horse racing, bowling, golfing, hockey, tennis, greyhound racing, track and field events, bicycling, and boxing.

The enormous growth in spectator sports has led to a concern about "spectatoritis." The twentieth century has also seen tremendous growth in sport *participation,* however. Over the last several decades, with the support of finances from the Land and Water Conservation Fund and other resources, a dramatic increase in the supply of leisure resources has occurred. This is reflected in the acquisition and development of parks, swimming pools, golf courses, ski slopes, stadiums, tennis and racquetball courts, and ice rinks. The continued emphasis on fitness and wellness in American society should continue to encourage active participation in sports.

Table 5.6 presents the total number of participants for a number of selected sports activities. Walking, swimming, bicycling, freshwater fishing, and bowling rank among the top activities in which Americans participate. The expenditures by sport listed in table 5.7 reflect the economic impact of involvement in sports.

Cultural Activities as Mass Leisure

Cultural activities, often seen as cultivation of the mind and spirit, historically have been referred to as *high culture.* In the past, the activities designated as high culture have rested in the domain of the wealthy and well-to-do and therefore consisted of activities in which only a few participated. A distinction traditionally made between mass culture and high culture defined high culture

TABLE

5.6 PARTICIPATION FIGURES FOR TOP TEN SPORT ACTIVITIES IN 2000

Sport	1993 (in millions)	2000 (in millions)
Exercise walking	64.4	86.2
Swimming	61.4	60.8
Exercising with equipment	34.9	44.8
Camping	42.7	50.0
Bicycle riding	47.9	43.1
Bowling	41.7	43.1
Fishing—freshwater	45.3	44.4
Billiards	N/A	32.5
Basketball	29.6	27.1
Hiking	N/A	24.3

N/A Not Available

Data from Data National Sporting Goods Association. 2000. *Statistical Abstacts of the United States.*

TABLE

5.7 SPORTING GOOD SALES BY PRODUCT CATEGORY 1980–2001

Sport	1980 (in millions)	2001 (in millions)
Athletic and sport clothing	10,130	11,570
Athletic and sport footwear	11,654	13,593
Athletic and sport equipment	11,964	21,931
Recreaton sport transport	14,502	27,309

Data from Data National Sporting Goods Association. 2000. *Statistical Abstacts of the United States.*

as ". . . recreational and cultural activities that are somehow more serious and more profound than mass and popular culture" (Kando, 1980, p.143). This attitude is slowly changing, however, as the arts and other types of cultural experiences just mentioned have begun to appeal more to the masses. According to Naisbett and Aburdene (1990) in their book *Megatrends 2000,* the arts will gradually replace sports as society's primary leisure activity. "The 1990s will bring forth a modern renaissance in the visual arts, poetry, dance, theater, and music throughout the developed world. . . . The affluent information society has laid the economic groundwork for the renaissance, creating new patrons . . . [who are] educated, professional, and increasingly female. . . . Today's consumer is sophisticated enough to appreciate the arts and can pay the price of admission" (Naisbett and Aburdene, 1990, p. 63). This growth in the arts is reflected in table 5.8.

The Environment and Mass Leisure

Most people have a broad definition of outdoor recreation—it entails any activity that takes place outdoors (e.g., playing football and tennis, attending outdoor sports events, and visiting amusement parks). A more specific definition, however, is needed to differentiate out-

TABLE

5.8	AMERICA'S INCREASING INVOLVEMENT WITH THE ARTS	
Performance Type	**Attendance 1985 (in millions)**	**Attendance 2000 (in millions)**
Broadway shows	7.3	11.4
Broadway road tours	8.2	11.7
Nonprofit professional theater	14.2	22.0
Opera	3.3	6.7
Symphony orchestra	24.0	31.7

Data from U.S. Bureau of the Census. 2002. *Statistical Abstracts of the United States.*

door recreation from such sports as football and tennis. In an attempt to create such a definition, Carlson (1960) notes that outdoor recreation is any enjoyable leisure time activity pursued outdoors or indoors involving knowledge, use, or appreciation of natural resources. This definition best fits the fastest-growing area of outdoor recreation and outdoor adventure pursuits.

Outdoor adventure pursuits have been defined as "a variety of self-initiated activities utilizing an interaction with the natural environment, that contains elements of real or apparent danger, in which the outcome, while uncertain, can be influenced by the participant and circumstance" (Ewert, 1989, p. 6). Specific outdoor adventure pursuits include such activities as backpacking, white water rafting, mountain biking, and rock climbing.

In the last twenty years, outdoor recreation (especially adventure pursuits) participation in the United States has increased. For example, in 1990, the National Park Service reported 258.7 million visitors; in 2000, the National Park Service reported 285.9 million. Nash (2004) reports on four major revolutions that have contributed to the increased levels of participation in outdoor recreation.

First, a revolution in equipment that is lighter, stronger, and smaller than ever before allows people more access to remote areas. Furthermore, the invention of new equipment has created new sports such as windsurfing, snowboarding, and mountain biking.

The second major revolution has taken place in transportation. Pristine outdoor areas are reached more easily than ever before. People can fly from New York to Portland in a matter of hours, then drive another two hours and be on a glacier on Mount Hood where they can enjoy year-round snow skiing. As Nash (1982) points out, the bush plane is Alaska's covered wagon, and the helicopter has replaced horses as the preferred means of transportation.

The third major revolution revolves around the ease of accessing information about new areas. Pristine areas receive positive publicity and become world famous. It took John Muir a lifetime to learn about the Sierra Nevadas; this information can be gleaned in a matter of hours by reading guide books or viewing CD-ROM disks about northern California.

The fourth and final revolution involves an intellectual change in how people view the wilderness. As Nash (1982) notes, today's appreciation of wilderness and the outdoors represents one of the most remarkable intellectual revolutions in human history. Historically, humans have viewed wilderness and the outdoors as something to fear, something to tame in order to survive. Today, however, these areas are appreciated on a different level.

Further, interest in outdoor recreation results from a growing concern for environmental issues and the need to reconnect with our biological roots. Americans have a long tradition of involvement with the outdoors, celebrating it in literature, music, and art. Highly valued, the outdoors is central to the quality of life in all communities across the United States.

> [Yet] . . . if there is a single word that describes Americans outdoors, it is diversity. We go outdoors for many reasons; to keep physically fit, for excitement, to have fun with family and friends; to get away from other people, to experience nature and to learn. Nearly 50 percent of Americans describe themselves as "outdoors people," and another 16 percent consider themselves a combination of indoors and out. It is a rare American who does not engage in some form of recreation outdoors. (PCAO, 1987, p.17)

The popularity of outdoor recreation is reiterated by the fact that in 1999 only two in ten Americans did not participate in some form of outdoor recreation at some point in the year (Raymond, 2000). Although there still seems to be a number of different participation rates based on demographic variables like education level and ethnicity, there does seem to be something for everyone in the great outdoors. Today seniors, equipped with their good health, an abundance of free time, and hefty retirement accounts, are seeking out more outdoor opportunities such as elderhostel or organized camping. Environmentally conscious baby boomers are flocking to exotic adventure travel destinations. Gen-Xers have spurred the development of nontraditional outdoor activities and the recreation of new recreational sites for snowboarding, in-line skating, motocross, and telemark skiing (Raymond, 2000).

This growth in outdoor recreation participation is well documented. In 1987 the President's Council on Americans Outdoors submitted its report, *American Outdoors: The Legacy, The Challenge,* which was commissioned to review private and public outdoor recreation opportunities, policies, and programs and to make recommendations to ensure the future availability of outdoor recreation for the American people. Two of the trends identified were that pursuit of physically outdoor recreation will increase, especially in the area of high-risk adventure activities, and outdoor recreation will grow more diverse.

Priest and Gass (1999) have reiterated the findings of the President's Council on Americans Outdoors, noting the growth in adventure-based programs and activities. They cite the increasing number of participants and increased revenues from outdoor recreation participation and also note that many of the fastest-growing sports, such as rock climbing, surfing, and sailing, are adventure based. In addition, Priest and Gass (1999) cite the increase in artificial adventure environments that are being built throughout the United States. These facilities include wave pools, climbing walls, ski slopes, kayak roll tanks, and white-water canoe chutes. As technology continues to advance, it will be interesting to note what other "outdoor environments" will be simulated for pleasure.

Americans' increasing participation in outdoor recreation, whether inside or outside, demonstrates the need to reconnect with the natural environment. As society becomes even more technical and advanced, this need will continue and will be met in a number of diverse outdoor activities—from fishing to white-water rafting, from hunting to outdoor photography, from sightseeing in one's car to backpacking in the wilderness.

Tourism as Mass Leisure

Whether it is a trip to a local museum or a trip around the world, most people have been or will be tourists at some point in their lifetime. In the later half of the twentieth century we saw tourism become the world's second-largest industry (behind the petroleum industry) with strong growth projected into the twenty-first century. Tourism has certainly become a major economic force in the United States, and the world. Consider the fact that, according to the World Tourism Organization, 698 million people traveled to a foreign country in 2000, spending more than $478

Hostelling: Fulfilling the Promise of Travel

People have seen the world grow smaller in the twentieth century. Advances in transportation and communication have connected everyone in a global network. These advances, combined with increased discretionary income of people in the developed world, have led to an explosion in international travel in the last twenty years. However, much of the travel is predominantly a one-way exchange as Western tourists travel to developing countries in search of "exotic experiences." When one browses through travel brochures and magazines, it becomes apparent that developing countries are increasingly the destination point for planes and cruise lines. This phenomenon has caused many critics to claim that tourism has become another form of dependence, a kind of economic colonialism, which has a lasting effect on native cultures and traditions. Yet this description seems unfair, failing to give recognition to the opportunities that travel and tourism can present to promote global understanding. One must realize travel is only a medium that can be used for good or ill. The challenge to the tourism industry and the individual traveler is to promote travel, which strives to be equally beneficial to all members of the global community, and brings about the realization that all nations share a "cultural parity" or cultural equality within diversity.

One organization working to help promote travel as education is Hostelling International-USA (HI-USA). For HI-USA, hostelling is "a way of traveling that unlocks opportunity. It offers a chance to see the world—to experience people and places different from what we've known. The end result can be greater understanding of a country or a culture, a deeper appreciation of the world's diversity, or a new perspective on our own lives" (HI-USA, 1999). HI-USA is a part of the global network of Hostelling International, which makes travel possible by providing an expansive system of hostel facilities and programs. HI-USA operates a network of hostels throughout the United States that are affordable, safe, and clean. Most important, however, is the fact that hostels are designed to foster interaction among guests. They include shared living space and common areas that give people from all over the world an opportunity to get to know one another.

HI-USA hostels are often found in unique and historic settings such as San Francisco's Fort Mason, an old lifesaving station on Nantucket Island, Pigeon Point Lighthouse in California, and Bear's Den Hostel on the Appalachian Trail. Hostels also provide a wide range of educational programs. These programs help travelers learn more about cities and towns, histories, and cultures of the surrounding areas, providing them a sense of place. HI-USA also offers a variety of programs for people in local communities. These programs range from travel seminars like "World Travel 101" and "Women Traveling Alone" to programs such as the Cultural Kitchen, which reaches out to local youth, helping them interact with travelers from around the world.

Although the mission of HI-USA focuses on young people, hostels are open to and widely used by people of all ages. In choosing hostelling as the means by which they travel, these people make a conscious choice to travel in an alternative manner and support the aims of hostelling, which HI-USA identifies as the following:

- Hostelling promotes world understanding— having a chance to see how people in other parts of the world live, and what's important to them can sometimes reshape a person's own values.
- Hostelling fosters discovery and learning.
- Hostelling supports community development.

Source: HI-AYH Annual Report, 1999.

billion U.S. dollars. International tourism receipts combined with passenger transport currently total more than $575 billion—making tourism the world's number one export earner, ahead of automotive products, chemicals, petroleum, and food (United Nations Environment Program, 2004).

In the United States, travel and tourism rank among the top three economic activities in thirty-two states as of 1999. Global travelers are expected to double to 1 billion by 2010, and expenditures are expected to top $1.6 trillion in that same year (Molitor, 2000). The United States ranked third behind France and Spain as the most visited country by international visitors. Revenues generated from international travelers in the United States are one of the true bright spots in the international trade accounts.

Since the terrorist acts on September 11, 2001, the tourism industry both in the United States and abroad has been hit hard. The immediate effect of the attacks was a sharp drop in the numbers of Americans venturing abroad. September 11th changed Americans' perception of the world, which they now see as more hostile, and led them to travel less.

On the flip side, stricter security and administrative measures for entry into the United States have decreased the number of tourists visiting the United States from abroad. Yet, the tourism industry is adapting and showing a slow rebound in the first three years since 9/11/2001, despite other setbacks such as the spread of SARS disease in the summer of 2003. There have been switches in destination and a clear shift for Americans from international travel to regional and domestic tourism.

The tragic results of 9/11/2001 also have shown the need for continued travel and learning about people from around the world. One organization, highlighted in a Leisure Line in this chapter, that is working to address the need for cultural understanding is Hostelling International-USA (HI-USA). The mission of HI-USA is "to help all, especially the young, gain a greater understanding of the world and its people through hostelling." They recently initiated a program entitled Opening Doors/Opening Minds (ODOM) as a response to the events of September 11, 2001. The bombing of the World Trade Center in New York and the continued mistrust between countries and regions of the world indicate the relevance of this mission today. The program is responsive to the deep fissures in understanding that exist among cultures and people. It is particularly responsive to young people's need to interact in a complex society filled with individuals from different ethnic, economic, and cultural backgrounds.

ODOM brings together the best of what HI-USA has to offer. Built on the foundation of the hostelling movement, this initiative combines mission-based programs and public awareness messages to reach today's young people and amplify their voices. It brings into sharp focus HI-USA's vision that hostellers can become caring world citizens who are catalysts in creating a more peaceful world. ODOM is an opportunity for today's youth to challenge their assumptions, increase their civic involvement, and expand the scope of their dreams.

Tourism as mass leisure includes the activities in which people engage during their travels. People may travel to large metropolitan areas in search of cultural activities or major sporting events. Likewise, people may travel to rural areas for opportunities to participate in eco-tourism—outdoor recreation and adventure pursuits. Or people may simply travel to visit friends or family in a distant place. Table 5.9 presents a number of specific characteristics of American travelers in 1998. From these characteristics two major travel trends seem to have emerged. The first of these trends sees the vacation patterns of American families changing. Americans want weeklong or monthlong vacations; however, pressed-for-time people take shorter and more frequent vacations rather than one longer annual vacation (Molitar, 2000). During these vacations they are often seeking recreational activities closer to home. The second trend focuses on emerging adventure tourism and eco-tourism markets.

TABLE

5.9	TRAVEL BY U.S. RESIDENTS BY SELECTED TRIP CHARACTERISTICS (1998)	

Characteristic	Percentage of the Total Trips Taken in 1998 (%)
Visiting relatives and friends	48
Major purpose was entertainment	35
Pursued outdoor recreation interests	15
Involved motor transport only (car, bus)	83
Included air transport	13
Stayed in hotels and/or motels (with an average stay of 3.6 overnights per trip)	41

Data from: Molitar, 2000.

As evidence of the growing demand of people to vacation closer to home, consider the amusement and theme park industry as well as the megaleisure complexes that are evolving. Although Disney is often regarded as the leader of the theme park industry, many smaller regional parks are springing up throughout the country. In 1998, Americans filled an estimated 900 million ride seats at some 450 amusement parks across the country (Gardyn and Fetto, 2000). Theme park revenues accounted for more than $6.1 billion in 1999 (Molitar, 2000). The rides at these parks grow bigger, faster, and more gravity-defying each year. As of May 2000, the Millennial Force roller coaster at Cedar Point amusement park in Sandusky, Ohio, is the world's tallest and fastest. This two-minute-plus ride climbs to 310 feet and plunges at a top speed of 92 mph.

In addition to amusement parks, mega-multiuse leisure complexes are being built throughout the world—places like the Mall of America in Minneapolis, which includes shopping, an indoor amusement park (Camp Snoopy), Lego Land, an aquarium, restaurants, theaters, and comedy clubs. Year-round sports complexes are also expanding. Consider Gotcha Glacier, a facility situated in Anaheim, California. The facility includes the first indoor snowboard and surf entertainment/sports attraction in America. Winter sports hosted include two snowboard half-pipes, beginner ski slopes, and an ice skating rink. Swimmers and surfers will be able to choose among six wave pools. These types of complexes attract people from throughout their region and in some cases develop a national reputation.

On the other end of the spectrum of humanmade theme parks and megafacilities, adventure tourism and eco-tourism are also continuing to expand at a rapid rate. These new industries are founded on the belief that travel is a form of education. For several decades, tourism has brought us closer to global (as well as national and regional) understanding and acceptance of various cultures. Not only does tourism stimulate economies and distribute wealth to less stable economies, it also encourages peace in this world. Tourism has been credited in part for the opening of China's borders, liberalizing Eastern Europe, and reducing international conflicts. When people from different cultures have the opportunity to meet one another and exchange ideas, inhibitions and misconceptions are destroyed (*Earth Journal*, 1993).

Although little consensus exists regarding exact definitions of adventure tourism and eco-tourism, these areas of the tourism industry encourage people of different cultures to interact and share common interests, such as concern for the environment or interest in a particular outdoor adventure pursuit. Adventure tourism (including eco-tourism) combines many of the trends of American society such as fitness, environmentalism, multiculturalism, and travel. In the last twenty years, adventure tourism has grown from a small segment of the travel industry to as much as one-fifth of the U.S. leisure travel market (Adler, Glick, King, Gorden, and Cohen, 1993, World Tourism Organization, 1998).

Mass Media and Leisure

The media has a tremendous impact on the leisure behavior of U.S. citizens. Television viewing, attendance at movies, listening to music, and other forms of mass media consume large blocks of leisure time of individuals. For example, the average American child (ages two to eighteen) spends five hours and twenty-nine minutes, seven days a week, watching TV, listening to music, or working on a computer at home, and most of this is done in isolation—in bedrooms that are fully media equipped with no parental supervision (Johnson, 1999). Not only does the mass media consume leisure time, it also greatly influences the leisure values of individuals. This section of the chapter discusses television viewing, movie attendance, and involvement with computers and other forms of mass media.

Television Viewing as Mass Leisure   Television is by far the most popular of all American pastimes: with the average American watching over four hours of television a day. Between 1965 and 1995 Americans gained an average of six hours a week in added leisure time, and we spent almost all six of those additional hours watching television. In short, Robinson and Godbey (1997) conclude, "Television is the 800-pound gorilla of leisure time" (p. 20). (See figure 5.2)

Figure 5.2

Mass leisure: The television viewer—an impact of passive mass leisure.

Top: CALVIN AND HOBBES copyright 1990 Watterson. Reprinted with permission of UNIVERSAL PRESS SYNDICATE. All rights reserved. Bottom: CALVIN AND HOBBES copyright 1992 Watterson. Reprinted with permission of UNIVERSAL PRESS SYNDICATE. All rights reserved.

Americans are not alone in their television viewing. In fact, television is growing in popularity in almost every country on the globe. In countries where many families cannot afford their own television, people congregate in the houses of friends and viewing becomes a social experience.

The TV-Turnoff Network has compiled a number of facts and figures about our television habit. These facts and figures are presented in table 5.10 and come from a wide variety of studies conducted between 1992 and 2003. These results clearly indicate the power of television in people's lives and the need to use this medium widely. Kubey and Csikszentmihalyi (1990) suggest that schools must begin to accept some responsibility for helping students be astute television viewers and helping them use their leisure wisely. As Brightbill (1960) notes, "The future will belong not only to the educated man [sic] but to the man who is educated to use . . . leisure wisely" (p. 94). Clearly television can benefit people, but to optimize this benefit it must be used wisely.

The television habits of individuals reflect their values and interests in many ways. Americans like to watch thirty-minute situation comedies that require little, if any, thinking by the viewer, and they enjoy television dramas where complex social issues are raised, addressed, and resolved in less than an hour. The comedies, often highly predictable, are entertainment in the clearest sense of the word. In many ways these shows also shape people's views and influence their leisure choices. What values do the shows you like to watch transmit about leisure?

What values does television transmit about American society? Television is often seen as the reality of life rather than as fantasy. This can create problems when viewers begin to feel that their lives do not live up to the standards they see on television. False perceptions also can be detrimental on a global scale.

Enormous audiences around the world view programs such as *Friends, Baywatch,* and *Dallas; Dallas* has aired in more than ninety countries (Kubey and Csikszentmihalyi, 1990). They note that "at a 1988 international meeting of television program buyers and sellers in Cannes, one estimate set U.S. television program sales to Europe at $2.7 billion for 1992" (p.xi). MTV, an invention of the American media, powerfully shapes culture in Hong Kong as much as it does in the United States and Canada. MTV Hong Kong, a dynamic form of entertainment, integrates American mass leisure in the form of MTV videos with rock videos produced in Hong Kong, China, Japan, and other Asian venues.

As we look to the future of television, we are on the brink of breakthroughs in creating more of an interactive television experience. We have been slowly moving to interactive television from the VCR to the remote control, DVDs, pay per view, digital television, and TiVo (a digital video recorder which allows viewers to record hundreds of hours of TV and watch programs at their convenience, often bypassing commercials). Television is also looking to include viewers in their programs through on-line polls and voting, catering to viewers' desires to participate, empathize, and enter the game (Deery, 2003). This trend will continue to engage viewers making television less of a finished product and more of a continued process in which the viewers, cast and producers are creating their own production (Deery, 2003).

Advertisers are already taking note of this trend and beginning to question the effectiveness of television advertising, favoring instead on-line advertising, which allows them to target the message to specific markets as well as target people during daytime working hours. Research is showing that as younger workers (who are more tech savvy) enter the workforce they are much more likely to surf the web for personal reasons while at work. At home, this same group is harder to reach on prime-time television.

The 18 to 34 year old group watches nearly an hour less of prime time television than the household average . . . there are no signs that point to a reversal in this trend. Prime time, the 8 pm to 11 pm hours that millions of people have faithfully devoted their evening to viewing sitcoms, adventures,

5.10 FACTS AND FIGURES ABOUT OUR TELEVISION HABIT

TV Undermines Family Life

- Time per day that TV is on in an average U.S. home: 7 hours, 40 minutes
- Amount of television that the average American watches per day: over 4 hours
- Time spent daily with screen media for U.S. children age 6 and under: about 2 hours
- Percentage of U.S. families with children age 0–6 with at least one television: 99
- Percentage of U.S. households with 3 or more TVs (2003): 50
- Percentage of parents who say that if they have something important to do, it is likely that they will use the TV to occupy their child: 45
- Percentage of Americans who always or often watch television while eating dinner: 40
- Percentage of Americans who say they watch too much TV: 49
- Time per week that parents spend in meaningful conversation with their children: 38.5 minutes
- Percentage of 4–6 year olds who, when asked, would rather watch TV than spend time with their fathers: 54

TV Harms Children and Hampers Education

- Average daily time American children under age 2 will spend in front of a screen: 2 hours, 5 minutes
- Average time per week that the American child, ages 2–17, spends watching television: 19 hours, 40 minutes
- Hours of TV watching per week shown to negatively affect academic achievement: 10 or more
- Percentage of children, ages 8–16, who have a TV in their bedroom: 56
- Percentage of television time that children ages 2–7 spend watching alone and unsupervised: 81
- Percent of total television time that children older than 7 spend without their parents: 95
- Percentage of parents who would like to limit their children's TV watching: 73
- Percentage of day care centers that use TV during a typical day: 70
- Hours per year the average American youth spends in school: 900
- Hours per year the average American youth watches television: 1,023
- Percentage of self-professed educational TV that has little or no educational value: 21
- Chance that an American parent requires children to do their homework before watching TV: 1 in 12
- Amount of time children age 6 and under spend daily, on average, reading or being read to: 41 minutes

TV Promotes Obesity

- Adults in United States technically obese: 1 in 3, or 62 million
- Percentage of American children who were seriously overweight in 1964: 5; 2003: more than 15
- Amount of daily moderate physical activity recommended for children: 60 minutes
- Percentage of young people who report having had no recent physical activity: 14
- Percentage chance that an overweight adolescent will become an overweight or obese adult: 70%
- Economic cost of obesity in the United States in 2000: $117 billion

TV Promotes Violence

- Number of violent acts the average American child sees on TV by age 18: 200,000
- Number of murders witnessed by children on television by age 18: 16,000
- Percentage of youth violence directly attributable to TV viewing: 10
- Percentage of Hollywood executives who believe there is a link between TV violence and real violence: 80
- Percentage of children polled who said they felt "upset" or "scared" by violence on television: 91
- Percent increase in network news coverage of homicide between 1993 and 1996: 721
- Percent reduction in the American homicide rate between 1993 and 1996: 20
- Percentage of programs that show the long-term consequences of violence: 16
- Percentage of violent programs that emphasize an anti-violence theme: 4

Source: RealVision, an initiative to raise awareness about television's impact on us, is a project of TV-Turnoff Network, www.tvturnoff.org.

news shows and reality programs for the past four decades, is rapidly eroding economic concept as new lifestyles and attitudes seems to be colliding head on with the old life stages and habits. As more tech savvy consumers enter the 18 to 34 year old age group, we expect even more of a drop in their prime time consumption as they continue to instant message friends, surf the internet, and game away hours, night, and day. (Brier, 2004, p. 15)

The future of television is certainly going to change as new technology becomes available. It remains to be seen how these changes will impact people's leisure behaviors and how these changes will be reflected in the information presented in table 5.10. What does appear to be the case is that the impact of television continues to be impacted by other forms of mass media, namely computers and the World Wide Web.

Computer Usage as Mass Leisure

The U.S. Census Bureau reports that 51 percent of U.S. homes were equipped with a computer in 2000, a fivefold increase since 1984, 80 percent of these households have Internet access, up from 50 percent on-line users in 1997. Families are using the Internet to get information, shop, play, chat on-line, play games, and so on. Retailers are recognizing the potential of the Internet as indicated by the 19 percent annual increase in Internet sales over the last five years, rising to 229 billion in 2008 from 95.7 million in 2003. On-line retail sales will account for 10 percent of total U.S. retail sales by 2008 (Rush, 2003).

Francese (2004) reports declines over the past five years in the time consumers spent with broadcast television, radio, newspapers, and consumer magazines. But in the same period, there has been a double-digit annual increase in the time spent with video games, home video, and of course, the Internet. In addition, Francese (2004) notes almost a 500 percent increase in Internet usage from 1997 to 2002 (see table 5.11). The Internet is changing how people access and use information. Of the total U.S. population, about one in three adults used e-mail from home and nearly one in four used the internet to search for information about topics such as business, health, or government services. Nearly one in five used the Internet to check on news, sports, or weather, and one in eight adults performed job-related tasks using a home Internet connection (U.S. Census Bureau, 2003).

These trends will continue as young children continue to become computer literate, as schools have leveled the playing field by giving computer access to children who do not have one at home. Now, nine in ten school-age children have computer and Internet access.

As computers and Internet usage continue to explode, it will be interesting to see how their use will impact people's leisure lifestyles. Will computers replace televisions as the "800-pound gorilla of leisure time," or will the computer continue to expand leisure choices and opportunities?

TABLE

5.11   AVERAGE WEB USAGE, UNITED STATES, JUNE, 2003

	Home	Work
Number of sessions/visits per month	30	63
Number of domains visited per month	53	95
Time spent per month	25.5 hrs	74.5 hrs
Time spent during Web visit	32.5 mins.	33.5 mins.

Movies and Mass Leisure   Big-screen cinema has a rich history in the United States. From the silent films at the beginning of the twentieth century to today's megahits, people hunger for the escape that only movies can provide. In the 1920s approximately seven to ten million people saw a movie every day. Dulles (1965) notes that by 1929 "weekly attendance jumped to an estimated 110 million—the equivalent of four-fifths of the entire population [of the United States] going to a show once a week throughout the entire year" (p. 299). The success of big-screen movies continued to rise until the early 1950s when television began to be mass produced.

With the creation of videos and the VCR, many people predicted the total demise of movie theaters. This, however, has not proven to be the case. Movie attendance steadily increased from 1975 to 1997. The Motion Picture Association of America reports that the number of theaters is increasing, with more than 32,000 movie theaters, 31,000 of which are walk-in; 1,000 are drive-ins. These figures represent an increase of over 100 percent since 1975. In 1997, Americans spent more than $6.3 billion at the box office, an increase of about 33 percent since 1990 (American Motion Picture Association, 1999).

Although Hollywood may never reach the peak it reached in the 1920s and 1930s, it is still a powerful force in people's lives and in the marketplace—its economic impact can be felt far from the box office itself. Through clever advance marketing, the 1996 hit *Independence Day* grossed $11 million in its first twenty-four hours of showing. Another 1996 hit *Pocahontas* displays an example of the economic power of a megamovie. Sales from toys, t-shirts, and other related merchandise reached well into the upper millions. Partnerships with fast-food restaurants and other commercial ventures to use picture-related packaging and products both promote the movie and increase related sales and profits. Having weathered the onslaught of television and the home video market, Hollywood continues to prosper and will be a major shaper of many of the fads and trends of the United States and Canada in the decades to come.

Other Forms of Media and Mass Leisure   Mass media includes several other mediums beyond those of television and movies. These additional mediums can be broken into two categories. The first, printed media, includes newspapers, magazines, comics, and books. The second category includes electronic forms of leisure such as radios, Nintendo, and other computer games.

The proliferation of mass media related to television, computers, movies, and radio sometimes makes it easy to overlook the impact of printed material. Yet people are reading and writing as never before. In 1999, Americans spent more than 30.8 million on books (Book Industry Supply Group, 1999). Beyond books, other forms of printed media (e.g., magazines and newspapers) are facing an uncertain future. The rising popularity of new forms of media and entertainment (e.g., Internet) is directly cutting into the demand for traditional printed media. Newspapers and magazines are struggling for ways to maintain their relevance today. They are reaching out in many ways, including how to integrate their services with Internet sites.

Technology has created a number of other forms of mass leisure and changed how we participate in certain activities, such as listening to music. From eight-tracks and records to cassettes, compact disks, and videos, the music industry is rapidly changing. Today, compact disk sales comprise the fastest-growing segment of the music industry, yet over the last three years, CD sales have declined rapidly. Many point to the faltering economy as well as file sharing on the Internet for the decline. Yet, in 2003, the music industry announced that the decline has slowed, falling 2.7 percent from the previous year. This still translates to revenues greater than 11.0 billion in 2003, compared with 11.6 billion in 2002 (*The Financial Times*, 2004).

With the combination of computers and television, Nintendo and other video games have evolved. Computer games such as "Where in the World Is Carmen Sandiego?" are also growing in popularity. Many computer games combine education with recreation as participants gain computer skills along with new knowledge and insights.

Future technological breakthroughs will continue to impact mass leisure. Initially, only a few can afford new technology, but as prices inevitably drop, participation and involvement increase. One of the newest and perhaps most far-reaching computer technologies, soon to be available en masse, is that of virtual reality. Virtual reality (VR) enables participants to experience "a through-the-looking-glass adventure in which they move freely in a three-dimensional space created by software" (Naisbitt, 1992, p. 7) by wearing fiber optic goggles and gloves, and sometimes earphones.

Application of this technology in entertainment includes an arcade where players can compete in video warfare, a Disneyland attraction entitled "Body Tours," a Universal Studio attraction entitled "Back to the Future," and virtual reality theaters in which the audience takes part in the video action. According to Naisbitt (1992), as computers become increasingly powerful, the development and use of virtual reality will accelerate. "VR probably will only begin to reach its full potential in the next 20 years, but within 30 years home VR systems could be as prevalent as television sets today" (p. 7).

Summary

In this chapter we have explored the concept of mass leisure and the activities in which the masses participate. As a shaper and a reflection of culture, leisure cannot be understood apart from the society in which it takes place. Although leisure is a personal matter, society encourages or discourages leisure behavior through its formal laws and regulations as well as through its unwritten values and traditions. As a result of this influence, various patterns of leisure behavior have developed and evolved. These patterns may be referred to as *mass leisure.* It is similar to popular or mass culture, which is defined as the most visible level of culture—the one found between the extremes of elite and folk culture. Within such popular culture, mass leisure is one facet of culture that reflects the everyday recreational activities of the majority of the population.

A number of factors have contributed to the proliferation of mass leisure in this century. First and foremost is the concept of time and mass leisure. Many people living in industrial societies today report a shortage of time, or "time famine," in their lives. People's views of time in the future will be critical to understanding leisure. Other factors influencing mass leisure that were identified in this chapter include an increase in discretionary income, the changing values of society toward mass leisure, improved infrastructure and technology, and the proliferation of the mass media.

The mass leisure activities explored in this chapter are diverse. These activities have been classified into several types of mass leisure that include *social activities*—done in a social context with other people; *sport activities,* including both active participation and spectator sports; *cultural activities*—participating in the arts; *outdoor activities*—interacting with the outdoor environment (includes outdoor adventure pursuits); *tourism activities,* including all activities people do during their travels; and *mass media,* including television, movies, music, printed media, and so forth.

Many of these activities are overlapping. For example, a sporting event is also a social event. This overlap highlights the interconnectedness of leisure activities—one category of activities can have a direct impact on many other types of leisure behavior. This interconnectedness is reflective of the growing dependency upon connections among all aspects of our daily lives. The challenge to leisure service professionals is one of promoting cooperation and collaboration between and among service providers to more effectively meet the needs of the individual.

Discussion Questions

1. Define mass leisure. In what types of mass leisure do you participate?
2. What is the difference between mass culture and high culture? In your opinion, is one better than another? Explain your answer.

3. What four revolutions have contributed to the growth of outdoor recreation activities?
4. What is a leisure democracy? What implications does this concept have for studying mass leisure?
5. What is time famine? Is this phenomenon evident in your life? Do you think society is running out of time? What implications might time famine have for delivering leisure services in the future?
6. What future technological breakthroughs are you anticipating? What impact will this new technology have on leisure?
7. Identify some of the ways television impacts your personal leisure lifestyle. What are some of the positive and negative ways that television can affect leisure participation?
8. Choose a recent popular movie and discuss its influence on the leisure behavior and consumption patterns of United States citizens.
9. Poll five of your friends as to the frequency and types of activities in which they are involved during their free time. How do the lists you generate compare to the activities listed in this chapter?
10. What forms of mass leisure might evolve in the future?

References

President's Commission on Americans Outdoors (1987). *Americans Outdoors: The legacy, the challenge with case studies.* Island Press.

Adler, J., D. Glick, P. King, J. Gorden, and A. Cohen. 1993. Been there, done that. *Time* (July 19), 42–49.

American Motion Picture Association. 1999. *Statistical Abstracts of the United States.* Washington, DC.

Americans Commission on Americans Outdoors.

Bammel, G., and L. Bammel. 1996. *Leisure and Human Behavior.* Dubuque, IA: Wm. C. Brown.

Book Industry Supply Group. 1999. *Statistical Abstracts of the United States.* Washington, DC.

Brier, N. R. 2004. Move over prime time. *American Demographics* (July-August), 14–19.

Brightbill, C. 1960. *The Challenge of Leisure.* Englewood Cliffs, NJ: Prentice-Hall.

Brown, R. 1978. Popular Culture, No. 4: Themes continue to be heard. *The Center Daily Times* (February 8).

Carlson, R. 1960, 1985. Outdoor recreation definition. Edited by N. T. Rillo, in *HPER* 542 Class Packet: Foundations Outdoor/Environmental Education. Indiana University: Unpublished Manuscript.

Coleman, J. 1988. Social Capital in the Creation of Human Capital. *American Journal of Sociology* 94, S95–S120.

Cutler, B. 1990. Where does the free time go? *American Demographics* (November), 36–39.

Deery, J. 2003. TV.com: Participatory viewing on the web. *The Journal of Popular Culture 37*(2), 161–183.

de Grazia, 1962. *Of Time, Work and Leisure.* Garden City, NY: Anchor Books.

DeGraaf, D., and Jordan, D. 2003. Social Capital: It's about community. Research Update. *Parks and Recreation 39*(2).

DeGraaf, J. 2004. *Take Back Your Time: Fighting Overwork and Time Poverty in America.* San Francisco: Berrett-Korhler Publishers.

Doherty, W., and Carlson, B. 2002. *Putting Family First.* Henry Holt Publishers.

Dulles, F. 1965. *A History of Recreation: America Learns to Play.* New York: Appleton-Century-Crofts.

Earth Journal. 1993. *Earth Journal: Environmental Almanac and Resources Directory.* Boulder, CO: Buzzworm Books.

Edginton, C., Husdon, S., Dieser, R., and Edginton, S. 2003. *Leisure Programming: A Service-Centered and Benefits Approach.* 4th ed. Dubuque, IA: McGraw-Hill.

Ewert, A. 1989. *Outdoor Adventure Pursuits: Foundation, Models, and Theories.* Scottsdale, AZ: Publishing Horizons.

Financial Times. Music Industry sales decline slows in U.S. *The Financial Times* (March 5, 2004).

Florida, R. 2002. *The rise of the creative class and how it's transforming work, leisure, community and everyday life.* New York: Basic Books.

Francese, P. 2004. Media blitzed. *American Demographics* (February), 40–41.

Gardyn, R., and J. Fetto. 2000. Off the beaten path: Looking for a good time. *American Demographics* (July), 72.

Gibbs, N. 1989. How America has run out of time. *Time* (April 24), 58–67.

Godbey, G. 2003. *Leisure in Your Life: An Exploration.* 6th ed. State College, PA: Venture.

Gunn, C. 1986. Philosophical relationships: Conservation, recreation, leisure, and tourism. In *A Literature Review: The President's Commission on Americans Outdoors,* 1–9. Washington, DC: U.S. Government Printing Office.

Hofferth, S. 1999. How American Children Spend Their Time. *Journal of Marriage and the Family 63*(January), 295–308.

Hostelling International—American Youth Hostels (HI-AYH). (1999). *Hostelling International—American Youth Hostels 1999 Annual Report.* Washington D.C. HI-AYH.

Johnson, P. 1999. TV grabs biggest share of kids' time. *USA Today* (November 18).

Kando, T. 1980. *Leisure and Popular Culture in Transition.* St. Louis: Mosby.

Kelly, J., and G. Godbey. 1992. *The Sociology of Leisure.* State College, PA: Venture.

Kelly, J. 1996. *Leisure.* 3rd ed. Boston: Allyn and Bacon.

Kubey, R., and M. Csikszentmihalyi. 1990. *Television and the Quality of Life.* Hillsdale, NJ: Lawrence Erlbaum.

May, H., and D. Petgin. 1928. *Leisure and Its Uses.* New York: A. S. Barnes.

Molitor, G. T. 2000, May 3. *Here Comes 2015: The Onset of the Leisure Era.* Speech delivered at the Travel Business Roundtable Annual Meeting, Crystal City, Virginia.

Naisbitt, J. 1992. *Trends Newsletter.*

Naisbitt, J., and B. Aburdene. 1990. *Megatrends 2000.* New York: Morrow.

Nash, R. 2004. *Wilderness and the American Mind.* 4th ed. New Haven: Yale University Press.

National Sporting Goods Association. 2000. *Statistical Abstracts of the U.S. 1995.* 115th ed.

National Sporting Goods Association. 2000. *Statistical Abstracts of the United States.* Washington, DC.

President's Commission on Americans Outdoors (PCAO). 1987. *Americans Outdoors, the Legacy, the Challenge.* Washington D.C., Island Press.

Priest, S., and M. Gass. 1999. Future trends and issues in adventure programming. J. Miles and S. Priest, eds. in *Adventure Programming,* 473–478. State College, PA: Venture.

Putnam, R. 2000. *Bowling Alone: The Collapse and Revival of American Community.* New York: Simon & Schuster.

Putnam, R., and Goss, K. 2002. Introduction. In R. Putnam (ed.), *Democracies in flux: The evolution of social capital in contemporary society* (pp. 3–21). New York: Oxford Press.

Ragheb M. and J. Beard. 1992. Measuring Leisure Interests. *Journal of Park and Recreation Administration, 10*(2), 1–13.

Raymond, J. 2000. Wild America. *American Demographics* (August), 54–58.

Recording Industry Association. 2000. *World Almanac and Book of Facts.* Mahway, NJ: World Almanac Books.

Robinson, J., and G. Godbey. 1997. *Time for Life: The Surprising Way Americans Spend Their Time.* University Park, PA: Pennsylvania State University Press.

Robinson, J. 2003. The incredible shrinking vacation. In DeGraaf, J. (ed), *Take back your time: Fighting overwork and time poverty in America.* San Francisco: Berrett-Korhler Publishers.

Robinson, J. P. 1989. Time's up. *American Demographics* (July), 33–35.

Robinson, J. P. 1990a. The time squeeze. *American Demographics* (February), 30–33.

Robinson, J. P. 1990b. The leisure pie. *American Demographics 12* (November), 39.

Robinson, J. P. 1991. Your money or your time. *American Demographics 13* (November), 22–26.

Rockerbie, D. 2004. The Economics of Professional Sports. University of Lethbridge, Alberta, Canada.

Samdahl, D. 1992. Leisure in our lives: Enhancing the common leisure occasion. *Journal of Leisure Research 24*(1), 19–32.

Schor, J. 1991. *The Overworked American: The Unexpected Decline of Leisure.* New York: Basic Books.

Schor, J. 2003. The (even more) overworked American. In DeGraaf, J. (ed), *Take back your time: Fighting overwork and time poverty in America.* San Francisco: Berrett-Korhler Publishers.

Searle, M. S., and R. E. Brayley. 2000. *Leisure in Canada: An Introduction.* 2d ed. State College, PA: Venture.

Spring, J. 1993. Seven Days of Play. *American Demographics* (March), 50–53.

Stein Wellner, A. 2000. The end of leisure. *American Demographics* (July), 50–56.

U.S. Bureau of the Census. 2002. *Statistical Abstract of the United States.* Washington, DC: U.S. Government Printing Office.

U.S. Bureau of Economic Analysis. 1995. *Statistical Abstract of the United States 1995.* 115th ed. Washington, DC: U.S. Government Printing Office.

U.S. Census Bureau. 2003. Report on Computer, Internet Access. U.S. Department of Commerce News: Washington DC. Retrieved from www.usembassy.it/file2001_09/akia/a1090605.htm.

U.S. Department of Health and Human Services. 1999. *Trends in the Well Being of America's Children and Youth.* Washington, D.C.: Department of Health and Human Services.

United Nations Environment Program. 2004. Economic Impacts of Tourism. Retrieved from http://www.unepie.org/pc/tourism/sust-tourism/economic.htm.

Van den Haag, E. 1964. A dissent from the consensual society. Edited by Norman Jacobs, in *Culture for the Millions? Mass Media in Modern Society,* 53–62. Boston: Beacon Books.

WTO Newsletter. 1998. *Ecotourism, Now One-Fifth of Market.* January/February. Retrieved from http://www.worldtourism.org/omt/newslett/janfeb98/ecotour.htm.

CHAPTER

6

Leisure and the Life Cycle

Leisure provides opportunities throughout the entire life span. Gardening is a significant activity among North Americans. Here, a man waters plants in his home greenhouse.

Introduction

How does the human life cycle relate to the concept of life satisfaction in leisure? Generally speaking, as individuals move through life, they grow, mature, gain wisdom and knowledge, and reflect leisure behaviors that result from their past experiences and development. As Erikson (1963) points out, the positive growth and development of individuals can lead to a life of fulfillment, characterized by trust, autonomy, initiative, industry, sense of identity, intimacy, and integrity. Successful leisure experiences can contribute to the positive growth and development of individuals.

According to Grey and Greben's benchmark article (1974), and underscored by the National Recreation and Park Association's Twenty-First Century Agenda (1992), the leisure movement in the United States must make the growth and development of participants a priority within its organizations and programs. Because it is freely chosen, the leisure experience can contribute in a unique way to growth and development throughout one's life. Yet during our lifetimes the activities we enjoy and participate in change. These changes are due in part to the process of development that is a part of the human experience.

This chapter addresses the life cycle and its relationship to leisure. It examines leisure throughout the life cycle, including a discussion of childhood, adolescence, adulthood, and older adulthood, and provides the reader with information regarding human development and its relationship to leisure.

Leisure throughout the Life Cycle

This section of the book discusses leisure and the life cycle along with a brief overview of the stages of human development and their relationship to leisure. This brief discussion provides a framework for understanding leisure and the life cycle in an overview of basic concepts and ideas related to the process of human development.

Lifestyles

Lifestyle is defined by *Webster's Encyclopedia Unabridged Dictionary* as "the habits, attitudes, tastes, moral standards, economic level, etc., that together constitute the mode of living of an individual or group." In addition to those demographic variables mentioned, lifestyle may also be influenced by other variables such as age, gender, social class, and more, including psychographic variables. Psychographics are those elements that define and reflect one's psychological state or disposition that may influence his or her behavior. For example, a person's degree of introversion or extroversion will impact his/her ability to interact with other people. One's propensity for risk taking may influence the types of leisure experiences they seek. Psychographics directly influence one's lifestyle. Sessoms (1985) defines the term *lifestyle* as "a person's mode of expression." The outward manifestation of lifestyle includes such items as dress, speech patterns, language, activity selection, living situation, social relationships, and religion. Most sociologists agree that each dominant lifestyle has an integrated core of activities associated with it. Those who share a similar lifestyle tend to form subgroups that reinforce their individual choices and set their behavior priorities. These are often referred to as subcultures.

Lifestyles are dynamic and therefore may change during the course of a lifetime. For example, as a student moves from high school to college and then into the working world, lifestyle changes can accompany each stage. Yet other aspects of lifestyle (e.g., religion, ethnic, or racial background) may cut across many age groups or life stages. Even within a dominant lifestyle, such as being a student, subgroups may appear, such as athletic teams or fraternity and sorority members. Although these two groups may share many common characteristics of being college students, unique differences surface between them. These subgroups, or subcultures, have the potential of establishing the norms and defining the underlying values and common behaviors for each of the individuals in them.

For example, the baby boom generation has been talked about and studied for a number of years as a cohort that shares a common lifestyle. This generation encompasses those who were born between 1945 and 1963—the post-World War II years. In 1998, however, the American Association of Retired Persons (AARP) identified five distinct segments (subgroups) among the baby boom generation (AARP, 2000). People who represent each of these subgroups share more in common with one another than with those who represent other segments.

The Strugglers   This subgroup constitutes 9 percent of the baby boom generation and is the lowest income group. It also has a large number of females (64 percent) in it. Those in this group find it difficult to save for retirement and have actually thought very little about it. A majority of Strugglers do not have an optimistic outlook about their later years.

The Anxious   The people representing this group also have a sense of apprehension when looking ahead to their later years. This group comprises almost one quarter of the baby boom group (23 percent) and they have limited means. They expect to *have* to work into retirement years. Anxious group members also have a great concern with coverage for health care in later years.

The Enthusiasts   Thirteen percent of baby boomers fall into this segment and include people who are eager to reach their retirement years. These people do not plan to work at all in retirement and envision plenty of money and plenty of time for recreation. Retirement is viewed as a time free from work.

Welcome to Virtual Leisure . . .

The following newspaper article appeared in newspapers around the country in April, 1996. The article reports an interesting trend in which people surround themselves with lifestyle ornaments they do not or cannot use.

A young sales manager has a kitchen that would make Julia Child's mouth water. But all the appliances are dusty. A woman buys a baby grand piano. But no one in the household knows how to play. Urban dwellers behind the wheels of their Range Rovers navigate nothing more demanding than traffic jams. The vehicles are capable of trouncing the Outback. Witness a growing trend in which Americans surround themselves with lifestyle ornaments they do not or cannot use. They create a living tableau of leisure in which they do not participate. Welcome to virtual leisure.

We sink onto the couch and watch "This Old House," but the prospect of actually stripping 16 layers of paint makes many of us sweat. We lose ourselves in Martha Stewart's books but don't emulate her. What's going on? Seismic lifestyle shifts have changed the way we spend our free time, experts say. We also may be measuring our lives against the model of our parents. When we watch a crafts show without lifting a finger, we may be feeling nostalgia for the days when people made things with their hands, rather than putting things on a credit card.

When we watch "This Old House" or follow Martha Stewart's projects, "we're vicariously participating in the baking of cookies, the growing of a garden, or going to a workshop," says Steven Kelly, head of the Direct Marketing Institute at DePaul University. Norm Abrams, the how-to hero of "This Old House" and "The New Yankee Workshop" agrees. "There is no sweat. There's no dirt. There's no bills to pay. They can watch a piece of furniture come together at 'Yankee Workshop' and they feel at the end of the show they've participated in some way."

Many people escape into virtual leisure because they are dissatisfied, theorizes TV fishing guru Babe Winkelman. "Most people are not happy with their lives. They're not happy with what they do for a living. They're not happy with the environment they're raising their children in." His fans tell him: "We fish through you."

"We've grown accustomed to watching instead of doing," Kelly said. "Television allows an involvement with what is going on that wasn't previously there," said Dr. Sidney Weissman of Loyola University Medical Center. Instead of going out dancing on Friday, we often turn to passive leisure, surfing the Internet or watching a video. "I'm sure more Nordic Tracks function as coat racks rather than exercise equipment," Weissman said.

Points to Ponder

- Within this article is the concept of virtual leisure positive or negative?
- What concerns or opportunities does this article raise for leisure service professionals?

The Self-Reliants The largest group of baby boomers (30 percent), Self-Reliants have the highest income and education levels of any group in this cohort. The 1 percent of people in this segment who envision themselves working some during retirement years plan to do so because of interest and enjoyment they find in the work.

Today's Traditionalists One quarter of the baby boomer generation comprises this segment and is traditional in many attitudes. Traditionalists express a stronger sense of confidence than the other segments in government retirement programs (Social Security, Medicare). In addition, people in this group intend to work and rely on government programs during retirement years.

One thing is clear among all five baby boomer segments. Most of this generation plan to work for pay after retirement. This has a large impact on the provision of leisure services for the older population. The new seniors will be active well into their later years.

A Perspective on the Life Cycle.

FRANK AND ERNEST reprinted by permission of Newspaper Enterprise Association, Inc.

The Life Cycle

Understanding leisure throughout the life cycle requires the realization that change is an integral part of life. This sort of developmental approach sees people as being in a constant state of becoming, changing, and developing by stages that are similar for most people. The concept of *stages* or *life stages* implies that life involves a series of connected stages, each influencing one another, but each being distinct (Sessoms, 1985). Education level, socioeconomic status, sex, and family status impact the nature of this cyclical process.

Within each life stage, age is not necessarily fixed as life stages overlap and vary widely in life situations. Life cycle does influence recreation and leisure choices. For instance, Kelly (1978, 1996) found that family life cycle proves to be a better indicator of participation in recreation than age. For example, the leisure activities of a twenty-five-year-old single person may well be different from a twenty-five-year-old married person with two children. Likewise, leisure patterns tend to rely more on the fact that a couple's children have left home than that the couple's age has advanced from forty to fifty years (Godbey, 1994). In these examples, parenthood plays a large part in leisure participation.

Other life cycle factors influence leisure participation. For instance, in your parents' and grandparents' generations, it was common for a person to complete grade school and either go to college or begin working. Between the ages of twenty and twenty-five, this individual would likely marry and continue to develop his or her work skills. Children would enter the family unit and this individual would remain with the same company for his or her entire work life. Today it is relatively common for a person to begin the same way (grade school, college, work), but then things change. Contemporary individuals are more likely to hold multiple jobs with multiple companies over the course of their work history, and it is not uncommon (particularly for men) to have two families—a first marriage with grown children and a second marriage with young children. One's participation in leisure is heavily affected by these types of cycles.

Stages of Human Development

The passage of individuals through various life stages involves all aspects of a person's development. According to Brill (n.d.), the five key aspects of human development are physical, social, emotional, intellectual, and spiritual. While many theories abound as to how people develop in each of these areas, one of the most accepted theories of personality development is Erikson's (1963) eight life stages (see table 6.1). Within each stage, individuals establish a new orientation to themselves and other people in their social world.

TABLE 6.1 ERIKSON'S LIFE STAGES

- **Infancy:**   **Trust versus Mistrust**

  Depending upon the quality of care received, the infant learns to trust the environment, to perceive it as orderly and predictable, or to be suspicious, fearful, and mistrusting.

- **Young Childhood:**   **Autonomy versus Doubt**

  The development of motor and mental abilities, and the opportunity to explore, encourage a sense of autonomy and independence. However, if the child is excessively criticized or limited in his/her exploration, it will lead to a sense of doubt over his/her adequacy and competency.

- **Middle Childhood:**   **Initiative versus Guilt**

  The manner in which adults respond to the child's self-initiated activities creates either a sense of freedom and initiative, or a sense of being an inept intruder in an adult world.

- **Late Childhood:**   **Industry versus Inferiority**

  The child has a concern for how things work and how they ought to operate, leading to a sense of industry in forming rules, organizing and ordering. However, if these efforts are rebuffed as silly, it may lead to a sense of inferiority. During this stage of development, outside influences begin to exert a greater influence on the child's development.

- **Adolescence:**   **Identity versus Role Confusion**

  The adolescent begins to develop the ability to see things from others' point of view. The youth must develop a sense of his or her own identity, as distinct from all others and personally acceptable, or he/she will be confused or settle on a "negative" identity, such as class clown.

- **Young Adulthood:**   **Intimacy versus Isolation**

  The consequences of the young adult's attempts at reaching out to make contact with others may result in a commitment to other persons or isolation from close personal relationships.

- **Middle Adulthood:**   **Generativity versus Self-Absorption**

  At this stage, one may become concerned about family, society, and future generations, or may become concerned with only material possessions and physical well-being.

- **Old Age:**   **Integrity versus Despair**

  One looks back at life with a sense of fulfillment and integrity, or despair, feeling that life has been misdirected.

From *Childhood and Society*, by Erik H. Erikson. Copyright 1950, © 1963 by W. W. Norton & Company, Inc., renewed © 1978, 1991 by Erik H. Erikson. Reprinted by permission of W. W. Norton & Company, Inc.

Each of the eight stages is characterized by a conflict that has two opposing outcomes. If the conflict is worked out in a constructive, satisfactory manner, the positive quality becomes part of the ego and enhances further healthy development (Salkind, 1985). If the conflict persists or is resolved unsatisfactorily, however, the negative quality is incorporated into the personality structure (Muuss, 1982). Table 6.1 presents each of these eight stages and the issues individuals must master within each level.

Erikson's eight stages serve as one model of life stages throughout the life cycle. Other researchers have developed their own stages. For example, Levinson (1978) identifies the following life stages: childhood, adolescence, early adulthood, middle adulthood, late adulthood, and old age.

Although the exact ages when people move from life stage to life stage may vary, most models of the human life cycle consist of three basic periods: preparation, establishment, and culmination. In the preparation period, learning and growing are the central tasks as young people prepare for adulthood. In establishment, individuals struggle with making a positive contri-

Figure 6.1

Leisure and the life span.

Relative Strength of the Tendencies to Seek Familiar and Novel Forms of Leisure throughout the Life Span

Relative strength

Seeking familiar leisure forms (structure, permanence)

Seeking new leisure experiences (novelty)

Infancy   Childhood   Adulthood   Retirement

bution to society and being accepted within a social group. In culmination, death is anticipated and individuals seek ways to place their lives in perspective. With these thoughts in mind this section of the chapter focuses on the following life stages: childhood (more specifically middle and late childhood), adolescence, adulthood (more specifically early, middle, and late adulthood), and older adulthood.

Within these specific life stages, research on leisure behavior demonstrates two interesting tendencies. First, while individuals seek stability and the familiar at some points in their lives, they also seek novel leisure experiences at other times (see figure 6.1). Second, the number of daily leisure activities that make up a person's leisure repertoire steadily increases, reaching a peak during early adulthood before the number begins to decline as a person reaches old age (see figure 6.2). Thus, during early and middle adulthood, one has the most leisure activities available to them and typically seeks the most novel.

Furthermore, Kleiber (1999) underscored that leisure experiences, in general, relate to human development in four principle ways. First, leisure is derived from other developmental processes and life circumstances. That is, leisure choices and behaviors are a result of developmental tasks and normative events. For example, the normative event of retirement can allow a person more time to being involved in leisure. Second, leisure is adjustive in allowing for some accommodations to developmental pressures and life events. Leisure activity can be a respite, buffer, or coping strategy to developmental changes or serious life events. For example, leisure can help adolescents develop an identity or deal with bodily changes that occur during puberty. Third, leisure is generative of development change. Leisure can serve as a context for generating growth and personal transformation. For example, control of attention during free-time activity (e.g., reading) can result in improving self-discipline that is necessary for success in other areas of life. Fourth, leisure is maladaptive, in some cases, hindering development. Although leisure provides many human development benefits (see Driver and Burns, 1999; Edginton, Hudson, Dieser, and Edginton, 2004), it can also impede human development. For example, a person can be so focused on a certain type of leisure experience (e.g., sport) that they do not spend enough time on developing a solid parent–son/daughter relationship. Likewise, escapist drug use is another example of leisure hindering healthy development.

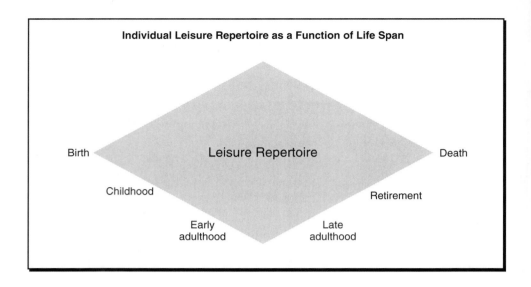

Figure 6.2

Relationship between leisure repertoire and life span.

Childhood and Leisure

In many ways there has never been a better time to be a child than during this era. Children have opportunities, rights, and status that have never before been awarded to them collectively. Yet being a child in today's world can also bring more pressures and decisions than ever before—dealing with working parents, access to an almost overwhelming variety of information through mass media and the Internet, and many more choices—forcing many children to mature faster than ever. Play and leisure opportunities have a major role in the development process. Play and games are the main forms of leisure activity during the period from birth to adolescence.

Play does not have to be taught or justified during this period of life. Play is a self-motivated behavior; one cannot force a child to play. However, for the child play is serious business. In his research, Huizinga (1962) identified the following characteristics of play: voluntary, steps outside of ordinary life, limited in time and space, not serious but consuming for participants, bounded by rules, and promotes cultural values and as such is an important means of learning for younger children. Children have much to teach adults about play.

Hansel (1979) refers to young children as midget gurus of play in that gurus teach people profound truths. He noted that infants and young children can teach us some of the following principles:

Total immersion. No matter what children do, they do it completely and do not worry about any inhibitions. They have the ability to let life hug them.

Total concentration. Children concentrate on one thing and one thing only. The Greek word for worry is *merimnao,* which means literally to divide the mind. Watch children and you will notice how free they are from this problem that plagues society.

Ability to bounce back. Their spirit is indomitable. Children are able to bounce back from failure to try again and again.

Total honesty and expression. Children have a wonderful sense of spontaneity, and they tend to be completely open and honest with their feelings.

Children can teach a "sense of wonder and uninhibitedness, of gratitude and spontaneity, of unimpeded trust and freedom to change, of imagination and creativity. . . . Children can

"Can Johnny come out and eat?"

show people how to see everything as if it were for the first time and to share as if there were no end, how to smell, and taste and touch life" (Hansel, 1979, p. 78).

The period of childhood itself can be divided in many ways including infancy and toddlers (birth to three), preschool children (four- to five-year-olds), younger children (six- to eight-year-olds), and older children (nine- to twelve-year-olds). The play and leisure of infants, toddlers, and preschoolers is primarily home based, although with working parents, younger and younger children are being introduced to organized programs. In fact, in 1999 it was reported that 54 percent of all children from birth through third grade received child care on a regular basis from a nonfamily member (Forum on Child and Family and Statistics, 2000). With this rise in the participation of very young children, leisure programmers need to be aware that early and middle childhood are considered two of the greatest developmental periods of life. During this time children develop both fundamental locomotor skills and basic social skills.

Table 6.2 presents the developmental characteristics of younger children. During this time period, children expand their social world beyond their immediate family. The gender differences reported in earlier research may be lessened in the twenty-first century, as girls and boys participate in a wider variety of activities as society becomes more sensitive to gender inequalities. Within Erikson's (1963) framework, children should be encouraged to be self-directed in initiating activities. Public and school playgrounds become a focal point for many children during this

TABLE

6.2 DEVELOPMENTAL CHARACTERISTICS OF YOUNGER CHILDREN (AGES 6 TO 8)

Characteristics

- Beginning to become competitive
- Relatively short attention span; frustrate easily
- Involved in the magical world of play
- Desire to impress leaders and peers
- Social rules are important
- Play and learning are an integrated process
- Motor development proceeds downward from head and outward from the center of the body; hand and eye coordination are developing
- Pleasure is gained from achievement
- Show pride and affection for parents
- Social skills developing; developing a sense of humor; more thoughtful of others

Program Implications

- Specific programs to help children experience varied activities that encourage peer interaction and motor development. Leisure activities for this group tend to be found in the public and private nonprofit sectors.
- Play is particularly important for this age group. Play offers intrinsically rewarding experiences that help children gain competence in both problem solving and creativity. Play is an important means of learning and socialization.
- Programs should emphasize gross motor activities including throwing, climbing, and rolling, as well as provide high-energy activities alternated with periodic quiet activities. In the later stages of this age span, programs should introduce cooperative activities such as new games.
- Programs tend to be more leader-directed. Staff need to be aware that they are role models for children, and they need to provide consistency and emphasize fairness.

Activities

- **Sports and Games:** Chasing games, singing games, individual games of skill (e.g., jacks), stunts, bike riding, and scavenger hunts. Some organized sports are introduced (e.g., baseball). Active hobbies (e.g., hiking, climbing) are often encouraged by parents.
- **Social:** Individuals are likely to interact with same-sex friends. Cliques are likely to form (e.g., treehouse club). Classes (e.g., karate, swimming, dancing), school, day camps—all foster socialization.
- **Miscellaneous:** Reading, board games, video games.

period as the bulk of leisure activities for this group tends to be found in the public and private, nonprofit sectors.

Leisure professionals should also be concerned with the physical fitness of youth. According to the United States Surgeon General (2001), "Overweight and obesity have reached nationwide epidemic proportions" (p. v), which are especially concerning among the youth. As Wechsler, McKenna, Lee, and Dietz (2004) noted:

> Since 1980, the percentage of children who are overweight has more than doubled . . . In 2002, 16 percent of 6-19-year-olds were overweight. Rates of overweight were higher among Mexican American boys (25.5 percent), non-Hispanic black girls (23.2 percent) and American Indian youth . . . In recent years, several weight-related conditions that were observed primarily among adults have been

Figure 6.3

Percentage of overweight youth in the United States in 2004.

Overweight Is a K–12 Issue

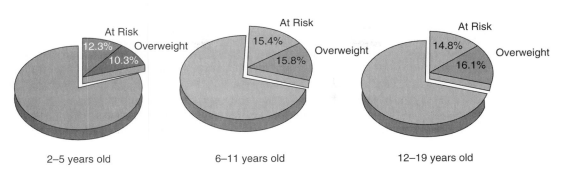

2–5 years old   6–11 years old   12–19 years old

Understanding Who Is at Greater Risk

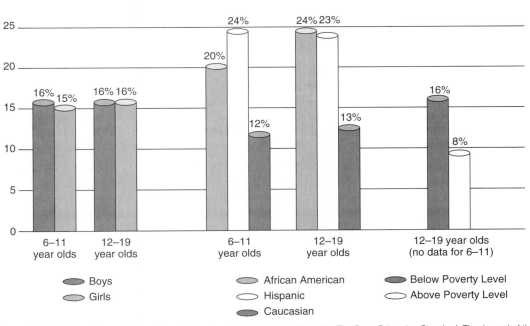

From: Trager, S. (2004). Preventing weight problems before they become too hard to solve. The State Education Standard: The Journal of the National Association of State Boards of Education, 5(2), 13–20.

increasingly diagnosed in young people. For example, 10 years ago type 2 diabetes was almost unknown among young people, but in some communities it now accounts from 50 percent of new cases of diabetes among children and adolescents. (p. 5)

Figure 6.3 reports percentages among overweight youth in the United States and table 6.3 underscores medical conditions associated with overweight and obesity in children.

6.3   MEDICAL CONDITIONS ASSOCIATED WITH OVERWEIGHT AND OBESITY IN CHILDREN

Medical Conditions Associated with Overweight and Obesity in Children

Type 2 (non-Insulin dependent) Diabetes	• An alarming increase in type 2 diabetes is seen in children and adolescents, a condition that used to only occur in adults and is more strongly associated with obesity than any other condition; • Risk increases approximately 25% after each additional BMI unit >22; • Hospital discharges for children with obesity-associated diabetes nearly doubled since 1979; • Up to 85% of children with type 2 diabetes are overweight or obese; • Total cost related to overweight and obesity is $98 billion (2001 dollars).
Glucose Intolerance	• A precursor to diabetes, glucose intolerance (pre-diabetes) is increasingly prevalent in children and adolescents; • Individuals with pre-diabetes are at an increased risk for heart disease and stroke.
High Cholesterol	• Poor diet, being overweight, and physical inactivity can increase blood cholesterol levels; • High cholesterol is a major risk factor for heart disease, the number one killer in the United States; • Overweight children are 2.4 times more likely than average-weight children to have an elevated total cholesterol level.
Hypertension (High Blood Pressure)	• Overweight children are 4.5 times more likely to have a higher systolic blood pressure and 2.4 times more likely to have a higher diastolic blood pressure; • Obese men and women have a relative risk of 2.1 and 1.9, respectively, for developing high blood pressure; • Direct cost related to overweight and obesity is $4.1 billion (1995 updated to 2001 dollars).
Coronary Heart Disease (CHD)	• Individuals who are overweight or obese have an increased incidence of heart disease (heart attack, congestive heart failure, sudden cardiac death, angina or chest pain, and abnormal heart rhythm); • 58% of overweight children (5-17 years old) have one additional cardiovascular risk factor, and 20% have two or more additional risk factors; • A sustained 10% reduction in weight could reduce the expected lifetime incidence of CHD by 12 to 38 cases per 1000; • The direct cost related to overweight and obesity is $8.8 billion (1995 updated to 2001 dollars).
Gall Bladder Disease	• Almost 50% of the cases of cholecystitis (inflammation of the bladder) in adolescents may be associated with overweight; • Hospital discharges for obesity-associated gallbladder disease tripled for children since 1979; • Total cost related to overweight and obesity is $3.4 billion (1995 updated to 2001 dollars).
Osteoarthritis	• For every 2-pound weight-gain, the risk of developing arthritis increases by 9-13%; • Overweight women and men have nearly 4 and 5 times the risk of developing knee osteoarthritis, respectively; • The total cost of osteoarthritis related to overweight and obesity is $21.2 billion (1995 updated to 2001 dollars).
Cancer	• Overweight and obesity are associated with an increased risk for certain types of cancer including endometrial, colon, gall bladder, prostate, kidney, and breast cancer; • 14% of cancer deaths for men and 20% of cancer deaths for women in the U.S. may be attributable to overweight and obesity; • Total cost related to overweight and obesity is $2.9 billion for breast cancer, $3.5 billion for colon cancer, and $933 million for endometrial cancer (1995 updated to 2001 dollars).
Sleep Apnea & Respiratory Problems	• Obesity is associated with a higher prevalence of asthma and approximately 7% of obese children have sleep apnea, one of the most severe conditions that can lead to learning and memory problems; • Hospital discharges for obesity-associated sleep apnea have increased five-fold for children since 1979.

6.3   CONTINUED

Medical Conditions Associated with Overweight and Obesity in Children (continued)

Liver Disease	• Studies have shown that 20%-60% of obese adults develop Nonalcoholic Steatohepatitis (NASH); • NASH is increasingly appearing in children—6% of overweight adolescents and 10% of obese adolescents presented with elevated alanine aminotransferases levels, an indicator of NASH; • Children with NASH risk progressive liver damage, including cirrohosis.
Psychosocial Effects	• Overweight children are often socially marginalized and isolated and experience mental health problems such as depression, lack of self-confidence, low self-esteem; • The likelihood of impaired quality of life for obese children is similar to that of a very sick child with cancer—5.5 times greater than for a healthy child.
Women's Reproductive Health	• Increased risk for reproductive health problems (menstrual irregularities, infertility, irregular ovulation) is evident for children who remain overweight into adulthood.
Death	• Poor diet and physical inactivity caused 400,000 deaths in 2000; • Compared with normal-weight individuals, obese individuals have a 50%-100% higher risk of death from all causes.

Source: *From:* Obesity in young children. 2004. *The National Institute for Health Care Management* (August), 1–12. Retrieved from: www.nihcm.org/pubsmain.html

According to Trager (2004), the two primary reasons for the overweight and obesity epidemic are poor nutrition/eating habits (e.g., processed and fast food) and decreased physical activity. In particular, Trager (2004) posited that decreased physical activity is related to:

- Less physical activity in school: Only 8 percent of elementary schools, 6.4 percent of middle schools, and 5.8 percent of high schools have daily physical education.
- Declining recreational and physical activity after school: 23 percent of children report no physical activity at all during their free time.
- More use of transit: Few children walk or ride their bikes to various places (e.g., friends' house, school).
- Electronic media: Children spend an average of 5.5 hours a day using electronic media, and preschoolers spend as much time with screen media as they do playing outside.

To this end, the Surgeon General (2001) has challenged families, community organizations, schools, health care organizations, media and communication facilities, and worksites to take action to prevent and decrease the overweight and obesity epidemic. Leisure, recreation, and play should be at the forefront of this challenge. Leisure-oriented programs such as active living and youth recreation sport can be used to help youth become healthier and in better overall shape. For example, the Youth Bicycle Education Network (YBEN) (www.yben.org) supports and strengthens organizations that use bicycles as a vehicle for youth development and community building. YBEN programs such as "Youth Cycle and Repair in Philadelphia, Free Ride Zone in Seattle, the Bicycle Action Project in Indianapolis, and others offer Earn-a-Bike programs where at-risk youth are awarded a bike for successful completion of bike mechanic courses that also teach work habits and communication skills" (Alvord, 2000 p. 156). Likewise, leisure education can target families to commit more time and energy toward physical activities among all members of a family (Edginton, Hudson, Dieser, and Edginton, 2004).

Another aspect that has serious health implications to children and adolescents, which is on the other side of the overweight and obesity spectrum, is cosmetic fitness. Although women and men are physically active, cosmetic fitness is focused solely on looking physically attractive and can often have serious health implications. For example, to look physically attractive (rather than being healthy), many women will use diet pills, self-induced vomiting, and starvation in conjunction with leisure and physical activity (Beals, 2000; Coakley, 2004). Furthermore, the dominant discourse for women to look like Barbie dolls can lead to a host of unhealthy actions, such as eating disorders, anorexia, and becoming addicted to unnecessary cosmetic surgery (Blum, 2003; Rogers, 1999). In addition, Coakley (2004) noted the following regarding the confusion between health-oriented physical fitness and beauty-oriented cosmetic fitness:

> Many girls and women hear confusing cultural messages that they should be "firm but shapely, fit but sexy, strong but thin" . . . These fashion images highlight thinness, bust size, waist size, lip shape, hairstyle, body hair removal, complexion, allure, and the clothes and accessories that together "make" a woman . . . They are told that men now like competent women, but they see men attracted to the NFL and NBA cheerleader and the latest celebrity models with breast implants and workout videos . . . . (p. 247)

In regard to male youth, to look physically attractive (rather than being healthy), many adolescents will combine leisure and physical activity with steroid use (Leshner, 2000) and suffer from muscular dysmorphia, which is the chronic preoccupation that a person is not sufficiently muscular (Driesen, 2005). Many men and women become confused between health and beauty, or physical fitness and cosmetic fitness, because the health industry sells fake and unhealthy body images as means to profit off people (Pronger, 2002; Thomsen, Bower, and Barnes, 2004).

Another area of potential development in leisure service organizations is that of youth sports. Often fraught with controversy because of the competitive nature of sport and athletics and the increase in sports-related violence, youth sports suggest more of a developmental orientation than in the past. Jordan (2001) suggests that youth sports should be implemented to enhance the emotional, physical, social, and educational well-being of children. Youth sports are also an opportunity for youth to be exposed to positive role models and healthy (drug- and tobacco-free) environments.

The lack of appropriate skills and the overemphasis on competition have driven many youth from sports programs. In fact, the number one reason youth play sports is to have fun (Ewing and Seefeldt, 1990). Contemporary youth sport programs operated by leisure service organizations recognize the importance of contributing to the growth of individuals at their own pace and consistent with their stages of development. They emphasize involvement in programs aligned to promote genuine opportunities for participation and skill development for everyone.

Youth sports produce a tremendous impact on the character and development of children. Consider the implications of Title IX legislation in the provision of youth sport programs for girls. Title IX, an Educational Amendement Act of 1972, was an antidiscrimination provision in which all physical education and athletic teams in high school and college were open to members of both sexes (Mechikoff and Estes, 2002). Limited opportunities have given way to a full range of youth sport services available to girls that can contribute in significant ways to their development. Leisure service organizations can play an important role in providing such services with a philosophical commitment to the development and growth of the individual. An estimated 35 million children and adolescents participate in youth sport programs each year (DiFiori, 1999). Municipal park and recreation departments, Little League baseball, Pop

Warner football, U.S. Ice Hockey Association, American Youth Soccer Organization, Boys and Girls Clubs, Girls Incorporated, Boy Scouts of America, YMCAs, YWCAs—all promote sport programs.

Some of the trends regarding youth sport programs follow:

- Participation in youth sport programs is highest in childhood (up to eleven years old) and young adulthood (eighteen to twenty-four years old) with a large decline in participation between the ages of twelve and seventeen years (National Sporting Goods Association, 2001).
- Younger children participate in sports to have fun, learn skills, and participate in a team atmosphere. Older children are more interested in competition (Carnegie Corporation, 1992).
- Financial support of school sports will continue to decrease, thus increasing the reliance upon municipal sports programs (Seefeldt, 1996).
- Many youth sport programs fail to integrate current knowledge of youth development principles into activities (National Alliance for Youth Sports, 2001).
- The need for volunteer assistance will continue to increase, although the threat of lawsuits will push youth sports programs to require certification of volunteer youth sport coaches (National Alliance for Youth Sports, 2001).
- Sports that permit the attainment of personal and individual styles of play will be increasingly popular; those that are highly regimented will decline (Seefeldt, 1996).
- Ethnic preferences will influence youth sports as sports like soccer, baseball, and basketball will continue to gain popularity while sports such as hockey, volleyball, racquetball, and swimming will decrease in popularity (Seefeldt, 1996).
- A gradual blending of youth sports for participants who are disabled and those who are able bodied will occur (National Alliance for Youth Sports, 2001).
- Boys are 1.5 times more likely to participate in youth sports than girls (Troiano et al., 1995).

The key to activities for infants and toddlers, as well as young children, involves offering a variety of appropriate activities that help them interact with peers in positive ways and assist in motor-skill development. Leisure service leaders should not push young children too intensely and should teach activities in a logical progression. DiFiori (1999) reports that 30 to 50 percent of all youth sport injuries are due to overuse. To minimize these types of injuries one should match physical abilities with the activity, allow adequate rest, teach and encourage complete conditioning, ensure the appropriate use of sports equipment and shoes, and monitor the social pressure applied by peers and adults on child athletes.

In the latter stages of childhood, life becomes more complex for children. Peers and school become increasingly important. Gender differences begin to become more pronounced, suggesting that males and females are learning social norms and values differently (Carlson, Uppal, and Prosser, 2000; Culp, 1998). Table 6.4 presents additional characteristics of this developmental stage. During this time, leisure continues to take place mainly in the public and private nonprofit sectors, although individuals begin to explore more school and commercially alternative opportunities.

Within Erikson's (1963) framework, youth throughout childhood need to achieve competency, a personal identity, and a feeling of closeness or intimacy with others within this process. As youth move through these stages, they ask and answer such questions as "Am I normal?" "Am I lovable?" "Am I competent?" "Am I loving to others?" As leisure professionals work with youth it is important to help them answer these questions with an emphatic yes.

During this time period, leisure professionals must be careful not to cater to some groups over others. Leisure organizations have sometimes been accused of sexism because they devoted more attention to males than females (Kelly, 1996). For example, almost twice as many

TABLE

6.4 DEVELOPMENTAL CHARACTERISTICS OF OLDER CHILDREN (AGES 9 TO 12)

Characteristics

- Girls are approximately one year more mature than boys
- Fitness improves as individuals gain more stamina; realization of personal limits (through peer comparison) occurs
- New interests develop; competitiveness lessens
- Selective memory is engaged
- Creative imagination along with the development of abstract logical thinking exists
- Pride in traditions
- Responses to various situations are more in control, less impulsive
- Good sense of humor
- Role models are extremely important; children are easily influenced
- Closeness of peers, focus on "best" friends; some arguments; can conceal hurt feelings
- Importance of peers increases dramatically
- Onset of adolescence; often more self-conscious about their bodies at this stage

Program Implications

- Individuals are beginning to establish themselves outside the family unit. Individuals are also beginning to be interested in members of the other sex. Leisure organizations should give participants opportunities to develop specific skills and to socialize with peers. Leisure continues to take place mainly in the public and private nonprofit sectors; individuals begin to explore more school opportunities and commercial alternatives (e.g., movies).
- Programs should offer opportunities for gradual acceptance of additional responsibility.

Activities

- **Sports and Games:** Team games, hobbies (camping with parents, organizations), physical sports, initiatives, spectator sports.
- **Social:** Clubs, social activities (dances), hanging out at the mall with friends, music becoming more important.
- **Miscellaneous:** Movies, video games, reading.

boys as girls participate in sports teams and leagues. This may be partly due to cultural norms, but it might also relate to the opportunities presented to males and females. Likewise, as team sports become more important, many of those less skilled are left out. Dynamic leisure programs need to address the needs of all children, giving them equal opportunities to participate.

Being committed to helping children grow and develop through leisure demands that professionals ask and answer many of the questions raised by studies such as the National Children and Youth Fitness Study II (Ross and Pate, 1987) and the Surgeon General (U.S. Department of Health and Human Services, 1996). Questions raised by these studies include: As parents, teachers, and members of society at large, do we encourage children to be active enough? Do we use television too often to control behavior? Are we pushing the few too quickly into competitive sports to the near exclusion of the many? Do we offer children the right options? Do we set the right example by our own lifestyle? What needs to happen to foster an individual commitment in children to grow and develop through their leisure pursuits? What needs to happen to foster in children a commitment to lifetime fitness?

TABLE

6.5 — DEVELOPMENTAL CHARACTERISTICS OF ADOLESCENCE (AGES 13 TO 21)

Characteristics

- Period of transition between childhood and adulthood
- Struggle over the lack of clearly defined role in society
- Search for personal identity and independence from parents
- Period of increasing freedom and access to resources
- Adolescents tend to be idealistic and egocentric
- Great confusion of values
- Affiliation and acceptance by peer group is of major importance
- Body experiences a number of internal biological changes as it begins to reach physical maturation
- Psychological reaction to bodily changes creates dissonance
- Interest in potential intimate relationships intensifies
- Have increased time for leisure

Program Implications

- Programs should provide opportunities for social interaction, development, and achievement as leisure experiences can provide the opportunity to establish relationships and desired independence. The majority of leisure opportunities take place in schools and the commercial sector. Some sports leagues are offered by public or private nonprofit organizations.
- Programs should help adolescents develop concepts of adequacy, self-respect, and self-confidence. Adolescents need a sense of who they are as they move from childhood to adulthood.
- Leisure service providers need to recognize that adolescents should be active and will be interested in trying out a wide range of activities; therefore, programs should offer variety and be sensitive to ongoing teenage fads. Areas for adolescents to safely "hang out" allow them to experiment with various roles and behaviors. Adolescent leisure provides a margin of freedom within institutionalized constraints.
- Programs can create opportunities for "rites of passage" into adulthood.

Activities

- **Sports:** Organized sports are very important. Greater emphasis should be placed on helping adolescents develop lifelong sport interests. Outdoor and adventure activities offer many adolescents opportunities for "rites of passage."
- **Social:** Music becomes important, dancing, places to "hang out" with friends, movies.
- **Miscellaneous:** Opportunities to help others, videos.

Adolescence and Leisure

The word *adolescence* comes from a Latin verb meaning "to grow into maturity." Thus, the period of adolescence is about the process of growing up. Table 6.5 presents some general characteristics of adolescence. In many ways, adolescence is a recent phenomenon, as modern society has altered the time whereby children participate fully in adult society. In the past, this transition came at an earlier age and resulted from some specific rite of passage into adulthood; today's adolescent experiences more time to become an adult. Yet this transition period can be difficult and confusing for adolescents—sometimes society expects them to act like adults, and other times encourages them to remain children. As a result, adolescents often seem to withdraw into their own separate society, drawing closer to their friends. In

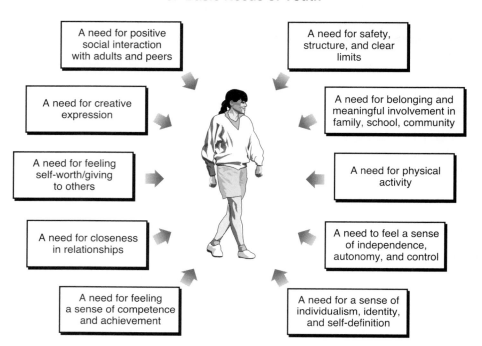

Figure 6.4
Needs that must be met for youth to grow into healthy adults.

Ten Basic Needs of Youth

A need for positive social interaction with adults and peers

A need for safety, structure, and clear limits

A need for creative expression

A need for belonging and meaningful involvement in family, school, community

A need for feeling self-worth/giving to others

A need for physical activity

A need for closeness in relationships

A need to feel a sense of independence, autonomy, and control

A need for feeling a sense of competence and achievement

A need for a sense of individualism, identity, and self-definition

this context adolescents often develop their own taste in music, clothing, hairstyles, social concerns, language, and attitudes.

The adolescent's need to be a part of a group and to "fit in" contrasts with the need to establish his or her own identity. Erikson (1963) notes that adolescents must develop a sense of their own identity, distinct from all others but still personally acceptable, or they will be confused and settle on a negative identity such as "class clown" or engage in even more negative behavior such as drug abuse or becoming a gang member.

Basic Needs of Youth   Various organizations, individuals, and groups have attempted to identify the basic needs of youth that must be met for them to develop into healthy and positive adults. Jaffe (1998) supports the ten basic needs of youth as defined by Pittman (1991) and Scales (1991). Figure 6.4 presents these factors. Leisure programs and services help meet these developmental needs as summarized here.

> *A need for positive social interaction.* Youth want to belong and need opportunities to form positive social relationships with adults and peers. We do this through sports, fine arts clubs, classes, and drop-in programs.

> *A need for safety, structure, and clear limits.* Expectations, structure, and boundaries are important for youth, so that they feel secure and also have a clear picture of the areas that they may or may not explore. Through the rules and guidelines we establish at our own agencies and organizations, youth come to know what is expected of them.

> *A need for belonging and meaningful involvement in family, school, and community.* Youth have a desire to be a part of and to participate in activities related to their families, schools, and communities. Service projects and opportunities such as 4-H often provide this type of involvement.

A need for creative expression. Youth need opportunities to express to others who they are and how they feel. Music, writing, sports, cooking, and other activities help to achieve this goal.

A need for feeling self-worth/giving to others. Involvement in meaningful and worthwhile efforts related to larger goals is extremely important to youth. Volunteer efforts such as community clean-up projects and visiting elderly shut-ins are examples of leisure outreach programs that help youth experience this.

A need for physical activity. Youth have tremendous energy and require a great deal of physical activity and time for fun. Leaders provide these opportunities in almost every program and event they offer.

A need to feel a sense of independence, autonomy, and control. Youth have a desire to mature, to become more independent and to exert some control and influence over their lives. Youth-led groups (music, reading, sports, etc.) provide young people with opportunities for independence and leadership.

A need for closeness in relationships. Youth need opportunities to form close relationships with peers and adults. They also have a need for relationships with caring adult role models. Thus, it is important for leisure services leaders to reach out to youth and establish trusting relationships.

A need for feeling a sense of competence and achievement. It is important for youth to have opportunities to achieve success and to receive recognition. Awards for service, trophies for success, and handshakes for a job well done carry great meaning for young people.

A need for a sense of individualism, identity, and self-definition. Youth need to have opportunities to become individuals and to define their sense of identity and self-concept, based on positive input from others. Opportunities for personal expression, whether it be the clothing one wears, the language one uses, or the activities in which one engages are embedded in leisure opportunities for youth.

Leisure service programmers who provide services in a manner that allows youth to have input, involvement, and ownership; a sense of achievement and recognition; opportunities for creative expression and physical activity; and opportunities for social interaction will find that youth will seek to participate. Further, these youth will show evidence of benefits from their participation.

Youth Development: A Program Framework As programmers identify and understand the needs of adolescents, a shift in delivering services to youth is being promoted. This shift toward a youth development approach encourages youth workers to see youth as resources to be developed rather than problems to be fixed. Whereas addressing the problems facing youth such as violence, substance abuse, and school failure is critical, it is not enough. Young people who are not on drugs, not dropouts, not in gangs, and not teen parents are viewed as "problem free," but are they prepared for work, for family, for citizenship? The commitment to prevention must be matched with an equal commitment to the promotion of positive personal and social development.

To this end, Edginton, Kowalski and Randall (2005), building upon the academic work of Edginton and de Oliveira (1995), developed a framework for youth programming that fosters the basic needs of youth and provides a structure for youth development competencies to grow. Their programming model is presented in figure 6.5 and consists of the following thirteen program areas:

- Peer-Mentoring: Youth providing guidance and counseling to other youth.
- Academic enrichment: Learning opportunities directed toward advancing knowledge, skills, or ability.

Figure 6.5

Youth
programming
model.

*From: Edginton,
C.R., Kowalski,
C.L., & Randall,
S.W., (2005). Youth
work: Emerging
perspectives in
youth development.
Champaign, IL:
Sagamore*

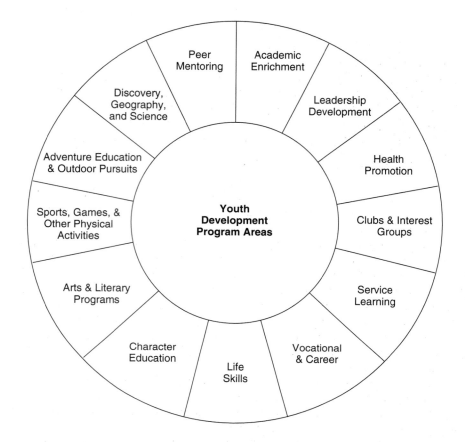

- Leadership development: Building leadership competencies and abilities.
- Health promotion: Encouraging positive healthy behaviors and lifestyles.
- Club and interest groups: Facilitating the need for youth to be with one another and engage in common activities.
- Service learning: Providing opportunities for youth to support community needs in a meaningful and learning way.
- Vocational/career: Assisting youth to find vocational interests and develop vocational/career skills.
- Life skills: Developing life skills that help youth meet daily challenges.
- Character education: Developing certain values and characteristics in youth.
- Arts and literary programs: Enabling youth to develop creative and cultural aspects of themselves.
- Sport, games, and physical activity: Developing of physical skills and endurance.
- Adventure education/outdoor pursuits: Exposing youth to risk and opportunities to gain an awareness of the self through adventure and outdoor pursuits.
- Discovery, geography, and science: Enabling youth to discover the physical environment.

Youth development is an ongoing process in which young people are engaged and invested. Throughout this process, young people seek ways to meet their basic physical and social needs and to build the competencies and connections they need for survival and success. Youth development is multidimensional, can be viewed from a variety of perspectives, and is marked by the acquisition

Five Competencies That Youth Should Master to Become Successful Adults

Citizenship competence
• Understand nation/community history/values

Personal/social competence
• Understand personal emotions
• Develop friendships
• Self-discipline
• Coping skills
• Judgment skills

Cognitive/creative competence
• Broad base of knowledge
• Creative expression
• Language skills
• Interest in learning

Health/physical competence
• Food/current health knowledge/skills to ensure future well-being

Vocational competence
• Awareness of vocational/career options
• Understand value of work/leisure

of a broad range of competencies and the demonstration of a full complement of connections to self, others, and the larger communities. With this in mind, Pittman and Wright (1991) note that there is no universally accepted definition of youth development, but rather it may be more profitable to focus on competencies that assist youth in their development.

Youth Development Competencies   In addition to these ten basic needs of youth, five basic areas of youth development objectives or *competencies* have been developed based on a review of the youth development factors that are seen as being important by youth-serving organizations (see figure 6.6). Five competencies that youth should acquire in order to be successful as adults, as adapted from Pittman (1991), Jaffe (1998), and Unger, Simon, Newman, and Montgomery (1998), include:

Health/physical competence. Youth need to have good current health status and appropriate knowledge, attitudes, and behaviors to ensure future health (exercise, good diet, nutrition).

Personal/social competence. It is important that youth gain intrapersonal skills (ability to understand personal emotions, have self-discipline); interpersonal skills (ability to work with others, develop friendships and relationships through communication, cooperation, empathizing, negotiating); coping skills (ability to adapt, assume responsibility); and judgment skills (plan, make decisions, solve problems) to be successful in a rapidly changing world.

Cognitive/creative competence. Youth need to develop a broad base of knowledge, the ability to appreciate/participate in areas of creative expression, good oral and written language skills, problem-solving and analytical skills, and the ability to learn along with an interest in learning and achieving throughout the life cycle.

Vocational competence. It is important for youth to develop a broad understanding and awareness of vocational (and avocational) options and of the steps necessary to act on their choices to make adequate career preparations, and to understand the value and function of work and leisure.

Citizenship competencies (ethics and preparation). Youth need to understand their nation's and community's history and values, and desire to contribute to their nation and community. All of society benefits from young people meeting this competency.

As youth move toward mastering these competencies, they also progress in their feelings of achievement and self-esteem. Youth need to be good at something to feel good about themselves. Parks, recreation, and leisure opportunities facilitate this development of self-concept.

However, it is important to remember that competency frameworks can be problematic if used universally or without caution. Although competency frameworks are often viewed as being attractive because they describe a variety of desirable traits and characteristics that our society wishes for its young people to possess, not all youth are the same—all youth come from different cultural and ethnic backgrounds, which hold diverse values (Edginton, Kowalski, and Randall, 2005). As such, it is important that leisure professional and youth service workers respect the cultural values of youth (Edginton, Kowalski, and Randall, 2005). While competency frameworks are useful for attracting support for the youth development movement, Magnuson (1999) highlighted five problematic aspects of competency frameworks: 1) they do not identify a normative moral criterion, 2) they make effectiveness a moral criterion, 3) they conflate moral commitment into obedience to rules, 4) they use lists of positive competencies that are arbitrary and relative, and 5) the skills, traits, and competencies they list present conceptual difficulties.

Leisure activities during youth can promote and maintain autonomy from parents while also strengthening the bond between friends. Leisure activities often provide opportunities for explicit learning about "forbidden" topics such as sexuality, tolerance for others, and a context where one can look back on youth with nostalgic sentimentality. Properly planned leisure options for adolescents can provide a margin of freedom within institutionalized constraints and can increase self-esteem. The social significance of leisure is great for adolescents. Leisure fosters opportunities for social contacts, development, and achievement.

Although adolescents comprise one of the most active groups in terms of leisure participation, they are also one of the most difficult groups to serve for public and private, nonprofit organizations. As public and private nonprofit organizations seek to better serve this group they should consider examining the success of the commercial sector in addressing the needs of adolescents. To meet their needs, programs and facilities should offer adolescents a safe place to hang out, places where teens can have the opportunity to establish sociosexual relationships, and desired independence. While programs should offer variety and be sensitive to changing teen fads, they need to invest in people who can build a relationship with teens. Many successful programs build on relationships with people whom teenagers feel they can trust and share confidences, rather than on activities or facilities.

An interesting framework in working with youth has been advanced by the Search Institute in Minneapolis, Minnesota. This organization has established a framework to identify the assets/deficits required in building a strong community foundation to support youth. Basically, they suggest that communities should identify their assets and deficits and then work to strengthen the former while diminishing the latter. There is a great deal of emphasis in the literature today focused on youth development that encourages the involvement of youth in community life in a positive way. The Search Institute's asset/deficit model enables communities to inventory their resources and then work to insure that youth have a positive environment within which to develop.

Adulthood and Leisure

Adulthood is considered a period of establishment for most individuals; however, the establishment process does not happen overnight. For some, the transition to adulthood happens abruptly with a first full-time job or a move out on their own. For others, this transition is gradual as families continue to help children during early adulthood (e.g., helping with college tuition or helping young adults become established in their first residence). The period of adulthood, the longest period in life, spans from approximately age twenty to death. Therefore, rather than considering adulthood as a single period, it makes sense to envision it as several periods with different preoccupations, interests, and changing patterns of leisure. The periods examined within this chapter are early, middle, and late adulthood. The characteristics of each of these periods are presented in tables 6.6 through 6.8.

TABLE

6.6	CHARACTERISTICS OF EARLY ADULTHOOD (AGES 21 TO 30)

Characteristics

- Establishes autonomy from parents while still seeking to maintain some type of connection
- Builds life structure (marriage, family, friendships)
- Completes formal schooling, concern for occupation increases, emphasis is placed on success in a career
- Develops an identification with social institutions
- Develops the ability to be intimate and to make commitments
- Structures a dream of the future

Program Implications for Leisure Service Organizations

- Early in this stage recreation is commercial and school based. As people establish families and settle down, however, recreation tends to be more home based, especially when children are young and money is tight. Public recreation agencies can become important as families are established. Leisure activities with new couples and young families can encourage interactions and development of shared commitments to a new life together.
- This stage can be a time of new experiences; organizations should attempt to offer variety and opportunities to try new things.
- Opportunities for continued sociosexual contact and activity are still important as are activities which have a strong physical component.

Activities

- **Sports:** Outdoor pursuits (rock climbing, waterskiing, backpacking), team sports (softball, basketball, volleyball) still important, starting to make the transition to lifelong sports such as tennis and golf. Spectator sports are enjoyed.
- **Social Activities:** Movies, concerts, music, dancing, dating and courting, and bars.
- **Miscellaneous:** Shopping, television, and videos.

TABLE

6.7   CHARACTERISTICS OF MIDDLE ADULTHOOD (AGES 31 TO 50)

Characteristics

- Settling down, established in career and family
- Self-reflection of goals and decisions, can be a period of skepticism and self-questioning
- Adjustment to aging parents; often involves some type of care for parents
- Career development becomes a predominant concern as individuals seek to fulfill their earlier dreams
- Physical maturity peaks in the early thirties and then begins to decline
- Deadline decade—the halfway point of one's life brings with it the realization of one's own mortality; that there is a limited amount of time left to find fulfillment in life, which can lead to midlife crisis
- Divorce and career changes can happen frequently as people search for fulfillment
- As culture bearers, norms and values of culture are passed on to maturing children
- Involvement in civic and community organizations increases

Program Implications for Leisure Service Organizations

- Leisure pursuits are among the significant means of achieving family growth as well as individual emotional health. Leisure is found primarily in the commercial sector with some involvement in public and private, nonprofit sectors (especially with children). The most frequent leisure activities are home and family centered.
- Physical activities are needed as the body starts to decline. Physical activities can improve a person's general well-being as well as improve work performance.
- Leisure service organizations should not be bound by stereotypes of what this group of people want to do in their free time. A variety of experiences need to be offered in innovative ways (e.g., time schedules, settings, bundling of services) to meet the varied needs of individuals and family units during this stage of life.
- Activities begun in the early thirties determine the quality of subsequent life. Attention should be paid to making an orderly transition into lifetime sports and other activities that can be enjoyed throughout the rest of one's life.
- Emphasis should be placed on self-directed rather than leader-directed activities.

Activities

- **Sports:** Golf, tennis, swimming, bicycling, volleyball, bowling, and exercising. Involvement in team sports continues to diminish. Spectator sports, car camping, hunting, and fishing become prevalent.
- **Social:** Social interactions become more prevalent and socializing becomes more important than sexualizing. Traveling becomes feasible again. Trips and tours can be important leisure outlets.
- **Miscellaneous:** Gardening, hobbies, crafts, driving.

For most young adults, issues revolve more around socialization than work. Erikson (1963) identifies the major theme of early adulthood as the quest for intimacy and personal identity, where individuals work to establish independence from parents and build lives of their own. This identity development is related to both the personal identity (who am I?) as well as social identity (how do I fit into society?) (Kleiber, 1999). Two major changes that usually occur within this time period dramatically influence leisure pursuits. The first is marriage or choosing a partner, and the second is the addition of children.

Marriage or choosing a partner tends to be the first step in settling down and scaling back on the wilder aspects of leisure. Drinking and carousing with friends are often curtailed and the dating games of "cat and mouse" cease. However, Kelly (1996) indicates that the arrival of the first child makes the most significant changes in lifestyle and leisure behavior.

TABLE

6.8 CHARACTERISTICS OF LATE ADULTHOOD (AGES 51 TO 65)

Characteristics

- "Empty nest syndrome" encourages couples to reconnect with each other; adjusting to being grandparents
- Fulfillment or failure of life goals
- Search for meaning in past living and current life
- Concern with unmet needs of self
- Start of physical deterioration: bodies take longer to recover from exhaustion and show lack of endurance
- Transition from job to retirement: anxiety over loss of work role. Increase in concern over issues such as social security, health care, and leisure activities during retirement
- Shift from body to intellect
- Assume role of mentor
- Involvement continues to increase in professional organizations, service, civic, and social clubs as well as religious organizations

Program Implications for Leisure Service Organizations

- Leisure serves three basic functions during this time: acceptance, dispel personal despair, and give structure to increasing free time. Majority of leisure takes place in the commercial sector during this time period.
- In some instances this group has an increase in free time as children leave the home. Leisure programs and activities can encourage individuals in this age group to volunteer and share their expertise in a variety of ways.
- Programming should continue to take a self-directed focus rather than a leader-directed focus although individuals need to be informed about the leisure/recreation opportunities that are available to them and educated about the importance of developing meaningful leisure pursuits for retirement.

Activities

- **Sports:** Spectator sports, fishing, bowling, golf, tennis, walking, exercise, bicycling, swimming. For the majority, team sports have come to an end.
- **Social:** Increased group participation and socializing; involvement in social organizations often increases.
- **Miscellaneous:** Gardening, relaxing, reading, church related activities, picnics, hobbies, travel, and service to others.

This results from several factors, including the additional planning required to participate in leisure opportunities and the decrease in income that may occur if one parent (traditionally the female) quits paid employment to care for the baby. Following the arrival of the first child, leisure becomes much more home based as the family becomes the focus of most leisure activities. Leisure is often used as a bonding experience for the development of family cohesion (Kleiber, 1999).

As individuals move into middle adulthood the focus shifts away from the issues of intimacy and establishment of a family to the establishment of a career. Levinson (1978) identifies two divergent themes of this settling-down period. One aspect of this period involves order, stability, security, and control. A second, contrasting element, is "making it": "This involves planning, striving, moving onward and upward, having an inner timetable that contains major goals and way stations by which they must be reached" (Levinson, 1978, p. 285). Many of those who fail to reach their professional goals turn to leisure as a way to find or add meaning to their lives. Many hobbies and avocations are begun or renewed at this life stage (Kleiber, 1999).

In the past, "making it" meant that the husband usually devoted time and attention to his occupation or profession while the wife's primary concern was for the family unit. These stereotypical roles have changed and continue to change as women pursue promising careers themselves, and men take a more active role in raising the family. As the desire to establish oneself in a career intensifies, leisure becomes an important outlet for achieving and maintaining marital and family stability and growth as well as maintaining individual emotional health.

Physical activities and exercise are important to maintaining good health as individuals begin to realize their mortality during this time. When a person reaches his or her thirties, the realization comes that one's body will not last forever, and the need to take care of it becomes paramount. Lifelong sports become increasingly important as participation in team sports begins to decline slightly. This age period exhibits a greater tendency toward a consumer model of leisure behavior—planned vacations, buying a boat or recreational vehicle, dining out, and the like. As a result, leisure takes place more in the commercial sector with limited involvement in public and private, nonprofit organizations due to their children's participation.

Toward the end of middle adulthood, the mid to late forties, many individuals experience midlife transition. For some this becomes a midlife crisis, while for others it becomes a time to rethink priorities, evaluate life, and make subtle changes. This period sees a number of major life changes. Children leave home for college and other endeavors, the career pinnacle may be reached, physical endurance and flexibility begin to decline, and bodies take longer to recover from exertion.

The role of leisure during this stage varies from person to person. Kleiber (1999, p. 53) states, ". . . more free time and greater financial security often provide ideal conditions for self-expression in leisure at this time." Furthermore, Kelly (1987) indicates:

> Some look back, settle for where they have been and what they have become, and seek security and acceptance. Others want something more in the limited time remaining and prepare to make changes in their priorities and allocations. . . . Dignity may most often be sought in what is known and safe. Autonomy may be sought in some new context, investment, or enterprise. What is evident is that leisure may rise in salience as options in other roles are closed off. (p. 85)

According to Gorden and Gaitz (1976), leisure can serve three basic functions during this stage. First, it can bring acceptance from others, replacing the earlier focus on establishment and achievement. Second, developing meaningful leisure helps avoid personal despair, which Erikson (1963) notes as a major problem of this life stage. Third, it structures time when people are beginning to reexperience more free time. Leisure continues to be commercially based and less home centered as decreasing financial responsibilities create more economic resources for leisure.

Leisure needs of adults vary; tables 6.6 to 6.8 present specific implications for leisure service professionals. However, some general considerations cut through the various stages of adulthood and should be considered in serving the leisure needs of this age group. These considerations include:

- Programs should be designed to encourage self-directed leisure behavior. Adults are generally more self-directed than at any other times in their lives. Their leisure behaviors are more likely to be self-motivated, experientially based, related to life tasks, focused on the present, and intrinsically motivated.
- Programs need to promote lifelong sports and activities as well as encourage new leisure behaviors early in adulthood. As evidenced in figure 6.2, people tend to seek less novelty and thus tend to participate in previously tried activities as they enter retirement. To ensure a varied leisure lifestyle during retirement, leisure service professionals should encourage new leisure pursuits throughout adulthood.

- A variety of experiences offered in innovative ways (e.g., time schedules, settings, bundling of services) will meet the varied needs of individuals and families during this stage of life. For example, Jackson and Scott (1999) and Lankford, DeGraaf, and Neal (1996) identify lack of time or conflicts with work schedules as major barriers to leisure participation. Innovative scheduling of programs could increase participation levels of adults in organized programs.

Older Adults and Leisure

Few days can cause so many people so much joy or so much anxiety as the day of their retirement. It is one of the milestones in life. It can signify freedom and the opportunity to pursue long-held dreams, or it can represent a feeling of uselessness, the beginning of the end. Growing old in a world infatuated with youth can be a frightening prospect to be sure, but many people also find retirement to be everything they have dreamed about and more. It is often perceived as time earned (through years of paid employment) to focus on one's self, one's family, and general happiness.

Older Americans comprise the most rapidly growing segment in the United States. Consider the following facts reported by the Administration on Aging (2000):

- In the United States, persons sixty-five years old or older represent approximately 13 percent of the population, about one in every eight Americans.
- By the year 2030, persons aged sixty-five or older are expected to represent 20 percent of the population.
- Eight out of ten persons over the age of sixty-five are women. Among the oldest old, there are 2.6 women for every man.
- Due to recent medical advancements the older population itself is getting older. The oldest old, aged eighty-five and older, are increasing at a faster rate than the total elderly population. In 1900, fewer than one in ten elderly persons was aged eighty-five or more. By 2045, the oldest old will represent one in five of the elderly.

The elderly, like other minority groups, fall victim to stereotyped images that are mainly based on misconceptions. Generally speaking, in the United States attitudes toward the elderly and the aging process are negative. Many believe that the elderly are sick, cognitively deficient, weak, and inactive. Thus, it is important to dispel some of the typical stereotypes of older people. See table 6.9 for many of the positive characteristics of old age.

Contrary to popular belief, only 4.3 percent of the 34.5 million U.S. citizens over sixty-five are confined to nursing homes and institutions. Fourteen percent of people aged sixty-five to sixty-nine need help with personal care such as eating, bathing, or toileting; 45 percent of people aged eighty-five and older need some degree of assistance (Administration on Aging, 2000). Over half of the elderly live with their spouses in independent households, usually in communities where they have roots; 31 percent live alone and only 13 percent live with their children. In addition, most older people are not poor and neglected. Although the number of elderly living at or below the poverty line (figure varies from 20 percent to 30 percent) is a major concern, the median net worth of older households in 1999 was $33,148, which was above the U.S. average of $32,000. Net worth was below $15,000 for 11.5 percent of the older households but was above $35,000 for 46.9 percent of this age group. In 1999, the United States recorded its lowest level of poverty among the elderly ever with only 9.7 percent of older Americans living below the poverty level (Administration on Aging, 2000).

According to Feldman (2003), the three most respected theories of aging are disengagement theory, activity theory, and continuity theory. Disengagement theory posits that late adulthood

TABLE

6.9   CHARACTERISTICS OF OLDER ADULTS (AGES 66+)

Characteristics

- Emphasis shifts from work to leisure: older adults want to stay active and feel good about themselves.
- Issues include integrity/integration vs. despair. In later stages of old age there is an attempt to maintain independence, self-direction, self-esteem, and self-concept.
- Life review and introspection occur during this stage.
- Coping with death, loss, and the prospect of widowhood.
- Physical health declines.
- Tendency to be alone increases.
- Decline in income; incomes often fixed.

Program Implications for Leisure Service Organizations

- The importance of leisure is most evident in offering seniors an identity and purpose for life. The majority of leisure takes place initially in the commercial sector. However, seniors increasingly turn back to public recreation programs. In the end the majority of leisure is home based.
- Meaningful integration is important for individuals in this stage. Opportunities should be created for intergenerational events as well as activities that encourage companionship and socializing.
- Meaningful and purposeful leisure is important rather than just trivial activities created to fill people's time. People want to feel needed; organizations can create opportunities for seniors to volunteer and share their skills and expertise.

Activities

- **Sports:** Spectator sports, golf, tennis, fishing, walking, bowling, swimming, bicycling.
- **Social:** Socializing with extended family and longtime friends, involvement in recreation centers, more activities are done alone. Many activities are centered around children and grandchildren.
- **Miscellaneous:** Gardening, relaxing, reading, church-related activities, picnics, television, hobbies, travel, museums, and board games and cards.

marks a gradual withdrawal from the world on physical, psychological, and social levels. Activity theory suggests that successful aging occurs when people maintain the interests, activities, and social interactions with which they were involved during middle age. Continuity theory holds that people need to maintain their desired level of involvement in society in order to maximize their sense of well-being and self-esteem. In regard to these three theories of aging, Kleiber (1999) underscored that leisure is associated with well-being in later life mainly because leisure opportunities are associated with meaningfulness and engagement. As such, leisure has a foundational role in activity theory and continuity theory.

In this regard, active people in later adulthood are a major market for leisure professionals (Freysinger and Kelly, 2004). Patterson (2002) posited that travel is the number one leisure activity that people want to engage in when they retire—especially among the baby boomers. In fact, older adults travel more often, further, and stay longer than younger adults (Leitner & Leitner, 2004). Teaff and Turpin (1996) reported that the travel priorities of older adults are:

- Visit new places (86.1 percent)
- Spend time with family (74.7 percent)
- Rest and relax (73 percent)

TABLE

6.10   BENEFITS OF LEISURE AMONG OLDER ADULTS

Physiological Benefits	Social/Psychological/Emotional Benefits
Improved circulation	Greater psychological well-being
Improved respiration	Higher quality of life
Greater flexibility	Higher morale and life satisfaction
Greater strength	Higher self-esteem, self-concept, and self-efficacy
Greater endurance	Keener mental ability
More energy	Feelings of achievement and accomplishment
Lower blood pressure	Greater optimism
Lower cholesterol	Greater levels of social interaction
Improved mobility	Laughter
Greater physical independence	Lower anxiety and hostility
Greater longevity	Lower incidence of loneliness and depression
Improved general health	Improved perceived health
Reduced risk of osteoporotic fractures	Reduced fear of falling
Reduced risk of falls	

Source: Leitner, M. J., and Leitner, S. F. 2004. *Leisure in later life.* 3rd ed. New York: Haworth Press.

- Escape everyday routine (68 percent)
- Experience new things (67.8 percent)
- Spend time with friends (64.7 percent)
- Visit museums and historical sites (62.6 percent)
- Visits festivals and special events (58.4 percent)

Leitner and Leitner (2004) remind us that providing leisure programs in later life is vast and can include leisure service in senior centers, social clubs, adult day care facilities, residential communities, outreach programs, nursing homes, and regular leisure sites, just to name a few. Furthermore, table 6.10, adapted from Leitner and Leitner, illustrates the many benefits that leisure activity provide for people who are in later adulthood.

For leisure service organizations that are concerned about the growth and well-being of the individual, it seems appropriate to ascribe to the activity theory the caution that programs should offer worthwhile activities rather than time-fillers. Programming for this life stage should emphasize:

Choice. Individuals want to be able to decide on their own activities and their own level of participation. Drop-in senior centers that offer a wide variety of flexible programming often meet these needs.

Participant involvement. Recreation professionals must provide opportunities for seniors themselves to be involved in the planning process. Their voices must be solicited, heard, and acted upon.

Integrated rather than segregated activities. In today's fast-paced world, generations are often isolated from each other. As a result, the old fear the young, the young don't understand their elders, and society suffers growing tensions between generations. Leisure can provide a forum to bridge these gaps.

Retiring Where the Mariachis Play

In Mexico, a retired couple can live luxuriously on $1,500 a month.

Retiring to Mexico may seem like an exotic, bougainvillea-filled dream, yet 1 million Americans and Canadians, both retired and working, already live there. Increased trade under the NAFTA treaty, along with the reasonable cost of living, are likely to increase the number of Americans who choose retirement Mexico-style.

That's the hope of FONATUR, the National Trust Fund for the Development of Tourism in Mexico. The organization's objective is to draw tourists to Mexico and to convert some of them—70 percent of whom are American—into residents.

To make moving to Mexico enticing to natives of the United States and Canada, FONATUR develops residential communities such as Loreto, which is in Baja California Sur, 660 miles from the U.S. border. More than 700 Americans already call Loreto home, according to Jim Moore, president of the research firm Moore Diversified Services (MDS) of Fort Worth, Texas. MDS was hired by FONATUR to determine what influences Americans to move to Mexico.

Americans who move to Mexico typically first experience the country as tourists, Moore says. They often repeat their visits to Mexico and finally settle on a favorite area for permanent or semi-permanent residency.

The cost of living in Mexico is not as low for Americans as it was ten years ago, but the U.S. dollar still stretches farther in Mexico than it does in the 50 states. The low cost of health-care services available in Mexico also attracts nonnative residents, especially retirees. The country lacks some sophisticated treatments, however, and this discourages some potential residents, according to MDS's research. In addition, in-home healthcare and assisted-living arrangements need to be more readily available.

Frequent visitors to Mexico aren't the only ones who consider retiring there. South of the Border Tour & Travel of Petaluma, California, has seen strong demand for its "retire to Mexico" tours since it started the program in April 1994, says Loujean LaMalfa, the company's president. LaMalfa started the tours after she had difficulty getting information to plan her own retirement to Mexico.

South of the Border coordinates tours to the Guadalajara-Lake Chapala region in west-central Mexico, which is one of the three most popular areas for American retirees. Cuernavaca and San Miguel Allende are the other two. The Lake Chapala area—including Guadalajara and the smaller communities of Ajijic, Chapala Town, and Tlaquepaque—is home to 40,000 Americans.

The majority of those taking the retirement tour are already retired. Many have tried life-in-the-sun cities of Florida and Arizona and are dissatisfied. "By the time they sign up for the tour, they've done their homework. Now they want a first-hand look at life in Mexico," says South of the Border's LaMalfa. She tries to give that to tour participants by including dinners in private homes with longtime American retirees to Mexico.

Although many retirees are couples, life in Mexico is attractive to singles as well. A single person with a monthly income of $900 can live quite comfortably, while a couple with $1,500 a month will have no trouble leading a luxurious life. In the Lake Chapala region, attractively furnished two-bedroom apartments rent for about $500 a month. Buying a retirement home in Mexico is also well within the reach of many retirees. Houses sell for $40,000 to $65,000.

Being innovative. Leisure service organizations should not be bound by traditional rules and expectations when providing activities for older adults, but rather can modify traditional sports and games to facilitate seniors' involvement.

Being sensitive. Leisure service organizations must be sensitive to the needs of older adults, with barrier-free and accessible facilities. Equipment and facilities should be user-friendly with something for everyone.

Summary

A number of variables impact leisure throughout the life cycle. This chapter examined generational and environmental factors, level of education, culture, and lifestyle, followed by an overview of leisure throughout the life cycle. The use of a developmental approach emphasizes an attempt by leisure professionals to understand the life stages of participants and create programs to assist individuals in their growth and development. The concept of stages, or life stages, implies that life involves a series of connected stages, each influencing one another yet each being distinctive.

Leisure service organizations play an active role in offering programs and activities to the public. These organizations must be innovative and creative in programming for individuals throughout the life cycle—as the individual participant changes and evolves, so must programs. In designing play spaces for children or creating programs for children or adults, leisure service professionals should note the following:

> We must remember that our field is experimental, should be experimental and will not survive unless it continues to be experimental. It is not written in stone what a playground should look like, or that there should be playgrounds. Nor can we say what a park should look like, how and to whom leisure skills should be taught or who should teach them. As Cranz (1982) so wisely observed, many recreation and park professionals have developed the mistaken idea concomitant with professionalization that providing park and recreation services is a matter of technology when in reality it is a process of cultural discovery. Said another way, it is a process rather than a product. (Godbey, 1991, p. 5)

If leisure professionals can be innovative and responsive in meeting the recreational and developmental needs of the people served, then the future looks bright for the profession.

Discussion Questions

1. Explain the stages of human development as they relate to understanding a person's leisure lifestyle throughout life.
2. Interview one of your friends, your parents, your grandparents, or an older family member; ask them to discuss what leisure means to them. What activities do they remember doing as a child? Compare and contrast these different views of leisure. In the people you interviewed, how does generation affect their leisure pursuits and attitudes?
3. What environmental factors (as defined in this chapter) would affect leisure in your city, state, province, or region?
4. How does education level affect leisure participation? Why do you think this is the case?
5. Define the term *lifestyle*. What factors make up an individual's lifestyle?
6. In understanding leisure behavior, why is the concept of life stage more important than age?
7. When is a person's leisure repertoire the greatest and why?
8. Visit a playground and watch children play for thirty minutes. What changes would you make in the playground to better meet the needs of the children playing there?
9. Interview three teenagers. Discuss the role of leisure in their lives. What could leisure service organizations do to better meet their leisure needs?
10. What are the major considerations in serving the leisure needs of people in the various stages of adulthood?

References

AARP. 2000. AARP/Roper Baby Boomer Study. [available on-line at
    http://research.aarp.org/econ/boomer_seg_3.html].
Administration on Aging. 2000. Profile of Older Americans 2000. [available on-line at www.aoa.dhhs.gov].

Alvord, K. 2000. *Divorce your car! Ending the love affair with the automobile.* Gabriola Island, BC: New Society Publishers.

Beals, K. A. 2000. Subclinical eating disorders in female athletes. *Journal of Physical Education, Recreation, and Dance 71*(7), 3–29.

Blum, V. L. 2003. *Flesh wounds: The culture of cosmetic surgery.* Berkeley, CA: University of California Press.

Brill, N. n.d. *Working with People: The Helping Process.* Philadelphia, PA: Lippincott.

Carlson, C., S. Uppal, and E. Prosser. 2000. Ethnic differences in processes contributing to the self-esteem of early adolescent girls. *The Journal of Early Adolescence 20*(10), 44–67.

Carnegie Corporation of New York. 1992. *A Matter of Time: Risk and Opportunity in the Non-School Hours.* New York: Carnegie Corporation.

Coakley, J. 2004. *Sports in society: Issues and controversies* 8th ed. Boston: McGraw-Hill.

Culp, R. 1998. Adolescent girls and outdoor recreation: A case study examining constraints and effective programming. *Journal of Leisure Research 30*(3), 356–379.

DiFiori. 1999. Overuse injuries in children and adolescents. *The Physician and Sportsmedicine, 27*(1), 22–27.

Driesen, J. J. 2005. Muscle dysmorphia. Retrieved January 26, 2005, from www.driesen.com/muscle_dysmorphia.htm.

Driver, B. L., and Bruns, D. H. 1999. Concepts and uses of the benefits approach to leisure. In E. L. Jackson and T. L. Burton (eds.), *Leisure studies: Prospects for the twenty-first century* (pp. 349–369). State College, PA: Venture.

Edginton, C.R., and de Oliveria, W. 1995. Youth development: A program framework. *PERS Review Hong Kong 1*(2), 22–27.

Edginton, C. R., Hudson, S. R., Dieser, R. B., and Edginton, S. R. 2004. *Leisure programming: A service-centered and benefits approach.* 4th ed. Boston: WCB McGraw-Hill.

Edginton, C. R., Kowalski, C. L., and Randall, S. W. 2005. *Youth work: Emerging perspectives in youth development.* Champaign, IL: Sagamore.

Erikson, E. 1963. *Childhood and Society.* New York: W. W. Norton.

Ewing, M., and V. Seefeldt. 1990. *American Youth and Sports Participation.* North Palm Beach, FL: Athletic Footwear Association.

Feldman, R. S. 2003. *Development across the life span.* 3rd ed. Upper Saddle River, NJ: Prentice Hall.

Forum on Child and Family Statistics. 2000. Quality of life indicators. [available on-line at www.childstats.gov].

Freysinger, V. J., and Kelly, J. R. 2004. *21st century leisure: Current issues.* State College, PA: Venture.

Godbey, G. 1991. Recreation and leisure in the 1990s: They are playing our song. *J. B. Nash Lecture.* Presented at the American Alliance of Health, Physical Education, Recreation and Dance National Convention, April 6. San Francisco, CA.

Godbey, G. 1994. *Leisure in Your Life: An Exploration.* State College, PA: Venture.

Godbey, G. 1997. *Leisure in the 21st Century.* State College, PA: Venture.

Gorden, C., and C. Gaitz. 1976. Leisure and lives: Personal expressivity across the life span. Edited by R. Binstock and E. Shanas, in *Handbook of Aging and the Social Sciences,* 310–332. New York: Van Nostrand Reinhold.

Grey, D., and S. Greben. 1974. Future perspectives. *California Parks and Recreation* 11–19 (June–July).

Hansel, T. 1979. *When I Relax I Feel Guilty.* Elgin, IL: David Cook.

Huizinga, J. 1962. *Homo Ludens—A Study of the Play Element in Culture.* Boston, MA: Beacon Press.

Jaffe, M. 1998. *Adolescence.* New York: Wiley.

Jackson, E., and D. Scott. 1999. Constraints to leisure, in Jackson, E. and T. Burton (eds.), *Leisure Studies: Prospects for the Twenty-first Century.* State College, PA: Venture.

Jordan, D. 2001. (2d ed.) *Leadership in Leisure Services: Making a Difference.* State College, PA: Venture.

Kelly, J. 1978. Leisure styles and choices in three environments. *Pacific Sociological Review 21*(4), 187–207.

Kelly, J. 1987. *Freedom to Be: A New Sociology of Leisure.* New York: Macmillan.

Kelly, J. 1996. *Leisure.* 3d ed. Boston: Allyn & Bacon.

Kleiber, D. 1999. *A dialectical interpretation: leisure experience and human development.* New York: Basic Books.

Kleiber, D. 1999. *Leisure experience and human development: A dialectical interpretation.* New York: Basic Books.

Lankford, S., D. DeGraaf, and L. Neal. 1996. A comparison of barriers to leisure and sport satisfaction in the United States: Implications for Hong Kong. *Hong Kong Recreation Review 8* (January), 343–346.

Leitner, M. J., and Leitner, S. F. 2004. *Leisure in later life.* 3rd ed. New York: Haworth Press.

Leshner, A. I. 2000. *Steroid abuse and addiction.* (NIH Publication No. 00-3721). Washington, DC: U.S. Department of Health and Human Services.

Levinson, D. 1978. *The Seasons of a Man's Life.* New York: Knopf.

Magnuson, D. 1999. *Social interdependence: The goal structure of moral experience.* Unpublished doctoral dissertation, University of Minnesota, Minneapolis.

Mechikoff, R. A., and Estes, S. G. 2002. *The history and philosophy of sport and physical education: From ancient civilization to the modern world.* 3rd ed. Boston: McGraw-Hill.

Muuss, R. 1982. *Theories of Adolescence*. New York: Random House.

National Recreation and Park Association. 1992. The 21st century, part 1, park and recreation agenda. *Parks and Recreation* (July), 53–57.

National Sporting Goods Association. 2001. www.usga.org/public/articles/details

Obesity in young children. 2004. *The National Institute for Health Care Management* (August), 1–12. Retrieved from: www.nihcm.org/pubsmain.html.

Patterson, I. 2002. Baby boomers and adventure tourism: The importance of marketing the leisure experience. *World Leisure* 44(2), 4–10.

Pittman, K. J. 1991. *Promoting Youth Development: Strengthening the Role of Youth Serving Community Organizations*. New York: Center for Youth Development and Policy Research.

Pittman, K. J., and M. Wright. 1991. *A Rationale for Enhancing the Role of the Non-School Voluntary Sector in Youth Development*. New York: Center for Youth Development and Policy Research.

Pronger, B. 2002. *Body fascism: Salvation in the technology of physical fitness*. Toronto, ON: University of Toronto Press.

Rogers, M. 1999. *Barbie culture*. Thousand Oaks, CA: Sage.

Ross, J., and R. Pate. 1987. A summary of findings of The National Children and Youth Fitness Study. *Journal of Physical Education, Recreation and Dance*, 51–56.

Salkind, N. 1985. *Theories of Human Development*. New York: Wiley.

Scales, P. 1991. *A Portrait of Young Adolescents in the 1990s*. Carborro, NC: Center for Early Adolescence.

Seefeldt, V. 1996. The future of youth sports in America. Edited by F. Smoll and R. Smith, in *Children and Youth in Sport: A Biopsychosocial Perspective*. Dubuque, IA: Brown & Benchmark.

Sessoms, H. D. 1985. Lifestyles and life cycles: A recreation programming approach. Edited by T. Goodale and P. Witt, in *Recreation and Leisure: Issues in an Era of Change*, 221–243.

Teaff, J. D., and Turpin, T. 1996. Travel and the elderly. *Parks and Recreation 6*, p. 1.

Thomsen, S. R., Bower, D. W., and Barnes, M. D. 2004. Photographic images in women's health, fitness, and sports magazines and the physical self-concept of a group of adolescent female volleyball players. *Journal of Sport and Social Issues* 28(3), 266–283.

Trager, S. 2004. Preventing weight problems before they become too hard to solve. *The State Education Standard: The Journal of the National Association of State Boards of Education* 5(2), 13–20.

Troiano, R., K. Flegal, R. Kuczmarski, S. Campbell, and C. Johnson. 1995. Overweight prevalence and trends for children and adolescents: The national health and nutrition examination surveys, 1963–1991. *Archives of Pediatrics and Adolescent Medicine 149* (October), 1011–1023.

Unger, J., T. Simon, T. Newman, and S. Montgomery. 1998. Early adolescent street youth: An overlooked population with unique problems and service needs. *Journal of Early Adolescence* 18(4), 325–348.

United States Surgeon General. 2001. *The Surgeon General's call to action to prevent and decrease overweight and obesity*. Rockville, MD: Office of the Surgeon General, U.S. Department of Health and Human Services.

U.S. Department of Health and Human Services. 1996. *Physical Activity and Health: A Report of the Surgeon General*. Atlanta: CDC.

Wechsler, H., McKenna, M. L., Lee, S. M., and Dietz, W. H. 2004. The role of schools in preventing childhood obesity. *The State Education Standard: The Journal of the National Association of State Boards of Education* 5(2), 4–12.

PART
TWO

Delivering Leisure Services

The leisure service delivery system in North America involves local, state, and federal agencies, non-profit organizations, and commercial businesses. Such agencies provide a vast array of programs and services.

CHAPTER

Delivery of Leisure Services: Local Government

Leisure activities and programs provide opportunities for families to enjoy one another. Here, a family hikes down a path in a local park.

Introduction

Evolving from needs created by the Industrial Revolution in the mid- and late-1800s in both Canada and the United States, the provision of local leisure services has contributed much to society. Local park and recreation and human service departments today provide a wide array of leisure activities, facilities, areas, and information. Organized and structured to meet specific community needs, such agencies vary tremendously in size, scope, and impact.

The term *local park and recreation services* refers to those public services that are provided at the subdivision of government with the closest relationship to the consumer. A local government can be a city, town, county, or other self-governed district. Such communities, usually incorporated, are granted powers via various types of laws to provide community services. Park and recreation services, from the turn of the century, have been considered to be an essential component of municipal services. Some of the services provided by local governmental agencies include police protection, fire protection, sewage, sanitation, community development, housing, protective inspection and regulation, public welfare, public works, corrections—and parks and recreation services.

This chapter explores a number of topics to help the reader gain a full understanding of and appreciation for the structure and processes of local park and recreation services. Initially, the characteristics of local park and recreation services are discussed, followed by a definition of the three types of governmental organizations within which park and recreation services are provided at the local level—municipal government, county government, and special districts. Further, a discussion of the types of services provided by local public park and recreation agencies—and professional roles and opportunities within them—is covered. Last, the current status and prospects for the future of this sector of the profession are reviewed.

Characteristics of Local Leisure Service Agencies

In terms of customer awareness, local park and recreation agencies are often perceived as the most obvious representation of the leisure service movement. People living in local communities relate, in a direct and tangible way, to their city's parks, swimming pools, playgrounds, community centers, and other leisure facilities and amenities. The availability of park and recreation services is often viewed as a strong determinant in the decisions made by large corporations to locate their businesses. As early as 1985 Naisbett and Aburdene noted in their book, *Re-inventing the Corporation,* that a major factor influencing the selection of an organization of an area in which to locate is the livability of the environment. Leisure amenities, as reflected in park and recreation opportunities, contribute significantly to the livability factor. This fact is reinforced by Kreck (2000), who cites a National League of Cities poll that found the most important qualities of a family-friendly city were, in order, education, community safety, recreation, and citizen involvement. Local park and recreation departments are often charged with increasing the quality of life of their citizens. This section presents a discussion of the goals, resource bases, orientation to customers, and other distinguishing characteristics of local leisure service agencies.

Goals and Functions

What are the goals of local park, and recreation agencies? In the broadest context, local park and recreation departments are primarily motivated by service to their customers. An organization categorized as a service provider has as its primary mission meeting the needs, wants, and desires of those target populations it serves. Individuals who provide public service are engaged in an activity for the general good—planning, organizing, staffing, and implementing activities that result in the provision of service to the general public.

Edginton (1978), Edginton and Neal (1983), Hastings (1984), and Howat and Edginton (1986) have conducted comprehensive studies of goals of local park and recreation departments. Over the past twenty years, these individuals have studied the goals of local park and recreation agencies in Australia, Canada, and the United States. The discussion here is limited to findings from Canada and the United States. In these studies, agency respondents rated fifty-nine goal statements in terms of actual or current importance and what the status of the goal should be in the future.

The major findings of these studies indicated strong concern for the maintenance of parks and other areas and facilities, along with general support for providing services to children, higher rankings for provision of services for seniors (in the United States), and higher rankings for providing services to people with special needs (in Canada). In both Canada and the United States "ensuring that their organizations received a fair share of the tax dollar" was ranked highly by directors. Concerns about securing fees and charges were more highly ranked in the United States than in Canada. Goal statements dealing with the realization of benefits or behaviors by participants were ranked low. The highest ranking item dealing with the realization of benefits by participants was to "enhance health and physical fitness" (Edginton, 1978).

Regarding the future level of importance of various goal statements, directors of local park and recreation departments ranked the following goals highly: (1) supplying adequate land for the future, (2) receiving a fair share of tax dollars, (3) effective management of staff, (4) long-range planning, and (5) maintaining parks, areas, and facilities. Goal statements

Park Box Donations Don't Cut It

The Des Moines Parks and Recreation Department is placing fifteen donation boxes in parks around the city. The first was installed this summer at Gray's Lake Park on Fleur Drive.

Some residents are disgusted by the idea. Parks aren't charities, they say, and shouldn't have "begging boxes" that make users feel guilty. Others argue that parks, like the art center, should have a donation box for those who want to give.

After all, grass must be mowed, parking lots plowed, flowers planted and gardens weeded, basketball hoops replaced, concrete cracks filled, and equipment kept safe.

All that takes dollars.

But donation boxes aren't the answer.

Rather, they're an act of desperation.

The answer is funding recreation. Des Moines has sixty-seven parks, open spaces, and strips of grass to maintain on fewer and fewer dollars. Government budgets are starved. The $20 to $50 collected each week in the box at Gray's Lake won't go very far. In fact, it might give the city an excuse to cut the park's budget more.

Instead of relying on boxes, Iowa should commit itself to recreation the way other states, the states that value green space, do. Missouri has a one-tenth of 1 percent sales tax dedicated to soil conservation and parks. That helps recreation at the state level. This program was so popular it led to the legislature passing a bill in 1995, allowing cities to dedicate up to a half-cent sales tax for parks and recreation. About 70 communities will have generated $250 million by the end of this year.

Missouri has the attitude that adequate public dollars should support recreation. They don't need donation boxes in Missouri.

Iowa cities shouldn't need them either.

Source: *Des Moines Register.* (2003). Park Box Donations Don't Cut It.

receiving lower rankings included the following: (1) providing direct financial aid, (2) providing leisure-counseling programs, and (3) enhancing intellectual growth. Interestingly, "enabling" types of services (assisting/facilitating people to organize their *own* services) was ranked higher by directors in Canada than in the United States (Edginton, 1978). The reason for these differences may result from the difference in philosophy between park and recreation departments in the United States and Canada. Local recreation departments in Canada tend to empower citizens to create their own programs, while local departments in the United States tend to plan and develop programs and then offer them to the public.

In the late 1990s, local park and recreation departments (supported by the National Recreation and Park Association [NRPA]) have turned to a benefits-based approach to meeting local goals and objectives. A benefits-based approach to park and recreation services involves identifying the benefits desired and realized by park, and recreation program participants, structuring opportunities to maximize benefit achievement, and assessing benefit achievement (Edginton and O'Neill, 1999). Jarvi (1993) states that public parks and recreation departments must "seek to discover the fundamental reason for the existence of our profession and be able to define it in the highly personal terms of those we serve. The key to our success as professionals will be found in the degree in which we can prove that we are relevant to the public we serve by being able to express what we do in terms that they can easily understand" (p. 16). A benefits-based approach encourages recreation providers to consider more of a medical model for explaining benefits in which managers understand the long-term benefits of participating in our programs. In this regard, benefits-based management (BBM) is turning out to be a major catalyst in helping dispel a popular myth: that recreation and leisure provide something of value but only as long as the pleasurable experience lasts. BBM moves the leisure profession forward a quantum leap by integrating within the concept that value which is added to people's lives following on-site recreation participation (Driver, Brown, and Peterson, 1991).

Fran Mainella, the NRPA president in 1997, accurately portrays the commitment to the benefits of parks and recreation as "much more than a campaign. It is a process, a philosophy and mindset that is critical to insure the future of the park and recreation movement" (NRPA, 1998). In implementing a benefits approach to delivering services, Edginton and O'Neill (1999) have identified three distinct components. The first is benefits awareness, which is an attempt to inform park and recreation professionals and the general public of the benefits of public parks and recreation programs. The second is benefits-based programming, which is programming using the benefits as the basis of programming, measuring them, and sharing the results. The third component of a benefits program is BBM, which is concerned with managing the benefits, especially marketing the benefits of the existing program to the public.

Resource Base

The resource base or revenue for municipal parks and recreation services is diverse and sometimes appears to be complex. Deppe (1983) writes that ". . . local units of government receive their revenue from two basic sources—local and external" (p. 18). The major source of local revenue has been, historically, property tax. External sources often include financial assistance from state and federal governments and other sources. The most comprehensive analysis of revenue types is a classification system developed by Hemphill. Hemphill (1985) suggests that there are four separate classifications of revenues available to public leisure service organizations—compulsory resources, earned income, contractual receipts, and financial assistance. Table 7.1 presents these classifications.

A brief description of each of these sources of revenue follows:

Compulsory resources. Some cash and noncash revenues occur, according to Hemphill (1985), as a result of the taxing and regulatory powers of a government agency. According to Brayley and McLean (1999), government sources of income have changed dramatically since the late 1970s when California voters passed Proposition 13, which cut property taxes by almost 50 percent. Since this legislation, governments have responded to the voter with massive tax cuts, which forced public parks and recreation departments to be more creative in financing their programs. Contrary to these authors, Crompton and Kaczynski (2003) have reported significant increases to local parks and recreation units, not only in terms of operating expenses, but also in terms of capital outlay. This will be discussed further in following paragraphs.

Earned income. These cash revenues, realized through fees and charges, have become an increasingly important source of income for park and recreation agencies. Fees and charges are most often levied for program activities, rather than access to areas and facilities.

Contractual receipts. These cash revenues accrue as a result of legal agreements between a park and recreation agency and other parties and can include revenues from leasing land, renting facilities, or concession operations at facilities. Public/private ventures form an increasingly important way to create mutually beneficial ways of building cash revenues for both parties.

Financial assistance. Brayley and McLean (1999) refer to this type of income as gratuitous income. Some external funds come from grant sources, entitlement, donations, or other

TABLE

7.1   REVENUE CLASSIFICATIONS AND TYPES

Classifications and Types

I. Compulsory Resources
  - A. Taxes
    1. property
    2. income
    3. sales
    4. franchise
  - B. Special assessments
  - C. Dedication ordinances/regulations
  - D. Fines/penalties

II. Earned Income
  - A. Fees and charges
    1. entrance fees
    2. admission fees
    3. rental fees
    4. user fees
    5. sales charges
    6. license/permit fees
    7. special service fees
  - B. Investment interest

III. Contractual Receipts
  - A. Land leases
  - B. Facility rentals
  - C. Operating concessions
  - D. Lease concessions
  - E. Lease, lease-backs
  - F. Sale, lease-backs

IV. Financial Assistance
  - A. Grants
    1. project
    2. block
  - B. Entitlements
    1. specific
    2. general
  - C. Special appropriations
  - D. Current donations
  - E. Planned gifts

From Stan A. Hemphill, "Revenue Management: Beginning with the Basics" in *Parks and Recreation, 20,* (12), December 1985, pp. 35–36. Reprinted by permission.

gifts. This financial assistance is often solicited from foundations or individuals, or gained from the acquisition of grants from various state or federal agencies and is usually received without the expectation of a return (see figure 7.1).

In general, three types of local government strategies provide park and recreation services—municipal, county, and special recreation district governments. A short presentation on the expenditures of these three types of governments for park and recreation services follows in this section. In 2000, $25 billion was spent for parks and recreation at the local level of government (U.S. Census Bureau, 2003). This compares with $23.4 billion in 1999

Figure 7.1
Major sources of local revenue.

(U.S. Census Bureau, 2003). This represents approximately 2 percent of all expenditures at the local level of government. Interestingly, Crompton and Kaczynski (2003, p. 124) report that from 1994–1995 to 1999–2000, average annual increases for parks and recreation at the local level of government average $595 million. This may be contrasted with the period of time evidenced by tax revolt in America from 1976–1977 to 1985 where there was an annual decrease of $13 million. These authors note that investments for capital projects for parks and recreation at the local level of government exceeded $70 billion between 1964–1965 and 1999–2000. In 2000, New York City spent $557 million for parks and recreation followed by San Francisco, California, with $255 million; Los Angeles, California, $252 million; Indianapolis, Indiana, $206 million; and San Diego, California, $174 million. Table 7.2 presents this information. In 1997, municipal governments in the United States expended more than $10.7 billion for park and recreation services. Expenditures by county government for park and recreation services for 2000–2001 exceeded $5 billion. (U.S. Census Bureau, 2003). This represents less than 1 percent of the total expenditures made for all services at the county level. However, when an additional $1.7 billion is added for capital improvement in the area of parks and recreation, this percentage is increased to nearly 2 percent. The total expenditures for county government were in excess of $247 billion. This compares to $3.9 billion in 1996–1997, or 1.9 percent of total expenditures for county governments, which was over $1.9 billion (U.S. Census Bureau, 1997b). Expenditures by special recreation districts' governments for park and recreation services amounted to nearly $3.8 billion in 2002. In addition, $1.5 billion was spent for capital projects. (U.S. Census Bureau, 2004). This compares with $2.1 billion in 1996–1997, which represented approximately 2.4 percent of the $52 billion of the total expenditures for special districts' government services (U.S. Census Bureau, 1997c). Note that the expenditures for special districts are less because this is not the most common form of organization for park and recreation service in the United States.

Characteristics of Professionals

The U.S. Census Bureau (2003) reports that there are 217,600 individuals employed at the local level in the park and recreation field. California, followed by Florida, Illinois, Texas, and New York have the largest number of park and recreation employees at the local level of government. These rates of employment do not necessarily directly follow the rank of each state regarding its size of population. For example, Florida has the second highest number of local government park and recreation employees, yet is fourth in population size; Illinois is fifth in population size yet has the third highest number of employees in parks and recreation in the

TABLE

7.2 PARK AND RECREATION EXPENDITURES BY CITY (IN MILLIONS OF DOLLARS)

City	Expenditures	Population Rank
New York, NY	$557	1
San Francisco, CA	$255	12
Los Angeles, CA	$252	2
Indianapolis, IN	$206	13
San Diego, CA	$174	6
Washington, D.C.	$172	23
Cleveland, OH	$171	28
Phoenix, AZ	$170	7
Dallas, TX	$153	9
Seattle, WA	$149	22
San Antonio, TX	$137	8
Honolulu, HI	$128	41
Houston, TX	$117	4
San Jose, CA	$116	11
Detroit, MI	$112	10
Oklahoma City, OK	$ 99	30
Denver, CO	$ 91	27
Philadelphia, PA	$ 90	5
Memphis, TN	$ 83	18
Portland, OR	$ 83	26
Columbus, OH	$ 80	15
Chicago, IL	$ 76	3
Austin, TX	$ 50	21
Tucson, AZ	$ 48	32
Baltimore, MD	$ 44	16
Ft. Worth, TX	$ 44	29
Charlotte, NC	$ 43	25
Las Vegas, NV	$ 41	37
Jacksonville, FL	$ 40	14
Long Beach, CA	$ 27	35
Boston, MA	$ 22	20
El Paso, TX	$ 22	17
New Orleans, LA	$ 21	31
Milwaukee, WI	$ 5	19

Source: U.S. Bureau of the Census. 2003. *Statistical Abstracts of the United States: 2003.* 123rd ed. Washington DC: U. S. Government Printing Office.

local level of government. Crompton and Kaczynski (2003) report that local government park and recreation units employed 145,000 individuals in 1977–1978. As one can see, when compared to 2003 that figure has increased dramatically. They also report that the number of part-time employees has increased from 26,000 to 172,000. This number does not include seasonal hires such as summer staff. Educational requirements for these jobs vary, however; for entry-

Leisure Line

Smoking Ban from L.A. Parks

Los Angeles, Calif.—First, they were kicked out of workplaces. Then banned from bars and restaurants. About the last place Los Angeles smokers have left to light up is the outdoors, and now even that may be restricted.

Los Angeles City Council members are contemplating a crackdown on smoking that would be tougher than any in the country; they may banish smokers from all public parks.

To groups struggling to protect smokers' rights, news that one of the nation's smoggiest cities would even consider each a move is a bit much.

"They're worried about a few wisps of second-hand smoke compared to the filthy L.A. air? That's ridiculous," said Enoch Ludlow, director of a national group fighting ordinances against smoking. "There's no good reason for this. It's just a concentrated effort to keep demonizing one-fourth of the population."

But community leaders in Los Angeles insist the bill before the council would have significant benefits. "We're not trying to be harsh," said Sonya Vasquez, chair of the Committee for Smoke-Free Parks, which represents about two dozen neighborhood groups. "We just want to create an environment that's healthy for the majority of citizens, especially in places where so many children play."

Such a step would not be entirely new. In recent years, dozens of American towns and a few large cities have imposed some limits on outdoor smoking. The movement is taking hold, especially in California, which has long led the nation in adopting strong anti-smoking rules. Still, most of these places have made only small no-smoking zones near building entrances at beaches or zoos, or in parts of their public parks or plazas.

What Los Angeles is talking about is much broader. The proposal would make every inch of the nearly 200 parks in this sprawling city off-limits to smokers and subject them to fines for lighting up.

Source: Sanchez, R. 2001. Smoking ban pushed for L.A. parks. *Washington Post* (October 31).

level professional positions, a college degree is important, and many administrative positions in large public recreation systems require a graduate degree.

Certifications also are becoming increasingly important for professionals working in government agencies (e.g., municipal recreation departments). Certification is offered by the NRPA National Certification Board. The NRPA, along with its state chapters, offers certification as a "Certified Park and Recreation Professional" for those with a bachelor's degree in recreation, park resources, and leisure services from an NRPA/AALR accredited program with no less than two years full-time experience, and as an "Associate Park and Recreational Professional" for those possessing an associate's degree and no less than two years of experience.

Frequently, certification as a community based therapeutic specialist is also required. Local park and recreation departments and special districts may require that individuals working with disabled persons possess certification as a Certified Therapeutic Recreation Specialist through the National Council for Therapeutic Recreation Certification.

In many ways, leisure professionals who work in government agencies see themselves as public servants promoting the common good through recreation spaces and programs. As with other individuals involved in public service, leisure professionals see themselves as altruistic, in that they are motivated primarily by service to others. Godbey (1997) identifies one of the three characteristics of successful leisure service organizations (whether public, nonprofit, or commercial) as having a service ethic.

A Benefits Approach in Advocating for Public Parks and Recreation

It costs approximately $30,000 to incarcerate a juvenile offender for one year. If that money were available to the Park Department, we could: take him swimming twice a week for 24 weeks, and give him four tours of the zoo, plus lunch, and enroll him in 50 Community Center programs, and visit Oxley Nature Center twice, and let him play league softball for a season, tour the gardens at Woodward Park twice, and give him two weeks of tennis lessons, and enroll him in two weeks of day camp, and let him play three rounds of golf, and act in one play, and participate in one fishing clinic, and take a four-week pottery class, and play basketball for eight hours a week for 40 weeks after which we could return to you: $29,125 and one much happier kid. (Bob Jennings, Naturalist Oxley Nature Center on the subject of Youth at Risk from the Tulsa Park and Recreation Department Marketing Plan, 1997–1998)

Source: National Recreation and Park Association. 1998. *Discover the Benefits*. Ashburn, VA: NRPA.

In promoting such a service ethic, park and recreation professionals often have a strong commitment to maintain the dignity and worth of those whom they serve. In addition, many individuals in the park and recreation field also have a strong commitment to the preservation and conservation of human resources. Connected with these types of values is having a high level of integrity. To support these types of values, the NRPA has developed and encourages its members to accept and promote a Professional Code of Ethics.

Beyond working to be a public servant, DeGraaf, Jordan, and DeGraaf (1998) urge park and recreation professionals to strive to be servant leaders in developing and implementing recreation programs. The term servant leadership was first coined in 1970 by Robert Greenleaf (1977) in an article entitled "The Servant as Leader." From this humble beginning, servant leadership is now in its third decade as a specific leadership and management approach. Spears (1995) has identified servant leadership as an approach that "attempts to simultaneously enhance the personal growth of workers and improve the quality and caring of our many institutions through a combination of teamwork and community, personal involvement in decision making and ethical and caring behavior" (p. 4). In describing the importance of servant leadership, Greenleaf (1977) states, "if a better society is to be built, one that is more just and more loving, one that provides greater creative opportunity for its people, then the most open course is to raise both the capacity to serve and the very performance as servant of existing major institutions by new regenerative forces operating within them" (p. 49).

In striving to become servant leaders and survive in today's workplace, Godbey (1997) has identified a number of personal strategies for those who will work in leisure services in the twenty-first century. These strategies, centered on being flexible and innovative in serving others, include the following:

- *Serve others.* An ethic of service will continue to distinguish leisure services in the public, private nonprofit, and commercial sectors. As a leisure services programmer the emphasis must always be on the people served and the benefits provided rather than the program itself.
- *Become an entrepreneur.* Entrepreneurs produce new ways of meeting needs, working to improve existing products and services, and responding to changing demographic conditions.

- *Seek continuous learning opportunities.* As the primary basis of the economy becomes knowledge, it becomes imperative that leisure service professionals stay current with the world around them through lifelong learning.
- *Become more flexible.* In a world of rapid and continuing change, the ability to adapt to changing circumstances is critical.
- *Call attention to the importance of what you do.* Leisure services professionals must believe in the power and potential of leisure programs to affect change in the lives of individuals and society. Leisure services are critical components of society, not just "frosting."

Orientation to Customers

Lappe and DuBois (1994), in their book *The Quickening of America: Rebuilding Our Nation, Remaking Our Lives,* put forth the idea that human service organizations (which include recreation and leisure) are moving away from simply providing services to creating a living democracy model whereby customers are viewed as partners in the planning process. Thus, community parks and recreation professionals must continue to build partnerships with customers—partnerships that link the professional and his or her skill with the needs, interests, and wants of the members of the community. This type of partnership focuses on solving common problems. Customers are viewed as clients; that is, they receive professional services and may participate in the problem-solving process.

To provide services, public park and recreation professionals tend to gather facts about problems and make decisions following the most rational course of action. In general, the population within the entire geographic boundary served by the park and recreation agency receives its services. Historically, a philosophy of providing the greatest good to the greatest number has prevailed. Because of limited organizational resources, however, park and recreation agencies have become more aware of the need to focus their activities on specific populations and services. Thus, they often apply marketing strategies to specific populations, such as children, people with disabilities, or older persons.

Park and recreation agencies increasingly are wed to the concept of quality. This is reflected in the use of such management strategies as Total Quality Management (TQM) and Continuous Quality Improvement (CQI). TQM focuses on the involvement of all organization members in the pursuit of quality as well as attention to the use of statistical measures as benchmarks, innovation, continuous improvement, anticipatory planning, and having a future orientation. With a commitment to quality, park and recreation professionals are increasingly seeking close communication with customers as reflected in an increase in the use of task forces, surveys, town meetings, and other ways of connecting with the consumer to improve quality.

Types of Local Governments Providing Park and Recreation Services

As mentioned, three basic types of local governments provide park and recreation services—municipal, county, and special district (see figure 7.2). All of these forms of government are close to the individuals served and also are characterized by their ability to be self-governed. Local park and recreation services derive their power from state government and must function within the laws established by it. Kraus and Curtis (1986) write,

> Under the American form of government, states have the authority to regulate governmental programs and various areas of human activity within their territories, except as limited by the federal Constitution or their own constitutions. This regulatory power is commonly known as "police power"

Figure 7.2

Expenditures for park and recreation services in the United States at the local level of government in 2001.

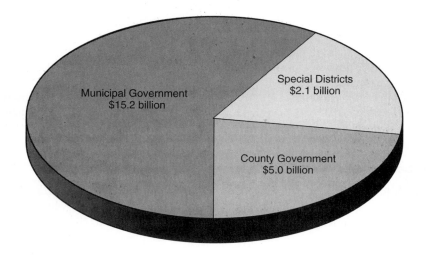

Municipal Government
$15.2 billion

Special Districts
$2.1 billion

County Government
$5.0 billion

and provides authorization to enact laws for the health, safety, morals, and general welfare of the citizens of each state. (p. 61)

Local leisure service organizations provide many public benefits. Hunt, Scott, and Richardson (2003, p. 1) have identified a number of benefits that can be provided by parks and recreation departments. Studying selected communities across the United States, they have identified the following as potential benefits, which are presented in order of importance. Benefits and the percentage response of participants toward these items are as follows: 1) enhance family recreation opportunities (93 percent), 2) make cities better places to live (93 percent), 3) increase community pride (91 percent), 4) preserve natural areas (86 percent), 5) help residents stay healthier (82 percent), 6) keep youth out of trouble (78 percent), 7) help residents meet other people (72 percent), 8) increase property values (72 percent), 9) bring tourists to the city (60 percent), 10) educate residents about the environment (58 percent), and 11) make businesses want to relocate here (56 percent).

Types of Legislation

The authority that states have given local governments to enable them to provide park and recreation services often occurs in the form of specific state statutes created to directly authorize the organization and implementation of such programs. Even without such specific legislation, local governments can operate park and recreation services by broadly exercising their police powers. Kraus and Curtis (2000) report five types of legislation (see figure 7.3) that have been created to assist in the establishment of local park and recreation services. They include the following:

Special park and recreation laws. These types of laws empower specific cities or communities to provide park and recreation services. In general, these laws set forth provisions for a governing structure, taxing powers, and methods and procedures to employ and supervise professional staff.

Regulatory laws. Regulatory laws control or monitor park and recreation services in order to protect those individuals affected by such activities. Such regulatory laws affect the management of facilities such as swimming pools, ice rinks, or programs in which risk

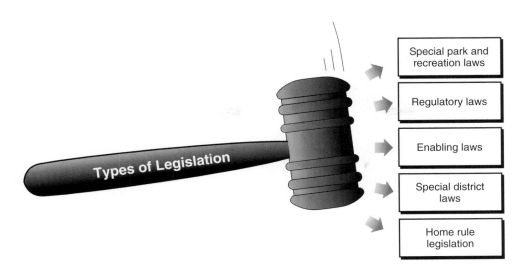

Figure 7.3

Types of
legislation that
can be used to
establish local
park and
recreation
services.

Special park and
recreation laws

Regulatory laws

Enabling laws

Special district
laws

Home rule
legislation

Types of Legislation

to the customer must be managed. Standards for sanitation of facilities also come under
the heading of regulatory laws.

Enabling laws. The most important type of legislation impacting on park and recreation
services is the enabling law. Enabling legislation specifies that a local branch of
government can own, operate, or manage park and recreation services. Enabling
legislation also usually provides for a governing body, spells out taxing powers, and so
forth. Such state laws, usually written in a permissive fashion, provide communities the
individual discretion to determine the size and scope of their services. Enabling
legislation does not mandate the establishment of services, as do special park and
recreation laws.

Special district laws. A large number of states have legislation that allows for the
establishment of special single-purpose local units of government. This can involve
park and recreation services as well as other services such as water, fire, electricity, and
sewage. These types of laws provide guidelines for acquiring areas and facilities, and
establishing programs, taxing powers, and governing structure.

Home rule legislation. Home rule legislation refers to the state statutes that provide local
subdivisions of government with the ability to determine their own form of government.
Communities that use this form of legislation often include park and recreation services
as a part of their basic structure.

Municipal Government

A common form of organizing leisure services in the United States falls under the jurisdiction
of a municipal government associated with a city or town. In this arrangement, park and recreation services become part of the community service offerings of the entire city government. A
city, basically a self-governing unit, derives its powers from state or provincial government.
The provision of leisure services within this structure, while not mandatory, is often provided
by a community as a part of its complete package of services.

A municipal government can provide leisure services in a number of ways. The most common form is a combined parks and recreation department. In this organizational arrangement,
the functions of park management and the creation and delivery of recreation activities merge

under one administrative unit. It is also possible to have these two functions separate from one another. In some communities, a variety of leisure activities, including libraries, cultural arts, and other specialized facilities such as zoos or aquariums, may be combined into a human services or community services department.

Boards are often established to govern these various types of departments that provide leisure services. *Park and recreation boards* exist to provide input into decision-making processes by interested, knowledgeable, and informed citizens. Individuals serving on park and recreation boards represent the citizens of the community. The three basic types of park and recreation boards include *policy-making boards, semi-independent boards,* and *advisory boards.* Policy-making boards, composed of elected or appointed individuals, make independent judgments in an autonomous fashion concerning the direction of the organization. Semi-independent boards have partial rather than full decision-making power. These boards oversee a specific area of government, such as parks and recreation. Semi-independent boards may be either elected or appointed. Advisory boards or commissions, usually appointed by a mayor or governing body such as a city council, provide nonbinding advice to either one or both of these appointing authorities.

No specific organizational format for park and recreation services can be applied universally in any community. Each community will create an internal organizational structure for the delivery of park and recreation services that best suits its needs. In general, however, combined park and recreation departments often address several major functions. According to Rodney and Toalson (1981), they include the following: (1) recreation programming; (2) management of special facilities; (3) construction and maintenance of parks; (4) business and finance; and (5) public relations. These functions are also depicted in figure 7.4. Rodney and Toalson further note that a park department might be organized according to the following functions: (1) engineering; (2) horticulture; (3) forestry and street trees; (4) botanical gardens; and (5) park police.

Figure 7.5 presents an organization chart for The City of San Diego (California) Park and Recreation Department. San Diego is a community of 1,223,400. The Park and Recreation Department is responsible for overseeing 36,300 acres of developed and undeveloped open space;

Figure 7.4

Major functions of combined park and recreation departments.

Figure 7.5

Organizational Chart.
Parks & Recreation, City of San Diego, California.

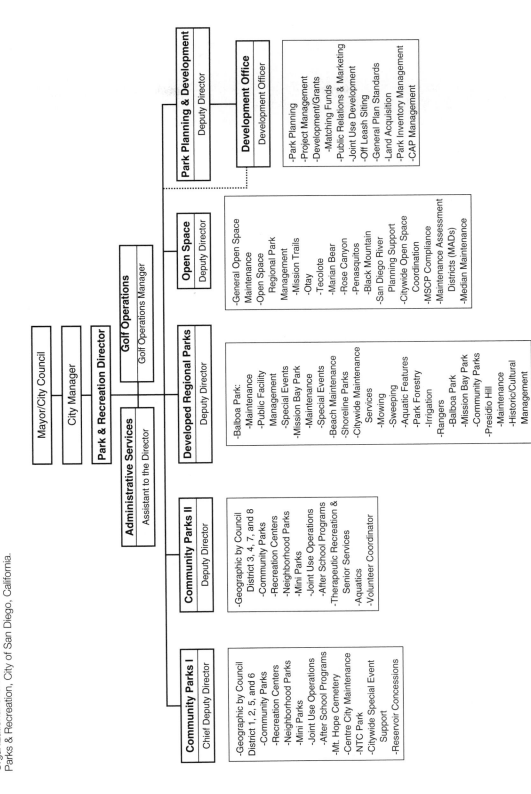

None of Twenty-Five Largest Cities Rates Five Stars in Report

The Trust for Public Land analyzed the park systems in the nation's twenty-five largest cities. Its ratings were based on fifteen factors, including percentage of parkland in each city and the availability of facilities such as pools, tennis courts, and recreation centers.

The cities were rated on a system of one to five stars against cities in the same population category. No cities received a five-star rating, which is the highest.

Four-Star Cities

Boston
Cincinnati
Minneapolis

Three-Star Cities

Chicago
Denver
New York
Phoenix
Portland, OR
San Diego
San Francisco
Seattle

Two-Star Cities

Atlanta
Baltimore
Dallas
Houston
Indianapolis
Kansas City
Los Angeles
Philadelphia
Pittsburgh
St. Louis
Tampa

One-Star Cities

Cleveland
Detriot
Miami

Source: Davis, K. 2000, August 10. 3 Cities Earn 4 Stars for Parks. *USA Today,* 3A.

337 parks including Balboa Park, Mission Trails Regional Park, and Mission Bay Park; 25 miles of shoreline from Sunset Cliffs to La Jolla; thirteen pools that are open year-round; three public golf complexes; fifty-one recreational centers; twenty-five tennis sites and more (http://www.sannet.gov/park-and-recreation/general-info/mission.shtml). As one can see viewing the organizational chart, there are multiple units, including community parks division, developed regional parks division, open space division, planning and development, golf course operations, and administrative services.

County Government

County governments also provide park and recreation services. A county is the next political unit that exists below state government. Rodney and Toalson (1981) discuss the functions performed by counties.

> The functions counties perform have become somewhat traditional and are similar in character. In most instances, counties build and maintain roads and bridges, care for the indigent, register land titles, preserve peace and administer justice, collect taxes and provide state and county elections . . . [In the 20th

century,] however, county functions have become somewhat liberalized to include services of an urban nature such as parks, recreation, libraries, drainage, sewage control, and the like." (p.197)

The development of county park systems occurred at the turn of the century in the United States. The first attempt to acquire lands that encompassed a broad area occurred in Boston in 1882. A metropolitan parks commission, established by the state legislature, encompassed thirty-six communities surrounding the city of Boston. The first actual system of parks established within a county occurred in Essex County, New Jersey.

The Essex County Parks Commission was founded in 1895, following legislation signed by the governor of New Jersey. Twenty of its twenty-six parks were designed by Fredrick Law Olmsted, Sr. His attention to creating landscapes that featured winding roads, natural blended water ways, open fields, and overlooks are all evident in these parks today. Today, the park system consists of 5,745 acres of green space, which includes reservations, parks, golf courses, tennis courts, ice and roller skating centers, and a zoo.

What types of services do county park and recreation departments provide? Answers vary because counties vary in geographic size and density of population; however, a county park system usually provides services that are commensurate with the needs of its residents. In general, a county park system offers the following services:

1. Regional park and recreation areas and facilities that combine some of the resources of other park and recreation departments to create a unified system (e.g., the creation of a regional park system).
2. Unique or specialized parks and recreation areas and facilities that emphasize particular natural resources or other special features (e.g., a rodeo, fairgrounds, zoos).
3. Recreation program services that are difficult, if not impractical, to offer in urban areas (e.g., resident camping programs, yachting classes).
4. Specialized recreation services that require a broader base of support and population (e.g., programs for disabled populations).
5. Recreation program services that meet the general needs of the population of the county (especially in rural settings not served by incorporated communities).

County park and recreation departments also may provide informational services regarding the public leisure resources within their political jurisdiction. County governments can play an important role in advancing the park and recreation movement by coordinating various activities between and among individual city service providers. County governments can also serve to stimulate the development of public park and recreation services in incorporated cities and towns.

The managing authority established for county park and recreation departments across the United States varies and depends upon state legislation. In some cases, the highway department or a conservation department manages the county park and recreation board. In other cases, it functions as a separate department, managed by a policy-making or advisory board. Still further, the county park and recreation board can function under the management of an elected county commissioner.

The organizational chart from the Lane County (Oregon) Parks Division serves as an example of the structure of a county park and recreation system (figure 7.6). The Lane County Parks Division manages more than 5,000 acres of park land. County parks have been established in both urban and rural areas and vary from well-developed, well-manicured park areas to park sites that are in a natural state. Facilities include marinas, beaches, playgrounds, and camp sites.

Figure 7.6

Organizational
chart, Lane
County Parks
Division.

Lane County
Parks Division
Organizational Chart

The amount of funds spent for county park and recreation systems varies a great deal from state to state. Large populous states like California, however, tend to spend more on their county park systems than smaller, less populated states. In 1997, California spent the most for county parks and recreation services, followed by Florida, Maryland, New York, Arizona, and Wisconsin (U.S. Census Bureau, 1997b).

Special Districts

Another approach to organizing park and recreation services involves the creation of a special district. A special district is an autonomous, separate function of government having a particular purpose, in this case the provision of park and recreation services. The key terms are *separate* and *autonomous*. Special districts are created in such a way as to be independent of other government bodies. A park and recreation special district is a legally organized subdivision of a state. It derives its power as a legal entity from the state statutes that provide for its incorporation. There are 1,314 special districts in the United States, established for the specific purpose of providing park and recreation services (Census of Governments, 2002). This compares with 1997, where there were 1,253, and 1987, where there were 1,002 special districts organized for the purpose of providing park and/or recreation services. (Bureau of Census, 1997c). As one can see, this represents a significant growth in the governmental body dedicated to this purpose. This is an increase of over 30 percent in this method of organizing local park and recreation services.

Figure 7.7 is an organizational chart for the Arlington Heights (Illinois) Park District. The Arlington Heights Park District was established in 1925 and is governed by a five-member board of commissioners. The district owns 450 acres, leases 260 acres of land, and has fifty-eight parks comprised of community parks, neighborhood parks, play lots, passive parks, and linear parks. Recreational facilities include five outdoor and one indoor swimming pool, five community centers (each with gymnasium and meeting rooms), a cultural arts center, historical museum, senior center, Forest View Racquet and Fitness Club, Heritage Tennis Club, Arlington Lakes Golf Club, Nickol Knoll Golf Club, Melas Park Softball Complex, Lake Arlington's 1.8 mile walk/bike path and fifty-acre boating lake, driving range, forty-six softball diamonds, three football fields, seventeen soccer fields, forty-one playgrounds, fifty-six outdoor tennis courts, twelve outdoor ice skating rinks, and thirty-nine picnic areas. The district provides a full range of activities and services all year. Major recreation programs include athletics, fitness, music, arts and crafts, performing arts, preschools, museum programs, swimming, tennis, senior programs, day camps, special events, trips, and, in cooperation with School District 25 and the Village of Arlington Heights, a before- and after-school program called the Northwest Special Recreation Association, and cosponsors the community band and many other special interest groups (http: www.ahpd.org/About Us/Profile.htm).

As one can see viewing the organizational chart in figure 7.7, the district is organized into three primary areas: parks and planning, finance and personnel, and recreation and facilities. In addition, there is a separate unit focused on golf course operations. Subunits within each of these areas further organize the work of the district into additional functional areas. There is no atypical way of organizing park and recreation services. Each community or local subdivision of government will organize its work in such a way as to provide appropriate managerial leadership to its programs, facilities, and support functions.

Generally speaking, special park districts have several unique characteristics. They include the following: (1) existence as an organized entity with a resident population and defined geographic area; (2) governmental character as a separate legal governing body; and (3) substantial autonomy to provide a service (parks and recreation) and the taxing power to raise part of their own revenue (U.S. Census Bureau, 1997c).

In other words, a park and recreation special district represents a specific population in a defined geographic area. The district has a governing body—usually an elected board of directors. This board is empowered to acquire land, provide recreation programs, hire employees, and collect taxes and other revenues. A special district operates with autonomy in decision making and is not encumbered by political interference from other governmental decision-making bodies.

Special districts can be established to focus on the general functions of parks and recreation or they may be delimited to a more specific area (for example, a district established to focus on the preservation of wilderness areas, seashores, or other natural resources). Most park and recreation districts, however, serve urban or suburban community needs.

A special district has a great advantage in that the central work of the agency is focused primarily on parks and recreation. Within municipal governments, park and recreation departments compete with all other services for tax dollars and other revenues. Special districts

Figure 7.7

Organizational Chart.
Arlington Heights Park District, Arlington Heights, Illinois

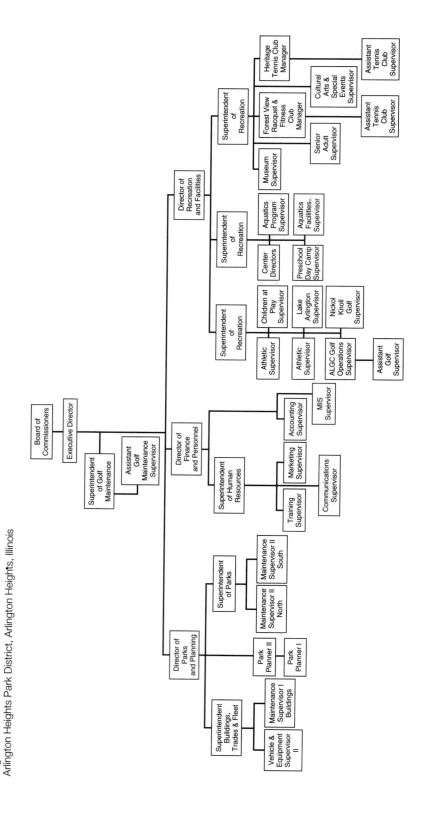

not only have the ability to tax, but they also control their funds, unlike municipalities where revenue generated may go back to the general fund. Sometimes the competition in municipal government leads to a reduction of funds for park and recreation services. The disadvantage of special districts is their lack of access to other city resources, such as police protection and public works. All of these services must be provided by the district itself, or contracted for with other agencies.

The Pleasure Driveway and Park District of Peoria, organized in 1894, was the first park system formed in Illinois. Seventy years later, in 1963, the City of Peoria Playground and Recreation Department merged with the Park District, thus expanding the potential program and facility responsibilities of the Park District. The Peoria Park District's boundaries encompass approximately fifty-seven square miles in Peoria County. Its park and open space holdings in the City of Peoria, Peoria Heights, and outlying townships approach 9,000 acres. Much of the land was acquired through matching grants from the federal Land-Water Conservation Fund, the Illinois Open Space Lands Acquisition and Development program, and many generous gifts and donations. The Peoria Park District ranks first in the state and is one of the top public park systems in the nation based on its ration of open-space holdings to population.

Illinois, by far, leads all states in the number of organized special recreation districts with 360 special districts in existence (U.S. Census Bureau, 1997c). As a result, Illinois also leads all states in expenditures of special districts services in the United States. Other states that favor the special district system as demonstrated by the number of special recreation districts in existence are North Dakota (240 special districts), California (164), Ohio (94), Washington (61), and Pennsylvania (60) (U.S. Census Bureau, 1997c). Undoubtedly, the preference in these states for special district systems is due to the influence of early legislation in Illinois (in the late 1800s) influencing the establishment of the Illinois Park District Code.

An excellent example of the special district organizational arrangement is the West Suburban Special Recreation Association (WSSRA) in Franklin Park, Illinois. This cooperative extension of local park districts and two villages came together in 1976 to create a special district to coordinate year-round recreation opportunities for individuals with special needs, disabilities, or handicapping conditions. By cooperating, the partner communities consolidate their resources and populations and hire staff who are trained to work with special populations (WSSRA, 1993).

The mission of WSSRA is to provide superior recreation services for persons with disabilities. This organization is dedicated to serving their customers with: 1) first class program opportunities, 2) responsive outreach, 3) distinctive customer service, 4) reliable transportation, 5) professional, caring staff, and 6) a safe and fun environment. The focus of WSSRA is each individual participant. Through WSSRA, residents of all ages can participate in year-round programming specifically designed to meet their individual needs. Residents of partner communities who have a disability or handicapping condition are eligible for WSSRA services. Services are available for preschoolers, school age children, teens, young adults, and senior citizens that live in the following communities: Berwyn Park District, Clyde Park District, Village of Elmwood Park, Park District of Forest Park, Park District of Franklin Park, Hawthorne Park District, Village of Harwood Heights, Norridge Park District, North Berwyn Park District, Park District of Oak Park, and River Forest Park District (http://www.wssra.net).

WSSRA offers a variety of programs that reflect the mood and activities of the changing seasons and resemble programs offered by partner park districts and recreation districts. WSSRA strives to provide programs in centralized locations as close to home and school as possible. WSSRA does not own or operate any recreation facilities and therefore coordinates with local park and recreation districts, churches, schools, and other private facilities to offer their programs. This serves to enhance the special district's philosophy of assisting in the normalization and mainstreaming process (WSSRA, 1993).

In addition to public funds used to operate WSSRA, parents of children with disabilities who live in the service district formed a not-for-profit corporation, the West Suburban Special Recreation Foundation. This corporation is dedicated to raising funds to purchase recreation equipment and offer programs for the WSSRA.

Recreation Services as a Part of a School District

A school district is a special district and, although the provision of park and recreation services is not its primary function, a school district may assist in the provision of park and recreation services as a corollary function. From a historical perspective, use of schools for recreation services was viewed as being a desirable, practical approach. Thus, a number of states, particularly Wisconsin, California, New Jersey, and Michigan, established enabling legislation for schools to coordinate their efforts to provide leisure services.

Recently, the community education movement, organized within various school districts in the United States, has strongly embraced the pursuit of leisure activities as an important component of their activities. The community education movement, built on a concept that promotes the use of various resources in a community to meet community needs, focuses on facilitating communication and cooperation between and among individuals. Community education, a process that encourages community involvement, also organizes a service delivery system. Thus, focusing on the leisure needs of people, community educators have encouraged school systems to actively engage in problem-solving processes related to leisure as well as actually providing leisure services.

Community educators, although using the entire community or given neighborhood as their resource, often work within a particular school. This school facility becomes a primary resource base for promoting community activities and providing leisure services. School facilities have gymnasiums, classrooms, meeting rooms, art studios, and wood and metal shops, as well as playing and athletic fields. This resource base provides areas and facilities that can be used in programming activities and services.

Types of Services

Park and recreation systems at the local level of government provide a wide array of services. The innovation and ingenuity of area and facility planners and recreation programmers have resulted in the creation of many outstanding park and recreation services. The range of such services moves from traditional programs, such as youth sports leagues, to more highly sophisticated uses of technology, including the production of videocassettes from acquisition of leisure skills. Leisure services offered by local governments, while difficult to categorize, often fall into four general classifications: recreation activities, areas and facilities, information, and leadership.

Recreation Activities The category of recreation activities includes the creation and delivery of classes, leagues, drop-in programs, special events, outreach programs, and others. These programs can be provided in a variety of program areas, including sports, outdoor recreation, performing arts (dance, drama, music), arts, new arts (use of technology), travel and tourism, crafts, literary and self-improvement, hobbies, social recreation, and voluntary services.

A review of the program offering of Indy Parks and Recreation, Indianapolis, Indiana, shows that the department provided a full range of programs. They offer sports leagues, outdoor movies, nature hikes, after-school program services, and much more. Table 7.3 highlights a select number of programs and services provided by Indy Parks and Recreation in its 2002 annual report.

TABLE

7.3 SELECTED PROGRAM HIGHLIGHTS INDY PARKS AND RECREATION

- served over seven million park visitors through expanded community center hours, open seven days a week into the evening
- developed the Urban Soccer Development Program to provide more than 75 clinics at 10 different locations
- held day camp programs at nine park sites, three of which were added in 2002, serving an additional 1,826 youth
- offered free, structured, supervised play programs to over 24,000 youth at 32 park sites through creative partnerships with neighborhood organizations, church groups, or other youth-serving agencies
- expanded the School With A Park (SWAP) program to serve seven elementary schools—approximately 13,000 students—in subjects such as bicycle, fire, and water safety
- began the "Indy in Motion" program, a partnership with Marion County Health Department and Natural Institute for Fitness and Sports, to provide new fitness and walking opportunities for over 800 participants
- held 82 special events, including a new event called YouthFest, at which over 5,000 attended
- held 14 clinics for skateboarding, BMX-Freestyle biking, and inline-skating to attract these specialized and extreme sport enthusiasts from around the nation
- sponsored and hosted the 2002 State Senior Olympic Games with over 400 athletes participating in 13 different competitions.
- hosted more than 1,000 athletes from Scarborough, Canada, for the 30th Anniversary Peace Games
- expanded the "Mayor's Symphony in the Park" series with the Indianapolis Symphony Orchestra to five performances
- marked the eleventh year of grant support from the Clowes Foundation for the Arts Services Presenters Tour. In total, this partnership has generated over $100,000 to service and inspire our day camps, after-school programs and other park activities
- offered a total of 20 free movies throughout different parks over the summer with a total attendance of over 50,000. Introduced new concert genres, including Latin and country music. Over 20,000 attended the Blues in the Hood and Jazz in the Park series
- conducted five theatre performances at four different park sites, attracting more than 500 audience members
- provided 84 free visual art classes at three sites, for over 2,200 people of all ages and abilities
- revived the Citywide Talent Contest to celebrate its fiftieth season after a four-year hiatus. The contest involved over 50 talented children and adult volunteers
- expanded both school day and after-school programming to engage over 50,000 students in field trips and outreach activities at Indy Park sites
- operated joint park/school programming sites at 21 schools, including 12 Indianapolis public schools, five in Pike Township, two in Warren Township, and two in Wayne Township. Participation topped 5,000 weekly in these programs
- provided opportunity for over 1,700 youth to go through the nationally recognized Stay in Bounds Character Discovery Challenge Education Program. The youth were exposed to the six RICHER principals of Respect, Integrity, Caring, Harmony, Excellence, and Responsibility
- offered character education in seven of the eleven school districts due in part to a supportive community development block grant. Partnered with Indiana University's Bradford Woods to assist with level five and six of the Character Discovery Program
- expanded the Recreation Adventure Program (RAP) at two public school sites from two days to four days a week through additional funding from the Mary Rigg Neighborhood Center and a federal grant
- completed design of the Environmental EdVentures Program to meet the Indiana Department of Education standards for academic excellence in science, math, language arts, and social studies. This gives Indy Parks and teachers the opportunity to enhance in science, math, language arts, and social studies. This gives Indy Parks and teachers the opportunity to enhance each other's programs and meet the needs of school-age children in grades pre-kindergarten through fifth grade

Source: Live, Learn, Explore Indy Parks and Recreation. 2002. Annual Report (Indianapolis, Indiana).

Areas and Facilities   Recreation activities often depend on specific facilities. Hence, the planning and management of areas and facilities plays an important part in a well-designed program. A *facility* may be defined as a structure that provides for or houses a recreation service. For example, a community center is a recreation facility. An *area* may be defined as an open space or a piece of developed land that is used for recreation purposes.

People commonly associate a number of areas and facilities with parks and recreation—swimming pools, parks, ball fields, and playgrounds. Many of these traditional facilities are still present, yet new technologies and customer demand are adding a great deal of variety to park departments today. In the past ten years we have seen a number of trends manifest themselves in recreation space and facility design. These trends include more multiple-use facilities, creativity in creating new open space in cities using public/private cooperation, more linked linear trail systems, increased accessibility for people with disabilities, and environmental-friendly design (Kraus and Curtis, 2000). These trends are evident in some of the following innovative uses of both facilities and open space:

Aquatic facilities. In recent years leisure pools have begun to replace traditional pools that were created primarily for exercise and competitive swimming. Public agencies are following the lead of commercial aquatic water parks and creating pools that are more conducive to family recreation. For example, in Springfield, Oregon, the Willamalane Park and Recreation District built an indoor aquatic facility that offers guests a wave pool, water slides, hot tubs, waterfalls, a long narrow lap pool, wide spacious decks (both inside and outside), snack bars, and locker rooms. The facility also has high ceilings, skylights, indoor plants, and open space, creating the illusion of being outdoors.

Climbing walls. Indoor climbing walls are increasingly found as a part of the facilities provided by local park and recreation departments. Such structures effectively simulate outdoor environments, providing individuals access to one type of high adventure activity. Programs often include instructional programs as well as drop-in services. Climbing walls are usually built with several levels of difficulty and the ability to change climbing routes to promote interest and provide new challenges for participants.

Fitness centers. Americans' increased awareness of fitness has created a boom for fitness programs and equipment. Municipal governments are building new facilities and refitting old ones to provide accessible space and equipment for fitness programs for people of all ages and abilities. In conjunction with these programs, circuit training has developed. Between the early 1970s and 1990 more than 700 paracourses (that is, circuit training courses) were installed in parks, schools, and recreation centers (Kraus and Curtis, 2000).

Rails-to-trails corridors. In 1916, the United States boasted the largest rail system in the world with nearly 300,000 miles of steel connecting every large city and small town into a massive transportation network. Today, that impressive system has shrunk to less than 150,000 miles. As more than 2,000 miles of track are abandoned each year, unused corridors offer a perfect backbone for another type of transportation system—rails to trails (Rails to Trails Conservancy, 1993). Local governments are combining with state and federal governments, as well as the private sector, to create recreation resources of local, state, and federal significance. Other possibilities for creating new green space and parks include utilizing other transportation corridors such as highways and rivers. One northwest town has created a number of covered basketball courts by placing them under highway underpasses.

Ecological recovery sites. As the United States and Canada struggle with environmental problems such as water pollution, many new strategies are being developed. One wastewater treatment plan for small towns can create new park resources for many local park and recreation departments. Towns such as Union, Mississippi, and Haughton, Louisiana, use swamps and marshes to treat town sewage. These small-scale water-treatment areas can be practical and beautiful and provide new places for local parks. Although these plans may never replace large metropolitan sewage systems (to replace metropolitan Boston's current sewage treatment plant would require a thirty-nine-square-mile marsh), this may be a cost-effective way for small governments to deal with water-waste management as well as provide wildlife areas that could be used as parks (Burke, 1992).

Urban forestry projects. "Trees are not just a nicety, an amenity, something we can do without. In fact, they make our cities livable. . . . Trees are nature's janitor" (Haurwitz, 1992, p.18). Yet, our urban forests are dying, and revitalizing them is imperative. The federal government provides some assistance to local government. Municipal governments are also fighting to reverse the urban forest decline. Cities and towns can become a part of the Tree City USA program. To qualify for the program a city must spend at least $2 a resident on forestry. In return, the city receives a flag, a plaque, and technical reports on planting and maintaining trees. About 1,600 communities have enrolled in the program. In many cities this program is coordinated through the park and recreation department. Tree-planting projects offer municipal governments opportunities to build partnerships with volunteer groups and the private sector. For example, a local group of the Telephone Pioneers of America, a group of phone company retirees, planted over 15,000 seedlings in 1991. Such projects beautify existing open spaces as well as help combat environmental problems such as global warming.

National Program for Playground Safety. The National Program for Playground Safety is focused on assisting schools, park and recreation systems, child care centers, and other locations with information about playground safety. Operated at the University of Northern Iowa, the program has developed a national plan that includes four primary goals: (1) the design of age-appropriate playgrounds; (2) the provision of proper surfacing under and around playground equipment; (3) the provision of proper supervision on playgrounds; and (4) properly maintaining playgrounds. Information regarding this program's activities may be accessed by contacting the University of Northern Iowa, or at the website www.uni.edu/playground (see figure 7.8).

Information Local governments also have a responsibility to provide public information concerning leisure pursuits. Most local park and recreation agencies disseminate information regarding their activities and resources and develop brochures emphasizing program offerings or focusing on unique facilities.

Some local park and recreation departments take an even more comprehensive approach to information dissemination, helping individuals become aware of available services throughout the entire community. Still further, a few parks and recreation departments have engaged in leisure education and leisure counseling. These two activities often aim at trying to influence the attitudes and behaviors of individuals. Some believe that cultivation of a positive leisure ethic and set of values contributes to a healthy lifestyle.

Figure 7.8

The National
Program for
Playground
Safety.

The
**National
Program for
Playground
Safety**

Keep Your Children Safe

A parent's quick checklist*

Place this list in a prominent area of your home for quick
reference. Then, before your children head out the door for the
playground, check that:

Supervision is present, but strings and rope aren't

*Adult presence is needed to watch for potential hazards, observe, intercede and facilitate play when
necessary. Strings on clothing and ropes used for play can cause accidental strangulation if
caught on equipment.*

All children play on age-appropriate equipment

*Preschoolers, ages 2–5, and children ages 5–12 are developmentally different and need different
equipment located in separate areas to keep the playground safe and fun for all.*

Falls to surface are cushioned

*Nearly 70 percent of all playground injuries are related to falls to the surface. Acceptable surfaces
include hardwood fiber/mulch, pea gravel, sand, and synthetic materials such as poured-in-place,
rubber mats or tiles. Playground surfaces should not be concrete, asphalt, grass, blacktop, packed
dirt or rocks.*

Equipment is safe

*Check to make sure the equipment is anchored safely in the ground, all equipment pieces are in
good working order, S-hooks are entirely closed, bolts are not protruding, there are no exposed
footings, etc. Safety checklists are available from the CPSC or the National Program for
Playground Safety.*

America's Playgrounds — Make them Safe

*This information was produced by the National Program for Playground Safety, University of Northern
Iowa, Cedar Falls, Iowa 50614-0161, 800-554-PLAY, http:uni.edu/coe/playgrnd.

An information brochure is found in figure 7.9. This brochure advertises self-directed
recreational and educational opportunities focused on natural history of the Cedar Valley Nature Trail. This area is a program of the Black Hawk County (Iowa) Conservation Board. The
brochure contains information concerning the woodlands, grasslands, and wetlands and geography found along the trail, including its flora, fauna, and wildlife. The brochure also includes a
map, which can be used for self-guided tours.

Leadership   Local park and recreation departments also provide leadership to communities.
This leadership occurs not only in the form of instruction or supervision of recreation programs but
also in a broader sense by helping communities to solve their leisure and social problems. Park and

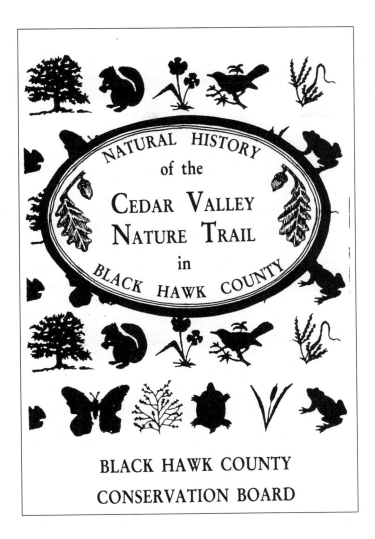

recreation personnel often play a key role in the identification and solution of community concerns. They bring to bear their expertise, knowledge, and experience to assist their community.

The leadership role played by professionals also includes promoting leisure values. In effect, the professional uses his or her expertise to influence community values concerning leisure. By promoting and interpreting the ideas and values of the leisure movement, professionals engage in leadership.

Professional Roles and Opportunities

Varied professional roles exist at the local level of government in the park and recreation area (see figure 7.10). In general, these professional roles can be divided into three classifications: direct service, supervisory, and administrative (Jordan, 2001).

Direct service professional roles involve the leading of activities, provision of information, or the operation or maintenance of a special facility. The majority of positions at the local level of government carried out on a part-time or seasonal basis fall into the direct service category.

Figure 7.10

Professional roles in the park and recreation field at the local level of government.

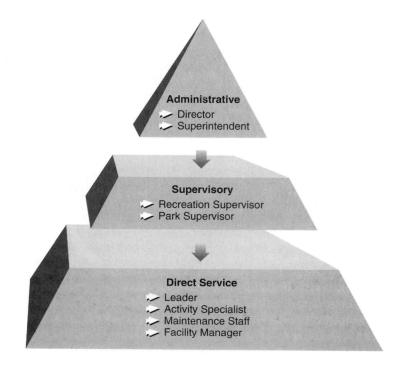

Administrative
- Director
- Superintendent

Supervisory
- Recreation Supervisor
- Park Supervisor

Direct Service
- Leader
- Activity Specialist
- Maintenance Staff
- Facility Manager

For example, a direct service provider in the position of a part-time or seasonal recreation leader would be involved in program leadership at a specific location such as a playground or community center. He or she would plan, organize, and lead groups in a variety of recreation activities. More specifically, the recreation leader might issue and collect equipment and supplies, teach recreation skills, perform simple maintenance tasks, and maintain records and activity reports.

Supervisory roles are middle-management functions within organizations. Park supervisors often manage a crew of workers or laborers, or maintain a cluster of areas or facilities. Recreation supervisors are employed for their specific knowledge of a program area or facility or for their general knowledge of recreation program development.

A recreation supervisor usually has primary responsibility for initiating and coordinating activity programs or managing a facility. In general, a recreation supervisor manages, oversees, and trains leaders and volunteers. She or he engages in such activities as planning programs with leaders, scheduling and coordinating activities, promoting and publicizing programs, and evaluating activities to determine whether they have met the needs of customers. The recreation supervisor is often called upon to speak publicly and to justify budget requests.

Another example of a supervisory role in the park and recreation field is that of a park supervisor. A park supervisor's work relates to the maintenance, construction, and landscaping of grounds and facilities and the supervision of work performed by semiskilled and unskilled personnel. In this role, a park supervisor would schedule jobs and work routines for maintenance, inspect areas to determine whether work met performance standards, and maintain basic time, material, and work records.

An example of an upper-level management position in the community parks and recreation field is described in figure 7.11 on pages 234 and 235. This position announcement describes the executive level position of Recreation, Parks and Arts Director for the City of Largo,

Florida. As one can see by reviewing the position announcement, the candidates must have graduated from accredited college or university with a degree in parks and recreation administration or a related area and possess five years of experience. This community seeks a leader in the parks and recreation field who will serve as an enthusiastic role model for the staff. Excellent oral and written communication skills are a requirement of the position.

Administrative roles, held by the senior managers of park and recreation organizations, include division heads as well as the head executive officer. These individuals primarily engage in long-range planning, public relations, budget analysis and control, and the supervision and direction of personnel.

A director of parks and recreation, for example, holds an administrative role. The head executive officer of a park and recreation agency is sometimes referred to as the superintendent of parks and recreation or the general manager. A park and recreation director administers the program and supervises all personnel within the department, either indirectly or directly. He or she establishes a program for the recruitment and selection of staff and controls all expenditures directly or indirectly. The director engages in long-range planning and carries out established organizational policy. A director also works with the public and/or other public or private agencies to determine community needs.

Career Opportunities in Public Parks and Recreation

In the 1960s, experts predicted that a gap would occur between the supply of college-educated workers trained in the public parks and recreation field and the positions available in the field. By the late 1980s, this gap had closed as the supply of college-educated workers had exceeded demand (Dunn, 1986). This trend has continued as the *Occupational Outlook Handbook* (2000) indicates that competition will remain keen for career positions in recreation.

Three factors have contributed to a decline in the number of opportunities that are available in the public park and recreation sector today. First, there has been phenomenal growth in the number of colleges and universities offering professional education in the park and recreation area. In the early 1950s, only a handful offered these curricula throughout the United States. At one point, in the 1970s, more than 400 institutions offered degree programs in the park and recreation area. In 2000 the number of accredited bachelor's programs in parks and recreation was 100. Second, public support for public park and recreation services has shown a general decline, although more recent trends seem to indicate park and recreation departments are growing with funding coming from a wide variety of sources. The third factor influencing the decline in opportunities in the public park and recreation profession is the decrease in the movement of professionals within the field today as compared with past years. In the public sector, individuals extend their careers for long periods, resulting in little turnover and a lack of movement to new positions.

The future outlook for public (local) agencies is good however, as opportunities for recreation professionals is "expected to grow about as fast as the average for all occupations through 2008, as growing numbers of people spend more time and money on leisure services. Growth in these jobs will also stem from increased interest in fitness and health and the rising demand for recreational opportunities for older adults in senior centers and retirement communities. In particular, jobs will increase in social services as more recreation professionals are needed to develop and lead activity programs in senior centers, halfway houses, children's homes, and day-care programs for people with special needs" (*Occupational Outlook Handbook,* 2000, p. 60).

Figure 7.11

Recruitment/position announcement for an upper-level position in recreation.

NOW RECRUITING

Recreation, Parks and Arts Director City of Largo, Florida

The City of Largo, Florida is seeking a proven professional to fill the executive level position of Recreation, Parks and Arts Director.

The City's anticipated growth due to annexation, along with the community's commitment to the importance of recreation, parks and arts, necessitates an effective Recreation, Parks and Arts Director who has outstanding visionary and communication skills, professional passion, creativity and innovation and community relations skills and involvement. The Director will plan, coordinate and administer comprehensive leisure and arts programs, a parks system and special athletic facilities. Currently the city operates four recreation centers, 2 aquatic facilities (one being a new family aquatic center), three community outreach centers, four athletic facilities, a cultural center, golf course, and tennis complex. The department also maintains 434 acres of park land. The largest area is Largo Central Park—a 170 acre park in the heart of town. Largo also has a new 35 acre Nature Preserve, as well as two other nature parks and a Dog Park. The City will soon be constructing a skatepark and an expansion of the aquatic center which includes a 28 foot slide.

Qualified candidates for the Recreation, Parks and Arts Director position will have graduated from an accredited college or university with a degree in park and recreation administration, community services, public administration or related field and have a minimum of five years of management experience. Professional certification and a Masters Degree are preferred. The successful candidate will be a leader in the field and an engaged and enthusiastic role model for department personnel, will place a high priority on continuous self-development and staff development, will assume responsibility for department operations and management, will be committed to fostering participation at all levels of the department and will be a team member supporting the overall mission of the City. The Recreation, Parks and Arts Director will be supportive of the City Manager and City Commission form of government. Excellent oral and written communication skills are critical.

The salary is negotiable to $82,000 depending on qualifications, and a generous benefits package is provided. Interested persons must submit the following application materials: a City application (completed in its entirety and signed), a resume, three professional references, and a letter summarizing your qualifications. Application materials must be received by March 14, 2003. More detailed information and the application are available on the website: www.largo.com/rec_dir.html.

Questions or requests for materials also may be directed to Human Resources. If accommodations are needed to receive or complete the application, please call. The City of Largo is an equal opportunity employer.

Photos:

Top: Largo Cultural Center- With over 133 performances per year and 341 rentals, the 24,000 sq. ft. facility is well-known as one of the area's premiere cultural centers.

Middle: McGough Nature Park is a beautiful park located along the Intracoastal Waterway. It includes nature trails, picnic areas and shelters, a playground, restrooms and a boardwalk which leads to a panoramic view of the Intracoastal.

Bottom: City of Largo Clock Tower. A city landmark located in the popular Largo Central Park. Many equate this structure as the Heart of Largo.

In 1905, residents built the county's first church and first school and incorporated a one square-mile city with fewer than 300 residents.

Through the years, tourism flourished throughout the Suncoast and many tourists decided to stay. Orange groves that had put Largo on the map gave way to housing and business development.

But some of old Largo remains and the City government and community groups are actively protecting historic structures and redeveloping the early downtown area.

With a population of nearly 70,000 year-round residents, Largo is the third-largest of the 24 municipalities in Pinellas County.

Quiet tree-lined residential streets, lots of wonderful recreation facilities, art events and parks make a true family atmosphere. It may be hard to imagine that this 15-square-mile city is part of a 2.2-million population metropolis.

We enjoy affordable housing, low property taxes and one of the lowest crime rates in the state, a healthy business economy and convenient transportation routes to the rest of the Suncoast . . . and the world.

Then there's the weather—from an average low of 59 degrees in winter to an average high of 82 degrees in summer. And it's clean air, too, thanks to breezes from the Gulf of Mexico.

A recent poll conducted by the St. Petersburg Times captured and published statements from a large majority of residents, all agreeing that quality Recreation, Parks and Arts is what makes living in Largo so special.

One interesting fact with respect to jobs for the future is that many retirements will occur in the next decade as a result of the retirements of the early years of the baby boom generation. As a result, there will be many mid-level management opportunities available in the very near future. Career progression should be accelerated as a result of this situation.

Individuals desiring a career in local government in the park and recreation field should follow several steps. First—and most essential—the student should attain a degree from an accredited institution in the park and recreation field. Second, individuals should seek paid seasonal, part-time, and voluntary opportunities in the park and recreation field. The more experience, the better, especially if it is diverse and of high quality. In addition, individuals should make an attempt to get acquainted with professionals in the field by joining professional associations or societies and attending conferences, meetings, and seminars. The key is to establish a network that will position the student prominently when opportunities are presented.

Challenges for the Future

Park and recreation professionals operating at the local level of government face many challenges. The rate of change in society is increasing. In the 1980s David Gray (1984) recognized this trend when he wrote,

> This is a time of great concern, uncertainty, ambivalence, and ambiguity in the recreation and park movement. It is a time of change. Change brings crisis and opportunity. In periods of rapid change, reforms are possible that could never be accomplished in periods of stability. Flexibility, recognition of opportunity, escape from pessimistic thinking, and leadership are required to respond to this period. (p. 47)

Change continues to be the norm as we begin the twenty-first century, and there is still a great deal of uncertainty for park and recreation professionals. The basic values and assumptions upon which the public park and recreation movement was built are being called into question. New approaches, strategies, and vehicles of service delivery will be required to meet emerging societal needs, as well as maintenance of the traditional values of the profession. This realization has led to a number of efforts to identify critical trends and issues in the field as well as to create an agenda for the profession in the future.

Innovative responses to specific trends and issues, as well as future needs and directions for public park and recreation departments, are the following:

- *Marketing Orientation.* Public parks and recreation programs are utilizing marketing techniques more to better respond to changing needs of those they serve. A marketing orientation requires a different way of thinking about the consumer than has been historically the case in the park and recreation field.
- *Fees and Charges.* Increasingly public parks and recreation departments are using fees and charges to finance programs. In 1974–1975 self-generated funds constituted 14.2 percent of total expenditures on park and recreation services, but by 1987–1988 this had increased to 24 percent (Crompton and McGregor, 1994). In addition, a survey of sixty small towns in the midwest and west found that the most frequently reported revenue source for parks and recreation was fees and charges (Weissinger and Murphy, 1993).
- *Quality Services.* Assuring the quality of their programs is an important task for park and recreation departments, and many organizations are turning to the concept of Total Quality Management (TQM) to help ensure quality outcomes. In addition, accreditation of leisure professionals is another means of quality assurance.
- *Building Partnerships.* Developing partnerships is one way of dealing with funding shortfalls. "Partnerships take many forms when it comes to protecting natural and cultural

resources and providing recreation opportunities. Regardless of the form, they do have some common elements. These include a shared vision, shared risks, and shared benefits. Without this shared approach, the success of the partnership will be questionable" (Walters, 1992, p. 2). An example of a partnership with a local park and recreation department is Hostelling International's Chamounix Mansion, Philadelphia Hostel. The mission of hostelling is "to help all, especially the young, gain a greater understanding of the world and its people through hostelling". The Philadelphia Hostel is situated in Fairmount Park in the Chamounix Mansion. Built in 1802, the Federal style mansion and surrounding property were taken over by the city in 1871 and incorporated into Fairmount Park, one of the largest urban parks in the nation. In 1954, the mansion stood desolate and the Parks Commission was contemplating demolition when a group of hostelling volunteers approached the Parks Commission with the idea of establishing a hostel in Philadelphia in the mansion. The Parks Commission agreed and provided funds to volunteers to help renovate the mansion. Over the last thirty years this hostel has been very successful. Today it has more than sixty beds for overnight guests and also serves as an active community center, hosting conferences, educational programs, young athletes attending sporting events, and much more (Krause, 1996).

- *Contracting Services.* Contracting and privatization are also becoming more commonplace as governments on all levels downsize. "Virtually anything and everything is up for grabs in the next decade" (Dickinson, 1996, p. 41). Eighty-three percent of city and county governments use private contractors to provide at least some form of service. Although core programs such as fire, police, and other social services (like recreation) are the least likely to be privatized, the possibility does exist as everyone continues to look for ways to shrink government and improve the quality of service.

- *Networking.* As public support in the form of tax revenues declines, park and recreation systems are generating revenue in other ways. Fees and charges generate considerable funds in support of park and recreation services. Park and recreation organizations are also working with other disciplines to find ways of sharing resources and problem-solving skills.

- *Diversity.* All demographic and census studies indicate that the population of the United States is becoming more multiracial and multicultural. African Americans, Hispanics, and to a lesser degree, Asian Americans are increasing in number (Kraus, 2000). This changing demographic picture will increasingly influence recreation and recreation resource demand. Park and recreation professionals will need to become increasingly aware of recreational preferences as well as to continue to develop programs that contribute to reducing racial tensions and discrimination and promoting respect for all groups in society (Kraus, 2000).

- *Inclusion.* Local park and recreation departments need to move to a more inclusive philosophy for delivering services to people with disabilities. Law mandates community park and recreation programs meet the needs of people with disabilities. This includes both integrating people with disabilities into traditional programming and providing specialized programs when necessary.

- *Child Care.* Increasingly, parks and recreation departments are creating child care programs that serve very young children. Furthermore, latchkey programs are being developed to serve the needs of children from the time they get out of school until their parents can pick them up.

- *Youth Development.* The youth development approach is a relatively new paradigm of research and service in dealing with children and adolescents. It is rapidly gaining

Child's Play, Adult Spin: A Level Playing Field

Chicago—If the ball in one corner of Brands Park in Chicago calls to mind the movie "Bend it Like Beckham," the ball in the opposing corner recalls another British export, TV's "Teletubbies."

As bouncy and banana-yellow as the Tubbie named Laa-Laa, the kickball in this game rarely plays hard to get, inviting contact to the same degree that the neighboring soccer ball seems to dodge it during a simultaneous match.

That accessibility helps explain why so many adults are regressing to a prepubescent pastime.

The Chicago Sport and Social Club's co-ed kickball league, introduced last fall with ten or twelve teams, sold out of slots this spring. More than fifty teams now play either on Mondays or Saturdays.

Separately, the World Adult Kickball Association, based in Washington, D.C., is branching out as it builds to 10,000 players across the country.

For more information on the World Adult Kickball Association's leagues, check out www.worldkickball.com

Source: Child's play, adult spin: A Level Playing Field. 2003. *Chicago Tribune* (June 19).

acceptance as the preferred approach when dealing with young people by a large majority of youth-serving organizations (including local park and recreation departments). Although there is no universally accepted definition of youth development, it can be viewed as an orientation, which involves shifting away from concentrating on problems, toward concentrating on strengths. A youth development approach strives to create a wide variety of programs that build competencies and assets in youth and fosters opportunities for adults and youth to develop caring, long-term relationships (see table 7.4). In summary, youth development can be viewed as a multifaceted approach to working with youth whereby young people seek ways to meet their basic physical and social needs and to build a broad range of competencies making connections with themselves, others, and the larger community.

The move to a youth development approach in dealing with youth creates many opportunities for local park and recreation departments through the programs and services they offer to youth. To assist local park and recreation departments in implementing a youth development orientation in their programs, the National Recreation and Park Association has launched NRPA 2000, Urban Youth Initiative. The goals of this initiative include (1) increasing public awareness of recreation programs and activities and the benefits they provide, (2) broadening the knowledge of youth in regard to the field of recreation and the many opportunities it presents, and (3) implementing partnerships that provide programs in urban areas that will concentrate on building awareness, confidence, and self-esteem in youth (NRPA, n.d., Urban Youth Initiative).

An example of a local park and recreation department promoting youth development that embodies many of the characteristics put forth in table 7.4 is the city of Austin's "Get R.E.A.L. (Recreation, Education, Activities, Leader) Program." Since its inception in 1998, eight roving leaders and their assistants have gone into the city's neighborhoods to work with youth who are particularly vulnerable to gangs, drugs, violence, and alcohol. "Their overall goal is to be a beacon to guide kids into healthy lifestyles and help them make good choices for the future" (Baker and Witt, 2000, p. 87).

- *Developing Social Capital.* As mentioned in Chapter 5, people today often feel isolated from their neighbors and feel that there has been a loss of community in recent years. This loss, described by Putnam (2000) as the loss of social capital, creates an opportunity for local parks and recreation departments. Putnam notes that in the past when America felt a loss of social capital, it was the parks and recreation movement that stepped in and created programs, facilities, and services, which helped bring Americans together again. Putnam's challenge to the park and recreation movement is this: "Let us find ways to ensure that by 2010 Americans will spend less leisure time sitting passively alone in front of a glowing screen [TV] and more time in active connection with our fellow citizens. . . . Henry Ward Beecher's advice a century ago to 'multiply picnics' is not entirely ridiculous today" (p. 410).
- *New Programs, New Facilities.* There will be a continued evolution of leisure programs, areas, and facilities. Florida (2002) suggests that leisure will reflect a more active lifestyle and individuals will experience more efficient use of their leisure. Areas and facilities that package or bundle multiple services will become the norm. Individuals will continue their "quest for experience." Creative people will live creative lifestyles.
- *Open Space.* The recreation needs of an expanding population require new facilities and open space. Yet open space areas are becoming harder to find. For example, in the Chicago area it is projected that most of the remaining open space opportunities will be lost in the next twenty years (Westfall, 1991). One innovative response to providing open space is creating long linear parks that connect existing open space. Such greenways often follow rivers, power corridors, or old railway corridors. Another way for park and recreation departments to be innovative in developing open space is through partnering with both public and private organizations that are promoting many of the concepts of new urbanism.
- *New Urbanism.* In the early 1990s, a new architectural and urban design movement began to take shape and move into the mainstream. This movement has been identified as *new urbanism.* Katz (1994) feels this movement is relevant because it addresses many of the ills of our current sprawl development pattern while encouraging the building of social capital and community. According to Katz (1994, p. x), "If the New Urbanism can indeed be shown to deliver a higher, more sustainable quality of life to a majority of this nation's citizens, we can only hope that it will be embraced as the next paradigm for the shaping of American communities". The principles of new urbanism include examining both the neighborhood and the region as a whole and making the scale of neighborhoods more community friendly. A critical component of new urbanism is the concept of public space. Public space should be a primary consideration rather than a residual thought for neighborhoods. As urban planners contemplate how to apply the concepts of new urbanism in an effort to promote a sense of community, public park and recreation professionals have a wonderful opportunity to incorporate the key values of park and recreation programs. To this end, park and recreation professionals must learn more about the concepts of new urbanism and look for ways in which to partner with city planners as they move forward in encouraging the development of social capital and a sense of community in our towns and cities.
- *Documenting Benefits.* Documenting outcomes provided by programs is becoming common practice. Park and recreation professionals must be able to identify and substantiate the benefits of their programs and services. For example, for park and recreation departments to move beyond a fun and games approach to a youth development approach in working with youth, they must document and begin to understand how their

programs impact youth. Caldwell (2000) reiterates this point and points out that if recreation services are not relevant to communities, and if the research that is conducted is not relevant, we may "go out of business."

The challenges and opportunities presented in this section will stretch park and recreation professionals in the next century to reach out and foster new partnerships with both the commercial and nonprofit sectors to forge a vision that will continue to address the quality of life issue for all Americans. In striving to meet these challenges of the twenty-first century, Hartsoe (n.d.), encourages professionals to keep in mind four central concepts that have fostered the growth of public parks and recreation over the last century:

1. Promoting the importance of parks and open spaces in creating a livable urban environment;
2. Stressing the need for positive recreation experiences for all citizens, particularly children and youth;
3. Emphasizing the essential role of recreation in improving individual health and well-being; and
4. Recognizing the central role that building strong local citizen support has had in developing successful park and recreation programs.

These types of responses provide insight for the future development of the public parks and recreation departments. The next several decades will be exciting and dynamic and will offer opportunities to redefine and reshape the very essence of the public parks and recreation movement.

Summary

Park and recreation services provided at the local level of government emerged as a result of social needs that occurred at the beginning of the Industrial Revolution in the United States. The phrase *local park and recreation services* refers to those public services that are provided at the subdivision of government that is closest to the customer. People view such services as important and necessary—and as a strong factor in the livability of an environment.

This chapter discussed the three basic subdivisions of government at the local level that provide park and recreation services—municipalities, counties, and special districts. Provision of park and recreation services under the jurisdiction of a municipal government is the most common form of organization. In this arrangement, services are offered as a part of the community service offerings of an entire city government. Counties, the subdivision of government just below state government, often provide park and recreation services in such a way as to link the resources of various cities, towns, and districts within their jurisdiction. Special park and recreation districts are autonomous and independent subdivisions of government. Their single focus on park and recreation services makes them an especially effective method for organizing services.

Individuals involved in professional positions in local park and recreation agencies often perceive themselves as working in partnership with the residents of their communities. They see themselves as service providers, as well as problem solvers, in identifying and analyzing community concerns. Individuals involved in public service also often see themselves as being altruistic. That is, they view themselves as being primarily motivated by service to others.

Professionals in local park and recreation agencies today face numerous challenges. The need to redefine basic values, adopt new management strategies, and seek innovative sources of funding make work opportunities in this area both exciting and challenging. Those individuals pursuing leadership, supervisory, and administrative roles in the local park and recreation area will often be rewarded with satisfying, stimulating, and creative professional opportunities.

Discussion Questions

1. Define the phrase *local park and recreation services.*
2. Identify sources of revenue for local park and recreation services.
3. Compare and contrast three types of governmental organizations providing park and recreation services at the local level.
4. Identify and define five types of legislation that can be used to establish local park and recreation services.
5. Identify five functions that may be performed by county park and recreation systems. Which do you believe is most important, and why?
6. Identify professional roles in the park and recreation field at the local level of government.
7. Discuss what you perceive as professional career opportunities in public parks and recreation.
8. Identify and discuss challenges facing professionals at the local level of government. How are they being addressed in your community?
9. Discuss how school districts are enabled to provide local park and recreation services.
10. What is the relationship of a local park and recreation agency to those whom it serves?

References

Baker, J., and P. Witt. 2000. Backstreet beacons: Austin's roving leaders. *Journal of Park and Recreation Administration 18*(1), 87–105.

Brayley, R., and D. McLean. 1999. *Managing Financial Resources in Sport and Leisure Service Organizations.* Champaign, IL: Sagamore.

Burke, W. 1992. A prophet of Eden. *Buzzworm 4*(2), 18–19.

Busser, J. 1999. Human resource management. Edited by B. van der Smissen, M. Moiseichik, V. Hartenburg, and L. Twardzik, in *Management of Park and Recreation Agencies.* Ashburn, VA: NRPA.

Caldwell, L. 2000. Beyond fun and games? Challenges to adopting a prevention and youth development approach to youth recreation. *Journal of Park and Recreation Management 18*(3), 1–18.

Crompton, J., and B. McGregor. 1994. Trends in the financing and staffing of local government park and recreation services. *Journal of Park and Recreation Administration 12*(3), 19–37.

Crompton, J.L., and Kaczynski, A. 2003. Trends in Local Park and Recreation Department Finances and Staffing from 1964–65 to 1999–2000. *Journal of Park and Recreation Administration 21,*(4), 124–144.

DeGraaf, D., R. Ramsin, J. Gassman, and K. DeGraaf. in press. *Camp Counseling: A Staff Development Approach.* Dubuque, IA: Eddie Bowers.

DeGraaf, D., D. Jordan, and K. DeGraaf. 1998. *Programming for Parks, Recreation and Leisure Services: A Servant Leadership Approach.* State College, PA: Venture.

Deppe, T. 1983. *Management Strategies in Financing Parks and Recreation.* New York: Wiley.

Dickinson, R. 1996. The rush to sell off government. *American Demographics* (February), 41.

Driver, B., P. Brown, and G. Peterson. 1991. *Benefits of Leisure.* State College, PA: Venture.

Dunn, D. 1986. Professionalism and human resources. *Leisure Today—Journal of Physical Education, Recreation, and Dance* (October), 50–53.

Edginton, C. 1978. Organizational goals—what directors think they should be and are. *Recreation Canada 5*(36), 33–35, 39, 41.

Edginton, C., and L. Neal. 1983. Park and recreation directors' perceptions of organizational goals. *Journal of Park and Recreation Administration 1*(1), 39–49.

Edginton, C., and J. O'Neill. 1999. Program, services and events management. Edited by B. van der Smissen, M. Moiseichik, V. Hartenburg, and L. Twardzik, in *Management of Park and Recreation Agencies.* Ashburn, VA: NRPA.

Florida, R. 2002. *The Rise of the Creative Class.* New York, Basic Books.

Godbey, G. 1997. *Leisure and Leisure Services in the 21st Century.* State College, PA: Venture.

Gray, D. 1984. Managing our way to a preferred future. *Parks and Recreation 19*(5), 47–49.

Greenleaf, R. 1977. *Servant Leadership: A Journey into the Nature of Legitimate Power and Greatness.* New York: Paulist Press.

Hartsoe, C. n.d. A foundation for the future. *The Millenium Vision: Exploring the Future of Parks and Recreation.* A supplement to *Parks and Recreation,* 38–42.

Hastings, M. 1984. *A Comparison of Canadian Municipal Parks and Recreation Director's Perception of Organizational Goal Importance in 1976 and 1984,* unpublished doctoral dissertation, University of Oregon.

Haurwitz, R. 1992. Soothing the city soul. *Buzzworm 4*(5), 18–19.

Hemphill, S. 1985. Revenue management: Beginning with the basics. *Park and Recreation 20*(12), 35–36.

Howat, G., and C. Edginton. 1986. A study of the goals for Australian local government parks and recreation. *Australian Parks and Recreation 22*(4), 12–15.

Hunt, K.S., Scott, D., and Richardson, S. 2003. Positioning Public Recreation and Park Offerings Using Importance-Performance Analysis. *Journal of Park and Recreation Administration 21*(3), p. 1–21.

Jarvi, C. 1993. Leadership to meet the demands of today's changing needs. Unpublished manuscript.

Jordan, D. 2001. *Leadership in Leisure Services: Making a Difference.* State College, PA: Venture.

Katz, P. 1994. *The New Urbanism: Toward an Architecture of Community.* New York: McGraw-Hill.

Kraus, R. 2000. *Leisure in a Changing America: Trends and Issues for the 21st Century.* Boston, MA: Allyn & Bacon.

Kraus, R., and J. Curtis. 1986. *Creative Management in Recreation, Parks and Leisure Services.* 4th ed. St. Louis: Times Mirror/Mosby.

Kraus, R., and J. Curtis. 2000. *Creative Management in Recreation, Parks, and Leisure Services.* 5th ed. Boston, MA: McGraw-Hill.

Krause, D. 1996. *Creative Partnerships: Private/Public Successes in Developing Hostels.* Washington, DC: Hostelling International—American Youth Hostels.

Kreck, C. 2000, January. Kid's-eye view of city's comprehensive plan: Looks at family issues. *Denver Post,* E.Z.

Lappe, F., and P. DuBois. 1994. *The Quickening of America: Rebuilding Our Nation, Remaking Our Lives.* San Francisco, CA: Jossey-Bass.

Mobley, T., and R. Toalson. 1992. *Parks and Recreation in the 21st Century: Part I.* Arlington, VA: NRPA.

Naisbitt, J., and P. Aburdene. 1985. *Re-inventing the Corporation.* New York: Warner Books.

NRPA. n.d. *NRPA 2000: Urban Youth Initiative.* Washington, DC: NRPA.

NRPA, 1998. *Discover the Benefits.* Ashburn, VA: NRPA.

Putnam, R. 2000. *Bowling Alone: The Collapse and Revival of American Community.* New York: Simon & Schuster.

Rails to Trails Conservancy. 1993. *Great Rail-Trails.* Washington, DC: Living Planet Press.

Rodney, L., and R. Toalson. 1981. *Administration of Recreation, Parks and Leisure Services.* 2d ed. New York: John Wiley and Sons.

Spears, L. 1995. Servant leadership and the Greenleaf legacy. Edited by L. Spear, in *Reflections on Leadership: How Robert K. Greenleaf's Theory of Servant Leadership Influenced Today's Top Management Thinkers,* pp.1–16. New York: Wiley.

Staff. 2000. *Occupational Outlook Handbook.*

U.S. Census Bureau. 1997a. *1997 Census of Governments: Volume 4, Government Finances—Finances of Municipal and Township Governments.* Washington, DC: U.S. Department of Commerce.

U.S. Census Bureau. 1997b. *1997 Census of Governments: Volume 4, Government Finances—Finances of County Governments.* Washington, DC: U.S. Department of Commerce.

U.S. Census Bureau. 1997c. *1997 Census of Governments: Volume 4, Government Finances—Finances of Special District Governments.* Washington, DC: U.S. Department of Commerce.

U.S. Census Bureau. 1999. *Statistical Abstract of the United States: 2003* (123rd ed.) Washington, DC.

Walters, W. 1992. Partnerships in parks and preservation. *Trends 29*(2), 2.

Weissinger, E., and D. Murphy. 1993. A survey of fiscal conditions in small town public recreation departments from 1987 to 1991. *Journal of Park and Recreation Administration 11*(3), 61–71.

Westfall, R. 1991. Emerging trends at the state level. *Trends 28*(2), 39–42.

Whyte, D. 1992. Key trends and issues impacting local government recreation and park administration in the 1990s: A focus for strategic management and research. *Journal of Park and Recreation Administration 10*(3), 84–106.

WSSRA. 1993. *West Suburban Special Recreation Association.* Franklin Park, IL: West Suburban Special Recreation Association.

Delivery of Leisure Services: State Government

State governments often provide natural resources such as lakes, parks, beaches, and historic and cultural areas.

Source: Department of Natural Resources. State of Iowa. Used by permission

Introduction

Prior to the turn of the twentieth century the involvement of states in offering amenities for their residents was relatively simple. Services such as education, health, and welfare were the concerns of private agencies such as the church. With the coming of the Industrial Revolution and the concentration of people in larger urban areas, each state gradually accepted responsibility for providing specific services for its residents. Today, recreation has become an accepted and even expected service provided by individual states.

The basis for involvement by individual states in providing parks and recreation opportunities is found in the Tenth Amendment to the Constitution of the United States. This amendment, also known as the states' rights amendment, was passed in 1925 and clarified the role of the state versus the federal government in providing services to its residents. The amendment states that "the powers not delegated to the United States by the Constitution, nor prohibited by it to the States, are reserved to the States respectively, or to the people." This amendment was originally regarded as the source of state powers in such areas as public education, welfare, and health services. As time progressed, states included recreation facilities and services as a part of their responsibility in meeting the needs of their residents.

The importance of state government in providing recreation facilities and programs is increasing. Many feel that federal programs have become "unmanageable, ineffective, costly, confusing, and unaccountable to the public" (Kraus, 1990, p. 226), and that states would do a better job of administering many programs, including recreation. Thus, this chapter examines the historical role of states in the provision of recreational facilities and services, current practices of states in the provision of recreational facilities and services, and future options of states in meeting residents' recreational needs.

Characteristics of State Leisure Services

This section of the chapter presents the characteristics of state and provincial governments as they pertain to leisure services. As Meyer and Brightbill (1950) stated nearly a half century ago, "State government is a foundation stone of the American way of life" (p. 1) and, "The aim and purpose of government should be to bring about the greatest good for the greatest number of people" (p. 2). Initially, the goals and functions of state government are discussed, followed by information concerning the resource base of state government. Finally, a review of the characteristics of professionals involved in the delivery of state and provincial government leisure services is presented.

Goals and Functions

The distinctions made between the functions of state government and the direct delivery of services are often difficult to understand. For the purpose of this chapter, however, the functions of state government revolve around the legislative process as well as the role state governments play in the coordination of services between federal, state, and local areas (see figure 8.1).

Legislation   One important function of state and provincial governments is the creation of legislative acts in support of the provision of park and recreation services. Such legislation can directly impact the provision of services by state government. The state government also plays an important role in creating enabling legislation for local and municipal governments to establish and provide recreation and parks programs. Such enabling legislation provides city, county, and special-district governments with the specific authority to acquire property, employ personnel, or impose taxes to support recreation; it is generally granted to municipal governments by constitutional, statutory, or charter provisions granted by the state legislature.

This type of legislation, often entitled *enabling legislation,* may range from simple authorization to fully detailed codes. According to Kraus (1990), enabling legislation can include such

Figure 8.1

Roles and functions of state government.

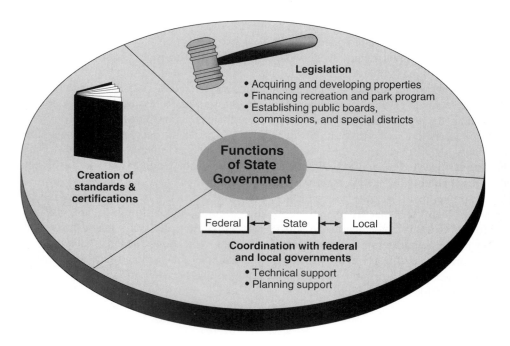

elements as the method of acquiring and developing properties, financing recreation and park programs, and establishing public boards, commissions, and special districts. Such legislation, as well as statutes and laws, vary from state to state as southern states like Florida do not need to be concerned with snow skiing or snowmobiling. Likewise, in states like Wyoming, issues about ocean beaches and saltwater fishing and boating are irrelevant.

Creation of Standards and Certifications The standards and regulations created by state governments to regulate many types of recreational providers also relate to the legislative process. For example, a commercial recreation provider, such as an organized camp, must adhere to the health and sanitation laws of the state. Likewise, the seating capacity for a sports event or a movie must conform to state or local laws and ordinances such as fire regulations. Other areas of regulatory laws include laws that specify facility standards, laws that ensure accessibility, and laws that regulate and/or prohibit certain types of recreation such as gambling or prostitution.

A growing number of states have also promoted and developed standards for recreation programs and leadership, influenced the development of new commercial recreation opportunities, and set up standards, certifications, and registration programs for specific positions in the field. For example, therapeutic recreation specialists are licensed in Georgia and Utah.

Coordination with Federal and Local Governments

The final report of the Outdoor Recreation Resources Review Commission (1962) encouraged states to assume the pivotal role of bridging the gap between federal and local services. At the beginning of the twenty-first century, this recommendation is even more timely. As government budgets on all levels shrink, due in many cases to citizen-initiated tax-cutting programs, it is increasingly important to coordinate existing services to avoid overlap and to stretch program dollars as far as they will go. Just as no governmental subdivision alone can clean up a polluted river or deal with such social issues as homelessness, the problems of recreation planning and programming must be approached in an integrated fashion. All levels of government need to be involved, and in many cases it appears that state governments are in the best position to fill this coordinating role.

State cooperation with the federal government has often centered around recreational planning. For example, through the Land and Water Conservation Fund Act of 1965, the federal government encouraged states to prepare an approved, comprehensive recreation plan. States that created such plans received matching funds for the acquisition and development of state recreation lands. The outgrowth of many of these planning efforts included proposals for wild and scenic rivers, historical preservation initiatives, and other grant proposals to improve both state and local recreation resources. In recent years, with the demise of the Land and Water Conservation Act, federal funds have diminished; however, many state governments are continuing this planning process in an effort to better coordinate resources for recreation. States also monitor federal resources and federal grants to expand recreation resources.

One of the first efforts at identifying the coordinating role of state government in promoting recreation and leisure on the local level was developed by Meyer and Brightbill (1950) in their book, *State Recreation*. These efforts can be summarized into two general areas, technical support and planning support. Technical support includes such things as assisting communities in organizing and improving local recreation systems, providing assistance in securing and improving local and state legislation and related legal recreation problems, providing research for good decision making as well as helping to prepare surveys and appraisals of statewide and specific recreation needs and conditions, and assisting in methods of financing and budgeting. Planning support includes such things as assisting in the preparation of long-range plans for recreation, creating a comprehensive recreation policy for the state, and investigating and helping meet recreation needs in special settings such as rural areas and state and local institutions.

Resource Base

State governments draw resources from a variety of sources to support the services they provide for their residents. An overview of revenues can be examined to highlight the specific revenue sources of leisure and recreation services. The more common methods of finance include the following:

Taxes. This type of financial resource comes from the general fund provided from tax revenues generated by state government. In general, these taxes occur as a result of levies against the income of individuals, corporations, or other units, as well as sales taxes from such commodities as gasoline, alcoholic beverages, tobacco, and other nondurable goods.

Fees and charges. Most state governments levy a fee or charge for exclusive use of an area or facilities. A good example of a fee is the levy charged an individual for the exclusive use of a campsite at a state park or forest for one or more nights. Another example of a fee or charge would be the levy required for entry into a specialized area such as a botanical garden, beach, marina, park, or other resource.

Federal funds. State governments use funds provided by the federal government to support acquisition and development of natural and other resources.

Endowments and trusts. State governments may receive gifts in the form of cash, natural resources, or other items of value. These may be placed in endowments or trusts that can be used to generate revenue in support of budgets of state governments. Most endowments or trusts specifically focus on maintenance, development, or acquisition of a specific resource.

Sales revenue from concessions and retail outlets. State governments can generate revenues from concessions on public lands. Sales of food, clothing, guides, books, pamphlets, and equipment may earn income for state government. Revenue is often also earned from the rental of equipment such as canoes, paddle boats, and beach umbrellas.

The majority of state government resources comes from taxes, followed by revenues generated from fees and charges. Like other leisure services provided by the government, state units increasingly generate revenues from sources other than taxes. As a result, those using the services of state governments often pay directly rather than having taxpayer-subsidized access to areas, facilities, and recreational programs and services.

Although the overall expenditure by state governments ($1.08 trillion) is approximately the same as for local governments ($996 billion), the percentage of expenditures by state governments for parks and recreation services is significantly less than at the local level of government. State governments spend approximately $4 billion for parks and recreation compared with $20 billion at the local level (U.S. Census Bureau, 2003).

For example, financing for state parks comes from a variety of sources. Wealthy individuals often help support state parks. In the United States, the federal government has in the past assisted in the acquisition of state park lands through the Land and Water Conservation Fund. Other means of financing both the acquisition and maintenance of park systems include state ability to

TABLE

8.1   REVENUE SOURCES OF STATE GOVERNMENT

Revenue Source	1996 Amount (million/US $)	2000 Amount (million/US $)
Taxes		
Includes: property, personal income, corporation, income sales, and gross receipts	399,222	539,655
Charges and miscellaneous fees	120,752	170,747
Includes: parks and recreation fees	1,000	1,132
Interest earnings	28,621	35,008
Motor vehicles and operator licenses	13,848	16,445
Death and gifts	5,320	7,998
Sale of property	5,320	476
Special assessment	209	81

Source: U.S. Bureau of the Census. 2003. *Statistical Abstracts of the United States: 2003.* 123rd ed. Washington, DC: U. S. Government Printing Office. U.S. Bureau of the Census. 1999. *Statistical Abstracts of the United States: 1999.* 119th ed. Washington, DC: U.S. Government Printing Office.

teach, resolve conflicts between individuals, negotiate, and manage. There is a need for natural resource managers to be socially sensitive in dealing with customers and staff. The narrow focus of some individuals working in these positions often produces a "technical narrowness" that may result in a lack of creativity, innovation, and imagination in decision making.

The U.S. Census Bureau (2003) reports that there are 36,100 individuals employed at the state level of government in the park and recreation field. California, with 3,500 state employees, and Georgia, with 3,100 state employees, have the largest number of state employees in the park and recreation field. Other states employing a large number of individuals at the state level of government in parks and recreation include Florida, Kentucky, Louisiana, Massachusetts, New Jersey, New York, Oklahoma, Pennsylvania, Tennessee, and Texas. Interestingly, the state of Kentucky employs more individuals at the state level than at the local level of government in the park and recreation field. Further, the relative number of employees in state government is not directly related to its population rank. For example, Georgia is ranked tenth in population, yet has the second highest number of state employees involved in parks and recreation in the United States.

Types of Direct Recreation Resources and Services Provided by States

States play an increasingly important role in providing park and recreation programs, areas, and facilities. Collectively, the states spent more than $4 billion for parks and recreation services and $15 billion for natural resources (U.S. Bureau of Census, 2003). Table 8.2 presents park and recreation expenditures by state compared with population rank. States with the largest expenditures for state parks and recreation are New York, New Jersey, California, Maryland, and Louisiana. When compared with their population ranking, states such as Maryland, Louisiana, Kentucky, and Arkansas spend more funds per capita for state parks and recreation than other states. States with lower expenditures per capita for state park and recreation include Texas, Wisconsin, and Indiana. Most of the funds for these two programs

TABLE

8.2   STATE PARK AND RECREATION EXPENDITURES (IN MILLIONS OF DOLLARS)

State	Expenditures	Population Rank	State	Expenditures	Population Rank
Alabama	$ 11	23	Montana	$ 4	44
Alaska	$ 9	48	Nebraska	$ 25	38
Arizona	$ 37	21	Nevada	$ 18	36
Arkansas	$ 75	33	New Hampshire	$ 7	42
California	$286	1	New Jersey	$317	9
Colorado	$ 59	24	New Mexico	$ 43	37
Connecticut	$ 41	29	New York	$495	3
Delaware	$ 48	45	North Carolina	$152	11
Florida	$141	4	North Dakota	$ 9	47
Georgia	$ 28	10	Ohio	$132	7
Hawaii	$ 46	41	Oklahoma	$ 61	27
Idaho	$ 21	40	Oregon	$ 41	28
Illinois	$141	5	Pennsylvania	$140	6
Indiana	$ 61	14	Rhode Island	$ 13	43
Iowa	$ 18	30	South Carolina	$ 56	26
Kansas	$ 8	31	South Dakota	$ 22	46
Kentucky	$112	25	Tennessee	$116	17
Louisiana	$168	22	Texas	$ 56	2
Maine	$ 10	39	Utah	$ 30	34
Maryland	$173	19	Vermont	$ 7	49
Massachusetts	$127	13	Virginia	$ 76	12
Michigan	$125	8	Washington	$ 64	15
Minnesota	$ 99	20	West Virginia	$ 55	35
Mississippi	$ 50	31	Wisconsin	$ 54	18
Missouri	$ 38	16	Wyoming	$ 11	15

Source: U.S. Bureau of the Census. 2003. *Statistical Abstracts of the United States: 2003.* 123rd ed. Washington, DC: U.S. Government Printing Office.

support partnership agreements, music, theatre, dance, media arts, and the visual arts. When all these funds are added together, one can see that a great deal of money is available for park and recreation services at the state level. Recreational programs and areas provided by state governments are well used by residents (see figure 8.2).

Furthermore, with the increasingly fast-paced lifestyles of most American families, vacation patterns are changing. People seek more frequent, shorter vacations rather than one longer vacation per year, with recreational opportunities closer to home (see figure 8.3). Findings of the President's Commission on Americans Outdoors (1987) indicate that states must prepare to meet the greater demands that will be placed on them in the years ahead. In providing recreation facilities and services, states should especially consider the following areas: outdoor recreation and resources, tourism promotion, promotion of the arts, and services for people with disabilities and other underserved groups.

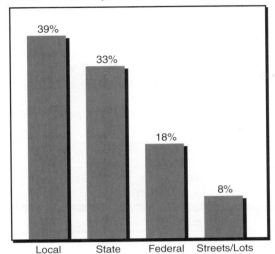

Places Where People Recreate Often: Public Areas

Figure 8.2

Use of recreation areas.

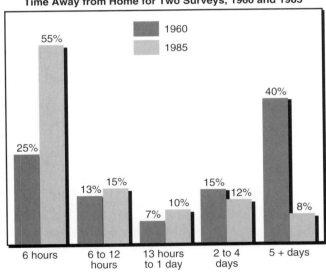

Comparison of Distribution of Visitors to Public Areas by Time Away from Home for Two Surveys, 1960 and 1985

Outdoor Recreation and Resources

States have long been involved in the management of outdoor resources. In the United States as early as 1626 the colony of Plymouth prohibited the cutting of timber on colony land without a permit. The Great Ponds Act of 1641 protected all bodies of freshwater of more than ten acres, about 2,000 sites, and assured public access to these ponds. By 1776, twelve out of the thirteen states had enacted closed seasons on certain game. In 1872, New York established the Adirondack Forest Preserve. In 1885, the federal government placed Niagara Falls under the care of the state of New York as the State Reservation of Niagara. This action resulted because of the uncontrollable commercial development of the areas surrounding the falls. According to Knudson (1984), "It was difficult to see the falls because of all the hucksters and makeshift commercial shops that lined the sides of the scenic wonder" (p. 86).

Much of this early legislation related to subsistence hunting and fishing. Nonetheless, these early laws could be looked upon as the beginning of state involvement in protecting natural resources (Foss, 1968). Following the 1885 action of New York surrounding Niagara Falls, state legislation for recreation purposes increased dramatically. Today, states own approximately 6 percent of the total area of the United States. The bulk of state-owned land is found in the west, primarily due to large state holdings in both Alaska and California. Management of state

TABLE

8.3 TERMS AND GUIDELINES FOR DEFINING STATE PARK RESOURCES

Term	Definition
State parks	Areas containing a number of coordinated programs for the preservation of natural and/or cultural resources and provision of a variety of outdoor recreation activities supported by those resources.
State recreation areas	Areas where a clear emphasis is placed on the provision of opportunities for primarily active recreation activities.
State natural areas	Areas where a clear emphasis is placed on protection, management, and interpretation of natural resources or features.
State historical areas	Areas where a clear emphasis is placed on protection, management, and interpretation of historical and/or archaeological resources or features.
State environmental education sites	Areas used exclusively or primarily for conducting educational programs on environmental subjects, natural resources, conservation, etc.
State scientific areas	Areas set aside exclusively or primarily for scientific study, observation, and experimentation involving natural objects, processes, and interrelationships; any other allowable uses are secondary and incidental.
State forests	Areas that, while under the direct administrative supervision and control of the state parks agency, are identified separately from the state park system and distinguished from state park units by having primarily a forest management and/or timber production role rather than a natural area and/or provision of recreation role.
State fish/wildlife areas	Areas under the administrative supervision and control of the state parks agency that are identified and managed primarily for the propagation and recreational taking of fish and/or game ("fishing and/or hunting areas").
State trails	Linear areas outside any other unit of the state park system that provide primarily for trail-type recreational activities (hiking, cycling, horseback riding, etc.) and normally do not contain any land areas large enough to support non-trail activities.
Other specified areas	Areas other than the above, that are considered special or significant enough in a particular state to warrant separate identification and treatment.
Miscellaneous areas	Areas other than the above, that are not easily categorized or distinguished, or are not considered significant enough to warrant the specification of "everything else."

Source: The National Association of State Park Directors. 2000. *Definitions.* www.indiana.edu/~naspd/statistics/definitions.html

lands often varies due to the type of land being managed and the philosophy of the managing agency. Basic classifications of land are managed by different state agencies—state parks, state forests, and state fish and wildlife reserves (see table 8.3). The National Association of State Park Directors (NASPD) has provided definitions for the various areas operated by state agencies. These are presented in table 8.3. As the NASPD points out, "While all of the fifty state park systems share common attributes, they nevertheless vary considerably from state to state. . . . Common denominators . . . allow a useful degree of comparison" (NASPD, 2000).

State Parks   The concept of land being owned by individual states for the enjoyment of its residents can be traced back to two events in the mid-1800s. The initial event centered around the federal government granting the territorial governor of the Arkansas Territory the right to withhold the Arkansas Hot Springs from private ownership in 1832 (Ibrahim and Cordes, 1993). This tradition continued in 1864 with the designation of Yosemite as the country's first state park. At this time the state of California was awarded a land grant for acquiring ten square miles in Yosemite Valley for "public use, resort, and recreation." Although both Yosemite and the Arkansas Hot Springs eventually were given back to the federal government to become national parks in 1890 and 1921, the idea of state parks had been established.

State park legislation increased at the turn of the century. Minnesota developed Itasca State Park; New York developed the Adirondack Wilderness; and Illinois established Fort Massac State Park in 1903. The establishment of Fort Massac was of particular importance because it facilitated a 1909 legislature-appointed commission to investigate the best way to manage state parks. This commission led to the establishment of the Illinois Division of Parks and Memorials within the Department of Public Works and Buildings in 1919. That same year Indiana also established a Division of State Parks within the Department of Conservation (Jensen, 1995). Many state park systems have achieved a level of maturity. For example, Wisconsin's state park system, which was founded in 1900, recently celebrated its 100th year of service. Today, more than eighty-five parks, forests, recreation areas, and trails are managed under the direction of the unit serving over a million people annually (see figure 8.4).

Figure 8.4

Wisconsin State Parks celebrates its centennial.

Economic Recovery Brings Some Relief to Tight State Budgets

Using phrases like "guardedly optimistic" and "notably—but cautiously—brighter," two new surveys report state budget conditions to be markedly healthier at the end of fiscal year 2004. After experiencing some of the most severe and widespread budget cuts in history during 2002 and 2003, many states seem to be, if not heading toward recovery, reaching the end of a very steep decline.

Budget projections for fiscal year 2005 anticipate more shortfalls, though less severe than those in the past. Five states expect budget gaps in excess of 10 percent and eleven more anticipate gaps above 5 percent. According to the National Conference of State Legislatures, the cumulative budget gap for 2005 will be $35.6 billion, 42 percent of which will be attributable to California's shortfall. The National Association of State Budget Officers

suggests a slightly more promising outlook for the future. According to their most recent *Fiscal Survey of States*, governors' proposed budgets for 2005 project continued revenue improvement and a continued decline in negative-growth budgets. State expenditures are expected to grow by a national average of 2.8 percent. This is up from the 0.6 percent growth experienced in 2003, but still far below the twenty-six year average of 6.2 percent. While the worst of the economic downturn seems to be in the past, many states still plan to proceed cautiously in the future. Demographic pressures will continue to drive up state expenses in health, education, and corrections categories. This means that competition for discretionary dollars that fuel all other state services—including the arts—will remain fierce.

Expenditures for Fiscal Year 2005

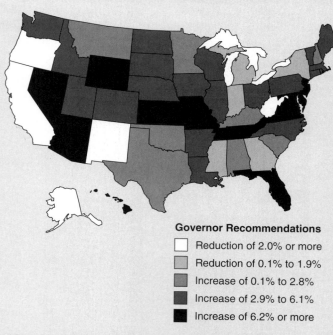

Governor Recommendations

- ☐ Reduction of 2.0% or more
- ◻ Reduction of 0.1% to 1.9%
- ▨ Increase of 0.1% to 2.8%
- ▦ Increase of 2.9% to 6.1%
- ■ Increase of 6.2% or more

Source: National Association of State Budget Officers. 2004. *State Budget Shortfalls Drop Dramatically According to New NCSL Budget Analysis. The Fiscal Survey of States.* National Conference of State Legislation 2004

When the National Park Service was established in 1916, its first director, Stephen Mather, saw the importance of the state park movement and promoted the idea strongly. In 1921 he organized the first National Conference on State Parks in Des Moines, Iowa. At this time only nineteen states had some type of state park or state forest system. The National Conference on State Parks became a permanent organization known today as the National Society for Park Resources (Ibrahim and Cordes, 1993).

Mather believed state parks formed an important link in saving America's natural heritage. As director of the National Park Service, Mather knew that his fledgling agency could not protect all appropriate areas. "Mather saw state administration as an alternative to protecting some of the prize areas until he could gather political and financial support to bring them into the national park system" (Jensen, 1995, p. 125). Mather also hoped that state parks would bring outdoor recreation closer to the masses who were not able to visit many of the national parks that had been established in the western part of the United States.

The depression years brought greater cooperation between the states and the federal government. Many of the Civilian Conservation Corps (CCC) projects benefited state as well as federal parks through the building of trails and facilities. Following World War II, visits to state parks increased dramatically. State park systems tried to keep pace with demand. These efforts were aided by the Surplus Property Act of 1944 and amended in 1948, which allowed certain federal land to be converted to state parks and recreation areas. Other major legislation that helped the state park movement included the Recreation and Public Purposes Act of 1954 and the Land and Water Conservation Act of 1965.

Today, all fifty states have park systems in place. Throughout the United States there are 5,655 areas designated as state parks that total 13 million acres. There are nearly 55,000 employees working on either a full-time or seasonal basis in state park systems. It is interesting to note that state parks represent less than 2 percent of the total outdoor recreation space available in the United States. However, visitors to state parks account for 29 percent of all visits to state and federal outdoor recreation areas. The National Association of State Park Directors (http://139.102.62.141/statistics.html) reported that there were 786 million visitors to state parks in 2001. This represents an increase from 1997, when 783 million individuals visited the state parks systems, and an increase from 1991, when state parks received a total of 737 million visitors. Interestingly, 91.2 percent of all state park visitors were daytime users, although overnight use still constitutes a significant portion of visits to state parks with 67 million visitors. Table 8.4 provides a report of state park visits, resources, and personnel for the year 2002.

Today's parks vary in many ways, including size, available facilities, the amount of development, types of administration, and financing. For example, in Oregon, the state's department of transportation administers the state park system, while in Michigan, state parks are administered by the Park Division of the Department of Natural Resources. Several factors enter into the many differences found in state park systems. These factors include historical events, political trends, intergovernmental relationships, and prevailing management concepts.

Yet state park lands also have many similarities. For example, land designated as state parks is mostly seen as intermediate areas, as contrasted to wild areas or municipal areas. This means that they are relatively close to large urban areas; provide activities such as picnicking, camping, swimming, hiking, fishing, and hunting; and are of medium size (hundreds to several thousand acres). Table 8.5 provides an overview of the type of state parks that exist in the United States today, and table 8.6 provides an overview of state park and recreation areas by state.

TABLE

8.4   STATE PARK FACTS AND STATISTICS

- 5,655 state park areas totaling 13 million acres
- 4,114 trails encompassing 32,225 miles
- Almost 210,000 campsites ranging from multiple hookups to primitive
- 6,592 cabins and cottages
- 124 lodges in 25 states with 6,695 rooms
- 127 golf courses
- 31 ski slopes
- 311 marinas
- 300 swimming pools
- 97 stable operations
- 323 million visitors to fee areas—435 million to non-fee areas
- 59 million campers
- 2.4 million lodge guests
- 3.9 million cabin guests
- 17.7 million campsites rented
- $312 million spent on capital improvements and land acquisition
- Operating expenditures totaling $1.8 billion—less than 50% from the general fund of states
- $665 million expended for capital expenditures
- Average share of the state budget—.25% (1/4 of 1%)
- 21,148 full-time state park personnel and 56,630 total personnel (part-time and seasonal)
  - 1 full-time person per 622 acres
  - 1 full-time person per 35,840 visitors
- Average starting salary—$21,048
- Average starting ranger salary—$24,856

Source: The National Association of State Park Directors. 2004. State Park Facts. Retrieved 6-11-04 from http://139.102.62.141/statistics.html.

TABLE

8.5   TYPES OF STATE PARK AREAS

Types	Number
Parks	1,906
Natural areas	336
Recreation areas	754
Historic areas	551
Water-use areas	548
Environmental education areas	19
Trail systems	23
Miscellaneous areas	314
Total number of areas	4,451

Source: C. Jensen, *Outdoor Recreation in America.* 2d ed. 1995.

TABLE

8.6   STATE PARK AND RECREATION AREAS BY STATE: 2002

State	Acreage	Rank by Acreage	Visitors	Rank by Visitor
Alaska	3,326	1	4,283	15
California	1,457	2	85,665	1
New York	1,159	3	56,864	2
Texas	668	4	17,090	9
Florida	592	5	17,735	8
New Jersey	377	6	15,040	10
Colorado	365	7	11,098	12
Illinois	306	8	43,623	4
Massachusetts	294	9	11,884	11
Pennsylvania	289	10	36,627	5
Michigan	285	11	25,297	7
Minnesota	267	12	8,076	14
Maryland	266	13	10,340	13
Washington	262	14	48,864	3
Ohio	205	15	29,030	6

Source: U.S. Bureau of the Census. 2003. *Statistical Abstracts of the United States: 2003.* 123rd ed. Washington, DC: U.S. Government Printing Office.

State Forests   Whereas the management philosophy of state parks is one of preservation, state forests operate under a multiple-use approach. Initially, when state forests were acquired, the major thrust was to protect land from erosion, to develop areas for timber, and to provide experimental and demonstration areas. The outdoor recreation potential of these areas was not considered until after World War II. Today the management priorities of state forests vary from state to state due to such factors as type and abundance of forest land and the philosophy of the state government as to how state forests should be used. Typically, the management of state forests includes some combination of the following concerns: outdoor recreation, natural resource management (e.g., timber management), watershed, and fish and wildlife management. According to the National Association of State Foresters, twenty-eight of the forty-seven state forest administrative agencies or departments have specific recreation departments, whereas the remaining states handle recreation in conjunction with their other duties (Jones, 1992).

With the exception of Kansas, Nebraska, and Oklahoma, all states have some type of state forest system. These systems are usually administered by an independent state agency (e.g., Department of Forestry). According to Jensen (1985) the best state forest systems appear in the eastern, southern, and midwestern states with high-quality forests and small amounts of federal forested lands. States in the Great Plains or the Southwest tend to have small systems because of the relatively small amounts of forested land.

Activities that take place in state forests typically include hunting, fishing, boating, camping, hiking, nature study, bird watching, rock climbing, horseback riding, and mountain biking. As a general rule, recreational facilities in state forests tend to be less developed than counterpart areas in state parks. For example, campsites are more primitive than in state parks and do not include as many conveniences, such as showers or water and sewer hookups.

TABLE

8.7   2001 WILDLIFE-ASSOCIATED RECREATION PARTICIPANTS AND EXPENDITURES

	Fishing	Hunting	Wildlife Watchers
Participants (thousands)	34,071	13,034	66,105
Days of participation	557,394	228,368	846,982
Total expenditures (millions $)	35,632	20,611	52,083
Food & lodging	5,881	2,450	4,819
Transportation	3,516	7,789	2,596
Other trip costs	5,259	1,013	748
Sport-specific equipment	4,618	4,562	7,354
Auxiliary equipment	721	1,203	717
Special equipment	11,625	4,597	15,469
Other expenditures	4,013	4,997	6,712

Source: U.S. Bureau of the Census. 2003. *Statistical Abstracts of the United States: 2003.* 123rd ed. Washington, DC: U.S. Government Printing Office.

In the future, the amount of land included in state forests will not likely increase or decrease a great deal as states do not wish to lose control of the lands they already have and there will be little opportunity to expand. Outdoor recreation will become increasingly important in state forests as people search for less-crowded areas that are still close to large urban areas. This increased demand may result in an improvement of recreation resources in state forests in the future.

State Fish and Wildlife Agencies   States have a long history dating back to before the Revolutionary War of being involved in the management of fish and wildlife populations. Today each of the fifty states has created a separate department or a major division within a department to administer a program of fish and wildlife management. One of the reasons for the importance of managing hunting and fishing resources within each state is the economic importance of fishing and hunting for state economies. In addition to licenses, expenditures by anglers, hunters, and other wildlife enthusiasts have significant economic impact throughout the country (see table 8.7).

It is interesting to note that wildlife recreation has been viewed as a possible economic incubator for rural communities. The Center for the Study of Rural America has strongly suggested that an important economic opportunity for small communities may be a focus on promoting hunting, fishing, and wildlife watching as an important form of tourism.

Although many state fish and wildlife agencies manage some specific areas, their responsibilities extend well beyond the boundaries of their land holdings. For example, because wildlife is considered to be a resource of the state (unless it is endangered or crosses state lines), wildlife on federal lands is still managed by each state's fish and wildlife agency. According to Jensen (1995), the major responsibilities of these agencies include the following:

- *Issuing licenses* for hunting, fishing, and trapping, and enforcing the laws and regulations pertaining to these activities. The income generated from the selling of these licenses is reinvested into propagating, protecting, and distributing game fish, birds, and animals.

Wildlife Recreation: Rural America's Newest Billion Dollar Industry

In today's search for the next billion-dollar industry to revitalize main streets, many rural leaders are again pinning their hopes on nature. New opportunities are not arising from traditional sources—commodity industries like agriculture or mining. Tomorrow's opportunity may well be wildlife-related recreation—already a $108 billion industry nationwide.

In many rural places, hunting, fishing, and wildlife watching have boosted rural tourism, spurred business growth, and contributed to strong land value gains. The brightest prospects, though, still lie ahead. Rural communities fortunate enough to have other amenities to complement their natural resource base are in the best position to reap new economic benefits from this booming industry.

Wildlife recreation offers even more promise for rural communities with existing entrainment amenities. Tourists, even wildlife recreationers, often prefer places with amenities beyond scenic landscapes and abundant wildlife. They eat at restaurants, sleep in hotels, and visit night spots. As a result, a growing number of hunting resorts that combine entertainment and wildlife are beginning to dot the rural landscape. To help draw customers, many of these resorts also offer off-season activities and promote other types of entertainment in the region. They clearly show that rural places with a regional identity that embraces both entertainment and wildlife amenities are probably in the best position to capture wildlife recreation's dollars.

Nature has always been a strong foundation for rural America. Now, wildlife recreation appears to be the newest opportunity. The industry may not be the answer for every rural community, but those with entertainment and wildlife may be able to leverage Mother Nature to spark new growth.

Source: Henderson, J. 2004. Wildlife Recreation: Rural America's Newest Billion Dollar Industry. *The Main Street Economist* (April). Center for the Study of Rural America, Federal Reserve Bank of Kansas City

- *Managing a variety of wildlife areas,* including reserves, sanctuaries, game farms, hatcheries, and special shooting grounds.
- *Assisting landowners,* both private and public, with habitat management.

Hunting and fishing are still the primary recreational activities that take place on land managed by state fish and wildlife agencies. A number of nonconsumptive recreational pursuits are becoming increasingly popular, also (e.g., such as camping, hiking, and photography). With more users now enjoying state fish and wildlife areas, a number of additional pressures make it difficult for fish and wildlife managers. These pressures include the following:

Increasing user conflicts between noncomplementary forms of recreation users. For example, hiking and hunting cannot be done in the same area because of the inherent danger of a hiker getting shot. These types of conflicts increase as the number of recreationists increase in a variety of leisure pursuits.

Decreasing resource base for wildlife habitat places greater hardships on the remaining areas available for wildlife. The majority of habitat is being lost in the private sector, and, as a result, more hunting and fishing participants use public lands. This increase in the number of users presents challenges to fish and wildlife managers. Specifically, managers must face the dilution of the hunting and fishing experience caused by the inability of the fish and wildlife base to meet the expectations of the increasing number of hunters and anglers (Jensen, 1985).

The times have changed. People no longer live in a world of surplus, and with the recent technological and communication advances the decisions of resource managers are highly scrutinized. People are more involved with decisions, and more interest groups want to be a part of the decision-making process.

Trail Systems   In the past several decades there has been a tremendous expansion at the state level of trail systems. State governments are often involved in providing support funds to local governments. For example, the State of Iowa has made a great investment for the development and construction of trails. The General Assembly of the State of Iowa has made funds available through the Rebuild Iowa Infrastructure Fund. In the past decade, over $40 million has been invested in the development of recreational trails. Table 8.8 provides a definition of the various types of trails. These types of trails could be developed on a local, regional, or even statewide basis. Again, they are often done with state support.

TABLE

8.8   TERMS AND GUIDELINES FOR TRAILS

Term	Definition
Backcountry Trails	Backcountry trails, sometimes called "single-track" or primitive trails, are generally unsurfaced natural routes that range from narrow treadways to carefully planned and elaborately constructed (but natural-looking) thoroughfares. Attention to slopes and effective drainage is essential for the long-term stability of this type of trail.
Recreational Greenways	A greenway is any linear open-space area along a natural corridor (riverfront, stream valley, ridgeline) or overland along a converted railroad right-of-way, canal, or scenic road (Little, 1991). As such, a greenway may or may not include a trail. A "recreational greenway" is a linear open space that contains a trail(s). Although a greenway trail can take any form, the term generally refers to a high-standard paved trail that accommodates multiple users.
Multiple-Use Recreation Trails	"Multiple-use recreation trails" or "multiuse trails" are generic terms for what many people call trails or greenways. These trails are built to high standards, are usually ten feet wide, asphalt or concrete paved, and designed for many types of use. Bicycling, walking, running, in-line skating, and other nonmotorized uses are typical on multi-use trails, and they are frequently very heavily used.
Rail-Trails	Rail-trails are trails constructed on abandoned railroad corridors converted to recreational use or "railbanked" for possible future rail use. They can be very short to hundreds of miles long. Typically surfaced in crushed stone or paved, their moderate grades make rail-trails popular with bicyclists, walkers, and others. Currently, there are more than 700 rail-trails totaling nearly 10,000 miles. With thousands of miles of rail corridor being abandoned every year, rail-trails offer tremendous potential for new trail opportunities. In fact, progress is being made on a coast-to-coast rail-trail.
Water Trails	Many people consider any corridor of open water used for recreational travel or string of lakes connected by portage to be a water trail. Camping accessibility by water along the route makes multiday travel possible. Canoeing, kayaking, and, in some areas, personal watercraft use are all popular ways to enjoy water trails.

Source: R. L. Moore and D. T. Ross. 1998, January. Trails and recreation greenways: Corridors of benefits. *Parks and Recreation,* 69–75.

An interesting example of a nonprofit organization that promotes the securing of areas for trails is the Rails-to-Trails Conservancy. The RTC is involved in securing multipurpose public paths that have been created from previous railroad passageways. This organization reports that since the 1960s throughout the United States almost 11,000 miles of rail-trails have been set aside. These types of developments promote environmental stewardship, tourism, and heritage management (see figure 8.5). This organization has acquired more than 650 miles of trails since 1993. Its goal is to find public agencies to own and manage these trails for public use.

Tourism Promotion

Figuratively, people saw the world grow smaller in the twentieth century. Advances in transportation and communication have created a global network. These advances, combined with increased discretionary income of people in the developed world, have led to an explosion in international and domestic travel in the last twenty years. Tourism ranks only behind oil as the world's second largest industry according to the United Nation's affiliated World Tourism Organization, which forecasts that tourism will become the world's most important global activity. States have seen the importance of promoting their lands as a potential tourist destination. Every state is actively involved in the development of tourist attractions and the promotion of tourism. "From the state's point of view there are two good reasons for promoting tourism: increased revenue from taxes and more jobs for the state's residents" (Jensen, 1995, p. 127).

TABLE

8.9 DOMESTIC TRAVEL EXPENDITURES

State	Expenditures (millions of U.S. dollars)	Market Share (percentage)	Rank
California	$63,709	13.0	1
Florida	$41,692	8.5	2
Texas	32,307	6.6	3
New York	29,269	6.0	4
Illinois	21,931	4.5	5
Nevada	19,518	4.0	6
New Jersey	14,756	3.0	7
Pennsylvania	14,726	3.0	8
Georgia	14,269	2.9	9
Virginia	13,294	2.7	10
Ohio	12,952	2.6	11
North Carolina	12,249	2.5	12
Michigan	12,063	2.5	13
Massachusetts	11,133	2.3	14
Tennessee	9,867	2.0	15

Source: U.S. Bureau of the Census. 2003. *Statistical Abstracts of the United States: 2003.* 123rd ed. Washington, DC: U.S. Government Printing Office.

In 2001, Americans spent more than $490 billion dollars on domestic travel in the United States (U.S. Bureau of Census, 2003). This compares with $396 billion in 1997, and $323 billion in 1993 (U.S. Bureau of Census, 1999, 1995). Table 8.9 shows the top states in terms of domestic travel expenditures. In viewing this table, one can see that California, followed by Florida, Texas, New York, Illinois, and Nevada account for over 50 percent of the market share.

Foreign visitors spent an additional $91 million in 2001. Again, this compares with 1997 when foreign visitors spent 73 million, and 1988 when $29 million was expended (U.S. Bureau of Census, 1999). Not too surprisingly, foreign visitors spent $103 million in the year 2000. Obviously, the impact of the terrorist attacks of 9/11/2001 caused a significant reduction in the number of foreign visitors to the United States and, therefore, on the foreign tourism expenditures in the United States. Conversely, expenditures for domestic travel by Americans increased (U.S. Bureau of Census, 1999). Foreign travelers focused their visits on Florida, New York, California, Hawaii, and Nevada (see table 8.10). The top cities visited include New York City, New York; Los Angeles, California; Miami, Florida; Orlando, Florida; San Francisco, California; Honolulu, HI; and Las Vegas, Nevada. This information and the market share are found in table 8.11. These cities account for over 80 percent of the total market share for overseas visitors. Although the private sector provides the majority of these jobs, state governments support the travel and tourism industry by promoting their state throughout the country.

The "war" to entice visitors as well as lure in-state residents to stay at home is increasing. Full-page advertisements in travel magazines, television ads, travel brochures, and magazines are all evidence of the increase in state budgets to promote tourism. Researchers are finding that leisure pursuits and outdoor recreation opportunities are an essential component of tourism. Ebberson (1983) found that opportunities to participate in certain activities were more important than a particular destination for vacationers.

TABLE
8.10 TOP STATES VISITED BY OVERSEAS TRAVELERS

State	Market Share Percent (percent)
Florida	24.1
New York	23.1
California	22.2
Hawaiian Islands	10.1
Nevada	7.2
Massachusetts	5.4
Illinois	5.1
Guam	5.1
Texas	4.3
New Jersey	3.7
Georgia	3.6
Pennsylvania	3.2
Arizona	2.9
Michigan	2.0
Louisiana	2.0
Colorado	2.0
Washington	1.8
Ohio	1.8
Virginia	1.5
North Carolina	1.4
Utah	1.3
Minnesota	1.3

Source: U.S. Bureau of the Census. 2003. *Statistical Abstracts of the United States: 2003*. 123rd ed. Washington, DC: U.S. Government Printing Office.

Several states have a separate department of tourism while other states have agencies in larger departments. For example, the Texas Travel Information Center is a part of the State Department of Highways and Public Transportation. In addition to having one main office, many states also have regional offices to facilitate the dissemination of travel information. States vary greatly in what they emphasize to potential visitors. Whereas Florida might market its beaches and warm climate in the winter, South Carolina highlights its "Southern hospitality" and Virginia capitalizes on its colonial history and Civil War involvement. Each state's emphasis differs as each tries to capture potential visitors and market its uniqueness. This is mainly dictated by geography, culture, and history; however, different states have also established different marketing techniques and target markets for their advertising. One aspect of the "Say Yes to Michigan" campaign is geared to Chicago residents who are looking to get out of the big city on weekends.

The Arts

According to Kreisberg (1979), state agencies for the arts are a relatively recent phenomenon; most have developed since 1965 in response to the legislation that created the National Endowment for the Arts. The Congressional Declaration of Purpose of this legislation stated, "It is necessary and appropriate for the federal government to complement, assist and add to programs for

TABLE

8.11   TOP CITIES VISITED BY OVERSEAS TRAVELERS

City	Market Share Percent (percent)
New York City, NY	22.0
Los Angeles, CA	12.9
Miami, FL	11.7
Orlando, FL	11.3
San Francisco, CA	9.0
Oahu/Honolulu, HI	8.0
Las Vegas, NV	6.9
Washington, DC	5.5
Boston, MA	4.9
Chicago, IL	4.9
Atlanta, GA	3.2
San Diego, CA	2.7
Tampa/St. Petersburg, FL	2.3
Ft. Lauderdale, FL	1.9
Houston, TX	1.9
Philadelphia, PA	1.9
San Jose, CA	1.9
Anaheim, CA	1.8
New Orleans, LA	1.8
Dallas/Ft. Worth, TX	1.6
Seattle, WA	1.6
Detroit, MI	1.3
Maui, HI	1.3

Source: U.S. Bureau of the Census. 2003. *Statistical Abstracts of the United States: 2003.* 123rd ed. Washington, DC: U.S. Government Printing Office.

the advancement of the humanities and arts by local, state, regional, and private agencies and their organizations" (Kreisberg, 1979, p. 180). State governments responded to this legislation by creating their own state agencies that could tap federal funds for the promotion of the arts.

A state agency for the arts exists in each of the fifty United States. The makeup and responsibility of these agencies differ from state to state. All state art agencies, however, administer certain federal programs and support the arts within their state. Most of the support provided by state art agencies takes the form of grants-in-aid to arts institutions, community arts agencies, production organizations, schools, and, in some cases, individuals (see table 8.12). State art agencies also provide technical assistance (e.g., workshops and seminars on topics such as fundraising) to arts programs and institutions within their state.

In many ways, the role of individual state governments is that of an enabler as the majority of direct services involving the arts and recreation will be carried out at the local level by public development agencies, private developers, arts organizations, municipal parks and recreation offices, nonprofit organizations, and commercial entrepreneurs. Yet, as pointed out by Peene and Shanahan (1990), states can make a significant contribution to linking arts and other recreation amenities to economic development in both supporting and leading roles. The starting

Disney World Tops Family Destinations

According to *Family Fun* magazine, Walt Disney World in Orlando, Florida, and Yosemite National Park in California are the top two destinations in the magazine's readers' poll.

This marks the second year in a row that the Disney theme park topped the list. Its California cousin, Disneyland in Anaheim, placed fifth.

Outdoor adventures also are crowd-pleasers: in addition to Yosemite, Yellowstone National Park in Wyoming, Montana, and Idaho; the Great Smoky Mountains National Park in Tennessee and North Carolina; and Acadia National Park in Maine all ranked in the top twelve.

Rounding out the list are Washington, D.C.; the San Diego Zoo; Monterey Bay Aquarium in Monterey, California; SeaWorld Orlando in Orlando, Florida; the Statue of Liberty in New York City; and New York's American Museum of National History.

Source: Iowa Life. 2002. *The Des Moines Register*. (March)

point is to acknowledge the role that the arts and other recreation amenities can have in the economic development of an individual state.

Assuming that those involved with the planning of the arts and state economic development can see the benefits of collaboration, opportunities exist to strengthen the performance of development programs through systematically including cultural and recreational resources. Drawing from Peene and Shanahan (1990), each state can benefit from doing at least some of the following, especially with regard to the arts:

- Incorporate information about art programs, cultural events, recreation resources, and other quality-of-life amenities when it tries to recruit new businesses. This information should be as prevalent as information provided about schools, taxes, and utility rates.
- Treat support for art institutions as opportunities to strengthen the state's investment climate.
- Make art institutions and art-related businesses eligible for state development financing programs.
- Encourage sound economic assessments before taking on major art projects, cultural event projects, or recreation projects that have economic development objectives.
- Involve artists in the planning and implementation of programs.
- Establish programs for strengthening the management of art institutions, as well as cultural events and recreation resources and programs.

Building on elements such as these can generate significant economic development for individual states as well as strengthen relationships between diverse areas within the state government. In many instances this will help states build the kind of partnerships discussed throughout this chapter.

Other State Services

Beyond the services mentioned in the preceding sections, state governments also provide a number of other services to their residents. The exact mix of services varies from state to state as governing bodies struggle to identify specific funding priorities for their state budgets. Yet many states recognize the provision of recreation programs as a legitimate responsibility. Some of the other major programs and facilities operated by state governments include the following:

TABLE

8.12 ARTS AND HUMANITIES—SELECTED FEDERAL AID PROGRAMS: 1980 TO 2001 (IN MILLIONS OF U.S. DOLLARS)

Types of Fund and Program	1980	1990	2000	2001
National Endowment for the Arts				
Funds available	188.1	170.8	85.2	94.0
Program appropriation	97.0	124.3	66.0	86.7
Matching funds	42.9	32.4	13.0	—
Grants awarded (number)	5,505	4,475	1,882	2,093
Funds obligated	166.4	157.6	83.5	92.5
Partnership agreements	22.1	26.1	33.4	36.1
National Endowment of the Humanities				
Funds available	186.2	140.6	102.6	106.8
Program appropriation	100.3	114.2	82.4	86.4
Matching funds	38.4	26.3	15.1	15.6
Grants awarded (number)	2,917	2,195	1,230	1,290
Funds obligated	185.5	141.0	100.0	105.7

Source: U.S. Bureau of the Census. 2003. *Statistical Abstracts of the United States: 2003.* 123rd ed. Washington, DC: U.S. Government Printing Office.

Correctional institutions. Therapeutic recreation and other leisure services form an important component of correctional institutions operated by states. For example, the State of Iowa operates a correctional institution—Iowa Medical and Classification Center—that employs several certified therapeutic recreation specialists. Programs include social activities, physical recreation, table games, small-group interaction, leisure education programs, and other activities.

State hospitals and institutions. State governments often provide a full range of hospital services to persons with disabilities, including those under psychiatric treatment, the developmentally disabled, persons with visual and hearing impairments, and others. Such hospitals and institutions often provide a full range of recreation and leisure services. These programs include such therapies as assertiveness training, leisure education, leisure skill development, socialization activities, and physical activities. Diverse job opportunities exist in this area of therapeutic recreation. For example, the State of Iowa hires certified therapeutic recreation specialists to work at such places as the Mental Health Institute in Independence, Woodward State Hospital in Woodward, and the Iowa Braille and Sightsaving School at Vinton.

Care and activity centers. State governments often establish standards and the licensing of care and activity centers for older individuals. Few state governments provide direct-care facilities; rather, they emphasize regulatory activities and the creation of standards in support of quality care. In addition, state and federal governments provide funds to local and county governments to create support services to older individuals, keeping them in their homes as long as possible to avoid the expenses of institutionalized care.

Substance-abuse and chemical-dependency rehabilitation programs. State governments also support substance-abuse and chemical-dependency rehabilitation programs. Such efforts vary from direct involvement in state institutions, such as prisons and mental health facilities, to providing financial subsidies, regulatory legislation, and other forms of support to governmental, nonprofit, and private organizations.

Budget Cut Opportunities

For some reason the philosophy in the public sector is, "When funds are cut, there's no other way but to cut services." But in my opinion, sometimes the best opportunities come because you're forced by budget cuts to find new ways to do things.

Source: David Osborn and Ted Goebler.

Museums. State and provincial governments in both the United States and Canada operate museums. Such facilities often develop along historical, cultural, natural history, or other themes, such as science, technology, and art. An outstanding example of a provincially supported museum is the Royal Ontario Museum (ROM) located in Toronto, Ontario. This facility provides historical, cultural, and other information concerning important factors in the development of Ontario and Canada.

Fairgrounds. Perhaps one of the most popular programs throughout the United States is the annual state fair. Such programs often take place using land and facilities operated by state government. Programs include exhibits, shows, displays, and amusements. Well-developed state fairgrounds are often used on a year-round basis for sporting events, flea markets, fairs, exhibitions, conferences, revivals, and other activities.

Cultural programs and facilities. State governments also provide direct and indirect support for the organization of cultural and historical events, programs, and activities. Such programs can take diverse forms—from a reenactment of an important historical event to the promotion of art exhibits and performing arts activities. State governments also provide support to local governments and nonprofit organizations by providing funding to seed activities such as theater groups, community events, and others. In Ontario, funds from provincial government lotteries can be directly committed to leisure-oriented cultural and historical pursuits.

Enabling legislation. States also provide legislative acts that enable, inhibit, or regulate behaviors related to parks and recreation. A good example of a legislative act supporting the acquisition of unique land areas is the state of Iowa's State Preserve Act. Legislation such as this works to support the continued provision and development of parks and recreation services. Other examples of state legislative acts that regulate park and recreation services are laws pertaining to regulating hunting and fishing in each state.

In addition to these direct services, most state governments have at least one state-supported institution of higher education that offers programs in recreation and park administration as well as tourism development. These programs support the state by providing qualified entry-level professionals. They also offer various state agencies technical assistance, interns, and professional growth opportunities such as conferences, workshops, and results of research focused on recreation.

States also provide legislative acts that enable, inhibit, or regulate behaviors related to parks and recreation. A good example of a legislative act supportive of the acquisition of unique land areas is the state of Iowa's State Preserve Act. Legislation such as this works to support the continued provision and development of parks and recreation services. Other examples of state legislative acts that regulate park and recreation activities are laws pertaining to regulating hunting and fishing in each state.

State Preserves Protect Iowa's Heritage

The State Preserves Act became law in Iowa in 1965, outlining guidelines for properties deemed so rare, so unique, or so utterly irreplaceable that they must be maintained for future generations.

"It's considered the highest and best use of the land," says Laura Jackson, a member of the state preserves advisory board, which determines what properties are included.

Since 1968, when the first nominees were dedicated, ninety-one sites have earned preserve status. The newest member of the family is Hartman Bluff State Preserve in Waterloo, which cleared the final hurdle in February 2005.

The preserve system is an exclusive club and only covers about 9,300 acres statewide. By comparison, Iowa's borders surround about 36 million acres.

Challenges for the Future

State governments face immense challenges in the twenty-first century. As the federal government continues to downsize, states must pick up the slack; yet most states face financial crises of their own. For most states the question is not whether they view many social and human services (including leisure and recreation) as important, but rather how to finance and pay for these services.

State funding for parks and recreation is changing. In the past, agencies had considerably more control over how they spent their appropriations. In the 1990s, agencies found that elected officials set agency funding priorities. Westfall (1991) indicates elected officials tend to favor new development projects over land acquisition, facility rehabilitation, natural resource protection and site operation, and maintenance. Each new development places increased demand on already-stressed agency operating resources and creates future rehabilitation needs. Agencies must now package and sell basic, less visible funding needs to state legislatures.

McLean, Hurd, Beggs, and Chavez (2000) have suggested that numerous trends are affecting state parks. Some of these include the following: (1) During the 1990s, state parks were models of slow growth (this was representative of the political tenor of the times—that of reduced or no government); (2) distribution of acreage and areas is not consistent with population distribution; (3) visitation is the most dramatic variable, often a result of weather and sometimes politics; (4) state support for state parks has, at best, been neutral, with few additional dollars being made available; (5) bond monies are becoming more available; and (6) legislatures, in some cases, are increasing operating funds.

Many states are cutting back on staff. In an effort to replace staff, agencies use technology as well as volunteers. For example, interactive computer information devices now orient many visitors to park resources and programs. Likewise, volunteers greet and help visitors in the campground host program. In this program private citizens (often retirees) serve as campground hosts in various state parks and forests. This often entails answering questions and dealing with minor problems in exchange for free camping from a week to several months.

States also use public-private partnerships to promote tourism and generate revenue. In Illinois, the state's first public-private resort was created in 1989 at Eagle Creek State Park. This privately developed resort includes a 130-room inn and an eighteen-hole championship golf course on Lake Shelbyville in central Illinois. The Illinois Department of Conservation contributed a cash incentive and infrastructure improvements to the venture, which was primarily financed and developed by the private sector (Westfall, 1991). Other possible partnerships include American Youth Hostels, which convert old buildings in public parks to provide low-cost travel accommodations. Hiking clubs help to maintain trails; local snowmobile clubs work with private landowners to develop trails and resting huts. In return, the snowmobile community has been instrumental in legislation providing liability protection for landowners. States need to find ways to create similar partnerships to increase recreation opportunities for their residents.

States also use fees and charges to finance their recreation programs. For example, in California, visitor and concession fees totaled $7.3 million in 1981; the fee target a decade later was ten times as high: $79.5 million (Myers, 1992). In response to many of these trends, agencies within each state cooperate with one another to develop a plan of action for the coming decade. Managers in outdoor recreation resources in Oregon, for example, created a list of priorities at the second Oregon Outdoor Conference. These priorities, which parallel the recommendations of the President's Commission on Americans Outdoors, are presented in table 8.13.

TABLE

8.13 PRIORITIES OF OUTDOOR RECREATION RESOURCE MANAGERS IN OREGON

- *Create an outdoor ethic in individuals.*
  "For the past 100 years, especially the last 25, we have emphasized the role of government in conservation and have given little attention to the individual. We have not developed a land ethic in the minds and hearts of citizens in a manner and scale that complements public programs" (President's Commission on Americans Outdoors [PCAO], 1987, p. 83). According to the PCAO (1987) "an outdoor ethic means personal involvement in the outdoors as an essential part of life. It means a sense of appreciation for an obligation toward the air, land, water, and living things of the earth" (p. 81). For many, the best way for creating such an outdoor ethic involves increasing the amount of environmental education in all levels of the school curriculum.

- *Create a state-dedicated trust.*
  Such a trust would help resource agencies purchase land and open space to meet the outdoor recreation needs of future generations. This trust fund could be set up similarly to the Land and Water Conservation Fund, which helped states acquire land and build facilities for outdoor recreation.

- *Create a state recreation information clearinghouse.*
  A clearinghouse would allow resource managers from a variety of agencies to cooperate in meeting the outdoor recreation needs of state residents.

- *Increase coordinated efforts concerning wildlife habitat.*
  Due to the increasing demands on wildlife habitat, agencies must work together to meet future demands and create more opportunities for nonconsumptive use of wildlife such as nature study and tracking for photography purposes.

- *Encourage public/private partnerships.*
  The key to successful partnerships is to match resources to achieve mutual goals. Partnerships can be encouraged between government agencies and the private sector or between nonprofit organizations.

- *Plan and budget for renovation and maintenance.*
  In the past century, Americans have invested heavily in public recreation facilities. A large portion of this investment took place in the 1930s, 1940s, and 1950s. These facilities now need major renovation and maintenance. The recreation infrastructure is aging, and agencies must find innovative ways to renovate and maintain areas and facilities.

- *Encourage volunteer participation.*
  For many state recreation agencies volunteers remain an untapped resource, which could greatly improve services to state residents. In a successfully run volunteer program, the campground host program developed by state parks, volunteers help manage state parks during the peak summer season.

- *Determine recreation needs of the public periodically.*
  To meet the recreational needs of residents and visitors, managers must identify and understand what those needs are. This could take the form of a recreational needs survey completed on a five- or ten-year cycle.

Source: The 2nd Annual Oregonian's Outdoor Conference, 1987, Salem, Oregon.

Summary

In many ways state involvement in recreation mirrors that of the federal government. States, responsible for vast amounts of public land, also serve as facilitators and enablers for local governments. The role of state governments in providing recreation for its citizens is increasing. More state and local involvement in recreation planning and program implementation encourages a more participatory approach to governments and allows local citizens to meet local and regional needs. This chapter discussed both the functions and direct services provided by individual state governments. Functions of state governments include drafting legislation, coordinating with both federal and local governments (especially in the planning process), and encouraging and creating standards for the field. Direct-service delivery for states revolves primarily around outdoor recreation resources while other direct services include tourism development, the promotion of the arts, and meeting the needs of such citizen groups as senior citizens, people incarcerated or institutionalized, and people with physical and mental disabilities.

Many state functions and services discussed in this chapter are interrelated. For example, the arts or outdoor recreation resources can play a role in tourism promotion. These functions and services also connect to other aspects of the state, such as economic development. Therefore, recreation agencies and organizations (or any other state agency) cannot be isolationists and expect to survive. Recreation agencies and organizations on both state and local levels must strive to create innovative partnerships within other aspects of government and the private sector to create multifaceted approaches to improving people's quality of life.

Discussion Questions

1. What is enabling legislation? What does it allow state governments to do?
2. Do you agree or disagree that states or provinces should take on greater responsibility in planning for the recreational needs of their citizens?
3. Identify a specific recreation business in your area and interview the owner. Identify all laws and standards that this business must adhere to in your state or province (specific to recreation). How does the owner of the business feel about the amount of state or provincial regulation? Should there be more or less regulation from his/her point of view?
4. What environmental issues are specific to your state or province? How do these issues affect the management of state or provincial land for outdoor recreation?
5. Find your state's or province's outdoor recreation plan in your school or local library. What are the management priorities of your state or province regarding outdoor recreation?
6. Identify the recreation resources (natural resources, cultural resources, festivals, and special events) that make your state or province unique. How are these resources marketed to entice both in-state or in-province and out-of-state or out-of-province visitors?
7. Identify one specific government partnership that is taking place in your state or province. What does the partnership entail?
8. Locate a leisure services professional working in state or provincial government and ask him or her to describe the technical and interpersonal skills required for his or her position.
9. What roles do state and provincial governments play that are not handled by either municipal or federal governments?
10. What are the skills needed to work in direct service at the state or provincial level? Evaluate your own skills in these areas.

References

Ebberson, A. 1983. Why people travel. *Journal of Physical Education, Recreation, and Dance—Leisure Today 54*(4), 53–54.

Foss, P. 1968. *Recreation: Conservation in the United States, a Documentary History.* New York: Chelsea House.

Ibrahim, H., and K. Cordes. 1993. *Outdoor Recreation.* Madison, WI: Brown & Benchmark.

Jensen, C. 1985. *Outdoor Recreation in America.* Minneapolis, MN: Burgess.

Jensen, C. 1995. *Outdoor Recreation in America.* 2d ed. Champaign, IL: Human Kinetics.

Jones, J. 1992. *The United States Outdoor Atlas and Recreation Guide.* New York: Houghton.

Knudson, D. 1984. *Outdoor Recreation.* New York: Macmillan.

Kraus, R. 1990. *Recreation and Leisure in Modern Society.* 4th ed. New York: HarperCollins.

Kreisberg, L. 1979. *Local Government and the Arts.* New York: American Council for the Arts.

McLean, D. D., A. Hurd, B. Beggs, and D. Chavez. 2000. *Trends in State Park Operations.* http://php.indiana.edu

Meyer, H., and C. Brightbill. 1950. *State Recreation: Organization and Administration.* New York: A. S. Baines.

Myers, P. 1992. Testimony before the subcommittee on energy and the environment. *Crisis in State and Local Recreation and Fiscal Year 1993 Budget for LWCF and UPARR.* Washington, DC: U.S. Government Printing Office.

The National Association of State Park Directors. 2000. *Definitions.* www.indiana.edu/~naspd/statistics/definitions.html

Outdoor Recreation Resources Review Commission. 1962. *Outdoor Recreation for America: A Report to the President and to the Congress.* Washington, DC: U.S. Government Printing Office.

Peene, L., and J. Shanahan. 1990. The role of the arts in state and local economic development. Edited by W. T. Pound, in *Economic Impact of the Arts: A Sourcebook.* Washington, DC: National Conference of State Legislatures.

President's Commission on Americans Outdoors. 1987. *Americans Outdoors: The Legacy, the Challenge.* Washington, DC: Island Press.

U.S. Bureau of the Census. 1995. *Statistical Abstracts of the United States: 1995.* 115th ed. Washington, DC: U.S. Government Printing Office.

U.S. Bureau of the Census. 1999. *Statistical Abstracts of the United States: 1999.* 119th ed. Washington, DC: U.S. Government Printing Office.

U.S. Census Bureau. 1999. *Statistical Abstract of the United States: 2003.* 123rd ed. Washington, DC.

U.S. Census Bureau. *Statistical Abstract of the United States: 2003.* (123rd edition) Washington, DC, 1999.

Westfall, R. 1991. Emerging trends at the state level. *Trends 28*(2), 39–42.

CHAPTER 9

Delivery of Leisure Services: Federal Government

Federal lands and other resources provide opportunities for many different types of leisure experiences. In North America, our natural resources abound. Here, a family resting during a hike pauses for a reflective moment.

Introduction

The United States and Canada are blessed with many unique natural land areas. Federal agencies administer most of these areas and have as a primary and secondary goal the provision of parks, recreation, and/or cultural services. The United States has majestic environmental areas that draw tourists from around the world. One need only think of Yosemite Valley, the geysers of Yellowstone, and the vistas of the Grand Canyon to appreciate this heritage of natural resources.

From a historical perspective, the United States has acquired more than 1,837,770,000 acres of land and water as a part of its public domain. The majority of this land and water was acquired between 1781 and 1867, with additional small acquisitions at the close of the 1800s and the beginning of the 1900s. These land masses provide the basis for many leisure opportunities and have resulted in the creation of a large number of federal agencies and institutions to manage parks and recreation services.

This chapter reviews the involvement of the federal government of the United States in the provision of parks, recreation, and cultural services. The number and types of areas, facilities, and services are diverse and do not lend themselves to a clean classification system. Some of the agencies discussed have the provision of parks and recreation services as a primary objective. Other agencies must contend with a variety of objectives under one administrative umbrella. Still other federal agencies provide recreation services in support of their primary mission. For example, the National Park Service's primary objective is to maintain preserves for the purpose of recreation, tourism, and preservation. The U.S. Forest Service has multiple objectives including timber management, watershed management, fish and wildlife management, range management, and recreation. Branches of the U.S. Armed Forces provide Morale, Welfare and Recreation Services in support of their primary mission of defense.

Characteristics of Federal Leisure Service Agencies

Kraus (1990) writes that more than ninety federal agencies, bureaus, commissions, and/or councils provide parks, recreation, and leisure services at the federal level of government. He suggests that the more than 300 federal programs have had little coordination or otherwise centralized planning. This involvement of the federal government has grown steadily since the late 1800s.

Goals and Functions

What are the goals and functions of federal agencies? The large number of federal agencies makes it difficult to specify the goals of the federal government with respect to leisure services. Nonetheless, Kraus (1990) identifies the following eight basic functions of the federal government in relation to parks, recreation, and leisure services (see figure 9.1):

1. *Direct management of outdoor recreation resources.* The federal government owns approximately one-third of the total land area in the United States; much of this land is used for a variety of outdoor pursuits. Thus, the federal government plays an immense role in providing outdoor recreation opportunities. Campgrounds, forests, parks, artificial and natural lakes, and other geographic areas come under the direct stewardship of the federal government and are managed by such agencies as the National Park Service, U.S. Forest Service, Bureau of Land Management, U.S. Fish and Wildlife Service, Tennessee Valley Authority, and the U.S. Corps of Engineers.
2. *Conservation and resource reclamation.* The federal government is involved in restoring land and water resources that have been damaged or destroyed and in conserving natural resources, including environmental management and wildlife conservation.

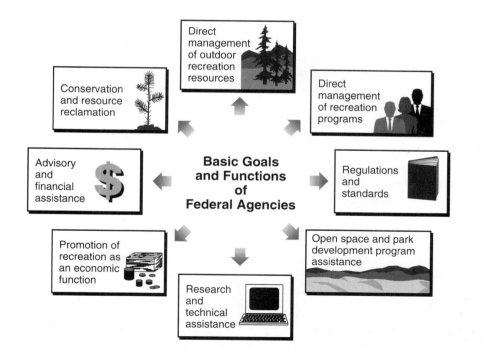

Figure 9.1

Eight basic functions of federal agencies related to leisure services.

Best Intentions . . .

. . . Estimated annual numbers of through hikers: starts and finishes

	Start	Finish
Appalachian Trail (2,158 miles)	1,200 to 1,500	180 to 225
Continental Divide Trail (3,000 miles)	6 to 8	2 to 3
Pacific Crest Trail (2,600 miles)	75 to 100	12 to 24

Source: Staff, "Best Intentions" in *Backpacker,* p. 17, June 1996.

3. *Assistance to open space and park development programs.* During the past several decades, the federal government provided funds to state and local governments to acquire and develop park and recreation resources. The most significant legislation was that of the 1965 Land and Water Conservation Fund Act. One of the priorities for the use of this fund, the rails-to-trails movement, transforms old railroad corridors into new walking and biking greenways.

4. *Direct management of recreation programs.* Several federal agencies provide recreation programs directly to participants. These include activities provided by the Veterans Administration, National Park Service, U.S. Armed Forces, and others. Many of these programs will be discussed later in this chapter.

5. *Advisory and financial assistance.* The federal government provides technical advice to community agencies and rural environments as well as leadership in the coordination of national recreation policy. From a historical perspective, the cooperative extension services in various states have provided this type of information and have been supported by federal funds.

Leadership direction for national recreation policy appears in such efforts as the National Outdoor Recreation Plans. Special federal commissions also have played major roles in shaping national policy. For example, three presidential commissions, examining the nation's outdoor recreation policy, were created in the 1900s. In 1924, President Calvin Coolidge initiated the first commission that dealt with outdoor recreation resources. Among other things, a National Conference on Outdoor Recreation resulted.

In 1958, the U.S. Congress appointed representatives to the Outdoor Recreation Resources Review Commission (ORRRC). This commission produced a twenty-eight-volume report that recommended major federal involvement in the outdoor recreation area. President John F. Kennedy presented the report to Congress, endorsing its findings. His endorsement encouraged a number of developments, including the establishment of the federal coordinating agency (Bureau of Outdoor Recreation) and funding program for outdoor recreation resources (Land and Water Conservation Act).

In 1985, President Ronald Reagan established a commission, the President's Commission on Americans Outdoors (PCAO), to review existing public outdoor recreation programs and opportunities provided by the federal government, state and local governments, and private organizations and entities. Table 9.1 presents an overview of the findings and suggestions of this commission.

In addition to coordination of policy and performing various advisory functions, the federal government also provides state and local governments, as well as nonprofit organizations, with financial assistance. Often this assistance takes the forms of grants. Two examples include the National Endowment for the Arts and the Administration on

TABLE

9.1 FINDINGS AND SUGGESTIONS OF THE PRESIDENT'S COMMISSION ON AMERICANS OUTDOORS

Purpose:

To create a comprehensive governmental appraisal of the nation's outdoor recreation policy and to examine the roles that government and the private sector should play in protecting outdoor recreation resources and meeting anticipated outdoor recreation needs.

Participants:

The Commission, composed of fifteen members including two senators, three representatives, one governor, one mayor, and several conservationists and leaders from the private sector, heard testimony from more than 1,000 Americans in eighteen hearings in every region of the United States. Ideas, concerns, and hopes for the future were shared. Findings and suggestions are presented in the book, *Americans Outdoors: The Legacy, the Challenge.*

Selected Findings:

- Americans place a high value on the outdoors. More than anything else, the Commission found a love for the land and a shared conviction that it is our legacy and our future.
- Outdoor recreation provides significant social, economic, and environmental benefits.
- Quality of the outdoor estate remains precarious. Americans are losing open space as well as wild and free-flowing rivers. Competition for available lands and waters is increasing.
- The quality of recreation services delivery is inadequate. Funding poses a problem, as do liability concerns. Inadequate funding for staff, development of facilities, and maintenance limits recreation use on public lands.

Suggestions:

- *Light a prairie fire of local action.* People on the local level know what their needs are. Grassroots efforts can make communities attractive places to live, work, and play, with maintained open spaces.
- *Develop an outdoor ethic.* Every American must develop a sense of ownership of the outdoors and a commitment to maintaining outdoor opportunities for the future. The nation needs an aware, sensitive, and activated outdoor constituency.
- *Establish education programs about the outdoors.* Local school systems should establish outdoor education programs to encourage appreciation of the outdoors—the 4 R's: Reading, 'Riting, 'Rithmatic, and Resources.
- *Create an Outdoors Corps.* Groups of youth and individuals of all ages should be encouraged to dedicate a portion of their lives to the stewardship of natural resources.
- *Create greenways.* Greenways, corridors of open space linking public and private lands and waterways, can put recreation open space within a short walk of everyone's residence. A network of scenic byways, including roadways and thoroughfares, should be established.
- *Develop innovative funding and management strategies.* Public-private partnerships should be encouraged, realizing the vital role that can be played by volunteers; innovative strategies including fees and charges, a dedicated trust, and other mechanisms should be established to fund future outdoor recreation development.
- *Protect endangered resources.* Protecting 2,000 rivers by the year 2000, as well as expending greater effort to protect wetlands and shorelines and providing for the recreation of people in large urban areas where open space is scarce, must be a priority.
- *Enforce environmental laws.* Outdoor recreation depends on healthy resources, and Americans must diligently protect the environment.
- *Improve the quality of services.* The quality of areas and programs can be improved.
- *Protect our investment.* A systematic plan of renovation and replacement for recreation facilities should be in place.
- *Develop better leadership.* Well-trained professional staff must be developed and educated.
- *Create a clearinghouse of information on the outdoors.* Informational material must be made available.

Source: The President's Commission on Americans Outdoors (PCAO). 1987. *Americans Outdoors: The Legacy, The Challenge.* Washington, DC: Island Press.

Ethnicity and the Great Outdoors

A recent survey on outdoor recreation patterns revealed that only 4 percent of frequent backpackers are African American, while Hispanics make up 19 percent, and whites just over 70 percent.

Source: Staff, "Changing the Face of Backpacking" in *Backpacker,* p. 16, May 1996.

Aging. The National Endowment for the Arts provides grants to individuals and organizations to promote the arts; the Administration on Aging provides funds for demonstration projects that meet the needs of seniors in unique ways and help older Americans avoid institutionalization.

6. *Promotion of recreation as an economic function.* Numerous examples exist of the federal government's involvement in promotion of recreation, leisure, and park concerns. Some of the federal agencies operating in this arena focus on the promotion of tourist attractions and opportunities for international tourists. The United States attracts large numbers of international tourists, and their economic impact is growing. As indicated in Chapter 8, in 2001, international tourists spent more than $91 million in the United States (U.S. Bureau of Census, 2003). In 1997, foreign visitors spent $73 million in the United States as part of their tourist-related expenditures. In 1988, the figure was $29 million. (U.S. Bureau of Census, 1999). This compares with 1998 when international tourists spent $38 million, and there was a deficit between the total travel expenditures of Americans abroad and receipts from foreign visitors. The federal government also helps to provide outdoor recreation opportunities that can generate significant economic opportunities. In 1996, wildlife-associated recreation expenditures totaled $87.5 million (U.S. Bureau of Census, 1999). This compares with 1991 when expenditures totaled approximately $54 million (U.S. Bureau of Census, 1993).

7. *Research and technical assistance.* The federal government supports a wide variety of research, especially in the area of outdoor recreation. Some of the research, in turn, is applied and is available in the form of direct technical assistance to businesses and other levels of government. Other research projects of the federal government include examining the recreation needs of special populations as well as examining the recreation resources available to inner-city youth.

8. *Regulations and standards.* The regulatory activities of the federal government have influenced ". . . pollution control, watershed production, and environmental quality" (Kraus, 1990, p. 212). In addition, legislation has impacted upon services for individuals who are disabled and physically challenged. For example, the Americans with Disabilities Act (ADA) signed in 1990 by President Bush prohibits discrimination against people with disabilities in employment and in public services, public and private transportation, public accommodations, and telecommunications services. This legislation has tremendous implications for leisure service organizations as it mandates equal opportunity and access to recreation opportunities for persons with disabilities.

Resource Base

The resource base or revenue for federal parks, recreation, and cultural services comes primarily from two sources. The first includes revenues that are made available through appropriated funds from the Congress of the United States. In general, these revenues are subject to executive approval, although they are legislatively mandated. In addition, federal agencies can collect revenues in support of services. These "nonappropriated funds" are often locally generated fees and charges at specific sites, and many agencies are able to keep these funds in direct support of their areas, programs, and services.

In the United States, approximately $3.1 billion is expended yearly at the federal level for recreation resources (U.S. Bureau of Census, 2003). This figure has more than doubled in actual dollars when compared with 1990. If one combined all of the federal funds dedicated to natural resources and the environment, the amount is over $30 billion. This figure does not include resources dedicated from other areas of the federal budget such as the Department of Defense or the Department of Veterans Affairs.

In 2001, nearly $4 billion in funds was available from appropriations, revenue from operations, and other sources to operate the National Park Service. This compares with nearly $3 billion in 1995 and $2.4 billion in 1990. Table 9.2 presents this information. Funding for the National Park Service provides an illustration of appropriations from Congress, as well as revenues generated from other sources, such as operations. In 1997, approximately $23 billion was available for park operations; of this amount $6 billion came from federal appropriations and the remainder from other sources such as fees and charges. It is interesting to note that revenues in 1990 available for park operations were $13 billion.

Characteristics of Professionals

The types and numbers of employees working for federal agencies vary tremendously. Due to the large number of classifications, it is not possible to include a list of all of them in this chapter. In general, however, employment in the federal system involves qualifying for a GS (Government Service) ranking. Individuals with a bachelor's degree in the parks and recreation field often enter federal service as a GS 7 ranking under the federal civil service system.

For specific information about examinations for positions with the federal government, one can contact the nearest Federal Job Information Center. Some Federal Job Information Centers also provide information concerning jobs in other governmental jurisdictions. There is a Federal Job Information Center in most major cities and in every state of the United States. Most permanent positions in the federal government are filled by an employment list of eligible candidates. This employment list is usually established as a result of some type of competitive review; some reviews require a written examination, whereas others do not. An individual interested in applying for a specific type of position should obtain and review the relevant position announcement from the local Federal Job Information Center. The position announcement includes the education, experience, and skill-level requirements for individual jobs. For additional information on jobs with the federal government, students are encouraged to visit their Web site at http://www.fedworld.gov/jobs/jobsearch.html.

Customer Orientation

The customer orientation of employees of the federal government is termed a *public servant* orientation. To be a public servant means to be *in the service of the public*. A public servant is one who holds the public's trust. He or she has the responsibility to act on behalf of and in the interest of the public's welfare. Public servants do not work to earn a profit but rather to provide a service that is of value to society.

TABLE

9.2 NATIONAL PARK SERVICE EXPENDITURES

No. 1249 National Park System—Summary: 1990 to 2002

[For year ending September 30, except as noted. (986 represents $986,000,000) Includes data for live areas in Puerto Rico and Virgin Islands, one area in American Samoa, and one area in Guam]

Item	1990	1995	1997	1998	1999	2000	2001	2002
Finances (mil dol.):[1]								
Expenditures reported	986	1,445	1,473	1,604	1,530	1,833	1,985	2,181
Salaries and wages	459	633	683	721	733	799	840	876
Improvements, maintenance	160	234	246	255	289	299	305	311
Construction	109	192	188	191	62	215	199	298
Other	259	388	356	437	446	520	641	678
Funds available	1,506	2,225	2,301	2,658	2,972	3,816	3,642	3,940
Appropriations	1,053	1,325	1,625	1,765	1,867	1,881	2,341	2,257
Other[2]	453	900	676	893	1,105	1,435	1,401	1,863
Revenue from operations	79	108	175	208	215	284	248	245
Recreation visits (millions):[3]								
All areas	258.7	289.8	275.3	288.7	287.1	285.9	279.9	277.3
National Parks[4]	57.7	64.8	65.3	64.5	64.3	66.1	64.1	64.5
National monuments	28.9	23.5	24.1	23.6	24.9	28.8	21.8	20.3
National historical, commemorative, archaeological[5]	57.5	58.9	63.0	74.2	72.6	72.2	66.7	70.2
National parkways	29.1	31.3	31.6	32.8	34.6	34.0	34.4	35.7
National recreation areas	47.2	53.7	51.6	53.0	52.8	50.0	48.3	48.2
National seashores and lakeshores	23.3	22.5	22.4	22.6	22.7	22.5	22.2	23.3
National Capital Parks	7.5	5.5	5.1	4.2	3.9	5.4	4.6	3.8
Recreation overnight stays (millions)	17.6	16.8	15.8	15.6	15.9	15.4	15.3	14.7
In commercial lodgings	3.9	3.8	3.8	3.6	3.7	3.7	3.8	3.5
In Park Service campgrounds	7.9	7.1	6.3	6.1	6.2	5.9	5.7	5.8
In backcountry	1.7	2.2	2.2	2.1	2.0	1.9	2.0	1.9
Other	4.2	3.7	3.8	3.9	4.1	3.8	3.9	3.5
Land (1,000 acres)[6]								
Total	78,362	77,335	77,457	77,854	78,166	78,153	78,943	78,811
Parks	46,089	49,307	49,384	49,416	49,859	49,785	49,882	49,639
Recreation areas	3,344	3,353	3,329	3,381	3,404	3,388	3,388	3,390
Other	26,929	24,695	24,744	24,877	24,903	24,980	25,693	25,782
Acquisition. nat.	21	27	61	95	44	222	20	17

[1]Financial data are those associated with the National Park System. Certain other functions of the National Park Service (principally the activities absorbed from the former Heritage Conservation and Recreation Service in 1981) are excluded. [2]Includes funds carried over from prior years. [3]For calendar year. Includes other areas, not shown separately. [4]For 1990, total. [5]Includes military areas. [6]Federal land only as of Dec. 31. Federal land acreages, in addition to National Park Service administered lands, also include lands within national park system or boundaries but under the administration of other agencies. Year-to-year changes in the Federal lands figures include changes in the acreages of these other lands and hence often differ from "net acquisition."

Source: U.S. National Park Service. Visits. National Park Statistical Abstract, annual and unpublished data. Other data are unpublished.

As an example, the mission statement of Community, Family, and Soldier Support Command-Korea outlines this federal organization's basic values and customer orientation. The mission statement indicates that its members will provide quality service in support of the mission of the military at a fair value to their customers. They pledge integrity and honesty in their dealings with customers. Furthermore, they point out the types of interactions that are desirable between themselves as public servants and their customers, suggesting that people be treated with respect and in a courteous manner (see figure 9.2).

Another example illustrates the public servant orientation of government employees. The U.S. Forest Service's pamphlet, *People Serving People* (n.d.), discusses the work of the U.S. Forest Service and points out that

> . . . the Forest Service, by definition, is devoted to serving the American public. . . . In order for the public's wants and needs to be known, sensitivity and responsiveness are required on our part. . . . Our public service attitude is communicated both directly and indirectly. For example, how available are forest service personnel to the public? Can someone be reached and information be obtained most of the time? In the forest, does the public feel safe and relatively protected by the presence of law enforcement staff? Is there a feedback system through which the public may indicate their desires or responses to existing services? All of these impressions convey to the public our role. Are we serving the public?

As Gifford Pinchot, founder of the U.S. Forest Service and the first native-born American to complete graduate training in forestry, indicated ". . . a public official is there to serve the public and not run them" (*People Serving People,* n.d.).

Types of Federal Agencies: United States

This section discusses major federal agencies providing parks, recreation, and cultural services in the United States. These agencies fall into the following groups: land-managing agencies, reservoir providers, and other major agencies providing direct services or support to parks and recreation.

The total area of the United States, including land and water masses, is 3.8 billion acres (U.S. Bureau of Census, 2003). Approximately 25 percent of this area is managed by various agencies of the federal government. These agencies include the U.S. Forest Service (part of the Department of Agriculture), and the Bureau of Land Management, National Park Service, U.S. Fish and Wildlife Service, and Bureau of Indian Affairs (which are all divisions within the Department of the Interior).

In addition to managing land areas, the federal government also manages a number of large reservoirs and, as a result, has become the nation's largest provider of inland water recreation opportunities. The importance of these recreation opportunities is heightened by the fact that many of these reservoir areas are close to large cities in the northeast, southeast, and south, whereas the majority of federally owned land is located in the western half of the United States. Three agencies within the federal government—the U.S. Corps of Engineers, Tennessee Valley Authority, and the Bureau of Reclamation—manage the majority of these water resources.

A number of additional agencies and programs within the federal government provide services in specific ways. These agencies include the work of the Veterans Administration in the area of therapeutic recreation as well as the involvement of the Morale, Welfare, and Recreation Services of the U.S. Armed Forces, the National Endowment for the Arts, and the National Endowment for the Humanities (see figure 9.3).

Figure 9.2

Service ethic.

*Source:
Community, Family,
and Soldier
Support
Command-
Korea, Eighth
United States
Army.*

Service Ethic

As a member of the Community, Family, and Soldier Support Command-Korea and in the spirit
of the highest standards of service and business responsibility

We Hereby Pledge to:

Programs Offered	Provide value in all the morale, welfare, and recreation programs we offer our patrons.
Service	Maintain courteous, attentive, and efficient service in a pleasant atmosphere and maintain a professional attitude at all times.
Clean Facilities	Meet and maintain all prescribed standards of sanitation service and remain constantly aware of our responsibility to our patrons.
Community Responsibility	Earn the respect of the military community and contribute to command and community life by supporting the programs that enhance the quality of life in the military community.
Fair Trade Practices	Operate with integrity in all operations and engage in fair and open competition based on truthful representation of services offered.
MWR Program Development	Contribute through dedicated service to our patrons toward the growth and development of better morale, welfare, and recreation programs.
Profit	Maintain the ability to earn a reasonable profit so that facilities can be renovated and value to our patrons can continue to be a primary objective.

U.S. Forest Service

In 1891, Congress was authorized by the President of the United States to establish forest preserves from forest and range lands in the public domain. These forest preserves were subsequently organized for the intent of protection and management as national forests. In 1905, the management of national forests was transferred to the U.S. Department of Agriculture, and what is known today as the U.S. Forest Service was established. Today, the Forest Service is the largest and most diverse agency in the U.S. Department of Agriculture, employing more than 30,000 permanent full-time and seasonal employees. It is America's largest conservation organization.

The mission of the U.S. Forest Service is to sustain the health, diversity, and productivity of the nation's forests and grasslands to meet the needs of present and future generations. Figure 9.4 presents the distribution of these resources across the United States. Table 9.3 presents highlights of the U.S. Forest Service for the year 2002. The Forest Service organization includes six forest and range experimental stations, the Forest Products Lab, the State and Private Forestry Northeastern Area, the International Institute of Tropical Forestry, nine National Forest System regions that include the 155 national forests and twenty national grasslands, and the national headquarters office in Washington, DC.

Figure 9.3

Major federal agencies providing parks, recreation, and cultural services.

U.S. Forest Service	National Endowment for the Humanities	U.S. Fish and Wildlife Service
National Park Service	National Endowment for the Arts	U.S. Corps of Engineers
Bureau of Land Management	MWR Services: U.S. Armed Forces	Soil Conservation Service
Bureau of Reclamation	Veterans' Administration	Bureau of Indian Affairs
	Tennessee Valley Authority	

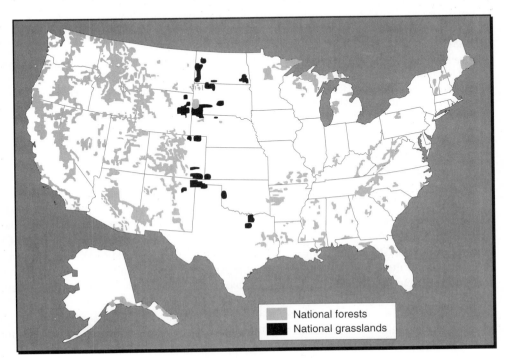

Figure 9.4

U.S. National Forest Service Reserves.

Source: Data from the U.S. National Forest Service Reserve, Natural Resources and Environment, U.S. Department of Agriculture.

National forests
National grasslands

TABLE

9.3 ANNUAL HIGHLIGHTS USDA FOREST SERVICE

- There are 155 national forests and twenty grasslands on the more than 192 million acres that make up the National Forest System, an area the size of America's original thirteen colonies.
- The U.S. Department of Agriculture Forest Service manages 35 million acres of designated wilderness and more than 50 million acres of wild backcountry, including vast tracts of old-growth forest.
- In forty-three states, 3,400 communities with a total population of more than 60 million people obtain at least a portion of their drinking water from watersheds located on national forests and grasslands.
- More than 1.3 million cattle and approximately 1 million sheep and goats are permitted to graze over 4.8 million tons of forage (grass, forbs, and shrubs) on National Forest System lands.
- More than 9,800 Forest Service land managers work together to reduce erosion, restore stability, and improve productivity of the soils, resulting in cleaner water, improved fish and wildlife habitat and enhanced recreational opportunities.
- Nearly 4 million Americans participate in conservation education programs and activities. This includes 1.5 million students, 90,000 educators, more than 500,000 visitors to national forests and grasslands, and 1.5 million members of the general public.
- The Forest Service sells about 240,000 Christmas trees, valued at about $1.4 million.
- More than 46 million anglers fish in national forest waters, making an economic contribution of $8.5 billion to the economy. Some 28 million people hunt on national forest lands, making an economic contribution of $6.1 billion to the economy.
- On National Forest System lands, 99 percent of unplanned and unwanted wildland fires are controlled during initial attack.
- On federal and non-federal lands, 1.8 million acres of forest and rangeland affected by insects, diseases, and invasive plants are treated.
- Permits are issued to remove about 400,000 cords of firewood, enabling people to supplement their heating throughout the winter months.
- Approximately 1.7 billion board feet of timber are harvested, at a value of $165 million.
- About 75,000 special use permits (lands and recreation use) generate about $46 million to the U.S. Treasury.
- More than 250,000 acres of habitat are treated or improved for wildlife species annually.
- More than 912,500 ounces of gold, platinum, and palladium are extracted from national forests and grasslands and used for commercial and hobbyist purposes.
- On national forests and grasslands, 81.5 million people hike or walk, 46 million fish, 150.7 million view natural features and/or wildlife, 23.4 million camp in developed campgrounds, 28 million hunt, 42.5 million pursue winter sports (downhill or cross-country skiing or snowmobiling), and 95 million spend time relaxing.

Source: Forest Service at a Glance: Annual Highlights U.S. Department of Agriculture, Forest Service. Retrieved on June 14, 2004, from http://www.fs.fed.us/plan/par/2003/final/html/fs_glance/annual_highlights.shtml.

The underlying philosophy of the Forest Service is conservation. Conservation suggests wise use of resources. It also suggests that resources are renewable (e.g., timber) and can be managed in such a way as to protect the values associated with them. Gifford Pinchot, Chief Forester of the Forest Service from 1898 to 1910, noted ". . . conservation of natural resources . . . is the key to the safety and prosperity of the American people and of all the people of the world for all time to come" (U.S. Forest Service, 1970, p. 1). A motto of the Forest Service (1986) is "caring for the land . . . serving the people."

The conservation mandate includes the idea of managing the land for multiple uses. The Multiple-Use Sustained Yield Act of 1960 identified the five primary uses of national forest land as outdoor recreation, watershed protection, grazing, timber production, and the propagation of fish and wildlife. Although these five basic uses are supposedly of equal importance, any one of them may be emphasized over the others in a particular area. For example, within wilderness areas outdoor recreation, watershed, and the propagation of fish and wildlife would be emphasized while timber cutting might be forbidden.

The Forest Service provides more outdoor recreation resources than any other federal agency in the U.S. government—the natural resources found in national forests provide a focal point for many outdoor recreation activities. For example, the Forest Service administers more than 120,000 miles of hiking and riding trails (Jensen, 1995). In addition, it maintains more than 10,000 recreational sites, including campgrounds, picnic areas, ski areas, and boat ramps. The combined capacity of all recreation areas administered by the Forest Service exceeds 1.5 million people at any given time. In 2002, over 465 million individuals used the forest service system for a variety recreational activities including hunting, fishing, hiking, walking, viewing natural features or wildlife, camping, or engaging in winter sports such as downhill skiing, cross-country skiing, or snowmobiling. In 1996, the Forest Service played to more than 341 million recreation visitor days (a visitor day is the recreational use of National Forest that aggregates twelve visitor hours) (U.S. Bureau of Census, 1999). This compares with 1980 when there were 233 million visitor days. The Forest Service has also been active in the creation and management of wilderness areas, including the first one established in 1924—the Gila Wilderness Area in New Mexico. Today the Forest Service manages more than 32 million acres of wilderness.

In the area of outdoor recreation, the Forest Service has three primary roles (U.S. Forest Service, 1983):

1. *Management, protection, and use of the national forest system.* This involves care of the lands and water areas that provide opportunities for recreation experiences and related services.
2. *Cooperation.* The Forest Service works with private interests and other governmental agencies to share its knowledge, resources, and capabilities to improve the delivery of recreation services.
3. *Research.* The Forest Service conducts research to improve opportunities for quality outdoor recreation experiences.

The U.S. Forest Service has clarified its role in providing a revision of its Forest Service Strategic Plan which was revised in the year 2000. The plan includes four goals including ecosystem health, multiple benefits for people, scientific and technical assistance, and effective public service. This strategy serves as the conceptual framework aimed at finding creative and imaginative ways to take advantage of outdoor recreation opportunities in the national forests by working with people. The ultimate goal of the strategy—to promote customer satisfaction with more high-quality recreation services—involves forging partnerships with state and local government as well as private enterprise, and developing the professionalism of recreation staff by creating standards and challenging career paths.

Partnerships between the U.S. Forest Service and the private sector date back to 1871. An example of a partnership is one existing between the U.S. Forest Service and the Hoodoo Ski Area in the Dechutes National Forest. The private sector operates campground concessions and ski areas on U.S. Forest Service land. This partnership, as well as others, has resulted in providing high-quality recreational experiences through improved and expanded facilities and excellent guest service.

Save Alaska's Rainforest

The world's largest temperate rainforest graces the long, narrow strip of Alaska that reaches southward to border western Canada. It's the Tongass National Forest, home to centuries-old trees and the array of bears, wolves, and bald eagles that they shelter. The forest is the prime attraction for cruise-ship tourists plying the inland passage. The trees protect watersheds containing the best fishing streams anywhere.

The Tongass trees are protected by the Roadless Rule, established in the Clinton administration to prohibit building logging roads into unspoiled portions of our national forests.

Now the Bush administration wants to wreck the rule and the forest. It would provide exemptions to allow logging of the Tongass and its northern neighbor, the Chugach National Forest.

Letters of protest have been signed by literally hundreds of organizations—not just tourism, sports,

and environmental groups but also some loggers. The Alaska forests "represent some relatively easy pickings but the building industry does not need or want to see this wood in our supply chain." Others joining the protest include KB Home and Staples Inc. *The Wall Street Journal* lists the three as major users of wood products.

The three-member Alaska congressional delegation, however, is firmly allied with loggers eager to blitz the forests. And the Alaska delegation, thanks to seniority, carries ponderous political clout.

The loggers have long argued that wrecking the forest is vital to U.S. homebuilding needs. Meanwhile, they quietly ship timber to Japan.

The Bush administration has the authority to reverse the Clinton policy. But if it happens, no authority on Earth is capable of reversing the damage to the Tongass.

Source: Save Alaska's Rainforest. 2003. *The Des Moines Register* (October), p. 6a.

The Bureau of Land Management

The Bureau of Land Management (BLM), created in 1946 as a part of the Department of Interior, has as its primary responsibility the management of lands within the original public domain. Lands within the public domain are those areas to which the public has right of ownership, rather than individuals. Although large parcels of land have been transferred or sold from the public domain to homesteaders, railroad corporations, in support of common schools, or have been otherwise dispersed, today the BLM manages an enormous portion of the United States—more than 341 million acres. Most of this area is in the western portion of the United States. Figure 9.5 shows the distribution of lands under the jurisdiction of the BLM.

Like the U.S. Forest Service, the BLM uses the principles of multiple use and sustained yield to manage its land holdings. The Federal Land Policy and Management Act of 1976 mandates the BLM to manage its land in accordance with the multiple-use and sustained yield concept. Much of the land managed by the BLM is arid or semiarid and found in the southwest; however, the BLM also manages large land areas in Alaska and the Pacific Northwest.

The BLM public lands provide visitors with a vast array of recreational opportunities. These include hunting, fishing, camping, hiking, boating, hang gliding, off-highway vehicle driving, mountain biking, birding, and visiting natural and cultural heritage sites. The BLM administers 205,498 miles of fishable streams, 2.2 million acres of lakes and reservoirs, 6,600 miles of floatable rivers, over 500 boating access points, 69 National Back Country

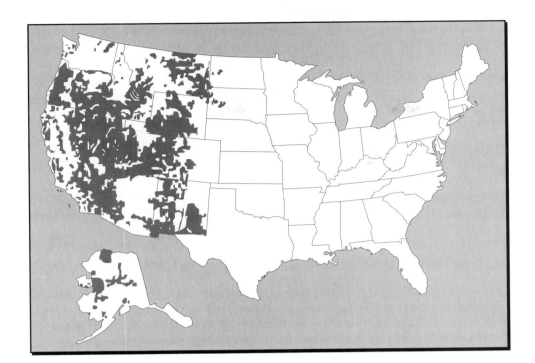

Figure 9.5

Areas under the jurisdiction of the Bureau of Land Management.

Source: Data from the Department of the Interior.

Byways, and 300 Watchable Wildlife sites. The BLM also manages 4,500 miles of National Scenic, Historic, and Recreational Trails, as well as thousands of miles of multiple-use trails used by motorcyclists, hikers, equestrians, and mountain bikers (http://www.blm.gov/nhp/what/index.htm#recreation).

The BLM's primary function in the area of recreation is to provide outdoor recreation opportunities to the public, particularly those not provided by other public or private entities. Its secondary goals include protecting resources, maintaining visitor health and safety, and helping resolve conflicts between users involving recreation resources. In general, the BLM provides resource-dependent types of outdoor recreation. It focuses on the provision of such activities as fishing, hunting, rock hounding, and other resource-dependent activities. The BLM also invests in the creation of special or more intensely managed recreation areas, such as recreation assistance facilities and visitor assistance programs like campgrounds, picnic sites, sanitation facilities, trails, and information displays. The BLM is involved in the management of such areas as San Pedro Riparian Natural Conservation Area, Gila Box Riparian Natural Conservation Area, Aravaipa Creek Wilderness Area, and other riparian areas.

The Bureau of Land Management Strategic Plan identifies one of its major goals as providing opportunities for environmentally responsible recreation. This strategic plan adopted in 2000 has a number of key goals focused on improving Special Recreation Management Areas (SRMA) administered by the BLM. The plan notes that in fiscal year (FY) 1995, 77 percent of BLM recreation users were satisfied with their recreation experience. For FY 2005, the plan calls for achieving 88 percent satisfaction rate among users in SRMA. In addition, the plan calls for 75 percent of physical facilities within SRMA to be in good or fair condition by FY 2005. Interestingly, this is a decline from the expectations of 80 percent in 2000. This goal is reduced based on anticipated increase in public use and the fact that resources will not keep pace with increasing demand.

National Park Service

The National Park Service was founded as a part of the Department of Interior in 1916. Some areas administered by the National Park Service, however, predate the actual creation of this integrated administrative unit. For example, the first national memorial, Montgomery Monument, was established in 1776. The first national park in the United States, and the world, was established in 1872 when Yellowstone was set aside as a "pleasuring grounds" of unique geographic character for future generations (Lee, 1972). When the National Park Service was established in 1916, its responsibilities were set forth as follows:

> . . . to conserve the scenery and natural and historic objects and the wildlife therein, and to provide for the enjoyment of the same in such a manner and by such a means as will leave them unimpaired for enjoyment for future generations. (Lee, 1972, p. 6)

Through the National Park Service, an incredibly diverse system of parks, monuments, historical sites, and recreation areas has been established for the enjoyment and education of the citizens of the United States. The National Park Service administered more than 388 individual units. Within its charge, the National Park Service administers national parks (e.g., Yellowstone and Yosemite); national preserves (e.g., Big Cypress and Glacier Bay); national reserves (e.g., City of the Rocks, Idaho); national monuments (e.g., Casa Grande and Death Valley); national historic sites (e.g., Abraham Lincoln's Birthplace and Martin Luther King's Birthplace); national historic parks (e.g., Valley Forge and San Francisco Maritime); national memorials (e.g., Lincoln Memorial and J.F.K. Center for Performing Arts); national recreation areas (e.g., Lake Mead), national seashores (e.g., Assateague Island and Padre Island); national lake shores (e.g., Indiana Dunes); national military parks (e.g., Gettysburg); national wild and scenic riverways (e.g., Rio Grande); national rivers (e.g., Mississippi River); parkways (e.g., Natchez Trace); national battlefield parks (e.g., Manassas); national scenic trails (e.g., Appalachian); international historic sites (e.g., Saint Croix Island); national battlefield sites (e.g., Brices Cross Roads); and others (e.g., National Capital Parks and National Mall).

National Park Service operations are guided by the philosophy of preservation of resources. That philosophy is embedded in a 1918 letter written from Secretary of the Interior, Franklin K. Lane, to the first director of the National Park Service, Stephen T. Mather. Lane, suggesting that a policy be developed to guide the work of the National Park Service, wrote the following:

> . . . the National Parks must be maintained in absolutely unimpaired form for the use of future generations as well as those of our own time; they are set apart for the use, observation, health, and pleasure of the people; and that national interest must dictate all decisions affecting public or private enterprise in the parks. (Albright, Dickenson, and Mott, 1987, p. 18)

The National Park Service still maintains this philosophy of preservation, although this mandate becomes increasingly strained as the parks play host to more and more visitors. In the twenty-first century, park officials will continue to face the challenges of finding the correct balance between preserving national treasures and making them available for the enjoyment of the American people.

Yellowstone Trails Lead Bison to their Death

While the Bush administration's decision to reverse the ban on noisy and antiquated snowmobiles from Yellowstone National Park will undoubtedly increase pollution in this pristine ecosystem, increase adverse impacts on wildlife, and escalate impacts on park employees and visitors, it will also escalate the very problem that originally started this snowmobile controversy: the killing of Yellowstone's bison.

The Fund for Animals' lawsuit in 1997 forced the National Park Service to conduct an environmental impact statement that revealed snowmobiles cause grave impacts to the park's air, water, and wildlife.

Bison use the groomed snowmobile roads in Yellowstone National Park, making it easier for them to leave the park in search of food. When bison step over the park boundary into the state of Montana, they are either gunned down or trucked to slaughterhouses by state livestock officials. More than 2,000 Yellowstone bison have been massacred in the last decade due to Montana's archaic fear of bison wandering into their state.

Under the Bush administration proposal, the National Park Service will continue to groom roads to facilitate access by snowmobiles and snowcoaches (large passenger buses) in Yellowstone. These groomed roads will continue to lead bison to their deaths and will continue to disrupt populations of imperiled species such as grizzly bears.

To protect wildlife and put an end to the bison controversy, Yellowstone must ban snowmobiles and terminate all road grooming activities.

Source: Markarian, M. 2002. (December), p. 10a. Yellowstone Trails Lead Bison to their Death. *The Des Moines Register*

In addition to its direct service responsibilities, the National Park Service also administers a number of other federal programs (see table 9.4). Many of these responsibilities require a great deal of coordination among many of the land-managing agencies of the federal government. For example, in managing the National Wilderness Preservation System, the National Park Service must work with a number of agencies. The Wilderness Preservation System, created by the 1964 Wilderness Act, defines wilderness in the following way: "A wilderness, in contrast with those areas where man [*sic*] and his works dominate the landscape, is hereby recognized as an area where the earth and community of life are untrammeled by man, where man himself is a visitor and does not remain" (The Wilderness Act, 1964). More than 474 wilderness units total nearly 91 million acres. Special attention to coordinating wilderness policy is needed as wilderness areas face a variety of high-priority issues. Cordell, Bergstrom, Hartmenn, and English (1990) identified the following issues for wilderness in the United States:

Allocation. Issues range from debating the appropriate size of wilderness to what types of ecosystems should be represented within the system.

Nontraditional wilderness. The issue is whether the National Wilderness Preservation System should be expanded to include aquatic and underground wilderness units (e.g., caverns).

Wilderness degradation. Can wilderness areas be protected from such natural phenomena as global environmental problems or human-imposed phenomena such as aircraft overflights or the introduction to exotic plant and animal species?

International cooperation. Can global cooperation be assured to protect areas of global significance such as the Everglades or portions of the Amazon rain forest?

TABLE

9.4 NATIONAL PARK SERVICE: PARTNERING AND MANAGING FOR EXCELLENCE

ISSUE:

The report, *National Park Service: Partnering and Managing for Excellence,* documents accomplishments in four major areas—Maintenance Backlog and Facility Management Excellence; Enhancing Partnerships, Volunteers, and Recreation; Resource Protection through Science and Cooperation; and Serving Visitors and Keeping Parks Safe. The document also highlights "next steps," which the NPS will take over the next two years to further improve and strengthen the NPS management and stewardship of the nation's national parks. This is the first document of its kind to be prepared in the twenty-first century.

BACKGROUND:

In May 2001, at Sequoia National Park, President Bush affirmed his commitment to "ensure proper care of our National Park System" and to "improve outdoor opportunities" through his National Parks Legacy Project.

As part of the President's National Parks Legacy Project, NPS Director Fran Mainella focused her efforts on the four major areas of: Maintenance Backlog and Facility Management Excellence; Enhancing Partnerships, Volunteers, and Recreation; Resource Protection through Science and Cooperation; and Serving Visitors and Keeping Parks Safe.

The NPS manages 388 park units that contain some of the nation's most significant cultural, natural, and historic treasures. Established in 1916 to conserve park scenery, wildlife and natural and historic objects, the national parks attract millions of visitors that hike, canoe, explore, and learn about our nation's history, culture, lands, and waters.

The President's National Parks Legacy set forth a vision of caring for and enhancing these special places. The President's leadership team is carrying out this vision through what Interior Secretary Gale Norton refers to as the 4 C's—conservation through cooperation, communication, and consultation. NPS Director Fran Mainella is overseeing NPS efforts, which are restoring old facilities, improving landscape health, enhancing opportunities for visitors to enjoy parks, and inspiring volunteers to participate in their care.

Serving Visitors and Keeping Parks Safe.

Source: Fact sheet, July 2, 2003.

Management coordination. Can management coordination and consistency between agencies with different management philosophies be assured?

Funding and training. Federal land-managing agencies are traditionally understaffed and underfinanced. Can resources for proper management be acquired?

Education. How can wilderness managers instill an outdoor ethic in the general public?

In addition to the Wilderness Preservation System, the National Park System administers the state portion of the Land and Water Conservation Fund, maintains the Nationwide Outdoor Recreation Plan, provides parks and recreation technical services, assists states in the development of comprehensive outdoor recreation planning, plans for the National Wild and Scenic River System, administers the National Trails System, and maintains the National Register of Historic Places, Historic American Building Survey, and the Historic American Engineering Record.

U.S. Fish and Wildlife Service

The U.S. Fish and Wildlife Service is responsible for conserving, protecting, and enhancing fish and wildlife and their habitats for the continuing benefit of humanity. The service was preceded by the Bureau of Fisheries established in 1871 and the Bureau of Biological Survey established in 1885. These two bureaus transferred their functions to the Department of the Interior in 1939 and were redesignated as the U.S. Fish and Wildlife Service in 1940. In 1956, the

Hetch Hetchy Valley: The First Environmental Battleground

Within the boundaries of Yosemite National Park lies the Hetch Hetchy Valley, which resembles the more famous Yosemite Valley. In the early part of the twentieth century this valley achieved national prominence as the nation decided the fate of the valley itself. The issue was whether the Tuolumne River should be dammed to create a reservoir to provide the people of San Francisco with drinking water. The valley, with its high walls and narrow entrance, made a perfect site for such a reservoir. As part of the National Park System, however, the valley was supposed to be managed in its natural state. The debate over the fate of the valley was led by two men: Gifford Pinchot and John Muir.

Gifford Pinchot, the first director of the United States Forest Service, was a conservationist who believed that America's resources must be managed to . . . "provide the greatest good for the greatest number in the long run." Pinchot strongly advocated damming the valley to provide water for the people of San Francisco.

John Muir, a famous naturalist and the first president of the Sierra Club, was a preservationist. He believed that the valley should remain in its natural state and should not be dammed.

After more than a ten-year struggle, Congress authorized the building of the reservoir in August, 1913. Most legislators said they appreciated the value of unspoiled nature but did not feel justified in voting against progress.

A footnote to this struggle appeared in 1987 when the Secretary of the Interior, Donald Hodell, proposed the "undamming" of the Tuolomne River and the restoration of the valley to ease the overcrowding being felt in Yosemite Valley. Although this proposal will probably never come about, it does demonstrate the need to be cautious in developing areas that could one day serve as valuable recreational resources.

Fish and Wildlife Act created the U.S. Fish and Wildlife Service and established within it two bureaus—the Bureau of Commercial Fisheries and the Bureau of Sports Fisheries and Wildlife.

The Fish and Wildlife Service manages the 95-million-acre National Wildlife Refuge System, which encompasses 544 national wildlife refuges, thousands of small wetlands, and other special management areas. In addition, it operates 69 national fish hatcheries, 63 Fish and Wildlife Management offices, and 81 ecological services field stations. More than 88 percent of the acreage in the National Wildlife Refuge System was withdrawn from the public domain. Eighty-three percent of the land is found in sixteen refuges in Alaska. The agency enforces federal wildlife laws, administers the Endangered Species Act, manages migratory bird populations, restores nationally significant fisheries, conserves and restores wildlife habitat such as wetlands, and helps foreign governments with their conservation efforts. It also oversees the Federal Assistance program, which distributes hundreds of millions of dollars in excise taxes on fishing and hunting equipment to state fish and wildlife agencies (http://partners.fws.gov/What_we_do/overview.html)

The U.S. Fish and Wildlife Service is responsible for protecting endangered species, migratory birds, marine mammals, and inland sports fisheries. The Service engages in research activities and is involved in the development of an environmental stewardship ethic. It is a preservation- and conservation-oriented organization that provides leadership in the protection and improvement of land and water resources. In addition, the Service improves and maintains fish and wildlife resources and manages the Wildlife Refuge System. The Wildlife Refuge System of the Forest Service is managed from the standpoint of the conservation

Restoration Accomplishments
U.S. Fish and Wildlife Service

- 639,560 acres of wetlands
- 1,069,660 acres of prairie and other uplands

- 4,740 miles of streamside and in-stream habitat
- 28,725 landowner agreements

Source: http://partners.fws.gov/What_we_do/overview.html

ethic. These vitally important areas provide habitat for approximately sixty endangered species as well as hundreds of birds and other animals.

From a recreation perspective, the U.S. Fish and Wildlife Service provides opportunities for hunters and anglers in the form of stable sources of fish and game, as well as providing opportunities for activities such as photography, bird watching, animal tracking, and wildlife study. Interpretive services, increasingly made available at wildlife refuges, are being widely used. Estimates suggest that approximately 30 million visits are made annually to wildlife refuges. The majority of individuals attending these refuges engage in sightseeing activities (65%) as opposed to hunting or fishing (35%). This demand for nonconsumptive forms of recreation within wildlife refuges creates a challenge for wildlife managers. As in the national parks, fish and wildlife managers strive to meet the challenge of tourists by providing more extensive outdoor experiences while protecting the wildlife for which the refuges were created.

Bureau of Indian Affairs

The Bureau of Indian Affairs, created as a part of the War Department in 1924, was later transferred to the Department of the Interior in 1949. Tribal lands in the United States now exceed 50 million acres. The Bureau of Indian Affairs assists native peoples in organizing and implementing programs to assist in their advancement. Often, the development of recreation resources, tourist attractions, and other leisure amenities offer opportunities for economic development.

Estimates show more than 800,000 visitor days spent fishing on Indian reservations and 300,000 visitor days spent hunting on Indian reservations. Total recreation visitations are estimated at over 3 million visitor days per year. Many Indian reservations have unique resources including lakes, rivers, mountains, and other natural areas. A number of tribes operate campgrounds, tourist resorts, hotels, and other recreation facilities that are based on these natural resources.

There are diverse leisure program and service offerings sponsored by native Americans and available on reservation land. For example, the Meskwaki Nation located in Iowa, as well as the Southern Utes Tribe in Colorado both operate casinos that provide a variety of gaming and entertainment venues. The Navajo Nation located in Arizona, Colorado, New Mexico, and Utah has developed several interesting programs. Their youth program is focused on assisting youth to acquire appropriate work and life skills to assist individuals in successfully transitioning into adulthood. "To help revitalize its economy, the Navajo Nation has recently undertaken steps to develop, strengthen and manage an ever-increasing tourism industry. Despite the fact that most tourists visit Arizona to see cowboys and Indians, it is estimated that only 7 percent of a nearly $550 million industry ever reaches the Navajo Nation. With the formation of the "Navajo Tourism Master Plan" it is hoped that the Navajo Nation will be able to reach more than 20% of tourism expenditures by the year 2000, creating some 5,000 jobs" (http://www.americanwest.com/pages/navajo2.htm).

U.S. Corps of Engineers

The U.S. Corps of Engineers was established in the earliest days of the United States as part of the Continental Army. In the early years, army engineers blazed trails for westward migration and cleared waterways and harbors for commerce. Today the Corps' duties include many of these same tasks as well as flood control, hydropower production, fish and wildlife management, and outdoor recreation. The U.S. Corps of Engineers is responsible for providing over 30 percent of the recreation opportunities found on federal lands. It is estimated that over 25 million individuals visit a corps of engineers project on an annual basis. There are many opportunities for volunteers to work with the corps of engineers by serving as a campground host, engaging in trail building and maintenance, building wildlife habits, dispersing information at visitors centers, providing interpretive tours, and/or presenting educational programs (see figure 9.6).

The U.S. Corps of Engineers manages approximately 12 million acres of land and water, with water resources as its main outdoor recreation resource. Such water resources provide opportunities for sailing, swimming, windsurfing, waterskiing, fishing, scuba diving, and pleasure boating. Many of the lakes developed by the Corps of Engineers for flood control, hydroelectric power, navigation, or other uses also serve outdoor recreation purposes. Eighty percent of these developments are within a fifty-mile radius of Standard Metropolitan Statistical Areas (cities with large populations).

The Corps provides access to the waterways and projects it manages and also provides natural resource amenities to complement them (e.g., campgrounds, marinas, picnic areas, parks, and sanitation facilities). Often, such land and water resources developed by the Corps of Engineers are leased to other public agencies for development and management. An illustration of this type of cooperative arrangement can be seen at Fern Ridge Reservoir, located west of Eugene, Oregon.

Figure 9.6

Historical photo of U.S. Corps of Engineers clearing a road for use in a California federal park.

Copyright © Corbis.

Leisure Line

A Happy Volunteer Is a Successful One— Crooked Creek Lake

Crooked Creek Lake, located in southwestern Pennsylvania, is a very scenic park that attracts a variety of visitors. The small flood control project attracts swimmers, sunbathers, trail hikers, recreational boaters, picnickers, campers, and groups for both the organized group campground and the Environmental Learning Center. Along with these park attractions come a variety of volunteers to the park.

Sandra and Harold Mason enjoy the park so much that they have volunteered as campground host since 1991. Sandra and Harold assign sites, answer park visitors' questions, inform campers of rules and regulations, issue rent-a-tent equipment, and perform light janitorial services at the comfort station during the week. They also pick up litter, clean fire grills, and rake the playground beds on a daily basis.

Sandra says, "I love Crooked Creek Lake! There is no place that I would rather be than here." Harold also likes to welcome both old and new visitors to the park. Both Sandra and Harold are very happy volunteers. They enjoy the job they do and that makes all the difference. A happy volunteer is a successful one!

Sandra and Harold have volunteered a total of 12,722 hours. The staff at Crooked Creek Lake is very proud of Sandra and Harold. Their dedication and efforts have made the park more enjoyable for all Crooked Creek Lake's visitors.

Source: Toman, P. and Mckee, R. 2004. A Happy Volunteer is a Successful One—Crooked Creek Lake. Retrieved June 14, 2004, from http://www.orn.usace.army.mil/volunteer/happy.htm.

Fern Ridge Reservoir not only protects the southern part of the Willamette Valley from flooding, but in cooperation with the Corps, has been the focus of several parks and recreation developments undertaken by public and nonprofit private organizations. Specifically, Lane County operates a major park facility in the area, and the Eugene Yacht Club provides a marina facility.

The recreation resource management orientation of the Corps encourages sustained public use, while maintaining the integrity of the natural resources. Recreation resource management, according to the Corps, suggests not only a natural resources ethic, but a people-oriented program of recreation services. The Corps of Engineers has developed a classification system to manage its water resources. This system not only helps protect the natural environment, but also encourages public use of facilities.

> To ensure sound management practices, the Corps has devised a land classification system which designates areas according to the primary use and types of management needed; these designations include natural areas, fish and wildlife management areas, and recreation areas with public facilities. Different types of public facilities and activity areas are separated by distance and natural barriers to maintain the recreation values of the resource, aid in management, and create the least possible conflict with other project purposes such as flood control, hydroelectric power production, navigation, and water supply. (U.S. Corps of Engineers, 1982, p. 6)

This classification system is managed through the employment of a group of professional managers, including people trained not only in biology, engineering, and forestry but also in outdoor recreation.

Tennessee Valley Authority

The Tennessee Valley Authority (TVA) is a public corporation that was established by an act of Congress in 1933. Basically, the TVA is an electric power program that is financially self-

Living History Programs

The Homeplace—1850

Living History programs, such as Civil War reenactments and living history farms, provide a first hand experience with the past. This form of educational experience is becoming more popular as a leisure opportunity both for the participants and those who come to watch and interact. Consider The Homeplace program in place at Land Between the Lakes.

Visitors to The Homeplace—1850 can go back in time to a nineteenth-century working farm. Dressed in period clothing, interpreters carry out the daily and seasonal work of the farm. The men can be found tending livestock, working the field, cutting wood, or doing any one of a number of other chores. The women might be preparing a meal on the cook stove or open hearth, spinning, gardening, quilting, or carrying out other domestic activities.

As visitors walk the farm at their leisure, they can see a single-crib cabin, double-crib house, ox barn, springhouse, and other buildings. Each of the buildings was restored and furnished to re-create a mid-nineteenth-century farm of the "between the rivers" region. Even the garden, fields, and patches are planted with crops and vegetables representative of those produced here in the 1850s.

Daily programs vary with the season but typically include activities such as buttermaking, fall plowing, tobacco firing, breadmaking, spinning, dyeing, weaving, and oxen working. During each of the demonstration programs, interpreters explain equipment used, techniques and processes, and importance to the culture.

Throughout the year (March through November), several special events take place at The Homeplace—1850, including an 1850-style wedding and Independence Day celebration. Several festivals, such as the Apple Festival, are also incorporated into the daily lives of the staff at The Homeplace.

Source: Tennessee Valley Authority (n.d.), *A Guide to Land Between the Lakes,* Tennessee Valley Authority, Golden Pond, Kentucky.

---

sufficient. The TVA constructed a system of dams on the Tennessee River for flood regulation, navigation, and hydroelectric power. The project also provided opportunities for outdoor recreation. In fact, TVA recognized the potential economic benefits of developing recreation resources in the 1930s and has worked to encourage a wide variety of outdoor recreation facilities and opportunities in the Tennessee Valley.

TVA projects have resulted in the creation of more than 500,000 acres of water resources and 11,000 miles of shoreline. These resources attract more than 70 million visitors for recreation purposes each year. The TVA emphasizes access to its resources and, as a result, features 500 public access points and more than 120 state, county, and municipal parks on the shores of TVA lakes, along with numerous private resorts, marinas, and boating facilities. The TVA has set aside a large number of natural areas for ecological study and annually conducts research and development programs in forestry, fish and game, and watershed protection.

In the western part of Kentucky and Tennessee, the TVA operates a national demonstration program known as the Land Between the Lakes. This program combines TVA's interest in outdoor recreation, environmental education, and natural resource management. The Land Between the Lakes program is situated between two of the largest human-made reservoirs in the United States—Lake Kentucky and Lake Barkley. This area consists of 170,000 acres of land, and the reservoirs include about 300 miles of shoreline.

The Land Between the Lakes program uses a multiple-use concept to promote both recreational and educational values. It is being developed as a public use area, where recreation can be enjoyed and people can gain a greater appreciation of the need for conservation principles and values. Activities in the Land Between the Lakes program include camping, fishing, hiking, horseback riding, hunting, nature study, and environmental education. Facilities include campsites, swimming areas, boat ramps, sanitation facilities, trails, an environmental education center, and an 1850s living history farm. In 1991, Land Between the Lakes was named the world's 300th biosphere reserve as part of the United Nations Educational, Scientific, and Cultural Organization's Man and the Biosphere program.

Bureau of Reclamation

In 1902, Congress passed the Reclamation Act, authorizing the Secretary of the Interior to establish a reclamation program to supply water to the semiarid lands of seventeen contiguous states in the western portion of the United States. As a result of this action, the Reclamation Service was established within the U.S. Geological Survey. Separated from that unit, in 1923, it was renamed the Bureau of Reclamation. The growth of the Bureau of Reclamation was directly tied to the expansion of population in the western United States. As the population grew in the West, so did the need for water resources. The Bureau's mission also expanded, and today it is not only responsible for providing water resources but also for the generation of hydroelectric power, river regulation, flood control, outdoor recreation, and the enhancement and management of fish and wildlife habitats.

Today, "the mission of the Bureau of Reclamation is to manage, develop, and protect water and related resources in an environmental and economically sound manner in the interest of the American public. The agency's program emphasis is on water conservation and reuse, environmental protection and restoration, and expansion of its customer base beyond agricultural interests to include rural and urban water users, Native American tribes, the environmental community, and recreationists." (Bureau of Reclamation, 2001)

The Bureau of Reclamation operates dams, power plants, and canals. The Bureau has constructed more than 600 dams and reservoirs. Although, recreation pursuits were not an original part of the mission of the Bureau of Reclamation, in 1965 the Federal Water Projects Recreation Act provided statutory authority for the planning and construction of recreation areas and facilities. The majority of recreation areas within the land area of the Bureau of Reclamation are managed, however, by other governmental agencies such as the National Park Service, U.S. Forest Service, and local, state, or county government agencies. These agencies provide a variety of predominantly water-based recreational opportunities. Support facilities often include campsites, picnic areas, sightseeing areas, sanitation facilities, marinas, and boat ramps. The Bureau of Reclamation manages, in partnership with non-federal entities such as state and county park and recreation systems, 308 recreation sites. More than 90 million people visit these water-based recreation areas on an annual basis. Still others are managed by federal agencies including the National Park Service and the U.S. Forest Service. The Bureau of Reclamation also seeks partnerships with nonprofit organizations to sponsor events and works with concessionaires to operate facilities and services such as marinas, campgrounds, swimming beaches, and golf courses.

Veterans Affairs

The Department of Veterans Affairs (formerly known as Veterans Administration) was established in 1989. The Veterans Administration was originally established in 1930 to provide benefits to veterans and their families. Today, Veterans Affairs operates 158 hospitals, 854 ambulatory care community-based outpatient clinics, 132 nursing homes, 42 residential rehabilitation treatment programs, and 88 comprehensive home programs. The concept of recreation therapy was developed as a part of the Veterans Administration and is the largest employer of therapeutic recreation specialists in the federal government. Recreation therapists working in Veterans Affairs health care facilities use a variety of modalities to provide treatment for individuals who are physically, mentally, emotionally, or socially disabled. The Department of Veterans Affairs uses recreation therapy to improve the quality of participants' lives and to facilitate their reentry into the community. Readjustment counseling programs as well as ones for alcohol and drug addiction and post-traumatic stress disorder are programs that have been expanded in recent years.

Programs focus on meeting the needs of a variety of veteran patient population groups, including those involved in cardiac rehabilitation, spinal cord injuries, drug and alcohol abuse, general medical and surgical conditions, chronic illness, psychiatrics, and geriatrics. Activities offered as a part of a typical recreation therapy program include games, sports, arts and crafts, music therapy, dance therapy, psychodrama, outdoor recreation, social activities, special events, leisure counseling, and community reentry.

The mission of recreation therapy within the Department of Veterans Affairs is to provide quality clinical treatment interventions for veterans and other beneficiaries. They are committed to the advancement of recreation therapy through on-going education, clinical training, and research.

In describing the functions played by individuals in providing the work of recreation, the Department of Veterans Affairs notes several key jobs, including the following:

1. *Rehabilitation.* The recreation therapist functions as a member of the medical team, has knowledge of the illness and problems of the physically, mentally, emotionally, and developmentally disabled and the geriatric patient; works with the team and prepares the patient for community reentry.
2. *Education.* The therapist provides education and counseling in coping with leisure time, particularly with regard to a patient returning to life in the community.
3. *Implementation.* Working with patients to develop an individualized treatment plan, the recreation therapist implements and organizes this plan, modifying activities when appropriate, and evaluates the success of a program for each individual patient.

In describing recreation therapy services in the Nursing Home Care Unit of the Department of Veterans Affairs Medical Center in San Francisco, Marcia Lizza, CTRS, Chief Recreation Therapist, has written the following:

What is Recreation Therapy? It is using recreation services to help people with potentially limiting conditions make the most of their lives, physically, mentally, emotionally and socially. Therapeutic recreation has a lot to offer. It is important for many reasons. It can help people of all ages and backgrounds to get well by contributing to a healthier mind and body. It helps people live well, by being as active as possible, and this makes life more satisfying and fun. Participating in therapeutic recreation can help maintain a sense of wellness. It helps people to help themselves so that they can enjoy life more each day.

Here in the Nursing Home Care Unit there are many recreation therapy groups and events. Residents enjoy keeping the ball in play during volleyball games. We listen to live music at parties and when Bread and Roses sends volunteer performers to entertain. We offer creative arts groups, Blackjack, and Bingo. Residents match wits playing trivia. Friendly dogs from the SPCA visit regularly. We participate in leading a group for the cognitively impaired, 'Living In The Moment.' We show travelogues, biographies, and National Geographic Videos. Through these activities we try to awaken old memories, encourage reminiscences and life review, and self exploration.

Here at the VA, we are also working with groups of veterans who are dealing with substance abuse issues and/or mental health issues. Recreation therapy focuses on self exploration, helping the veterans restructure their lifestyle to promote a style of wellness, one that does not include drugs or alcohol. They learn to replace substance abuse with new leisure skills. Through groups, outings in the community, art therapy, and leisure planning, they gain knowledge and experience for sober leisure, helping them learn healthy coping skills with leisure as the modality.

We help to exercise mind and body, encourage individuals to make choices and promote creative expression. We help people learn to play and have fun again. The groups listed above all contribute in some way to these goals. (Lizza, 2004, http://www.sf.med.va.gov/events/Wellness/recreationtherapy.htm)

The Department of Veterans Affairs provided health care services to 4.8 million individuals and disability compensation, death compensation, and pension to an additional 3.4 million individuals. The recreation therapy function has been transformed from its early image of diversionary fun and games to one of serious therapy and treatment (see table 9.5).

The recreation therapy function has been transformed from its early image of diversionary fun and games to one of serious therapy and treatment.

TABLE

9.5 RECREATION/CREATIVE ARTS THERAPISTS

Recreation/Creative Arts Therapists perform professional work requiring application of either 1) knowledge of the concepts, principles, and practices of recreation therapy and the use of various interventions to treat physical, social, cognitive, emotional conditions associated with illness, or chronic disability; 2) a knowledge of the concepts, principle, and practices of a specialized creative arts therapy (i.e., art, dance, music, and psychodrama) and the use of appropriate specialized treatment modalities to improve and maintain physical, cognitive, emotional, and social functioning, preventing secondary health conditions, enhancing independent living skills and overall quality of life.

These therapists evaluate history, interests, aptitudes, and skills of patients by interviews, inventories, tests, and measurements, and use such findings, along with medical records and therapy orders of physicians, to develop and implement recreation therapy or creative arts therapy activities for individual patients. These several therapy approaches are directed toward achieving such therapeutic objectives as achieving and maintaining optimal levels of independence, productivity, and well-being, and entering/re-entering the mainstream of community life:

- Creative Arts Therapist (Art)
- Creative Arts Therapist (Dance)
- Creative Arts Therapist (Music)
- Creative Arts Therapist (Psychodrama)

Using various modalities appropriate to the particular therapy approach involved, therapists in these specializations seek to achieve and maintain optimal levels of independence, productivity, and well-being through therapeutic art, dance, music, drama, or recreation activities and services.

Source: Recreation/Creative Arts Therapists. Department of Veterans Affairs. Retrieved June 15, 2004, from http://www1.va.gov/health/Natrecth/Crea_art.html.

Morale, Welfare, and Recreation Services, U.S. Armed Forces

The United States military has control over large preserves of land that are used for recreation purposes for military personnel and their dependents. Each branch of the armed services—the U.S. Army, the U.S. Air Force, the U.S. Marine Corps, and the U.S. Navy—have well-developed recreation areas, facilities, and programs. Furthermore, some of these areas and facilities are open to the public to pursue recreational interests. Each branch of the services refers to its units in a slightly different way. For example, the U.S. Marine Corps refers to its units as "Community Services," the U.S. Navy refers to its organizations as "Morale, Welfare, and Recreation Departments," the U.S. Army refers to its units as "Community and Family Support" and the U.S. Air Force refers to its units as "Service Squadrons." In this section we refer to all these units collectively as Morale, Welfare, and Recreation.

Morale, Welfare, and Recreation (MWR) activities provided by various branches of the armed forces offer a variety of social, recreational, and welfare activities, programs, and services. Morale, Welfare, and Recreation services can include management of such facilities as arts and crafts centers, bowling centers, entertainment programs, golf courses, libraries, outdoor recreation programs, multipurpose recreation centers, sport programs, and child and youth activities. MWR services also include the management of clubs, newspapers, museums, skeet and trap ranges, skating rinks, gift shops, snack bars, and music and theater programs. Military bases may be viewed as small American communities that offer all the recreation amenities of a small city in the United States.

Policies and procedures for the implementation of MWR programs vary by service (Army, Marines, Navy, or Air Force). For example, the U.S. Navy's policy is designed to promote/provide a well-rounded recreation program to ensure the mental and physical well-being of its personnel. The recreation program of the Navy is designed to assist in attaining and sustaining a high level of morale among Navy personnel and their families. The Navy does not use an absolute set of standards for each installation's recreation programs. On the other hand, the U.S. Army is very specific in its written policies and procedures for operating MWR programs and services. U.S. Army programs are operated, maintained, and funded as an integral part of the quality of life of the Department of the Army. Objectives of the Army MWR program follow:

1. Maintain among personnel a high level of esprit de corps, job proficiency, military effectiveness, and educational attainment.
2. Promote and maintain the mental and physical fitness and well-being of Department of the Army personnel, primarily active duty personnel.
3. Encourage Department of the Army personnel to use their time constructively and creatively by taking part in programs that help develop and maintain motivation, talent, and skills that will help them discharge their duties as responsible citizens.
4. Aid in recruitment and retention by making service with the army an attractive career.
5. Assist military personnel in adjusting from civilian life to the military environment upon entry into the service.
6. Assist in providing a community support environment to Department of Army personnel and their families. This is most important when military sponsors are on unaccompanied tours or maneuvers or involved in armed conflicts.
7. Create a vital self-sustaining military community.

Figure 9.7

Organizational chart of the MWR Department, Yokosuka.

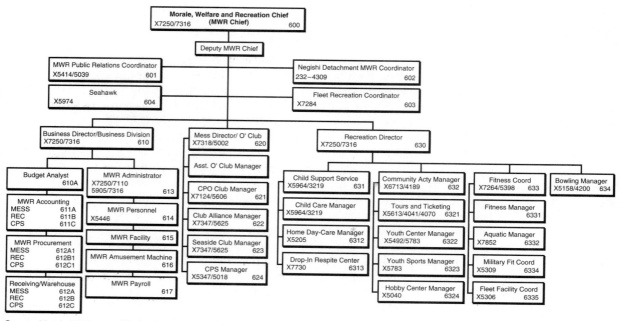

Source: Morale, Welfare, and Recreation Department, U.S. Naval Fleet Activities, Yokosuka, Japan

8. Provide programs that appeal to soldiers as members of their units.
9. Increase combat readiness and effectiveness (Department of the Army, 1988).

The organizational chart presented in figure 9.7 represents the services and staffing patterns of the Morale, Welfare, and Recreation Department, U.S. Naval Fleet Activities, Yokosuka, Japan. The organizational chart presents the various activities provided by this unit. They range from provision of a newspaper, *The Seahawk,* to a myriad of recreation services including clubs, child support, community centers, tours and ticketing, youth activities, hobby clubs, fitness programs, bowling, aquatic services, and others. Figure 9.8 is a brochure describing the summer aquatic programs offered at Carney Park Pool. Carney Park is a recreation area managed by the Morale, Welfare, and Recreation Department of the U.S. Navy in Naples, Italy. This Olympic-size swimming pool sits in a multi-purpose recreation area that includes a host of recreation areas and facilities. The Carney Park programs and services are available to service members and their families.

National Endowment for the Arts

The arts play an important part in the leisure domain. The National Endowment for the Arts has as a goal, the fostering of professional excellence for the arts in the United States. The endowment has been established to help nurture and sustain the arts and develop a climate in which the arts may flourish. The goals of the National Endowment for the Arts are the following:

1. To foster individual creativity and excellence;
2. To foster institutional creativity and excellence;

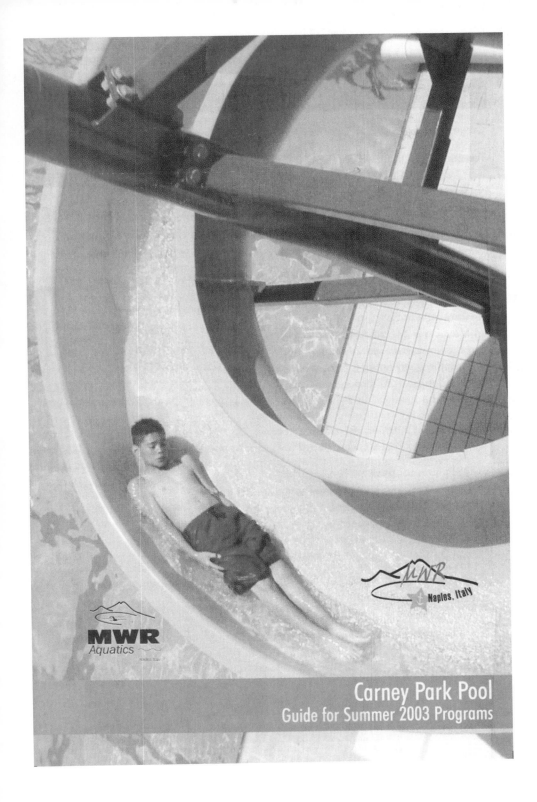

Figure 9.8
Carney Park
Pool Summer
Guide.

*Source: MWR
Department, NAS
Naples, Italy.*

3. To preserve the artistic birthright of present and future generations of Americans by supporting survival of the best of all art forms that reflect the American heritage in its full range of ethnic and cultural diversity;
4. To ensure that all Americans have a true opportunity to make an informed, educated choice to have the arts of high quality touch their lives; and
5. To provide leadership on behalf of the arts.

The majority of funds spent by this agency provide endowments to specific projects, artists, programs, and museums. The funds for the National Endowment have grown rapidly in the last several decades. In 2001, the National Endowment for the Arts awarded $92.1 million to 2,093 project award winners. This compares to 1995 when $147.9 million were available and 3,685 projects were awarded funds. (U.S. Bureau of Census, 2003). This is a drastic reduction when compared with 1980 when $188 million was disbursed to 5,500 projects with the largest amount coming between 1995 and 1996. These funds have made an important contribution to the arts in the United States by bringing an awareness to Americans of the importance of art in their lives.

National Endowment for the Humanities

This independent agency, established by Congress in 1965, supports research, education, and public programs in the humanities. The term *humanities* refers to the study of language; linguistics; literature; history; jurisprudence; philosophy; archaeology; comparative religion; ethics; the history, criticism, and theory of the arts; and the portions of the social sciences that have humanistic content. The Endowment provides grants to help increase understanding and appreciation of the humanities. In 2001, the National Endowment for the Humanities awarded $86.4 million in funds to 1,290 project award winners. This compares to 1995 when $125.7 million in funds were available and 1,871 projects were awarded funds (U.S. Bureau of Census, 2003). Again, when compared with 1980 this is a dramatic reduction in projects supported where $186 million was previously available and supported over 2,900 projects. Many of the projects supported by the endowment are leisure related, including museums, libraries, public agencies, and nonprofit organizations.

Challenges for the Future

Federal agencies in the United States face many challenges. Decade by decade, the demand for services provided by the federal government in this area has increased dramatically. Massive governmental programs will positively impact upon the environment and increase outdoor recreation resources. The future holds numerous challenges, however. They include the following:

Decrease in the level of funding. The federal funding in the United States is a challenge in terms of continued provision of services. Agencies must find innovative strategies to finance services or they will be forced to cut back. In addition, more interagency coordination will be required to determine the most appropriate and cost-effective use of federal resources. As a result, partnerships are being encouraged on a federal level.

Continue the Land and Water Conservation Fund. The success of the Land and Water Fund has been documented in this chapter. Efforts must be made to sustain such a trust for the acquisition and development of outdoor recreation resources. In addition to land acquisition and development, funds for maintaining existing resources and facilities must be assured.

Competition over the use of resources. There is competition for the same resources. Environmental concerns often conflict directly with the need for economic development. Even various types of recreation use create conflict (e.g., snowmobilers often conflict with cross country skiers). With new technology generating new outdoor pursuits such as windsurfing, these conflicts will increase. Resolution of these conflicts will become a responsibility of federal agencies and the courts.

Overuse of resources. The demand for selected outdoor recreation resources challenges basic preservation-conservation precepts. There is a need to find strategies to control use of resources to ensure their preservation for future generations.

Lack of consistency in the political environment. The federal government must develop consistency in its approach to managing the environment on a long-term basis. Changing political conditions often challenge long-term strategies. A strong environmental ethic needs to become a part of the political agenda in America. This includes educating people about the need for such an agenda. In many ways urban dwellers have lost their connection with the land. They have a strong idea that they want to preserve land, yet they are also the biggest consumers in the world. For example, American urbanites want to preserve free-flowing rivers, but they also like to water their lawns, wash their cars, and clean the driveway. In many ways Americans have created a paradox of preservation—people want to both preserve and use the resources as they wish. Resource managers are being asked to provide both resources (e.g., timber, oil, minerals, and grazing land) and amenities (e.g., clean air and water, places for outdoor recreation, wildlife refuges, and wilderness areas). Collectively, U.S. citizens must develop a sustainable lifestyle both for themselves and for the millions of people still aspiring to a better way of life in developing countries.

Consumptive vs. nonconsumptive recreation pursuits. In light of the paradox of preservation, what kind of activities should recreational professionals provide for individuals? Dustin, in his article, "Recreational Limits in a World of Ethics" (1984), raises the question: "Should park and recreation professionals serve popular tastes for recreation or should they try to elevate them?" To Dustin the answer is clear: "We have a responsibility not only to educate recreationists but to encourage them to recreate in a way that reflects a more sensitive, a more caring attitude toward the earth" (p. 50). As recreational professionals face global environmental problems and the overuse of resources, the question of how to elevate recreation tastes without impeding personal freedom will become even more critical.

Accessibility issues. The Americans with Disabilities Act encourages federal managers to make accessibility for people with disabilities a priority. The accessibility issue continues to be a financial strain for many federal managers.

These challenges and others stretch the mental, physical, and financial resources of future managers of federal agencies. The future of federally managed leisure programs and services hinges upon the ability of present and future managers to effectively resolve these and other emerging concerns.

Summary

The federal governments in the United States play a vital role in the provision of parks, recreation, leisure, and cultural services. The United States has unique natural areas that provide opportunities for leisure services, especially outdoor recreation. America is large geographically and has small populations compared with its land mass. As a result, Americans have had the opportunity to set aside large tracts of land for preservation and conservation purposes.

Numerous federal agencies in the United States provide parks, recreation, and leisure services. Some of the larger agencies are the U.S. Forest Service, the National Park Service, the Bureau of Land Management, the U.S. Fish and Wildlife Service, the U.S. Corps of Engineers, the Bureau of Reclamation, and the Tennessee Valley Authority. These agencies manage the land and water resources that fall within public domain. Other federal agencies that provide people-oriented recreation programs include the Veterans Affairs, the U.S. Armed Forces, the National Endowment for the Arts, and the National Endowment for the Humanities.

Discussion Questions

1. What are the goals and functions of federal agencies?
2. Explain the fiscal resource base of federal agencies. What is the difference between appropriated and nonappropriated funds?
3. Discuss what you feel is the customer orientation of employees working for the federal government.
4. Identify three presidential commissions that have influenced the development of outdoor recreation resources in the United States.
5. Identify five federal agencies in the United States providing outdoor recreation services.
6. What is the difference between the philosophy of conservation and the philosophy of preservation?
7. What does multiple-use of resources imply? How does this affect the management of land and water resources managed by the federal government?
8. Discuss the role of federal agencies in America in providing recreation, parks, and leisure services.
9. Identify and discuss future challenges to the management of federal land and water agencies in the United States.
10. Contact a federal agency mentioned in this chapter to determine its current operating and capital budget, as well as current status of services.

References

Albright, H., R. Dickenson, and W. Mott. 1987. *National Park Service: The Story Behind the Scenery.* Las Vegas, NV: K.C. Publications.

Bell, B. 1984. *Medical Center Memorandum 117* (August 28), 9.

Bureau of Land Management. 1988. *Recreation 2000: BLM National Outdoor Strategy.* Washington, DC: U.S. Government Printing Office.

Bureau of Reclamation. 2001. www.usbr.gov/main/what/index.html

Cordell, H., L. Bergstrom, L. Hartmenn, and D. English. 1990. *An Analysis of the Outdoor Recreation and Wilderness Situation in the United States: 1989–2040.* Fort Collins, CO: U.S. Department of Agriculture Forest Service General Technical Report.

Department of the Army. 1988. *The Administration of Army Morale, Welfare, and Recreation Activities and Nonappropriated Fund Instrumentalities.* Army Regulation 215-1, 7. Washington, DC: Department of the Army.

Dustin, D. 1984. Recreation limits in a world of ethics. *Parks and Recreation 57* (March), 49–51.

Ibrahim, H., and K. Cordes. 1993. *Outdoor Recreation.* Madison, WI: Brown & Benchmark.

Jensen, C. 1995. *Outdoor Recreation in America.* 5th ed. Champaign, IL: Human Kinetics.

Kraus, R. 1990. *Recreation and Leisure in Modern Society.* 4th ed. New York: HarperCollins.

Land Letter. 1991. The Land and Water Conservation Fund. *Land Letter* (September 20), 1–6.

Lee, R. 1972. *Family Tree of National Park System.* Philadelphia, PA: Eastern National Park and Monument Association.

Little, C. 1991. *Greenways for America.* Baltimore: The Johns Hopkins University Press, 237.

Lizza, M. 2004. Recreation Therapy. U.S. Department of Veterans Affairs. Retrieved June 15, 2004, from http://www.sf.med.va.gov/events/Wellness/recreationtherapy.htm

Lothian, W. 1977. *Extract from a History of Canada's National Parks.* Vol. 1, 9. Parks Canada.

President's Commission on Americans Outdoors (PCAO). 1987. *Americans Outdoors: The Legacy, the Challenge.* Washington, DC: Island Press.

Searle, M. S., and R. E. Brayley. 2000. *Leisure Services in Canada: An Introduction.* 2nd ed. State College, PA: Venture.

Staff. 1992. *Canada Year Book.* Ottawa: Information Canada.

Statistics Canada. 1999. *Culture, Tourism, and the Centre for Education Statistics.*

U.S. Bureau of the Census, 1999. *Statistical Abstract of the United States 1999,* 119th ed. Washington, DC: U.S. Government Printing Office.

U.S. Corps of Engineers. 1982. *1980–1981 Statistical Summary of the U.S. Corps of Engineers,* 6.

U.S. Forest Service. 1970. *Forest Service Objectives and Policy Guidelines.* U.S. Department of Agriculture, Forest Service, U.S. Government Printing Office.

U.S. Forest Service. 1983. *What the Forest Service Does.* (Pamphlet FS-20). U.S. Department of Agriculture, Forest Service.

U.S. Forest Service. 1986. *The USDA Forest Service.* (Pamphlet FS-402). Washington, DC: U.S. Department of Agriculture, Forest Service.

U.S. Forest Service. 1993. *The Urban Tree House—A Tree for All Reasons.* (Pamphlet). Washington, DC: U.S. Department of Agriculture, Forest Service.

U.S. Forest Service. n.d. *People Serving People.* (Pamphlet) U.S. Department of Agriculture, Forest Service.

Wilderness Society. 1984. *The Wilderness Act Handbook.* The Wilderness Society.

10

Delivery of Leisure Services: Nonprofit

Private, nonprofit organizations often provide leisure programs that promote youth development. Such programs have strong educational components as well as providing opportunities for fun and enjoyment.

Introduction

Nonprofit leisure service organizations form a large and important segment of the leisure service industry. Nonprofit organizations provide a wide variety of programs and services. Such organizations pursue multiple goals, including the character development of individuals, the pursuit of worthwhile leisure experiences, and the development of community interest. Drucker (1999, p. 9) has written that the greatest growth among organizations will be among nonprofit organizations. He has suggested, ". . . as far as we can predict the growth sector of the 21st century in developed countries . . . is likely to be the nonprofit sector."

In 2004, the Independent Sector reporting on employment in the nonprofit sector suggests that it employs an increasing larger segment of America's workforce. As indicated in the Nonprofit Almanac Facts and Findings Web site:

> The nonprofit sector in America employs a steadily increasing segment of the country's working population. According to the latest measures, the average annual growth rate in employment for nonprofits (2.5%) was significantly higher than for business (1.8%) or government (1.6%). The number of Americans employed in the nonprofit sector has doubled in the last 25 years. Nonprofit employment represents 9.5 percent of total employment in the United States, with total employees numbering 12.5 million. (www.IndependentSector.org, 2004) See table 10.1, figure 10.1, figure 10.2, and figure 10.3.

Oleck notes that "far more Americans now participate in the activities on nonprofit organizations than those of profit-seeking organizations" (1988, p. 2). Again, Drucker (1999) suggests that a growing number of individuals will seek opportunities to develop parallel careers and/or retire early. He feels that many individuals doing so will be drawn into nonprofit organizations. Many individuals will become "social entrepreneurs" developing nonprofit enterprises to "keep on doing what they have been doing all along, though they spend less and less of their time on it . . . they start another, and usually nonprofit activity" (Drucker, 1999, p. 191).

10.1 NUMBER OF EMPLOYEES IN NONPROFIT BUSINESS, AND GOVERNMENT SECTORS 1977–2001.

Sector	1977	1982	1987	1992	1997	2001
Total All Sectors (millions) (In millions, 82.4 = 82,400,000)	82.4	89.4	102.3	108.6	122.6	131.8
Nonprofit	6.0	7.0	8.0	9.7	11.3	12.5
Independent sector	5.5	6.5	7.4	9.1	10.6	11.7
Other nonprofit	0.5	0.5	0.6	0.6	0.7	0.8
Business (for-profit)	61.3	66.6	77.3	80.2	91.7	98.4
Goods	24.3	23.8	24.8	23.2	24.9	24.9
Services	37.0	42.8	52.5	57.0	66.8	73.5
Government	15.1	15.8	17.0	18.7	19.6	20.9
Federal (civilian)	2.7	2.7	2.9	3.0	2.7	2.6
State	3.4	3.6	4.0	4.4	4.6	4.9
Local	9.0	9.5	10.1	11.3	12.3	13.4

Source: Independent Sector. (2005, March). The New Nonprofit Almanac and Desk Reference. Retrieved from: www.Independent Sector.org.

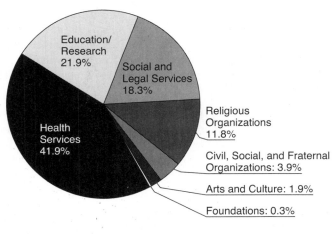

Figure 10.1

Nonprofit Employment by Subsection

Source: Independent Sector. (2005, March). The New Nonprofit Almanac and Desk Reference. Retrieved from: www.Independent Sector.org.

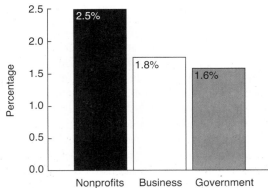

Figure 10.2

Employment Growth Rates 1997-2001.

Source: Independent Sector. (2005, March). The New Nonprofit Almanac and Desk Reference. Retrieved from: www.Independent Sector.org.

Figure 10.3

Where Americans Work: Employment Distribution by Major Sector.

Source: Independent Sector. (2004). Employment in the Nonprofit Sector. Nonprofit Almanac: Facts and Figures. Retrieved June 20, 2005.

	1977	1982	1987	1992	1997	2001
▲ Private nonprofit	7.3	7.9	7.8	9.0	9.3	9.5
■ Business (for profit)	74.4	74.4	75.6	73.8	74.8	74.6
◆ Government	18.3	17.7	16.6	17.2	15.9	15.9

Figures denote percentage of workers employed by major sector.

Nonprofit leisure service organizations in the United States have great impact—consider nonprofit organizations that provide leisure services as a primary and/or secondary purpose. Churches, clubs, golf courses, fraternal organizations, sport groups, hobby clubs, condominiums, museums, social service organizations, hospitals, and many other types of associations can, and do, plan, organize, and deliver leisure services. The outgrowth of nonprofit leisure service organizations is a natural extension of the attitudes that Canadians and U.S. citizens hold toward volunteerism and community involvement.

> Americans of all ages, all stations of life, and all types of dispositions are forever forming associations . . . religious, moral, serious, futile, very general and very limited, immensely large and very minute. . . . Americans combine great individualism with an attitude toward community action that knows no counterpart in the world. Altruistic volunteerism . . . runs throughout all of the history of nonprofit enterprise and community service of the American "nation of joiners." (Oleck, 1988, p. 1)

Steckel and Lehman (1997) have explored the work of nonprofit organizations. They have found many to be the best managed and operated organizations in the United States when compared with businesses or government agencies. Describing why viewing the best managed nonprofit organizations can be valuable for professionals, they have suggested the following:

- There are admirable organizations worthy of consideration, ones that promote the highest caliber of standards for charitable activity regardless of their geographic location, mission, or size. Many of these are run like the world's most respected corporations: efficiently, creatively, and with a clear vision for the future.
- There are fresh concepts about the roles nonprofit organizations should play in American society, including ideas for sustainable earned-income generation, employee benefits and incentives, and innovative leadership styles.
- There are insights shared by Americans active in the nonprofit world that can encourage better understanding of the organizations to which we contribute our time and money. These individuals suggest questions we can ask that make us a better-educated constituency for charities working in our communities. (Steckel and Lehman, 1997)

Surging Payroll: Nonprofit Job Growth Outpaces Business, Government

Nonprofit jobs have doubled in twenty-five years to 12.5 million, or nearly one in ten jobs in the United States and are expected to grow another 2.5 million by 2010, a new study says.

In the five years through 2001, nonprofit jobs grew 2.5 percent a year, on average, compared to 1.8 percent for business and 1.6 percent for government, says the study by Independent Sector, a nonprofit coalition in Washington, D.C.

In that same period, which included the start of the recession in March 2001, social-services nonprofits added more than 300,000 jobs, a gain of more than 17 percent, while health services nonprofits added nearly 300,000 jobs, up more than 6 percent.

The nonprofit sector "remains a place that people can turn to for employment," says Diana Aviv, Independent Sector president.

Employment in the so-called "independent sector," which includes charitable, advocacy, and religious groups, totals 11.7 million workers, or 9 percent of the U.S. workforce, up from 5.5 million in 1977, the study says.

When other tax-exempt organizations such as business trade groups, labor unions, and homeowner associations are included, nonprofit employment overall totals 9.5 percent of the U.S. workforce.

Of the total "independent sector" payroll, the study says, health-services nonprofits employ 42 percent, mainly in nonprofit hospitals, while education nonprofits employ 22 percent.

Citing a report by the Bureau of Labor Statistics, the study says several industries closely associated with nonprofits are expected to grow in the ten years through 2010, including 2.8 million new jobs in health services, and 1.2 million new jobs in social and human services, mainly among nursing, hospital, and residential care facilities.

Citing a separate report in the Monthly Labor Review in October 2001, the study also says some industries such as health services and social services that are closely tied to nonprofits "gained jobs impressively" in the twelve months ending June 30, 2001.

While recessions can cause job slowdowns in the business sector, the Labor Review reported, some industries closely associated with nonprofits are "slightly countercyclical, gaining jobs faster during recessions than in normal times," the study says.

Source: Philanthropy Journal. 2004. Surging payroll: Nonprofit job growth outpaces business, government. Retrieved May 26, 2004, from www.philanthropyjournal.org.

It is evident that nonprofit organizations play an important role in North American society. Further, it is evident that their influence will increase in the immediate decades to come.

This chapter explores the work of nonprofit organizations delivering leisure services and discusses the characteristics of these types of organizations, including their goals, resource bases, and other distinguishing characteristics. Of particular importance will be a discussion of nonprofit organizations that deliver youth and voluntary services; several different types of nonprofit youth and voluntary service organizations have provided the historical backbone for leisure services to children and youth, as well as adults, in the United States and Canada.

Characteristics of Private, Nonprofit Leisure Service Organizations

Nonprofit leisure service organizations share a number of distinguishing features. In general, nonprofit organizations follow guidelines that have been established by state statutes and laws to provide for their existence. According to Wolf (1990), the ". . . term *nonprofit organization* refers to those legally constituted nongovernmental entities, incorporated under state law as charitable or not-for-profit corporations that have been set up to serve some public purpose and are tax exempt" (p. 6). In other words, nonprofit organizations are legal entities that promote, in some way, a public service orientation or mission. Nonprofit organizations have three basic characteristics. First, they are designated, specifically, as nonprofit entities when established. Second, a nonprofit organization may not divide its assets among its members, officers, or directors. Third, nonprofits may only pursue those activities that they have been established to promote.

There are many different types of nonprofit organizations. The National Taxonomy of Exempt Entities (NTEE) provides a classification system for identifying nonprofit organizations. This classification system identifies twenty-six different types of nonprofit organizations. The system enables organizations to be sorted by major purpose, program focus, and the primary beneficiary of the organization. Many of the types of organizations in the classification system are related to leisure, recreation, the environment, youth services, and other concerns that are indirectly related to the aforementioned (see table 10.2).

TABLE

10.2 CLASSIFICATIONS OF NONPROFIT ORGANIZATIONS

Type of Organization

Arts, Culture, Humanities

Educational Institutions and Related Activities

Environmental Quality, Protection, and Beautification

Animal-Related

Health: General and Rehabilitative

Mental Health Crisis Intervention

Diseases, Disorders, Medical Disciplines

Medical Research

Crime, Legal-Related

Employment, Job-Related

Food, Agriculture, and Nutrition

Housing, Shelter

Public Safety, Disaster Preparedness, and Relief

Recreation, Sports, Leisure, Athletics

Youth Development

Human Services: Multipurpose and Other

International Foreign Affairs and National Security

Civil Rights, Social Action, Advocacy

Community Improvement, Capacity Building

Philanthropy, Voluntarism, and Grantmaking Foundations

Science and Technology Research Institutes, Services

Social Science Research Institutes, Services

Public, Society Benefit: Multipurpose and Other

Religion-Related, Spiritual Development

Mutual Membership Benefit Organizations, Other

Unknown (Not Yet Classified)

Source: National Taxonomy of Exempt Entities. *National Center for Charitable Statistics.* (As cited in Hodgkinson, V., and Weitzman, M. (1996). (1996–1997) Nonprofit Almanac: Dimensions of the independent sector. San Francisco: Jossey-Bass.

What are the distinguishing characteristics of nonprofit organizations? How do they differ from business and government organizations? Perhaps the best way to identify the distinguishing characteristics is to point out the differences between nonprofit and profit and government organizations. A nonprofit organization does not earn a profit that is returned to its owners or members, and it often receives its primary financial support from charitable contributions, donations, and user fees. Government organizations rely on taxes and fees; profit-oriented or commercial organizations rely primarily on charges paid by customers for services.

Some of the distinguishing characteristics of nonprofit organizations are reflected in the following:

1. *Altruistic.* Most nonprofit organizations operate with altruistic motives. In fact, most nonprofit organizations' dominant themes are focused on altruistic, ethical, moral, or social values (Oleck, 1988).
2. *Public service mission.* According to Wolf (1990), an essential characteristic of a nonprofit organization is that it has a public service mission. In other words, nonprofits have the public interest at heart. Mason (1996) writes that nonprofit organizations hold different values than government or profit-oriented organizations. Some of the core values found in nonprofit organizations include *accountability, caring, citizenship, excellence, fairness, honesty, integrity, loyalty, promise-keeping, respect, fidelity, democracy, frugality, pluralism, stewardship, volunteerism, prudence, proportion, contextualism, consensus, community, openness, noblesse oblige (obligation to community) charity, service,* and *others.*
3. *Tax-exempt.* Nonprofit organizations are organized according to Internal Revenue Service guidelines that enable them to be tax-exempt. Section 501 (c) and 501 (d) provide exemptions for organizations from federal taxation. These types of organizations must meet the criteria of performing a service of social value, rather than promoting private ends (profit).
4. *Governance.* The governance structure of nonprofit organizations is established in such a way as to preclude self-interest and private financial gain (Wolf, 1990).

Mason (1996) suggests that there is a wide range of nonprofit organizations. In defining nonprofit organizations, he suggests that they can be distinguished by comparing and contrasting them to business and governmental organizations. As he notes, ". . . the primary goal of business is to be instrumental in making money. The goal of government is to be instrumental in governing. Nonprofits take their generic name not from their goals, but from the fact that distributing profits is not one of their goals" (p. 32).

Mason defines a nonprofit as an organization that is ". . . *usually self governed by local representative boards that achieve compliance by normative means rather than an exchange of wages for work or by coercion, or supported by contributions for member or public benefit and have instrumental and/or expressive purposes*" (p. 31). Mason views nonprofits on a continuum, along the expressive and instrumental dimensions, as follows.

- *Expressive.* Both the stated purposes and activities of purely expressive organizations involve the doing of the action itself. Examples are chess clubs, fraternities, and garden clubs.
- *Expressive-instrumental.* Expressive-instrumental organizations combine the purposes and activities of organizations at the extreme ends of the present continuum, but overt expressive values predominate. Examples are civic clubs and charismatic congregations.
- *Instrumental-expressive.* Instrumental-expressive organizations combine the purposes and activities of organizations at the extreme ends of the present continuum, but instrumental production activities predominate. Examples are hospital auxiliaries, parent-teacher associations, and the Literacy Volunteers of America.

Grassley Plans Hearing on Charitable Giving Problems, Best Practices

Sen. Charles E. Grassley (R-IA), chairman of the Senate Finance Committee (http://www.finance.senate.gov/), and Sen. Max Baucus (D-MT), the committee's ranking member, have announced that they will convene an oversight hearing on tax-exempt organizations on Tuesday, June 22.

According to a statement issued by Grassley's office, the hearing will consider the governance and best practices of charities; problems and abuses in the donation of tangible and intangible property; and potentially abusive situations involving tax shelters. In addition to receiving testimony from IRS commissioner Mark Everson and various state officials, the committee expects to hear from individuals with firsthand knowledge of problems and abuses in the sector as well as from leaders on issues of best practices and governance. According to the statement, the committee hopes the hearing will serve as a basis for consideration of legislation that addresses governance and best practice issues in the charitable sector, while highlighting the importance of the nonprofit community to the nation.

"We have a responsibility to conduct oversight of the tax system," said Grassley. "Lately, more and more tax problems involving charitable giving have come out. Our oversight should include which transactions are in keeping with the intent and spirit of the tax code, which may be inappropriately exploiting charities' tax-exempt status, and which may be unfairly enriching individuals and corporations."

United States Senate Finance Committee

Source: Retrieved from www.finance.senate.gov, June 1, 2004.

- *Instrumental.* The purposes and activities of the purely instrumental nonprofit organization focus on producing something of value for people outside of the organization, and any expressive aspect is incidental or distractive. Examples are nursing homes, private schools, and hospices.

One of the key factors influencing the work of nonprofit organizations in the provision of leisure services is the reliance on the use of volunteers for the delivery of services. Many nonprofit leisure service organizations depend on volunteers to serve as board members, supervisors, and leaders in the delivery of services. Take, for example, youth sports programs. Such programs require coaches, scorekeepers, officials, fundraisers, and individuals in other positions in order to ensure their success. Most, if not all, nonprofit youth service organizations depend on volunteer leadership to organize programs, conduct meetings, plan special events, and, in general, ensure the continued management and maintenance of the organization. Thus, an additional distinguishing characteristic of many nonprofit leisure service organizations is reliance on volunteers.

Goals and Functions

Nonprofit organizations often serve different groupings, often with divergent needs. Oleck (1988) suggests three basic orientations that nonprofit organizations take:

Public benefit. Nonprofit organizations can be organized to promote the public welfare. In general, this type of organization appeals to a wide variety of individuals. Although these organizations may have a specific focus (such as a specific age group, philosophy, and character development), their general purpose is to promote the common good. Organizations such as hospitals, museums, and schools often fit into this category.

Increasing Opportunities for Service for Youth

While no state and only a small percentage of districts as of 1990 required community service for high school graduation, the climate is largely working to promote that eventual development. Service and opportunities for community connection, as noted earlier, are among the key recommendations in practically all the blue-ribbon commission reports on "at-risk" youth, and the National and Community Service Act was signed into law in late 1990. The $125 million program, the only one of dozens of service bills that included young adolescents as eligible participants, would stimulate a host of service efforts around the country. The more we can encourage this service, apparently, the better: a Gallup survey reported that teenagers fourteen to seventeen are not only volunteering slightly more than adults (58% to 54%), but that 69% of those whose schools encouraged service actually volunteered, versus just 44% in schools where service was not especially encouraged.

There are endless examples of how we can provide as well as promote caring and a sense of community among young people. The following is just a sampling of the many efforts being conducted across the country.

- The Magic Me program in Baltimore pairs at-risk middle-grade youth with nursing home residents (for the school year).
- In the Valued Youth Partnership in San Antonio, the Coca-Cola Company and the Intercultural Development Research Association are serving a primarily Mexican American population through a mentoring initiative. Seventh and ninth graders, as well as high school students, are given extra help to sharpen their math and reading skills and then work, at minimum wage, at a nearby elementary school with younger Latino students. Instead of an expected dropout rate of 45% among these youth, only 4% of the tutors have dropped out of school.
- The principal of the Challenger Middle School in Colorado Springs created HUGSS—Help Us Grow Through Service and Smiles. The school of 900 is divided into nine academic teams, with each team adopting a community agency for school year service projects. The academic curriculum is realistically woven around these community service experiences.
- In Alaska, many of the Governor's Commission on Children and Youth recommendations that resulted in new funding were developed from the testimony of young people from around the state, including ten- to fifteen-year-olds, and the Commission awarded $30,000 in funds to youth-designed and -led prevention programs in junior and senior high schools.
- In Washington, high school seniors who have been through the Governor's Summer Citizenship School work with at-risk middle school students and their teachers/advisors to design and conduct community leadership projects that run throughout the school year.
- The Lutheran Brotherhood has developed a social studies program, Speak for Yourself, that encourages seventh and eighth graders across the nation to reflect on current issues and then share their opinions with government leaders.
- Now in a number of communities, the Early Adolescent Helper Program works with schools to place ten- to fifteen-year-olds in service settings such as Head Start or senior citizen centers. The program has documented the positive effects on Head Start children, and its success has led to its expansion as the National Center for Service Learning in Early Adolescence.
- In Detroit, young adolescents are caring for each other in Twelve Together, a program of the Metropolitan Detroit Youth Foundation. Hundreds of at-risk ninth graders are organized into peer helping groups of a dozen each who, with adult volunteers, hold thirty meetings during the school year, including one parent reception and six monthly academic forums. Peer counseling occurs in the offices of businesses that have adopted each group. Four years later, the graduation rate of these Twelve Together youth is 12% to 16% higher than that of control groups.

—continued

Increasing Opportunities for Service for Youth—continued

- The Teen Outreach Program of the Association of Junior Leagues combines curriculum-based life-skills instruction for seventh to twelfth graders with volunteer community service. A study of its impact across thirty-five sites showed that although program participants entered the program with more problems than comparison youths, they exited with fewer problems, such as involvement in a pregnancy, school course failure, or suspension from school.
- The Indiana Black Expo, Inc., designs programs that empower adolescents to help themselves, including holding Youth Empowerment Summits on economics, politics, African American culture, education, and the entertainment industry, and Youth Financial Literacy Workshops aimed ultimately at helping Indiana's youths create their own Youth Credit Union.

- The Children's Museum in Boston has an Early Adolescent Program for nine- to fifteen-year-olds, including adolescent-designed exhibits, a Youth Advisory Board, and after-school and Friday evening free workshops on rap music and recording, video improvisation, fitness, job opportunities for young artists, and much more.
- There are numerous KidsPlaces around the country. These boards of eleven- to fifteen-year-olds examine the conditions of growing up in those communities and make recommendations to the community leaders about how to improve the communities. For example, Minneapolis is setting its children's agenda through a communitywide City's Children: 2007 initiative. In May 1990, the Seattle KidsPlace hosted a national gathering of scores of these city- and state-based children's efforts.

Mutual benefit. Organizations formed to serve a more exclusive group of individuals for mutual benefit defines this category. Fraternal clubs, hobby groups, art associations/guilds, and the like are examples of these types of nonprofit associations. In general, these organizations promote the welfare of their constituents.

Private benefit. Organizations can form as nonprofit units for private benefit, such as golf clubs, swim and tennis associations, and others. These organizations promote an exclusive use of an area, facility, or service, or provide opportunities for a group of people to interact with one another for the exclusive benefit of that group. Numerous private, nonprofit leisure service organizations have formed to promote the interests of a more select group of individuals.

The benefit structure of a given nonprofit organization impacts its goals, programs, and membership.

What are the goals of nonprofit leisure service organizations? The answer to this question is as varied as the nature of the organization. Like public leisure service organizations, nonprofit organizations primarily promote the interests of those they serve. Their primary mission is *not* to make a profit, but, rather, to serve society in such a way as to promote the general welfare. Some nonprofit organizations have broadly defined goals such as promoting the development of youth, whereas others, more specifically focused, direct their work toward the provision of a specific program, facility, or area that benefits a more narrowly focused group of individuals.

The goals of nonprofit organizations are often difficult to measure or quantify. In the commercial sector, an organization's financial status is a quantitative measure stated in profit or

Nonprofits: America's Largest Employer

ew people are aware that the nonprofit sector is by far America's largest employer. Every other adult—total of *80 million-plus* people—works as a volunteer, giving an average of nearly five hours each week to one or several nonprofit organizations.

This is equal to 10 million full-time jobs. Were volunteers paid, their wages, even at minimum rate, would amount to some $10 billion, or 5 percent of GNP (Gross National Product).

Source: Peter F. Drucker, *Managing for the Future: The 1990s and Beyond,* 1992.

TABLE

10.3   MISSION STATEMENT: GIRLS, INCORPORATED

The mission of Girls, Incorporated is to assist affiliates in meeting the needs of girls in their communities; to help girls and young women overcome the effects of discrimination and to develop their capacity to be self-sufficient, responsible citizens; and to serve as a vigorous advocate for girls, focusing attention on their special needs.

Source: Girls, Incorporated, New York, NY. Reprinted by permission.

loss. The measurement of the goals of nonprofit organizations creates a greater challenge. Nonprofit organizations often state their goals in terms of promoting "quality of life," "enhancing the general welfare," "pursuing excellence," "promoting equity," and other statements that are difficult to quantify. The greatest challenge to nonprofit organizations lies in the development of goals that have clarity, purpose, and focus. Such clarity provides an opportunity to nonprofit organizations to clearly articulate and measure the benefit structures which they pursue.

An example of the goals of a nonprofit organization is that of Girls, Incorporated. This organization, dedicated to assisting girls to develop themselves as individuals, has a broad mission statement that promotes the general welfare of its targeted population. Its mission statement is found in table 10.3.

Obviously, the goals of Girls, Incorporated are broad in nature. Overcoming discrimination, developing self-sufficiency, advocating for girls, and focusing on the specific needs of girls provide a level of specificity in this statement that offers direction to the organization.

Another example of a goal statement is that of the Big Brothers/Big Sisters program. The Big Brothers/Big Sisters organization provides stable role models to children on an individual basis. Its mission statement is direct, focusing on promoting the welfare of children. Table 10.4 presents the mission statement. This mission statement focuses on defining the benefits to be derived from participation in the Big Brothers/Big Sisters program.

Resource Base

The resource base for nonprofit leisure service organizations is as diverse and complex as it is for other types of organizations. Depending on the philosophy and nature of the nonprofit organization, resources are sought both externally and internally, with an attempt to generate programs and

TABLE

10.4 MISSION STATEMENT: BIG BROTHERS/BIG SISTERS

Big Brothers/Big Sisters is a universally recognized youth development force that empowers children to reach their potential through supported dynamic mentoring relationships.

Source: Big Brothers/Big Sisters of America, Philadelphia, PA. Reprinted by permission.

Figure 10.4
Revenue sources available to nonprofit organizations.

services that produce revenues. Resources found in the "support" category are derived from contributions made by individuals, corporations, foundations, and the government (see figure 10.4). The "revenue" category shows income from membership fees, interest, dividends, and funds from special events.

In general, a number of revenue sources are available to nonprofit organizations, including the following:

Membership fees. Often, nonprofit leisure service organizations charge a basic membership fee for participating in the organization. For example, summer memberships at the Black Hawk County (Iowa) YMCA ranges from $408 for basic services for children to $624 for whole-family memberships. Figure 10.5 presents information regarding the membership fee structure for a family YMCA. Included is a discussion of membership information describing types of membership services available.

Program fees and tuition. Program fees/tuition are the charges assessed for participation in a specific program. For example, the Palo Alto (California) YMCA offers several family camping options. A father/child weekend camping program costs $98 per person. This YMCA also provides hiking trips for facility members at a no-cost basis and $10 for program members. See figures 10.6 and 10.7.

Government grants. Nonprofit organizations are eligible to receive funding from the state and federal government. Such support often enables nonprofit organizations to provide meal functions, program development, and other services.

Figure 10.5

2004 Membership Rates.

Source: Black Hawk County (Iowa) YMCA.

2004 Membership Rates

Membership Type	Activation Fee	Full Pay Start Up	Autochecking Monthly	Autochecking Start Up
Youth up to 18 Code 400	NA	$108	$9	$18
College Code 500	NA	$20/month	NA	NA
Basic Code 600	$48	$408	$30	$108
Fitness Center Code 601	$48	$552	$42	$132
Basic Family Code 800	$72	$624	$46	$164
FC Family Code 802	$72	$852	$65	$202
1 Parent Basic Family Code 900	$72	$504	$36	$144
1 Parent Fitness Center Family Code 901	$72	$648	$48	$168
65 & Better Code 660	$38	$290	$21	$80
65 & Better Family Code 760	$58	$394	$28	$114

Fitness Center Laundry—$120 for a person per year or $10 per month

Fitness Center Tall Locker—$96 for a person per year or $8 per month

All membership prices subject to change without notification

Corporate gifts. Donations by corporations comprise a substantial portion of the budgets of national youth service organizations. When seeking such gifts, nonprofit organizations must match their interests with the philosophy of the corporations' giving programs—and often submit a prospectus outlining the programs and services to be offered.

Donations and gifts. Individual giving provides an important source of support for nonprofit organizations, which can seek unrestricted contributions from individuals, local businesses, and other groups. Often these donations result from annual gift-giving programs organized by peer groups or community-service organizations. Donations also come in the form of bequests. A bequest is established in a person's will and allows an organization to use the individual's assets after his or her death. Another form of gift is the purchase of a life insurance policy with the death benefits assigned to a nonprofit organization.

Figure 10.6

Family Campus
Brochure.

*Source: Palo Alto
(California) Family
YMCA.*

Palo Alto Family YMCA
YFAMILY CAMP™

We build strong kids, strong families, strong communities.

YMCA
Family
Camps

The vacation you'll cherish forever!

Weekend or week-long trips, campfires, family time, fun activities and opportunities to meet other families.

Palo Alto Family YMCA
3412 Ross Rd, Palo Alto, CA 94303
(650) 856-9622

Figure 10.7

Hiking Trips
Brochure.

*Source: Palo Alto
(California) Family
YMCA.*

Palo Alto Family YMCA
HEALTH & FITNESS™

We build strong kids, strong families, strong communities.

Palo Alto Family YMCA
Hiking Trips

Come and join in the fun!
Aerobic hikes, scenic hikes, beach
hikes, forest hikes and much more!

Facility Members free,
program members $10
(plus annual membership fee)

Next Hike Fri, April 23

Palo Alto Family YMCA
3412 Ross Rd, Palo Alto, CA 94303
(650) 856-9622

Foundation grants. Foundations often supply considerable revenue for nonprofit organizations. Using resources such as the Foundation Grant Index or the Foundation Directory can help identify the vast network of foundation support in the United States and Canada. Foundations provide large restricted-grant support that organizations can use for program development or to focus on targeted populations. Foundations, interested in the ability of organizations to deliver services, need to know what problem is being addressed, the capability of the organization, anticipated evaluation strategies, and the resources required.

Interest and dividends. Nonprofit organizations sometimes have established endowments or trusts. Such financial arrangements enable an organization to earn interest or dividends on the principal that has been invested.

Scholarships. A scholarship may be thought of as aid or funds given to an individual to enable participation in a program. For example, an individual, group, or business could provide scholarships to enable a selected number of individuals to participate in a program such as a day camp. Scholarships often target financially disadvantaged individuals and, as a result, help provide equity.

Sales revenue. Nonprofit organizations can sell equipment, clothing, food, and other items that generate revenue for the enterprise. Over the years, the Girl Scouts of the U.S.A. and Camp Fire Boys and Girls, Inc. have generated great support for their endeavors through the sale of cookies and candy. Such fundraising activities have become institutionalized and are a part of popular culture.

Admissions. Admission fees to areas and facilities, another source of potential revenue, can be assessed for specific programs as well as for the use of facilities and equipment.

Rental fees. Income derived from the short-term, temporary, exclusive use of an area, facility, or piece of equipment is called a rental fee. Individuals and groups often rent facilities for meetings, special events, receptions, and other activities.

These and other miscellaneous sources of revenue provide the revenue base of nonprofit leisure service organizations. Nonprofit organizations work diligently to promote sources of revenue in order to prosper. Often, they organize internal programs directed toward raising their own funds. If they are a part of a national organization, they can participate in national or regional fundraising programs.

Fundraising   Nonprofit organizations depend on motivating individuals to provide financial support for their programs. As such, almost all nonprofit organizations have some type of fundraising program in place. Fundraising provides an opportunity for individuals to engage in philanthropic activity, which is the voluntary sharing of wealth. Canadians and U.S. citizens are extremely generous and contribute for various reasons, including out of their sense of moral responsibility to promote community welfare. There is also great personal satisfaction in assisting others by providing support.

Most nonprofit organizations have some type of annual fund campaign. Such campaigns generate funds to support the operation of nonprofit programs and services on a year-to-year basis. Fundraising campaigns are also organized in support of capital developments for new facilities or facility improvements. Among the many ways of soliciting funds from individuals, by far the most preferred means is the direct contact method. This method involves direct personal contact with potential donors. Other forms of fundraising include direct mail, telephone solicitations, special events, and other methods.

It is evident that a major source of revenue for nonprofit organizations is the charitable contributions made by donors. In 2002, nearly $241 billion was given in charitable contributions. The American Association of Fundraising Counsel reports that the vast majority of these funds were given by individuals (76.3%), followed by foundations (11.2%), bequests (7.5%), and corporations (5.1%) (see figure 10.8). By far, the vast amount of charitable giving goes to religious organizations. (See figure 10.9 for a breakdown of charitable giving.) It is estimated

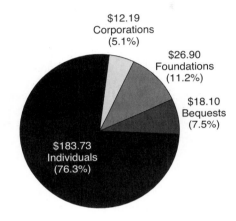

**2002 CONTRIBUTIONS: $240.92 BILLION
BY SOURCE OF CONTRIBUTIONS**

$12.19
Corporations
(5.1%)

$26.90
Foundations
(11.2%)

$18.10
Bequests
(7.5%)

$183.73
Individuals
(76.3%)

All figures are rounded
Total may not be 100%.

Figure 10.8

2002 Source of Philanthropic Contributions.

Source: American Association of Fundraising Counsel (AAFRC) Trust for Philanthropy Giving USA 2003.

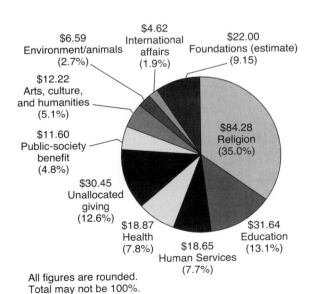

**2002 CONTRIBUTIONS: $240.92 BILLION
BY TYPE OF RECIPIENT ORGANIZATION**

$6.59
Environment/animals
(2.7%)

$4.62
International
affairs
(1.9%)

$22.00
Foundations (estimate)
(9.15)

$12.22
Arts, culture,
and humanities
(5.1%)

$11.60
Public-society
benefit
(4.8%)

$84.28
Religion
(35.0%)

$30.45
Unallocated
giving
(12.6%)

$18.87
Health
(7.8%)

$18.65
Human Services
(7.7%)

$31.64
Education
(13.1%)

All figures are rounded.
Total may not be 100%.

Figure 10.9

2002 Philanthropic Contributions by Type of Recipient Organization.

Source: American Association of Fundraising Counsel (AAFRC) Trust for Philanthropy Giving USA 2003.

Giving Up in 2003

Charitable giving in the United States in 2003 rose to the highest rate in three years, according to a national survey released today.

The giving USA annual report said donations by individuals, estates, foundations, and corporations totaled $240.7 billion in 2003. Researched by the Center on Philanthropy at Indiana University, the survey showed a 2.8 percent increase over 2002, when giving amounted to 234.1 billion.

Adjusted for inflation, donations rose only 0.5 percent in 2003, hovering at about the same rate of growth of 0.6 percent in 2002.

However, the estimated contributions amounted to 2.2 percent of the country's gross domestic product, falling just short of the nation's all-time charitable giving high of 2.3 percent GDP in 2000.

Of the 1,369 organizations that responded to the survey, 55 percent reported an increase in donations, while 8 percent reported stable levels of giving and 37 percent reported a decline in 2003. A year earlier, about half the organizations reported increases and the other half reported decreases.

While donations from individuals, estates, and corporations increased, gifts from foundations fell slightly. Individual contributions, which comprised of 74.5 percent of total giving, rose 2.5 percent to $179.4 billion, up from just over $175 billion in 2002.

that 89 percent of all households in America make some kind of charitable contribution annually, and the average annual contribution is $1,220. Fifty-two percent (52%) of all households give to both religious and secular organizations.

Obviously, a major source of revenue for nonprofits is the volunteer efforts of the individuals. Many individuals serve as leaders, coaches, and/or instructors providing a huge labor resource to nonprofit organizations, especially those dealing in the leisure and recreation field. It is estimated that 44 percent of all Americans volunteer. Women are more likely to volunteer than men. The volunteer workforce in American represents over 9 million full-time employees, valued at nearly $240 million.

Partnerships and Building Collaborative Efforts The twenty-first century will be an age of alliances (Austin, 2000). It will be important for businesses, government agencies, and nonprofit agencies to link together in partnerships to provide quality services and programs. Building collaborative relationships between various entities will be essential. Such collaborations will enable the sharing of organizational resources including areas, facilities, staff, information technology, marketing strategies, and numerous other concerns.

Building partnerships and collaborative efforts will be essential in the years to come for many reasons. Economic factors alone are forcing government agencies to think in new and innovative ways. Businesses seeking to build community goodwill are extending themselves and their resources to assist in the provision of community services. Nonprofit organizations are often underfunded to meet the demands they face and seek to increase their resource base.

There are numerous benefits for businesses, government agencies, and nonprofits to partner with one another. Austin (2000) has suggested the following are benefits for partnering:

- *Cost savings.* By cooperating, organizations can eliminate duplication of cost and also decrease unneeded resources.
- *Economies of scale and scope.* By working together, organizations can build a larger base to serve similar customer populations.

- *Synergies.* Collaborations promote greater thinking, problem solving, and solutions to community concerns.
- *Revenue enhancement.* By combining various organizations' resources, revenue is enhanced.
- *Strategy enrichment.* By collaborating, organizations are viewed as contributing to the welfare of the society.
- *Human resource management.* By combining human resources, organizations can enhance opportunities for leadership, community involvement, culture building, and so on.
- *Culture building.* Community service is a way of life for many individuals within organizations. Collaborative efforts enable this type of culture to thrive.
- *Business generation.* Collaborative relationships may create new markets by linking with potential new customers. Certainly it creates a sense of goodwill, which enhances business opportunities.

Clearly, there are numerous benefits to building collaborative partnerships. In the future this will become a key element in the success of professionals working in nonprofit organizations as well as businesses and government agencies.

Characteristics of Professionals

The nonprofit sector varies in terms of the types of organizations that deliver leisure services. As a result, it is difficult to analyze professionals in the industry with a great deal of precision. Nonetheless, a profile has emerged regarding the nature of employees in this sector, educational levels, salary structure, and job satisfaction. In general, the nonprofit area employs more women than men, particularly in positions focused on the delivery of program activities and/or the management of facilities.

The employees working in this segment of the industry, interestingly, express high job satisfaction. In fact, studies conducted comparing the nonprofit sector with the commercial and public sectors suggest that the level of satisfaction among this group ranks highest. Nonprofit sector workers express a high level of satisfaction with their work. They also note a high degree of satisfaction with the amount of control they have over their work life, with management, career progress, and even pay. Mason (1996) has written that paid staff members in nonprofit organizations:

> . . . enjoy their jobs for the sake of the work itself, and their ideal reward is more work with more responsibility. They enjoy a collegial environment and gain satisfaction from their work. They tend to be better educated than their business counterparts and tend to think of their work as being more important than any material rewards. (p. 33)

It is also interesting to note that individuals in this area indicate a long-term commitment to their profession. Furthermore, individuals stay with their careers and on average spend nine years at one work site, suggesting that this area is very stable.

Range of Personnel   Nonprofit organizations require a full range of individuals who contribute to the success of these types of endeavors. Nonprofit organizations have many different types of stakeholders who share in the success of the endeavor. As stakeholders, they all contribute to the organization, but in different ways. Mason (1996) notes that some of the types of salaried staff and unpaid volunteers often associated with nonprofit organizations include the following:

- *Founders.* These individuals are the originators of the nonprofit organization. Such individuals are often visionary, charismatic, driven, and intensely committed individuals.

- *Chief executive officers/managers.* Individuals occupying the roles of CEO or manager of a nonprofit organization provide overall managerial leadership to the organization, or a component of the organization, on a day-to-day basis. Such individuals have skills in fiscal resource management, human resource management, programming, and providing strategic direction and supervision to the work of an organization.
- *Program personnel.* These individuals are responsible for supervising a program area, facility, or age grouping, or some combination of these. They are responsible for the planning, promotion, implementation, and evaluation of specific programs in their assigned area. Duties may include the creation and implementation of direct services and/or programs that offer opportunities for enabling activities such as providing consultation and/or information.
- *Development personnel (fundraisers).* Nonprofit organizations must raise their own funding. They are dependent upon membership drives, donations, gifts, grants, endowments, trusts, and other forms of fundraising. Often, a nonprofit organization will secure the services of an individual who will, as a part of her/his responsibilities, or as her/his primary role, organize this effort within an organization.
- *Support staff.* As Mason (1996, p. 36) writes, ". . . support staff are those who file, drive, type, keep books, operate computers, clean and attend to other technical or administrative details, much as do their business counterparts. They may or may not exhibit strong commitment, and their pay and work are often quite similar to that in comparable business positions."
- *Volunteers.* As mentioned earlier, nonprofit organizations often rely heavily on the use of volunteers to carry out the work of the organization. There are three types of volunteers. First are individuals who serve as members of a *board of directors.* A board of directors provides oversight governance, helping define ". . . an organization's mission . . . establish its policies, and . . . [determine] . . . the control mechanisms it will use to allocate power, establish decision-making processes and set up procedures for performing specific tasks" (Mason, 1996, p. 36).

    The second type of volunteers are those who assist in providing *direct face-to-face leadership or general supervision* to programs. Such volunteers often serve as coaches, scout leaders, teen specialists, program hosts, teacher aides, and other roles. The third type of volunteers are those who assist with *administrative or support functions.* These individuals aid in the activities of the organization that often involve their annual fundraising campaign, registration activities, clerical activities, or other support functions as mentioned previously.
- *Rank and file members.* Many nonprofit organizations are membership organizations; that is, they are dependent upon and seek a membership base that meet selected criteria. Such criteria may be broad or specific. The membership of an organization may contribute to the governance of the agency, support its financial goals and, in general, contribute to its well-being. Members are instrumental in recruiting new members, recommending program enhancements, paying dues, fundraising, and providing leadership to the nonprofit organizations.
- *Contributors.* Individuals, organizations, or agencies may support the goals of a nonprofit organization with various forms of contributions. As Mason (1996, p. 40) notes ". . . individuals, governments, businesses, foundations and unaffiliated individuals can and do support . . . [nonprofit] organizations." People contribute to nonprofit organizations because they value the work of a group, because it is consistent with their interests, or because they have respect for its efforts. Further, contributors often give simply because they are asked.

Types of Youth and Voluntary Nonprofit Leisure Service Organizations

Many voluntary, charitable, and social welfare organizations exist in the United States. According to the National Center for Charitable Statistics, there are nearly 1.4 million nonprofit organizations in the United States. These can be divided into several categories, including the following: 1) health services; 2) education research; 3) social and legal services; 4) religious organizations; 5) civic, social, and fraternal organizations, 6) arts and culture; and 7) foundations. These types of organizations can be further subdivided into two classifications. One is known as the "independent sector" and includes 501(c)(3), charitable organizations, and 501(c)(4), social welfare organizations and religious organizations. The second category is simple referred to as "other nonprofits." In viewing these types of nonprofit organizations, the largest is health services, followed by education/research, social and legal services, and religious organizations (see figure 10.10). Many of these organizations are involved in recreation and leisure in a variety of ways. This section of the chapter presents an overview of many specific nonprofit organizations, grouped according to the participants they serve: youth serving organizations (both nonsectarian and religious), religious organizations, organizations serving special populations (including people with disabilities), relief and social service organizations, conservation organizations, and service and fraternal clubs.

Table 10.5 presents information regarding nonprofit organizations related to leisure in the United States. As one can see from viewing this table, a diverse number of nonprofit organizations provide leisure or related services. Between 1985 and 1997 the number of nonprofit organizations has grown dramatically.

Youth Serving Organizations

A large and important part of the nonprofit segment of the leisure service industry is dedicated to providing youth services. The Carnegie Corporation (1992) estimates that more than 400 national organizations provide services to youth. Table 10.6 provides information concerning a variety of these types of organizations, ranging from sports groups to fraternal organizations with youth programs.

One of the developments among such organizations involves the movement away from traditional programs which focus exclusively on recreation, to those that consider principles of education and youth development within leisure programs and services. The Carnegie

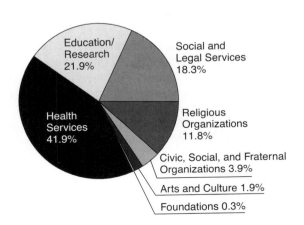

Figure 10.10

Nonprofit Employment by Subsector.

Source: Independent sector. (2005, March). The new nonprofit almanac and Desk Reference. Retrieved from: www.Independent Sector.org

TABLE

10.5 NONPROFIT ASSOCIATIONS RELATED TO LEISURE

Type	Number of Associations			
	1985	**1990**	**1995**	**1997**
Cultural	N/A	1,886	1,918	1,918
Social welfare	1,450	1,705	1,885	1,934
Fraternal	462	573	552	541
Religious	953	1,172	1,230	1,230
Patriotic	281	462	686	745
Hobby/avocational	1,311	1,475	1,549	1,548
Athletic sports	787	840	838	836
Fan clubs	N/A	581	460	491

Source: R. Famighetti (ed.), 1996. *World Almanac and Book of Facts*. Mahwah, NJ: Funk and Wagnalls, U.S. Bureau of the Census. 1999. *Statistical Abstracts of the United States: 1999*. 119th ed. Washington, DC: U.S. Government Printing Office.

TABLE

10.6 YOUTH SERVED BY MAJOR NATIONAL NONPROFIT ORGANIZATIONS

Organization	Total Youth Served
Boy Scouts of America	3.2 million
Boys & Girls Clubs	4.0 million
Camp Fire USA	735,000
4-H Youth for America	6.8 million
Girls Scouts of the USA	2.8 million
Girls, Inc.	525,000
Junior Achievement, Inc.	4.0 million
YMCA of the USA	8.5 million
YWCA	2.0 million

Corporation (1992) also reports ". . . greater emphasis being placed on building specific skills and competencies rather than self-esteem and self-confidence" (p. 44). The characteristics of these organizations depend on the mission and philosophy of the organization. Several unique components of youth serving nonprofit organizations, as reported by the Carnegie Corporation, appear in table 10.7.

While religious organizations sponsor and support many youth organizations, others are nonsectarian. The nonsectarian organizations often have goals connected to social development and good citizenship.

Nonsectarian-Sponsored Organizations The goals and objectives of nonsectarian-sponsored organizations supply an overview of youth development objectives that they would promote. Youth serving organizations that are committed to youth development all

TABLE 10.7 UNIQUE CHARACTERISTICS OF YOUTH SERVING NONPROFIT ORGANIZATIONS AS REPORTED BY THE CARNEGIE CORPORATION

- Some organizations are facility-based, others are organized around a specific group or troop, and still others rely on a one-to-one match between a young person and an adult mentor. The programs offered by these organizations are often led by volunteers; others (usually the facility-based organizations) rely primarily on paid staff.

- Troop or group-based agencies tend to meet once a week, for an hour or two, while facility-based agencies generally offer services for twenty to thirty hours per week (although the extent to which individual members make use of the entire array of services varies).

- Program content and approaches vary. Some organizations offer a comprehensive "core" program, while others focus on one or two aspects of overall youth development, such as academic enrichment or leadership skills.

- The demographics of service populations can differ in composition in terms of socioeconomic status, race and ethnic background, age, and gender and in total number of youths served.

- Some organizations are well funded (e.g., Boy Scouts of America and Girl Scouts of the U.S.A.) while others struggle. Some national troops rely heavily on affiliate dues and on revenues from the sale of equipment, products, and supplies; others receive the bulk of their support from government or charitable contributions.

- Every organization defines its membership differently—in general, the national organizations try to maximize their membership numbers occasionally by including leaders and others.

- Most organizations try to encourage active youth participation at the local level, but they seldom permit young people to take part in genuine decision making. Only a few national organizations appoint youth members to their boards or commissions. (p. 44)

Source: *A Matter of Time: Risk and Opportunity in the Nonschool Hours,* a report of the Carnegie Council on Adolescent Development. Copyright© December 1992 by Carnegie Corporation of New York.

have related objectives toward which they focus their efforts. The organizations described include 4—H Clubs, Boy and Girl Scouts, Junior Achievement, Camp Fire Boys and Girls, Inc., Girls, Inc., Boys and Girls Clubs of America, and Big Brothers/Big Sisters of America.

4—H for Youth of America   The national 4—H program is part of the U.S. Department of Agriculture's Cooperative Extension Service program. The four Hs of the 4—H program, which was founded in 1924, stand for *Head, Heart, Hands,* and *Health* and represent the organization's emphasis on education and living a healthy and productive life. Its main goal is to create a learning environment for youth that stimulates the development of particular life skills: (1)competency—developing skills and knowledge; (2) coping—dealing with stress; and (3) contributory—learning to help others. The 4—H program serves young people ages five to nineteen. The 4—H program operates in more than 3,000 counties in the United States, District of Columbia, Puerto Rico, Virgin Islands, Guam, American Samoa, and Micronesia. Estimates show that there is an enrollment of over 6.8 million boys and girls in 4–H programs. Most live in rural areas, although the program now operates in suburban and urban areas as well.

The 4–H program operates a variety of services including clubs, projects, activities, outreach, and international programs. The 4–H program depends on more than 500,000 volunteer leaders who give an average of 220 hours per year. The 4–H program provides opportunities for youth to work with adult volunteer leaders on one or more projects. The club program forms the backbone of 4–H, and most activities are carried out in this format. 4–H projects are grouped in the areas of animal science, plant science, home economics, natural science, mechanical science, and expressive arts. These programs provide real-life experiences for participants. Activities provided by 4–H include opportunities for individuals to participate in fairs, contests, camps, tours, exchanges, and special events. The 4–H program also operates on extensive outreach effort. 4–H materials are used in schools, seen on television, and used in other formats. International 4–H programs provide opportunities for exchanges for young adults to live and work with families in other countries.

Boy Scouts of America   Scouting, a program that covers the globe, was founded in Britain by Lord Baden Powell. The Boy Scouts of America was founded in the United States by William D. Boyce in 1910. The purpose of the Boy Scouts is to provide an educational program for boys and young adults to build character, to train in the responsibilities of participating citizenship, and to develop personal fitness. In general, the Boy Scouts of America program pursues three purposes: (1) character development, (2) citizenship training, and (3) personal fitness. Scouting units are sponsored by churches, schools, and civic groups. Sponsoring groups form a partnership with local Boy Scout Councils that help train, supervise, and deliver services. "Community-based organizations receive national charters to use the Scouting program as a part of their own youth work. These groups, which have goals compatible with those of the BSA, include religious, educational, civic, fraternal, business, and labor organizations; governmental bodies; corporations; professional associations; and citizens' groups" (www.scouting.org/factsheets/02-501.html).

The scouting program is organized into several units: 1) Tiger Cubs, 2) Cub Scouts, 3) Webelos Scouts, 4) Boy Scouting, 5) Varsity Scouting, and 6) Venturing. Tiger Cubs is a year-round family and home-centered program that encourages the ethical decision-making skills for first grade (or seven-year-old) boys. These boys participate in the program with their adult partners. The program emphasizes shared leadership, learning about the community, and family understanding (www.scouting.org/factsheets/02-501.html). Cub Scouts is a year-round family and home-centered program that develops ethical decision-making skills for boys in the second through fifth grade (or who are eight, nine, and ten years old). Activities emphasize character development, citizenship training, and personal fitness (www.scouting.org/factsheets/02-501.html). Webelos Scouts is a year-round family and home-centered program that develops ethical decision-making skills for fourth and fifth grade (or ten-year-old) boys. Webelos Scouts participate in more advanced activities that begin to prepare them to become Boy Scouts (www.scouting.org/factsheets/02-501.html). Boy Scouting is a year-round program for boys eleven through seventeen designed to achieve the aims of Scouting through a vigorous outdoor program and peer group leadership with counsel of an adult Scoutmaster. (Boys also may become Boy Scouts if they have earned the Cub Scouting Arrow of Light Award and have completed the fifth grade.) (www.scouting.org/factsheets/02-501.html) Varsity Scouting is an active, exciting, year-round program for young men fourteen through seventeen built around five program fields of emphasis: advancement, high adventure, personal development, service, and special programs and events (www.scouting.org/factsheets/02-501.html). Venturing is a year-round program for young men and women who are fourteen (and have completed the eighth grade) through twenty years of age to provide positive experiences through exciting and meaningful youth-run activities that help them pursue their special interests, grow by teaching others, and develop leadership skills (www.scouting.org/factsheets/02-501.html).

Girl Scouts of the U.S.A.   The Girl Scout organization was established in 1912 and founded by Juliette Gordon Lowe, who organized the first group of girls in Savannah, Georgia. This program for girls ages five to seventeen builds on an informal educational foundation. The

Girl Scouts Want 'Cool' Image

Leslie Walter meets with three seventh graders several times a month in her Urbandale home.

She used to meet with fourteen girls in her Girl Scout troop. But as those girls aged, that number dropped to eleven, then seven, and now Troop 522 has three members.

Walter's troop recently started a new less-structured program—Studio 2B—with her seventh graders designed specifically to retain older members.

Nationwide, the ninety-one-year old Girl Scouts of the United States of America has fewer senior members than it once did. Iowa troops are part of the trend that shows that older members find the group to be "uncool" and leave.

Older members in Iowa are part of the decline. Of the 2.8 million members nationwide, only 12 percent are over age eleven. To survive, the organization has had to find ways to be "cool," including changes in uniforms and the new program, called Studio 2B.

The decrease in older members is important, Scout leaders say, because the group's mission is to teach leadership and build self-esteem through high school.

In an attempt to improve the image of older members, uniforms got a makeover. Girls can now wear cargo pants and skirts, t-shirts, and hats. Before, they wore blue, brown, and green jumpers and berets.

A more concerted effort was put toward creating Studio 2B, designed to project opportunities and values in a more contemporary, flexible, and in-depth manner.

In Studio 2B, the leader takes less of a role in the instruction. Instead, a volunteer expert in the area initiates the activities.

Along with the traditional patches, the girls in Studio 2B earn rewards, such as charms, for reaching their goals in leadership training, programming, and career exploration.

So far, the effort to be "cool" is helping Troop 522.

Source: Westendorf, B. 2003. Girl Scouts Want 'Cool' Image. *The Des Moines Register* (November), pp. 1–2B.

Girl Scouts of the USA have positioned themselves as the world's preeminent organization ". . . where in an accepting and nurturing environment, girls build character and skills for success in the real world. In partnership with adult volunteers, girls develop qualities that will serve them all their lives, like leadership, strong values, social conscience, and conviction about their own potential and self worth." A congressional charter was conferred on the Girl Scouts of the U.S.A. in 1950 by a special act of Congress. This charter provides the basic guidelines for the operations of the Girl Scout programToday, Girl Scouts serves more than 3.8 million individuals, including 2.9 million girl members and 986,000 adult members. Most of the funding for the Girl Scout program comes from two basic income streams: (1) revenue generated from membership dues, uniform sales, books, and other equipment, and (2) local United Way contributions, corporate gifts, foundation grants and gifts, and individual philanthropic efforts.

The program of the Girl Scouts centers in the five following areas: (1) personal well-being and fitness, (2) awareness of other cultures, (3) exploring new technologies, (4) the arts, and (5) the out-of-doors. The program is organized in to the following: Daisy Girl Scouts are five to six years old, Brownie Girl Scouts are six to eight years old, and Junior Girl Scouts are eight to eleven years old. Girls, ages eleven to seventeen, may participate through the STUDIO 28sm program design. Most Girl Scout programs operate in the troop/group format. Girl Scout programs include a variety of activities, including opportunities for camping, skill-development activities, trips and tours, and exchanges. The Girl Scout program promotes adventure in learning with activities focused on helping girls address both their current interests and future roles in society. The United States has more than 300 Girl Scout councils. The Girl Scout program is offered in over 100 countries and the Girl Scouts of the U.S.A. are affiliated with the World Association of Girl Guides and Girl Scouts.

Junior Achievement   Junior Achievement, established in 1919, assists youth in gaining knowledge about the business world and prepares them for roles as entrepreneurs or professionals in the future. The Junior Achievement Program involves more than 4 million youth a year in various activities. The Junior Achievement program uses volunteers to provide services to youth and, on a yearly basis, sees 100,000 individuals support the programs and services offered by the organization. The mission of Junior Achievement is ". . . to promote economic literacy and understanding of business and competitive private enterprise among young people through hands-on experience" (Carnegie Corp., 1992, p. 146). Junior Achievement is a nonprofit, tax-exempt organization that is international in scope with programs in every major city in the United States. Also, the program operates in nearly 100 countries throughout the world.

Junior Achievement offers a variety of programs focused on the elementary, middle school, and high school levels. At the elementary school level, programs include seven sequential themes where students can learn basic concepts of business and economics. The themes include: 1) Ourselves, 2) Our families, 3) Our Community, 4) Our City, 5) Our Region, 6) Our Nation, and 7) JA Enterprise Village. The middle grade and high school programs focus areas include: economics, personal finance, business and entrepreneurship, and work preparation. Themes pursued for these grades include: 1) Our World, 2) JA Enterprise in Action, 3) The Economics of Staying in School, 4) JA go Figure! Exploring Math in Business™, 5) The International Marketplace™, 6) JA Global Marketplace™, 7) JA Job Shadow™, 8) Personal Economics, and 9) JA Finance Park™. High school programs emphasizing economics concepts and continuing in school include: 1) JA Company Program, 2) JA Economics, 3) GLOBE, 4) JA Go Figure!, 5) JA Job Shadow, 6) JA Personal Finance, 7) JA Titan, and 8) JA Success Skills. J. A. Company, is directed toward high school students and enables them to develop a mini-business. Youth elect their own officers, sell stock, manufacture and market a product or service, and manage financial activities, including paying shareholders of the organization.

Camp Fire USA   The Camp Fire USA program was founded (as Camp Fire Girls) by Luther and Charlotte Gulick. Today, the program provides all-inclusive, co-educational programs that include youth leadership, self-reliance, after-school groups, camping, environmental education, and childcare. The program serves youth from birth to age twenty-one. Camp Fire USA takes pride in its long-standing commitment to providing fun programs and services to all children and families in America. They operate in an inclusive manner, open to all persons in the communities they serve. Camp Fire USA welcomes children, youth, and adults regardless of race, religion, socioeconomic status, disability, sexual orientation, or other aspect of diversity. Camp Fire USA's programs are designed and implemented to reduce sex-role, racial, and cultural stereotypes to foster positive intercultural relationships (www.http:campfire.org/all_about_us). Camp Fire USA, like other youth service organizations, depends on adult volunteer leaders. Such individuals provide guidance and support for most programs. Because Camp Fire is coeducational, it offers opportunities for female and male teams to provide leadership to the programs and services of Camp Fire.

Camp Fire USA's basic mission is to build caring, confident youth and future leaders. Five core values are drawn from the mission statement to provide direction for its program offerings. They are: 1) we are youth-centered; 2) we engage the entire family in fun, rich activities; 3) we are welcoming and inclusive; 4) we build youth and adult partnerships; and 5) we provide service to others. Camp Fire USA organizes its programs into five core areas. These are: 1) small-group clubs and mentoring opportunities, 2) leadership development, 3) camping and environmental education, 4) child care, and 5) self-reliance and service learning. In addition to these core values, the following twelve guidelines are used in the development of programs. These guidelines are; 1) we believe that children and youth are our most precious resources; 2) we believe in an approach to youth development that builds assets and empowers individuals; 3) we believe that the best youth development occurs in small groups where children and youth are actively involved in creating their own learning; 4) we are committed to coeducation, providing opportunities for boys, girls, and families to develop together; 5) we provide caring, trained mentors to work with children and youth; 6) we are inclusive, welcoming children and adults regardless of race, religion, socioeconomic status, disability, sexual orientation, or other aspect of diversity; 7) we respect and celebrate nature; 8) we foster leadership, engaging children, and youth to give service and make decisions in a democratic society; 9) we provide safe, fun, and nurturing environments for children and youth; 10) we enrich parents' and other adults' lives by expanding their skills and encouraging them to share their talents and build relationships with children and youth; 11) we respond to community needs with our programs and expertise; and 12) we advocate on behalf of children, youth, and families (http://www.campfire. org/al_about_us/core_values.). Camp Fire USA involves more than 735,000 youth each year. Today, the distribution of participants is 54 percent female and 46 percent male. As this organization has transformed its mission to one focused exclusively on girls to a coeducational agency, it appears that the transition has been a successful one.

In addition to the club program, Camp Fire USA offers camping and environmental education programs, child-care programs, self-reliance programs that promote acquisition of life skills, and leadership development activities that are aimed at empowering youth. program involves more than 738,000 children each year. The majority of these participants are female (54%), which may reflect the founding mission of the organization.

Girls, Inc. Girls, Inc., founded in 1945, was initially established at the Girls Clubs of America and offers programs through a network of 1000 sites throughout the United States. The program is supported by a national headquarters and regional offices. Girls, Inc., has framed itself as a nationwide research education and direct advocacy organization with a mission of "inspiring all girls to be strong, smart, and bold." The organization provides services to girls ages six to eighteen and encourages its participants to take risks, mastering physical, intellectual, and emotional challenges. The program serves over 525,000 participants annually through its neighborhood centers, partnering organizations, Web sites, and organizational educational products. Girls, Inc., is focused on girls of color who come from single-parent households. Forty-seven percent of its members are African American/Black and 53 percent come from single-parent households with very low incomes. It is evident that its focus is on girls in high-risk/under-served areas. Most of its support comes from corporations, foundations, government grants, and individuals. The remainder comes from affiliate dues, fees, interest, and dividends.

1) Girls Incorporated; 2) Girls, Inc., Operation SMART[sm]; 3) Girls, Inc., Preventing Adolescent Pregnancy[sm]; 4) Girls, Inc., Media Literacy[sm]; 5) Girls, Inc., Project Bold[sm]; 6) Girls, Inc., Economic Literacy[sm]; 7) Girls, Inc., Friendly PEERsuation[sm]; 8) Girls, Inc., Sporting Chance[sm]; and 9) Girls, Inc., Discovery Leadership[sm]. The Girls, Inc., Web site provides a definition of each of these programs (www.www.girlsinc.org). Operation SMART[sm] builds girls' skills and interest in science, math, and technology. Hands-on activities give girls the opportunity to explore, ask questions, and solve problems. Components of Operation SMART include: Eureka!,

GirlsLink^{sm}, GirlsLink Gets SMART, Girls Dig It, and Career Action. Girls, Inc., Preventing Adolescent Pregnancy^{sm} helps girls identify ways and reasons to avoid early pregnancy. The program fosters girls' communication skills, provides basic health education, and encourages girls to plan for the future through four age-appropriate components: Growing Together^{sm}, Will Power/Won't Power^{sm}, Taking Care of Business^{sm}, and Health Bridge^{sm}. The first two components have been translated into Spanish as Crecer Juntas and Querer/Poder Decir "no". Girls, Inc., Media Literacy^{sm} encourages girls to think critically about media messages and fosters their awareness of the scope and power of the media and its effects on girls and women. Girls gain media literacy skills that enhance their ability to critically examine and advocate for change in entertainment, news, and advertising media. Girls, Inc., Project Bold^{sm} strengthens girls' abilities to lead safer lives. Girls develop strategies for self-defense (including physical techniques), seeking out and talking with caring adults about personal violence, and advocating on violence issues for girls and young women. Age-appropriate components include Kid-Ability!™ (Kid Jr.), Action for Safety^{sm}, and Taking Action. Girls, Inc., Economic Literacy^{sm} introduces girls as young as six to basic financial concepts, including money management and investment. The program explores how money affects us locally and globally as it fosters development of the skills needed to be financially self-sufficient. Girls, Inc., Friendly PEERsuasion^{sm} builds girls' skills for resisting pressure to use harmful substances such as alcohol, tobacco, household chemicals, and other drugs. The two-part substance abuse prevention program teaches girls ages eleven to fourteen healthy ways to manage stress and confront peer, media, and other pressures. The girls then assume roles as PEERsuaders for younger girls. Girls, Inc., Sporting Chance^{sm} builds movement and athletic skills, cooperative and competitive spirit, health awareness, and interest in all sports as girls explore career opportunities related to sports and experience the benefits of healthy risk taking. The program lays a foundation for a lifetime of sports participation through two age-appropriate programs: Steppingstones^{sm} and Bridges^{sm}. Girls, Inc., Discovery Leadership^{sm} partners girls and women in community action projects chosen by girls, building leadership skills and creating lasting change. This leadership development program for girls ages nine to eleven celebrates the heritage of girls and women as leaders and fosters girls' awareness of themselves as community resources and trustees of the common good.

Girls, Inc. offers several specific programs directed toward helping individuals gain skills, have fun, and meet with friends. Programs, offered in the centers operated by Girls, Inc., include the following:

Boys and Girls Clubs of America   The Boys and Girls Clubs of America, founded in 1906 as the Boys Club of America, changed its name in 1990 to reflect a coeducational philosophy. The Boys and Girls Clubs operate in centers and, in that sense, are often facility based. The mission of Boys & Girls Clubs is to "inspire and enable all young people, especially those from disadvantaged circumstances, to realize their full potential as productive, responsible and caring citizens." Boys & Girls Clubs are organized to provide the following: 1) a safe place to learn and grow; 2) ongoing relationships with caring, adult professionals; 3) life-enhancing programs and character development experiences; and 4) hope and opportunity. Today, the Boys & Girls Clubs of America serve over 4 million youth at some 3,400 club locations with 42,000 trained professional staff. Boys & Girls Clubs are located in all fifty states and in Puerto Rico and the Virgin Islands. There are many Boys & Girls clubs located on U.S. Military Bases in the continental United States and in overseas locations. In addition, the Boys & Girls Clubs are aggressively partnering with Native American tribes to provide services.

The Boys & Girls Clubs have built their program on what they define as seven timeless, simple, and straightforward principles. These principles are as follows: 1) a mission of hope and opportunity—Boys & Girls Clubs are designed to inspire and enable young people to become responsible, productive, caring citizens; to assure that every young person has the opportunity to share in the American Dream; and to provide young people with the resources to succeed; 2) a focus on young people from disadvantaged circumstances—Boys & Girls Clubs serve all school-age youth, especially those from disadvantaged circumstances who have the fewest resources and face the greatest obstacles. Young people from difficult economic, social, and family situations are our first priority. If we do not serve them who will? 3) a unique system of informal guidance—clubs are more than a building or a program. They are a unique form of informal guidance, where kids are free to make their own choices and encouraged to openly seek assistance from adults who only want the best for them; 4) ongoing relationships with caring adults—club staff who work with young people are youth development professionals. Their first job is to develop positive relationships and serve as role models. Above all, youth development professionals help young people become responsible, productive, caring citizens; 5) youth development philosophy—club staff fosters members' self-worth by encouraging a sense of belonging, competence, usefulness, and influence; 6) a commitment to character—clubs must teach—through word and deed—the importance of living honorably. Through programs, activities, and everyday interactions, clubs reinforce service and selflessness, caring and compassion, honesty and integrity, freedom and fairness, inclusion and diversity, and knowing right from wrong; 7) fun, diverse, and interesting experiences—one of the most important principles of the Boys & Girls Club experience is having fun. Along with personal relationships, fun activities bring young people into the club and keep them coming back. Fun is essential to the business of Boys & Girls Clubs (Boys & Girls Clubs, 2003).

There are varied and numerous programs offered by the Boys & Girls Clubs. In fact, the organization offers more than twenty-five programs in the areas of education, environment, health, the arts, careers, alcohol/drug and pregnancy prevention, gang prevention, leadership development, and athletics. There are six basic program areas including: 1) character and leadership—these programs assist youth in becoming responsible, caring citizens and acquire skills for participating in the democratic process, developing leadership skills and providing opportunities for planning, decision making, community building, and celebrating our national heritage; 2) education and career—this program cluster is focused on helping youth create aspirations for the future, providing opportunities for career exploration and educational enhancement; 3) health and life skills—this area is focused on helping youth achieve and maintain healthy and active lifestyles; 4) the arts—this program area assists youth in enhancing their self-expression and creativity, as well as exposure and skill development in crafts, visual arts, performing arts, and literary arts; 5) sports, fitness, and recreation—these programs promote fitness, positive use of leisure time, reduction of stress, appreciation for the environment, and social and interpersonal skills; and 6) specialized programs. The Boys & Girls Clubs operate many different types of programs that are packaged at the national level and available at the local level. Some of these include: TEENSupreme Keystone Clubs, National Youth of the Year, Torch Club, Project Learn, Power Hour, SMART Moves, SMART Girls, Passport to Manhood, Act SMART, Kids in Control, Street SMART, Career-Launch, ClubService, Fitness Authority, Jr. NBA/Jr. WNBA, Athletic Director University, Teen Sports Clubs, Sectional Sports Tournaments, Reviving Baseball in Inner Cities (RBI), and Gang Prevention/ Intervention Through Targeted Outreach.

Big Brothers/Big Sisters of America Big Brothers/Big Sisters of America was founded in 1904 and is designed to match children and youth one-on-one with adults. Originally established for fatherless boys who were facing legal action, it is believed to be one of the earliest prevention programs aimed at reducing juvenile delinquency in the United States. The first Big Sisters program started in 1908 for delinquent girls. Over the years the program has served to help match a child, usually from a single-parent family, with an adult who serves as a support, friend, mentor, and positive role model. The one-to-one friendships established in the Big Brothers/Big Sisters program serve as a highly effective way of supporting children and can curb problems that might later lead to more serious criminal activity.

The program annually serves over 200,000 children ages five to eighteen in 5,000 communities across all fifty states through a network of 470 agencies.

Adult volunteers in the Big Brothers/Big Sisters program provide guidance, companionship, and emotional support. Volunteers must be at least eighteen years old and evidence a stable lifestyle. They usually commit between three and six hours a week, working with a little brother or little sister aged seven to thirteen. The Big Brother or Big Sister does not act as a substitute parent or child-care provider, but as a friend. Adult volunteers are screened in a stringent application and reference checking process that includes a police check. Volunteers are further oriented through Empower, a child sexual abuse education and prevention program, and Alternatives, a substance abuse education and prevention program.

Big Brothers/Big Sisters operates a number of programs. Their basic program is a community-based one where adults cultivate relations and unstructured outings with youth. In addition, they operate a program in the schools with volunteers providing one-on-one time and attention to assist individuals in discovering ways to make school and learning fun. Other programs include: Amachi Big Brothers Big Sisters, AARP Big Brothers and Big Sisters, Alpha Phi Alpha BBBS, Club-based Big Brothers and Big Sisters (Up2Us), Corporate Volunteers, High School Bigs, and BBBS Partnership with Four Leading Service Clubs.

Religious-Sponsored Organizations   Religious organizations have traditionally cared about the development of children and youth. Some organizations are connected with a specific church or denomination, while others are connected to various religions throughout the world. The larger youth serving organizations with religious affiliation in the United States include the Young Men's Christian Association (YMCA), Young Women's Christian Association (YWCA), the Catholic Youth Organization (CYO), Young Men's Hebrew Association (YMHA), and the Young Women's Hebrew Association (YWHA). Although this list is not inclusive, it does represent a cross section of the types of programs offered by youth serving organizations with religious affiliation.

Young Men's Christian Association   The YMCA movement was established in England in the early 1800s by Sir George Williams. In the United States, the first YMCA was established in 1851 in the city of Boston. From a historical perspective, the YMCA programs were established to meet the spiritual needs of young men. Today, that philosophy, while intact, has broadened considerably in terms of the types of services and programs offered. The mission statement of the YMCA is "To put Christian principles into practice through programs that build healthy spirit, mind, and body for all." (www.ymca.net). In support of the mission of the YMCA, a vision of "building strong kids, strong families and strong communities" has emerged. This vision is reinforced by core values of the YMCA focused on caring, honesty, respect, and responsibilities. Today, YMCA uses an asset-building strategy in meeting the needs of the local communities in which they serve.

In the United States, there are more than 2,500 YMCAs. The YMCA frames itself as the largest nonprofit service organization focused on meeting health and social service needs of Americans. YMCAs are open to people of all faith, races, abilities, ages, and incomes. Each YMCA is organized to reflect the unique needs of the community it serves. The decision about what programs and services will be offered and how they are operated is made in each local venue.

YMCA programs are facility centered. Individuals or families buy a membership that covers the use of basic services such as a gymnasium, exercise area, swimming pool, locker rooms, game rooms, and lounge. Members also receive reduced fees on other programs. For example, YMCAs run extensive resident and day camp programs for children. In fact, the YMCA was a pioneer in the camping movement, with its first camp established in New York in 1885. Further, YMCA activities for youth include sports clinics, volleyball, health enhancement, karate, gymnastics, swimming programs, dance classes, tennis instruction, fitness and aerobic activities, racquetball, youth and adult sports leagues, and teen programs.

The range of services provided by many YMCAs is virtually unlimited. Some of the programs that may be available at a local YMCA include the following: 1) Adventure Guides—strengthening the relationships between parents and children; 2) Aquatics—swim lessons, scuba, water fitness, national competitive swimming, and many others; 3) Arts and Humanities—writing, performing, visual, and more; 4) Camping—day, overnight, outdoor education, and more; 5) Child Care—infant, toddler, preschool, school-age, and other combinations; 6) Community Development—job training, drug abuse prevention, economic development programs, and more; 7) Family—family nights, support groups, programs, and more; 8) Health and Fitness—group exercise, strength training, walking, yoga, personal fitness, and more; 9) International—educational exchanges and programs, international fairs, and more; 10) Older Adults—health and fitness, social clubs, volunteering, and more; 11) SCUBA—the history of national dive training in the United States began with the development of the YMCA SCUBA Program. Let us teach you to enjoy the underwater world; 12) Sports—for youth and adults in basketball, soccer, baseball/t-ball, and more; 13) Teen Leadership—clubs, adventure programs, Black Achievers, Earth Service Corps, Leader Clubs, Hi-Y, Youth and Government, Model United Nations, middle-school programs, and more.

Young Women's Christian Association of the United States of America The YWCA of the U.S.A. was established in 1858. Today the YWCA has more than 4 million members. The program, historically rooted in the Christian religion, focuses on drawing together women and girls of ". . . diverse experiences and faith, that their lives may be open to new understanding and deeper relationships, and that they may join in the struggle for peace and justice, freedom and dignity for all people" (Carnegie Corp., 1992, p. 151). Today the mission of the YWCA seeks to empower women and eliminate racism. The YWCA operates 300 associations throughout the United States, and local YWCAs are supported by a national association that provides support to each of the units.

The services of a local YWCA, both varied and diverse, depend on the local needs and conditions of various communities. Programs include services for women in crisis, refugee women, single parents, displaced homemakers, homeless women, women in prison, ex-offenders and women coping with substance abuse, as well as others in the general population. The YWCA runs programs for teens directed toward the development of self-reliance, self-esteem, and acquisition of life skills. A strong component works toward supporting programs in the areas of health, physical education, and recreation. Leadership activities promote volunteer training, as well as teen leadership development. Sample programs operated by a midwestern YWCA include a young mother's support group, women in transition, day camp for children, child care, mother's support center, cake decorating, candy making, hiking club, book discussion group, fitness and aquatics, parent/teen communication skill development, teen educational multicultural awareness, and trips and tours.

Catholic Youth Organization The Catholic Youth Organization is the leading Catholic organization concerned with meeting the spiritual, social, and recreational needs of young people in the United States. The CYO, officially established in the early 1950s as a component of the National Council of Catholic Youth, implements its programs on a parish level and relies on the leadership of a local priest as well as volunteers from the parish. Youth are encouraged to become involved in such activities as retreats, sports programs, service programs, religious workshops, and educational classes.

Young Men's and Women's Hebrew Association/Jewish Community Centers According to Kraus (1991) the YMHA and YWHA do not regard themselves as recreation agencies, but rather as community organizations devoted to social service, with a strong Jewish cultural component. The YM-YWHA identifies social work as its major professional discipline. Staff try to create opportunities for participants to meet their physical, social, and emotional needs while stimulating individual growth, leadership, and responsibility.

From a historical prospective, YM-YWHA/Jewish Community Centers created a space where individuals could "exercise your body, exercise your mind, and exercise your value and culture." One YM-YWHA/Jewish Community Center states its focus as follows: Our mission is to be a central force in the Jewish Community, responsive to the needs of its individuals and families, by providing, in a Jewish ambience, quality services that promote the social, cultural, recreational, physical, and intellectual needs of our members and users.

Programs offered by YM-YWHA/Jewish Community Centers offer a broad range of programs focused on health and fitness, community and educational services, and camps. The Jewish Community Center of Louisville, Kentucky, offers a full range of programs and offers its members "38 fitness classes a week, 130 pieces of exercise and fitness equipment, aerobics, Cycle Reebok classes, use of sauna, whirlpool, steam room, fitness track, racquetball courts, tennis courts, indoor swimming pool, bubble pool, Olympic size outdoor family pool, kiddie pool (on a full filter system), basketball, volleyball, and open gym" (see figure 10.11).

The YM-YWHA operate a number of recreation centers and camps primarily concentrated in the northeast portion of the United States.

Religious Organizations

Beyond serving youth, many churches of various denominations and other religious organizations plan, organize, and implement a variety of recreation and leisure services for families, seniors, and other special groups. These programs usually have either one or two broad purposes—to provide activities to promote fellowship with one another and to encourage involvement within the organization. For example, the Church of Jesus Christ of Latter Day Saints has a strong program of organized events for church members of all ages. These activities help church members meet their spiritual, social, cultural, physical, and emotional needs. Activities include such services as competitive sports, scouting, cultural arts, drama, camping, art, hobbies, crafts, music and dance, fitness, home improvement skills, single adult programs, genealogy, and special events.

Recreation activities also provide a means of bringing others into the organization and serve as a means to help others. For example, the Salvation Army is a religious organization committed to promoting a ministry of religious activities combined with social service work, education, training, fellowship, and recreation. The Salvation Army operates most of its center programs in disadvantaged areas and generally targets its services to meet the needs of the disadvantaged population. The Salvation Army serves nearly 38 million people annually. The

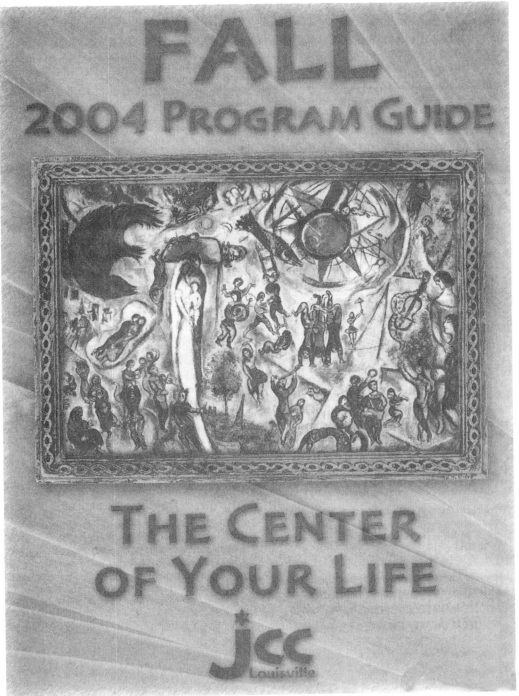

Figure 10.11

Fall 2004
Program Guide.

*Source: Jewish
Community Center,
Louisville,
Kentucky.*

greatest participation occurs in camping programs, boys' and girls' clubs, and community centers. Membership fees for participants are nominal, usually under ten dollars. The Salvation Army programs, while usually driven by local needs, sometimes receive support for individual centers and programs from a national headquarters and four regional offices.

While exact purposes differ, these organizations base the philosophy of service on their religious beliefs. For Christian churches and organizations, this means infusing a strong moral ethic based on the Judeo-Christian credo, as well as merging their specific doctrine and beliefs with their recreation and leisure program offerings. An organization based on Islamic principles would integrate teachings of the Koran and Arabic customs with the activities it offered. For example, Christian organizations may structure many activities and events around Easter or the Christmas holidays, Jewish organizations would organize events and activities around Passover or Purim, and Islamic organizations might emphasize a holiday season such as Ramadan.

Organizations Serving Special Populations

Beyond serving youth, a variety of organizations serve other specific groups. Some groups have been created to meet the needs of enlisted personnel in the U.S. Armed Forces (e.g., USO); some organizations work with people with specific disabilities (e.g., Recreation Center for the Handicapped, Inc.); still others work with youth who are adjudicated as delinquent (e.g., Eckerd Foundation). This section profiles several of these types of organizations.

USO   The United Service Organization, Inc. (USO), formed in 1941, provides a broad range of programs for U.S. Armed Forces and their families throughout the world. The USO is a private nonprofit voluntary organization that is congressionally chartered; it receives no funding from the federal government, but rather is supported by private donations, including contributions from the United Way. At 121 locations throughout the world, the USO provides various types of programs through Family and Community Centers, Fleet Centers, Airport Centers, Intercultural Programs, and Celebrity Entertainment. The USO mission is "to provide morale, welfare, and recreation-type services to uniformed military personnel. The original intent of Congress—and enduring style of USO delivery—is to represent the American people by extending a "touch of home" to their military members. Thus, although some USO programs/services are similar to those provided by other agencies, the hallmark of the USO has been and will continue to be *how,* as much as *what* services are provided" (USO-We Deliver America, 2001).

The USO operates a wide variety of human services, including many involving recreation and leisure. For instance, the USO operates Family and Community Centers in fourteen states, as well as Puerto Rico, the Virgin Islands, and the District of Columbia. In addition, the USO operates similar facilities in eight foreign countries. These centers help individuals adjust to new surroundings and provide information and program services concerning employment opportunities, parenting, nutrition, budgeting, and children's recreation programs.

The USO also operates Fleet Centers serving the United States Naval Fleet worldwide. When the fleet makes a port call, the USO is poised to provide services—maps, directions, currency exchange, language assistance, hotels, travel connections, and family exchange programs. All of these services are available to members of the fleet. Probably the best-known USO activity is the Celebrity Entertainment program—USO shows around the world feature a variety of entertainment, from sports celebrities to musical reviews.

The Janet Pomeroy Center (formerly RCH, Inc., Recreation Center for the Handicapped)   This renowned center was established in 1952 in San Francisco, California as a community-based facility serving individuals of all ages and disabilities. Today, the organization provides therapeutic recreation, locational rehabilitation, child and adult development, and respite care programs for individuals from ages five through senior adults. The center was founded by Janet Pomeroy, a leading pioneer in recreation for disabled persons. Today, the program serves over 2,000 children, adults, and seniors with developmental disabilities and acquired brain injuries each week.

The Janet Pomeroy Center facilities include a therapeutic swimming pool, gymnasium, computer lab, kitchen, stage, program rooms, multi-purpose area, playground, community garden with greenhouse, and a day camp. Recreation programs include: children and teen services, adult recreation, senior recreation, brainstorm program, Marin Center, Theatre Unlimited, adaptive computer lab, and respite care services. Vocational rehabilitation services include Able Gardners, adult development, assessment and training, integrated work services, personal and social adjustment service, placement services, point of transition, SF TBI Net, TBA Case Services, vocational and leisure services, and vocational services. The center currently employs over 200 full-time and part-time individuals providing services. Funding for the Janet Pomeroy Center comes from state and federal agencies, as well as grants, private contributions, and income generated from special events.

Eckert Family Foundation & Eckert Youth Alternatives The Eckert Family Foundation is focused on supporting programs and organizations whose work reflects principles of positive youth development. More specifically, the mission of the foundation is to award grants to nonprofit organizations that provide and support innovative educational, preventive, and therapeutic and rehabilitative programs for youth and their families. Although the Eckert Family Foundation was established in 1998, it traces the philanthropic commitment to the efforts of Jack and Ruth Eckert when they founded Eckert Youth Alternatives. At that time, they established a therapeutic wilderness camp for troubled youth in Florida.

The program provides year-round residential therapy in a nurturing wilderness environment. Groups of ten children and two counselors work together to construct their own shelters, cut their own wood for campfires and cooking, repair their equipment, arrange their own recreation and meal plans, and do all the things necessary to live in the outdoors. Participants stay in the program for nine to twelve months and receive extensive aftercare upon release from the program. Research shows that such opportunities can create a sense of accomplishment, self-worth, and cooperation within the participant.

Many nonprofit organizations provide programs and services for the increasing number of youth involved in some form of socially deviant behavior. Many of these programs have developed outdoor components designed to either prescribe treatment for, reduce, or prevent the socially deviant behavior of youth who are labeled as juvenile delinquents. This often means addressing some of the variables that seem to contribute to juvenile delinquency, such as low self-esteem, emotional problems, inadequate socialization, lack of moral judgment, and consistent failure in school (Laurence and Stuart, 1990). Examples of these types of programs may be found throughout the United States and include long-term residential therapeutic camping, stress/adventure experiences based on a modified Outward Bound model, and school-based programs following the Project Adventure model.

Today, Eckert Youth Alternatives serves approximately 8,000 children and youth, operating services in Florida, Georgia, North Carolina, Tennessee, Rhode Island, Vermont, and New Hampshire. Although no longer an entity tied to the Eckert Foundation, Eckert Youth Alternatives provide services for boys and girls ages eight to eighteen who are at risk or exhibit emotional or behavioral problems at home, at school, or in the community. Eckert Youth Alternatives has been viewed as a pioneer in therapeutic treatment in outdoor settings. In addition,

Treats

Creating magic moments for children is becoming a worldwide endeavor as nonprofit organizations around the world try to brighten a child's day through recreation and play. For example, TREATS, a nonprofit organization based in Hong Kong, strives to integrate children of different backgrounds and abilities in a recreation setting to help promote better understanding of one another and to provide them with enjoyable ways of learning life skills. TREATS' emphasis on inclusion and integration as well as its experience in partnerships and collaboration with other organizations are fine examples of the type of programs that can evolve in response to knowing and understanding the needs of the local community.

Hong Kong, a city of 6.2 million people, can be a scary place to grow up, especially for children from disadvantaged backgrounds. TREATS was established in 1979 when very little was being done to promote recreation and play in Hong Kong and play facilities were scarce. Initially the aim of TREATS was simply to give children a fun and happy day—a treat—a day away from their noisy, crowded urban environment. Trips were organized for children living in institutions, special schools, and crowded settlement estates to overnight camps in the countryside. There were also day trips to the beach and other special locations and events.

In the late 1980s, with greater awareness of the importance of recreation in the overall well-being of children and the development of recreation facilities throughout Hong Kong, TREATS began its own recreation program.

The aim of TREATS is still to provide fun and enjoyment by providing well-organized, well-executed, and caring youth development services, but additional goals have been added to include an emphasis on integrating children with and without disabilities.

TREATS works closely with Hong Kong's Education Department, Social Welfare Department, Youth and Community Centers, and other nongovernmental organizations to reach a wide variety of children including children with special needs, children living in institutions and small group homes, children who have recently immigrated from China, children on public assistance, children with only one parent, and children living in crowded public temporary housing. Within TREATS programs, children from two or more of these diverse targeted groups are brought together in a camp setting and through games and activities encouraged to communicate, understand, respect, and trust one another. In 1995, TREATS programs reached a total of 4,498 children in both day and resident camps as well as cooperative games sessions at schools throughout Hong Kong.

Eckert Youth alternatives provide specialized residential treatment and community-based treatment for juvenile offenders and early intervention curriculum for grade schools. Outdoor therapeutic treatment programs include residential treatment, developing social skills, managing behavior, experiential education, transitional services, and program locations. Juvenile Justice Programs include day treatment programs, non-secure residential treatment, and secure residential treatment. ReEntry Programs include community-based transition services. Early Intervention and Prevention Programs include school-based programs. Today, Eckert Youth Alternatives employs over 1,400 individuals.

Relief Organizations

Recreation services form a vital part of many relief organizations. In relief organizations such as the Red Cross, programs are offered to make many recreation activities safer, and, because of the voluntary nature of the Red Cross, many volunteers donate their leisure time to provide these programs.

American Red Cross   The mission of the American Red Cross is to "improve the quality of human life; enhance self-reliance and concern for others; and to help people avoid, prepare for, and cope with emergencies. Its services are governed and directed by volunteers consistent with a congressional charter" (Carnegie Corp., 1992, p. 141). The American Red Cross values impartiality, volunteerism, humanitarianism, service excellence, and internationalism.

American Red Cross organizations are community-based voluntary organizations that are governed, supported, and principally staffed by volunteers who work in conjunction with paid staff members. The American Red Cross helps to provide and support the delivery of recreation and leisure services from a number of different perspectives; for example, the Red Cross provides training courses in areas such as boating and water safety. Additionally, the Red Cross provides recreation events to veterans, members of the Armed Forces, and their families. Furthermore, the American Red Cross operates a large youth services program.

Perhaps the most well-known program operated by the American Red Cross has been the Aquatics Safety program. This program, designed to provide individuals with a full range of courses, helps increase aquatic fun while promoting safety. The Red Cross operates standardized courses for individuals of all ages and swimming abilities. Many public parks and recreation agencies, as well as other private voluntary organizations, use the American Red Cross system to provide aquatic programs.

The American Red Cross also operates Boating Safety courses. These courses aim to teach individuals the fundamentals of safe canoeing, kayaking, rowing, sailing, and use of outboard motor boats. The American Red Cross courses provide individuals with lectures, discussions, and hands-on experiences directed toward improving competence in the water.

Another program operated by the American Red Cross is the Leadership Development/Volunteerism program. The American Red Cross offers many direct-service opportunities for individuals to use their leisure time to volunteer. As indicated in the American Red Cross publication *Youth, a Timeless Resource,* ". . . there is no better way to help young people learn about the value of caring for others than by introducing them to volunteerism through Red Cross service projects." Other Red Cross programs aimed at helping youth gain leadership opportunities include the International Understanding program and Leadership Development program.

Social Service Organizations

Social service organizations have traditionally viewed recreation as a social instrument. Historically the provision of wholesome recreation served as a central part of the settlement-house movement, discussed in chapter 3, established to ease the transition to urban living for thousands of persons immigrating to the cities of America during the Industrial Revolution. Metropolitan Family Services, a local social service organization, has incorporated recreation into its overall program.

Metropolitan Family Services   Metropolitan Family Services offers a variety of social services throughout the metropolitan Chicago area, including a camping program at Camp Algonquin. This year-round camping program enables campers to acquire and/or strengthen skills that will help them to cope more effectively with their life situations in the city. In addition, the program provides campers with a sustained positive experience with people of diverse ethnic groups and generations whereby stereotypes and prejudices can be diminished. The camp setting removes many of the constraints of the city and provides a place where campers of all ages can interact, test new behaviors, and plan future directions. To assist in this process the camp program includes traditional camp activities as well as professional social work interventions such as family assessments, group discussions, and crisis counseling.

Conservation/Preservation Organizations

Many nonprofit special-interest organizations seek to educate the public and influence governmental policy in the areas of conservation and outdoor recreation. In the areas of conservation, organizations range from radical organizations like the Sea Shepherd Conservation Society to conservative organizations like the Nature Conservancy. The Sea Shepherds advocate sabotage to prevent the killing of dolphins in the tuna industry and to protect whales from the whaling industry. On the other hand, the Nature Conservancy uses a businesslike approach to purchase threatened areas. The Nature Conservancy is a nonprofit organization that was founded in 1951. Its mission is to "preserve the plants, animals, and natural communities that represent the diversity of life on Earth by protecting the lands and waters they need to survive" (The Nature Conservancy, 2001).

The Appalachian Mountain Club and the National Rifle Association are examples of nonprofit special-interest organizations involved in the promotion of various aspects of outdoor recreation. For example, the Appalachian Mountain Club advocates conservation efforts throughout the northeast and maintains trails and a network of huts and shelters, publishes guides, and promotes programs for developing outdoor leaders. The National Rifle Association carries on extensive lobbying efforts involving gun control and also sponsors firearm instruction, safety training, and shooting tournaments. Many of these conservation organizations combine conservation and outdoor recreation initiatives. For example, the Sierra Club is a well-respected conservation organization as well as being the nation's largest skiing and hiking club, and the Yellowstone Association supports the continued preservation and interpretation of Yellowstone National Park.

Sierra Club   The Sierra Club, founded in 1892, resulted from the passion of a small group of people for the mountains of California. Its first president was the famous preservationist, John Muir. The purpose of the club is to explore, enjoy, and protect the wild places of the earth; to practice and promote the responsible use of the earth's ecosystems and resources; to educate and enlist humanity to protect and restore the quality of the natural and human environment; and to use all lawful means to carry out these objectives.

In the 1992 centennial celebration, *Sierra Magazine* noted,

> The Sierra Club's first century comes to a close with our view having widened from the mountains of California to all seven continents, and on into the highest reaches of the atmosphere. Our second century may well see that gaze embrace still broader horizons, as all that we learn about the environment—and humanity's niche within it—provides further proof of John Muir's maxim: 'When we try to pick out anything by itself, we find it hitched to everything else in the universe.' (p. 73)

The Yellowstone Association   The Yellowstone Association operates in partnership with the National Parks Service. Its primary mission is to promote and foster the public's understanding, appreciation, and enjoyment of Yellowstone National Park and its surrounding ecosystem by funding and providing education products and services. Founded as a nonprofit organization in 1933, the Association provides a variety of educational, scientific, and historical programs. The Yellowstone Association Institute operates five different types of educational programs: lodging and learning, wildlife ed-ventures, custom courses, field seminars, and backcountry courses. Members of the organization receive discounts on these classes and field

Engineering Satisfaction Among Constituents

In the nonprofit sector, marketing is the engineering of *satisfaction* among a variety of groups including users of an organization's services, funders, trustees, regulators, and others who can influence the success of the organization—such as the media and even the general public.

One of the most important aspects of marketing is called *market segmentation.* In the nonprofit sector, market segmentation refers to the various constituencies whose satisfaction must be addressed. In most cases different strategies need to be developed for each group, but many nonprofit organizations do not correctly identify all their constituencies.

This was certainly the case with Abbott Academy, which had stated publicly and quite explicitly that the single constituency to which it needed to address itself was its students. The . . .

catalogue of the school began with the following words: "Abbott Academy was founded with the express intent of providing an outstanding education to young people. It is to our students, therefore, that we devote our attention, our resources, and our energies."

From a marketing point of view, students were not the only constituency whose needs had to be addressed if Abbott was to be successful. Other groups included parents, college representatives, potential applicants/prospective students, minority representatives, faculty, trustees, and other donors. . . . Each of these constituent groups could have been a vital link in helping Abbott Academy solve its problems, achieve its goals, and remain fiscally healthy. Yet, by focusing on only one group—its students—the school's leadership paid a very high price.

Source: Thomas Wolf, *Managing a Nonprofit Organization,* 1990, Fireside, NY.

courses as well as items including books, clothing, and other products sold in visitor centers, by mail or over the Internet. In addition, the Association published a quarterly newsletter entitled *Yellowstone Discovery* and *Yellowstone Parks* quarterly newspaper.

Service Clubs

Service clubs, often made up of various professional and business organizations within a community, have a twofold involvement in recreation and leisure. First, many of these organizations provide recreation, fellowship, and service opportunities for their members. Second, many of these organizations, such as the Kiwanis, Lions, or Junior League, sponsor recreation programs for other groups within the community. They promote diverse programs that include sports programs, programs for disadvantaged children and youth, programs for the arts and other cultural activities, and camping for children with disabilities.

Challenges for the Future

Nonprofit organizations face many challenges today. Like other leisure service organizations, nonprofit agencies face an increased demand for the services they provide while funding dollars become more difficult to obtain. Nonprofit organizations serving youth are being challenged to expand their services to younger children and promote outreach programs while at the same time they must deal with shrinking resources and increasing incidences of litigation. Meanwhile, the changing needs of youth require program expansion, including providing more job training, promoting diversity and tolerance of differences in terms of religion, ethnicity, physical abilities, and sexual orientation, and taking a more holistic approach to youth development.

Other issues affecting nonprofit organizations include effective fundraising; attracting, training, and managing volunteer workers; creating staff development opportunities for paid staff; and developing partnerships with both the public and private sector.

Summary

Nonprofit organizations form an important part of the leisure service industry. They focus their services on a variety of constituents of all ages and of both sexes. Some nonprofit organizations have a commitment to a broad segment of the population, whereas others serve specific groups and promote a specific set of goals, such as the character development of youth. Estimates suggest that the nonprofit sector spends nearly $15 billion a year. Among youth serving organizations, some 400 agencies deliver leisure services to youth either exclusively or as a part of their mission.

In general, nonprofit organizations can be subdivided into three major categories—public benefit, mutual benefit, and private benefit. Public benefit nonprofit organizations have a broad focus and serve the general welfare of the public. Nonprofit organizations that focus on the mutual benefit of their membership are organized to bring together individuals and/or groups with complementary or mutual needs and interests. A private benefit nonprofit organization usually has a more exclusive membership, focuses on an activity, or provides the opportunity for individuals to interact in some type of social environment, such as a swim, tennis, or country club.

Nonprofit organizations have four primary elements. First, a nonprofit organization must operate with a degree of altruism. In other words, nonprofits are not in the business of making money. Second, most nonprofit organizations have at their core a public-service mission—they promote the general public welfare in some way. In addition, nonprofit organizations fall under special tax-exempt considerations for organizational purposes; they do not pay taxes on their assets. The last element of nonprofit organizations relates to the organization of their governance structure. Most have boards of directors that serve to promote the altruistic values reflected in the mission statement.

Discussion Questions

1. What is a nonprofit organization? What are its distinguishing characteristics?
2. Compare and contrast expenditures for nonprofit, government, and commercial leisure service organizations.
3. Identify three basic types of nonprofit organizations.
4. What are some of the ways of financing nonprofit organizations?
5. Locate three nonprofit organizations in your community; identify and detail their fundraising programs. Do they sell a product? Seek donations? Sponsorships? Gifts?
6. Profile a local professional working in a nonprofit organization. How does this individual's characteristics equate with the general information presented in this section of the book?
7. Locate a nonprofit organization in your community and detail its organization, budget, programs, and methods of publicity.
8. The Carnegie Corporation states that youth serving organizations pursue not only recreational ends, but also consider the principles of education and youth development. How might this influence the work of a youth serving organization?
9. Churches, as nonprofit organizations, provide recreation services as a secondary component to their spiritual endeavors. Locate two different churches in your community and compare and contrast their recreation-related program services.
10. Develop a charter for a new nonprofit youth service organization. What would be its mission? Scope of programs? Methods of funding?

References

Austin, J. E. 2000. *The Collaboration Challenge.* San Francisco: Jossey-Bass.

BSA at a Glance. 2004. Retrieved June 21, 2004, from www.scouting.org/factsheets/02-501.html.

Boys & Girls Clubs of America. *Lessons of Hope.* 2003 Annual Report.

Carnegie Corporation of New York. 1992. *A Matter of Time: Risk and Opportunity in the Non-School Hours.* Woodlawn, MD: Wolk Press.

Drucker, P. F. 1999. *Management Challenges for the 21st Century.* New York: HarperBusiness.

Girls, Inc. Retrieved June 21, 2004, from www.girlsinc.org.

Hodgkinson, V. A., and M. S. Weitzman. 1996. *Nonprofit Almanac 1996–1997.* San Francisco: Jossey-Bass.

Kennedy, D., R. Smith, and D. Austin. 1991. 3d ed. *Special Recreation.* Dubuque, IA: Wm. C. Brown.

Kraus, R. 1991. *Creative Management in Recreation Parks and Leisure.* St. Louis: Mosby.

Laurence, M., and T. Stuart. 1990. The use of adventure in reducing and preventing socially deviant youth behavior. Edited by J. Miles and S. Priest, in *Adventure Education.* State College, PA: Venture.

Mason, D. E. 1996. *Leading and Managing the Expressive Dimension.* San Francisco: Jossey-Bass.

The Nature Conservancy: Saving the Last Great Places. 2001. http://nature.org/aboutus/

Oleck, H. L. 1988. *Non-Profit Corporations, Organizations and Associations.* New York: Prentice Hall.

Steckel, R., and J. Lehman. 1997. *In Search of America's Best Nonprofits.* San Francisco: Jossey-Bass.

Staff. 1993. *1993 Earth Journal.* Boulder, CO: Buzzworm Books.

U.S. Bureau of the Census. 1997. *Statistical Abstract of the United States, 1997.* 117th ed. Washington, DC: U.S. Government Printing Office.

USO-We Deliver America. 2001. www.uso.org/about_uso.htm

Wolf, T. 1990. *Managing a Nonprofit Organization.* New York: Fireside.

C H A P T E R

Delivery of Leisure Services: Commercial

Commercial recreation venues provide many opportunities for leisure. Waterslides and water parks are among the most popular commercial leisure facilities.

Introduction

By far, the majority of organizations delivering leisure services in the United States today are commercial ventures. In fact, nearly 90 percent of all expenditures made for leisure goods and services takes place in the commercial sector (U.S. Bureau of the Census, 1999). Business opportunities in the area of commercial leisure services range from managing retail outlets that distribute leisure apparel to working in large theme or amusement parks. This chapter discusses the delivery of commercial leisure services.

Working in the commercial leisure business sector presents unique challenges and opportunities. The ability to develop and successfully manage a commercial leisure service venture requires knowledge of marketing, management, and finance, as well as a keen understanding of the leisure field. Individuals who are involved in the creation and delivery of commercial leisure services often seek the opportunity to operate in an independent fashion. Professionals in this area care about service and quality, as well as producing a profit for their effort.

This chapter reviews a number of specific topics. First, it defines and describes the distinguishing characteristics of commercial leisure service organizations, followed by a discussion of the three major types of business ownership and the major categories of commercial leisure services. The next section includes a discussion of professional roles and responsibilities in commercial leisure service businesses. The chapter concludes with a review of the current status of commercial leisure services as well as prospects for the future.

Characteristics of Commercial Leisure Services

In spite of the great growth of government and private nonprofit leisure services in the last century, private enterprise in the United States delivers by far the largest segment of leisure ser-

Figure 11.1

Comparison of the orientations of commercial and nonprofit leisure service organizations.

vices. The private sector differs from both public and nonprofit organizations in many ways. This section discusses these differences in terms of goals, fiscal base, personnel, orientation to the customer, and other distinguishing characteristics.

Goals and Functions

The primary objective of a commercial leisure service organization is both simple and complex. Most commercial leisure service organizations have, as their primary goal, earning a profit. To earn a profit, however, a commercial leisure service organization must meet the needs of its customers. Figure 11.1 shows the relationship of customer service, profit, and outstanding satisfaction, comparing commercial leisure services with public or nonprofit leisure service organizations.

Successful commercial leisure organizations attempt to build a strong bond between themselves and their customers. This ensures a sense of loyalty on the part of customers. For a commercial leisure service organization to be successful and profitable, it must not only initially attract and serve target customers, but also retain them. So, while the goal of commercial leisure service organizations is to make a profit, serving the needs of customers ensures long-term profitability.

Who benefits from the efforts of a commercial leisure service business? At first glance, it appears that the profit earned by a business primarily benefits its owner(s) by increasing wealth. Profits also assist in the growth and expansion of a business, however, and pay dividends to stockholders. Most commercial leisure service businesses reinvest a portion of their profits in improving their quality of services, thus serving to benefit their customers.

Resource Base

Unlike the public sector that relies heavily on tax dollars to support its operations, commercial leisure service organizations must generate their own funds. When establishing a new commercial leisure service organization, two basic approaches can be taken to acquire the funds (capital) necessary to start the business—*equity* and *debt financing*. Equity financing involves the investment of an individual's own financial resources. Debt financing involves borrowing money from another source, which must eventually be repaid, in order to start a business venture.

According to Bullaro and Edginton (1986), six basic sources of capital can be used in establishing a new commercial leisure service business. These include personal savings; commercial bank loans; trade credit (credit on goods purchased for the business); equipment loans and leases; and funds from friends, relatives, and local investors (often known as venture capitalists). According to Crossley and Jamieson (1993), typical start-up costs for commercial leisure enterprises involve such things as legal and professional consultants, insurance, incorporation expenses, tax deposits, licenses and permits, cost of obtaining loans, land and buildings, equipment, vehicles, machinery, remodeling and decorations, fixtures, displays, signs, salaries, utilities, staff development, supplies and equipment, inventory, maintenance expenses, advertising, and reserves.

The amount of capital necessary to operate a leisure service business varies according to the size, scope, and type of services provided. A key to obtaining capital and building and maintaining a successful business is the development of a *profit plan.* This detailed report about a proposed business venture shows potential sales (revenues) and costs (expenditures). A variety of factors must be taken into consideration when developing such a plan, including types of services to be offered, changing market conditions, customer preferences, the influence of governmental regulations, the cost of labor, estimates of profitability, and other factors (Bullaro and Edginton, 1986; Crossley and Jamieson, 1993).

Not only does the commercial leisure service organization need to generate start-up capital, but it also must generate sufficient income to maintain itself, through the sale of its products or services. In other words, it must carefully calculate the cost and worth of its service or product and affix a price. This price must reflect the cost of production, take into consideration the willingness of people to consume the product or service, and the need to produce a profit.

Characteristics of Professionals/Owners

Although it is difficult to distinguish between professionals working in public, private nonprofit, and commercial leisure service organizations, some unique characteristics generally apply to entrepreneurs in the commercial leisure service sector. In general, these individuals, especially in small businesses, perceive themselves as being goal-oriented, self-reliant, and self-motivated (Pinchot, 1985). They like moderate risk and see themselves as the creator of needs. They also view themselves as being action-oriented and see mistakes and failures as learning experiences. Crossley and Jamieson (1993) write that entrepreneurs ". . . come from a family value system that emphasizes an independent work life, leadership and a strong educational background" (p. 22). Furthermore, they note that goals of accomplishment, self-respect, freedom, family security, honesty, independence, competence, and ambition, as well as the desire to serve others, are a part of the makeup of entrepreneurs in the leisure services area.

Orientation to Customers

Discussing the role of commercial leisure service organizations and their relationship to consumers, Bullaro and Edginton (1986) write,

> Organizations that are wedded to their consumers are, by and large, more successful than those organizations that are not. It is therefore essential that primary importance be placed on serving people. This involves placing consumers first, ensuring that they are greeted with respect, dignity, courtesy, thoughtfulness, and ensuring that their welfare is utmost in the mind of the commercial leisure service professional. . . . This is accomplished by having a philosophy of service to people.
>
> What is the relationship between a commercial leisure service organization's philosophy regarding service to people and its profitability? Basically, people must perceive that a product or service has value to them . . . or they will not purchase it. In other words, they must feel that they will derive some benefit from the service. If the commercial leisure service organization is able to cultivate this type of feeling in its consumers, then with good management profitability will follow. (p. 5)

THE FAR SIDE By GARY LARSON

Chronicle Features, 1983 Larson

Obviously, it is in the best interest of the commercial leisure service organization to place customer needs first. Although all types of leisure service organizations now implement some type of marketing information, commercial organizations must use marketing strategies to meet customer needs if they are to survive in a competitive environment.

Marketing concepts suggest organizations must first determine their target markets—discrete clusters of homogeneous customers. In other words, a group of individuals who have a common set of characteristics or needs that can be satisfied by the provision of a particular product or service comprise a target market. For example, teens aged fourteen to nineteen whose parents earn more than $100,000 a year comprise a target market for expensive stereo equipment, trendy clothing, or DVDs. Figure 11.2 presents an example of a vendor not accurately determining his target market—young children like ice cream, not liver and onions.

In using a marketing strategy, commercial leisure service organizations focus on creating, communicating, and delivering a product that satisfies customer needs in a way that also results in profitability for the organization. Numerous psychological and sociological factors influence the needs of customers. Psychological factors include an individual's perceptions of the quality of a specific program, the motivation to participate in certain recreational activities, and the needs and attitudes of specific groups. Sociological influences include cultural factors, social class, and cohort groups. For example, a person's choice of recreation could result from the likes and dislikes of his or her social group.

Figure 11.3

Types of business ownership.

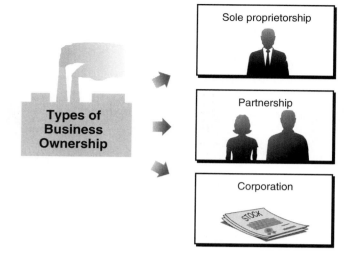

Types of Business Ownership

Each of the three basic forms of business ownership—sole proprietorship, partnership, and corporation—has certain merits. Any individual who decides to establish a leisure service business must first consider the relative advantages and disadvantages of each and determine which form best meets the business needs. In addition, as a business grows, the type of business ownership might evolve and change. This portion of the chapter deals with the characteristics of each of these three forms of legal organization (see figure 11.3).

Sole Proprietorship

A sole proprietorship—the simplest and least costly form of business ownership to establish—occurs when one person owns a business and is legally responsible for its debts and legal obligations (Crossley and Jamieson, 1993). In other words, the sole proprietor controls all of the assets of the organization and also is responsible for any of its liabilities. A sole proprietorship is the most common form of business ownership in the United States with 72 percent organized as such (U.S. Bureau of Census, 2003). Figure 11.4 shows the relationship of the percentages of types of business organization in the service industries.

Sole proprietorships provide individuals with a great deal of flexibility and latitude in the management of a business. One person makes the decisions about the types of products or services to be provided and the way in which these are marketed. The sole proprietor takes all of the risks associated with the business venture and also has, as a major advantage, the opportunity to reap the profits that are derived from it. On the other hand, the sole proprietor also faces the risk of personal loss, extending to loss of personal assets, should the business fail.

Advantages of this form of ownership of a commercial leisure service organization include high personal incentive, freedom to act, less cost to establish, private financial statements, opportunity for tax savings, and the ability to be dissolved quickly. Some of the disadvantages of a sole proprietorship result from limited capital, limited talent (due to just one owner), unlimited liability, lack of continuity (if the owner dies or sells the business), and possible heavier taxation (Bullaro and Edginton, 1986).

Figure 11.4

Forms of legal organization in service-type industries.

Source: Data from the Statistical Abstract of the United States, Washington, DC 2003 (123 ed.).

Corporation
20%

Partnership
8%

Sole proprietorship
72%

Partnerships

A business partnership results when two or more people voluntarily decide to pool their funds and abilities and to go into business for profit (Crossley and Jamieson, 1993). The reasons for forming partnerships vary. A partnership allows two or more individuals to couple their skills, talents, and abilities to more effectively manage a commercial enterprise. It also offers a way to provide more capital to establish and maintain the venture. Partnerships are not as widespread as sole proprietorships; as depicted in figure 11.4, only 8 percent of all business use this method of organization.

What makes a partnership successful? A successful partnership brings together individuals with complementary knowledge and skills that provide value to the enterprise. In the case of a commercial leisure service organization, one person might have a great deal of technical knowledge, while the other partner brings good managerial skills. For example, in a river rafting business one partner might have the technical skills necessary to plan and implement a series of adventure-oriented rafting trips. This person's knowledge of the outdoor environment would be essential to the success of the business. On the other hand, another partner might possess skills in the area of marketing, management, and accounting. This person would collect and receive monies, promote the program, and recruit staff. The combination of the talents of these two individuals would contribute to the success of the business as a whole. Without either of the partners, the business might be in jeopardy.

As is the case with sole proprietorships, partnerships also have advantages and disadvantages. Some of the advantages of a partnership are the possibility of greater capital, improved credit standing, more talent, and few legal restrictions. Some of the disadvantages of a partnership include the potential for management conflict, unlimited liability, constraints on capital, difficulty in withdrawing financial investment, and problems with the continuity of the business (Bullaro and Edginton, 1986).

Corporations

A corporation may be thought of as a separate legal entity. It is, as Chief Justice John Marshall of the United States Supreme Court defined it in 1819, an "artificial being, invisible, intangible, and resting only in the contemplation of the law." This means that a corporation has rights and privileges under the law, similar to those of an individual. A corporation can transact business, buy and sell property, sue and be sued, and engage in other activities as defined in its bylaws. The corporation itself is responsible for the liabilities that are incurred as a result of its actions, whereas in sole proprietorships and partnerships, the owners are legally responsible for the obligations incurred by the business.

Corporations are owned by stockholders—those individuals who own shares of stock in them. Individuals who own the majority of the shares of a corporation's stock control its direction. Stockholders, rewarded when the business succeeds, earn dividends on their shares based on the profits earned by the corporation. In the United States today, corporations are generally more profitable than sole proprietorships or partnerships. Twenty percent of businesses are organized as corporations. However, corporations generate by far a greater percentage of the total receipts of service-type industries in the United States (over 70 percent).

Organizing as a corporation has a number of advantages and disadvantages. The principal advantage of a corporation is the limited liability of its owners (stockholders). In other words, individual investors are only liable for the amount that they have invested in the organization. Some of the other advantages of corporations include their ease in raising capital (through selling shares of stock), the ability to transfer ownership easily (also through the selling of shares of stock), and the fact that corporations enable continuity of operations.

The disadvantages of corporations as a form of organization include the higher costs involved in establishing them (higher than either a sole proprietorship or a partnership), possible double taxation of shareholders, and the fact that corporations must disclose information concerning their financial affairs.

A form of organizing as a corporation, known as the *S Corporation,* presents the stockholder with limited liability and taxes the profits of the corporation as if it were a partnership. This form of organization has a number of legal advantages. As Crossley and Jamieson (1993) note, "This form is very popular among small businesses where the owners desire the legal protection of the corporation but the flexibility and tax treatment of a partnership" (p. 79).

One leisure service organization organized as a corporation is Magic Theater Video. This commercial leisure service business was developed as a result of the expansion of home entertainment and was first conceptualized as a graduate class project. One of the first questions the initiators of this business, Marsha and Tom Johnson, asked, "was what form of legal organization would be most appropriate?" Because they used their personal savings as their primary source of capital, they decided to establish the business as a corporation. This enabled them to limit their personal liability for any losses that the business might incur. It also enabled them to receive capital from investors (two other stockholders) and certain tax benefits.

According to Marsha Johnson, the couple's motivation to develop Magic Theater Video was to become involved in a perceived rapid-growth industry, to control their own destiny (be their own boss), and to enjoy the excitement of making and acting on decisions in a rapidly changing marketplace. In its first two years of business, Magic Theater Video doubled its inventory and quadrupled its sales.

Types of Commercial Leisure Services

With so many commercial leisure services, it becomes difficult to classify all of them. Crossley and Jamieson (1993) propose a classification system that includes the following commercial leisure services: travel/transportation industry, hospitality industry, local commercial recreation industry, and facilitators. Chubb and Chubb (1981) list the following businesses as examples of commercial recreation services: shopping facilities; food and drink services; participatory facilities; amusement parks; museums, gardens, and parks; shows, trips, and tours; stadiums and racetracks; camps, hotels, and resorts; and farms and estates. Kelly (1996) suggests that commercial leisure services may be categorized to include travel, sports, popular culture, the arts, and others. Types of commercial leisure resources identified by Kelly (1996) include destination attractions, travel support, community activity centers, outdoor sports provisions, spectator sports, skill acquisition, outdoor resource sites, mechanized activities, equipment and service retailers, popular culture, high culture, gambling, food and drink provisions, and equipment manufacturing.

The Play Station located in Cedar Rapids, Iowa, provides a playground environment where children can have fun while developing mental, physical, and social skills. This is done with accompanying adults. Figure 11.5 is a flyer outlining group trip opportunities to Play Station Family Fun Center. Still another example of this type of enterprise is the Playfair Discovery Center located in Duluth, Minnesota. Promoting family activities, this operation provides opportunities to explore the similarities and differences between Americans and families who dwell in various countries including Japan, Russia, Canada, and Sweden. Programs include art projects, role playing, cooperative games, storytelling, and live performances.

Figure 11.5

Play Station Family Fun Center flyer.

Play Station Information

We welcome you to The Play Station family fun center!

We offer a fun and imaginative 3 level play center specially designed for kids 12 and under. It's a safe place where children and adults can spend quality time together playing, pretending, challenging, and giggling.

The Play Station's purpose is to build physical fitness, enhance imagination and boost self-confidence in a stimulating and fun-filled environment.

Kids will increase their physical fitness and challenge their imagination as they climb, crawl, bounce, and slide through our colorful indoor play land with over 12,000 square feet of excitement! The fun will double when Mom and Dad play along!

The Play Station is open for fun 7 days a week, 360 days of the year. Stop in:
Monday - Thursday 10am - 8pm
Friday - Saturday 10am - 9pm
Sunday 11am - 6pm

ADMISSION RATES:
General Admission...............$5.50 + tax
Children 12 - 36 mths. ....$4.50 + tax
Children under 1 yr..............FREE
Parents/Adults.....................FREE
Perpetual Player Card..........$44.00 + tax
(10 Admissions for price of 8,good for one year)

*Monday - Friday 10am - 4pm

PLAY STATION GIFT CERTIFICATES MAKE GREAT GIFTS!...........Play Station gift certificates are available all year long at our front desk -- good for one free admission.

We are located at 200 Collins Rd. NE; behind Lindale Mall, west of K-Mart. Call us at 373-1111. All play participants must wear socks!

Best Birthday Parties

Our birthday parties are led by your very own Personal Party Coach who will make your child feel extra special on their big day! Party time includes fun and games in our huge indoor playground and game depot, plus cake and refreshments in a private partyroom. Maximum fun for kids, minimum fuss for parents! We take care of the entertainment, party supplies, tokens, favors, and clean-up!

LOCK - INS

Bring the whole gang for a Play Station overnight! The ultimate in slumber party fun, play from 10pm - 7am! Your group of 40 or more can play till the cows come home for just $14.95 per child. Price includes overnight admission, free pop all night donut and milk in the morning, organized games. Reservations, deposit and chaperones required.
Call for more info!

SPECIAL GROUP RATES

Our field trips make the perfect outing for your class, troop, team, or group. With reservations for your group of 10 or more you can share the fun with special discounted rates. Call for more information! 373-1111

FUNraisers

We offer easy FUNraisers for non-profit organizations with no hassel, tons of fun and great success! The Play Station will sponsor your school or charitable group for a fun-filled weekday evening and donate 25% of the admissions for your cause. Call for more information! 373-1111

FACILITY RENTALS

Searching for a unique activity for your company or large group party? The Play Station can be yours alone for a private party. Just $375 gets your group of 100 guests unlimited soda and 2 hours of fun. $3.00 per additional guest, Pizza buffet available, extended parties and special catering or entertainment options negotiated.

Figure 11.6

Seven types of
commercial
leisure service
businesses.

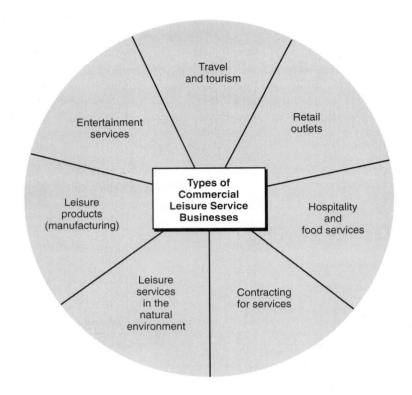

This section of the book presents major categories or types of commercial leisure services, including travel and tourism, hospitality and food services, manufacture of leisure products, entertainment services, contracting for services, retail outlets, and commercial leisure services in the natural environment. Figure 11.6 graphically represents the categories of commercial leisure services presented in this book.

Travel and Tourism

Tourism ranks as one of the most vital industries in the United States today. Between 1990 and 2001, the number of foreign visitors admitted for pleasure trips to the United States increased from 39.3 million to 44.8 million (U.S. Bureau of Census, 2003). The number of visitors in 2000 was 50.9 million, and obviously there was a reduction due to the terrorist attacks of September 11, 2001. Likewise, the number of individuals traveling from the United States abroad also has increased. In 1990, 44.6 million individuals traveled abroad, compared with 57.9 million in 2001 (U.S. Bureau of Census, 2003). Again, the number of U.S. travelers to foreign countries was 60.8 million in 2000; the reduction was most likely due to the events mentioned previously. The Travel Industry Association of America reports that the number of pleasure trips to places of fifty miles or more from an individual's home increased from 301.2 million in 1985 to 331.9 in 2002 (U.S. Bureau of Census, 2003).

The statistics on travel and tourism activities in the United States are staggering. Bullaro and Edginton (1986) report that travel ranks as the second-largest retail industry in the United States and the second-largest private employer. They further note that the highly diversified

Disney World Tops Family Destinations

According to *Family Fun Magazine,* Walt Disney World in Orlando, Fla., and Yosemite National Park in California are the top two destinations in the magazine's readers' poll.

This marks the second year in a row the Disney theme park topped the list. Its California cousin, Disneyland in Anaheim, placed fifth.

Outdoor adventures also are crowd pleasers. In addition to Yosemite, Yellowstone National Park in Wyoming, Montana, and Idaho; the Great Smoky Mountains National Park in Tennessee and North Carolina; and Acadia National Park in Maine all ranked in the top twelve.

Rounding out the list are Washington, D.C.; the San Diego Zoo; Monterey Bay Aquarium in Monterey, Calif.; SeaWorld Orlando in Orlando, Fla., the Statue of Liberty in New York City; and New York's Museum of National History.

Source: Disney World tops family destinations. *The Des Moines Register.* March 19, 2002, Page 6B.

travel and tourism industry has more than 1 million component companies, ranging from small agencies to large hotel chains. Most, however, can be classified as small business.

The travel and tourism industry exists primarily to provide services to tourists and people traveling for business purposes. A tourist is an individual who moves from one location to another, primarily for the purpose of experiencing leisure. The dictionary defines a tourist as an individual who "travels for pleasure." Tourism can be defined as the business of serving tourists, and travel is the movement of a person from one place to another. Most definitions of tourists suggest that individuals must be away from home overnight, for a twenty-four-hour period of time. Zabel (1992) notes that the U.S. Travel Data Center defines travel and tourism as synonymous terms—". . .the actions and activities of international and domestic travelers taking trips to places outside their home communities for any purpose except commuting to and from work or attending school" (p. 96).

The travel and tourism industry concerns itself with the movement of people to and from destination areas. Destination areas may be thought of as resources, whether natural or artificial, that attract people to spend time and money in an area. Disneyland and Disney World are examples of artificial structures that attract tourists; Yosemite, Yellowstone, and Crater Lake national parks are natural resources. Destination areas can also refer to events, such as the Rose Bowl and Rose Parade in Pasadena, California, that attract tourists.

Hospitality and Food Services

An industry closely aligned with the travel and tourism industry is the food and hospitality industry, concerned with the lodging and feeding of people. As the tourism industry has grown, so has the hospitality and food industry. Food franchises have become the fastest-growing franchises in the United States today. In 1955, 25 percent of the food dollar spent by each family was spent away from home. By 1985 that figure increased to 40 percent (Gottschalk, 1986). Estimates suggest that this growth continues.

Ritzer (2000) reports that there has been a wholesale movement associated with the fast-food industry that has ". . . reverberations extending far beyond its point-of-origin in the United States." In fact, it has influenced a wide range of undertakings, indeed, the way of life of a significant portion of the world. Of course, the leaders of this movement worldwide have been

Missing in Action. Survey: North American Theme Parks Struggle to Attract International Thrill Seekers

Attendance at North American theme parks fell by 3.2 million visitors this year, largely due to a sluggish world economy that kept international visitors at home, according to an industry survey.

Attendance at the fifty most visited theme parks in North America this year was 170 million, down from 173.2 million in 2001, according to the annual survey by *Amusement Business*, a trade magazine. Almost three-fifths of those parks showed attendance decreases from last year. The decline amounted to a drop of just less than 2 percent.

"Attendance at regional parks was stagnant, partly because many smaller parks were reluctant to build new rides, given the uncertain economy and unpredictable travel habits," said Tim O'Brien, the magazine's senior editor.

"Visitors to regional parks made last-minute travel plans rather than planning months ahead, making it difficult for operators to plan," said Pete Owens, a spokesman for Dollywood in Pigeon Forge, Tennessee, which had 2.3 million visitors and ranked twenty-seventh on the North American List.

"There was no rhyme or reason to travel this year," said Owens. "Typically, once a season starts, you get into a consistent pattern of travel. That didn't happen."

Overall, International visits to Walt Disney World were down about 20 percent, according to analysts. In Orlando, home to seven of North America's best-attended parks, international traffic at the airport was down almost 25 percent for the year.

U.S. theme parks seeking to make up losses from fewer international visitors began marketing directly to people within driving distance.

At Universal Orlando, for instance, Florida residents saved $25 on a two-day, two-park ticket by bringing in specially marked Coca-Cola products. Sea World Orlando and Busch Gardens Tampa Bay offered Florida residents unlimited free return trips for buying a one-day admission ticket.

Worldwide, theme and amusement parks performed a bit better in North America. A record 250 million visitors went to the world's top fifty theme parks, an increase of 285,000 visitors over last year.

Source: "Missing in Action. Survey: North American theme parks struggle to attract international thrill-seekers." *Waterloo/Cedar Falls Courier.* December 24, 2002, P. B5.

McDonald's and TRICOM (Pizza Hut, Kentucky Fried Chicken, and Taco Bell), which have 53,800 restaurants between them worldwide. Subway has 13,000 outlets.

The hotel and lodging industry has experienced slight increases over the past several years when viewed in its totality. However, the actual number of hotels and motels has decreased. The average occupancy rate for these rooms was 65.2 percent. This compares to 2001, when there were 45,972 hotel and motel rooms available, reporting an occupancy rate of 60.3 percent. In 2001, hotels and motels earned $88.4 million. This represents a decline from 1996. However, it is an increase when compared to 1985. When viewing annual receipts of hotels and motels, they earned $90.7 billion in 1996. This compares with 1985 when hotel and motels earned $45.4 billion (U.S. Bureau of Census, 1999). Domestic overnight leisure trips by U.S. citizens increased from 310.2 million in 1997 to 331.9 million in 2002. (The average number of nights per trip remained constant at 4.2.) Of these travelers, 43 percent stay in a hotel or motel while on a trip (U.S. Bureau of Census, 2003).

Between 1980 and 1998, sales for eating and drinking establishments, including restaurants, nightclubs, and other establishments, rose from $90 billion to $247 billion (U.S. Bureau of Census, 2003). Obviously, people are not cooking at home. We also can look at the growth of these types of establishments in terms of the number of establishments, employees, and the amount spent on their payrolls. In 1996, there were 466,000 eating and drinking places in the United States employing 7.4 million individuals with a payroll of $69 billion, compared with 402,000 in 1990, employing 6.4 million individuals with a payroll of $49.6 billion.

The numerous types of hospitality and food businesses each cater to specific target markets. Resorts, hostels, hotels, motels, restaurants, bed-and-breakfast inns, and convention centers all fall within the hospitality and food service industry. A brief description of each of these types of commercial leisure service businesses follows:

Resorts. Resort facilities serve people who go to them primarily to experience leisure. In addition to lodging and food services, resorts also have recreation areas and facilities and, often, leisure programs and services.

Hostel. A hostel is a lodging place usually designated for young people. Hostels often cater to individuals who use other than motor transportation, such as bicycles or hiking. Guests are charged a nominal lodging fee and are expected to help with housekeeping chores. While hostels have traditionally served younger people, many cater to a diverse clientele. For example, some hostels even provide family rooms.

Hotels. Hotels supply sleeping accommodations, usually have some type of dining area, and may have recreation areas, pools, and fitness centers.

Motels. Motels, like hotels, supply sleeping accommodations and, often, food to tourists and other individuals. Motels can be distinguished from hotels in that their units can usually be entered directly from an outdoor court or parking lot.

Restaurants. Restaurants allow people to purchase and consume meals. Many restaurants are designed to facilitate unique leisure experiences. For example, pizza parlors with a gay nineties motif provide both food and a fun leisure atmosphere.

Bed-and-breakfast inns. These types of accommodations provide individuals with lodging and breakfast—breakfasts range from light continental fare to several courses of country cooking. Bed-and-breakfast inns are found in renovated houses, barns, and other buildings that evoke an old world or homey atmosphere.

Convention centers. Many communities have facilities to accommodate conventions and conferences. Typically, these complexes offer meeting facilities, lodging facilities, and restaurants within close proximity to one another.

Casino resorts. Family casino resorts have created a new trend in the leisure service industry. Several areas in the United States—Atlantic City, Reno, Lake Tahoe, Las Vegas, and others—have constructed elaborate family resorts that include gaming facilities, theme parks, entertainment, shopping malls, and special events.

The hospitality and food service business presents many challenges. As the margin of profit in the food and hospitality industry is narrow, these types of businesses must employ careful planning and management techniques.

Leisure Products (Manufacturing)

A myriad of recreation products is manufactured and sold in the United States today. As Kelly (1996) indicates, no list of all those "things" is possible. Leisure products, so evident in everyday life, have a tremendous impact not only on recreational pursuits, but in other aspects of life as well. Leisure apparel—shorts, tennis shoes, and athletic apparel—influences how people dress and, in a sense, their self-concept.

In 2001, the total expenditures for personal consumption for recreation were $593.9 billion. This compares to total expenditures for personal consumption for recreation in 1996, which was $431.1 billion, and in 1990, when the figure was $281.6 billion. This represents 8.5 percent of the total dollars spent for consumption by Americans. The figure has increased steadily since 1990, when 7.4 percent of expenditures were made for recreation (U.S. Bureau of Census, 2003). Further, in 2002, Americans spent over $75.3 billion on sporting goods. This compares with $66 billion in 1998.

The production of finished leisure goods and products from processed raw materials is a secondary process of manufacturing. Manufacturing involves the planning and controlling of human resources, machines, and materials in such a way as to efficiently and effectively create desired products. In general, individuals who manufacture leisure products are concerned with producing a quality product in the right quantity at the right time. Products that do not meet consumer expectations in terms of quality will be at a disadvantage in the competitive market place. Furthermore, manufacturers must produce enough products to meet consumer demand. Today, people look for quality products of high value at a reasonable cost. Thus, those who produce leisure products must carefully consider costs and the break-even point for each product. Table 11.1 presents a partial listing of leisure products available in the marketplace today.

Kelly (1996) writes that six types of leisure products exist—namely sports, services, arts, technology-based, hobby-based, and market segment-oriented. He also indicates that a new product may be viewed as either an improvement, innovation, or invention (Kelly, 1985). Most newly developed products are actually improvements on existing ones. For example, recreation vehicles improved upon travel trailers. Travel trailers improved upon tents. A product innovation occurs when a substantial change is made to a piece of equipment or other product that significantly influences the leisure experiences. Kelly explains, "The introduction of fiberglass boats not only reduced maintenance and prolonged life, but also increased performance. It made boating quite different and more accessible" (Kelly, 1985, p. 343). A product invention

TABLE

11.1 A PARTIAL LIST OF LEISURE PRODUCTS

Toys	Food preparation equipment
Games	Musical instruments
Sports equipment	Arts and crafts supplies
Leisure apparel	Camping equipment
Computers	Tools
Home entertainment units	Hobby products
Televisions	Gardening supplies
Stereos	Video/audiotapes
Recreation vehicles	Records
Water-based equipment	Cooking supplies
Cars	Fabrics/sewing supplies
Bicycles	Books
Playground apparatus	Magazines
Fitness/exercise equipment	Needlework/knitting supplies
Photography supplies	Electronic equipment

Disney's New Adventures

The sun never sets on the Disney Empire. But for more than forty-five years, Disneyland—the first house of the Mouse that roared—has had to soldier on while more money and attention were paid to its younger siblings, first Florida's Walt Disney World and later Tokyo Disneyland and Disneyland Paris. Next month, all that changes when the California Disney facility that invented the concept of the modern theme park reinvents itself.

And just two months later, Walt Disney World in Florida debuts perhaps the most innovative resort hotel in the Disney system—Disney's Animal Kingdom Lodge—located near the fourth and newest Walt Disney World theme park, Disney's Animal Kingdom. Many of the guest rooms look out over a thirty-three-acre savanna where more than 200 mammals and birds will be on view, much like an African game preserve. Both the California and Florida constructions signal Disney's intent to continue expansion of its U.S. parks.

On February 8, the doors swing open to Disney's California Adventure, centerpiece of a ten-year, $4 billion effort to revitalize and expand the Disneyland Resort and the surrounding city of Anaheim, coordinated by Disneyland Resort, the city of Anaheim, Orange County, the state of California, and a number of federal agencies. The result will pair the two adjacent parks with a variety of other Anaheim developments to create an extended-stay resort destination expected to attract visitors from around the globe.

The newly expanded Disneyland Resort in Anaheim includes six components: Disney's California Adventure, a new fifty-five-acre, $14 billion theme park adjacent to the original Disneyland celebrating California's culture, spirit, and natural beauty in three distinct themed "lands"; the original Disneyland park, created in 1955 and now sprawling over eighty-five acres; Downtown Disney, a public esplanade of shops, restaurants, and entertainment venues centrally located between the two park entrances and near surrounding hotels; Disney's Grand California Hotel, a 750-room hotel located within California Adventure, the first Disney hotel inside a theme park; Disney's Paradise Pier Hotel (formerly the Disneyland Pacific Hotel), a 502-room hotel that overlooks the Paradise Pier themed area inside Disney's California Adventure; and Disneyland Hotel, the original 990-room hotel that already serves the Disneyland park.

"This is a very different kind of experience, much more pop culture and MTV-like," says Barry Braverman, Disney Imagineering's creative director for the California designs and iconographies. "As visitors approach, they'll feel like they're walking into a postcard of California."

The entrance features massive freestanding letters spelling the state's name, a hand-glazed ceramic wall mural, a sixty-foot mirrored heliostat that continuously tracks and reflects the sun, and gates that open beneath an overarching Golden Gate Bridge. The park itself is composed of three lands that represent various California cultural and natural icons.

First is Hollywood Pictures Backlot, a mock studio that mimics the architecture and film-industry structures of Hollywood while immersing visitors in movie-making attractions, rides, and films. Themed movie sets and interactive animation displays let visitors take part in the creative process. A 2,000-seat, state-of-the art theater will host live shows.

The park's second land is The Golden State, a section that pays tribute to California's natural beauty and microclimates. Visitors can sample California produce and take part in wine tastings next to actual on-site Robert Mondavi vineyards. Dominating the land is Grizzly Peak, a constructed mountain with rock formations at the summit shaped to look like the head of a growling grizzly bear. The most popular ride in the new park is likely to be Soarin' Over California, a mock hang-gliding experience that lifts visitors forty feet up and into the concavity of a huge surrounding projection screen. Visitors will "fly" above twelve different California locales, including Yosemite, Lake Tahoe, and Napa Valley.

Paradise Pier, the third section, is a tribute to California oceanfront amusemant park piers and beach culture. The area will contain classic amusement park rides such as the 150-foot-tall Sun Wheel ferris wheel and the California Screamin'

—continued

Disney's New Adventures—continued

roller coaster. Rounding out Paradise Pier will be midway games, street musicians, and artists.

Beyond the Disney facilities, the city of Anaheim has completed a $177 million expansion of nearby Anaheim Convention Center, which, with the Disney properties, is part of the 1,100-acre Anaheim Resort District. Citywide construction projects are improving residential areas, parking, mass transit, and retail and commercial areas.

Three thousand miles away, Florida's Walt Disney World is opening Disney's Animal Kingdom Lodge in April. The 1,293-room, six-story hotel features hand-carved furnishings, a semicircular *kraal* African village design, and views of an expansive grassland filled with birds and free-roaming mammals, including giraffes, zebra, Thomson's gazelle, ostrich, and ibis.

The viewing areas and walkways are intended to make guests feel as though they are in Africa. The lodge features three African-inspired restaurants, a thatch-roofed lobby with a massive mud fireplace, and an indoor flowing stream.

Source: Bateman, S. 2001, January. Travel trends: Disney's new adventures. *Hemisphere Magazine*, 42, 44.

occurs when someone creates a new product that heretofore did not exist—the invention of magnetic tape and its resultant application to home entertainment have revolutionized home-based leisure pursuits.

Entertainment Services

American citizens, like other people throughout the world, like to be entertained. In the entertainment industry, professionals actually deliver entertainment or entertainment services, or support individuals providing entertainment. Participation in such services ranges from viewing professional sporting events to attending community festivals. The production of entertainment services may involve live performances and/or the creation of productions that are electronically or technologically reproduced through the media. Entertainment services also encompass the management of such attractions as theme and amusement parks, circuses, gaming establishments, race tracks, and live concerts.

As the entertainment industry is vast, it is difficult to identify discrete categories within it. Some of the more obvious general categories within the entertainment industry, however, include the following:

Professional sports. This involves the management and promotion of a wide variety of professional men's and women's sports activities, including baseball, football, basketball, hockey, figure skating, tennis, golf, and soccer.

Gaming establishments. Many types of gaming establishments exist in the United States, and their impact is enormous. For example, the number of total ticket sales for lotteries increased from $2.3 billion in 1980 to $41.9 billion in 1998 (U.S. Bureau of Census, 2003). The bulk of the proceeds support educational endeavors, although some proceeds in various states support infrastructure development, recreation concerns, and the environment. Casino gambling, pari-mutuel betting, and lotteries—including the nationwide Powerball"—fall in this category.

Horse racing and dog racing. Due to attendance, thoroughbred, harness, and greyhound racing rank among the top ten spectator sports in the United States.

Automobile racing. Automobile racing is the number one spectator sport in the United States, drawing more than 50 million people a year.

Circuses and carnivals. The circus and the carnival have long been standbys in the entertainment industry in the United States.

Theme and amusement parks. Theme/amusement parks have become one of the dominant forms of entertainment in the United States. Disneyland, Disney World, Six Flags, Great America, and Knott's Berry Farm all serve as examples of this component within the entertainment industry.

Special events and festivals. These activities contribute to community morale. They are built around a variety of different themes, including geographic, historic, and cultural ones. The Rhododendron Festival in Florence, Oregon, illustrates this concept. Festivals generate funds for a community, including many leisure-oriented businesses within it, and impact its economic well-being.

Live, filmed, taped, or broadcasted performances. Plays, operas, concerts, movies, television broadcasts, compact disks (CDs), tapes, and DVDs are all examples of products and services that relate to this component of the entertainment industry to produce a unique blend of entertainment services. When looking at the composite of this area, which could include motion pictures, entertainers, commercial sports, sports clubs, and amusement parks as well as others mentioned, the growth is spectacular. In billions of dollars, these combined areas generated $177.1 billion in receipts in 2000, compared with $156 billion in 1997, and $52.7 billion in 1985 (U.S. Bureau of Census, 2003).

Shore Excursions Can Take Budget Off Course

The price of a cruise is often such a bargain that you hardly can refuse, but the add-ons add up to sticker shock. And, typically, that happens when it's too late to do much about it.

Anne Campbell, editor of the consumer Web site Cruisemates.com, said she recently got a distraught phone call from a couple who had just returned from a one-week Caribbean sailing. They were astonished at checkout time to learn they had run up $900 in on-board charges, almost as much as they had spent for the cruise itself. They are moderate drinkers and gamblers who skip art auctions and bingo. So where did the money go?

A look at their final bill showed 25 percent of the charges were spent in the spa (one fifty-minute massage: $110 plus tip), and the remainder went for shore excursions. Not exactly profligacy for the average cruiser.

Hardly any line lets you get away with just the cost of a stateroom. Many, including some upscale ones, charge even for orange juice if you ask for it at a shipboard bar, though it's free in your cabin. In fact, of the forty best-known cruise lines, just luxury line Silversea comes close to being all-inclusive. The line charges nada for extras, including gratuities, alcoholic beverages, and, on some sailings, even a shore excursion or two.

Though cruising used to be close to all-inclusive, these days it's far from that. Expect to pay for everything, and if it turns out you don't have to, you'll be pleasantly surprised.

The trend of charging for little extras surfaced years ago, when Princess introduced a fee of about $4 for "premium" ice cream. The line successfully deflected the inevitable criticism and, eventually,

most lines followed suit—if not with ice cream, then with cappuccino, pie by the slice and, yes, water.

Charges also creep in where you least expect them. On some ships, if you open that disposable camera in your cabin, $17 will appear on your bill.

So far, no line charges for meals per se, unless you count those ubiquitous alternative restaurants. Norwegian Cruise Line pioneered the trend in 1988 when it introduced the concept on Seaward. These days, such eateries on all ships levy surcharges ranging anywhere from $5 to $35. Today, with Norwegian's Freestyle Dining, the line is virtually pay-as-you-go for meals, with most of the ten restaurants on its newest vessels carrying a la carte prices.

In other economic innovations, Holland America—a line that has long touted its "tipping optional" policy—recently succumbed to the trend of billing tips to your on-board account, a strategy now entrenched on several lines, including Princess and Carnival. In this permutation, it's up to you to muster the courage to ask the purser to delete the charge.

Things could get worse. Industry expert George Devol, publisher of Ocean Cruise News, says first-time cruisers attracted to big new ships "will not be as taken back by the extra cost items as would a longtime cruiser." He predicts that "once the concept of having many extra cost items takes hold, it will open up a number of features for those traveling on these ships. Dining will mostly be at an extra cost (although some very basic food might still be included), but with a number of the restaurants being run and operated by well-known shoreside establishments rather than by the cruise lines." In fact, that already has come to pass on some ships, such as the Crystal Serenity and the QM2.

Source: "Shore excursions can take budget off course." *Waterloo/Cedar Falls Courier*. February 29, 2004, Page E7.

Home Entertainment. In the past several decades, there has been tremendous growth in the home entertainment industry as a result of new technological applications. The computer, enhanced sound systems, DVD technology, the use of LCDs, coupled with other forms of technology, have provided an array of opportunities for individuals to "cocoon" in their home environments.

Cruise Vacations. Cruise ships provide opportunities for activities for all ages. In the United States, ports for cruise ships include California, Florida, Hawaii, New York,

Louisiana, Texas, Washington, Massachusetts, and Alaska. Nearly 8.3 million individuals take vacations on cruise ships. Themed trips, family focused cruises, as well as programs emphasizing knowledge and skill acquisition classes are among the latest trends in this industry.

Malls. Mega malls, such as The West Edmonton (Alberta) Mall and the Mall of America in Minneapolis, Minnesota, provide unique leisure opportunities combining various entertainment venues. For example, such malls often feature an amusement park, eating establishments, and other leisure-focused activities including special events such as concerts and performances in addition to the shopping activities that are available.

Retail Outlets

Retail outlets provide a way of moving leisure products to consumers. Some businesses provide leisure products as one line in their total merchandising effort, whereas other retail outlets specialize exclusively in leisure products. For example, many stores focus exclusively on the provision of sports equipment and apparel. The Sports Line, a retail outlet located in Cedar Falls, Iowa, sells only sports apparel from professional athletic teams and sports hobby cards (e.g., baseball cards). Play It Again Sports in Stillwater, Oklahoma, focuses its retail business on buying and selling both used and new sporting goods. Some of the retail outlets often associated with leisure products include radio, television, and stereo outlets; bicycle shops; athletic equipment stores, including shoes and apparel; outdoor stores; bookstores; toy and hobby stores; photography stores; video rental outlets; and catalog sales (e.g., L. L. Bean and Patagonia).

Retail outlets can generally be categorized into two classifications—store and nonstore outlets. Nonstore outlets, as contrasted with store outlets, bring their products to the customer's home, for example, in the case of catalog sales. Some of the different types of store and non-store outlets that distribute commercial leisure products and services include the following:

Specialty store. Offering merchandise in a specific area, such as athletics, outdoor recreation, and music or art supplies, specialty stores provide the customer with an opportunity to purchase a particular type of item.

Variety store. These moderately priced retail outlets provide a wide variety of merchandise, usually inexpensively.

Department store. While department stores also provide a wide variety of merchandise, they often target their lines to particular income levels or target markets. Their merchandise is often of a higher quality than the variety store.

Full-line discount store. This type of retail outlet provides merchandise at discount prices. Discount stores focus on price and value, as contrasted with quality and value (as might be the case in a department store).

Retail catalog showroom. This type of store, often self-service, usually offers its products at a discount.

Factory outlet. The purpose of this type of retail outlet is to sell factory seconds and factory overruns.

Flea market. A flea market is a leisure experience in and of itself, with many different products offered for sale in a festive atmosphere.

Video ordering system. Recently there has been a growth in the ordering of merchandise via the use of cable television. Individuals can see products on television and order them over the phone.

10 Great Places to See the USA the Scenic Way

If you like taking the road less traveled, try America's National Scenic By-ways—25,000 miles of pavement that features unique regional characteristics. Hit the road on May 10, named "SeeAmerica Day" by the Travel Industry Association and Federal Highway Administration (which designates scenic byways). It's part of SeeAmerica's Byways, a broader national promotion (www.seeamerica.org) to celebrate and encourage exploration of America's scenic drives, historic attractions, and rural culture. Favorite byways:

- Acadia Scenic Byway, Maine
- Columbia Gorge Scenic Byway, Washington and Oregon
- San Juan Skyway, Colorado
- The Great River Road and Grand Rounds, Minnesota
- Pacific Coast Highway, California
- U.S. Route 9, New York
- U.S. 17 Coastal Byway, Georgia
- Ohio River Trail, Ohio
- The Blue Ridge Parkway, Virginia and North Carolina
- George Washington Heritage Trail, West Virginia

Source: "10 Great Places to see the USA the Scenic Way." *USA Today.* May 2, 2003, p. 3D.

World Wide Web. Use of the World Wide Web as a mechanism to order goods and services has grown exponentially. It is now possible to order on-line nearly any product or service one desires.

Retail outlets fall into a number of ownership categories—independent, corporate, and/or a chain of stores. Most retail trade in the United States is organized as sole proprietorship (76%), while 4 percent are organized as partnerships and 20 percent as corporations (U.S. Bureau of Census, 2003).

Leisure Services in the Natural Environment

American citizens enjoy many leisure activities in the natural environment such as swimming, hiking, boating, camping, backpacking, hunting, waterskiing, diving, fishing, and skiing. While many of these activities take place on public land, private entrepreneurs often provide the equipment, instruction, guide services, and so forth to meet the demand for leisure experiences in the natural environment.

The United States has nearly 700,000 private outdoor enterprises in operation. Some of these agencies control their own natural resources in terms of land and water; however, most use public resources. Many outdoor recreation services are seasonally based. This creates a challenge in terms of return on investment and year-round financial planning, staffing, and marketing. This influences profit, work schedules, and promotional activities.

People who want to work in commercial leisure service organizations in the natural environment have many work opportunities; these include owner, manager, marketing director, instructor, guide, concession operator, ticket seller, clerk, site attendant, and maintenance manager. Direct-service positions (face-to-face) often require a high level of skill, knowledge, and competency in specific areas. For example, outdoor leaders must not only have technical knowledge related to the out-of-doors, but must also know how to interact positively with people.

Dolphin Dive a Peaceful Trip

PORT LUCAYA, Bahamas (AP)

An open hand brings Romballa the dolphin sidling up for a stroke of her silky skin. Holding up a rubber ring will prompt her to scoop it up and take it to the next person.

For those who wish Sea World offered season tickets, or who get excited by reruns of the *Flipper* television show, the Dolphin Experience on Grand Bahamas Island offers a chance to swim with the beloved marine mammals in the open ocean.

Chris Allison, president of the Dolphin Experience, said about 50,000 people a year visit his nine-and-a-half-acre dolphin center in Sanctuary Bay to interact with seventeen trained dolphins, either by just sitting on the dock, swimming with them in shallow water, or scuba diving with them off the coast. "What we are providing is a safe and controlled interaction with the dolphins, where the dolphins know and understand the interaction," Allison explains.

Allison says the dives offer an opportunity to fulfill a fantasy in a way that protects both the divers and wild dolphins. The United States and the Bahamas have outlawed swimming with wild dolphins, which have been known to attack people who get too close.

"Everyone relates to dolphins." Allison says. "By the time they leave us, everybody realizes not only how important dolphins are, but how important the whole eco-structure is, what great responsibilities we have to take care of the ocean."

Source: *Waterloo-Cedar Falls Courier,* Sunday, April, 2, 2000, E-8.

Commercial leisure service activities and businesses that depend on the natural environment fall into five general categories: land-based, water-based, air-based, historically/culturally-based, and geographically-based. Their descriptions follow:

Land-based. Land-based activities in the natural environment include touring, mountain climbing, rappelling, backpacking, spelunking, skiing, camping (tent, trailer, RV), bird watching, hiking, hunting, and driving off-the-road vehicles. Many types of commercial leisure service businesses support these activities, such as commercial campgrounds (e.g., Thousand Trails and KOA), RV rentals and sales, trail guide businesses, and outdoor schools.

Water-based. Water-based activities in the natural environment range from luxurious cruises to wind surfing. Other water-based activities include canoeing, fishing, rafting, boating, kayaking, snorkeling and diving, swimming, waterskiing, and surfing. Some of the commercial leisure service businesses supporting these activities are cruise lines, commercial fishing boats, river guides, boating equipment and sales, and training schools for diving and snorkeling.

Air-Based.   There are increasing activities that occur in the air, such as flying, ballooning, hang gliding, parasailing, base jumping, heli-skiing, and parachuting. All of these activities have related commercial leisure services businesses that support them in terms of training and sales of equipment.

Historically and culturally-based. Some commercial leisure service businesses manage, for profit, historical or cultural sites. The exhibition of the Queen Mary in Long Beach, California, is an example of a historically based commercial leisure service business operating in the natural environment.

Geographically-based. Some commercial leisure service businesses manage natural habitats for profit. Sea Lion Caves in Florence, Oregon, an example of this type of commercial leisure service business, bases its business on the natural environment. These types of businesses often have food, lodging, and souvenir services associated with them.

Entrepreneurship, Opportunities, and Challenges

Working in the commercial leisure service area provides many opportunities and involves risk. Approximately 95 percent of all small businesses fail within the first five years of start-up. Constant shifts in demand for services and products result in great entrepreneurial activity and opportunity, but also involve certain challenges. This section discusses the concept of entrepreneurship and the opportunities and challenges in the commercial leisure service sector.

What Is Entrepreneurship?

This is an age of entrepreneurship. Increasingly, the economies of the United States rely on the ability of small businesses to flex in response to rapid shifts in the marketplace. Individuals who seek risk and have the desire to operate independently and creatively are often referred to as entrepreneurs. Entrepreneurs make an investment or take a risk to start a new enterprise. If the business succeeds, these people benefit from their activity. Entrepreneurs often create perceived need through effective marketing, and people often view them as decisive and action-oriented.

Peter Drucker, a noted management theorist, writes that entrepreneurship involves systematic innovation. According to Drucker (1985), systematic innovation consists of the purposeful and organized search for changes and a systematic analysis of the opportunities such changes might offer for economic or social innovation. Thus, entrepreneurship deals with change, innovation, and a systematic analysis of conditions. While entrepreneurs do take risks, Drucker points out that entrepreneurs take calculated risks that minimize their exposure to failure and enhance their opportunity for success.

What key entrepreneurial skills do people need to succeed? First, they must have a firm commitment to the free-enterprise system; they believe that each individual has the freedom to use his or her own resources, talent, time, and energy to pursue a vision. Edginton, Carpenter, and Chenery (1987) observe a number of key entrepreneurial skills that enhance success in managing a commercial leisure service organization (see figure 11.7).

Vision. Vision, often thought of as forward thinking, is the ability to move in a new direction with purpose, to see a new reality.

Creativity. Creativity is the ability to be imaginative, inventive, resourceful, or constructive. Creative entrepreneurs generate new ideas and bring them to fruition.

Idea generation. An idea is a mental image, a thought, or an opinion. Generating ideas involves brainstorming, reflecting, reasoning, and imagining. Idea generation is closely related to creativity.

Problem solving. Problem solving involves the ability to overcome barriers and obstacles and create solutions. Problem solvers use creativity, idea generation, and other resources to move forward even in the face of great difficulty.

Decision making. Entrepreneurs tend to be independent decision makers who learn from their mistakes. Because entrepreneurs can see a need that may not exist, decisions often involve risk and must be done in a thoughtful yet decisive manner.

Figure 11.7
Six key
entrepreneurial
skills.

Change management. Change management involves the ability to move into organizations and unfreeze ideas, structures, values, opinions, attitudes, methods, and procedures that influence the way people live and work. This often requires an ability to communicate effectively and persuasively.

A new entrepreneurial spirit has apparently emerged in the United States, reflected partly by the number of new jobs that have emerged over the past several decades; for example, between 1980 and 2002, there was a net gain of employment in the United States of 37.1 million jobs (U.S. Bureau of Census, 2003). In 2002, it was reported that there are 136,485,000 individuals in the workforce. By the year 2005, it is projected that there will be 150.5 million individuals in the workforce, an anticipated gain of 67.7 million jobs when compared with 1970. These new jobs primarily result from entrepreneurial ventures in the service and information sectors of society, with many in the leisure area. Entrepreneurs serve as pacesetters of opportunity, a challenging and demanding role. Their work is dynamic, diverse, inventive, and creative. Entrepreneurs produce new ways of meeting needs, work to improve existing products and services, and respond to changing demographic conditions.

Opportunities in the Commercial Leisure Services Sector

The size of the commercial leisure service market is staggering when compared with the delivery of public leisure services. As indicated, the expenditure for recreation in 2001 was

$593.9 billion (U.S. Bureau of Census, 2003). Expenditures for state and local government were $25 billion, with $2.8 billion at the federal level (U.S. Bureau of Census, 2003). If we add $25 billion from nonprofit organizations focused on youth and family leisure services, then there is a total of approximately $646.7 billion being spent for recreation in America. We estimate that somewhere between 85 percent and 95 percent is spent in the commercial sector. All indications suggest that this area will continue to grow.

Prospects for Profit   The leisure industry is one market area in which profits have grown dramatically. In a study of the top 1,000 businesses in the United States, *Business Week* reports that a composite of the top leisure industries showed a significantly higher change in profits than other businesses. In 2004, profits in the leisure services industry, including hotels and restaurants, increased by 15 percent when compared to 2002 (*Business Week,* 2004). Over a three-year average, profitability increased by 7.6 percent. This compares to an average profit margin of 6.5 percent in 1999 (*Business Week,* 1999) and 4.7 percent in 1992 (*Business Week,* 1993).

The Top Leisure Industries   How do the top leisure industries in the United States rank in terms of profit? Table 11.2 presents, in rank order, these large corporations; it does not reflect the many small businesses providing leisure services. Among the companies listed are International Game Technology, Starbucks, Carnival, McDonald's, YUM! Brands, Wendy's International, Harrah's Entertainment, Darden Restaurants, Marriott International, Starwood Hotels & Resorts, and Hilton Hotels. If the media group is added to the leisure industry, this list would include corporations such as Walt Disney, McGraw-Hill, Omnicom Group, Clear Channel Communications, Tribune, Univision Communications, Gannett, Time Warner, Meredith, Viacom, Comcast, Knight-Ridder, New York Times, Dow Jones, and Interpublic Group. The Walt Disney Corporation increased its profits by 112 percent when compared with 2002. It's three-year average change in profitability was 42 percent. The media industry's average change in profitability over a three-year period was 25.1 percent.

In the food and lodging industry, franchising has become an important means to deliver goods and services. By the year 2005, franchising will have become a $1 trillion-a-year industry—about

TABLE

| 11.2 | TOP LEISURE INDUSTRIES IN TERMS OF PROFITS EARNED—HOTELS, RESTAURANTS, AND LEISURE |

Rank	Company	Market Value (millions of dollars)
1	International Game Technology	13598.3
2	Starbucks	14799.3
3	Carnival	36083.8
4	McDonald's	35915.5
5	YUM! Brands	10812.8
6	Wendy's International	4664.7
7	Harrah's Entertainment	5720.8
8	Darden Restaurants	4021.5
9	Marriott International	10320.0
10	Starwood Hotels & Resorts	7872.7

Source: Author. 2004. The Standard & Poor's Five Hundred. *Business Week* (April 5).

double the current level—and will account for half of all retail sales (Pettsinger, 1987). Tables 11.3 and 11.4 show the fastest-growing franchises in the United States. It is interesting to note that in 1995 the fastest-growing franchises dealt with leisure and related areas such as fast-food establishments and hotels and motels. There are still a number of fast-food and other eating establishments identified on the current list. We suspect that list changes very rapidly from year to year depending on demands in the marketplace.

Small Leisure Service Businesses   The United States has more than 15 million small business owners. Of all businesses in the United States, more (perhaps as many as 81%) could be defined as small businesses (U.S. Bureau of the Census, 1995). Bullaro and Edginton

TABLE

11.3   TOP LEISURE INDUSTRIES IN TERMS OF PROFITS EARNED—MEDIA

Rank	Company	Market Value (millions of dollars)
1	Walt Disney	53412.9
2	McGraw-Hill	14977.4
3	Omnicom Group	15542.1
4	Clear Channel Communications	26494.6
5	Tribune	16395.2
6	Univision Communications	11481.0
7	Gannett	23303.2
8	Time Warner	78249.4
9	Meredith	2519.2
10	Viacom	67062.7

Source: Author. 2004. The Standard & Poor's Five Hundred. *Business Week* (April 5).

TABLE

11.4   TOP LEISURE INDUSTRIES IN TERMS OF PROFITS EARNED—TOP TEN FRANCHISES

Company	Type of Business	Startup Costs
Subway	Sandwiches & salads	$86K–213K
Curves	Fitness & Weight Loss Center	$36.4K–42.9K
Quizno's	Sandwiches, soup & salads	$208.4K–243.8K
7-Eleven	Convenience Store	$65K–227K
Jackson Hewitt Tax Service	Tax preparation service	$47.4K–75.2K
UPS Store	Postal/business/communications	$131.1K–237.7K
McDonald's	Hamburgers, chicken, salads	$506K–1.6M+
Jani-King	Commercial cleaning	$11.3K–34.1K+
Dunkin' Donuts	Donuts and baked goods	$255.7K–1.1M
Baskin-Robbins USA	Ice cream & yogurt	$145.7K–527.8K

Source: Author. 2004. *Entrepreneur's* 25th Annual Franchise 500. *Entrepreneur.* Retrieved from www.entrepreneur.com/francishe500.

(1986), discussing commercial leisure services, suggest that this rate is even higher, noting that 95 percent of all businesses are small businesses. They suggest that small businesses can uniquely respond to the emerging diverse leisure lifestyles and cultural patterns. Since they do not have the same constraints as large businesses or corporations, small businesses can respond more quickly to innovations and fluctuations in the fad-oriented leisure service market. Significant growth has occurred in the number of new entrepreneurial ventures in the last thirty years.

In reviewing the state of small business in the United States, The *Wall Street Journal* reported that the fastest-growing small businesses dealt with amusement and recreation services, resulting, no doubt, from the growth of leisure in an era of change. A great deal of entrepreneurial activity exists, and much of it focuses on the creation of new ways to meet people's needs, including their leisure needs. Such businesses range from providing play and motor learning opportunities for young children to fantasy camps for adults. Growth in the areas of arts, entertainment, and recreation services continues. Actual employment in 1997 was 1,572,000. In 2001, this figure increased to 1,780,000. Thus, one can see that there is continuous growth in terms of numbers of employees in this area. Further, the number of establishments providing arts, entertainment, and recreation services as well as actual payroll, also increased. This was also the case for the area of accommodations and food services. Employment areas such as agriculture, mining, utilities, construction, and manufacturing decreased.

Challenges to the Entrepreneur

The owner or operator of a commercial leisure service enterprise faces many challenges. Not only must commercial leisure service providers remain responsive to customer needs, they also must carefully price and market their services and products to ensure profitability. Furthermore, ethical considerations come into play when providing leisure services in certain environments, especially the natural environment. Some of the challenges that a commercial leisure service entrepreneur may face include the following:

Responsiveness to changing conditions. Leisure interests are often fad-oriented, changing rapidly. Most leisure service organizations, to remain competitive, must constantly change, upgrade, or enhance their products or services.

Capital. Difficulty can arise when commercial leisure service organizations need capital to start new enterprises. They must be creative and innovative, yet have a practical, well-thought-out profit plan. In addition, cash flow into a leisure business is often irregular and requires a keen sense of fiscal management.

Seasonal factors. Many leisure activities are seasonal in nature. For example, businesses that cater to skiing in the winter, water activities in the summer, or various types of sports all require seasonal adjustments in staff, cash flow, and promotion.

Ethical considerations. The leisure service field has, as core values, the preservation and conservation of the environment and the wise use of leisure. Commercial businesses can meet ethical considerations when they focus on values, quality, and service, as well as fair profit, within the framework of the foundational ethics of the profession.

Risk management. Issues surrounding liability, especially as related to high-adventure recreation programs, are increasing. Businesses need to identify major risks and establish a program to effectively manage risk, either by purchasing insurance, avoiding the high-risk activities, establishing preventive measures, or other means.

Social responsibilities. Owners and managers have a responsibility to invest in their communities—a practice that is also "good business." It often involves contributing to community projects and activities with the resources of the organization, in terms of money, time, personnel, or other resources.

Consumer protection. Successful commercial leisure service organizations provide safe and satisfying leisure experiences for their customers.

Knowledge of consumers. Knowledge of consumers and consumer markets can make the difference between success or failure. To gain this knowledge, the business might engage in market research and acquire information that will help in making decisions.

Lack of personal time. Running a small commercial leisure business can result in a lack of personal or leisure time. The challenge is one of finding a balance between the two.

Inadequate managerial skills. Few small commercial leisure service business professionals have all of the skills necessary to operate an enterprise effectively and efficiently. This challenge can be met by finding ways to augment one's abilities and skills—for example, through business assistance programs, taking on a partner, hiring a consultant, or taking classes.

Overregulation. Governmental regulations can be burdensome. They can put undue constraints on the operation of businesses and may impact on profits.

These challenges need not deter the entrepreneur from succeeding. When faced squarely, they become opportunities for an interesting and stimulating work environment. A key to excellence involves understanding the challenges that exist and then anticipating them with a planned strategy that produces successful results.

Summary

Commercial leisure service ventures make up a large proportion of the entire leisure market. In fact, estimates indicate that over 90 percent of all expenditures for leisure goods and services occur in the commercial leisure service sector. Commercial leisure service organizations have, as their primary objective, earning a profit. They also work, however, to build strong bonds between themselves and their consumers. This loyalty often results in sustained profits over a long period of time.

While there are numerous ways to classify commercial leisure service organizations, this chapter identifies six major classifications: travel and tourism, hospitality and food services, leisure products, entertainment services, retail outlets, and leisure in the natural environment. Each type of service has unique patterns of organization, management, and marketing and can be legally organized as a sole proprietorship, partnership, or corporation.

Most commercial leisure service organizations are organized as small businesses. In fact, the fastest-growing small businesses in the United States deal with amusement and recreation services. The management and organization of small businesses are often conducted by individuals referred to as entrepreneurs. Entrepreneurs, individuals who seek systematic innovation, often perceive themselves as being goal-oriented, self-reliant, and self-motivated. Some entrepreneurial skills include vision, creativity, idea generation, problem solving, decision making, and change management. Individuals who work in the commercial sector show a high degree of job satisfaction related to such variables as pay and control over job environment. As in any business, however, owners and managers of commercial leisure service businesses face a number of challenges. These challenges provide opportunities for forward thinking and planning and impact on the managing, marketing, and pricing of services and products.

The commercial leisure service sector holds many opportunities for success and great promise for individuals wishing to pursue careers in this area. The commercial leisure service sector involves a full range of products and services from amusement/theme parks to leisure apparel. Individuals wishing to pursue professional careers in this area should acquire a foundation in areas such as leisure, marketing, financial management, and entrepreneurship.

Discussion Questions

1. From your perspective, what opportunities are available in the commercial leisure service sector today? List as many as possible.
2. What are the primary motives of commercial leisure service organizations? How do they contrast with those of public and nonprofit leisure service organizations?
3. What are the types of legal ownership of commercial leisure service organizations? What are their advantages and disadvantages?
4. Identify six major categories of commercial leisure service organizations.
5. Choose one leisure service organization and describe it in terms of its products, services, target markets, and form of ownership.
6. What is entrepreneurship? What skills does an entrepreneur need to be successful?
7. Why is entrepreneurship important in the delivery of leisure services?
8. Discuss the current state of the leisure service industry in the United States and Canada.
9. Identify what you think will be the fastest-growing commercial service industries in the United States in the next decade. Why do you believe this?
10. Identify and describe eleven challenges to individuals working in the commercial leisure service sector.

References

Bullaro, J., and C. Edginton. 1986. *Commercial Leisure Services: Managing for Profit, Service, and Personal Satisfaction.* New York: Macmillan.

Chubb, M., and H. Chubb. 1981. *One Third of Our Time.* New York: Wiley.

Crossley, J. C., and L. M. Jamieson. 1993. *Introduction to Commercial and Entrepreneurial Recreation.* 2d ed. Champaign, IL: Sagamore.

Cutler, B. 1990. Where does the free time go? *American Demographics* (November), 31–32.

Drucker, P. 1985. *Innovation and Entrepreneurship.* New York: Harper & Row.

Edginton, C. R., G. Carpenter, and M. F. Chenery. 1987. Educating for entrepreneurship in leisure services. *SPRE Annual on Education 2,* 30–58.

Gottschalk, E. C., Jr. 1986. Dining out chic to chic. *The Wall Street Journal* (April 21), 2D.

Grover, R., R. Vamos, and T. Mason. 1987. Disney's magic. *Business Week* (March 9), 62.

Kelly, J. 1985. *Recreation Business.* New York: Wiley.

Kelly, J. 1996. *Leisure.* 3d ed. Boston: Allyn & Bacon.

Naisbitt, J., and P. Aburdene. 1986. *Reinventing the Corporation.* New York: Warner Books.

Pettsinger, T. 1987. So you want to get rich. *The Wall Street Journal* (May 15), 2–15.

Pinchot, G. 1985. *Entrepreneuring.* New York: Harper & Row.

Ritzer, G. 2000. *The McDonaldization of Society.* Thousand Oaks, CA: Pine Forge Press.

Staff. 1987. The top U.S. companies ranked by industry. *Business Week* (April 17), 127.

Staff. 1993. The top U.S. companies ranked by industry. *Business Week* (April 7), 182–183.

Staff. 1996. The Business Week 1000. *Business Week* (March 25), 106.

Staff. 2000. The S&P 500 *Business Week* industry rankings. *Business Week* (March 27), 112.

U.S. Bureau of the Census. 1995. *Statistical Abstract of the United States: 1995.* 115th ed. Washington, DC: U.S. Government Printing Office.

U.S. Bureau of the Census. 1999. *Statistical Abstract of the United States: 1999.* 119th ed. Washington, DC: U.S. Government Printing Office.

U.S. Bureau of the Census. 2003. *Statistical Abstract of the United States: 2003.* 123rd ed. Washington, D.C.: U.S. Government Printing Office.

Zabel, D. 1992. The literature of travel tourism. Edited by N. Herron, in *The Leisure Literature.* Englewood, CO: Libraries Unlimited.

Delivery of Leisure Services: Therapeutic Recreation

Sports offer individuals opportunities to participate in activities and events that promote competition, sportsmanship, and a healthy and vigorous lifestyle.

Introduction

Whereas the other chapters in Part Two of this book classify leisure service delivery systems in terms of the type of funding they receive (public, nonprofit, or commercial), this chapter discusses a program area of leisure services—therapeutic recreation. Therapeutic recreation programs are found in public, private, nonprofit, and commercial organizations. This specialized form of organized recreation programming involves professionals and organizations that either use recreation activities as a means to intervene in people's lives to accomplish desired ends (therapeutic recreation) or provide recreation opportunities for people who are part of special populations (inclusive recreation).

Over the last half of the twentieth century, there was an increased recognition in the potential of recreation as a treatment modality as well as the need to provide inclusive or special recreation programs for people with disabilities. Persons with disabilities are becoming more vocal about their needs and desires, and society is recognizing that meeting this increased demand is the "right thing to do." Therapeutic recreation professionals have contributed to these changes, advocating for the rights of people with disabilities and empowering people of all abilities to improve their quality of life through leisure.

This chapter chronicles the growth and development of the therapeutic recreation profession and provides insights into the goals, resource base, characteristics of professionals, and orientation to customer of therapeutic recreation specialists. In addition, it describes the diverse and varied settings where therapeutic recreation specialists work and the future challenges of providing inclusive programs and therapeutic recreation programs.

The Emergence of Therapeutic Recreation as a Profession

The use of recreation as a tool to address social problems in the United States can be traced to the late 1800s as social reformers used play and recreation to address the problems and needs that grew out of the Industrial Revolution. For instance, the first playground, the Boston Sand Gardens, was established to meet the play needs of disadvantaged children. Also, many of the first organized camps were designed for "sickly boys." Further, the settlement house movement used recreation as a means to ease the transition of immigrants to life in large urban American cities. Sessoms and Stevenson (1981) have written that

> Adult education, recreation, and social group work all have a common heritage. Each is a product of the social welfare reforms that occurred in our cities and industries at the turn of the nineteenth century. Their founders shared a belief—they were concerned with the quality of life and believed that through the "proper" use of leisure it could be achieved. (p. 2)

As public recreation departments grew, the philosophy that views recreation as an end in itself was adopted by most public recreation agencies across the country (Gray, 1969). In other words, public recreation drifted away from a social welfare model, and a basic gap in the continuum of recreation services emerged. This gap was filled by professionals who were the forerunners to therapeutic recreation specialists today. Thus, the beginning of therapeutic recreation as a profession can be attributed to developments that took shape in the early part of the twentieth century and have continued into today. These developments include the need for specialized services for people with special needs, the influx of wounded soldiers from various wars and military conflicts, the emergence of professional organizations, and the number of landmark legislative bills that became law throughout the twentieth century.

The Need for Specialized Services

During the early history of the United States, those with mental illness and physical disabilities did not pose much of a challenge for communities. Population density was low and most communities were predominately rural and agricultural. The few cases of special needs that did become evident were addressed on a case-by-case basis by the family or the community. For the most part, communities became involved only when an individual seemed to threaten public safety or had no means of support. For example, in 1694 Massachusetts enacted "An Act for the Relief of Idiots and Distracted Persons." Under this provision all persons who had special needs and did not have family to take care of them were aided by the state. In 1699, Connecticut followed Massachusetts' lead; other colonies such as New York and Vermont passed similar laws.

The responsibility of taking care of those with mental illness when family care was unavailable fell to public almshouses. Almshouses typically provided a minimal level of food and shelter to a mixed grouping of persons who were able-bodied poor, ill, and disabled. An almshouse was in existence in Boston as early as 1662. The physical environs of almshouses were said to have been dungeonlike; the emotional environment was not any more humane. Records show that these places provided bizarre entertainment for the community. Cruel treatment, including the use of chains for restraints, led to the eventual outcry that demanded changes be made in caring for the people with disabilities.

The first documented medical institution in the United States was the Pennsylvania Hospital in Philadelphia, which was established in 1751. The services provided at this hospital included programs for mentally ill persons who had been previously denied treatment. The first U.S. hospital devoted exclusively to the care of the mentally ill was established in Williamsburg, Virginia, in 1773 to make provisions for the "Support and Maintenance of Idiots, Lunatics, and Other Persons of Unsound Minds." As the United States moved into the 1800s, hospitals and custodial care facilities were constructed for the mentally ill, deaf, blind, mentally challenged, and physically disabled. Private voluntary charity blossomed in the late 1800s to take care of the poor, the ill, the elderly, and the disabled. These institutions often became warehouses for individuals who had been shunned by society and contributed to the negative attitudes toward "people who were different." Many of these attitudes were perpetuated late into the twentieth century. The first private school to educate severely retarded individuals opened in Massachusetts in 1848. Many of the early reformers and proponents of the forerunner of modern rehabilitation services are presented in table 12.1.

Many of these early institutions began to offer recreation opportunities in both formal and informal programs. In the case of mental patients, the conviction grew that occupations of various kinds would be helpful in overcoming mental illness and restoring rational functioning. As a result, mental patients in the late 1800s were allowed to dance, take part in outdoor sports, and use "airing courts," rocking horses, and other special equipment (Kraus and Shank, 1992).

Carter, Van Andel, and Robb (2003) have identified a number of developments of the late nineteenth and early twentieth centuries that set the stage for the development of specialized services for a variety of people with special needs. These developments include the following:

- Health care reform that emphasized the dignity of all persons and the therapeutic value of humane treatment that included the social and environmental stimulation of recreation activities;
- Private and public hospital systems that created the structure for health care providers to experiment with programs and services that included recreation activities as a component of care; and
- The playground movement that reemphasized the role that play activities and spaces serve in social and environmental reform. The playground movement also spawned professional associations that supported therapeutic recreation.

The Influx of Wounded Soldiers from the World Wars

Following the Civil War, the importance of recreation for wounded soldiers was acknowledged. Florence Nightingale, in her 1873 text on nursing, "urged nurses to pay attention not only to the patient's body but also to his mind and morale. She urged that music and conversation be encouraged, that beautiful objects be placed in patient wards, that the family be encouraged to visit and that patients keep small pets. Under her leadership, so-called bedside occupations were introduced in military hospitals to cheer up injured soldiers" (Kraus and Shank, 1992, p. 7).

Yet, it was not until the sudden influx of traumatic and permanent injuries into American society as a result of the World Wars that we begin to see a slow change in attitudes toward people with disabilities and improved recreation programs in hospitals and long-term treatment facilities (Crawford, 1996). Under the leadership of the American Red Cross, the use of recreational activities to treat those who sustained various injuries in military combat during World War I was expanded.

As a result of the success experienced by the American Red Cross, in the 1920s and 1930s recreation services began to appear in other settings such as state mental hospitals (Carter et al., (2003). The Easter Seals Society began providing day and residential camp programs in the 1930s. These types of programs continued to expand, and with the outbreak of World War II therapeutic recreation became an important element in the rehabilitation of wounded soldiers.

TABLE

12.1 EARLY REFORMERS IN PUBLIC HEALTH CARE AND THERAPEUTIC RECREATION

Phillippe Pinel (1745–1826)

A French physician who advocated for the humane treatment of persons with mental illness and the economically disadvantaged, Pinel believed these people were capable human beings who deserved to be treated with compassion and dignity. His approach became known as moral treatment and included purposeful recreational activity and work experiences to restore mental and physical health (Carter, Van Andel, and Robb, 1995).

Benjamin Rush (1745–1813)

One early reformer addressing the needs of the mentally ill at the end of the 1700s was Benjamin Rush, an influential physician. Rush was a signer of the Declaration of Independence, member of the Continental Congress, Surgeon General to the Continental Army during the Revolution, Treasurer of the United States Mint, passionate reformer, brilliant physician, and the first important American psychiatrist. After joining the staff of the Pennsylvania Hospital in 1783, he became the first American physician to develop a comprehensive course of study in mental disease. Rush wrote the first textbook on mental health in 1812 (Crawford, 1996).

Dorothy Dix (1802–1887)

The most famous and influential psychiatric reformer of the nineteenth century was Dorothy Dix. A woman who dedicated her life to the proper care of the mentally ill, her influence spanned three decades (1840s to the 1870s). By the close of her career she had been responsible for founding or enlarging over thirty mental hospitals in the United States and abroad (Crawford, 1996).

Florence Nightingale (1820–1910)

A British nurse in military hospitals who was a pioneer of modern nursing, Florence Nightingale was a strong advocate for improving the rehabilitation environment of hospitals. She organized classes, reading rooms, and recreation huts to combat the negative side effects of being a wounded soldier. In 1873, she wrote a book that included guidelines for visitor conversation, promoted the psychological benefits of music and pets, and highlighted the need for variety in both the objects and the color of hospital environments (Avedon, 1974).

Howard Rusk (1901–1989)

Physician and international authority on physical rehabilitation who believed that both individual and group recreation had a direct and positive relationship upon recovery, Rusk helped to establish the credibility of recreation as an adjunctive therapy (Crawford, 1996).

Paul Haun (1906–1969)

A physician/advocate in the 1940s and 1950s whose writings and presentations supported recreation as a therapeutic modality able to create a desirable psychological state within the patient, Haun was a respected leader in the field (Crawford, 1996).

Eunice Kennedy Shriver (1921-   )

Founder of the Special Olympics movement under the auspices of the Joseph P. Kennedy, Jr. Foundation in 1968, Shriver helped to spread recreation as formal community movement throughout community-based programs for people with developmental disabilities (Crawford, 1996).

The increase in therapeutic recreation programs is evident in the over 1,800 recreation leaders the Red Cross trained and employed during World War II (Frye and Peters, 1972). After the war these leaders became the core of young professionals who pushed the field of therapeutic recreation into other community and clinical settings.

Professional Organizations

As the ranks of hospital workers grew in the mid-1940s, several organizations began to emerge. Carter, Van Andel, and Robb (2003) report that the first effort toward professionalization came from the American Recreation Society (ARS) in 1948 when members laid the groundwork for the establishment of the Hospital Recreation Section (HRS) within ARS. Early members of this section represented hospital recreation workers from military, veterans, and public institutions.

In the early 1950s an organization emerged from within the American Alliance for Health, Physical Education, Recreation and Dance—the Recreation Therapy Section (RTS). Members of this organization felt that HRS was too closely aligned with the community recreation movement and did not adequately represent the recreational therapy perspective. The interests of the membership focused on developing recreation and physical education programs in schools, serving students with disabilities, and adapting physical education programs in integrated schools (Carter et al., 2003).

A third organization emerged in 1953 to meet the needs of recreational therapists from state hospitals and schools serving persons with mental illness or mental retardation. The National Association of Recreational Therapists (NART) became involved in the development of standards for professional education, outlining professional qualifications for clinical practice and defining the role of the profession (Carter et al., 2003).

These three organizations (ARS, RTS, and NART) merged in 1966 to form the National Therapeutic Recreation Society (NTRS) within the National Recreation and Park Association (NRPA). The combined resources and energies of these three organizations pushed the field of therapeutic recreation to new heights in the areas of credentialing, accreditation, and personnel and program standards. In the mid-1980s friction concerning the governance of the organization and the development of a definition and philosophical statement for the organization contributed to the formation of a new professional organization—the American Therapeutic Recreation Association (ATRA) (Carter et al., 2003).

Although the goals of ATRA are similar to NTRS, the process of pursuing these goals is different. Today, ATRA advocates recreation as a form of treatment, hence recreation therapy. This philosophy represents the view of professionals who work in health-care settings where "professional services are more likely to be judged by their effectiveness in improving the functional capacity, health status, and/or quality of life of the client" (Carter et al., 2003 p. 58), whereas NTRS has advocated more for community-based recreation services for persons with disabilities. Together, these two perspectives provide a comprehensive continuum of services to serve the total person; they are discussed in more depth later in this chapter.

Legislation

In the latter half of the twentieth century, the concern for the equal rights of all Americans (including those with disabilities) has increased. This concern has been translated into action as legislation pertaining to equal access and rights to educational and recreational services has evolved. Legislation affecting the delivery of recreation services to persons with disabilities is listed in table 12.2. These laws have led to the passing of the most powerful

TABLE

12.2   LEGISLATION AND OTHER EVENTS AFFECTING RECREATION FOR SPECIAL POPULATIONS

1932   **The Bill of Rights for the Handicapped.** Adopted by the White House Conference on Child Health and Protection, it provided an important endorsement of recreation for disabled children.

1936   **The Social Security Act.** A compilation of laws, including numerous amendments over the last several years related specifically to the elderly and disabled, it includes provisions for physical education and recreation through formal procedures for review of professional services, establishes funds to states for self-support services for individuals, and gives grants to states to provide community-based care.

1963   **Vocational Rehabilitation Act.** This Act provided training and research funds for recreation for the ill and handicapped. This was the first recognition by a specific federal agency of the importance of recreation services in rehabilitation.

1963   **National Outdoor Recreation Plan,** PL 88–29. Directing the formulation and maintenance of a comprehensive nationwide outdoor plan, this plan was completed in 1973 and included an emphasis on compliance with PL 90–480 (see below). Concerns for the handicapped were listed as a priority area.

1967   **Education for Handicapped Children Act,** PL 90–170. This law established the unit of physical education and recreation for handicapped children within the Bureau of Education for the Handicapped; it became the largest federal program for training, research, and special projects related to recreation for special populations.

1968   **Architectural Barriers Act,** PL 90–480. Simply stated, this law indicates that "any building or facility, constructed in whole or part by federal funds, must be accessible to and usable by the physically handicapped."

1971   **Developmental Disabilities Services and Facilities Construction Act,** PL 91–517. Developmentally disabled persons are specifically defined and recreation is listed as a specific service to be included as a fundable service in this federal law.

1973   **Rehabilitation Act,** PL 93–112. This Rehabilitation Act was a comprehensive revision of the 1963 Vocational Rehabilitation Act that included an emphasis on the "total" rehabilitation of the individual.

1974   **Rehabilitation Act Amendment,** PL 93–516. This law authorized the planning and implementation of the White House Conference on Handicapped Individuals. The final report noted the importance of recreation for individuals with disabilities and called for the expansion of recreation services, as well as an increase in the number of professionally trained individuals employed in the field of recreation.

1975   **Education for All Handicapped Children Act,** PL 94–142. By mandating free and appropriate education for all handicapped children, this law identified physical education as a direct service and recreation as a related service to be offered to those with disabilities. Mainstreaming in the school system is usually viewed as an outgrowth of this Act providing the legislative leverage for disabled children and their families to gain access to often denied educational services.

1978   **Rehabilitation Act,** PL 95–602. As with many federal programs, the 1973 Rehabilitation Act and the programs it authorized expired at the end of five years. In 1978, legislation was introduced to extend and amend the 1973 Act. This renewal called for recreation and leisure services to be a part of the rehabilitation process.

1981   Designated by the United Nations as the **International Year of Disabled Persons,** the theme chosen for 1981 was "the full participation of disabled persons in the life of their society."

1986   **Education of the Handicapped Act Amendment,** PL 99–457. This law emphasized the development of comprehensive statewide programs for early intervention services for handicapped infants, toddlers, and families. A multidisciplinary team to develop an individualized family service plan was advocated. Recreation was cited as a related service in this amendment.

1990   **Americans with Disabilities Act,** PL 101–336. Probably the best known of all the laws protecting those with disabilities, the ADA provides comprehensive guidelines banning discrimination against people with disabilities. It is an omnibus civil rights statute that prohibits discrimination against people with disabilities in sectors of private and public employment, all public sectors (including recreation), public accommodations, transportation, and telecommunications.

From D. R. Austin and M. E. Crawford (eds.), "Organization and Formation of the Profession" in *Therapeutic Recreation: An Introduction,* 3rd edition, 2001. Copyright © 1996 by Allyn and Bacon. Reprinted by permission.

legislation pertaining to persons with disabilities, the Americans with Disabilities Act of 1990 (ADA, PL 101–336). ADA is a civil rights law that extends the same protection against discrimination now provided by other federal civil rights laws to people with disabilities. It is the purpose of the act

- to provide a clear and comprehensive national mandate for the elimination of discrimination against individuals with disabilities;
- to provide clear, strong, consistent, enforceable standards addressing discrimination against individuals with disabilities;
- to ensure that the federal government plays a central role in enforcing the standards established in this act on behalf of individuals with disabilities; and
- to invoke the sweep of congressional authority, including the power to enforce the 14th Amendment and to regulate commerce, in order to address the major areas of discrimination faced daily by people with disabilities.

The ADA has offered certified therapeutic recreation specialists (CTRSs) and others working in recreation settings a powerful tool to advocate for the rights of people with disabilities to receive the services and support they need to improve the quality of their lives. The ADA provides the basis to demand full and equal access by persons with disabilities to all types of government and private facilities and programs (restaurants, theaters, stadiums, museums, parks, amusement centers, or other places of recreation). For example, Casey Martin used the ADA to win his right to use a golf cart in Professional Golf Association (PGA) events due to disability (i.e., congenital circulatory disorder) that prevents him from walking long distances (*Golf Magazine,* March 31, 1998). Despite the many strides that have occurred due to the ADA, many Americans are still unaware of the implications of the ADA. As one poll found, 54 percent of individuals over age sixteen with disabilities who took part in the survey did not know that the ADA existed (Farrell, 1998 as cited in Smith, Austin, and Kennedy, 2000).

The legislative history in the United States is encouraging, but old stereotypes and attitudes do not die easily. All too often, people with disabilities are still marginalized and deprived of equal opportunities due to unnecessary barriers and fears. The legislation discussed in this section is not the end of discrimination but it does serve as the beginning where individuals (such as CTRSs) can work to make the dream of equal opportunities for people with disabilities a reality.

Characteristics of Therapeutic Recreation: People with Disabilities Today

The 2000 Census identified 49.7 million people with some type of long-lasting condition or disability; this represents 19.3 percent of the U.S. population over five years of age or nearly one person in five. More specifically, the 2000 Census found:

- 9.3 million people (3.6 percent) with a sensory disability involving sight or hearing
- 21.2 million people (8.2 percent) with a condition limiting basic physical activities, such as walking, climbing stairs, reaching, lifting, or carrying
- 12.4 million people (4.8 percent) with a physical, mental, or emotional condition causing difficulty in learning, remembering, or concentrating
- 6.8 million people (2.6 percent) with a physical, mental, or emotional condition causing difficulty in dressing, bathing, or getting around inside the home
- 18.2 million of those aged 16 and older with a condition that made it difficult to go outside the home to shop or visit a doctor (8.6 percent of the 212.0 million people this age)
- 21.3 million of those aged 16 to 64 with a condition that affected their ability to work at a job or business (11.9 percent of the 178.7 million people this age) (U.S. Census, 2000).

With many of these disabilities come activity limitation that confines their ability to fully participate in a wide range of life opportunities ranging from education and employment to marital and family involvement, as well as recreation participation. Although many of these

Therapeutic recreation is important for people with disabilities to help them learn new skills, get involved in community, and to provide them with a sense of accomplishment.

Copyright © Digital Vision.

disabilities are apparent, others are not. Disabilities such as HIV, dyslexia, or being subject to seizures are not always apparent. All disabilities (hidden or apparent) are often heightened by society's response to people with disabilities and from their own lack of a positive self-concept and confidence in meeting society's challenges.

Therapeutic recreation programs and services serve a wide range of individuals. Programs can help individuals in numerous ways to develop skills, contribute to self-concept and awareness, and, in general, contribute in a positive way to a higher quality of life through the constructive use of leisure. In discussing the ways in which therapeutic recreation can help people of all ages reach their goals, Carter, Van Andel, and Robb (2003) have identified how programs can help individuals with varying disabilities.

People with Physical Disabilities. Therapeutic recreation can help people with physical disabilities, sensory impairments, or other health-related disabilities to learn new skills and/or modify old ones to compensate for abilities they have lost; practice self-care skills; get involved in community recreation programs; and feel a sense of accomplishment.

People with Developmental Disabilities. Therapeutic recreation can help people with mental retardation, cerebral palsy, or other developmental disabilities to develop and use their physical and intellectual abilities to the fullest; develop independence; gain confidence in themselves; and interact with others and participate in community recreation activities.

People with Mental Illness. Taking time to "play" is an important part of good mental health. Therapeutic recreation gives people an opportunity to feel good about themselves and their accomplishments; improve relationships with others; relieve tension; develop healthy coping techniques; and express and communicate their needs.

Older Adults with Limitations. Services can help older adults continue to be involved socially; express themselves creatively; maintain independence; and live fully in spite of any limitations they may have.

People Dependent on Alcohol or Other Drugs. Therapeutic recreation can help people who abuse chemical substances to learn new skills that will enhance their self-esteem to find healthy alternatives to substance abuse, and to feel fit and appreciate the value of wellness.

At-Risk Youth, and Juvenile and Adult Offenders. Therapeutic recreation can provide healthy outlets for energy and activity—recreation is a way to release tension that can be destructive if it remains bottled up; teach people to cooperate with others—through group activities, individuals can learn to work and play together; and improve self-esteem—people need to feel good about themselves before they can feel good about others.

Homeless and Destitute. According to Carter, Van Andel, and Robb (2003, pp. 459–460), therapeutic recreation can serve to assist in "assessment of social and functional capacity to behavioral change and acquisition of coping strategies for daily living" for individuals who are homeless and destitute. Autonomy, control, self-esteem, independent functioning, self-awareness, decision making, planning, and participation in socially valued roles can be enhanced through therapeutic recreation.

Barriers to Success in Leisure

As can be surmised, to be successfully integrated into society, people with disabilities must overcome a number of barriers. Smith, Austin, and Kennedy (2000) have identified three categories of barriers preventing individuals with disabilities from full leisure participation. We have added additional items to their lists. These are found in table 12.3.

Leisure service professionals working with people with disabilities must strive to create an environment whereby many of these barriers can be overcome or negotiated. In the process, it is important for leisure service professionals to work "with" persons with disabilities, empowering them and working together to improve their quality of life. Specifically, leisure service professionals need to create accessible programs and facilities, promote inclusive programs whereby people from different backgrounds and abilities can interact together, and facilitate open communication.

Leisure service programs can offer a valuable experience to people with disabilities. The modifications that are needed to integrate individuals who have special needs is usually very minimal. "These modifications should result in the individualization of the activity and should be taken into account when planning for all peoples. The modifications may require a change in the rules to make the activity more or less challenging. It may require a change in the time allowed for completion. Equipment may need to be modified. The process may need to be stressed instead of the product" (Eller and Mulroy, 1996, p. 6). In the end, being committed to creating integrated programs means

- knocking down the barriers and roadblocks that may exist so that everyone, regardless of ability or background, feels welcome at your program;
- having staff and volunteers who are aware, trained, and ready to facilitate an integrated program;
- promoting a process in which each individual is seen and respected as an individual with strengths and abilities;
- encouraging both physical and social inclusion in all aspects of the program; and
- creating a supportive environment where everyone feels both physically and psychologically safe to participate. This means that specific supports are available for individuals with disabilities or medical needs to ensure that they have equitable opportunities for involvement (Blake, 1996).

TABLE

12.3   BARRIERS/BEHAVIORS

Attitudinal Barriers

These behaviors are usually intentional and obvious. They clearly inform the individual that he or she has less value than individuals without disabilities. An obvious example would be mocking or ridiculing a person with a visible disability while a more subtle example would be avoiding a person with a disability.

Paternalistic Behaviors

Head patting, giving undue or excessive praise, and providing help when it is not needed are examples of paternalistic behaviors. Unlike negative behaviors, paternalistic behaviors arise out of a desire to show the person with a disability that you care or that you have a favorable view of a person with a disability. Unfortunately, the message conveyed is that people with disabilities lack competence, maturity, and the capacity for independence.

Apathetic Behaviors

People who are apathetic toward individuals with disabilities express no feelings of sympathy, understanding, or caring toward people with disabilities.

Intrinsic Barriers

These barriers result from an individual's own limitations and may be associated with a physical, psychological, or cognitive disability. These barriers may be associated with the disability but may also arise from other factors such as parental overprotection or inadequate educational opportunities. Regardless of their cause, intrinsic barriers are permanent or temporary limitations that reside within the individual. Intrinsic barriers include lack of knowledge, social ineffectiveness, health problems, physical and psychological dependency, and lack of skill.

Environmental Barriers

Barriers that result from many of the external forces that impose limitations on the individual with a disability are considered to be evnironmental. No matter how well a person with a disability copes with intrinsic barriers to recreation participation, he or she is faced with other forces that are out of his or her control. These barriers are often complex and require a great deal of cooperation to solve. As a result, these issues can be frustrating to people with disabilities as they are out of their control. Environmental barriers include attitudinal barriers, architectural barriers, transportation barriers, ecological barriers, economic barriers, rules and regulations, and barriers of omission (i.e., failure to publicize adequately those programs that offer appropriate service to people with disabilities).

Communication Barriers

Those factors that block interaction between the individual and his or her social environment are part of communication barriers. These barriers cannot be thought of as either intrinsic or environmental. Communication barriers result from a reciprocal interaction between individuals with disabilities and their social environment.

Goals and Functions

Therapeutic recreation programs serve a variety of different age groups with a wide range of characteristics. As a result, it is difficult to pinpoint one definition that encompasses all aspects of therapeutic recreation. However, it is possible to provide a broad framework for understanding the goals and functions of therapeutic recreation. This framework is evident in the following excerpt of the philosophical statement of NTRS (1996). The purpose of this statement is not to suggest how to practice therapeutic recreation, but rather to articulate a value structure for the profession. The statement includes three broad values:

- *The right to leisure.* The right to leisure is grounded in the notion that the individual is entitled to the opportunity to express unique interests and pursue, develop, and improve talents and abilities because of his/her abilities. The right to leisure is a condition for human dignity and well-being.
- *Self-determination.* Self-determination holds that leisure is an arena of action wherein the individual can express unique abilities and preferences that are encompassed within leisure experiences.
- *Quality of life.* The quality of leisure of persons with disabilities contributes to their quality of life. Leisure should be fun, enjoyable, or satisfying regardless of the participant's abilities. Quality of life also extends beyond the idea of fun. Leisure activities may help prevent illness and secondary disabilities. Within the context of leisure, quality of life also includes prevention of illness within the context of preexisting impairments and promotion of health and functional abilities through leisure.

From this statement, we can see that therapeutic recreation promotes the rights of persons with disabilities to have leisure as well as encourages therapeutic recreation specialists to use leisure and other means to improve individuals' overall quality of life. A number of models in therapeutic recreation have been developed to accomplish this purpose. Two such models are presented in figures 12.1 and 12.2. The model presented in figure 12.1 is one of the foundational models of therapeutic recreation and is called the Leisure Ability Model. It was developed in the late 1970s and revised in the late 1990s. The model is based on the concept of identified client need related to leisure involvement (Peterson and Stumbo, 2000). The overall intended outcome of this model is a satisfying, independent, and freely chosen leisure lifestyle.

The model includes three components—functional intervention, leisure education, and recreation participation. Therapy is directed at improvement of functional behavior that may impede leisure involvement or using leisure to help individuals reach other treatment-related goals. Leisure education teaches new recreation and social skills to help expand a person's leisure repertoire or assist in adapting his or her interests and hobbies into a new situation (e.g., a basketball player learning how to play wheelchair basketball after a spinal injury). The last component, recreation participation, concerns the provision of self-directed leisure participation for individuals with disabilities. In a recent critique of the Leisure Ability Model, Ross and Ashton-Schaeffer noted that "conceptually, the leisure ability model demonstrates a high degree of merit and worth. There are still concerns regarding its theoretical framework and its relevance to setting where only functional outcomes, rather than leisure, are the foci" (p. 169).

Figure 12.2 presents two models that complement each other—the Therapeutic Recreation Outcome Model and the Therapeutic Recreation Service Delivery Model developed by Van Andel in the late 1990s. Within the Therapeutic Recreation Outcome Model, the goal of therapeutic recreation is to assist the client in achieving the highest possible level of health and well-being through leisure and non-leisure experiences (Van Andel, 1998). The key to this model is that quality of life, identified as feelings of satisfaction, contentment, joy, self-determination, well-being, and mastery is interrelated to functional capacities and wellness (Ross and Ashton-Schaeffer, 2002).

Similarly, the goal of therapeutic recreation within the Therapeutic Recreation Service Delivery Model is to empower the client to achieve his or her goals and optimally experience a sense of fulfillment, satisfaction, mastery, and well-being (VanAndel, 1998). Within this model, the scope of the therapeutic recreation services component includes diagnosis/need assessment, treatment/rehabilitation, client education, and prevention and health promotion.

The two models presented in figure 12.2, when used together, are both leisure and therapy oriented; that is, the end product or outcome—the highest possible level of health and well-being—includes leisure and the means of achieving these outcomes may or may not involve

Figure 12.1

Leisure ability
model.

*Source: Peterson,
C. and Stumbo, N.
2000. Therapeutic
Recreation
Program Design:
Principles and
Procedures.
Boston, MA: Allyn
& Bacon, p. 26.*

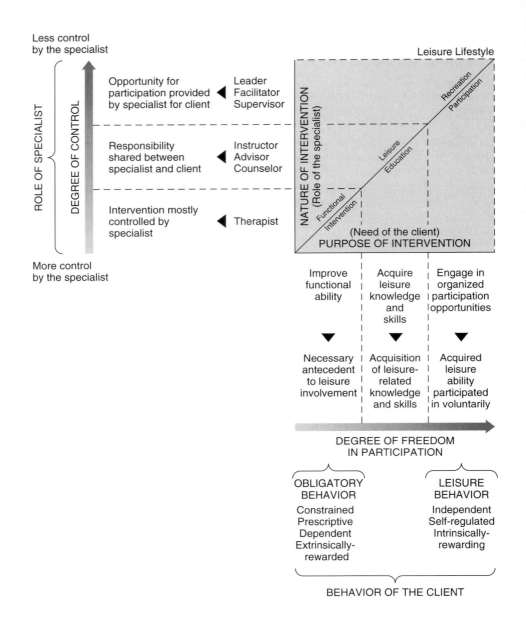

leisure. These models provide therapeutic recreation specialists with a strong theoretical foundation that connects the developmental contributions of leisure to functional outcomes, as well as provides a solid direction for both practice and research in therapeutic recreation (Ross and Ashton-Schaeffer, 2002).

As can be seen in both figures 12.1 and 12.2, professional services in therapeutic recreation can be viewed on a continuum. The purpose of including these two models (for those entering therapeutic recreation, you will be studying many others) reflects the growth of therapeutic recreation. The Leisure Ability Model focuses on recreation and leisure as the only means to move individuals to increased wellness, while the Therapeutic Recreation Outcome model and the Therapeutic Recreation Service Delivery Model broadens the role of therapeutic recreation

Figure 12.2

(a) Therapeutic recreation Service Delivery Model and (b) the Therapeutic Recreation Outcome Model.

Source: Carter, M.J., Van Andel, G.E., & Robb, G.M. (2003) Therapeutic recreation: A practical approach (3rd ed). Prospect Heights, IL: Waveland Press.

A

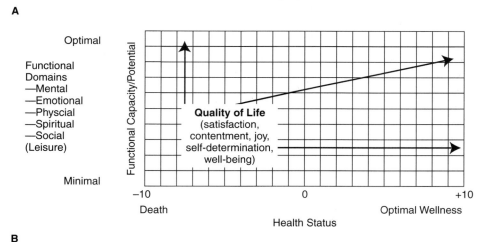

B

specialists to include other interventions (beyond leisure) to increase functional capacity to improve clients' quality of life.

Within these two models and other therapeutic recreation models, two components continually emerge as being important: treatment and recreation (Smith, Austin, and Kennedy, 2000). Within the treatment mode, therapeutic recreation specialists use leisure and other means as a purposeful intervention designed to help clients relieve or prevent problems and to assist them in personal growth in an effort to achieve the highest level of health possible. This is what ATRA emphasizes in its philosophical statement that states "the primary purpose of treatment services, which is often referred to as recreation therapy, is to restore, remediate, or rehabilitate in order to improve functioning and independence as well as reduce or eliminate the effects of illness or disability" (Carter, VanAndel, and Robb, 2003, p. 56). Strong proponents of recreation as therapy and the role of therapeutic recreation specialists in increasing functional capacity often feel that the provision of community recreation for people with disabilities should be the responsibility of community recreation and park personnel who are trained to assist individuals in adapting these activities to their unique needs.

Viewing therapeutic recreation as purposeful intervention does not diminish the importance of providing recreation opportunities for everyone in society. Such programs referred to as inclusive or special recreation programs are equally important if the continuum of services (presented in figure 12.1 and figure 12.2) is to be complete. In many ways the term *inclusive recreation* is being used to describe full inclusion of persons with disabilities into the recreation mainstream whereby equal and joint participation of persons with and without disabilities can take place (Smith et al., 2000). In contrast, *special recreation* programs refer to special or adapted activities, such as Special Olympics and wheelchair sports, through which special needs are met. The emphasis on inclusive and special recreation programs demonstrates the increasing importance for recreation providers in all areas of the economy (public, nonprofit, and commercial operators) to provide recreation services for persons with disabilities. As these types of programs continue to grow, there is a need for therapeutic recreation specialists to help organizations meet the diverse needs of all people in the community.

Resource Base

The resource base or revenue for therapeutic recreation services is diverse. Therapeutic recreation services may be found in public organizations (e.g., federal, state, county, and municipal government), private nonprofit organizations (e.g., group homes, advocacy groups), as well as commercial organizations (e.g., for profit hospitals, nursing homes). In addition, today's competitive health-care environment is encouraging a number of innovative collaborative projects between public, private, and commercial organizations. As a result, funding may be a complex issue for many therapeutic recreation programs.

Insurance payments further compound the issue of funding for therapeutic recreation services. Although third party billing is not a reality for many agencies devoted to therapeutic recreation, insurance companies often pay for related services such as therapeutic recreation in inpatient and outpatient care in medically-based facilities. Within the funding framework, one constant is clear: Therapeutic recreation specialists need to be creative to continue funding programs at the needed level because the rising costs of medical care are shrinking health-care dollars.

To remain competitive, therapeutic recreation specialists are constantly looking for opportunities to document the outcomes of their programs (Coveliers, Milliron, Page, and Rath, 1996). Programs are developed with specific benefits, values, and goals in mind. It is only through an underlying commitment to fostering these benefits that they will be achieved. One of the results of such an analysis is identifying the benefits associated with various programs. In many areas of the parks and recreation field, professionals are embracing such a benefits-based approach to providing services.

Characteristics of Professionals

In 2002, there were approximately 27,000 recreation therapists employed throughout the United States. About one-third of salaried jobs for therapists were in nursing care facilities and almost another third were in hospitals. Others were employed in state and local government agencies and in community care facilities for the elderly, including assisted living, community mental health centers, adult day care programs, correctional facilities, substance abuse centers, and community programs for persons with disabilities. A small number of therapists were self-employed, generally contracting with long-term care facilities or community agencies to develop and oversee programs (U.S. Department of Labor, 2004).

The overall job outlook for therapeutic recreation specialists varies depending on the type of setting in which one is interested in working. For example, overall employment of recreational therapists is expected to grow more slowly than the average of all occupations, but employment of therapeutic recreation specialists who work in community care facilities for the elderly and in residential mental health and substance abuse facilities should grow faster than average (U.S. Department of Labor, 2004).

To be a certified therapeutic recreation specialist (CTRS), one must have at least a bachelor's degree in therapeutic recreation. In addition to a college degree, CTRSs must have completed an internship (of at least 480 hours) under the supervision of a CTRS, passed a certification exam, and maintained a program of continuing education as set forth by the National Council for Therapeutic Recreation Certification (NCTRC). NCTRC is an important organization for aspiring therapeutic recreation specialists. The mission statement for NCTRC is presented in table 12.4, while additional information about NCTRC can be found at its Web site (http://www.nctrc.org).

In addition to these educational and certification requirements, the U.S. Department of Labor's *Occupational Outlook Handbook* (2004) states that "recreation therapists should be comfortable working with people who are ill or who have disabilities. Therapists must be patient, tactful, and persuasive when working with people who have a variety of special needs. Ingenuity, a sense of humor, and imagination are needed to adapt activities to individual needs" (p. 221).

In an empirical study examining the competencies that entry-level recreational professionals should possess to serve people with disabilities, Austin and Powell (as cited in Smith, Austin, and Kennedy, 2000) identified eighty-six different competencies. These competencies were then organized into clusters. The highest-rating cluster related to attitudes (i.e., understands how to

TABLE

12.4 MISSION OF NCTRC

To protect the consumer of therapeutic recreation services by promoting the provision of quality therapeutic recreation services by NCTRC certificants.

To Achieve this Mission we. . .

- Develop standards for certification.
- Establish standards of conduct and apply a disciplinary process.
- Conduct entry, recertification, and reentry testing.
- Maintain an up-to-date job analysis.
- Liaison with professional organizations with regards to standards of practice.
- Verify certification for employers.
- Conduct research and development.
- Provide recertification and reentry.
- Liaison with educators to provide information and develop opportunities for student acquisition of education and experience necessary for certification.
- Provide information to the public regarding standards, disciplinary processes, and certification.

Source: NCTRC, 2004. Retrieved from http://www.nctrc.org/about/mission.html.

promote positive attitudes toward people with disabilities through recreation programs). The second cluster related to areas and facilities (i.e., understands the frustration experienced in an inaccessible environment). The third cluster related to having a philosophical position that advocates for the recreation needs of people with disabilities. The fourth cluster related to leadership issues in which recreational professionals know how to facilitate integrated recreational groups.

In related research connected to the characteristics of leaders who make a difference in the lives of youth, a variety of studies have identified the need for leaders to focus on the potential of youth rather than on their problems, focusing on the needs of clients first, having a passion for one's work, and finding a personalized style in working with youth (DeGraaf, Ramsing, Gassman, and DeGraaf, 2001). Although many of these characteristics relate specifically to youth leaders, they are also transferable to working with other populations, including those with disabilities.

Types of Therapeutic Recreation Programs/Settings

As previously discussed in the goals and functions section, there is a difference between therapeutic recreation and special or inclusive recreation, and each stands alone as an important element in meeting the needs of all members of a community. While distinct, these two entities often overlap. Overlap occurs when a therapeutic recreation program offers a client an accompanying benefit of a recreative experience, or when a special or inclusive recreation program serves as an intervention, bringing about a desired therapeutic benefit (Smith et al., 2000). This overlap may also be seen in the variety of agencies that offer both therapeutic recreation programs as well as special/inclusive recreation. Kraus and Shank (1992) and the NTRS (1993) have identified several types of agencies or settings that provide a variety of programs along the continuum presented in figure 12.1.

Outpatient clinics. Outpatient clinics provide a number of therapeutic recreation services and programs. In general, outpatient programs provide services for individuals who do not stay overnight. Length of treatment can vary, as can the number of hours per day that patients are involved in treatment. For example, outpatient programs may be offered to support and treat individuals with substance abuse problems. Such programs may include counseling, information, small-group discussion, and a variety of leisure activities and services.

Group homes. A group home is usually thought of as a residential facility that houses six or more individuals. These types of residential care units provide therapeutic recreation programs and services such as sports, trips and tours, arts and crafts, aquatics, literary self-improvement, and others. In addition, group homes provide leisure education programs that prepare individuals to live more independently and/or improve their leisure skills. A group home is a controlled, strongly supervised environment.

Home health care agencies. Such organizations provide in-home care and associated support services for individuals. For example, the hospice concept found in many communities throughout the United States provides in-home health care and other support services for terminally ill individuals and their families. For example, the Cedar Valley (Iowa) Hospice has as its mission a commitment ". . . to providing quality palliative and support services to help meet the physical, psychological, social and spiritual needs of dying persons and their families, during the patient's illness and throughout bereavement."

Substance abuse facilities. There are several different types of settings in which therapeutic recreation services are offered as a part of a substance abuse program. Some of these include acute care hospital programs, residential care, and outpatient services. Programs include self-help, education, counseling, therapy (e.g., milieu, psychotherapy, group therapy, etc.), and others. The purpose of therapeutic recreation in these types of settings is to help individuals find a ". . . healthy means to satisfy needs previously met through drug-taking . . . TR can facilitate new learning related to social and free-time choices, and provide a natural but supportive environment to practice new skills and pursue positive alternative ways of behaving." (Kunstler, 2001, p. 97)

Vocational training centers. These types of settings provide individuals with training and counseling focused on an individual's work or career goals. For example, Goodwill Industries of America provides career training while offering social skills development, medical management, and leisure education. Vocational training centers are often associated with treatment or rehabilitation programs. Such programs provide opportunities for involvement in action-oriented therapies such as art, dance, music, occupational, and, of course, therapeutic recreation.

Camps. Numerous day and residential camp programs are targeted specifically for individuals with disabilities. Camp Courageous in the state of Iowa provides opportunities for individuals with a full range of disabilities to participate in a wide variety of therapeutic recreation programs including outdoor adventure, camping, sports, arts and crafts, aquatics, and others. This organization is a nonprofit, year-round, recreational, and respite care facility for individuals with disabilities.

Centers for independent living. Usually, facilities for independent living are supervised residential facilities for one or more individuals. These arrangements are clustered in several combined units such as an apartment complex. Centers for independent living provide opportunities for individuals to continue their career training while engaging in activities for social skill development and leisure education. Following a stay in a halfway house, an individual might transition to a center for independent living.

Sheltered workshops. This type of setting provides a protective environment in which individuals engage in meaningful work experiences and learn job skills. Sheltered workshops may provide therapeutic recreation services as a part of their support for participating individuals. An example, Adults, Inc. in Waterloo, Iowa, uses therapeutic recreation to enhance its clients' social and recreational skills.

Community mental health centers. Gallagher (1980) refers to a community mental health center as a program that provides partial (day) hospitalization for individuals with psychiatric disorders. These types of centers may provide inpatient and outpatient services, partial hospitalization, emergency services, consultation, and education. Therapeutic recreation services vary, but usually emphasize community recreational activities such as sports, drama, trips, camping, outdoor pursuits, and others. For example, the Merced (California) County Mental Health program offers all of the previously mentioned services as well as conducts a fully developed therapeutic recreation program staffed by certified therapeutic recreation specialists and aides.

Adult day-care centers. An adult day-care center ". . . is a community-based group program designed to meet the needs of functionally impaired adults through an individual plan of care. It is a structured, comprehensive program that provides a variety of health, social, and related support services in a protected setting during any part of the day, but less than 24-hours . . ." (Behren, 1986, p. 2).

Senior centers. These types of settings provide opportunities for individuals to pursue leisure activities as a major focal point of their effort. As Teague, McGhee, and Hawkins (2001) write, "senior centers provide a place for older adults to come together for socialization, leisure activity and other services" (2001) (p. 242) Nearly every community in the United States provides some type of support for such a program. Activities found in these types of programs include current events, literature, trips, genealogy, art, fitness, social recreation, and numerous others. Programs also provide information, referral services, and treatment programs related to the needs of participants.

Psychiatric facilities. Therapeutic recreation programs in psychiatric facilities focus on rehabilitation, education, and participation (Peterson and Gunn, 1984). In these environments, the role of the therapeutic recreation specialist is ". . . to help the individual free himself from the constraints that are limiting his personal growth and healthy choices in behavior . . . typical settings include inpatient, outpatient, partial or day settings, transitional settings, and individualized settings . . ." (Austin and Crawford, 2001).

Hospitals. Hospitals are housed under various sponsorship such as the Veterans. Administration, military, public health (federal, state, county, municipal), nonprofit hospitals, sectarian, and proprietary. Many of them offer therapeutic recreation services as a part of patient rehabilitation.

Nursing homes. Nursing homes can be described as long-term care facilities for ill or disabled (and often, senior) citizens who can no longer function in the community or reside with their own families. Nursing homes are increasingly admitting younger patients who may be profoundly mentally retarded or have head injuries, strokes, or other traumas, and who cannot live independently.

Settings serving elderly persons. There are increasing numbers of residential centers for seniors who cannot or choose not to live independently or with their families, do not require intensive nursing or medical care, and meet many of their own needs independently. These types of programs/settings include municipal, county, or state homes for the elderly; residential centers sponsored by sectarian or service organizations; low income housing projects with special units for the aging; and commercially developed retirement centers. In the future, this type of setting may also include senior day-care programs as well as in-home care programs that may be offered to seniors who live in their own homes.

Schools or residential centers for those with specific disabilities. These institutions permanently house people with physical disabilities (e.g., visually impaired, hearing impaired, orthopedically or neurologically impaired), those with mental retardation, or emotionally ill persons. These centers offer "full service programming" with schooling, recreation, religion, and living skills all a part of the services provided.

Penal institutions and other programs for socially deviant persons. These types of institutions include adult penal institutions such as prisons, jails, and other detention centers, as well as work camps, reformatories, therapeutic camps, wilderness programs, and special schools for youth who have been committed by the courts for delinquent behavior. In addition, special schools and shelters for emotionally disturbed children and youth, or for those from broken families or families incapable of providing adequate care, are included here.

Centers for physical medicine and rehabilitation. Often these types of facilities are found in close proximity to hospital complexes, universities, and/or medical schools and serve as treatment centers for a variety of people who have suffered serious physical injury. Such people are no longer under treatment for the acute phase of their illness or injury and are receiving varied forms of physical, psychological, vocational, and social rehabilitation to facilitate their return to their families and community life.

Programs of voluntary agencies. A number of national organizations have been established to promote services for specific groups of people with disabilities such as cerebral palsy, orthopedic or neurological disorders, and mental retardation. Special Olympics International and Easter Seals (which provides special camping programs) are two examples of the growing number of these types of programs. National youth serving organizations are also increasing their programs targeting specific groups of children and adolescents facing specific risks (e.g., gangs, violence, pregnancy, drug abuse).

Public recreation and parks departments. Governmental leisure service agencies on every level—federal, state, and local—have increasingly accepted responsibility for providing recreation for persons with disabilities. In some cases the sponsor may offer segregated activities for customers with severe disabilities while encouraging opportunities for fully integrated participation for others. With the emphasis on integration and mainstreaming, and with the support of legislation such as the Americans with Disabilities Act, more emphasis will be placed on creating inclusive recreation opportunities for all.

Challenges for the Future

As we have moved through the 1990s and into the twenty-first century, we have seen tremendous change in health care. Therapeutic recreation specialists in both clinical and community settings are facing a work environment that is constantly changing. On one hand professionals are being asked to document outcomes, respond to the needs of the customer, and provide quality services, while on the other hand they are being asked to deal with budget cuts and staff reductions. Managers and staff everywhere must meet the challenge of doing more, doing it faster and better, and with fewer resources.

Little, Lankford, DeGraaf, and Tashiro (1995) used a nominal group process technique to identify the issues and trends with which therapeutic recreation professionals were most concerned. Specifically, participants viewed the related issues/trends of budget cuts, health care reform, and reduction of staff as the most important changes related to the field of therapeutic recreation. (See table 12.5 for the shifts in approaches to health care.) "Lack of awareness of therapeutic recreation by political leadership" and "salary equity of therapeutic recreation workers" also ranked high. Other issues identified included transportation and mobility issues for people with disabilities, the need for staff (and volunteer) training, need for services in developing countries, motivating staff, having less time to assist patients to re-enter the community, fundraising, promotion of community outings for residential patients, lack of qualified personnel, deinstitutionalization, the impact of ADA, need for certification, value of TR in general hospital setting, and the lack of opportunities and funding for continuing education units (cells).

As all agencies deal with the rising costs of health care, it will be increasingly important to document the effectiveness of therapeutic recreation in clinical and community settings and to increase programs and find innovative funding sources and partnerships. For example, home-based recreation services will serve a wide range of populations, especially an increasing number of senior citizens. Home health care in the United States is expanding because it reduces health-care costs while helping individuals to maintain some of their independence.

TABLE

12.5 HEALTH SHIFTS—CHANGES IN ALL ASPECTS OF HEALTH CARE

Shifts From	To
Doctor Care	Self-Care
Treatment	Prevention
Sole Provider	Health Promotion Team
Exercise and Fitness	Wellness
Looking Good	Living Well
The Years in Your Life	The Life in Your Years

Source: Trends Action Group, 1993, National Recreation and Park Association.

Documenting Outcomes

Today's complex world demands that all recreation professionals understand societal changes as well as the specific benefits customers expect from programs. This is especially true for therapeutic recreation specialists as they look to partner with other medical disciplines to serve clients and patients as well as work to find funding to deliver their services. One approach to document outcomes that is being embraced by park and recreation departments as well as therapeutic recreation programs is a benefits-based approach to providing services.

A benefits approach to leisure has evolved from benefits-based management (BBM) theory, which encourages therapeutic recreation specialists to consider a broad model for explaining benefits in a way such that funders and managers understand the long- and short-term benefits of participating in therapeutic recreation programs. Within such a model, benefits are defined as:

- The realization of desired and satisfying on-site psychological experiences;
- Changes that are viewed to be advantageous or improvements in condition (gains) to individuals (i.e., psychological and physiological), groups, society, or even to another entity such as an endangered species; and
- The prevention of a worse condition (Driver, Brown, and Peterson, 1991).

In this regard, benefits-based management is moving the recreation profession (including therapeutic recreation programs) forward by integrating the concept that value is added to people's lives *following* on-site recreation participation (Driver, Brown, and Peterson, 1991). According to Driver and Bruns (1999) the fundamental question raised by a benefits approach to leisure is:

> [W]hy should a particular leisure service be provided? The answer to this question is formulated in terms of clearly defined positive and negative consequences of delivering that service with the objective being to optimize net benefits—or to add as much value as possible. To do this, leisure policy analysts and managers must understand what values would be added by each leisure service provided, articulate those values, and understand how to capture them. (p. 4)
>
> Thus, it is important for therapeutic recreation professionals to understand the immediate and potential long-term benefits connected to their programs and work to maximize these benefit opportunities. This includes understanding the role of therapeutic recreation services in assessment, treatment, education, and prevention/health promotion. As therapeutic recreation specialists do a better job in

documenting the positive outcomes of their services, the easier it will become to justify funding and defend programs and services in times of tight budgets.

Dealing with Assistive Technology

Keeping current with technological breakthroughs is a constant challenge for therapeutic recreation professionals today. New technologies to assist individuals with disabilities enhance their quality of life are developed everyday. Simply stated, assistive technologies include all devices that increase independence and enable people with disabilities to enjoy learning, living, working, and playing more fully. "Assistive technology is any device or piece of equipment that can be used by a person with a disability to become less dependent. Examples of assistive technology include the following: computers, seating systems, communication devices, magnifiers, beeper balls, sit skis, assistive listening devices, and many, many more" (Bullock and Mahon, 1997, p. 430). As can be seen from this list, assistive technology does not necessarily mean high-cost, complex technology items. Rather, assistive technology is any item that enhances the lives of people with disabilities.

In dealing with assistive technology, Broach, Datilo, and Deavours (2000) have suggested that CTRSs and other recreation professionals remember the following suggestions:

- Focus on the person rather than on the technology.
- Focus on a person's abilities rather than his or her limitations when using technology.
- Provide technology—assistive technology cannot provide empowerment or access unless it is made available. Many people do not access technology due to a lack of community services and funding. As a result CTRSs and other recreation professionals need to be strong advocates for the development of inexpensive and versatile technology and providing this technology to the people who need it.
- Encourage independence, as dependence may result when technology does too much for individuals with disabilities, thus discouraging them from reaching their potential.
- Develop competence in assistive technology—one of the barriers to using assistive technology is lack of knowledge and how to select appropriate devices. CTRSs and other recreation professionals who are knowledgeable about new technology and how to use the technology are a tremendous resource to people with disabilities as they attempt to learn about and incorporate assistive technologies into their lives.

Addressing Social Problems

CTRSs must continue to serve those outside of the mainstream. It is easy to serve those outside the mainstream in times of affluence, but when resources begin to dwindle, a conflict in values can result. For while good times provide increased options and encourage the free play of individual interests, hard times diminish options and create competition for resources. Professionals in the field of therapeutic recreation must seek out connections with other fields and social service agencies. Professionals need to build bridges between fields, especially in community therapeutic recreation programs. Expanding an agency's role in the community increases political strength for, and public awareness of, the therapeutic recreation profession. Through collaboration and partnerships therapeutic recreation can be involved in addressing a variety of social problems that include the following:

- *AIDS.* AIDS affects three groups: those with clinical cases of AIDS, those with AIDS-related complex, and those who are infected with the AIDS virus but are asymptomatic. CTRSs may work with persons with AIDS in a variety of clinical and community settings including hospitals, long-term care facilities, prisons, substance abuse centers, and hospices. Because there is no cure for AIDS, individuals will need activities that provide immediate gratification as well as those that assist them in coping with the demands and uncertainty of the disease. Persons with AIDS and related illnesses need opportunities to learn coping and leisure skills that are appropriate to their health status and emotional needs.

- *Brain Injured.* Therapeutic recreation professionals need to be sensitive to a new population created due to technology. For example, whereas twenty years ago the majority of brain-injured people died soon after the injury, today 95 percent of people with head injuries survive—technology helps keep people alive. An estimated 15 percent of survivors of brain injury are left with permanent deficits that prevent them from returning to their previous school, job, or relationships. Responding to this group of people means providing programs in all areas of the service continuum: therapy, leisure education, and recreation.
- *Homeless.* According to the Department of Housing and Urban Development, homelessness is "a condition of being without a regular dwelling place whereby a person or family lives outside on the streets, tries to find a public or private shelter at night or sleeps in a makeshift dwelling such as a car or a train station" (Kunstler, 1991, p. 31). In 2003, the U.S. Conference of Mayors conducted a survey of twenty-five large cities throughout the United States. They found that the number of people served in homeless shelters increased in the majority of American cities and that length of time people remained homeless (average five months) also increased. Other findings of this study found that single men comprised 41 percent of the homeless population; families with children, 40 percent; single women, 14 percent; and unaccompanied youth, 5 percent. An average of 23 percent of homeless people in cities are considered mentally ill, 30 percent are substance abusers, 17 percent are employed, and 10 percent are veterans (U.S. Conference of Mayors, 2003).
- *New Poor.* Lahey (1991) has identified three groups that are the hardest hit by today's growing inequity in the health-care system who should be of major concern for all recreation professionals. These groups include children living in poverty, the working poor (an alarming number are homeless and without medical insurance), and the frail elderly. By strict clinical/medical definitions, these groups would not qualify for services until the difficulty of their situations brings them to the point of hospitalization and short-term intervention. As recreation professionals continue to look for ways to develop preventative approaches rather than reactive programs, those living in poverty should not be overlooked. One example of a organization reaching out to this segment of the population through recreation programs is Degage, a nonprofit organization in Grand Rapids, Michigan, that attempts to reach out to the poor and dispossessed and create a safe harbor where friendships are formed and community begins. Affectionately nicknamed "the living room" of the Heartside community, Degage offers an informal space for leisure, recreation, and connecting with others.
- *Gangs.* Gang activity remains a problem for many American cities. The latest data from the Centers for Disease Control and Prevention show that, in 2001, 2,911 children and teens were killed by gunfire (1771 homicides, 928 suicides, 182 accidental shootings, and 30 other means). Although these numbers are down from the mid-1990s, the numbers are still too high. The role of firearm deaths among children under fifteen is twelve times higher in the United States than in twenty-five other industrial countries combined (Children's Defense Fund, 2004). Many of these violent deaths are related to gangs. One example of a public recreation department reaching out to gangs can be found in the city of

Phoenix Parks, Recreation, and Library Department. This department has created an At-Risk Youth Division, which supports, develops, and maintains community resources for partnerships and coordinates direct services for youths (City of Phoenix, 1999). One specific program offered is the X-TATTOO: Tattoo Removal Program, which provides former gang members an opportunity to remove tattoos on their face, neck, and hands that pose a significant barrier to leaving their former life. In partnership with local plastic surgeons, youth can have tattoos removed free of charge in exchange for community service and their attendance in educational classes.

Recreation professionals have much to offer as communities search out multidimensional solutions to gangs. As society moves toward a more holistic youth development model for dealing with young people, recreation professionals must see youth as a resource to be developed rather than as a problem to be fixed. Such an approach to youth development creates programs where youth can acquire a broad range of competencies and demonstrate a full complement of connections to self, others, and the larger communities.

This list is not all-inclusive of the problems facing our communities but it does demonstrate the need for CTRSs to continue to look for ways to extend our services. The possibilities are everywhere; using cooperative arrangements with other social service agencies, we can continue to meet the changing needs of everyone, including people with disabilities.

As therapeutic recreation professionals look to the future, the challenges can seem overwhelming. There is opportunity in change, however, and the profession must move forward. In the words of Broida (1996), "Now is the time for us to mobilize our creativity and meet our professional challenges in positive, proactive ways. We need to communicate our ideas with others so that we all benefit from the expertise of our colleagues. This probably means losing some ego, letting up on the protection of our 'turf' and having everyone in the field commit to move the professional toward the unified goal of better services for our customers" (p. 37).

Summary

Oliver Wendall Holmes once said, "The great thing in this world is not so much where we are, but in what direction we are moving." This chapter has documented the movement of society in providing recreation opportunities for everyone. Much still needs to be done, but the field of therapeutic recreation is moving forward in the right direction. With the increased recognition of the potential of recreation as a treatment modality as well as the increasing need to provide inclusive or special recreation programs for persons with disabilities, the field of therapeutic recreation has grown tremendously.

Therapeutic recreation emerged over the last century as a result of a number of different factors including the influx of wounded soldiers from both World War I and World War II, the emergence of professional organizations, and a variety of federal legislation. Despite the growth of services for people with disabilities, a number of barriers still exist in truly integrating them back into society. This chapter discusses two types of barriers—physical and attitudinal. Professionals in the field of therapeutic recreation are constantly advocating for their clients and assisting them in overcoming these barriers.

Within the field of therapeutic recreation, two distinct aspects of the profession remain. The first is often referred to as therapeutic recreation, which is a purposeful intervention designed to help clients grow and to assist them to relieve or prevent problems through recreation. A second aspect of the profession, often referred to as inclusive or special recreation programs, provides recreation services for people with disabilities. With the growth of legislation (like ADA), it is becoming increasingly important for all recreation providers (public, private, nonprofit, and commercial) to provide recreation services for people with disabilities.

The growth in services for people with disabilities and increased awareness of society to meet the needs of people with disabilities translate to a bright future for those interested in both therapeutic recreation and inclusive recreation. Yet many challenges exist, ranging from financing and assuring quality in program development to meeting the program needs for new disability groups and growing social problems. As therapeutic recreation professionals look to the future, the challenges can seem overwhelming; yet, if one looks how far the profession has come, one realizes that anything is possible.

Discussion Questions

1. Define therapeutic recreation and inclusive recreation. Why is there a need for both types of services?
2. How do the philosophical statements of NTRS and ATRA differ?
3. What are the barriers people with disabilities face in participating in leisure and recreation? What are three specific things that could be done to make community recreation programs more inclusive?
4. Identify several of the major types of sponsors of therapeutic recreation service (e.g., nursing homes) and clarify the role recreation can play in the lives of the people they serve.
5. How did the U.S. Armed Forces assist in the development of therapeutic recreation programs?
6. As people move more to a wellness approach to medical care, how will the role of therapeutic recreation change?
7. In your own words, explain the impact of the ADA on the provision of recreation services.
8. Identify five or more disabling conditions and discuss how therapeutic recreation services can assist individuals to improve their quality of life.
9. Discuss the emergence of therapeutic recreation as a profession.
10. Identify and discuss successful leadership strategies and characteristics of leaders who work with people who have disabilities.

References

Austin, D. R. 2001. The therapeutic recreation process. Edited by D. R. Austin and M. E. Crawford, in *Therapeutic Recreation: An Introduction*. Boston, MA: Allyn & Bacon.

Avedon, E. M. 1974. *Therapeutic Recreation Service: An Applied Behavior Science Approach*. Englewood Cliffs, NJ: Prentice Hall.

Behren, R. V. 1986. *Adult Day Care in America: Summary of a National Survey*. Washington, DC: The National Council on Aging and National Institute on Adult Day Care.

Blake, J. 1996. Opening doors: Integration of persons with a disability in organized children's camping in Canada. *Leisurability 23*(2), 3–9.

Broach, E., J. Datilo, and M. Deavours. 2000. Assistive technologies. Edited by J. Datilo, in *Facilitation Techniques in Therapeutic Recreation*. 99–132. State College, PA: Venture.

Broida, J. K. 1996. Innovation in therapeutic recreation. *Parks and Recreation 31*(5), 371.

Bullock, C., and M. Mahon. 1997. *Introduction to Recreation Services for People with Disabilities: A People Centered Approach*. Champaign, IL: Sagamore.

Carter, M. J., G. E. Van Andel, and G. M. Robb. 2003. *Therapeutic Recreation: A Practical Approach*. Prospect Heights, IL: Waveland Press.

Carter, M., VanAndel, G., and Robb, G. 2003. *Therapeutic Recreation: A Practical Approach*. Prospect Heights, IL: Waveland Press.

Children's Defense Fund. 2004. *Protect Children Instead of Guns, 2004*. Washington, D.C.

City of Phoenix. 1999. *Making a Difference in Phoenix*. Phoenix, AZ: Phoenix Parks, Recreation, and Library Department.

Coveliers, L., T. Milliron, G. Page, and K. Rath. 1996. Advancement of therapeutic recreation through "creative administration." *Parks and Recreation 31*(5), 54–57.

Crawford, M. E. 1996. Organization and formation of the profession. Edited by D. R. Austin and M. E. Crawford, in *Therapeutic Recreation: An Introduction*. Boston, MA: Allyn & Bacon.

DeGraaf, D., R. Ramsing, J. Gassman, and K. DeGraaf. 2001. *Camp Leadership: A Staff Development Approach.* Dubuque, IA: Eddie Bowers.

Driver, B. L., and Bruns, D. H. 1999. Concepts and uses of the benefits approach to leisure. In E. L. Jackson and T. L. Burton, eds., *Leisure studies: Prospects for the twenty-first century.* State College, PA: Venture Publishing, Inc.

Driver, B. L., Brown, P. J., and Peterson, G. L., eds. 1991. *Benefits of leisure.* State College, PA: Venture Publishing, Inc.

Eller, C. L., and M. T. Mulroy. 1996. *Developmentally Appropriate Programming for School-Age Children.* Available at www.exnet.iastate.edu/pages/nncc/SACC/dev.approp.sac.html.

Frye, V., and M. Peters. 1972. *Therapeutic Recreation: Its Theory, Philosophy and Practice.* Harrisburg, PA: Stackpole Books.

Gallagher, B. J. 1980. *The Sociology of Mental Illness.* Englewood Cliffs, NJ: Prentice Hall.

Goldman, C. 1987. *Disability Rights Guide: Practical Solutions to Problems Affecting People with Disabilities.* Lincoln, NE: Media Publications.

Gray, D. E. 1969. The case for compensatory recreation. *Parks and Recreation 4*(4), 23–24.

Kraus, R., and J. Shank. 1992. *Therapeutic Recreation Service: Principles and Practices.* Dubuque, IA: Wm. C. Brown.

Kraus, L., S. Stoddard, and D. Gilmartin. 1996. *Chartbook on Disability.* Washington DC: National Institute on Disability and Rehabilitation Research.

Kunstler, R. 1991. There but for a fortune: A therapeutic recreation perspective on the homeless in America. *Therapeutic Recreation Journal 25*(2), 31–38.

Kunstler, R., *Substance Abuse* in Austin, D. R., and M. E. Crawford, eds. 2001. *Therapeutic Recreation: An Introduction.* Boston, MA: Allyn & Bacon.

Lahey, M. p. 1991. Serving the new poor: Therapeutic recreation values in hard times. *Therapeutic Recreation Journal 25*(2), 9–19.

Little, J., S. Lankford, D. DeGraaf, and A. Tashiro. 1995. An exploratory study of issues and trends in therapeutic recreation: A recreation perspective. *Journal of Applied Recreation Research 20*(4), 269–282.

National Therapeutic Recreation Society. 1993. *About Therapeutic Recreation.* South Deerfield, MA: Channing L. Bete Co.

National Therapeutic Recreation Society. 1996. *Philosophical Position Statement of the National Therapeutic Recreation Society.*

NCTRC. 2004. Mission statement retrieved from http://www.nctrc.org.

Peterson, C. A., and S. L. Gunn. 1984. *Therapeutic Recreation Program Design: Principles and Procedures.* Englewood Cliffs, NJ: Prentice Hall.

Peterson, C., and N. Stumbo. 2000. *Therapeutic Recreation Program Design: Principles and Procedures.* Boston, MA: Allyn & Bacon.

Ross, J. and Ashton-Shaeffer, C. Therapeutic Recreation Practice Models. In Stumbo, N. (ed) *Professional Issues in Therapeutic Recreation: On Competence and Outcomes.* Champaign, IL: Sagamore.

Sessoms, H. G., and J. L. Stevenson. 1981. *Leadership and Group Dynamics in Recreation Services.* Boston, MA: Allyn & Bacon.

Smith, R., D. Austin, and D. Kennedy. 2000. *Inclusive and Special Recreation: Opportunities for Persons with Disabilities.* Boston, MA: McGraw-Hill.

Staff. March 31, 1998. Martin to use cart for U.S. Open qualifier. *Golf Magazine* online found at: www.golfonline.com/tours/caseymartin/usopencart0331.html.

Staff. (2004). *Occupational Outlook Handbook.* Washington, DC: U.S. Government Printing Office, U.S. Department of Labor.

Teague, M., McGhee, V., and Hawkins, B. *Geriatric Practice* in Austin, D. R., and M. E. Crawford, eds. 2001. *Therapeutic Recreation: An Introduction.* Boston, MA: Allyn & Bacon.

Trends Action Group (TAG). 1993. *Trends Being Tracked.* Presented at the National Recreation and Park Association national conference, San Jose, CA.

U.S. Bureau of the Census. 2000. Statistical Abstract of the United States. Retrieved from http://www.census.gov/hhes/www/disable/disabstat2k/disabstat2ktxt.html.

U.S. Conference of Mayors. 2003. *Hunger and Homelessness Survey: A Status Report on Hunger and Homelessness in American Cities.* Retrieved from http://usmayors.org/uscm/home.asp

U.S. Department of Labor. 2004. *Occupational Outlook Handbook.* Washington, DC: U.S. Government Printing Office.

Van Andel, G. 1998. TR Service Delivery and TR Outcome Models. *Therapeutic Recreation Journal 32,* 180–193.

Issues, Trends, and Professional Practice

Leisure service professionals manage a wide array of programs and activities that require continuous learning and development to respond to the ever-changing needs of individuals.

CHAPTER 13

Leisure Programming: Promoting Quality Services

Here, a father and son enjoy the exhilaration of a quality play experience.

Introduction

Leisure programming, creating leisure experiences and benefits, is central to the work of the profession. It has become a primary focus of professionals because of increased emphasis on accountability and a desire to provide more relevant, meaningful programs and services to customers. The key to successfully meeting customer needs is to provide services of quality and value. All individuals involved in leisure service organizations touch the customer, either directly or indirectly. Those who are involved in the area of programming work *directly* with customers and plan, organize, implement, and evaluate services. Speaking to the importance of programming, Stenger, Ryan, and Jordan (1999, pp. 28, 39) have written:

> Programming is often perceived as the heart of the field of leisure services. At the very least, we could probably all agree that programming is a common denominator of leisure entities, no matter the setting, philosophy, or funding sources. . . . Programming serves as the common denominator among all parks, recreation and leisure service delivery programs.

As Johnson-Tew, Havitz, and McCarville (1999, p. 2) have noted, ". . . leisure programming is dynamic. It is characterized by ongoing planning, implementation, and refinement."

Programs, the products produced by programmers, enable individuals to receive the outcomes and benefits of leisure participation. Knowledge of programming and its relationship to the leisure experience is important to the leisure service professional. Furthermore, a keen awareness of the importance of quality in leisure programming forms an essential building block of professional success.

This chapter, divided into four major sections, first discusses information about the importance of providing quality services. The next section focuses on strategies used in developing a customer service orientation. The third portion of this chapter defines the various types of programs and suggests a cyclical program planning process. The last section discusses different

396

types of direct-service leadership roles found in public, private, nonprofit, and commercial leisure service organizations.

Promoting Quality and Value

Quality and value have become important elements of the work of leisure service professionals, as well as the yardstick by which customers measure the success of their involvement in terms of time, money, and commitment. Quality—a perception of excellence—is the extent to which the services received by the customer equal or exceed expectations. The term *quality services* suggests that individuals have engaged in thorough planning, have attempted to anticipate the needs of consumers, and have brought the sum of their resources to bear as effectively as possible on meeting those needs.

Value can be thought of as the extent to which the return on one's investment in leisure services and programs—as measured in time, money, or other factors—equals or exceeds the investment made. Value involves providing people with an effective return on their investment so that their monetary investment equals the services received. Leisure service organizations may also increase value by providing customers with a return on investment that is perceived to be greater than expected. This builds consumer commitment and loyalty as customers make comparisons with other competitive providers. Quality and value are hallmarks of successful organizations.

To be successful, leisure programmers must understand the expectations of their customers (McCarville, 1993). They must understand the characteristics that influence the perceptions of customers concerning issues related to quality in the delivery of leisure services. Zeithaml, Parasuraman, and Berry (1988) have identified the five following distinct characteristics or dimensions to evaluate service programs in terms of quality:

- *Tangibility*—physical cues provided by staff, other users, facilities, and equipment;
- *Reliability*—consistently providing the promised service;
- *Empathy*—caring and individualized attention;
- *Assurance*—knowledgeable staff able to convey trust and confidence; and
- *Responsiveness*—willingness to provide prompt attention.

In the leisure services field, Crompton and McKay (1989) studied these dimensions and their relationship to program satisfaction. These researchers found that reliability—the ability to consistently deliver a service with great quality—consistently ranked as the most important characteristic desired by individuals. For example, at a well-organized, clean, welcoming, contemporary theme park such as Disney World, customers can depend on the delivery of high-quality services in a consistent fashion each time they visit the park environment.

Another important dimension in the delivery of quality leisure services is the management of leader-customer interfaces—where the leader communicates and interacts with customers in person or on the telephone. According to Swell and Brown (1990), appropriate training must be provided to professionals and others who manage these key encounters. The ability of leaders to respond with empathy and relevance in a timely fashion often contributes greatly to the perception of quality.

Commitment to quality requires the leisure service programmer to find better ways to serve customers. It involves a commitment to creating better leisure services by working in a way that leads to innovation, reduction of mistakes, a positive attitude, attention to detail, and other factors. Commitment to quality requires leaders to develop their expertise and knowledge through continuous development.

The leisure services programmer who uses principles of quality and value produces technically and developmentally sound programs and creates programs that *exceed minimum requirements,* that is, programs that create a special intangible quality that inspires customers, provides heightened insight, introspection, development, and is meaningful (Edginton and Edginton, 1993a). A quality program produces positive experiences that will be locked into the minds and emotions of customers and serve as a beacon for future positive leisure behaviors.

Building a Commitment to Quality

The leisure services professional has a responsibility to build staff training and program efforts around the idea of commitment to quality. This focus on quality must permeate the organization thoroughly. Leisure service professionals must work toward eliminating poorly organized services, poor attitudes toward customers, use of poor equipment/materials, and willingness to live with mediocrity.

A philosophy of excellence focuses on high-quality programs and services; it should be applied vigorously in the area of leisure services. The hallmarks or guidelines that are used by organizations and leaders with a strong commitment to quality follow (Edginton and Edginton, 1993b):

Innovation. Success in programming stems from a commitment to innovation. No program should be the same from one year to the next; rather, programs should constantly evolve to meet the needs of customers. Innovative organizations are constantly looking for new and different services, equipment, areas, and facilities that improve the quality of services to customers.

Future orientation. Leisure service professionals who address quality issues not only of today but also of tomorrow will be successful. Leisure service organizations that invest in the future invest some of their resources in ensuring that their programs and services are successful and vibrant in months and years to come.

Getting things right the first time. Perhaps the most efficient way to promote quality within an organization is to do things right the first time. Sloppiness and a "seat of the pants," last-minute approach to planning often lead to having to redo activities or services. This is not only costly, but often results in poor performance. Some activities and programs cannot be corrected if they are not planned effectively, and the opportunity they presented is lost.

Continuous improvement. The best way to achieve quality is to improve the processes associated with creating leisure services. The job of any leisure service programmer should be to find ways to continuously improve programs and services. Programmers constantly search out new ways of doing things better, more cost-efficiently, and/or in a way that is more meaningful to customers. In addition, quality recreation programmers often establish a goal of making one small change in every program every week to improve the quality. This is a never-ending dynamic process; it should not be thought of as a one-time event.

Continuous education. The continuous development of the leader's knowledge and skills is essential to achieving quality. Good people make good programs, but the needs of customers are dynamic and changing, requiring continuous education and development. Recreation leaders should seek ways to improve their knowledge base.

Space Tourism Industry Faces Safety Regulations Hurdle Before Taking Off

Thrill seekers are plunking down six figures to ride rockets that haven't even been built yet, and a new airline called Virgin Galactic promised to be up and soaring in the next three years. Still, the budding space tourism industry faces a myriad of safety concerns—in the sky and on the ground—that must be resolved before any paying passengers take off.

The rules that will govern the industry in the United States remain under discussion between federal regulators and rocket developers, and legislation is still before Congress.

The pace of negotiations and the ultimate shape of the regulations could determine whether the sky-high enthusiasm for space tourism—fueled by the historic suborbital flights of SpaceShipOne—grows or wanes, especially among investors.

Federal Aviation Administration chief Marion Blakey this week visited Xcor Aerospace, a rocket developer just down the Mojave Airport flight line from SpaceShipOne's home. She talked of partnership with the new industry and said it was important for the United States to be the world leader.

She made clear, however, that broad safety issues are the agency's number one topic.

"Our first concern will be the safety of the uninvolved public, making sure that as this grows and develops that we're doing everything we can to protect the folks on the ground, to make sure that the people who go into space understand the risks," she said. "It will be a risky business for many years to come, no doubt."

The FAA for several years has been studying what the average passenger will face from G-force and psychological factors and what type of medical fitness he or she will require, Blakey said.

There is also a question of what information a passenger should have about safety records, for example, to assess risk and make a meaningful informed-consent statement.

Patti Grace Smith, associate administrator for the FAA's office of commercial space transportation, indicated passenger awareness is one of the "hurdles" in the way of making space travel as routine as aviation.

"The kind of threshold that we will have to figure out how to achieve is the cognizance issue: How do we know that they understand the risk that they are taking? How do we know that they understand what they're doing?" she said.

Source: Author. "Space tourism industry faces safety regulations hurdle before taking off." *Waterloo Courier* (October 7, 2004). p. C8.

Attention to detail. Success in programs is painted in small steps as well as broad strokes. The little things make a program of high quality and make the difference between superior services and mediocre ones.

Pride. Belief in what you are doing is contagious. Pride is having a high opinion of yourself and your work. Pride comes from doing a job competently as well as having ownership in the effort.

Anticipatory planning. Do not merely respond to the needs of customers as they are expressed from moment to moment. Learn how to anticipate needs in advance and meet them before they are requested. Anticipatory planning requires the leader to think in advance (days, weeks, months) and to visualize services as they will likely unfold, and to anticipate actions that may be needed.

Performance measurements. Find ways to record progress toward achieving quality by creating performance measurements. Determine how to chart progress toward the achievement of quality. Graphs and charts provide opportunities for discussion and focus on opportunities for change, and they may lead to the development of new programs and/or better methods and procedures. Participant numbers, customer outcomes related to performance measures, program costs, participant use hours, and participant survey results are all sources of data for charts to measure performance. Measuring achievement over a period of time enables the leisure services programmer to see the gains in quality and performance and possibly to justify future program developments.

Elimination of mistakes. Mistakes are costly to an organization both in terms of funds and image. Mistakes made in program planning are costly to participants in terms of opportunity for development. If play/leisure is powerful enough to help customers, it is powerful enough to hurt them. When mistakes in program planning impact the quality of services, they also impact customers. Eliminating mistakes helps improve quality, morale, cost-effectiveness, and other critical factors.

Elimination of negativeness. Positive attitudes are important in the delivery of leisure services. Programmers should strive to be enthusiastic, energetic, and zestful. If you enjoy what you are doing, that quality will rub off on others; the reverse is also true. Positiveness is a "can do" attitude that promotes a willingness to find ways to effectively serve customers with quality programs.

Assume personal responsibility for quality. The old way to get quality was to supervise and inspect services and manage change from the top down, or from without. The new way of promoting quality is to build it from within. The best way to promote quality from within is to ensure that each individual assumes personal responsibility and accountability for making sure that services are provided in an excellent, high-quality manner.

Teaming: Doing what it takes to get the job done. The leisure services programmer as well as other staff must be willing to do what it takes to get the job done, and to get it done right. The "quality" approach depends upon teamwork, cooperation, and supportive behavior. It is not "your job" or "my job" but, rather, "our job." All staff should be focused and have their eyes and efforts directed toward the primary goal, that is, providing the very highest quality service for customers, and they should be willing to do what it takes to make that happen.

The leisure services professional who is committed to excellence and who follows the guidelines that are discussed in the preceding section will outperform those who are not committed to excellence. The committed leisure service professional's programs will likely have a greater impact on customers.

Developing a Service Orientation

Leisure service professionals operate within an occupational area known as a service area. As indicated in Chapter 4 dealing with historical concepts, service-related industries have seen great growth since society has progressed from the industrial era to the technological/information era. One of the important distinguishing characteristics of a service industry is that it does not deal in the manufacturing of products, but rather delivers experiences to customers.

Today, the golden arches of McDonald's may more accurately symbolize America than does the industrial heartland. As a society that is immediate- and convenience-oriented, Americans require the delivery of products and services in ways that match the nature of their lifestyles—fast-paced, efficient, dynamic, changing, and immediate. For example, we may not have time to cook our own foods, to maintain our own gardens, to clean our own homes, or to organize our own leisure. DINKS (double income, no kids), FLYERS (fun loving youth en-route to success), YUPPIES (young, upwardly mobile professionals), DENKS (dual employed, no kids), and DEWKS (dual employed, with kids) often require other individuals to provide basic services, which in other eras were achieved through self-sufficiency.

What Is a Service? A Product?

The fast-growing service sector includes a vast array of business services and a wide variety of personal services, including the provision of leisure experiences. What is the difference between a service and a product? A service is a process whereby arrangements are made to provide something desired, useful, or necessary, often an experience. A product is a tangible item. For example, to participate in skiing, individuals must have proper equipment and clothing. They also need skills, lodging, food, transportation, a ski run, and other support services in order to participate. The equipment and clothing constitute products, whereas the organization and management of the support services that enable the leisure experience come within the service domain. Interestingly, the actual sales process of equipment and clothing (the products) also falls within the service sector.

McCarville (2002, p. 2) has discussed the movement of marketing to goods to services to ideas and experiences. As he points out, ". . . goods are physical in nature. They can be seen, touched, and manipulated. The marketing of such goods is relatively straightforward. Goods are designed to be reproduced, reproduced to be transported, transported to be displayed, and displayed to be sold."

On the other hand, services provide, according to McCarville, ". . . unique challenges to the service marketer" (2002, p. 2). He suggests that there are four primary ways that services can be distinguished from goods. They are:

1. *Services are perishable.* Unsold services cannot be stockpiled. The opportunity to sell an empty seat in a theatre is gone forever once the show has begun. It cannot be set aside and sold later as can a manufactured product.
2. *Services are intangible.* Unlike manufactured goods, services typically lack substance. This poses a dilemma for both the producer and the participant. Providers find it difficult to convey service characteristics to potential participants. As a result, they may struggle in their attempts to appeal to potential clients. One of the most difficult tasks facing any service provider is to "tangiblize the intangible."
3. *Services reflect inseparability.* Services are consumed as they are produced. In other words, the client and the producer typically meet, and together they both produce and consume some the service.
4. *Service encounters are dynamic (heterogeneity).* Like all interactions, they evolve from one instant to the next, from one encounter to the next. Heterogeneity introduces an infinite variability to the service encounter. Each encounter is unique. The challenge for the service provider is to ensure that services are consistent enough to guarantee unfailing quality, but flexible enough to adjust to ongoing change.

As one can see, there are significant differences between leisure goods and services. However, service is the primary focus of any leisure service organization. Since service is not a single-dimension item, however, it can be difficult to define. Most products that customers purchase may be categorized as single-item commodities. A service, on the other hand, may have many dimensions. Someone may sell the service, another person may deliver it, and still another person may evaluate its effectiveness.

Services are less tangible than products. Whereas products usually are evaluated in terms of concrete quality and production standards, the quality, caliber, and effectiveness of a service can be more difficult to measure. Services often involve transmittal and exchange of knowledge, information, or the creation of an emotional state (e.g., excitement within an experience). Many variables are difficult to control and predict in producing a leisure experience. For example, each individual comes to a leisure experience with a unique set of expectations, experiences, values, and attitudes; this makes it difficult to produce and/or replicate a leisure experience consistently across all types of participants.

Albrecht and Zemke (1985), writing in a book entitled *Service America!,* suggest that a service can be thought of as "any incident of doing for others for a fee" (p. 36). The fee for services does not necessarily have to be paid by the individual; it can be offset by taxes, donations, gifts, or in-kind contributions. Following are characteristics of services:

1. A service is produced at the instant of delivery; it *cannot be created in advance* or held in readiness.
2. A service cannot be centrally produced, inspected, stockpiled, or warehoused. It is usually *delivered wherever the customer is* by people who are beyond the immediate influence of management.
3. The "product" *cannot be demonstrated,* nor can a sample be sent for customer approval in advance of the service; the provider can show various examples, but the customer's own haircut, for example, does not yet exist and cannot be shown.
4. The person receiving the service *has nothing tangible;* the value of the service depends on his or her personal experience.
5. The experience *cannot be sold or passed on to a third party.*
6. If improperly performed, a service *cannot be "recalled."* If it cannot be repeated, then reparations or apologies are the only means of recourse for customer satisfaction.
7. *Quality assurance must take place before production* rather than after production, as would be the case in a manufacturing situation.
8. Delivery of the service usually *requires human interaction* to some degree; buyer and seller come into contact in some relatively personal way to create the service.
9. The receiver's expectations of the service are integral to his or her satisfaction with the outcome. Quality of service is largely a *subjective* matter.
10. The more people the customer must *encounter during the delivery of the service,* the less likely it is that he or she will be satisfied with the service (Albrecht and Zemke, 1985, pp. 36–37).

Albrecht and Zemke (1985) note that not all of these characteristics necessarily appear in all services. Their assumptions have not been tested in leisure service organizations, but can help to clarify the differences between products and services. Leisure service professionals must recognize the challenges and opportunities that providing quality leisure services presents.

Organizing a Strategy to Provide Services

Outstanding leisure service organizations do not just happen. Successful organizations have a strong vision or direction for their actions. In other words, they develop a strategy that guides the work of the organization in terms of the quality of its services.

What necessary elements will ensure effective service delivery and profitability? Three quality factors are essential in the successful provision of services. The first is the organization's definition of what is unique or different about its services, called *value-added service*

Characteristics of Servant Leaders

Listening
Traditionally, leaders have been valued for their communication and decision-making skills. Servant leaders must reinforce these important skills by making a deep commitment to listening intently to others. Listening, coupled with regular periods of reflection, are essential to the growth of the servant leader.

Empathy
Servant leaders strive to understand and empathize with others. People need to be accepted and recognized for their special and unique spirits. The most successful servant leaders are those who have become skilled empathetic listeners.

Healing
Learning to heal is a powerful force for transformation and integration. Many people have broken spirits and suffered from a variety of emotional hurts. Although this is a part of being human, servant leaders recognize that they have an opportunity to help make whole those with whom they come in contact.

Awareness
General awareness, and especially self-awareness, strengthens the servant leader. Awareness also aids in understanding issues involving ethics and values. It enables one to view most situations from a more integrated position.

Persuasion
Servant leaders rely on persuasion rather than positional authority in making decisions. Servant leaders seek to convince others rather than coerce compliance. The servant leader is effective at building consensus within groups.

Conceptualization
Servant leaders seek to nurture their abilities to dream great dreams. Servant leaders must seek a delicate balance between conceptualization and day-to-day focus.

Foresight
Foresight is a characteristic that enables servant leaders to understand lessons from the past, the realities of the present, and the likely consequence of a decision for the future.

Stewardship
Stewardship is defined as holding something in trust for another. Servant leadership, like stewardship, assumes first and foremost a commitment to serving the needs of others. It also emphasizes the use of openness and persuasion, rather than control.

Commitment to the growth of people
Servant leaders believe that people have intrinsic value and must be included in decisions affecting their lives.

Building community
Servant leaders are aware of the need to build community and actively seek to involve people in the process.

Source: Spears, L. 1995. Servant leadership and the Greenleaf legacy. In L. Spear (ed.), *Reflections on Leadership: How Robert K. Greenleaf's Theory of Servant Leadership Influenced Today's Top Management Thinkers,* 1–16. New York: Wiley.

delivery. The second factor involves the *promotion of positive customer relations.* The third area includes *organizational policies and procedures* that create an attitude that the organization exists to meet customers' needs rather than the reverse.

Value-Added Services   Individuals have certain expectations for the level of service they expect prior to engaging the service. The value-added concept involves adding a dimension or quality of service that goes beyond the customer's basic expectation. In other words, the organization attempts to give customers or clients a better service than they expected. This strategy effectively ensures long-term customer loyalty. By adding to a service and improving its quality, efficiency, attractiveness, convenience, format, and intensity, an organization focuses clearly on the needs of the customers to be served. This approach to providing leisure services creates unique market niches and is the hallmark of any successful public, private, non-profit, or commercial organization.

Examples of the value-added concept in successful organizations abound. Tom Peters (1987), speaking to managers at the Hult Center in Eugene, Oregon, relates the story of a gas station in the San Francisco Bay area that employs the value-added concept and whose sales are thirteen times higher than the average gas station in the United States. As Peters relates this story, he says that he sent an associate to investigate this phenomenon. Upon returning, the associate declared that having a vehicle serviced while purchasing gas at this particular service station is as close as one could come to being in a pit stop at the Indianapolis 500. The gas station attendants not only pumped the gas (self-service stations predominate in California), washed the windows in the front and back and on the inside and on the outside but also vacuumed the inside of the car in the front and back and topped it off by giving him a cup of coffee and a newspaper. As Peters notes, the gas being sold in this station is no different from the gas being pumped in any other gas station. The major difference, resulting in increased sales and consumer loyalty, is the "value-add-ons" to the basic commodity.

How do organizations create value-added leisure services? The process requires continuous work, with constant improvement, innovation, and evaluation of the ways in which services are delivered. Peters (1987) notes that every organization should "add at least value-increasing 'differentiators' to each service every ninety days" (p. 50). He suggests that no matter how mundane a product or service, it can become a highly value-added product or service. Using the illustration of the gas station, pumping gas is usually perceived as a mundane activity; however, the Bay area gas station made it a highly unique, visible, dynamic, and differentiated service.

Which value-added items can be added to services within leisure service organizations? The following areas within leisure service agencies could benefit from the value-added concept:

1. *Features.* Every service can be augmented or enhanced by adding specialized, unique features that cannot be obtained elsewhere. The Louisville Redbirds minor league Triple A baseball team augments its basic entertainment service, the baseball game, by providing other unique entertainment and food-service features. Bands, family picnic areas, infant care areas, fireworks, and daily steam-cleaned stadium seats all contribute to an environment that results in this organization's annually attracting over 1 million participants.

2. *Customer-leader interaction.* No other area offers a greater opportunity to add value than in the customer-leader interaction. On a day-to-day basis, the way frontline service providers interact with customers greatly impacts their perception of the organization. Acts of courtesy, helpfulness, sincerity, generosity, as well as inspired instruction, direction, and supervision—all these areas of value influence the delivery of services within a leisure service organization. Leisure service organizations must focus constant attention and effort toward improving these interpersonal relations.

Anshin: Understanding the Customer

*A*nshin is the Japanese word for . . . security and comfort. Increasing the comfort level of your associates and customers in Japan goes far beyond providing quality products delivered on time and at the right price. Japanese want to feel comfortable and "in touch" with their suppliers and business partners. There is a human dimension to this desire along with the business side.

Japanese want to know you can be trusted and are as interested in their success as you are in your own. The first order of *anshin* is to understand the customer's needs: Response to customer demands is an obligation. This takes time and close relations. Two-way obligations between customers and suppliers are built over many years, and go far beyond traditional American expectations.

Source: Jim and Jeffrey Morgan, *Cracking the Japanese Market.*

3. *Image.* Organizations can add value to a service in several ways by enhancing or improving the image of an activity or event. First, and perhaps the simplest and most inexpensive, is using contemporary and up-to-date terms to define activities. In describing the work of a textile manufacturer, the Millikin Company, Peters (1987) notes that it does not make "rags," but rather is in the "shop towels" business. The simple change in terms adds distinction and value to the perceptions of customers with regard to this commodity. Another way to enhance the image of services involves paying close attention to pricing strategies since individuals often equate quality with price. Leisure services are often underpriced, especially those offered by public service agencies.

4. *Order and cleanliness.* An impressive hallmark of Disney theme parks—Disneyland, Disney World, Tokyo Disneyland, Disneyland Resort Paris—is the cleanliness maintained at these facilities. People far more prefer a clean, orderly leisure environment to one that is cluttered, dirty, and disorganized. Organizations can quickly add value to any service by ensuring that standards for orderliness and cleanliness are upgraded and maintained. This applies to the maintenance of areas and facilities, and even more to the grooming and dress of employees. Interestingly, this results in a cost-effective approach over the long term; individual behavior regarding cleanliness tends to support or correspond to the status quo—in other words, if consumers sense that cleanliness and orderliness are a priority, they will respond in kind and help to keep things clean.

Positive Customer Relations Leisure service professionals must remember that their business emphasizes service and relies on the goodwill generated between customers and providers. There is no secret to providing positive customer relations; it simply means operating so that the customers' "current situation, frame of mind, and needs are addressed" (Albrecht and Zemke, 1985, p. 39). A customer-oriented professional operates with a high degree of "responsiveness, attentiveness and willingness to help others" (Albrecht and Zemke, 1985, p. 39). Being customer-oriented means being attentive to the details that make leisure activities enjoyable and leisure facilities and areas hospitable and attractive. As Siegenthaler (2000, p. 101) has written, "Leisure service providers are in a competitive market to attract and retain customers; therefore, customer service must be a priority."

Miller (2000, p. 61) notes that in delivering quality customer services, leisure service professionals must "continually examine and evaluate existing policies, procedures, signage, staff

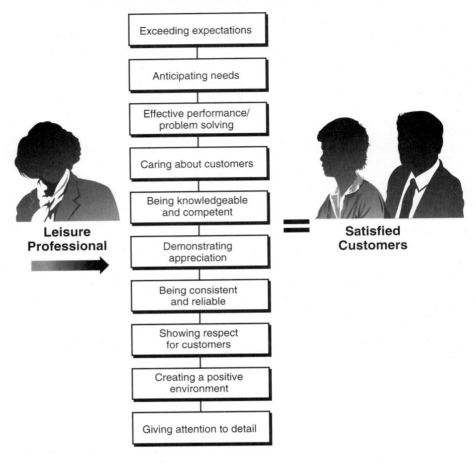

Figure 13.1

Employee behaviors that result in positive customer service.

An Emphasis on Customer Service Builds Customer Satisfaction and Loyalty

Exceeding expectations

Anticipating needs

Effective performance/ problem solving

Caring about customers

Being knowledgeable and competent

Demonstrating appreciation

Being consistent and reliable

Showing respect for customers

Creating a positive environment

Giving attention to detail

Leisure Professional

=

Satisfied Customers

training, mission and goal statements, and how to turn negative situations into a 'win-win,' customer friendly" one. He notes that customer service is a two-way street and that we must seek out both positive and negative feedback in order to learn about ourselves and our image.

An organization should not assume that its employees will be positively oriented toward customers. It must teach, encourage, and reinforce its values and reward employee behavior that leads to positive customer relations.

Key employee behaviors that produce positive customer relations include the following (see figure 13.1):

1. *Exceeding expectations.* People like to feel that when they communicate their needs the provider is attentive. People hate to be ignored or made to feel that their needs are not important. Being responsive means listening carefully and attending to people's needs in a timely fashion and in a way that exceeds their expectations.
2. *Anticipating needs.* It is not enough to merely respond to customers' needs; one must anticipate those needs and meet them as they occur. Anticipatory behavior is central to producing a satisfied customer.

FISH: An Approach to Customer Service

The combination of fish and chlorinated pool water may sound like a deadly one, but the Roseville (Calif.) Parks and Recreation Department aquatics division's FISH approach to customer service is alive and swimming. There was the stuffed fish pillow being thrown out the concessions service window at a customer. If the lucky customer caught the fish pillow, he or she was treated to a gummy worm, a favorite snack of fish-catchers. There was the fish decoupage megaphone awarded to the day's best lifeguard. There were the fish key chains given to staff who were caught displaying above-and-beyond-the-call-of-duty customer service. There were fish stickers, fish squirters, and fish decorations. It was a fishy summer.

The FISH philosophy to customer service contains four basic concepts: (1) *Play*—It's about having fun, enjoying yourself for your customers and co-workers. Make it a day to remember; (2) *Make their day*—It's about doing something special for your customers and coworkers. Make it a day to remember; (3) *Be there*—It's about being totally focused on the moment and on the person or task with which you are engaged. When we are fully present with our customers and with each other, we are listening deeply and important opportunities do not escape us; and (4) *Choose your attitude*—It's about accepting full responsibility for all of our choices, even our attitudes at work. A positive attitude is a decision we make moment to moment.

Source: Pritchard, A. 2000, February. Go fish. *Parks & Recreation 35*(2), 64–67.

3. *Effective performance.* A service, effectively performed, greatly enhances positive customer relations. In fact, there is no substitute—effective performance is the bottom line, and people will often forgo some of the other elements mentioned if the service is delivered in an effective, reliable, and consistent manner.
4. *Caring about customers.* Responding to individuals with polite and thoughtful behavior is essential. Courtesy also includes kindness, generosity, and supportive behavior.
5. *Being knowledgeable and competent.* The way an organization provides information about services impacts customers. People should be set at ease about asking questions that require direction and interpretation. Accuracy and thoughtfulness in providing such information can influence the success of a leisure experience. The initial contact a customer may make with a leisure service organization often involves requests for information or clarification. First impressions are lasting ones.
6. *Demonstrating appreciation.* People like to feel that their business is valued and that they are appreciated. Thanking a person is good business. Sometimes organizations place an ad in the paper or mail holiday cards, but even more important is the day-to-day interaction between the customer and the provider.
7. *Being consistent and reliable.* Cooperating with customers in a positive, reliable, and consistent manner is vital to customer satisfaction. Customers should be able to count on the same excellent service every time they interact with the organization.
8. *Showing respect for customers.* Enthusiasm, energy and zestfulness are important elements in successful leisure experiences. No matter how many times a professional has successfully implemented a given service, he or she should approach each new customer and each new situation with the same level of respect, intensity, and positiveness— qualities that will rub off on the customer.

9. *Creating a positive ambiance and environment.* Creating a positive feeling or mood greatly influences perceptions of quality. This mood may be one of warmth and relaxation or one of excitement and risk. Whatever the intent, the achievement of a mood needs to be carried out through careful planning and organization.

10. *Giving attention to detail.* The little things make a difference between superior organizational effort and mediocre performance. Attention to detail requires thought, planning, and a creative nature. A wrapped piece of chocolate on a pillow at a resort is a thoughtful act that represents attention to detail.

McChesney (1999, p. 6) has suggested that a focus on customer service is an important element in the effective management of leisure service organizations. He has indicated that "customer loyalty can be promoted and nurtured via customer service, resulting in added value to the business exchange, reduced cost of doing business, and customer acceptance of less than perfect program delivery." According to this author (McChesney, 1999), important characteristics required to promote customer service include the following:

1. Assisting customers takes precedence over all tasks.
2. Customers are satisfied when they perceive value—give it to them.
3. Complaining customers are an opportunity for us to learn about our company.
4. Always look at situations through the eyes of the customer.
5. The purpose of your job is to satisfy the customer!
6. Realize you don't have a job without customers!
7. "I don't know" should never be said without "I'll find out."
8. If a customer is dissatisfied, it's not enough to just give them what you should have provided in the first place. Give them something extra.
9. Be positive when you interact with customers—smile!
10. Follow up!

The Disney Company has made thoughtful, attentive behavior toward consumers a hallmark of the services it provides. At Disneyland, customers are treated as guests—hospitably, courteously, with employees placing the needs of these guests first. This action results in services of a superior nature, a model for the leisure service industry.

Organizational Policies and Procedures To promote positive consumer relations, values must be backed with organizational policies and procedures. In other words, an organization must have a system in place to ensure compliance with its vision. Policies and procedures can deal with a variety of topics, including how to approach customers, how to handle complaints, how facilities are to be used and maintained, safety regulations, and others. McChesney (1999) has suggested that there are five important customer service strategies that are important and can be applied to any leisure service organization. These strategies are (1) hiring practices, (2) customer service training, (3) frontline responsiveness, (4) customer response networks, and (5) management by walking around. The first strategy suggests that you have to get the right people in place, people who enjoy working with others. The second element suggests that the training of employees should be done from the perspective of the customer of the organization. Frontline responsiveness is about ensuring that individuals at the frontline are empowered to make important decisions influencing customer satisfaction. A customer response network refers to the way a leisure organization communicates with its customers. How are complaints handled? How are customers shown appreciation for their participation? The last strategy, management by wandering around, suggests that leisure service professionals should be hands-on, listening to customers, employees, and others who influence the work of the organization.

Camp Adventure™ Youth Services, a contracted youth developement service between the University of Northern Iowa and the U.S. Armed Forces, provides guidelines for staff working in resident and day camp situations. These guidelines govern the day-to-day interactions and behaviors that are expected between the providers and the customers. For example, staff are expected to use positive reinforcement, serve as positive role models, teach new skills, work as a part of a team, provide effective communications, be prepared and organized, make a genuine commitment to youth, establish a warm and caring atmosphere, anticipate and thereby prevent problems, provide a structure in which children can be successful, provide an atmosphere for learning, and treat each child as an individual. Individuals who participate in leading this program are reminded that *Camp Adventure*™ *Youth Services* is a business and that its primary reason for engaging in the activity is the success of the business enterprise. Policies and procedures for *Camp Adventure*™ *Youth Services* are documented in written form in the *Camp Adventure*™ Staff Handbook. In addition, the policies and procedures are systematically taught and reinforced to service providers. By understanding and adhering to the expectations concerning consumer relations, students participating in this program have made it an outstanding success and a model for this type of contractual effort.

Programs: The Services of Leisure Service Organizations

Programs may be thought of as the raison d'etre of any leisure service organization. Programs are created to deliver something of value—a benefit or the expectation of a benefit—to a customer or group of customers. Edginton and Rossman (1988) write that "by organizing, promoting, and delivering programs, leisure managers help their constituents experience leisure" (p. viii).

Programming involves arranging social, physical, and natural environments in such a way as to produce leisure experiences. For example, leisure programmers may create situations where social interaction between individuals is arranged, heightened, or encouraged. Programmers also build facilities and make natural areas accessible in order to support the leisure experience. All of these actions help individuals to engage in positive leisure opportunities. Bullaro and Edginton (1986) suggest that the work of programmers "may involve planning and organizing, assembling materials and supplies, providing leadership and other actions that create opportunities for leisure" (p. 12).

Programmers may create highly structured activities or they may enable individuals to experience leisure opportunities. The programmer's intervention can range from nearly total control of all of the elements of planning, organizing, and implementing the chosen event or activity to teaching or enabling participants to assume control of the experience. From an organizational perspective, planned intervention results in agency control. On the other hand, enabling services place a great degree of control and responsibility with the participant.

Types of Programs

Leisure service organizations provide many types of programs. Edginton and Rossman (1988) write that "programming involves the creation and distribution of activities, areas and facilities, information and leadership opportunities" (p. viii). In other words, programming involves more than the creation of activities or events (see figure 13.2). Programs can be far-reaching and involve a high level of sophistication, depending on the nature of the event to be produced or the facility to be developed. Listed here are four general categories of programs that can be offered by a leisure service organization:

1. *Activities.* Activities or events include those services that occur primarily in social settings. Activities often involve assisting individuals to acquire new knowledge or skill or arranging social situations to promote fun, enjoyment, and/or companionship. Activities may also include testing or demonstration of skills. Some examples include festivals, tournaments, leagues, lessons, drop-in programs, dances, clubs, parties, carnivals, and other special events.
2. *Areas and facilities.* An area is an open space that provides opportunities for individuals to experience leisure. A park, a ball diamond, picnic area, soccer field, playground, hiking trail, bicycle path, jogging trail, lakes and ponds, and other areas suitable for recreational use fall within this category. Facilities are artificial structures used for leisure, not necessarily confined to indoor usage. Gymnasiums, recreation centers, skateboard parks, ice rinks, tennis courts, racquetball centers, roller skating rinks, bowling centers, and theaters are all examples of leisure facilities.

Figure 13.2

Types of programs provided by leisure service organiztions.

Programming involves four components → Activities

Areas and facilities

Information

Leadership

3. *Information.* Leisure service organizations provide individuals with information about their own services, as well as other services that may contribute to the consumer's general satisfaction and well-being. Public agencies and private, nonprofit organizations often build customer awareness about various leisure opportunities. Leisure service organizations also develop and disperse interpretive material such as information regarding historical and cultural events or sites and information about the natural environment. Face-to-face interpretation, often presented by volunteer tour guides, requires great skill in bringing alive past history or the uniqueness of an environment area.

4. *Leadership.* Some leisure service organizations focus on the development of individuals as leaders. Youth serving voluntary organizations, in particular, engage in leadership development of youth participants and adult volunteer leaders. A number of program formats also require leaders to emerge from the participating group itself. Athletic teams and leagues require captains to exhibit leadership. Leisure-oriented clubs also require self-generated leadership.

Not all leisure service organizations provide a full range of programs and services. Often they specialize in one particular area or a combination of areas. For example, McKay and Crompton (1988) write, ". . . no longer do public recreation agencies aim to deliver a full range of recreation programs. Rather, they realize increasingly that they are only one small component of the total recreation system" (p. 53). They suggest a different system of categorizing leisure programs that focuses primarily on identifying and meeting the needs of participants. These categories include (1) the nature of the service, (2) the relationship between the programmer and the customer, (3) potential for customization, (4) the nature of the demand for a program, (5) attributes of the program, and (6) program beneficiaries. The major benefit of this classification system results from more succinctly differentiating or defining the target market.

Factors Influencing Leisure Program Planning

A number of variables should be considered by leisure program planners. In an effort to help individuals grow and develop, leisure professionals must understand these factors and how they impact leisure pursuits. Some of these variables include generation, environmental factors, level of education, and cultural background. This section briefly discusses each of these factors as well as the program planning process.

Generation Each person belongs to an *age cohort or generation,* and as a cohort, individuals face different circumstances and events that shape their perceptions. Thus, one generation of teenagers may gain a perspective of the world differently from teenagers of a different generation as they grow up in different "worlds." Today's newest generation or cohort faces a world of technology that earlier generations could only dream about. Advances in computers, electronics, transportation, and communication have created many new opportunities for young people, as well as problems and issues with which to cope.

One's age cohort provides a frame of reference from which to view the world. Someone who was born and lived through the Great Depression of the 1930s has a vastly different outlook on life than someone who grew up in the more liberal 1960s. For example, those born in the 1930s might have difficulty feeling comfortable buying on credit and spending money that has not yet been earned, while children of the 1960s use credit readily. In many respects, these changing frames of reference cause the generation gaps between older and younger people.

Seniors Travel the Information Superhighway

For years, senior centers have been seen as places where older adults can gather to play Bingo or cards. This image, however, is continually changing. Older adults are not moving slowly and cautiously but are racing into the computer age.

Ten years ago, seniors were interested in the computer; they were curious. They wanted to be informed and desired to be able to understand computer terminology. The ability to carry on an informed conversation with their children and grandchildren was important. However, the hands-on experience was intimidating at times.

The Park Ridge Senior Center in Park Ridge, Illinois, got its start when a computer company called and offered free introductory lessons to any interested senior. We coordinated the onslaught of registrations. Twelve sessions with ten students apiece made the center's staff and the computer company realize that this was only the beginning.

Many participants went on to purchase their own computers, while some inherited older models from their children. They were enthusiastic and aggressive in learning the skills necessary to use the computers for practical matters and also wanted to have some fun with them. They were using their computers primarily for word processing, record keeping, and paying bills.

Years later, the center approached with an idea for further computer classroom experience. A center member came forward with the idea of a computer discussion group. It was to be an information-sharing group for those who had some computer expertise. Once again, there was tremendous response. However, the members found the format too limiting. It was only for people who knew something about computers, and there was no opportunity for hands-on experience. Left out were those who had no idea how to turn on the computer and those who knew the basics but needed some practical instruction.

Source: Pritchard, A. 1998, June. Seniors travel the Information Superhighway. *Parks & Recreation 33*(6), 70–74.

The older generation was born before 1940. For the most part this generation lived through the Great Depression and World War II. Many are immigrants or first-generation Americans and Canadians who grew up in rural areas. This generation views leisure as a way to re-create themselves for more work. They played so they could work better.

The middle generation was born between 1940 and 1960. This generation entered adulthood during a period of affluence and optimism about the future. Such events as Vietnam and Watergate changed this generation, however, making it skeptical of big government. This generation viewed leisure as a central aspect of life and worked only to get to the weekend. Leisure was viewed as an end in itself rather than as a reward for working hard.

The younger generation was born after 1960. This generation was born into an affluent society that now struggles with what is next. This is the first generation where individuals may not be better off than their parents. It faces global environmental problems as well as the role of America in a post–cold war period. In many cases, leisure has become a major form of self-expression. This group works hard, plays hard, and tries to have it all, while wondering what the future holds.

America's newest generation has a number of interesting characteristics. It has high-tech literacy, is diverse, has high discretionary income, seeks independence, is action-oriented, and wants to return to traditional family values.

Environmental Factors   Environmental factors include such things as place of residence and financial resources. For example, a person living in Florida often participates in different leisure pursuits than does someone living in Montana. While influenced largely by climate, these differences also result from topography and leisure opportunities. People living in Florida participate in many year-round water-based leisure activities (e.g., fishing, boating, waterskiing, windsurfing, scuba diving), whereas individuals living in the Rockies participate in more winter sports (e.g., snow skiing, hockey, skating).

Likewise, people living in rural areas and small towns have different day-to-day leisure patterns than people living in large metropolitan areas. Rural residents often travel farther to participate in organized recreation. Urban residents often try to escape the city and participate in such outdoor recreation as bicycling, swimming, and waterskiing, whereas people who live and work outdoors on a daily basis may seek other forms of leisure and recreation.

A second environmental factor affects leisure participation: income. Leisure does not have to cost money—the old adage says, "The best things in life are free." Yet, in an increasingly materialistic society, money has great impact on leisure patterns. The *Third Nationwide Outdoor Recreation Plan* (Department of the Interior, 1979) reported a positive association between increased leisure participation and rising incomes. Howard and Crompton (1984) identified the factor "it cost too much" as an obstacle to participation by respondents in three large metropolitan areas in the United States. Lankford (1990) found that money was one of the top five barriers to leisure participation in Oregon and Washington. Jackson (1994) identifies cost of participating as one of the constraints to leisure participation, including the cost of transportation, cost of equipment, lack of transportation, and admission fees/other charges.

Income affects a person's leisure in a variety of ways: neighborhood and type of housing, the purchase of leisure equipment, and the type and affordability of leisure activities. Those of low income do not constitute a viable market for many leisure programs or provisions. Hence, lower-income individuals must rely on public and quasi-public leisure facilities and programs.

Level of Education   According to Godbey (1985), education stimulates interest in many forms of leisure activities. Individuals with higher levels of education often experience more leisure variety and are encouraged to try a variety of leisure activities. Specifically, studies show that individuals with higher levels of education participate in more outdoor recreation, sports, high-culture activities (e.g., the arts), and tourism. An educated person, often due to higher income, is able to follow through on leisure wishes and desires. Yet, even when the effects of age and income are taken into account, education itself often has a distinct bearing on leisure participation.

Within specific types of leisure activities, such as sports and outdoor recreation, certain activities are strongly associated with low or high education groups (Godbey, 1985). For example, hunting and fishing are associated more with individuals with lower education levels (*Nationwide Outdoor Recreation Survey,* 1984), whereas activities such as backpacking, nature study, kayaking, and adventure recreation are associated more with individuals with higher levels of education.

Cultural Background   Culture—defined as the attitudes, beliefs, values, ideas, and assumptions that a group passes on from generation to generation—is influenced by environment and history. People absorb their culture at an early age; they learn the habits and rules of behaving and how to do things, along with standards of right and wrong, beautiful and ugly, valuable or unimportant. For example, an open and friendly attitude toward new people may result from a history of moving frequently and constantly needing to make new friends to survive. These habits

U.S. Life Span Hits Record 77.2 Years

Life expectancy has reached an all-time high of 77.2 years in the United States, with men and women and Blacks and Whites setting new records. But in a sign of the times, federal health officials have added a new official death category: homicide by terrorism.

Life and death trends are tracked by the Centers for Disease Control and Prevention's National Center for Health Statistics. Its latest report shows numbers from 2001.

The average American life span rose exactly nine years between 1950 and 2001, including two-tenths of a year from 2000 to 2001. Women still outlive men, and the gap remained the same—5.4 years. Life expectancy increased from 74.3 years in 2000 to 74.4 years in 2001 for men and from 79.7 years to 79.8 years for women.

Life expectancy was 75 and 68.6 years for White and Black men, respectively, and 80.2 and 75.5 years for White and Black women, respectively.

Source: Author. U.S. Life Span Hits Record 77.2 Years. "*Des Moines Register.* (March 16, 2003)."

become so much a part of a person that he or she considers them natural or "just the way things are." As Godbey (1985) notes, leisure is a product of culture, and to some extent, culture is a product of leisure.

Another cultural difference centers around how people view time. Most Americans come from a large land mass situated in a temperate zone with four seasons. The four seasons have caused the cultures to develop the notion of future-mindedness, planting, harvesting, and storing. In addition, the transportation system, beginning with the railroad, placed punctuality high in the spectrum of cultural values. People from island countries, such as the Philippines, do not have four seasons. Many Filipinos see no need to slice their time into distinct periods and do not place punctuality high in their value spectrum. In the past, when a canoe sailed from one island to another, the sailors had a general idea of how long the trip would take but the specific time depended on the wind and waves. Therefore, the notion of general time still prevails today.

People often judge different cultures by their own value system, which can result in ethno-centrism—an attitude that one's culture is superior to others. In today's multicultural world (by the year 2000 California had no majority ethnic group), leisure professionals must learn to understand the cultural values of those they serve.

Cultural pluralism emphasizes the role of leisure as anything the individual chooses to do for pleasure. The limits of such behavior are defined only by laws, with activity representing an expression of personal interest, or lifestyle, rather than one's culture. Fads and created leisure needs may cause more innovation, a speeding up of the consumption of leisure experience with a corresponding questioning of what is worth doing. One resolution to this uncertainty is to try to do nothing, but a more prevalent reaction is to try to do everything. (Godbey, 1985, p. 115)

A pluralistic society must develop programs and experiences that help people to value their own unique culture while celebrating and respecting the cultures of others.

The Process of Program Planning

Current literature dealing with leisure programming suggests that planning occurs in a cyclical fashion. Leisure service professionals engage in a step-by-step process to produce services. Most program models suggest that program planning involves the following processes:

(1) development of program goals, (2) needs assessment, (3) program planning, and (4) program evaluation.

Development of Program Goals   Organizations have broad goals and their programs and services reflect that broad mission. In addition, leisure service organizations often develop particular goals and objectives to guide the development and implementation of specific programs and services. Such goals and objectives help to identify specific behavioral outcomes by participants engaging in specific programs and services. These types of statements are referred to as *performance* or *behavioral objectives.*

The development of performance or behavioral objectives plays an important role in measuring the impact of program services and is usually stated in quantifiable (measurable) terms. For example, an individual working with physically challenged individuals in a learn-to-swim program may develop a behavioral objective that describes specifically the outcomes that should result from participation in the activity—"The participant will demonstrate success in swimming by treading water for three minutes without needing assistance."

Needs Assessment   Most cyclical models of programming recommend the use of a needs assessment, either preceding or following the development of program objectives. Discussing needs assessment, Russell (1982) suggests that the "*identification of needs, interest and problems* of the program constituency is a logical place to start the planning process" (p. 68). She further notes that needs assessment helps in "[establishing] program form and content" (p. 68).

Needs assessment involves discovering information about participants' leisure needs, interests, value states, behaviors, and attitudes. Such information helps to determine the most appropriate programs and services. Howe and Qui (1988) suggest that leisure service professionals can approach needs assessment in two ways. First, public service providers primarily use a process of systematic inquiry. Second, the problem-solving approach involves identifying problems and barriers that prevent individuals from having successful leisure experiences. Edginton and Edginton (1993a) suggest that the programmer should consider some of the broad issues presented in figure 13.3 when engaged in needs assessment and program planning for youth. The model refers to some of the underlying needs of youth for leadership and achievement, youth involvement, family involvement, achieving youth development competencies, meeting the needs of the whole person (within the context of school, health issues, and other factors), clarifying values, and others.

Program Planning   Once needs and objectives are determined, the next step involves planning for the program's implementation and includes locating the site for the service, arranging for leadership, promoting the activity, and developing the program content. A vast array of potential program areas can be provided to meet the leisure needs of individuals. Some of these program areas include the following:

1. *Visual arts.* Visual arts refer to decorative objects that are created for their own sake (fine art) or for some utilitarian purpose (a craft).
2. *Performing arts.* The performing arts include music, drama, and dance. The human being is the creative mode of expression.
3. *New arts.* New arts involve the use of contemporary technology to create art, such as photography, computer, synthesizers, and so forth.
4. *Hobbies.* Hobbies, activities pursued in an intense way over an extended period of time, include four types—collecting, creative, educational, and performing.

Figure 13.3

Youth-centered programming.

Issues to Be Considered
When Planning Programs for Youth

Planning includes a base of youth development competencies/needs: health/physical, personal/social, cognitive/creative, citizenship/ethics, vocational

Youth have opportunities for leadership and achievement

Programming meets the needs of the youth, not the leader

Leader understands that youth learn and grow through leisure activity

Youth involvement in program selection, planning, and implementation

Program planning encourages family involvement

Programming promotes positive values

Programming is tied/coordinated with other youth serving agencies to serve the "whole" youth

5. *Sports, games, and athletics.* Sports, games, and athletics are activities that involve the use of fine and gross motor skills. Sports, more sophisticated than games, require a higher degree of organization, skill, and endurance. Athletics are often characterized by their competitive nature.

6. *Outdoor recreation.* Outdoor recreation activities depend on the natural environment. Mountaineering, spelunking, hiking, windsurfing, and others serve as examples.

7. *Social recreation.* The primary function of social recreation is to promote social interaction among people. Parties, carnivals, festivals, social gatherings, and picnics are examples of social recreation.

8. *Volunteer services.* Volunteering during one's leisure can be a creative, fulfilling, and valuable experience. As a program area, volunteering involves work in leadership roles, such as coaching, and as activity leaders, hosts, and guides.

9. *Literary and self-improvement programs.* Popular programs that contribute to the development of individuals intellectually, socially, or spiritually fall within this program area. Book discussion groups, parent groups, toastmasters, and others serve to illustrate this area.

10. *Travel and tourism.* Leisure service organizations often manage destination points (featured attractions). In addition, leisure service organizations often manage travel and tour activities.

Several different program formats or forms can be used to organize services for delivery. It is extremely important to use an appropriate format. For example, in contemporary society individuals increasingly require programs with convenient, intense formats. People trying to pack more and more into less and less time are challenging leisure service organizations to provide more accessible and efficient formats for their services. Some potential program formats include the following:

1. *Leagues, tournaments, and contests.* This program format emphasizes competition. There are basically three types of leagues, tournaments, or contests—self-perpetuating, round robin, and elimination.
2. *Drop-in programs.* Drop-in activities provide areas, facilities, and equipment with little structured leadership so that participants can engage in self-directed activities.
3. *Instructional classes.* Classes help people acquire specific leisure competencies, skills, or knowledge. There are two approaches—humanistic and systems—to instruction. The humanistic approach focuses on growth and development of each individual, whereas the systems approach measures minimal standards of competence.
4. *Clubs.* Clubs provide an opportunity for self-directed leadership to flourish. Clubs are often built around special themes, age groups, hobby interests, education endeavors, and political activities.
5. *Special events.* Special events, programs organized in a unique manner deviating from the routine, can take months of planning but can be implemented in a matter of hours or even minutes.
6. *Seminars, workshops, and conferences.* These involve short, intense instructional efforts aimed at providing concise information. Such formats are gaining in popularity due to the desire for convenient and efficient services of short duration.
7. *Outreach programs.* These programs are taken to customers in their own locale. This type of program format may involve mobile recreation equipment and roving leaders and often occurs in densely populated urban areas where entire programs can be organized and implemented on site.

Two of the greatest barriers to participating in leisure are lack of convenience and time commitments. A program's format has a direct bearing on its attractiveness and accessibility to its intended audience.

Program Evaluation   Program evaluation refers to the measurement of the effectiveness and efficiency of program services. Leisure service organizations usually attempt to measure or evaluate two specific areas—impact and process. The first type of evaluation attempts to assess the impact—behaviorally, socially, and economically—of the program on its participants. The second evaluation or measurement concerns the process that is used to produce the program. In other words, evaluation focuses on the step-by-step procedures used in constructing and implementing the program. For example, it addresses such questions as "Are the promotional materials communicating the intended message?" and "Was the format the right length?"

Generally speaking, two methods are used in measurement and evaluation—formative and summative. *Formative evaluation* takes place on a continuous basis throughout the life of the program. All programs require constant, ongoing monitoring, and such evaluation often results in midcourse corrections in the program. *Summative evaluation* takes place at the conclusion of the program. It provides a final assessment and "sums up" the impact and process of the program effort.

Roles of Leisure Programmers

Generally speaking, professionals in leisure service organizations perform three roles—management, supervisory, and direct service. Although organizing the program effort involves all of these roles to one degree or another, the supervisory and especially the direct-service levels carry out the actual organization and implementation of program services. Professionals occupying *direct-service* roles actually meet face-to-face with customers to provide activities, manage facilities, provide information, and train leaders. *Supervisory* responsibilities regarding

Reese. . .

I'm glad I've got Reese. He says don't bother with "Mister." He goes to the same church as us. He likes kids so he does things for them. My friends from school were on Reese's baseball team last summer, but I didn't join because I didn't think I'd be any good. But they all had fun and were league champions so I signed up this year.

I like Reese because he takes time to show you the right way to do things, instead of just telling you. Like when I couldn't hit a fastball and kept striking out, he never yelled when I struck out, he practiced with me more. He pitched fastballs until I could hit them with my eyes closed. The first time I got a hit off one, he cheered like it was the World Series or something. When someone messes up Reese doesn't give them any grief. He says, "maybe next time you will catch it."

Reese is the world's greatest coach. When it was time to pick the All Stars of the church league, he said, "no way—my team is All Stars." He doesn't want anyone to feel left out. Mrs. Reese had an All Star picnic at their house and Reese gave us plaques of things we'd done. I got one for a triple play. Mom hung it over the fireplace.

The other thing about Reese is he helps you out if you're having problems. He's more like a friend, even though he's old. When dad couldn't drive me to the playoffs Reese did. He has a lot of energy and he always has enough time for you. He loves all kids like they were his own.

programming involve identifying needs, establishing program goals, and, often, hiring, training, and supervising direct-service staff to implement services. This discussion focuses on the direct-service provider roles.

Direct-Service Roles

Literally thousands of different types of direct-service roles are carried out by professionals and others. Coaches, ride operators, tour directors, ballet instructors, camp counselors, teen leaders, convention hosts, lifeguards, leisure counselors, interpretive naturalists, park rangers, referees, drama directors, playground leaders, therapeutic recreation specialists, and craft instructors are but a few of the direct-service roles that can be found in leisure service organizations. These direct leadership roles all help bring about the leisure experience. Leisure service organizations also have other support roles, such as receptionists, cashiers, concession attendants, and others who back up the work of those actually delivering the service.

Direct-service program roles fall into a number of categories. Edginton and Ford (1985) suggest six types of direct face-to-face leadership roles—direct program leadership, team leadership, instructional leadership, counselor, outreach worker, and host/guide. Niepoth (1983) writes that the responsibilities of direct face-to-face leaders include a number of tasks such as (1) providing opportunities for people to engage in recreation behavior, (2) promoting interpersonal relationships between people, (3) leading, (4) teaching, and (5) referral and advocacy. Leaders perform diverse functions and carry out a wide variety of tasks.

What special skills or competencies do direct-service personnel need on an entry-level basis to perform effectively? Niepoth (1974) suggests fifteen core processes that enhance the effectiveness of direct-service personnel. The following criteria describe the skills necessary to perform effectively in the direct-service personnel role:

1. *Communication.* Entry-level direct-service personnel should be able to communicate effectively, both orally and in writing.

2. *Leadership.* Knowledge of leadership skills and the ability to use them appropriately and effectively is a key skill that should be possessed by direct-service personnel.
3. *Planning.* Direct-service personnel engage in effective program planning, as well as long-range and short-range organizational planning.
4. *Teaching.* Teaching is an important function carried out, either directly or indirectly, within most direct-service personnel roles. This type of leader should have knowledge of various teaching strategies and should know which strategies are most effective in different types of teaching situations.
5. *Organization.* Entry-level direct-service personnel should be able to organize available resources, as well as their own time and energies, in an effective and efficient manner.
6. *Evaluation.* The ability to effectively evaluate programs (operations) and staff is a skill that should be possessed by direct-service personnel.
7. *Management.* The entry-level direct-service provider should possess the skills necessary to manage organizational resources effectively and efficiently, including fiscal resources, personnel, facilities, and supplies.
8. *Group dynamics.* Direct-service personnel should possess knowledge of group dynamics. It is vital that this type of leader work well with different types of groups.
9. *Problem solving.* The ability to use independent problem-solving techniques is another skill that is important for the direct-service provider to have.
10. *Information gathering.* The entry-level direct-service provider should have skills in the area of information or data gathering. In other words, this type of leader should be able to assimilate relevant information about the population and community served that has potential for influencing service.
11. *Interpersonal skills.* The ability to interact positively and effectively with professional and community groups is an important skill that direct-service personnel should possess.
12. *Relevant legal knowledge.* Entry-level direct-service personnel should have sufficient knowledge of the law as it pertains to their professional area to ensure that they are able to operate well within legal and safety regulations.
13. *Professional philosophy.* The direct-service provider should have a personal and professional philosophy on which to base professional practice.
14. *Professional vernacular.* The entry-level direct-service provider should have a working knowledge of the "special language" or vernacular associated with the profession.
15. *Professional skills.* The entry-level direct-service provider should possess a variety of technical skills. (Niepoth, 1974)

To effectively serve in the direct-service program role requires a wide variety of skills and knowledge.

Types of Direct-Service Leadership

A number of types of direct-service leadership roles exist and can be categorized into nine general areas drawing upon Edginton, Hudson, and School (2005) six direct-service roles. These include direct program leadership, team leadership, instructional, official/referee, host/guide/interpreter, counselor, outreach worker, facility operator, and sales personnel. Some leisure service organizations employ all of these different types of leaders; others employ one or a combination of several. A short discussion of each of these nine types of direct-service leadership roles follows.

Direct Program Leadership The direct program leadership role involves helping individuals participate successfully in some type of activity. Direct program leadership, often general in nature, can require many skills, including serving as a teacher, coach, counselor, and/or group organizer. Direct leaders usually develop skills in scheduling, organizing special events, and promotion, and they often exhibit enthusiastic, energetic qualities.

Direct program leaders often plan programs and then lead the activities associated with these programs. Thus, they usually have specific technical knowledge related to the program. Leaders must guide and direct participants, maintain group cohesion, and at the same time create a leisure environment that is consistent with the goals of the program and organization. Direct leaders in this role often handle and inventory supplies, materials, and equipment.

Team Leadership Team leadership involves working with a group of individuals, usually in some type of competitive format. Team leadership, often associated with athletics and the team coach or captain, is not necessarily confined to this area. Individuals occupying these roles often exert a great deal of influence, either positively or negatively, over team members.

What do team leaders do? What do coaches do? The coaching function is one of teaching, clarifying values, and inspiring individuals to their highest levels of performance. The coach teaches basic skills to team members by organizing practice sessions, meetings, and study guides. The motivation and direction activities usually take place daily in practice sessions and also help the team develop a strategy to successfully compete with its opponents. This strategy becomes apparent when specific plays are implemented during a game.

Instructional Leadership This type of leadership involves organizing a learning environment that helps individuals acquire specific skills, knowledge, or competencies. The leader serves as a teacher. Instruction is a process of communicating with individuals so that learning occurs.

The learning process can be organized in both a formal and an informal manner. Teachers use a variety of instructional strategies, including lectures, demonstrations, role playing, problem solving, guided readings, and experiential activities. Teachers often develop lesson plans that identify course objectives, the course content, and instructional strategies.

Official/Referee Leaders often officiate or serve as referees in leisure service programs. The official/referee helps maintain the integrity of the event. In other words, the official or referee enforces the rules and regulations of the event or game. Officials or referees must be well schooled in the technical aspects of the activity they oversee. In addition, they must have good human relations skills because of the potential conflicts between individuals during the course of an event.

What types of skills do officials need? They must know much more than the rules of the game. An official or referee should maintain a calm and confident demeanor. Officiating also often requires a great deal of physical exertion. Furthermore, good officiating involves the use of common sense; different game situations require judgments based on common-sense application of the rules and regulations. Last, the official/referee must be consistent and fair in both judgments and behavior.

Host/Guide/Interpreter This direct-service role provides information to participants regarding a particular site, event, or thing and helps participants feel comfortable about their involvement in a particular activity or facility. As a host or guide, the leader must be courteous and anticipate participants' needs. As an interpreter, the leader should convey information in a lively, enthusiastic, and interesting manner. Interpreters often bring the subject matter to life—whether it is natural history or cultural or historical events.

The host/guide/interpreter must have a pleasant personality, have specialized knowledge, and understand the work of the organization in general. These individuals must genuinely love people and desire to make the participant's activity or stay at a facility more enjoyable and hospitable. This role requires highly organized individuals who research the topic or site prior to engaging with participants, anticipate contingencies, and plan for them.

Counselor   Counseling takes place in a variety of leisure service settings. Although the camp counselor may predominate in this area, persons in the positions of leisure counselors and leisure educators (as well as other leaders) also engage in the counseling process. The leisure service counselor helps people understand, discover, or define their leisure interests and potential. Counseling not only involves the act of exchanging of ideas and values, but it also may involve providing advice to people.

Most counseling activities involve either values-clarification or values-development exercises or the planning and designing of programs to help individuals. A leisure service counselor works with individuals to help them define their values as related to leisure. In addition, these counselors help people learn to make decisions and to discover and examine alternative leisure choices independently. They help individuals act and behave in accordance with the choices they make in life. A camp counselor serves as a parent, teacher, friend, and confidant to campers (Edginton and Ford, 1985).

Outreach Worker   Outreach workers extend themselves into neighborhoods, communities, or situations in order to provide leisure services. An outreach worker reaches out and assists individuals who are unreceptive, have been excluded, or lack information about a leisure service organization's program. Outreach workers operate in a variety of settings and use a variety of strategies to provide services. Mobile swimming pools, libraries, and playgrounds are a few of the services that might be extended through an outreach program. Outreach workers often work with groups of disadvantaged individuals and/or those who exhibit delinquent behavior.

The outreach worker's role closely resembles the roles of other activity leaders and counselors—it involves direct, face-to-face leadership. The major differences are the setting and the population being served. These factors make the work of the outreach worker intense, requiring specialized skills in interacting with hard-to-reach individuals whose problems may require specialized, creative solutions and program strategies. Outreach workers also sometimes undertake the role of advocate for the needs of disadvantaged groups.

Facility Operator   Leisure service organizations often manage areas and facilities. Facility operators differ from activity leaders in that they focus on the operation and maintenance of a particular facility rather than activity organization. The facility is the "program" in this case. For example, a person who manages a marina does little in terms of activity management; however, this individual keeps the boat docks and support services in excellent running condition in order to maintain a high-caliber leisure environment.

Facility operators, like other leaders, must work well with people and have technical knowledge related to their particular facility. The swimming pool operator, for instance, must understand the fundamentals of pool sanitation, filtration, and so forth. Facility operators also support staff such as cashiers, clerks, and maintenance personnel.

Sales Personnel   In commercial leisure service organizations, sales personnel serve as direct-service providers. They help customers make choices about leisure products or services. For example, an individual working as a convention or event planner at a hotel or resort assists the customer in making decisions about types of facilities, activities, and perhaps food services required for an event. This person might also be involved in the selection of entertainment. A tour or travel agent also works as a salesperson. The individual in this role helps identify points of interest and options in transportation, lodging, and food.

Good sales personnel have a thorough knowledge of their products or services. They must enthusiastically support or endorse the products and be flexible enough to customize services to meet individual needs. Like other leaders, a salesperson must learn to anticipate the needs of the customer, demonstrating a genuine interest in his or her welfare. Effective salespersons are friendly, courteous, and efficient.

Summary

This chapter focused on the development of leisure programs and services. Leisure programs are vehicles that help individuals experience leisure. Those involved in programming work directly with customers and engage in the planning, organizing, and implementation of services. Leisure service organizations fall within the service industry.

An important process in the operation of any leisure service organization, the development of a service orientation or strategy, requires the consideration of three factors: value-added service delivery, positive customer relations, and supportive policies and procedures. Value-added service delivery advocates providing an additional dimension of quality to a program to enhance the attractiveness of the service. Organizations build positive customer relations by having professional staff members who anticipate customers' needs, are courteous, pay attention to detail, are responsive, create a positive environment, demonstrate appreciation, cooperate, demonstrate pride, perform effectively, give out reliable and timely information, and maintain a positive attitude. Building supportive policies and procedures helps reinforce the basic service strategy.

Leisure service organizations provide a number of programs that fall into four general categories: activities, areas and facilities, information, and leadership. The creation of such programs occurs in a cyclical fashion initiated by the development of program goals, followed by needs assessment, program planning, and program evaluation.

Programmers engage in a number of roles. This chapter identifies nine specific direct-service program roles that are common in public, private, nonprofit, and/or commercial leisure service organizations. These include direct program leadership, team leadership, instructional leadership, official/referee, host/guide/interpreter, counselor, outreach worker, facility operator, and sales personnel. Some general requirements of these roles include the ability to work successfully with people, technical competence in the program area assigned, and program-planning and organizational skills.

Discussion Questions

1. Why are leisure services considered a part of the service industry?
2. Explain what is meant by *service*.
3. Define the term *value-added services*. What can a leisure service organization do to add value to its programs and services?
4. What key behaviors produce positive customer relationships?
5. How can such behaviors be taught, reinforced, and maintained in a leisure service organization?
6. What is a leisure service program? What are the different types of leisure service programs?
7. Discuss the cyclical process of program planning. Outline the steps in this procedure.
8. Identify ten program areas. Identify seven program formats.
9. What is the difference between formative and summative evaluation?
10. Identify and describe nine key direct-service roles operating in leisure service organizations.

References

Albrecht, K., and R. Zemke. 1985. *Service America!* Homewood, IL: Dow Jones-Irwin.
Bullaro, J., and C. Edginton. 1986. *Commercial Leisure Services.* New York: Macmillan.

Crompton, J., and K. McKay. 1989. Users' perceptions of the relative importance of service quality dimensions in selected public recreation programs. *Leisure Sciences 11,* 367–375.

Department of the Interior. 1979. *Third Nationwide Outdoor Recreation Plan.* Washington, DC: U.S. Government Printing Office.

Edginton, C. R., and J. P. O'Neil. 1999. Program, services, and event management. Edited by B. van der Smissen, M. Moiseichik, V. J. Hartenburg, and L. F. Twardzik, in *Management of Park and Recreation Agencies.* Ashburn, VA: National Recreation of Park Association.

Edginton, C. R., and S. R. Edginton. 1993a. Agile leisure programming. *Management Strategy 17*(3), 1.

Edginton, C. R., and S. R. Edginton. 1993b. Total quality programming planning. *Journal of Physical Education, Recreation and Dance 64*(8), 40–43.

Edginton, C. R., and S. R. Edginton. 1993c. Total quality program planning. *Journal of Physical Education, Recreation and Dance 64*(9), 41–42.

Edginton, C. R., and P. Ford. 1985. *Leadership in Recreation and Leisure-Service Organizations.* New York: Wiley.

Edginton, C. R., S. L. Little, and D. G. DeGraaf. 1992. Just-in-Time programming: Just for you. *Parks & Recreation 27*(11), 68–72.

Edginton, C. R., Hudson, S. D., and School, K. G. 2005. Leadership for Recreation, Parks and Leisure Services, (3rd ed). Champaign, IL: Sagamore.

Edginton, C. R., and R. Rossman. 1988. Leisure programming: Building a theoretical base. *Journal of Park and Recreation Administration 6*(4), viii.

Glancy, M., J. E. Coles, D. Detzel, L. B. Luck, and S. Rupe. 1994. Lessons for managers: Thinking lean with just-in-time management principles. *Journal of Park and Recreation Administration 2*(2), 1–13.

Godbey, G. 1985. Nonuse of public leisure services: A model. *Journal of Park and Recreation Administration 3*(2), 1–12.

Howard, D., and J. Crompton. 1984. Who are the consumers of public recreation services? An analysis of the users and non-users of three municipal leisure service organizations. *Journal of Parks and Recreation Administration 2,* 38–42.

Howe, C., and Y. Qui. 1988. The programming process revisited: Assumptions underlying the needs-based models. *Journal of Park and Recreation Administration 6*(4), 14–27.

Jackson, E. L. 1994. Activity-specific constraints on leisure participation. *Journal of Park and Recreation Administration 12*(2), 33–49.

Johnson-Tew, C. P., M. E. Havitz, and R. E. McCarville. 1999, Spring. The role of marketing in municipal recreation programming decisions: A challenge to conventional wisdom. *Journal of Park and Recreation Administration 17*(1), 1–20.

Lankford, S. V. 1990, November 5. *Barriers to leisure participation—a future problem.* Presentation to the 1990 Oregon Parks and Recreation Society Annual Conference. Springfield, OR.

McCarville, R. E. 1993. Keys to quality leisure programming. *Journal of Physical Education, Recreation and Dance 64*(9), 34–37.

McCarville, R. 2002. *Improving Leisure Services through Marketing Action.* Champaign, IL: Sagamore.

McChesney, J. C. 1999, October. Strategies for improving customer service in leisure organizations. *NIRSA Journal 23*(2), 6–13.

McKay, K., and J. Crompton. 1988. Alternative typologies of leisure programs. *Journal of Park and Recreation Administration 6*(4), 53.

Miller, R. D. 2000. Customer service for the new millennium. *NIRSA Journal 24*(1), 61–67.

Morgan, J., and J. J. Morgan, (1991). *Cracking the Japanese Market: Strategies for Success in the New Global Economy.* New York: The Free Press.

Nationwide Outdoor Recreation Survey. 1984. Washington, DC: Heritage Conservation and Recreation Service. U.S. Department of the Interior.

Niepoth, W. 1974. *Competency Assessment Processes in Curricula, 1973–74.* Long Beach, CA: Office of the Chancellor, California State University.

Niepoth, W. 1983. *Leisure Leadership.* Englewood Cliffs, NJ: Prentice Hall.

Peters, T. 1987. *Thriving on Chaos.* New York: Knopf.

Russell, R. 1982. *Planning Programs in Recreation.* St. Louis: Mosby.

Siegenthaler, K. L. 2000, April. Hello operator: Front-line staff performance reflects the entire organization. *Parks & Recreation 35*(4), 100–103.

Stenger, T., B. Ryan, and D. Jordan. 1999, November. Positive programming: The common denominator. *Parks & Recreation 34*(11), 28–40.

Swell, C., and P. Brown. 1990. *Customers for Life.* Toronto: Pocketbooks.

Zeithaml, V., A. Parasuraman, and L. Berry. 1988. *Delivering Quality Service: Balancing Customer Perceptions and Expectations.* New York: The Free Press.

Professional Career Development

Professionals bind together in associations and other forums to advocate and promote quality-of-life issues.

Introduction

So you have read the chapters in this book and you have been introduced to the connection between leisure and life satisfaction, as well as how various organizations are delivering leisure services, yet the question remains: How do I get involved in the life satisfaction business? How do I become a part of this exciting and dynamic field? We believe that a professional career in the leisure services field can provide meaningful, challenging, and valuable work and life experiences. Yet, to be successful as a leisure service professional requires forethought and planning; it doesn't just happen. This chapter explains the ongoing process of becoming and growing as a leisure service professional.

A leisure services professional has mastered a body of knowledge and, as a result, can provide a unique and valuable service to society. Leisure services professionals possess knowledge related to the behavior of people during leisure, management techniques, and strategies used to provide leisure services. They have a value structure or philosophy that promotes such ends as the wise use of leisure, preservation and conservation of resources, and the promotion of human dignity. Possessing such knowledge, leisure services professionals are, in fact, uniquely equipped to plan, organize, provide, and evaluate the impact of leisure experiences.

Success in pursuing a professional career requires consideration of a number of key factors related to professional practice. A person acquires some professional knowledge and competencies through formal and informal educational programs and gains others from valuable on-the-job experience. In addition, one's professional career can be enhanced by endorsements through programs of certification. This chapter examines information concerning the common elements of a profession along with information about membership and association with professional organizations. It also presents the key elements in pursuing a professional career.

Common Elements of a Profession

The first step in becoming a part of the leisure services field is to understand the common elements of any profession and the specific traits that make the leisure services profession unique. All professions possess four common elements: an organized body of knowledge, organizations and institutions that exist to transmit professional knowledge, creation of professional authority as a result of public sanction, and a code of ethics and standards to guide professional practice.

An Organized Body of Knowledge

One of a profession's primary requisites is that it serve society in some specific way. In order to perform a unique function, a profession must have a distinct body of knowledge. The leisure services field tends to be eclectic in that it draws from a number of different disciplines in providing services. Edginton, Hudson, Dieser, and Edginton (2003) identify three components of the professional knowledge needed in the leisure service field: *information drawn from the scientific disciplines, appropriate values,* and *applied or engineered skills.*

Information drawn from the scientific disciplines includes such areas as sociology, anatomy and physiology, psychology, anthropology, business, biology, and botany. Information from biology and botany assists leisure professionals in understanding the environment and how to interact with it. Information from sociology, psychology, anatomy and physiology, and anthropology assists leisure services professionals to examine and understand the human movement and the human experience. The information we gain from business impacts parks and recreation professionals in terms of economics and management issues.

The values leisure professionals profess include enriching the quality of human life, advocating for the rights of all people to have access to leisure experiences, assisting people in the wise use of leisure, and working for the conservation and preservation of natural resources. These values give professionals a strong ethical framework through which to filter empirical information and advance the profession.

Applied or engineered skills are the practical skills that leisure services professionals must have to perform their jobs. Examples of these skills include knowing how to lead and program activities, understanding the budgeting process, managing park resources, facility management, and knowing how to use public media to promote leisure programs. These skills also are referred to as technical skills.

The uniqueness of the profession's body of knowledge results from application of this knowledge to planning, implementing, and evaluating leisure services. As Edginton and colleagues (2003, p. 61) note, "The relationship between general scientific knowledge and professional practice is a linear one. As new bodies of knowledge are produced, the applicable or useful knowledge is incorporated into a professional framework (sometimes with modification due to professional values). This process results in the development of *quasi*-theories of professional knowledge." Leisure service professionals can find these theories and other new knowledge in a variety of sources, including books, magazines, journals, manuals, technical and research reports, conferences, and statements by professional associations, agencies, and individuals.

Organizations and Institutions that Exist to Transmit Professional Knowledge

Organizations and institutions play an important role in organizing and transmitting the leisure service profession's body of knowledge in a systematic way. In the late 1930s and 1940s, colleges and universities developed formalized curricula focused on parks and recreation. In 2004, the National Recreation and Park Association (NRPA) lists over 350 schools offering course-work or degrees in parks, recreation, leisure tourism, and natural resource management in the United States (see the NRPA Web site at: http://www.nrpa.org). These numbers have held steady and NRPA, in cooperation with the American Association for Leisure and Recreation (AALR), developed standards of accreditation for the four-year programs. Approximately 100 of these four-year programs are currently accredited. An additional 100 graduate degree pro-grams are in place in the field of parks and recreation (NRPA, 2004). Professional organiza-tions also play a major role in the advancement of a profession. The role of professional or-ganizations is discussed later in this chapter along with profiles of specific organizations within the leisure field.

Creation of Professional Authority as a Result of Public Sanction

Public sanction implies that an occupation is given authority to operate as a profession. Accord-ing to Edginton and colleagues (2003), one may view professional authority from two perspec-tives. First, the public at large may grant authority for an occupation to intervene on behalf of or in concert with, the customer without assuming full responsibility for its actions. Second, as an occupation achieves full professional status, it monopolizes services. Thus, the profession gains considerable authority, since it is the only occupational group with acknowledged ability in a given area of demand. The professional authority of leisure professionals does not appear to be widely recognized in the United States at the current time. Leisure services professionals have not monopolized services, nor has the work of the leisure practitioner been sanctioned to any great extent. Yet this is changing as the profession has established procedures to certify professionals in a variety of areas—exams are now in place for both certified therapeutic recre-ation specialists (CTRSs) as well as certified park and recreation professionals (CPRPs). In ad-dition, depending on their area of specialization, leisure services professionals may be certified as certified recreational sports specialists (CRSSs) certified commercial recreation profession-als (CCRPs), and certified pool operators (CPO).

Ethics and the Leisure Services Profession

Every profession has a set of ethics. Those who practice the profession make ongoing attempts to maintain a professional identity supported by those ethics. Ethics involve the study and prac-tice of an intellectual endeavor, which leisure service professionals believe must include atti-tudes and behaviors that add dignity to life. A professional, as one who lives the ethics of the field, knows that a moral action is greater than one without moral foundation (Fain, 1985).

Ethics are an integral part of all human services professions; members of the profession deal with political climates, the well-being of many individuals, and social issues, all of which involve ethics. Professional and ethical behaviors go hand in hand—professional actions up-hold a certain level of ethics, and ethical actions uphold professionalism (Stumbo, 1985). Issues such as privacy, privilege, autonomy, and other values of leisure dictate a moral position.

The parks, recreation, and leisure services profession believes that all people have the right to personal autonomy, to be self-governing, and to be morally free to make the choices that di-rect their lives (Sylvester, 1985). The dignity of self-determination should be preserved. Leisure professionals particularly value autonomy because it is fundamental to the free choices associated with play, recreation, and leisure (Shank, 1985). Most leisure philosophies also hold that people benefit from play and recreation opportunities, with an underlying belief structure that leisure and recreation contribute to the quality of life of participants.

Many professionals in leisure service organizations (especially those in public and nonprofit recreation organizations) have a passion for public service. Public service represents the act of doing something valuable and worthwhile for society (Brewer and Selden, 1998). Knapp and McLean (2003) have identified the importance of public service and the intrinsic benefits it provides professionals in the field of public park and recreation. They note that the positive feedback received from the community helps form a sense of accomplishment that has facilitated the development of a public service ethic. Knapp (2000) noted the fulfillment of personal values, such as making an impact on an individual's life and providing for the greater good of the community, were key components to their jobs (as cited by Knapp and McLean, 2003). Consider the following quote from a public park and recreation professional in Knapp's (2000) study:

> I feel in love with my work in parks and recreation. It was everything that I had hoped for and more. I immediately knew that this was the place for me. I really enjoy seeing people recreate. I feel that, when I drive by or through a park, that in some small way I am responsible for the experience that these people are having. It makes me feel wonderful. Also, there have been kids that have come to me ten years after participating in our programs and say, "You really saved my life" or "you made such a difference." Those are the things that you can't ever put a price tag on. It is that satisfaction of knowing that you are doing something good for people and the community. I really like the public aspect: I really do. (cited in Knapp and McLean, 2003, p. 28)

Code of Ethics

A code of ethics develops from the key values of the leisure profession. Some of these key values include: enriching the quality of human life, advocating for the rights of all individuals to have access to leisure experiences, assisting people in the wise use of leisure, and working for the conservation and preservation of natural resources. A set of ethics or standards develops from these values and governs the relationship between the professional and those he or she serves.

The leisure services field has been lethargic in the development and enforcement of behavioral standards. Not until 1960 did the American Recreation Society (a forerunner to the NRPA) establish a code of ethics. It was updated and rearticulated in 1995 and reaffirmed in 2000 by NRPA (see table 14.1). Other organizations have followed suit; for example, the code of ethics for the American Therapeutic Recreation Association can be found at http://www.atra-tr.org/ethics.html. Professionals are becoming aware of the document and investigating how the code might be used as a mechanism for self-control. While many leisure services organizations have developed specific statements for use within their organizations, the development of ethics and standards requires further work in the leisure services field. Specific branches of the field (e.g., parks and recreation, therapeutic recreation, campus recreation, commercial recreation) must continue their work on developing codes that reflect their uniqueness. It is not enough simply to have a code of ethics; leisure services professionals must commit to the ideals presented in the code.

Commitment to Professional Ideals

What professional ideals does the leisure services profession hold? Does it promote a commitment to the natural environment, diversity, dignity of life, program quality, or self-expression? Should it? These questions reach the heart of the leisure services profession. Professionals must respond to these questions from their own source of personal and professional ethics. Furthermore, professional standards affect every aspect of the profession—programming, leadership, the provision of facilities, and administrative practices.

14.1 NRPA PROFESSIONAL CODE OF ETHICS

The National Recreation and Park Association has provided leadership to the nation in fostering the expansion of recreation and parks. NRPA has stressed the value of recreation, both active and passive, for individual growth and development. Its members are dedicated to the common cause of assuring that people of all ages and abilities have the opportunity to find the most satisfying use of their leisure time and enjoy an improved quality of life.

The Association has consistently affirmed the importance of well informed and professionally trained personnel to continually improve the administration of recreation and park programs. Members of NRPA are encouraged to support the efforts of the Association and profession by supporting state affiliate and national activities and participating in continuing education opportunities, certification, and accreditation.

Membership in NRPA carries with it special responsibilities to the public at large, and to the specific communities and agencies in which recreation and park services are offered. As a member of the National Recreation and Park Association I accept and agree to abide by this Code of Ethics and pledge myself to:

- Adhere to the highest standards of integrity and honesty in all public and personal activities to inspire public confidence and trust.
- Strive for personal and professional excellence and encourage the professional development of associates and students.
- Strive for the highest standards of professional competence, fairness, impartiality, efficiency, effectiveness, and fiscal responsibility.
- Avoid any interest or activity that is in conflict with the performance of job responsibilities.
- Promote the public interest and avoid personal gain or profit from the performance of job duties and responsibilities.
- Support equal employment opportunities.

From D. Clark, "A New Code of Ethics for NRPA" in *Parks & Recreation Magazine 30*(8), pp. 38–43, 1995. Reprinted by permission of National Recreation and Park Association, Ashborn, VA.

As we continue to discuss and identify our professional ideals, it is interesting to note the continued importance of hanging on to the central mission of what we do. For Mobley (2004), this mission is to improve the quality of life for all of our citizens through creative, meaningful leisure experiences. Almost everything we do should focus on this mission. "It is obviously broad in scope and provides for comprehensive opportunities and diversity. It also becomes the philosophical basis for our fields" (Mobley, 2004, p. 24).

Professional Associations

Professional associations play an important role in the work of professionals. They advocate on behalf of the interests of a group, the members of which share some common interest. Membership in such organizations provides a means to network with others, gather new information, and promote the interests of the organization. Some professional organizations have a narrow focus or are limited to a region or state; others represent the leisure services movement on a nationwide or international basis. For example, the NRPA strongly advocates conservation, preservation, and leisure concerns to a national and international audience.

Holding a membership in one or more professional associations is important to one's professional life. Often, a person first asks, "What benefits or services does membership bring to me personally?" However, another perspective about whether or not to join a professional organization deserves consideration. Membership in a professional association offers opportunities to serve, as well as to promote and further one's own professional interests. In other words, many people give talent, time, and energy to the work of a professional organization in order to promote important ideals.

Professional associations serve as vehicles to advance the interests of their membership. In that context, a professional should seek membership in an appropriate organization, one within which to advocate, to promote ideals, and to serve other professionals. In short, membership in a professional association provides an opportunity for individuals to give to their profession and at the same time receive various benefits. Professional associations serve multiple ends, with the following among them (see figure 14.1):

Advocacy. Professional associations work to promote their ideals and to convince their constituency of the worthiness and value of their activities. Advocacy activities often include providing testimony, information, and lobbying for important pieces of legislation that can impact on the work of the profession. Most professional associations provide a platform for their membership to promote common interests through advocacy activities. Such activities help to establish and maintain the value and worth of a profession to society.

Educational opportunities. Professional associations provide educational opportunities for their members, often in the form of conferences, workshops, institutes, and seminars. Large national associations provide conferences that feature educational presentations and sessions and also display and demonstrate the latest and most innovative equipment, supplies, programs, and services.

Written and electronic communication. Most professionals agree that the most important benefit of association membership is the professional magazine, newsletter, or other written and electronic communication. Such communication provides information

Figure 14.1

Benefits of membership in professional associations.

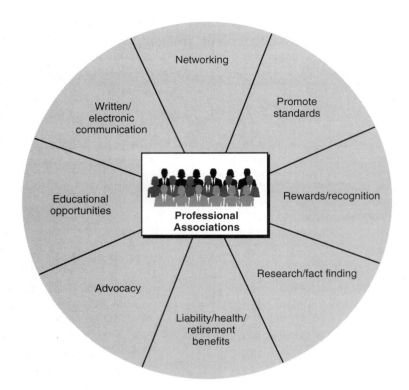

concerning the activities of the association, job opportunities, information about current trends and issues, and new knowledge as reflected in articles, research briefs, and legislative notes.

Networking. Membership in professional associations allows individuals to meet and interact with other professionals. Networking with people who have common interests provides a means to learn about new and improved ways of delivering services, identification of common problems and potential solutions, and, perhaps most important, an opportunity for individuals to reaffirm their commitment to a set of similarly held ideals and values. With the rise in access to computer technology, networking opportunities exist in two formats: directly through face-to-face contact and indirectly through Internet listserves.

Promote standards. Professional associations often work to promote higher standards of practice, as reflected in the creation of programs of voluntary registration, certification, and licensing. Professional associations often create codes of ethics that serve as standards of practice to guide individual action, and they influence the quality of educational institutions by establishing and administering programs of accreditation.

Rewards and recognition. Professional associations provide a means for recognizing the outstanding work of individuals, associations, and groups. Not only do professional associations reward and acknowledge the work of their own membership, they often acknowledge other individuals and groups that have contributed toward common values. Some national associations regularly acknowledge a legislator whose work has positively influenced their professional area of interest. Professional associations often provide scholarships to outstanding students to help defray costs associated with attending a college or university, or to attend a professional meeting or conference.

Research and fact finding. Many professional associations conduct research and fact-finding surveys, and some study the status of the profession on a yearly basis. Such studies provide valuable baseline information that is used to compare the growth or progress of the profession from one year to the next. Further, professional associations often devote resources toward solving emerging issues and specific problems. Such activities may involve the creation of task forces or special study groups that focus on specific issues and recommend courses of action.

Liability, health, or retirement benefits. Professional associations often serve their membership by providing benefits such as individual and group insurance—retirement, liability, health, and others. A professional association can often purchase services at a reduced cost on a group basis and then make these services available to individual members. These association packages provide financial savings and also meet the specific needs of the professional membership.

The value of these benefits and services to an individual depends on his or her position within the profession. Individuals in entry-level positions often find that conferences and workshops provide valuable information and opportunities to network for the purposes of socializing, job hunting, and meeting others in the profession. More seasoned professionals view the same conferences as an opportunity to pursue legislative initiatives, plan for future professional endeavors, and promote the interests of their profession.

Again, professional associations provide an opportunity for individuals to serve as well as to derive meaning from their work. Joining one or more professional associations or societies offers numerous benefits to members. Individuals should carefully consider which professional association(s) best serves their interests and ideals.

Types of Professional Associations

Since the leisure services field is so diverse, a large number of professional societies and associations exist to represent the varying nature and character of the profession. Many associations are referred to by their initials. For example, the American Camping Association is often called the ACA. While it is not possible to include all professional associations related to the field of leisure services here, some of the more common professional associations that employ individuals in the leisure services field include those mentioned in the following section. World Wide Web addresses have been provided for those associations that have Web pages. Readers should be aware that street and Web addresses change over time—it is good policy to double-check information before attempting to contact a professional association.

American Alliance for Health, Physical Education, Recreation and Dance (AAHPERD)

1900 Association Drive
Reston, VA 22091
www.aahperd.org

AAHPERD is dedicated to promoting professional activities for those who have interests in health and safety education, intramurals, aging, fitness research, physical education, athletics, sport, dance, outdoor education, and recreation. The organization, founded in the late 1800s, provides publications, research, and special projects consistent with the needs of its membership. While AAHPERD publishes several magazines and journals, its major publication is the *Journal of Physical Education, Recreation and Dance.* It also offers a job bulletin to both members and nonmembers, as well as other resources related to the profession.

The organization operates by promoting the work of a number of affiliate associations, including the American Association for Leisure and Recreation (AALR); the National Association for Sport and Physical Education (NASPE); National Association for Girls and Women in Sport (NAGWS); Association for the Advancement of Health Education (AAHE); National Dance Association (NDA); and American Association for Active Lifestyles and Fitness (AAALF).

American Association for Leisure and Recreation (formerly The American Association of Lifelong Recreation, Physical Activity and Fitness)

1900 Association Drive

Reston, VA 22091

www.aahperd.org/aalr.html

In 2004, American Association for Leisure and Recreation (AALR), in collaboration with the American Association for Active Lifestyles and Fitness, proposed a merger between the two organizations. The new organization to be created will be called the American Association for Lifelong Recreation, Physical Activity Fitness. The mission of the organization is "dedicated to enhancing quality of life by promoting creative and active lifestyles through meaningful recreation, physical activity, and fitness experiences across the lifespan." It was proposed that the organization will provide services to members by: 1) developing quality programs and products for the continuing education and certification of professionals and future professionals; 2) establishing opportunities for networking and collaborating; 3) linking professionals and future professionals with career opportunities; 4) providing a forum for professionals, students, and organizations to process, debate, educate, and exchange information and ideas; and 5) establishing and promoting a professional code of conduct and ethics. In addition, the organization will provide service to the profession and society by: 1) increasing public awareness, understanding, appreciation, and support for lifelong recreation, physical activity, and fitness programs and services; 2) encouraging, developing, publishing, and advancing scientific knowledge and research; 3) establishing and disseminating guidelines and standards for professional practice of programs and organizations and assessing the achievement of such standards; 4) ensuring the development of quality professional preparation programs; and 5) advocating for meaningful recreation, physical activity, and fitness programs.

The merger occurred in Chicago, Illinois in April of 2005. This new organization is an affiliate of AAHPERD. Information regarding this merger from AAHPERD is as follows:

> In a landmark vote during the 2005 AAHPERD Alliance Assembly, delegates approved the formation of the American Association for Lifelong Recreation, Physical Activity and Fitness. The new association, approved in Chicago, represents a consolidation of the American Association for Active Lifestyles and Fitness (AAALF) and the American Association for Leisure and Recreation (AALR). The new association, dedicated to enhancing quality of life by promoting creative and active lifestyles through meaningful recreation, physical activity, and fitness experiences across the lifespan predominantly through community-based programs, represents a total combined membership base of nearly 8,300 members. (http:www.aahperd.org/aahperd/template.cfm?template=new_assocation.html)

American Camping Association (ACA)

Bradford Woods

5000 State Road 67N

Martinsville, IN 46151

www.aca-camps.org

The ACA works primarily to increase the quality of the organized camping movement. Membership in ACA is open to individuals and organized camps that promote camping activities, including those involved in providing camping programs at private, youth serving, church, and in agency/nonprofit organizations. As an organization, ACA accredits camps and conference centers. In addition, ACA holds an annual convention and produces *Camping Magazine* as its primary publication. Another important publication of the ACA is the *ACA Guide to Accredited Camps.* This guide includes information about camps all over North America, describing programs, fees, staffing structures, and the like. ACA also offers an extensive bookstore with a wide variety of professional publications.

American Therapeutic Recreation Association (ATRA)
1414 Prince Street, Suite 204
Alexandria, VA 22314
www.atra-tr.org

The ATRA, one of the newest professional organizations related to our field, was founded in 1984. As a nonprofit organization, its primary purpose is to promote the needs of therapeutic recreation professionals in health care and human services. Among other things, ATRA is very active in legislative lobbying efforts to advance the therapeutic recreation profession. Professional education efforts include an annual and midyear conference, and the ATRA Academy, which offers training opportunities on a regional basis. Publications include a newsletter, job bulletin, *Treatment Networks* where professionals can share treatment ideas for a particular population, and other resources that address professional ethics issues such as reimbursment, and concerns related to professional practice. ATRA's primary publication is the *Therapeutic Recreation Annual.*

Association for Experiential Education (AEE)
3775 Iris Avenue, Suite #4
Boulder, CO 80301-2043
www.aee.org

The AEE was formed in 1972 as a nonprofit, international association. Today the association has a membership of some 1,600 individual and organizational members in over 30 countries committed to furthering experience-based teaching and learning. AEE members include people involved in adventure programming, ropes courses, schools, recreation programs, human service providers, correctional and mental health institutions, youth servicing agencies, programs for people with disabilities, environmental centers, outdoor adventure organizations, and universities. Each year AEE hosts an international conference as well as regional conferences across the country. Membership benefits include receiving the *Journal of Experiential Education,* newsletters, a job bulletin, and discounts on AEE publications and conferences.

The International Ecotourism Society (TIES)
733 15th St NW Suite 1000
Washington, DC, 20005
www.ecotourism.org

This nonprofit organization was founded in 1990. It serves tour operators, conservation professionals, park managers, government officials, lodge owners, guides, and other professionals who promote eco-tourism worldwide. Eco-tourism, a growing phenomenon, finds individuals traveling to remote and unspoiled areas without the luxuries associated with most vacation travel. The Ecotourism Society provides publications, workshops, training programs, and an evaluation program for areas and facilities to its membership.

International Festivals and Events Association (IFEA)

2601 Eastover Terrace

Boise, ID 83706

www.ifea.com

The IFEA is a membership organization for special events; its Web site reports over 2700 members. IFEA assists festival and event professionals with fundraising as well as the production and delivery of festivals, civic celebrations, and special events. The IFEA shares information with its members related to event sponsorship, marketing, operations, working with volunteers, and management. It also provides a variety of services to its membership, including regional seminars, an annual convention and trade show, publications, travel discounts, internship placement, and a resource center. The primary magazine is *The Business of Internations Events*. In addition, the IFEA offers a certification for festival administrators called the Certified Festival And Event Certificate (CTEE).

Employee Services Management Association (ESM Association)

2211 York Road, Suite 207

Oak Brook, IL 60523-2371

www.esmassn.org

ESM Association primarily serves corporate recreation and fitness directors, personnel managers, and human resource development specialists. The Employee Services Management Association (ESM Association) is a nonprofit association that serves as an information resource network for nearly 2,000 members nationwide. These members are responsible for implementing and maintaining a diverse range of employee services. ESM Association believes that employee services and practical solutions to work/life issues are essential to sound business management. These programs improve relations between employees and management, increase overall productivity, boost morale, and reduce absenteeism and turnover. Primary vehicles for dissemination of information include national and regional conferences, a monthly magazine entitled *Employee Services Management Magazine,* newsletters, and research data.

National Intramural-Recreation Sports Association (NIRSA)

4185 SW Research Parkway

Corvallis, OR 97333-1067

www.nirsa.org

NIRSA is a nonprofit organization devoted to the promotion of quality recreation sports programs and services. This organization provides up-to-date information and resource materials for colleges, universities, and other institutions that are involved in providing intramural sports, campus recreation, and community recreation services. Through national and regional conferences, NIRSA seeks to be a strong advocate, resource, and professional network for this area, and publishes the *NIRSA Journal*. In addition, NIRSA provides standards and professional ethics as guides for its members. One element of this is the Certified Recreational Sports Specialist (CRSS) certification.

National Recreation and Park Association (NRPA)

22377 Belmont Ridge Road

Ashburn, VA 20148

www.nrpa.org

State Park and Recreation Societies & Associations

Alabama Recreation and Parks Association	Mississippi Recreation and Park Association
Alaska Recreation and Park Association	Missouri Park and Recreation Association
Arizona Parks and Recreation Association	Montana Recreation and Park Association
Arkansas Recreation and Park Association	Nebraska Recreation and Park Association
California Park and Recreation Society	Nevada Recreation and Park Society
California Association of Park and Recreation Commissioners and Board Members	New Hampshire Recreation and Park Association
	New Jersey Recreation and Park Association
Colorado Parks and Recreation Association	New Mexico Recreation and Park Association
Connecticut Recreation and Parks Association	New York State Recreation and Park Society
Delaware Recreation and Park Society	North Carolina Recreation and Park Society
District of Columbia Recreation and Park Society	North Dakota Parks and Recreation Association
Florida Recreation and Park Association	Ohio Parks and Recreation Association
Georgia Recreation and Park Association, Inc.	Oklahoma Recreation and Parks Society
Hawaii Recreation and Park Association	Oregon Recreation and Park Association
Idaho Recreation and Park Association	Pennsylvania Recreation and Park Society
Illinois Association of Park Districts	Rhode Island Park and Recreation Society
Illinois Park and Recreation Association	South Carolina Recreation and Park Society
Indiana Park and Recreation Association	South Dakota Park and Recreation Association
Iowa Park and Recreation Association	Tennessee Recreation and Park Society
Kansas Recreation and Park Association	Texas Recreation and Park Society
Kentucky Recreation and Park Society	Utah Recreation and Park Association
Louisiana Recreation and Park Association	Vermont Recreation and Park Association
Maine Recreation and Park Association	Virginia Recreation and Park Society
Maryland Recreation and Park Association	Washington Recreation and Park Association
Massachusetts Recreation and Parks Association	West Virginia Park and Recreation Association
Michigan Recreation and Park Association	Wisconsin Recreation and Park Association
Minnesota Recreation and Park Association	Wyoming Recreation and Park Association

For many, the NRPA is the major professional association of the parks and recreation profession. It traces its heritage to the late 1800s. This amalgamation of professional associations merged in 1965 to form a nonprofit service, research, and educational organization. Its membership consists of professionals, volunteers (lay citizens), students, and organizations. NRPA holds an annual congress and provides a variety of services and publications consistent with the needs of branch members, including a job bulletin. Its major publication is *Parks and Recreation*, although it also publishes *Therapeutic Recreation Journal,* and others.

Currently, NRPA conducts many of its activities through a number of branch affiliates including:

- National Therapeutic Recreation Society (NTRS) serves members interested in therapeutic recreation. NTRS was discussed in detail in Chapter 12.
- Society of Park and Recreation Educators (SPRE) serves individuals involved in educating current and future recreation professionals. Activities sponsored or co-sponsored by SPRE include the Research Roundtable (presented at the annual NRPA congress); organizing a teaching institute every two years; organizing the leisure

research symposium (presented annually at the NRPA congress); and managing SPRENET, the branches listserv.

- American Park and Recreation Society (APRS) serves over 7,000 members. Its purposes include: to be advocates for parks and recreation in the United States and Canada; foster professional growth and development of park and recreation personnel, thus improving the delivery of leisure services; providing advice to NRPA in achieving overall organizational goals; to gather and disseminate information on significant park and recreation issues.
- National Society for Park Resources (NSPR) represents National Recreation and Park Association members working in natural resources, parks, and conservation. Their mandate includes assuring resource accessibility today and in the future while providing high-quality outdoor recreation experiences for all.
- Armed Forces Recreation Society (AFRS) represents NRPA members working in military recreation. It serves "a network of more than 100,000 highly trained professionals, students and military commanders in the business of providing recreation programs and services to the Armed Forces worldwide. It is a professional organization providing and coordinating training and professional development, networking, program recognition, and new program initiatives while providing a voice for Armed Forces recreation professionals to the national boards and to public action forums" (NRPA, 2004).
- Citizen Board Member (CBM) represents National Recreation and Park Association members serving on boards and commissions nationwide. In 2004, there were over 8,600 members of CBM branches. Resources provided by CBM include research and legislative updates, representation in Washington on legislation impacting parks and recreation, and training and development to become a national citizen voice to advance parks and recreation at all levels.
- National Aquatic Branch (NAB) serves aquatic professionals—from pool managers to executive staff. There are an estimated 205,000 swimming pools and 5,000 beaches owned, operated, managed, and maintained by NRPA-represented park and recreation systems. In 2004, there are over 1,000 members of NAB. Resources for members include: a National Aquatic Management School, a National Aquatic Conference, a branch newsletter, and the National Aquatic Facility Operator (AFO). It's Certification Course has trained over 5,000 AFOs and continues to become the nation's top training opportunity for pool operators and aquatic managers (NRPA, 2004).
- Student Branch (SB) represents NRPA members attending post-secondary institutions, giving future park and recreation professionals an opportunity to get involved with the profession.

In addition to these branches, NRPA also includes two sections—Commercial Recreation and Tourism Section (CRTS) and the Leisure and Aging Section (LAS). In conjunction with AALR, NRPA accredits university curricula and certifies individuals as Certified Parks and Recreation Professionals.

Resort & Commercial Recreation Association (RCRA)

www.r-c-r-a.org

One of the newest professional associations, RCRA, promotes the interests of the resort and commercial recreation area. RCRA holds regional and national conferences, a Program Leadership Workshop, and provides a number of services to its members, including a job-placement service, job fair, internship placement opportunities, and a newsletter. The RCRA publishes recreation program standards for commercial and resort recreation programs, as well as books related to this specialty area of the leisure services field. In addition, RCRA conducts and disseminates research information and offers a Certified Commercial Recreation Professional (CCRP) certification.

World Leisure Organization
203 Wellness/Recreation Center
University of Northern Iowa
Cedar Falls, Iowa 50614
www.worldleisure.org

World Leisure, a nonprofit, nongovernmental worldwide agency, promotes leisure and recreation around the globe. The organization was founded in 1956 and has been in the forefront of efforts to promote awareness of recreation and leisure as a basic human need in all countries and regions of the world. The organization publishes its magazine, *World Leisure Journal* four times a year. Its conference attracts professionals, educators, and interested individuals from throughout the world. WLRA has a consultative status with the United Nations—it is considered a nongovernmental organization (NGO). In this capacity, World Leisure performs its services in cooperation with other international organizations, specialized agencies of the United Nations, affiliated national associations, and organizations in more than 100 countries.

In addition to these organizations, nearly every state has its own state park and recreation societies and organizations. For example, the Michigan Recreation and Park Association (MRPA) was established in 1935, as a nonprofit association. Today, it has over 2,000 members representing the public and private sectors of the recreation and park profession. MRPA is comprised of a diversity of professionals and agencies from a variety of backgrounds including tourism, recreation, parks, therapeutics, senior citizens, resorts, arts, athletics, education, business, and industry. MRPA represents the interests of leisure service professionals and citizen advocates throughout Michigan. It publishes a magazine, *Michigan Parks & Recreation Magazine,* holds an annual conference, and sponsors a wide variety of programs throughout the state of Michigan.

Other examples of state organizations include the Illinois Park and Recreation Association (IPRA), the California Park and Recreation Society (CPRS), and the Florida Recreation and Park Association (FRPA). IPRA provides a full range of benefits to its membership, including an annual conference, educational seminars, video library, technical assistance library, leadership opportunities, government and media representation, annual salary survey, statewide marketing campaign, cooperative purchase program, packaged tours, discount tickets, investment fund, and multiple publications, including *Illinois Parks and Recreation, Leisure Review, Management Strategy, Get the Message,* and *Membership Directory.* IPRA operates several special-interest sections to meet membership needs, including those dealing with administration and finance, facility management, parks and natural resource management, recreation programming, therapeutic recreation, and a student section.

The CPRS also provides a full range of services to members, including an awards program, annual conference, publications such as *California Parks and Recreation, Leisure Lines, Job Line, CPRS Directory Service,* and other services. CPRS has nine special interest sections that offer training, publications, and network opportunities, including administrators, aging, armed forces, commercial, educators, park operations, recreation supervisors, students, and therapeutic recreation.

The FPRA also provides a broad range of services, including conferences, workshops, legislative representation, voluntary certification, liaison services, networking opportunities, scholarships, employment opportunities, special discounts and programs, and publications, including

Florida Recreation and Park News. Special-interest groups include aquatics, athletics, commercial/exhibitors, community centers, ethnic minorities, leisure arts, parks and natural resources, and resort/commercial and therapeutic recreation. Special committees and categories represent retirees, students, and military personnel.

In addition to state parks and recreation associations, many recreation and leisure services departments in colleges and universities have student recreation clubs. These clubs offer students opportunities to get involved with their chosen profession while they are still in school. Other benefits of such organizations include opportunities to gain experience, network, and learn more about the profession. For example, Club QOLLA (Quality of Life, Leisure Administrators) at the University of Northern Iowa provides an awareness of the human and leisure services profession by promoting growth opportunities through community service, education, and social experiences.

Three other types of leisure service professional organizations provide services and serve as a forum for advocacy activities. They include special-interest groups, trade associations, and futurist groups.

Special-Interest Groups Organizations such as the Sierra Club, National Audubon Society, Izaac Walton League, World Wildlife Fund, Earthwatch, and the Nature Conservancy— all special-interest groups—provide opportunities for individuals to participate in an organization with a specific focus. Such organizations do not perceive themselves as professional societies or associations, but rather as advocacy, information, and support groups. There are as many national and international special-interest groups as there are people with interests. One can find special-interest groups that relate to serving the needs of people with disabilities, the environment, special activities such as hot air ballooning, and the like.

Trade Associations Another type of organization, the trade association, provides information and services related to a specific element of an industry. These organizations often do not have members, but interested individuals and/or organizations purchase their services as products. For example, Athletic Business Publications, Inc., a trade association, publishes a magazine, *Athletic Business*™, on a monthly basis and distributes it without charge to athletic, recreation, and fitness professionals. Its annual conference features in-depth, well-developed presentations and exhibits. This group provides up-to-date information about athletic, fitness, and recreation areas by providing a professional directory and identifying the most current and contemporary concepts related to products, equipment, and professional services.

Futurist Groups Futurist groups are organized in different ways, depending on their orientation. Some provide services on a consulting basis, such as Brain Reserve, a highly respected consulting group, chaired by Faith Popcorn. Others provide cutting-edge information about the future of the leisure service industry. *Leisure Watch,* a quarterly publication of *Future Focus,* provides information about the leisure service industry that reflects innovations and issues that will dramatically affect the future of leisure in America. Another publication, *Leisure Industry Digest,* provides information on "futures" activities.

The decision to participate in professional organizations or activities is an important one. Such associations provide an invaluable opportunity for individuals to contribute to their profession, as they receive the benefits of membership. Professional involvement in activities offers stimulation and excitement; attendance at an exciting national conference can shape one's professional future in a dramatic way.

Obviously, an individual must select an appropriate professional association in which to become a member. Guidelines to follow in pursuing membership include:

1. *Be selective.* Write to different professional associations and ask for their literature. Investigate their services and the avenues for participation through your library and connections on the Internet.
2. *Start locally.* Perhaps the best way to begin participation in a professional association is to seek membership in your local university's professional leisure club or society; membership in state associations also can be helpful.
3. *Look for opportunities for membership involvement.* Look for associations that actively promote membership involvement—many encourage high levels of involvement in their affairs. Committee assignments, conference presentations, and legislative activities offer opportunities for new members. By becoming involved, one can better understand the needs of the profession and his or her role in it.
4. *Align interests.* Align your interests with professional associations that are consistent with your focus and reflect your career path. In this way, you can network with appropriate individuals and understand the underpinnings of your particular interest area.
5. *Be aware of discount memberships.* A number of professional associations provide discount memberships for students or organizations. Such membership fees provide access to the services of an organization at a reduced cost with no reduction in services.

Membership in a professional organization forms an essential part of one's professional career. Potential employers look for evidence of professional involvement on an individual's portfolio or resume. In part, professional involvement indicates a commitment to the profession as well as one's own professional development. Furthermore, joining a professional organization provides rewarding and worthwhile opportunities to serve one's profession in a positive and meaningful way and provides many useful benefits to the individual.

Pursuing a Professional Career: Key Elements

When considering a professional career, many individuals wonder where to begin. "How do I find the right position in a professional setting that will meet my needs and interests? What challenges will I find in the job market?" These complex questions require careful examination.

As seen in earlier chapters of this text, the leisure services field is highly diverse, with a number of different career pathways available. An individual must carefully assess his or her interests, desires, and career aspirations in order to establish an appropriate plan. Parts of the leisure services industry are competitive, with many seeking employment for similar jobs. Without proper planning and preparation, it may be difficult to achieve a position with the most desirable agencies. On the other hand, opportunities always exist for individuals who have prepared themselves and who have planned effectively for the future. Figure 14.2 humorously illustrates the results of failing to plan carefully.

This portion of the chapter discusses the process of career assessment and exploration. In addition, it presents information concerning education, professional experiences, and certifications. Lastly, the chapter emphasizes the importance of lifelong education and continuous professional development. All of these are essential elements in pursuing a professional career (see figure 14.3).

Career Assessment and Exploration

Each person considering a career as a leisure services professional must ask, "Where shall I focus my professional career endeavors? How do I know what professional direction to take?" Individuals must find a professional focus to assist them in decision making. First, one

Figure 14.2

Making life decisions.

Source: CALVIN AND HOBBES copyright 1990 Watterson. Reprinted with permission of UNIVERSAL PRESS SYNDICATE. All rights reserved.

Figure 14.3

Essential elements in pursuing a professional career.

needs to determine whether or not to seek employment in the leisure services field. The next step is to hone in on the area of greatest interest. The leisure services field presents a number of opportunities, with many potential career ladders. It is impossible to climb all of them simultaneously. Rather, a person should concentrate on particular career options and strive to do well in them.

Previous chapters discussed professional opportunities available: working in government (local, state, federal), nonprofit organizations (youth serving organizations, voluntary agencies, clubs), the private commercial sector (resorts, theme parks, hospitality industry, travel, and tourism) and/or therapeutic recreation arena (clinical- or community-based). Each of these sectors requires a specific strategy for career development—a unique set of educational competencies or a combination of professional work experiences. Certain sectors of the profession require detailed certification procedures. Different sectors of the profession conduct their professional business through their own professional associations. Knowledge of and membership in a particular association are important.

It is important to plan ahead in career development. Some students graduate from college or university and say, "OK, I've graduated, now what do I do?" This lack of planning puts the person at a professional disadvantage. Rather, an individual should establish options and then choose between desirable alternatives. Wise students lay the appropriate groundwork so that multiple options are available upon graduation.This groundwork can be laid in a variety of ways, from getting a wide range of experiences in a number of different leisure service organizations to working extensively in one specific setting. The key is getting experience early during summer vacations as well as during the school year. Students who have a plan have answered these types of questions: Will I choose a full-time position in the public, nonprofit, or commercial sector? How can I get the skills and/or certifications I need to be successful in my job search? Where does graduate school fit into my future?

Education

Perhaps the most important element in developing a professional career in leisure services is to study at a college or university that offers an appropriate degree in parks, recreation, or leisure services, preferably one accredited by the National Recreation and Park Association/American Association for Leisure and Recreation's Council on Accreditation. One can obtain a list of accredited programs by writing to either of these two professional associations or accessing the NRPA Web site at www.nrpa.org.

What makes higher education so important? A career in the leisure services area requires unique foundational knowledge best acquired by enrolling in an undergraduate program that offers the appropriate degree. Usually, the Bachelor of Arts or Bachelor of Science degree serves as the key entry-level requirement for employment. One's educational experience blends theoretical knowledge, applied or engineered skills, and professional values. The information presented in an undergraduate degree program enables a student to develop the basic knowledge, competencies, and skills required for entry-level positions.

Many colleges and universities provide specialized courses and degree offerings that have a particular focus, such as therapeutic recreation, travel and tourism, community recreation, sports management, resource management, youth development, and others. An advanced degree—Master of Arts or Master of Science—provides additional opportunities for specialization and focused study.

Professional Experience

Another essential element—experience—gives an aspiring leisure services professional a great advantage. The leisure services field has numerous opportunities available for part-time or seasonal professional work experiences. For example, nearly every community parks and recreation department offers extensive summer employment. Commercial resorts, theme parks, camps, and other settings provide similar opportunities. In addition, volunteer opportunities are widely available in a wide variety of human service settings. For example, working as a volunteer in organizations such as the Big Brothers/Big Sisters program and Boys and Girls Clubs of America can provide invaluable insight into dealing with children who are at risk.

Preprofessional experiences, which are often part-time or voluntary in nature, provide the foundation for one's professional values, strategies, and interests. For example, *Camp Adventure™ Youth Services Program,* operated by the University of Northern Iowa, provides contracted youth services to U.S. military installations worldwide. In addition to providing high-quality, high-impact youth services, the program dedicates itself to providing students with a hands-on orientation to the profession. *Camp Adventure™*, a value-driven program, strongly emphasizes quality in all that it does. This value structure translates into students who are highly motivated, as they participate in a model program of excellence. Such foundational experiences guide the professional endeavors of participating students as they pursue careers (see www.uni.edu/campadv/).

When leisure agencies, businesses, and organizations seek individuals to employ they will, invariably, look for relevant experience with all aspects of a job. For instance, in many organizations, computer skills (knowledge of word processing, spreadsheets, graphics) are a must. Almost all organizations will also look for previous experience in the field where a student has had practice in direct leadership or programming settings. Many college and university curricula require organized field study programs, practicums, and internships as a part of their degree offerings. Participation in such activities provides the minimum requirements for entry-level professional positions. Individuals should enhance their backgrounds by actively seeking these and similar opportunities. Part-time summer jobs, volunteer activities, and other experiences provide necessary real-life opportunities to increase relevant professional experience.

Another way to gain professional experience is through your internship. The internship is usually the final requirement of a student completing a degree in parks, recreation, or leisure services. The internship is typically one semester long and requires students to complete between 500 and 600 hours working in a park, recreation, or leisure service organization. The design of the internship provides students with a full time-structured learning experience in a recreational setting of the student's choice. The internship offers students an opportunity to bridge the gap between theory and practice as well as move from being a student to a professional. Table 14.2 presents some 'ips and resources to students to help them find the right internship.

Networking

Meeting and interacting positively with other professionals also comprises a key element in developing a professional career. The networking process starts immediately upon entering an academic program, since professors are usually the first important contacts with the profession. These individuals should know their students and have the ability to analyze their strengths and weaknesses effectively. They prepare and can promote students' initial entry into the profession. Also, supervisors of part-time, voluntary, and seasonal positions become important contacts. These people can provide an analysis of opportunities and often have other professional contacts who may help in professional career development. Certainly, such individuals can provide a perspective on the quality of professional work.

Involvement in professional associations also creates important opportunities to network. Attending conferences, meetings, greeting professionals, and serving as an advocate for professional interests are important elements of professional career development. For example, the Florida Recreation and Park Association has developed a student and professional mentoring program that seeks to connect students enrolled in parks, recreation, leisure studies, tourism,

TABLE

14.2   TIPS FOR FINDING INTERNSHIPS

1. **Network.** Talk to family and friends and see if they, or anyone they know, might be able to help you find an internship in your desired field.

2. **Surf the Web.** The Internet is a great source for finding internships and information about various careers. There are tons of helpful sites geared towards students that have internship postings as well as helpful information on how to update résumés and prepare for interviews.

   Some good sites to check out include:

   MonsterTRAK.com—This site is similar to Monster.com, only it's geared toward college students. There are many great internship and entry-level positions posted here, as well as tips on how to prepare for interviews and update your résumé.

   GetThatGig.com—An excellent site that states it will help you get that "cool gig." This site offers a lot of internships and jobs in various fields, including unique and hard to find jobs.

   WetFeet.com—Offers international internship opportunities for those who like to travel.

   WDWCollegeProgram.com—Provides all the information you need to apply for the Walt Disney College Program. This is a unique paid internship available for students of all majors. Students get to work in one of four theme parks, more than twenty resorts, three water parks, or Disney's dining/entertainment/retail complex.

3. **Take advantage of your school's resources.** Talk to a counselor at your school's career center for advice on how and where to look for an internship. Also, go to career fairs held at your school and talk to the attending employers about their internship programs.

4. **Don't be afraid to approach a company.** If there's a company you really want to work for, approach them and ask about getting an internship. Even if they don't have an internship program, you can offer to work there for free (most internships are unpaid anyway) for a couple days a week. The main thing is to gain the experience and references that you will need later.

Source: Jennifer Grubb, Virginia Tech University (http://youngmoney.com/careers/internships_seasonal/030127_03)

sports management, special event programming, and other related fields with professionals in the field.

There are two goals of the program. One goal is to create an interest in and better understanding of the many values and opportunities in a community parks and recreation department as a lifetime career opportunity. The second goal of the program is to introduce the students to the Florida Recreation and Park Association, increase the number of student members, and ultimately increase the number of future professional members. For additional information contact, the Florida Recreation and Park Association at the following Web site, www.frpa.org/profDevMentoring.html. In addition, at NRPA congresses, formal mechanisms are established for a practitioner to take a student to lunch and engage in mentoring and networking.

Individuals should consider joining one or more professional associations. Such organizations provide opportunities to better understand the profession and stay abreast of professional developments, and for networking by helping to identify job opportunities and other useful services.

Certifications

Certification, licensure, and registration often are viewed as hallmarks of a profession. As such, they attest to the fact that the holder is committed to the profession and has achieved certain levels of knowledge and skill. Certification is the chosen method of attesting to one's knowledge or skill that is being used by leisure services professional organizations. As the field of

Career Growth Timeline

Here's where a career in parks and recreation can take you—

While in College

- Join state and national association: (800) 626-6772
- Join campus recreation and leisure club

Within One Year After Graduating

- Secure an entry-level job in the field
- Apply to become professionally certified
- Attend state conferences and workshops

Within Two to Three Years After Graduating

- Speak at state conferences and workshops
- Become professionally certified
- Volunteer for state association

Within Five Years After Being on the Job

- Promoted to first line Supervisor/Program Manager
- Volunteer for State Association
- Attend regional workshops, schools, and seminars
- Be a mentor to young professionals
- Attend the NRPA Congress
- Be a community volunteer
- Attend graduate school
- Maintain professional certification
- Write and/or meet your legislators

Within Ten Years of Being in the Profession

- Promoted to Division Manager/Area Supervisor/Community Supervisor
- Be an officer in your state association
- Be an advocate for recreation and parks within other associations
- Publish in the NRPA *Parks and Recreation* magazine
- Ongoing community volunteering

Source: NRPA 2004.

- Serve on NRPA Task Forces and Committees
- Attend NRPA Executive Development School
- Present at the NRPA Congress
- Continue as a mentor to young professionals
- Lobby your local, state, and national legislators
- Be an expert in some facet of the field

Within Fifteen Years of Being in the Profession

- Promoted to Director of Parks and Recreation of a small to medium agency or a Division Director or a large agency
- Be an adjunct instructor at a university/community college
- Volunteer for NRPA and other human services organizations
- Be a board or council member for an NRPA Branch or Regional Council
- Continue to mentor young professionals
- Be a resource to your local, state, and national legislators and write letters and give testimony at legislative hearings
- Continue to serve your state association
- Publish articles on a regular basis in state and national publications
- Maintain your professional certification

Within Twenty or More Years in the Profession

- Become the director of a large park and recreation agency
- Teach as an adjunct instructor
- Present at other state, regional and national conferences
- Become a member of the NRPA Board of Trustees
- Continue to serve your state association
- Sponsor a young professional to a state or national conference
- Present at international conferences and workshops
- Continue to contribute to your state and national associations

leisure services continues to evolve, certification is becoming increasingly important to those employed in the profession. In addition, it is a statement about one's commitment to the development of the leisure services profession, and of one's concern for a baseline of competence.

After receiving a degree from an accredited university, persons in the field of leisure services are eligible to become certified as a certified parks and recreation professional (CPRP). Those in the area of therapeutic recreation are eligible to be certified as both a CPRP and as a CTRS, a certified therapeutic recreation specialist. The CTRS, similar to the CPRP, affirms that the holder possesses certain standards of knowledge necessary to effectively and safely conduct job functions. The CTRS certification is administered by the National Council for Therapeutic Recreation Certification. To maintain professional certifications, one must continue to seek out educational experiences (Continuing Education Units—CEUs) to perpetuate the addition of knowledge, and thus, the profession.

Technical Certification   Other common certifications sought and gained by those committed to the delivery of leisure services include some form of advanced first aid, cardiopulmonary resuscitation (CPR), mandatory child abuse reporting certification, certification in the handling of blood-borne pathogens, ropes course facilitation, wilderness first aid, and certification as a aquatic facility operator (AFO). Once gained, maintaining these certifications through recertification courses and CEUs is desirable.

Lifelong Education and Professional Development

The half-life of knowledge in the area of management is seven years; in physics, four. In the leisure services field, the half-life of knowledge is perceived to be ten years. What does this mean? Basically, it means that half of the knowledge that one learns becomes obsolete in a short time. Society is constantly challenged by change, with new products, new processes, and new methods of delivering services. All of these require the constant attention of the successful professional. Therefore, all professionals should dedicate themselves to lifelong education and professional development.

Lifelong education and continuous professional development mean constant involvement with and commitment to learning throughout life. Professional success requires attendance at professional conferences, intensive seminars, workshops, and institutes. Enrolling in college and university courses also upgrades a professional's development, knowledge, and skills. For example, the NRPA provides extensive, in-depth management and program institutes for parks and recreation professionals in the areas of risk management, playground safety, public golf course management, park maintenance, finance and revenue, aquatics, therapeutic recreation and inclusion, and administration.

Continuous review of electronic and written communications also serves as a valuable source of new information. A leisure services professional not only should read from within the leisure services field but also should review materials outside the profession; for example, management literature, human resources, current events, and philosophy. An organization can promote its staff's professional development by organizing preservice, in-service, and development programs. Such staff development initiatives may draw on internal resources, external consultants, colleagues, and others.

The Use of a Professional Portfolio

The importance of lifelong education and professional development cannot be overstated. Professionals must constantly be looking to improve and become better in everything they

The Ten Questions that Can Transform Your Life

We think of life as having three dimensions: being, doing, and having. Often we attempt to live our lives backwards. We try to have more money in order to feel we can do more of what we want, so we can be happier. The way it actually works is the reverse. We must first be who we really are, then do what we feel guided to do, in order to have what we want. Shakti Gawain

As you look to develop yourself as a person and as a professional, it is important to look inward. The first step in becoming an effective leader is to look in the mirror. Master the art of leading yourself and you will lay the foundation for helping others to do the same. In exploring the concept of self leadership, Marshall and Rawlins (2003) presented a session at the 2003 NRPA conference that looked at the Ten Questions that can Transform Your Life. These questions are presented here and offer you, as a student, a starting place for examining who you are and where you are going.

1. What did I accomplish?
   - Maybe no one noticed your finest moments over the past year, but you did. Think about the times when you were proud of yourself, did something well, or solved a problem. List these.
2. What were my biggest disappointments?
   - Recall the times you disappointed yourself or were disappointed by others. What dreams didn't come true? What expectations weren't fulfilled? List these
3. What did I learn?
   - Look back at your answers to the first two questions. What worked? What would you do differently? Based on what you noticed, set some guidelines for the next year.
4. How do I limit myself and how can I stop?
   - More than anything, you can be stopped from achieving your dreams by the thoughts and beliefs you have about your chances of success. By thinking through the following questions, you'll discover some of the hidden ways you prevent your own success. (a) How do I limit myself? (b) What do I say about myself to explain these limitations? Does what

we say to ourselves shape our chances of success? Listen to what you say to explain the limitations you listed in question A. (c) What is my new paradigm for my best year yet? What new perception or view of yourself could replace the old one?

5. What are my personal values?
   - Values are deeply held beliefs that live in our hearts and souls. To home in on yours, think about the end of your life, how do you want to be remembered? What do you want to be admired for? Think about your values and write them down.
6. What roles do I play in my life?
   - Think about the roles you currently play in your life. Are these roles you like to play? What other roles would you like to play in the future? What roles need more focus in your life right now?
7. Which role is my major focus for the next year?
   - Identify the major roles in your life. Select one of your roles as your major focus of attention over the next year.
8. What are my goals for each role?
   - People who have goals achieve more results. So when you set your own goals, make them powerful and specific, using acting verbs such as: earn, join, plan, choose, invest, achieve, learn, make. Your goals must also be measurable. How many? How big? How often? For how long?
9. What are my top ten goals for the next year?
   - Quickly preview your responses to the first seven questions. Remember what you've learned about yourself and what's most important to you. Think about the guidelines you've established for your next year. Remind yourself of your new paradigm and the prioritized goals you have set for the next year.
10. How can I make sure I achieve my goals?
    - The key to achieving your goals for the year is visibility. Keep your plan where you'll see it and read it every day. Consider identifying an accountability partner and develop a way to reflect on your goals on a regular basis.

Source: Presentation at the NRPA Congress, St. Louis, Missouri, 2003.

do. It is also important to document individual professional growth and development. One specific way to document these experiences is by utilizing a resource file and portfolio system. A resource file and subsequent portfolios will assist students in developing the needed skills to interpret an individual student's experiences to a specific person, group, or agency (DeGraaf and Jordan, 1996).

A portfolio development system is designed to assist students in the ongoing process of compiling and organizing the resources needed to interpret their preprofessional and professional experiences (academic and experiential) to others both inside and outside the profession. This process takes place throughout one's academic and professional career.

There are two elements within a portfolio development system—a resource file and a portfolio. A resource file is a collection of documents, papers, pictures, certificates, letters, work samples, references, recommendations, professional involvement logs, course descriptions, creative endeavors, and other pertinent materials that relate to the educational and career goals established by the student or professional. Students would be wise to begin collecting these items early in their academic, volunteer, and work careers.

A portfolio is a smaller collection of materials purposely drawn from the resource file to meet a particular purpose (e.g., to apply for a position as a programmer in a municipal recreation organization or to provide documentation in a specific skill area). Viewed as a professional self-portrait, a portfolio should illustrate an individual's proficiency in areas deemed important to being a professional in leisure services. The portfolio is an authentic measurement or assessment strategy that allows individuals to document their unique skills and abilities related to lifelong learning (DeGraaf and Jordan, 1996). In other words, a portfolio is an evolving tool that helps individuals to exhibit their talents and experiences. Using a portfolio enables one to document the technical skills, human resource skills, and conceptual skills needed to succeed in a specific career. In addition, a portfolio could be used to reflect on past experiences to develop a philosophy of delivering services to customers, as discussed in Chapter 4.

A portfolio can be organized in any number of ways. One consideration to bear in mind as it is developed is the intended reader or reviewer. Keep the presentation and layout simple and easy to follow (indexed in some fashion). Wisely utilize graphics and monitor the amount, type, and style of language. A professional appearance is important—remember, the reviewer is gaining an impression of the type of person you are and the type of employee you might be. Attention to detail is a hallmark of people who care about their work. One way to organize a portfolio would be to highlight various types of work experience. For instance, one might have direct leadership, programming, supervisory, and administrative skills or work experience. Within each of those categories one might choose to highlight his or her technical, interpersonal, and conceptual skills. A wise preprofessional is one who begins development of his or her portfolio materials early and continually reviews and updates those materials.

As we continue to move into the digital age, students can also consider creating electronic portfolios. Electronic portfolios are selective and purposeful collections of student work made available on the World Wide Web. They represent a learning history. As our use of the Web continues to expand, it will be interesting to see how it can be used to document competencies and present professionals to potential employers.

It is never too early to begin this documentation process. Undergraduate students should pay particular attention to beginning a documentation system that assists them in identifying strategies to meet specific professional goals as well as interpret experiential learning to potential employers. Such a system could be adapted to document lifelong education and professional development through one's professional career.

Summary

The leisure services field provides many diverse and challenging work opportunities. Preparing for one's career involves a process of planning and decision making in order to successfully locate an entry-level professional position. In developing a career path, individuals should focus their efforts in a specific direction. The leisure service field has many career ladders; the best employment opportunities require focused attention on only a few.

The first step in becoming a part of the leisure service field involves understanding the characteristics of the profession, the common elements of any profession, and the specifics that make leisure services unique. Four common elements all professions possess include: an organized body of knowledge, organizations and institutions that exist to transmit professional knowledge, creation of professional authority as a result of public sanction, and a code of ethics and standards to guide professional practice.

In crafting a professional career in the leisure services field, one must acquire foundational knowledge. This can be most effectively achieved by enrolling in a college or university in an accredited degree program. Part-time, seasonal, or voluntary work experiences often provide a long-standing foundation for one's career. Networking with practicing professionals, joining professional associations, and interacting with professionals in the field also play an important role. Professionals should seek appropriate certifications and credentials that attest to their competence, capability, and knowledge.

Professionals have a responsibility to be involved in professional organizations. Such organizations serve multiple ends, including providing opportunities for advocacy, education, communications, networking, promotion of standards, rewards and recognition, research and fact finding, and others. Membership in professional associations should be selective; it may be better initially to join a state or regional group. Membership in professional associations also provides opportunities for individuals to give back to their profession.

Discussion Questions

1. Identify the key elements in pursuing a professional career in the leisure services area.
2. What benefits result from attending a college or university whose program is accredited by the NRPA/AALR Council on Accreditation?
3. Discuss the importance of lifelong education as a part of the process of one's professional career development.
4. What are the common elements of all professions?
5. After reading some of the core values of the leisure field, what five standards would you like to see become a part of a code of ethics for the profession?
6. Identify the types of experiences (volunteer and paid) you think you need in the next three years to enhance your ability to get a job when you graduate.
7. Identify the courses you should take within your institution to graduate with a degree in recreation or leisure services.
8. What common functions do professional associations share?
9. Identify four or more professional associations, find their Web sites and look for pertinent information concerning membership services, fees, and other activities.
10. What is the difference between a professional association, special-interest group, trade association, and/or futurist group? Of what value is it to belong to these types of groups?

References

Clark D. 1995. A new code of ethics for NRPA. *Parks & Recreation 30*(8), 38–43.

DeGraaf, D., and D. Jordan. 1996. The use of a portfolio system as a pedagogical tool. *SCHOLE 11,* 37–45.

Edginton, C., Husdon, S., Dieser, R., and Edginton, S. 2003. *Leisure Programming: A Service-Centered and Benefits Approach.* 4th ed. Dubuque, IA: McGraw-Hill.

Fain, S. M. 1985. The art of teaching professional ethics. *Therapeutic Recreation Journal 19*(4), 68–74.

Knapp, J., and McLean, D. 2003. The passion for public service. *Park and Recreation* (May), 24–30.

Mobley, T. 2004. Observations on the future of parks, recreation and leisure services. In Edginton, C., ed., *Papers of the American Leisure Academy.* Cedar Falls, 1A: University of Northern Iowa. pp. 23–26.

NRPA. 2004. Retrieved from http://www.nrpa.org/ (section on NRPA/AALR Council on Accreditation).

Shank, J. W. 1985. Bioethical principles and the practice of therapeutic recreation in clinical settings. *Therapeutic Recreation Journal 19*(4), 31–39.

Stumbo, N. J. 1985. Knowledge of professional and ethical behavior in therapeutic recreation services. *Therapeutic Recreation Journal 19*(4), 59–67.

Sylvester, C. D. 1985. An analysis of selected ethical issues in therapeutic recreation. *Therapeutic Recreation Journal 19*(4), 8–21.

15

Leisure and Cultural Diversity

These youth learn the value of diversity while enjoying an outdoor celebration.

Introduction

As society increasingly becomes multicultural, it is important that leisure services professionals understand and value pluralism or diversity. By understanding the dynamics of differences and the processes used to develop perceptions and assumptions, one can examine and analyze the accuracy and validity of such assumptions. The concept of diversity presented in this chapter implies sensitivity to differences of physical qualities and abilities, race and ethnicity, gender, age, and sexual orientation—*unity without uniformity*. People also differ on socioeconomic status, religion, educational levels, and others. A positive focus on the multicultural populations of the United States highlights the benefits of a multicultural population.

The leisure service professional has a responsibility to create a climate that advocates diversity, gains accurate information about difference, and evaluates those differences in a context of mutual respect. American leisure lifestyles and choices, a mosaic of many cultures, exhibit the influences of Native people, Hispanics, Mexicans, Latinos, Asian, and African Americans as well as those of Norwegian, Irish, Scottish, Canadian, German, Slovakian, and other cultural groups in games, sports, festivals, arts, music, and other leisure forms. Leisure service professionals must move from a point of merely acknowledging differences to a place of assigning merit and worth to these differences. However, to do this, leisure professionals must be aware and skilled in diversity competencies. Wheeler's (1994) four-stage educational and training model posits that all professionals, including leisure professionals, go through four sequential levels of cognizance regarding diversity issues and competencies. The first level, unconsciously incompetent, holds that professionals do not know that they are ignorant about diversity issues and competencies. The second level, consciously incompetent, suggests that professionals become aware that they are ignorant about diversity issues and competencies. They begin to understand that they lack knowledge about diversity issues and skills when working with people from diverse cultural backgrounds. The third level, consciously competent, maintains that professionals have gained knowledge and skills in regard to working with people from diverse backgrounds. The fourth level, unconsciously competent, suggests that professionals become so grounded in diversity competencies (e.g., knowledge and skills) that it becomes part of their everyday professional lives. This chapter is a beginning step regarding how administration, leadership, and programming can lead leisure professionals to be consciously competent and unconsciously competent in regards to diversity issues.

Future Trends: A Dramatic Increase in Diversity

The third millennium, punctuated with rapid social, economic, political, and cultural change, will present opportunities and challenges to leisure services professionals. The increasing diversity of the population will greatly impact leisure services organizations. To be effective as a leisure services professional, one must have knowledge in the area of diversity, as well as skills to manage diversity in terms of customers, staff, and the community at-large.

Trends for the twenty-first century show an increasingly multicultural population and labor force, an increase in women in the workforce, a trend toward a more mature workforce, and opportunities for previously underused segments of the workforce. All of these trends have implications for issues of diversity. Chapter 16 presents a summary of statistics related to these trends; however, this chapter briefly mentions these trends to provide a foundation for this topic and to underscore the importance of this issue.

Ethnic minorities. In late 2000, California reached a milestone where no one ethnic group is in the majority (more than 50% of the population). This trend will continue across the United States.

Women. In the next decade two out of three new workers will be women, and women will constitute approximately 48 percent of the workforce in the year 2008 (Ameristat, 2000).

Individuals with physical disabilities. Computer-aided technologies will allow individuals with physical disabilities to compete more effectively for employment within leisure services organizations. In addition, the Americans with Disabilities Act will continue to impact this group in a positive fashion.

Older individuals. The number of people sixty-five and older who will remain in their jobs is predicted to increase in the next decade, partially due to the fact that U.S. Congress banned forced retirement in 1986.

People who are gay or lesbian. In 2000, Vermont became the first state to officially recognize same-sex civil unions, which carry the same legal benefits as marriage.

These trends will impact all leisure services organizations. Some of the emerging organizational considerations related to these trends include equal opportunity, child care, flexible work schedules, staff development in the area of diversity, and others. Following is a brief outline of potential organizational outcomes if the trend toward increased diversity continues as anticipated.

• To remain competitive and retain employees, leisure services professionals must be increasingly sensitive and responsive to issues related to diversity, including age, gender, ethnicity, disability, and sexual orientation.
• As the workforce becomes almost half female, there will be pressure on leisure services professionals to respond to the increased need for adequate child-care programs, parental leave, flexible hours, and innovative child-care options. Equity issues also will be important.

Women Do Not Speak with One Voice

Women do not speak with one voice. Each voice represents her own unique experiences of culture, religion, race, class, family, environment, and sexuality. Circumstances of birth contribute to who she is and who she will become. Women are as distinctive as the stripes of zebras. When viewing a herd of zebra, each zebra's unique markings are not seen. In much the same way, women are often seen as similar when looking at them as a group.

Each woman sings uniquely—soprano, alto, or contralto. When blended together in harmony, the collective choir of sopranos, altos, and contraltos provides sounds which are quite different from men's voices in harmony. Each woman speaks uniquely and in a way that is different from a man's.. . . [There are] . . . distinctive differences between women's and men's values as they relate to morality. Choices made as a result of these differences in value orientation represent many of the differences in our voices.

Source: Pritchard, A. 1997, Fall. Challenges for women in sport in the new millennium. *The Journal of the International Council for Health, Physical Education, Recreation, Sport and Dance 33*(1), 15–18.

- Leisure services professionals must respond to the values, needs, and desires of a diverse constituency. Cultural competence will be demanded of staff at all levels.
- Equal opportunity issues will persist for people of color as they seek promotion within organizational hierarchies and own their own businesses.
- In terms of both customers and staff, the leisure services professional must deal with issues of discrimination regarding HIV infection and AIDS, rights to privacy, and rights of noninfected customers and staff.
- Staff development will continue to play a key role in responding to issues related to the broad spectrum of diversity.

Issues related to increasing diversity continue to challenge leisure services organizations and leisure service professionals to develop policies and procedures to guide the direction of their organizations in a positive and responsive manner. This begins with a personal understanding of diversity by each leisure services professional, as well as the organizations in which we work.

This discussion of trends has laid the groundwork for the realization that diversity is an important issue in the leisure services field. The next section of the chapter, which deals with foundational perspectives, attempts to determine what diversity is—the dimensions, definitions, and terms that describe diversity and contribute to a greater understanding of the topic.

Diversity: Foundational Perspectives

The term *diversity* suggests a variety of topics—affirmative action, racial or ethnic issues, and sometimes simply difference. A discussion about diversity requires a conceptual framework and working definitions in order to operate from a common starting point.

Words can have a tremendous impact on self-esteem, the way one views the world, and the perspectives of others. Language is not static; it changes constantly. Common meanings for terms change and become acceptable or not as the culture evolves and grows. Even the language in this book will become outdated and require revision to maintain original meanings. However, the definitions provided in this section help establish a framework for communica-

Women: A Critical Mass

... Women have reached a critical mass in the professions. No longer are they a token minority. ... Since 1972, the percentage of women physicians has doubled. In 1966, fewer than 7 percent of MDs were granted to women. By 1987 it had reached 32.3 percent, nearly one third. In 1966 women were awarded an even tinier proportion of law degrees . . . a mere 3.5 percent. But by 1987, women were taking home 40 percent of all law degrees. . . .

Women have achieved, if not a majority, a substantial proportion of the previously male-dominated careers in the information and service industries. ... Women hold some 39.3 percent of the 14.2 million executive, administrative and management jobs, according to the Bureau of Labor Statistics . . . nearly one third of computer scientists are women. . . . Male or female, the effective leader wins commitment by setting an example of excellence: being ethical, open, empowering and inspiring.

tion. We discuss terminology related to culture, discrimination, and prejudice and look at the role of power in the formation of "isms" (e.g., racism, ageism, and other forms of discrimination) in order to set the framework for understanding.

Culture

Culture permeates everything that people do, think, and feel. The concept of culture includes the values, traditions, norms, customs, rituals, and ways of viewing the world of a group of people who are tied together by common factors. These factors may include a common history, geographic location, language, food, music, social class, and/or religion (Schwartz and Conley, 2000). In addition, leisure as a construct (what it means to different people) and as an activity also forms a component of culture.

We know that culture consists of at least two levels: surface culture and deep culture. *Surface culture* consists of those elements of culture that are visible to others—food, dress, appearance, music, use of gestures, and so on. We tend to draw conclusions about people based on what we see and think we know about them. *Deep culture* includes the elements of an individual that are not necessarily visible to others, yet are incredibly important in terms of self-identity. Examples of these are worldviews, social systems, beliefs, values, and unstated norms (Guirdham, 1999).

It is common for most people to belong to one primary culture and one or more subcultures. For instance, a typical college student might belong to the Panhellenic subculture (a sorority/fraternity), be considered middle class, and be of African American descent. Each subculture influences the individual's attitudes, thoughts, and actions. Leisure activities both produce subcultures and are the products of subcultures within society. Golfers, fantasy football team owners, country western line dancers, collectors of baseball cards, curlers, and quilting groups are all subcultures associated with leisure.

Some groups have been *marginalized* by society—pushed by the dominant culture to the *margins* or fringes of society in terms of social and economic resources (power). As Healey (1997) notes, minority status has more to do with the distribution of resources and power than

Outdoor Sports for People with Disabilities

AccessAdventure is a service that designs outdoor adventure challenge programs that challenge existing notions of what is achievable; designs programs with people with disabilities, rather than for people with disabilities; ensures the program is "tailor made" and that the challenges are proportional to the skills of the individuals; offers people with disabilities the opportunity to learn and develop skills that will help enhance quality of life; and facilitates outdoor adventure challenge activities in an atmosphere of care, support, and fun. HEAD OFFICE: Physical Difference, PO Box 216, Kurrajong NSW 2758.

Quad Rugby, or wheelchair rugby as it is also called, is a sport with roots going back to wheelchair basketball and ice hockey, which is not surprising, since it was developed by three Canadians from Winnipeg, Manitoba, as a quadriplegic equivalent to wheelchair basketball. The sport was originally called murderball due to the aggressive nature of the game. It was introduced in the United States in 1981 by Brad Mikkelson, who with the aid of the University of North Dakota's Disabled Student Services, formed the first team, the Wallbangers, and changed the game's name from murderball to quad rugby.

In 1979, a team from Winnipeg organized an exhibition at the regional track meet held at Southwest State University in Minnesota. Canada went on to play their first national championship that same year. The first quad rugby match in the United States was between North Dakota and Minnesota, as an exhibition game at the 1982 National Wheelchair games, also held at Southwest State University. This same year, the University of South Dakota hosted the first international tournament, with participating teams from Manitoba, Saskatchewan, North Dakota, and Minnesota.

In 1988, the United States Quad Rugby Association (USQRA) was formed to help regulate and promote the sport on both a national and international level. Since its introduction Quad Rugby has grown to become a truly international sport, with teams now competing from around the globe. There are now more than forty-five organized teams in the United States with many others in the developmental stage. In addition to the teams in the United States, there is estimated to be at least twenty international teams from as far away as Australia in addition to those in Canada. Without question, quad rugby is the fastest-growing wheelchair sport in the world today.

Who Can Play?

Players may have various disabilities that preclude their play in able-bodied sport competition. Players must have a combination of upper and lower extremity impairment to be considered as eligible to participate. Most of the players have sustained cervical-level spinal injuries and have some type of quadriplegia as a result. Players are given a classification number from one of seven classifications ranging from 0.5 to 3.5. The 0.5 player has the greatest impairment and is comparable to a C5 quadriplegic. Of those eligible to participate, the 3.5 player has the least impairment and is similar to a C7-8 incomplete quadriplegic. Both males and females are encouraged to play, and because of the classification process gender advantages don't exist.

The Game

Four players from each team are allowed on the court at a time. Classifications of the four players on the court must total no more than 8.0 points at one time. The action occurs on a regulation-sized basketball court with some minor changes. During the games team players pass a volleyball back and forth while advancing into the opponent's half court and then crossing over the goal line with the ball in one player's possession. While the offense is trying to advance the ball, the defense is trying to take it away and keep the opposing team from scoring. Certain restrictions apply in the key area. One restriction is that only three defensive players are allowed in the key, and if a fourth enters, a penalty can be assessed or a goal awarded. Another restriction is that an offensive player can only stay in the key area for ten seconds. Otherwise a turnover will be assessed.

with simple numbers. He suggests five characteristics that are part of the definition of a minority: (1) the members of the group experience a pattern of disadvantage or inequality; (2) group members share invisible traits or characteristics that differentiate them from other groups; (3) the minority group is a self-conscious social unit; (4) membership in the group is usually determined at birth; and (5) members tend to marry within the group.

Thus, marginalized or minority groups generally consist of individuals from outside the dominant, or most common, culture. Leisure programs and events can promote certain leisure outcomes that enable marginalized or minority individuals to maintain their cultural integrity and take advantage of opportunities for self-expression. This is important, because people are more likely to adjust to a new culture (i.e., immigrants) when they have contact with compatriots; people who share a culture affirm one another's cultural identity and validate the everyday realities of the acculturation process (Kurtz-Costes and Pungello, 2000). For example, celebrations such as Cinco de Mayo, a festival that is part of the Hispanic culture, offer opportunities to celebrate diversity and maintain traditions. While anyone might attend Cinco de Mayo and learn something about the Hispanic culture, the festival helps to maintain the Hispanic cultural identity. Marginalized groups often use leisure to affirm their cultural identity and values, and to promote their traditions and heritage.

Prejudice

Prejudice is an attitude or opinion that indicates a preconceived judgment, made before all information has been gathered. It is irrational and based on myth, fiction, and misinformation rather than fact. This negative bias against a person or group limits understanding of individuality and may constrain an individual from reaching his or her potential. Humans all have prejudices and prejudices interfere with the ability to perceive reality accurately. Table 15.1 offers a case in point regarding prejudice and illustrates the way people can react, physically and emotionally, and sometimes stereotype individuals who are "different."

TABLE

15.1	UNDERSTANDING PREJUDICE

Prejudice: A Case in Point

Many of our prejudices about others are unfounded; that is, they are not based in fact. Society, media, and culture have programmed us to accept stereotypes of others. Thus, it is important to acknowledge our prejudices and the danger of faulty stereotypes. The following two scenarios illustrate this point:

Scenario One: It is 3:00 A.M. and a white college student is walking down a dark street alone; there are no other people in the vicinity. He/she sees a group of five black youths coming from the opposite direction. They are talking loudly. What do you think the initial reaction of the white college student will be?

Scenario Two: It is 3:00 A.M. and a black college student is walking down a dark street alone; there are no other people in the vicinity. He/she sees a group of five white youths coming from the opposite direction. They are talking loudly. What do you think the initial reaction of the black college student will be?

We all have been programmed in a way that encourages us to react emotionally to situations like the one above, without foundation of fact. Based on societal stereotypes the two college students in the scenarios above will likely experience feelings of concern, possibly panic, and physical symptoms that usually accompany danger. Have either of the individuals, however, had time to make a logical or rational assessment of the situation? Isn't it possible that the two groups of five individuals are simply having a good time and are individuals of good character and values?

TABLE

15.2 MANY LEISURE PROGRAMS/ACTIVITIES MEET CRITERIA FOR REDUCING PREJUDICE

Contact Conditions for Reducing Prejudice

1. *Equal status.* Creating conditions to make all people feel equal may reduce prejudice; for example, individuals wear similar clothing, casual clothing, uniforms (e.g., sports). Individuals leave their rank, status, level of authority outside. Group use of identity markers, such as logos, uniforms, and other items that publicly attest to membership may also be effective.

2. *Positive perceptions of other group occurs.* Positive, successful images of all types of people, including women, people of color, and older people, are shown.

3. *Other majority group members are involved.* Majority group members offer support and indicate by their behavior and actions that valuing diversity is the right thing to do. Strong role models are important.

4. *Activities require intergroup cooperation.* To achieve goals, individuals must cooperate (e.g., organizational projects, sports, games). A sense of belonging is reinforced through rituals such as ceremonies, songs, and group cheers, as well as public commitment to vision and mission statements, codes of conduct, values, and other expressions of unity and loyalty.

5. *Situations entail interdependence of superordinate goals.* Individuals have a common goal or purpose as a group, for example, in the military or on sports teams. Goals tied to a base of moral action may be effective in binding people together.

6. *Contact is more intimate than casual.* Contact is more than just "Hello, how are you?" Individuals experience meaningful interaction that may involve goals, sharing, developing new strengths, clarifying values.

7. *Social climate promotes intergroup contact.* A social climate is created that promotes the ideal that diversity is an asset and that it enriches the effort.

8. *Contact is pleasant or rewarding.* When contact is fun, exciting, stimulating, and meaningful, these feelings contribute to the reduction of prejudice.

9. *Engaging in service to others.* As a group, serving prosocial ends and demonstrating altruistic behaviors can break down barriers and create common bonds. These types of behaviors are seen in Camp Fire, Scouting, 4-H, Rotary, and other groups for adults and youth. Service learning programs for youth provide this opportunity.

Source: Adapted from Yehuda Amir. 1976. The role of intergroup contact in change of prejudice and ethnic relations. Edited by Phyllis A. Katz (ed.), in *Towards the Elimination of Racism,* Chapter 8, pp. 245–308. New York: Pergamon Press.

Contact Conditions for Reducing Prejudice Many leisure services and programs contain elements, identified by Amir (1976) and presented by Hayles (1989), that meet criteria for reducing prejudice. By facilitating positive interaction, these factors reduce many of the barriers that may interfere with meaningful communication. These factors, depicted in table 15.2, contribute to reducing prejudice. Conditions such as equal status (e.g., individuals dressed similarly), intergroup cooperation (e.g., dramatic play, games), interdependence or superordinate goals (e.g., sports), intimate contact, service to others, and pleasant/rewarding contact all exist within a number of leisure programs and activities. Leisure programs and services offer an effective vehicle for promoting values related to diversity. Virtually all of the criteria cited may be easily and consistently applied within the leisure service setting.

Discrimination

Discrimination describes the action(s) that accompany prejudice—the actions that hinder equal access to economic resources, educational systems, and leisure opportunities. Unfounded discrimination leads to the various "isms" in society (e.g., racism, ageism, heterosexism, ableism, classism, sexism). The lack of access to power is a recurring theme of discrimination.

The Role of Power   Power has several definitions depending on its context. In discussions about discrimination, power refers to an individual's ability to influence and enforce decisions in the community. Power comes in many forms: economic power, social power, personal power, political power, and spiritual power (Kraus, 1994; Loden and Rosener, 1991; Nieto, 1992).

Those with access to the various forms of power can "use" or neglect those without that access. In a social system built on stratification, such as is found in the United States, power differentials exist. Some people and/or groups of people have power, others have less, and others essentially have none. As may be seen in various states and provinces, minority groups have made some strides in the area of political influence. There are larger numbers of minority elected officials now than there have been in previous times in history.

Discrimination cannot exist in the absence of power (Loden and Rosener, 1991). While one can try to act in a discriminatory way, the lack of power to support that discrimination renders it simply prejudice. However, both prejudice and discrimination damage society because they impact the way people view themselves and others. The most damaging aspect of discrimination and prejudice appears at an institutional level, where prejudice and discrimination are so pervasive that discriminatory policies and actions become "acceptable" business operations. Institutionalized discrimination creates social policies that perpetuate the inequities while appearing to be "good."

Status   Status crosses the boundaries of society and influences the lives of every person. All people have a concept of their own status or place in society, and they usually recognize the relative status of others. In a stratified society (every society has different "layers" of people based on some aspect—economic status, family connections, level of education, and so on), society as a whole attributes varying degrees of worth, esteem, respect, and prestige to different groups of people (Kraus, 1994; Nieto, 1992). Status is the amount of esteem and prestige that one can elicit from others in society. That status might be based on any of the primary and secondary characteristics that form the dimensions of diversity.

Dimensions of Diversity

To ensure fair treatment of the topic of diversity, the leisure services professional must examine its many dimensions. Diversity consists of much more than simply race or ethnicity—within-group differences are as important as between-group differences. For instance, as a group, Hispanic people differ from Asians; however, within the Hispanic culture some identify with a Mexican heritage, others with a Latin heritage, and still others with a Cuban tradition. These all represent distinct cultures with differences in beliefs, values, customs, and social patterns.

Discussion in this section focuses on two major categories of characteristics of individuals—*primary characteristics* and *secondary characteristics* (Loden and Rosener, 1991). Figure 15.1 depicts these characteristics. Primary characteristics (such as ethnicity, sex, age) may appear obvious upon meeting an individual, and secondary characteristics (such as education, religion, economic status) are revealed later. Each characteristic has a related "ism"—actions and attitudes that express the interrelationship of status and attributions of value or worth, and the discriminating characteristic. These actions and attitudes imply worth, normalcy, and a sense of rightness in society.

Isms are perpetuated in and through every aspect of society—television commercials and shows, magazine advertisements and articles, sports (types of people who play certain positions or sports), religious leadership, and education (students being tracked into certain fields of study). While those who receive advantages from discrimination may believe it to be morally wrong, they often do not want to give up the benefits of being "on top."

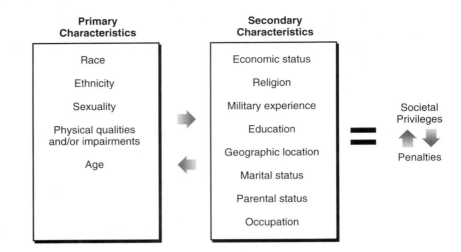

Figure 15.1

Examples of dimensions of diversity.

Source: Adapted from data from M. Loden and J. Rosener, 1991. Workforce America: Managing Employee Diversity as a Vital Resource, Professional Book Group. Burr Ridge, IL.

Primary Characteristics

Race

Ethnicity

Sexuality

Physical qualities and/or impairments

Age

Secondary Characteristics

Economic status

Religion

Military experience

Education

Geographic location

Marital status

Parental status

Occupation

Societal Privileges

Penalties

Five characteristics, identified as the primary dimensions of diversity, generally are obvious when meeting others, and they tend to generate the strongest emotional response. People tend to refine their judgments of others based on secondary characteristics that become apparent with further personal interaction.

Primary Characteristics

Primary characteristics generate first impressions and are things, generally, over which people have no control. They include race and ethnicity, sex and gender, physical and mental qualities and/or impairments, sexual orientation, and age (Loden and Rosener, 1991). Primary characteristics have a tremendous impact on how an individual is socialized from birth. These primary dimensions, found throughout every culture, generally have varying levels of status associated with them. Differing status attributions lead to discrimination and acts of prejudice solely based on that trait. The discrimination might manifest itself in negative actions (people of color being denied housing) or positive actions (treating the elderly with more respect than younger people).

Race and Ethnicity   Although used interchangeably by many, race and ethnicity have been perceived as different, yet related constructs. Race has implied the biological differences of a group of people that are transmissible by descent (skin pigment, eye folds). Ethnicity, on the other hand, is typically used to define the common qualities, language, history, customs, and traditions of a people. Ethnic groups cross racial boundaries (Kraus, 1994; Loden and Rosener, 1991; Nieto, 1992). Scientists are now beginning to believe that race is a sociological construct, rather than a biological one; therefore, ethnicity is the more accurate term to connote differences between cultural groups.

Racism basically involves the manifestation of a system of penalty and privilege based on race or ethnicity. It is based on the belief that one race or ethnic group is inherently superior (are born superior), and it presumes that other races or ethnic groups are inherently inferior (Loden and Rosener, 1991). The belief is that it is "only natural" for the better (smarter, richer, stronger, etc.) ethnic group to have access to more and better resources (Naylor, 1998).

One of the difficulties in addressing racism (and all isms) results from this system of penalty and privilege—one group is penalized for its assumed inferiority; another is privileged for its assumed superiority. This system of social comparison perpetuates feelings of self-esteem at the expense of others (Pelled, Eisenhardt, and Xin, 1999). Due to the institutionalized nature of racism, however, most of those in the privileged group and many of those in the penalized group do not recognize the privileges and penalties. Examples of privileges of being White include being able to

- obtain housing in a reasonably priced and well-maintained neighborhood,
- go to the mall without fear of being followed by security or asked to leave stores if nothing is purchased,
- go into almost any salon for a haircut or style, and
- swim in a public pool without fear of "chasing" others out (adapted from McIntosh, 1991).

Sexuality   Although gender, sexual orientation, and sexual identity are often viewed as separate concepts, Aitchison (2003) underscored the interdisciplinary nature of these concepts and explained how the concept of sexuality is developed ". . . through a variety of leisure forms, activities and locations, including literature and film, street culture and body fashion." Gender is the psychological construct a society forms to describe and explain masculinity and femininity. In Western culture, "real" men and boys are characterized by hegemonic gender stereotypes of physical strength, toughness, aggression, competition, individual achievement, and looking muscular (Aitchison, 2003; Wearing, 1998). As such, leisure services often error by providing programs for men and boys that reinforce hegemonic gender stereotypes (e.g., highly competitive sports, high adventure outdoor activities) and forget to provide programs for men and boys that fall outside of hegemonic gender stereotypes (e.g., crafts, photography, tap dance). In Western culture, "real" women and girls are characterized by hegemonic gender stereotypes of being passive, nurturing, and sexualized. For example, Wearing (1998) highlighted how mass leisure activities such as television watching or reading popular magazines provide a dominant representation that women should be sexualized and look like a Barbie doll. Numerous studies (e.g., Henderson and Vickers, 1995; Rogers, 1999; Schultz, 2004; Thomsen, Bower, and Barnes, 2004) have highlighted how powerful the Barbie doll image is for female sexuality and have underscored the damaging health results of this unrealistic image among women (e.g., eating disorders). As such, leisure services often err by providing programs for women and girls that reinforce hegemonic gender stereotypes (e.g., passive recreation like crafts and scrapbooking, cosmetic fitness) and forget to provide programs for women and girls that fall outside of hegemonic gender stereotypes (e.g., highly competitive sports, high adventure outdoor activities).

Discrimination or prejudice against a person based on sex or gender is defined as sexism or gender discrimination. As power is an integral part of any "-ism", many instances of sexism negatively impact women. Over the years, women have been considered less physically capable and less intelligent than men; too emotional and, therefore, unsuitable for certain situations; and more sexual than is good for them (Henderson, Bialeschki, Shaw, and Freysinger, 1996). Men are also negatively impacted by sexism (e.g., men should earn money, men should be physically strong). Examples of sexism include:

- Use of language that denigrates or puts down women (e.g., calling adult women "girls")
- A lack of paid parental leave for men
- Peer and social pressure that keeps girls and women from participating in activities such as rugby or rebuilding cars
- Peer and social pressure that inhibits boys and men from participating in activities such as sewing or cooking
- Tax breaks for legally married heterosexual couples, yet not for same-sex civil unions
- A lack of available child care in leisure facilities and centers

Mental and Physical Impairment and Qualities Those with mental and physical impairments include a variety of people with varying degrees of inconvenience and challenge. Some use wheelchairs, some use canes, some walkers. Some people wear thick corrective eyeglasses, others use a dog to help them see. Others live in a group home and work at a sheltered workshop. Some have less visible disabilities such as mild mental retardation, epilepsy, or learning disabilities. People with disabilities differ from one another just as any other people do.

Ableism is the act of discrimination or prejudice against those who are physically or mentally impaired (Nieto, 1992). As with racism, ableism implies a superior worth to able-bodied individuals. It extends the system of penalty and privilege to one's physical and mental abilities. Examples of ableism include:

- a refusal to remodel stairs into ramps because of the cost,
- a lack of signage in Braille in public and private facilities,
- a restaurant refusing service to a double-arm amputee who must eat with his feet, and
- refusing to hire an obese person as a front desk worker based strictly on appearance.

Individuals also differ in physical qualities: Some are tall, others short, some are thin, others obese. People tend to respond more favorably to those whom they consider attractive than to those who do not meet the societal or cultural standards of beauty. This inequity can be considered a form of prejudice.

Age Although many people overlook the influence of age on the treatment of people and the expectations placed on them, age comprises an important dimension of diversity. Western cultures tend to glorify youth and disparage age. Reactions to age change with culture as well as the age of the group. Children, adolescents, young adults, mature adults, and seniors all command different levels and degrees of respect based on culture and situation.

Ageism includes acts of prejudice and discrimination against people based on their age. Western societies tend to discriminate against both ends of the age continuum perhaps because of the tremendous value placed on success and achievement in the workforce. An ongoing struggle for the rights of children works to ensure that although legally minors, they are considered worthwhile and viable beings. On the other end, the elderly are also discriminated against. Examples of ageism include:

- calling or referring to elderly leisure participants as "cute,"
- ignoring the concerns of children in planning and developing leisure facilities for youth,
- not hiring or promoting older workers strictly due to their age, and
- assuming that all adolescents prefer to hang out on street corners rather than participate in structured activities.

Secondary Characteristics

Secondary characteristics of diversity impact judgments about people as further interaction takes place. These traits can often change, yet they still influence judgments and affect socialization. People ascertain these traits after getting to know someone and adjust their thoughts and biases accordingly. Secondary traits play an extremely important role in the way that they interact with primary characteristics to result in both overt and covert forms of discrimination (Loden and Rosener, 1991). Secondary traits include economic status, religion, military experience, education, geographic location, marital status, parental status, occupation, and other demographic characteristics.

Economic Status One's access to material wealth and family history combine to influence social status. As economic wealth tends to translate directly into better health, education, and political influence, it affects other dimensions of diversity as well.

Classism is discrimination or prejudice against a person based on socal and economic status (Nieto, 1992; Schwartz and Conley, 2000). As power forms an integral part of any ism, most instances of classism focus on those who are at or below the poverty line. Therefore, members of the working class or the poor experience the negative effects of classism from some individuals who have economic power.

Religion Societies differ in the religions they value. In most societies, the dominant culture establishes its religion as the norm. Individuals who participate in religions outside the cultural norm may experience a high degree of prejudice and persecution (e.g., Hasidic Jews in the United States, Christians in Saudi Arabia).

Military Experience The impact of military experience on one's social situation tends to change with the atmosphere of culture. In the United States, veterans of World War II and maybe the Gulf War received a hero's welcome while many Vietnam War veterans were ostracized and denigrated.

Education One's level of education and where it is received affect social status. Attendance at elite schools generates prestige, and the lack of a high school education has a detrimental impact on one's social status.

Geographic Location Both the current residence and a person's place of origin impact social status—from the side of town where one lives to the part of the country or world one considers home. Geographic location influences speech (e.g., accent, word usage, intonation), dress, attitudes, thoughts, and behaviors. Society as a whole makes judgments based on geographic location.

Marital Status Societies attribute different values of merit and worth to people based on their marital status—single, married, divorced, widowed, or domestic partnership whether it be gay or straight. The age at which one married, number of marriages, and other factors also influence social judgments.

Parental Status Many aspects of parental status impact individuals—whether one has children or not; the number of children; the age of the parents; whether it was a traditional birth, through artificial insemination, a surrogate mother or adoption; and parental status combined with marital status.

Occupation Reflected in levels of education and economic status, a person's job influences societal status. Whether one is a blue-collar worker, unskilled laborer, professional, or volunteer may all have an impact on how one is perceived by others. Even the days of the week, the hours of work, and insurance coverage affect social ranking.

Interaction of Primary/Secondary Characteristics

No one falls within just one primary or secondary dimension of diversity; people are composites with many different characteristics. Each trait or dimension of diversity carries with it its own social penalties and privileges. An individual's combined characteristics affect penalties and privileges and may serve to either mitigate negative sanctions and increase privilege, or increase negative sanctions and lessen the effects of privilege (Loden and Rosener, 1991).

At different times in one's life and in society some dimensions of diversity have greater effects than others. For instance, an African American female may experience discrimination because of her ethnicity; at other times her sex could prevent her from access to resources, even within her own ethnic group. The combined action of dimensions lessens the impact of some; for instance, a Hispanic person might receive negative social reactions based on ethnicity alone. However, economic success and a Harvard education usually generates a positive response. A sixty-two-year-old Native American with a twelfth-grade education and who is a retired construction worker will probably experience accumulated sanctions: racism, ageism, and classism.

Cultural Sensitivity: Valuing Differences

Becoming culturally sensitive involves the awareness of one's own ethnicity and differences and acknowledging and respecting differences in others. While tolerating differences may mean enduring or putting up with them, it does not imply a positive approach to cultural diversity. Leisure service professionals should understand the way in which individuals reach a point of valuing all cultures and ethnic groups.

A Process for Valuing Differences

Some individuals do not want anything to do with "different" people. Others think that all people are really just like them. Yet others strive to learn about a wide variety of differences. These individuals are developing skills to enhance their cultural competence and are at the beginning stages of the process of valuing diversity. This process leads one through many phases progressing toward the belief that all cultures and ethnic groups have value.

Figure 15.2 offers a model of these processes. The model represents a continuum of behavior in terms of awareness and valuing diversity—progressing from an ethnocentric stage (other groups/cultures are inferior) to an ethnorelative stage (all cultures/ethnic groups have equal value). At the bottom of the figure, an individual in a *denial state,* or stage, does not want to have anything to do with those who are different. In the next step (*defense*), the individual struggles with differences, although on the surface he or she appears to value diversity.

On the next level, the individual engages in *minimization,* mistakenly believing that "different people are *really* just like me." Although often intended as a gesture of goodwill, this attitude values others, but denies their diversity. An underlying foundation of affirmative action characterizes the *acceptance* stage. As the *adaptation* stage is reached, the individual attempts to create win/win situations and to be flexible, perhaps, for example, by supporting an employee's time off for a significant cultural event. *Integration/inclusion* is reached when the individual acknowledges that all cultures/ethnic groups have value, and results in actions based on selecting the best from diverse cultures.

Implications of Diversity for Leisure Services Professionals

Issues of diversity impact all levels and aspects of leisure services organizations and the profession as a whole. Administrators can establish management systems that effectively recruit and hire people of color, women, people with disabilities, and other individuals from underrepre-

A Process for Valuing Differences
Moving from a monocultural, ethnocentric mind-set to
one of understanding, awareness, integration/inclusion

Figure 15.2

How we respond
and relate to
differences.

*Source: Data from
Milton J. Bennett,
"A Developmental
Approach to
Training for
Intercultural
Sensitivity" in
International
Journal of
Intercultural
Relations, Vol. 10,
No. 2, pp 179-196.*

Ethnorelative Stages
(all cultures or ethnic groups
have equal value; no culture
is superior to another)

Integration/inclusion
(taking the best of a variety of ways)

Adaptation
(flexibility, synergy occurs)

Acceptance
(foundation of affirmative action)

Minimization
(belief that people are really alike;
ignoring part of the person)

Defense
(putting up positive appearances;
reality is negative)

Ethnocentric Stages
(other cultures/ethnic groups
are inferior to your culture)

Denial
(not wanting to have anything to
do with people who are different)

sented groups. Leisure services professionals in program and leadership roles who see leisure as basic to life should provide leisure services that are culturally relevant to all people.

The leisure services professional can no longer assume that everyone has similar leisure needs and desires or pretend not to be an active member of a system that perpetuates racism, classism, sexism, and other forms of oppression. Practitioners must journey back to the roots of the leisure services profession and again serve those who need opportunities and encouragement to reach their full potential. We must remind ourselves that every individual has a right to an ethnic identity and respect for that ethnic identity regardless of the cultural traits associated with that identity. This viewpoint can aid parks and recreation professionals in their growth toward cultural competence (Goldberg, 2000). Cultural competence refers to the ability to provide professional services in a way that is congruent with behavior and expectations that are normative for a given community (Green, 1995 as cited in Goldberg, 2000).

Although many view valuing diversity as a moral/ethical issue, other compelling forces provide motivation to support diversity. The following section discusses such factors as enrichment, demographic trends, external forces, and internal forces that speak strongly to the need for continued growth and development in multiculturalism and diversity within leisure service organizations.

Enrichment of the organization. Diverse individuals bring with them experiences and add
viewpoints that enrich the organization. For example, it has been suggested that male-
female work teams operate more effectively than all-male or all-female work teams,
because the synergy of both sexes strengthens the team (Hayles, 1996). In addition,
diverse work groups tend to develop more creative ideas and have increased work
efficiency (Knouse and Dansby, 1999).

Response to demographic trends. The population from which the leisure services organization will recruit applicants continues to show sharp increases in diverse groups. Increases in minority populations due to immigration as well as birthrates will continue to significantly change the potential workforce as well as constituent groups.

Acknowledgment of external forces. Leisure services organizations are accountable to the larger community, which is increasingly more diverse. The needs of constituent groups in the community must be addressed.

Response to internal forces. Individuals within leisure services organizations seek respect, equity, and opportunities for promotion and advancement.

Diversity also applies to administration, leadership, programming, and facilities design. Tools can be used in staff development, communication, guidelines for interactions, and other activities to support diversity.

Administrative Practices

Leisure organizations need to become antidiscriminatory work sites by promoting diversity within the organization (Allison, 2000). In this regard, Dahl (2000), building upon the academic work of Cox (1994), suggested five administrative strategies that can be used to help develop a leisure organization that promotes diversity. First, create a climate in which members of all identity groups excel. As such, organizational leadership must be committed to change, which has a clear vision by developing a formal diversity action plan. Second, leadership must establish an active agenda for change. For example, leisure organizations can broaden screening and selection criteria in hiring and promoting people who are different and embrace new paradigms of social change. Third, eliminate institutional biases. This can include such actions as developing an explicit commitment to diversity in a mission statement and reinforce values of diversity in reward and appraisal processes. Fourth, eliminate the relationship between culture group identity and job status. This can include supporting programs and training that foster respect and understanding, developing affirmative action programs, or embracing flexible work arrangements based upon cultural values. Fifth, eliminate bias in management systems. This can include cultural audits, survey feedback, or creating a task force on diversity. The following section of this chapter will further explain how administrative strategies can be used to help develop a leisure organization that promotes diversity.

Much can be done "at the top" to ensure cultural equity in the administration and provision of leisure services. Administration and management have a tremendous impact on the organizational culture and conduct. Effective administration and management of diversity includes a statement of beliefs, adherence to affirmative action and Equal Employment Opportunity (EEO) guidelines, appropriate staff development, and policies and practices that have impact.

Mission An agency's mission, philosophy, and vision statements set the stage for its activity. These statements serve as the foundation for all other administrative and programmatic functions and initially express the commitment to diversity. Consider the following component of the mission statement from the Leisure, Youth, and Human Services Division at the University of Northern Iowa:

> The Leisure, Youth and Human Services Division envisions a world where people are accepted and valued for their strengths and abilities rather than the way they look, speak, think, or live their lives. To that end the Leisure, Youth and Human Services Division strives to prepare students to meet the challenges of a diverse world through empowerment and diversity. In a rapidly

changing world, it is critical that each individual be empowered to take charge of their lives and assist others; this philosophy is based on the concept of fully valuing selves and others . . . and is committed to studying and learning about differences . . .

Rules and Regulations The rules, regulations, policies, and procedures within an agency or organization serve as its agents of action. Some regulations and rules are mandated by law, and agencies should actively promote the ideals of affirmative action.

> *Equal Employment Opportunity (EEO) regulations.* Equal employment regulations require that leisure service organizations eliminate all existing discriminatory conditions whether purposeful or inadvertent. The regulations further require the examination of employment and other policies to make sure that they do not operate to the detriment of persons in terms of ". . . race, color, gender, national origin, religion, age, marital status, disability or handicap status, veteran status, sexual orientation, or any other extraneous consideration not directly related to performance."

> *Affirmative Action.* Affirmative action refers to proactive efforts to achieve a diverse workforce. It often makes use of goals to increase participation of underrepresented groups. It also requires the leisure services organization to do more than ensure employment neutrality—it must attempt to recruit, hire, and advance qualified group members who were previously excluded.

> *Title IX.* In the United States in 1972, Title IX of the Educational Amendments Act was passed to ensure equal rights for girls in sports at any agency or program that received federal support. Shortly after that time, girls' involvement with physical activity skyrocketed. Leisure services organizations should promote the ideals of Title IX, ensuring that both girls and boys may engage in activities as they wish.

> *Americans with Disabilities Act (ADA).* The Americans with Disabilities Act (ADA) "establishes a clear and comprehensive federal prohibition of discrimination against persons with disabilities in private sector employment and ensures equal access for persons with disabilities to public accommodations, public services, transportation and telecommunications" (Stein, 1993).

The ADA has a broad scope and impacts building contractors, service providers, employers, and others. Individuals within leisure services organizations must plan accordingly in terms of building modifications, programming, employment, and other relevant factors. Of interest and importance to those in the leisure services profession are the edicts that state and local governments shall not

- deny a qualified person with a disability the opportunity to participate or benefit from services (every opportunity) available to people without disabilities;
- provide opportunity for a qualified person with a disability that does not equal the opportunity for those without disabilities;
- offer less effective opportunities to the disabled;
- provide different or separate aids, benefits, or services for people with disabilities, unless such are necessary to make services available and enjoyable;
- aid or perpetuate discrimination;
- deny a person the opportunity to serve on a board or committee;
- select sites that result in the exclusion of people with disabilities;
- administer testing, licensing, or certifications that discriminate, or
- charge a higher fee or surcharge to a person with a disability for the cost of delivering services in compliance with the ADA.

The ADA also states that state and local governments shall

- make reasonable accommodations for a qualified person with a disability to enable the full enjoyable use of services, programs, and facilities; and
- administer services, programs, and activities with the most interaction possible.

As mentioned, those providing public access and accommodations (most leisure services agencies and organizations fall into this category) may need to change rules, policies, and practices to enable persons with disabilities equal access to services. Transportation and architectural barriers may require adaptation, and the program delivery may require alteration.

Policies, Procedures, and Practices

Administrative policies and leisure service practices require periodic scrutiny to determine their relative impact on issues of diversity. This is sometimes referred to as a *cultural audit* and is one way to conduct an internal review of policies, procedures, and norms to determine their impact on perceptions of diversity acceptance (Dreachslin, 1999; Jordan, 2001). These issues affect such elements as:

- personnel recruitment, employment, and promotion;
- program development, implementation, and evaluation;
- facility use;
- registration for programs;
- promotional techniques, materials, and avenues;
- accessibility, both considering the buildings themselves as well as accessibility related to location of facilities;
- the times that programs are offered;
- fee structures; and
- in-service and ongoing educational opportunities for staff.

Another policy that can be used to help ensure that members of diverse cultural backgrounds feel welcomed in leisure programs is to follow the "I" Triad. According to Chavez (2000), the "I" Triad, which is present in figure 15.3, is a three-step process to leisure programming that is oriented toward allowing all people to be part of the leisure planning stage. In this model, leisure professionals are to invite, include, and involve people from diverse cultures to use leisure services and be part of planning future leisure programs. This can include making sure that marketing and promotion strategies include diverse and minority populations in the photographs. Likewise, this can include asking people from diverse cultural backgrounds to be part of community discussions or become members of committees that are important to leisure organizations (e.g., board of directors).

Figure 15.3

"I" Triad

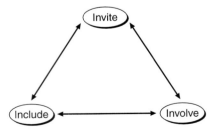

From: Chavez, D. J. (2000). Invite, include, and involve! Racial groups, ethnic groups, and leisure. In M. T. Allison & I. E. Schneider (Eds.), Diversity and the recreation profession: Organizational perspectives (pp. 179–194). State College, PA: Venture.

TABLE

15.3 COMMUNICATION PATTERNS: A POTENTIAL SOURCE OF MISCOMMUNICATION

The way in which individuals use words, the way they interact physically in terms of touch, their attire, and other factors can influence communication—they can even be a source of communication problems between individuals. Effective intercultural communication depends on knowledge and awareness of the factors that underlie communication within different cultural groups. Some of the factors that may cause communication problems follow:

Use of words. Cultures differ in how they use words. For example, some cultures do not like to use the word "no" or to say "I don't know." In some Asian cultures, an individual would not want to say "I don't know" if asked for directions by a passerby and might attempt to circumvent the original question, rather than just saying "I don't know." In addition, some words may have more than one meaning, opening up the possibility of miscommunication. Some cultures use many emotional phrases, and others make great use of adjectives. Some cultures consider it rude if a conversation does not start out with an exchange of personal information and questions before business is discussed.

Tone of voice. The tone of voice used for communication may vary from culture to culture. Some cultures speak loudly, some softly, some in a monotone. In some cultures it is appropriate to speak very softly to those in authority; in other cultures this appears as a sign of weakness. For example, some Chinese dialects have a wide range of tones from high to low, with the meaning of words changing as the tone of voice changes.

Type of attire. Different cultures place greater or less emphasis on formality of attire, modesty of dress, and other factors. Americans are fairly casual in much of their attire. In some cultures, immodest dress serves as grounds for abusive verbal or physical action by passersby.

Degree of physical contact and personal space. Different cultures are comfortable with varying degrees of touching and amount of personal space. Some cultures are very comfortable with touching, and women or men hold hands in public. Some cultures like to be in close proximity to others, with little distance between them while talking; others feel more comfortable if a speaker is at least a few feet away.

Facial gestures. The meanings of facial gestures may change from culture to culture. In particular, eye contact has different impact in different cultures. For example, direct eye contact may mean interest and attention to one culture, but may be a sign of disrespect or a direct challenge in another culture. For some cultures it is not appropriate to make eye contact in public. The degree of animation of the face when communicating may vary greatly between cultures.

Body gestures. Different cultures vary in types of body movements—slow and deliberate, tense and highly directed, fast-paced, or relaxed and social. Certain gestures may also be expected. For example, removing one's shoes in Japan or bowing at an appropriate level to show respect are two such expected gestures.

Characteristics of speech. Different cultures may communicate differently in terms of the speed of speech, the degree of feedback to communication, the degree of directness and frankness of communication, and use of silence. Whereas in the American culture, silence may be perceived to be an insult, in other cultures, silence may be a form of individual privacy or may indicate a feeling of well-being and fullness of life. In addition, in American culture laughter usually indicates happiness; however, in some cultures it may be a sign of embarrassment or loss.

Differences in communication between cultures requires consideration of the impact such factors have on the communication process. Within the leisure services workplace, as different cultures attempt to communicate with one another, individuals must realize that these differences exist and will affect the communication process. An effective organization offers informational vehicles that address communication patterns within the workplace so that communication can be enhanced.

Methods of Communication   Individuals from different cultures and different ethnic groups have unique methods and styles of communication. For example, many Anglo-Americans are frank, direct, and look other people in the eye. Individuals from some other cultures may find this disconcerting. For example, in Japan it is rude to begin talking business immediately. It is more appropriate to speak to one another first about personal matters, such as family, establishing personal contact, and then move on to business topics. Different cultures also have different personal space needs and other communication considerations. Table 15.3 presents information regarding a

15.4   SUGGESTED STAFF DEVELOPMENT TOPICS   CURRICULUM MODEL: MANAGING FOR DIVERSITY

I. Benefits and challenges of diversity

Valuing diversity. How does diversity enhance the leisure services organization's synergy, productivity, and impact?

Benefits and challenges of diversity. What does the leisure services manager need to know to effectively meet the challenges and reap the benefits of a diverse workforce?

Manager's role. How is the leisure services manager's role different when managing diversity as compared with implementing Affirmative Action and EEO?

II. Affirmative Action and EEO

Compliance issues. Management problems and issues associated with compliance/lack of compliance with affirmative action and EEO laws that impact upon the workplace: Guidelines for the leisure services manager, definition of terms, legal framework.

Policies and practices. How does diversity relate to organizational policies and practices?

III. Trends analysis: Workforce 2000

Workforce 2000. The emergence of demographic trends that will offer opportunities/challenges to the leisure services manager.

Diversity issues in the workplace. New management methods and approaches that can be used to respond to Workforce 2000 issues in a way that enhances the leisure services organization.

IV. Cultural awareness

Perceptions and worldview. Helping the leisure services manager solve problems related to employees' different perceptions and worldview, based on age, ethnicity, background, religion, gender, and other variables.

Increasing cultural awareness. Strategies that the leisure services manager can use to increase cultural awareness among employees—values, communication styles, stereotyping, accommodation styles.

Critical issues. Helping the leisure services manager become informed about critical issues related to different groups—gender, race, disability, age, religion, and others.

V. Managing diversity

Applications. What the leisure services manager can learn and apply from other organizations, models of multicultural development and cross-cultural management.

Tools. Available tools to help the leisure manager assess needs related to diversity: Employee/management surveys that assess needs, interests, attitudes.

Supporting diversity. What the leisure services manager can do to promote the values of diversity within the organization: Supporting diversity through mentoring, merit structure, management of the formal and informal organization, cross-cultural skills and communication.

VI. Maximizing benefits and minimizing challenges of diversity

Setting goals and objectives. Helping the leisure services manager set program goals and objectives to maximize benefits and minimize challenges related to diversity.

Source: S. Edginton, "PAC 10 Higher Education Institutions: Training for Managers in the Area of Diversity," 1991, University of Oregon.

number of communication patterns to help the leisure services administrator or manager communicate more effectively with diverse constituents and employees.

Staff Development Model The administrator or manager can arrange for a number of staff development activities to support diversity. Effective orientation programs, ongoing staff-development programs, release time to attend off-site diversity training, and other types of

TABLE

15.5   SUGGESTED ACTIONS TO PROMOTE DIVERSITY

Diversity: What Are the Best Organizations Doing?

- Pay for performance regarding diversity
- Strong affirmative action
- Organization-supported networks
- Mandatory diversity training at all levels
- Line leadership
- Diversity councils, boards, and task forces
- Outreach, interns, scholarships
- Events celebrating diversity
- Address more than protected classes
- Address both organizational climate and numbers
- Develop internal talent to do lead work

From Robert Hayles, 1989, Arizona Affirmative Action Association 14th Annual Conference. Phoenix, AZ. Reprinted by permission of Robert Hayles.

staff development serve as appropriate tools. Table 15.4 presents a model for staff training based on a review by Edginton (1991) of the diversity training programs of several top U.S. corporations and PAC 10 universities.

The model offers a comprehensive list of topics; the leisure services administrator may select those relevant to the organization's needs. The topics include: benefits and challenges of diversity, affirmative action and EEO, trends, cultural awareness, managing diversity, maximizing benefits, and minimizing challenges of diversity. Leisure services organizations should have a consistent, ongoing program of diversity training in order to (1) continually reinforce commitment to and support of diversity; (2) ensure continuity of training, expectations, and goals across the entire organization; and (3) ensure that all employees have access to informed supervisors and managers.

Actions Related to Diversity in "Best" Organizations   In addition to adhering to defined rules, regulations, policies, and procedures and engaging in staff development, other actions can be taken to promote diversity. Hayles (1989, 1996), consultant to a number of major U.S. corporations, presents a list of actions that are being carried out by what he terms the "best" organizations. These actions range from events celebrating diversity, to outreach, pay for performance regarding diversity (e.g., pay for attending diversity training), organization-supported networks, diversity councils, and others. Table 15.5 presents this list of actions that leisure services professionals can apply throughout their agencies.

Leveraging Pluralism for Competitive Advantage   Pluralism or diversity can be leveraged in a way that benefits the organization in terms of competitive advantage (Hayles, 1996). This author notes that the advantages of supporting pluralism or diversity work occur on two levels:

> The goal of pluralism work at a *personal level* is to create an environment in which everyone feels included and valued—just as they would if they were among people they considered to be like themselves. The goal of pluralism work at the organizational or *systems level* is to leverage diversity to

TABLE
15.6 ADVANTAGES OF PLURALISM WITHIN ORGANIZATIONS

Personal effectiveness. People who learn to live and/or work in integrated settings develop stronger interpersonal, communication, and negotiation skills. Employees become more effective inside and outside of the workplace.

Response to social and demographic changes. Social and demographic changes when ignored lead to reduced effectiveness in social and government services and mixed opportunities for business growth. Organizations that become more multilingual and multicultural will be the most successful in the global marketplace; those that accurately predict change and embrace it will outperform their competitors.

Fairness and equity. When individuals or groups perceive that they have been treated unfairly or inequitably, they seek justice. Peaceful means are used when people feel that they will be listened to; more disturbing approaches are taken when people feel they are not being heard. Pluralism creates a climate of fairness and equity for all.

Litigation avoidance. Lawsuits are painful as well as expensive. Fear of litigation is a powerful but unhealthy motivation for promoting workforce pluralism. It is reluctantly included here only because it reflects reality.

Productivity. Well-managed, diverse teams typically outperform homogeneous teams in terms of quantity, creativity, and quality of results. Diverse teams see more aspects of each issue and make fewer mistakes. For example, the team with a Spanish-speaking member would not try to market a car called "Nova" in Spanish-speaking countries where "no va" translates to "no go." Complex problems are best solved by multidisciplinary or cross-functional teams.

Profitability. The profitability case for pluralism has become increasingly clear. Investment clubs of women and men significantly outperform clubs composed only of men. When the five-year, ten-year, fifteen-year, and twenty-year financial performance of companies engaged in pluralism and related progressive human resource work is compared with the performance of those that are not doing such work or are doing it poorly, the former companies significantly outperform the latter in terms of sales growth, profit growth, and performance in a downturning economy.

Source: Hayles, 1996.

achieve exceptional performance. The work recognizes similarities and differences while focusing on unity without uniformity.

A list of six advantages of pluralism or diversity work within organizations, as adapted from Hayles (1996), includes the following: personal effectiveness, responsiveness to social and demographic changes, promotion of fairness and equity, avoidance of related litigation, productivity, and profitability. These advantages are described in more detail in table 15.6.

An organization that has implemented administrative strategies to develop diversity-oriented inclusion in the workforce is the Arizona branch of the Bureau of Land Management (BLM). Arizona state director for the Bureau of Land Management, Denise Meridith (2000), provided a twelve-step program to increase pluralism and diversity in her branch of the BLM. These twelve steps include:

1. Recognition that there is a diversity problem in your organization
2. Develop a central message to be committed to organizational diversity that is supported by stakeholders (e.g., leadership teams, chief executive officer)
3. The chief executive officer or director needs to explain his/her rationale for a commitment to diversity (e.g., understanding the benefits of a diverse worksite)
4. Communicate diversity changes to potential market groups (e.g., ethnic communities or clubs)
5. Recruit potential diverse employees from organizations that support diversity (e.g., advertise vacant positions in Asian newspapers or Native American colleges)
6. Set goals, timetable, and funds to diversity initiatives (e.g., recruitment strategies for hiring employees)

7. Do not neglect your onboard workshop—enlist their participation (e.g., members of hiring committees)
8. Listen to your current employees' thoughts and comments
9. Be committed to regular diversity training
10. Strengthen ties with members of minority cultures in your community
11. Benchmark techniques to implementing diversity programs and publicize positive results
12. Implement the change

Beyond these important organization strategies, Dieser and Wilson (2002) suggest that organizations can challenge professionals, as individuals, to learn more about diversity by: 1) field-trips and bicultural observations of ethnic communities, 2) role playing and role reversals with members of ethnic minority cultures, 3) panel or individual discussions with ethnic minority professional, 4) critical incident and case study workshops, and 5) immersion in an ethnic culture.

Diversity and Leadership

Leadership and programming, the most visible functions of leisure services organizations, exhibit the important commitment to diversity and celebration of differences. Program design, leadership, marketing practices, and other aspects of leisure services make continual statements to the public about values and belief structures.

Leadership Considerations for Diverse Groups

Face-to-face leadership holds many opportunities to directly impact the lives of leisure services customers. Leisure services professionals must examine verbal and nonverbal customer treatment, ways of showing respect, and the inadvertent perpetuation of stereotypes through behaviors and programs.

If leisure services professionals promote only basketball to African American youth because "that is all they want," discourage girls from participating in football because they might get hurt, discourage boys from entering a ballet class because the other children might tease them, have user fees so high that many cannot afford the cost, or allow children to call each other derogatory names, then they are not meeting professional obligations. Examples of how professionals can respond to the dimensions of diversity follow:

- Use pictures of people who are old, young, in wheelchairs, girls, boys, and of a variety of racial and ethnic backgrounds in literature.
- Structure user fees to meet the needs of people from different economic backgrounds.
- Assist with community celebrations of religious and cultural holidays (e.g., Martin Luther King Day, Kwanzaa, Rosh Hashanah, Cinco de Mayo, see figure 15.4).
- In skill-development programs, particularly sport programs for youth, use equipment that equalizes ability levels (e.g., t-ball instead of baseball, bowling ramps).
- Monitor behaviors that perpetuate sexism (or any type of ism). For example, when a young girl gets hurt we tend to nurture her, bandage her, and give her a hug before sending her back to play. When a young boy gets hurt, we tell him to "stop crying, it's not that bad," pat him on the back, and send him out. All hurt children need nurturing.
- Watch language when leading groups (e.g., when asking that people sit cross-legged on the floor, ask for people to sit cross-legged on the floor, not "Indian style").

These examples show how cultural sensitivity among leisure services customers and staff can be increased. Professional obligations require the provision of a sense of safety—physical,

Figure 15.4

Kwanzaa: An event celebrating diversity.

In recognition of heritage

A celebration to recognize and strengthen contributions to the unity, preservation and development of the African family, community and culture will take place on the Northern Iowa campus for the first time this Thursday.

Kwanzaa—Swahili for "first fruits"—is an African-American holiday conceptualized 26 years ago by Dr. Maulana Karenga of Los Angeles. The idea was to develop a non-religious holiday for African-Americans which did not center around a "hero," but did honor and commemorate the heritage.

Although Kwanzaa is scheduled as a one-day event at UNI, the holiday is traditionally celebrated December 26th to January 1st. Through the week, each day focuses on one of Kwanzaa's Seven Principles: umoja (unity), kujichagulia (self-determination), ujima (collective work and responsibility), ujamaa (cooperative economics), nia (purpose), kuumba (creativity), and imani (faith).

Symbolic items, such as candles of different colors, fruit, and a unity cup, are usually placed at the family meal table to represent the struggles and achievements within the heritage and to foster family discussion in this area.

Jim Johnson, director of the Ethnic Minorities Cultural and Educational Center, notes that while Kwanzaa symbols and rituals are rooted in African tradition, at the same time, they are meant to address the concerns of urban-based black people living in 20th century America.

KWANZAA

A CELEBRATION OF FAMILY, COMMUNITY AND CULTURE

Thursday, December 3
7:00 p.m.
Maucker Union Expansion
Food, Music, Entertainment

Kwanzaa is free
and open to the public.

Sponsored in part by:
Ethnic Minorities Cultural
and Educational Center,
Union Policy Board,
UNI Entertainment Committee,
Ethnic Student Senate,
and the Office of the
Vice-President of Academic
Affairs.

**Funded in part by
Student Activity Fees.**

emotional, and psychological—to all potential constituents. The professional must also facilitate programs and environments that encourage all customers to freely choose their leisure experiences.

Impact of Leader Expectations   In addition to examining how people are addressed and how their needs are met at the direct-service level, recreation and leisure leaders will want to examine their own expectations of others. According to Scales (1991), "Large and small scale data alike show that African American, Latino, Native American and Alaska Native youth believe that their teachers and [leaders] do not expect much of them." These low expectations often translate into low performance. Bannon (1973, p. 53) notes:

> In every successful . . . program with youth, a major reason for success was that the . . . [leaders] . . . *expected* the youth to do well, involved them in the planning and implementation of the program, learned as much about the youths as possible, and held him [her]self responsible if the program[s] failed.

This comment about leader expectations of youth may be extrapolated to leader expectations of all participants. As the leisure services professional works with diverse groups, he or she should examine how "leader expectations" might affect the quality and character of the interface between leader and participant. The degree to which the leader has high expectations and standards for *all* people will influence the success of programs and services.

Equity Issues: Actions Speak Louder Than Words   A number of important equity issues involve the role of the leader and his or her impact on diversity. A leader imparts values, either intentionally or unintentionally. No situation is value-free. Therefore, the leader must carefully consider his or her values and their impact on others. Five leadership issues follow:

TABLE

15.7 | LEADERSHIP GUIDELINES FOR THE LEISURE SERVICES YOUTH LEADER RESPECTING CULTURAL DIFFERENCES

1. Get to know youth.
2. Take the time to learn about the culture(s) of youth.
3. With sensitivity to cultural values, get to know youth as *individuals* who may or may not fit the norms of their culture. Do not make assumptions or judgments based on stereotypes or cultural generalizations about their group.
4. Adapt policies and practices to allow for cultural differences. Make room for treating youth fairly and equitably while respecting their different motivations, values, styles, and traditions.
5. Help youth communicate with one another to understand their cultural differences and to work more productively together.
6. Understand your own culture and the assumptions that result from your upbringing. Learn about your cultural influences your assumptions of others, as well as the assumptions others have of you.
7. Build on individual and cultural differences to enrich the creativity and productivity of your youth center.

Source: Originally developed by the University of California at Los Angeles: Office of Affirmative Action and Diversity Education, *Understanding and Managing a Diverse Workforce,* October, 1990. Adapted by S. Edginton, University of Northern Iowa, 1993.

Customer composition. The leadership of programs and activities should resemble as closely as possible the composition of the organization's constituency. Customers, particularly youth, need leaders who resemble them as role models.

Dialogue. The way in which the leader speaks to participants impacts the comfort level of the interaction. Leaders should interact with youth in a variety of ways, using different types of dialogue—not just the traditional Anglo-Saxon forms of greeting.

Leader tone and body language. Estimates suggest that an individual's words have an impact of just 7 percent on the listener while the other 93 percent of communication results from body language, tone of voice, and other factors.

Consistency. The leisure services leader must be consistent with rewards and negative consequences. Participants pick up on inequitable treatment based on race or other factors.

Program choices. The leader's choices in terms of programs, activities, and events that promote diversity have great impact.

These and other factors demonstrate the leader's influence in providing a creative climate that benefits all individuals. Table 15.7 presents additional guidelines for the leisure services leader in terms of respecting the cultural differences of participating youth. (Note: These same guidelines can be adapted and used to facilitate interaction between leisure services managers and their employees.)

Use of Language   Language—whether verbal, symbolic, or written—affects people. Professing belief in equal rights for everyone, but taking no action when racial or other slurs are used by others sends a contradictory message. If "silence is complicity," then ignoring injustice makes one an accomplice to it—and as guilty as the offender. Verbal language includes terms used to describe people (gays, gimp, hick), their titles (Ms., Mr., Mrs., ma'am, sir), and general references to people by position or job title (the director as he, the secretary as she, fireman, policeman). Terms can perpetuate the system of inequities; helping others reach their full potential requires care in naming and identifying others.

The leisure services profession also uses symbolic language—logos on team T-shirts, graphics on promotional literature, and photographs in annual reports. Do those logos, graphics, and photographs represent society at-large in a positive fashion? Do they promote a feeling of inclusion? Do they help to break stereotypes and the attendant biases and prejudices? How are the graphics and logos we use perceived by those in the general public?

Leisure services professionals use the written word extensively in annual reports, fliers, staff manuals, and newspaper announcements. Rules posted in facilities and posters help motivate people in the healthy use of leisure. Does the language invite all segments of society? Does it encourage participation by everyone? Is it exclusionary by omission? Continual examination of language helps to promote an atmosphere of inclusion and welcome.

Diversity Programming: Building Self-Esteem

A number of programs and activities can be selected by the leader to promote and support diversity. These activities contribute to fun and enjoyment, and they help build self-esteem and respect for others. A well-developed program of activities related to diversity involves all constituent groups. Cultural celebrations, special events, arts and crafts, food, music, dance, and books can all be used by the leisure services programmer to support diversity.

Esteem-Building Activities Feelings of prejudice toward others often occur in persons who do not feel good about themselves. *Camp Adventure™ Youth Services* has developed materials that offer instruction for self-esteem-building programs and activities that support positive interaction. Table 15.8 presents several small-group activities that support diversity and promote the building of self-esteem. A good programmer engages in research and uses a variety of sources to build a repertoire of culturally and ethnically relevant activities within all programs.

TABLE

15.8 ACTIVITIES THAT BUILD SELF-ESTEEM

I Spy, FBI. Youth set up an FBI adventure lab using an ink pad and paper and then conduct a fingerprint investigation. Each youth makes a set of his/her fingerprints. Youth are then encouraged to examine the different fingerprints to see how each person is individual and unique and no two sets of prints are the same (a magnifying glass is useful). The point can also be made that each person not only has unique fingerprints, but that each individual has unique talents and abilities that he/she can bring up to the group. Youth can also use fingerprint art to create individual or group creations or collages.

You Are the Star! Take a picture of each child and then have each child make a poster about him/herself that includes his/her picture within a large star in the middle of the poster. Have the child leave room on the poster for each of the other children to write a positive comment about the rising "star."

Hollywood Minute. Have youth write and produce a video in which each youth has an opportunity to express him/herself. Youth can tell about themselves, their hopes and goals; they can sing or dance or bring items from home that are important to them to tell about and other things that they want to share.

Time Capsule. An extension of Hollywood Minute, Time Capsule has youth reviewing the video that they made about themselves six months later, a year later, or even at a later time. Youth discuss how they have changed, how their goals have changed, and what is important to them both in terms of themselves and others.

You Are Special. Each member of the group, in turn, tells the person who is "it" why he or she is special and what attribute they most admire.

"Me" Baggie. Each youth is given a large, gallon size Ziplock® bag with his/her name on it in magic marker. They take the baggies home and fill them with things that tell about who they are as people. The bags might include things they collect, treasures, things they have made, their favorite book, a poem. When baggies are brought back to the youth program, youth can share what they have brought. Or baggies can be put on a table, name side down, and youth can guess whose baggie is whose. This activity helps address issues of individual and cultural awareness.

Program Design for Individuals with Disabilities

Schleien and Green (1992) suggest a continuum of leisure services options for persons with disabilities. This framework can be adapted for the primary characteristics of diversity. Noninvolvement serves as the first aspect, followed by segregation, integration, and accessibility.

Noninvolvement   In noninvolvement, individuals feel barriers of omission (people simply don't think to include them), negative attitudes from others (e.g., "old people shouldn't be here"), and a community or organizational stigma ("gay people are less than whole beings").

Segregation   At the segregation level, people may participate in "special recreation" (a somewhat patronizing approach), stay in homogeneous groups (segregated to be with their own kind), must have a prerequisite skill development (can be in Special Olympics if a basic skill level exists), utilize segregation as a stepping-stone for personal advancement, and view leisure as therapeutic intervention (people's value improves as they engage in activity).

Integration   Integration has mixed-ability groups (able-bodied and disabled) participating together, a focus on the participating individual, leisure experience as an ongoing process, and views leisure as activity participation.

Accessibility   Accessibility provides for all people to have multiple opportunities and freedom of choice and to interact in an interdependent manner. It allows individuals to experience a self-satisfying leisure lifestyle and views leisure as a state of mind.

Leisure services professionals must examine the leadership and programming functions of their services. Can all skill levels participate to their fullest potential? Do programs, activities, and events reflect the cultural aspects of diversity? Do the activities perpetuate or help to break down stereotypes? In some communities, dwarf tossing is still an acceptable leisure activity. Pseudo-Sumo, a fad in the United States, mocks the religiously based Sumo wrestling. Leisure services professionals must respect their customers—people from all walks of life.

Marketing Practices

Every leisure services organization must market its programs and services in order to survive financially and meet its mission. Many decisions must be made about marketing and promotions; serving all potential constituents requires open and sensitive marketing endeavors. Leisure services professionals must carefully consider marketing to ensure diversity throughout all promotional efforts. Do needs assessments reach all possible constituents? Does newspaper advertising reach both sexes, all ages, ethnic, and different socioeconomic groups? Do the wording, graphics, and photographs used in promotional materials reflect society? Does the professional promote an air of inclusion, of accessibility?

Other Considerations

Other aspects of leisure services can be designed to enhance commitment to diversity. Leisure services professionals must consider the various constraints to leisure and attempt to mitigate them. For instance, adequate, inexpensive, and convenient or on-site child care eliminates one barrier to full and free participation in leisure for parents with children, especially single parents. Similarly, leisure programs and facilities should consider the scheduling needs of both nine-to-five workers and those employed with shift work. Those who work nontraditional hours and days tend to be working-class people with limited economic resources for leisure experiences.

Summary

Leisure services professionals have an opportunity and responsibility to promote diversity. Leisure serves as an excellent vehicle to promote and encourage diversity as it touches the lives of everyone. Leisure, a universal human experience, is perceived as a fundamental human right. The topic of diversity requires a definition of such terms as culture, prejudice, discrimination, and status. Wide diversity exists among different cultures and people and encompasses both primary and secondary characteristics. Every society has dominant cultures and subcultures, and leisure provides opportunities to participate in the activities of many cultures while also pursuing activities of various subcultures.

Leisure services professionals must deal with a variety of issues related to diversity. Discrimination issues affect the way people are perceived in society and how they experience leisure. Forms of discrimination—sexism, ageism, ableism, heterosexism, racism, and classism—all ascribe penalties and privileges to individuals. These isms create barriers that prevent individuals from experiencing the freedoms associated with leisure. An organization can counter discriminatory activities by crafting an appropriate mission statement, following sensitive administrative practices and policies, and ensuring staff development related to diversity, marketing, leadership, and programming.

The celebration of diversity is more than a social responsibility. It encourages proactive response to individual needs and facilitates leisure experiences through careful planning. Interestingly, the discovery of our differences also reveals common ground—activities differ, but people find similar benefits such as joy, freedom, and happiness.

Discussion Questions

1. Why is the pursuit of diversity important to leisure services professionals today?
2. Define the concept of culture and identify leisure values, norms, or attitudes that influence it.
3. Identify three individuals who are members of three distinct subcultures and profile their unique leisure characteristics.
4. Identify forms of leisure in which you have personally experienced some form of discrimination in terms of racism, ageism, sexism, heterosexism, ableism, or classism. Describe the situation.
5. Identify the primary and secondary dimensions of diversity that most directly impact your life. How has your leisure been affected by these traits?
6. Locate a community leisure services agency and profile any programs that promote the concept of cultural diversity. How are those programs determined? How do they impact the community? How do they affect the subcultures they are intended to serve?
7. Select a leisure services agency and ask the director how he/she keeps its programs free of the many forms of discrimination.
8. Develop a mission statement for a leisure services organization that promotes cultural diversity.
9. Explain how you could use the "I"-Triad model to promote diversity in leisure service organizations.
10. Using the model presented by Schleien, discuss how to implement leisure services options for a person with disabilities.

References

Aitchison, C. C. 2003. *Gender and leisure: Social and cultural perspectives.* New York: Routledge.

Allison, M. T. 2000. Diversity in organizational perspective. In M. T. Allison and I. E. Schneider, eds., *Diversity and the recreation profession: Organizational perspectives* (pp. 3–16). State College, PA: Venture.

Ameristat. 2000. Minority statistics in the U.S. [available on-line at http://www.ameristat.org].

Amir, Y. 1976. The role of intergroup contact in change of prejudice and ethnic relations. Edited by Phyllis A. Katz, in *Towards the Elimination of Racism,* New York: Pergamon Press.

Bannon, J. 1973. *Outreach: Extending Community Service in Urban Areas.* Springfield, IL: Charles C. Thomas.

Chavez, D. J. 2000. Invite, include, and involve! Racial groups, ethnic groups, and leisure. In M. T. Allison and I. E. Schneider, eds., *Diversity and the recreation profession: Organizational perspectives* (pp. 179–194). State College, PA: Venture.

Cox, T., Jr. 1994. *Cultural diversity in organizations: Theory, research, and practice.* San Francisco: Berrett-Koehler.

Dahl, R. F. 2000. Intercultural dynamics and organizational models of change. In M. T. Allison and I. E. Schneider, Eds., *Diversity and the recreation profession: Organizational perspectives* (pp. 225–234). State College, PA: Venture.

Dieser, R. B., and Wilson, J. 2002. Learning to listen: Cross-ethnic therapeutic recreation service delivery. *Parks and Recreation 37*(5), 54–59.

Digital Equipment Corporation. n.d. Corporate Finance Newsletter.

Dreachslin, J., and J. Saunders. 1999. Diversity leadership and organization performance. *Journal of Healthcare Management 44*(6), 427–439.

Edginton, S. R. 1991. *PAC 10 Higher Education Institutions: Training for Managers in the Area of Diversity.* University of Oregon, Eugene, OR.

Goldberg, M. 2000. Conflicting principles in multicultural social work. *Families in Society 81*(1), 12–21.

Guirdham, M. 1999. *Communicating Across Cultures.* West Lafayette, IN: Ichor Business Books.

Hayles, V. R. 1989. Arizona Affirmative Action Association 14th Annual Conference. Phoenix, AZ.

Hayles, V. R. 1996. *Leveraging Pluralism for Global Competitive Advantage,* December 9, 1996, Effectiveness/Diversity. Arden Hills, MN.

Healey, 1997. *Race, Ethnicity and Gender in the United States.* Thousand Oaks, CA: Pine Forge Press.

Henderson, K. A., M. D. Bialeschki, S. M. Shaw, and V. J. Freysinger. 1996. *Both Gains and Gaps: Feminist Perspectives on Women's Leisure.* State College, PA: Venture.

Henderson, L., and Vickers, P. 1995. Health or beauty? A survey of Dundee women's attitudes to body size. *Health Education Journal 54,* 61–75.

Jordan, D. 2001. *Leadership in Leisure Services: Making a Difference.* 2d. ed. State College, PA: Venture.

Knouse, S., and M. Dansby. 1999. Percentage of work-group diversity and work-group effectiveness. *The Journal of Psychology 135*(5), 486–494.

Kraus, R. 1994. *Leisure in a Changing America.* New York: Macmillan.

Kurtz-Costes, B., and E. Pungello. 2000. Acculturation and immigrant children: Implications for educators. *Social Education 64*(2), 121–125.

Loden, M., and J. Rosener. 1991. *Workforce America!: Managing Employee Diversity as a Vital Resource.* Homewood, IL: Business One Irwin.

McIntosh, P. 1991. White privilege: Unpacking the invisible knapsack. *Matrix,* 5–6.

Meridith, D. P. 2000. Stepping toward a more diverse workforce. In M. T. Allison and I. E. Schneider, eds., *Diversity and the recreation profession: Organizational perspectives* (pp. 19–27). State College, PA: Venture.

Naylor, L. 1998. *American culture: Myth and reality of a culture of diversity.* Westport, CN: Bergin & Garvey.

Nieto, S. 1992. *Affirming Diversity: The Sociopolitical Context of Multicultural Education.* New York: Longman.

Pelled, L., K. Eisenhardt, and K. Xin. 1999. Exploring the black box: An analysis of work group diversity, conflict, and performance. *Administrative Science Quarterly 44*(1), 1–28.

Rogers, M. 1999. *Barbie culture.* Thousand Oaks, CA: Sage.

Scales, P. 1991. *A Portrait of Youth Adolescents in the 1900s.* Carborro, NC: Center for Early Adolescents.

Schleien, S., and F. Green. 1992. Three approaches for integrating persons with disabilities into community recreation. *Journal of Park and Recreation Administration 10*(2), 51–66.

Schultz, J. 2004. Discipline and push up: Female bodies, feminity, and sexuality in popular representations of sports bras. *Sociology of Sports Journal 21,* 185–205.

Stein, J. U. 1993. The Americans with Disabilities Act: Implications for recreation and leisure. Edited by S. J. Grosse & D. Thompson, in *Leisure Opportunities for Individuals with Disabilities: Legal Issues,* 1. Reston, VA: AAHPERD.

Thomsen, S. R., Bower, D. W., and Barnes, M. D. 2004. Photographic images in women's health, fitness, and sports magazines and the physical self-concept of a group of adolescent female volleyball players. *Journal of Sport and Social Issues 28*(3), 266–283.

Wearing, B. 1998. *Leisure and feminist theory.* Thousand Oaks, CA: Sage.

Wheeler, M. L. 1994. Diversity Training. A research report. New York: The Conference Board.

Future Trends

Leisure experiences often involve inter-generational activities. A grandfather shares his wisdom with his grandson who reflects his hope for the future.

Introduction

Forecasters study present movements and trends to make projections into the future. Examining current issues and attempting to forecast their impact has great value to leisure services professionals. Current issues in the United States influence the local provision of services, agency missions, and understanding of participant life satisfaction as it relates to leisure services.

Information and projections about future trends enable leisure services professionals to rethink and reexamine many aspects of their organizations—business practices, program offerings, scheduling, promotional strategies, and facilities maintenance. Similar to weather forecasting, a knowledge of trends offers practitioners information about new opportunities, pitfalls to avoid, potential problems regarding consumers, new twists to the provision of services, and environmental concerns. In addition, trends can redefine the nature of leisure services, helping to determine whether leisure services should operate from a social service perspective, an entrepreneurial approach, have a youth or adult focus, or simply provide leisure opportunities.

This chapter examines trends within society, including social trends, health trends, environmental concerns, educational issues, technological influences, and economic trends. We discuss environmental issues, such as resource depletion, overuse of outdoor recreation areas, and ongoing conflicts between the economy and the environment. The educational arena also holds new trends in the public educational system, effects of desegregation and open enrollment, and the impact of varying levels of education on the future of leisure and life satisfaction. Consumer-friendly technological changes greatly impact society in both positive and negative ways. Globally, as well as locally, evolving political situations affect leisure services. Economics also affects every aspect of leisure services and life satisfaction.

A New Era in American Society: Future Trends in Leisure Services After September 11, 2001

Since President George W. Bush took office in 2000, there has been dramatic change in the United States. The events of September 11, 2001 (9/11), when the World Trade Center and Pentagon were attacked in the United States, changed the United States and the world. In response to 9/11, the United States became militarily involved in Afghanistan and in Iraq and created the Department of Homeland Security. On the domestic side, President George W. Bush made sweeping tax cuts, implemented the No Child Left Behind (NCLB) policy in k–12 education, walked away from the international Kyoto protocol on global warming, attempted to stop Affirmative Action across the United States, selected the first African American woman as Secretary of State, and is attempting to revolutionize Social Security and the New Deal era in what he has dubbed the "ownership society." The following section will explain how 9/11, federal tax cuts (ownership society), and NCLB have future implications for leisure services.

9/11

The events of 9/11 changed American society. It is no surprise that recreation and leisure service delivery also have been affected. For example, the World Tourism Organization (2002) suggested that the events of 9/11 have restructured travel habits of Americans—tourists are favoring destinations that are closer to home, more familiar, and accessible using a means of transportation that is perceived to be safer than mass transportation.

Although leisure behaviors are changing as an outcome of 9/11, in regard to future trends leisure services and sites will continue to help in the aftermath of 9/11 (Edginton, Hudson, Dieser, and Edginton, 2004; Hamilton, 2002). For example, parks will increasingly be used as memorials to remember the events and deaths that occurred on 9/11. The Monmouth County Park 9/11 memorial leisure line provides a case study of how the Monmouth County Park System in New Jersey is using parks and leisure services to remember the events of 9/11. As such, leisure services and sites will provide community spaces to commemorate 9/11 and, in the process, help people heal.

In commenting about the role of leisure after 9/11, Williams, Dustin, and McKenney (2004) suggested that leisure has the power to transform, create, and do something good in society: "devoting ourselves to something meaningful not only wards off the negative but carries positive effects as well" (p. 13). Edginton, Hudson, Dieser, and Edginton (2004) provided a case study of a group of people who devoted themselves to something meaningful and good to help families deal with 9/11:

> . . . a group of volunteers in Varina, Iowa, developed the Freedom Quilt project after the World Trade Center building was attacked in New York City on September 11, 2001. On the first-year anniversary of the terrorist attacks, the Freedom Quilt project had given away 2,800 quilts to families who lost loved ones on that dreadful day. This leisure group is still planning on making 4,000 to 5,000 more quilts to donate to families of the September 11th attacks. The Freedom Quilt project has helped individuals deal with the terrorist attacks and has contributed to community unit. (pp. 2–3)

In addition, Hamilton (2002) posited that during national crises, "people instinctively flock to recreation areas . . ." (p. 45). Leisure is a means to cope and buffer stressful life events (Mannell and Kleiber, 1997). The following quotation by the Board of the National Society for Park

The Monmouth County Park 9/11 Memorial

The Monmouth County Park System in New Jersey is in the process of developing a memorial to remember individuals lost from Monmouth County on 9/11. As explained by the Monmouth County Park System (www.monmouthcounty911memorial.com), the path leading to the monument will provide a chronology and interpretation of 9/11. As visitors come to the top of the hill, the walk will lead to a plaza area where they will see a large, circular paved area, and a map of Monmouth County carved into the stone. In the center will be a round table twelve feet in diameter and forty inches high. The table will be covered with a shiny dark stone, like polished black granite, and the names of the individuals lost from Monmouth County will be carved into that piece.

The victims will be grouped under the names of their hometowns, and their ages at the time of death also will be carved into the stone. On the floor of the walkway around the table, poems and sayings that reflect thoughts about the events of that day will be carved. In the center of the table, the memorial will have sculpture (carved in light-colored Indiana limestone) of an eagle ascending to a better world. The eagle will be larger than life size with a nine-foot wingspan, grasping and lifting off with a piece of rubble from the WTC site, an actual piece of steel recovered from the site. This Monmouth County Park was chosen for its breathtaking views of lower Manhattan and because it is the highest elevation along the eastern seaboard.

Resources (2004) highlights how leisure sites and services can be used as a means to deal and buffer stressful life events:

> When, in the course of human events, fear, anxiety or anger become too much to bear, we seek places for solace, healing and refreshment. Often we turn to nature's healing power, which can be found everywhere in our parks, forests, natural preserves, lakes, seashores, monuments, battlefields, wildlife refuges and wilderness areas. These places are nature's cathedrals, and they're there for us in our times of need . . . Shortly after the terrorist attacks in 2001, Secretary of the Interior Gale Norton reminded us that "From Maine to Hawaii, Alaska to the U.S. Virgin Islands, our public lands tell America's stories—stories we can draw lessons from. Let us take time to . . . reconnect with our land and our heritage, and together we can find unity, hope, and healing." (p. 8)

We believe that local leisure services and sites will continue to have an important and serious place in the aftermath of 9/11 and will continue to provide healthy ways to deal with the stress that comes with living an era of potential terrorist attacks.

Federal Tax Cuts (the ownership society)

Due to the escalating cost of the war in Iraq and Afghanistan, the development of the U.S. Department of Homeland Security, federal tax cuts, and President George W. Bush's vision of an "ownership society," many current government-run or funded leisure service programs have been cut or reduced. This trend will continue in the future. From a strictly program and funding perspective, the 2001 enacted tax cuts by President George W. Bush have hurt leisure services by eliminating services, programs, and jobs. The National Recreation and Park Association Division of Public Policy (2003) suggested that the Bush Administration Fiscal Year 2004 budget eliminated funding related to important programs and support in parks, recreation, and leisure services. For example, the 21st Century Community Learning Center Program (Department of Education), which is a funding source for many leisure and youth-oriented after-school programs, received a cut of $400 million. Other important programs that received reduced funding were: Youth Opportunity Program (Department of Labor), Title V Local Grants for Delinquency (Department of Justice), Urban Parks and Recreation Recovery Program (Department of Interior), and Special Recreation Programs for Individuals with Disabilities (Department of Education).

At the time this chapter was being revised into its fourth edition, President George W. Bush has proposed his Fiscal Year 2006 budget to be approved by Congress, which seeks spending restraints and more tax cuts. Although the Fiscal Year 2006 budget may not be approved by Congress, tax cuts and spending restraint will still be a future trend in American society. The National Recreation and Park Association Division of Public Policy (2005) has highlighted that the 2006 budget request proposes to terminate the Land and Water Conservation Fund (LWCF). The LWCF, which became effective in 1965 from the 1962 Outdoor Recreation Resource Review Commission Report, is a paramount matching federal funding source for developing outdoor recreation resources throughout the United States (Crompton, 1999). The LWCF (1) is a major funding source for the National Park Service, U.S. Fish and Wildlife Services, U.S. Forest Service, and (to a lesser extent) the Bureau of Land Management, and (2) provides grants-in-aid to states and, through them to local jurisdictions, for the planning, land acquisition, and development of outdoor recreation facilities (Crompton, 1999). Even if Congress opposes terminating the LWCF, this program has already lost over $65 million in state aid grants from federal tax cuts under the Bush Administration (Dolesh, 2004). National Recreation and Park Association Executive Director John Thorner commented that the National Recreation and Park Association will make every effort to convince Congress to appropriate $100 million for reinvestment in state and local public parks (National Recreation and Park Association Division of Public Policy, 2005).

Furthermore, the Fiscal Year 2006 budget calls for the elimination of many programs that have recreation and leisure program implications funded by the U.S. Department of Education (2005a), (see http://preview.ed.gov/about/overview/budget/budget06/summary/edlite-section3.html).

The following is a sampling of some of the programs that have implications to leisure services:

- Reduction of $35.6 million in Arts in Education (program to encourage the integration of the arts into school curriculum)
- Reduction of $225.1 million in Even Start (program for low-income families to develop family literacy)
- Reduction of $2.5 million in recreational programs (programs that use recreation to help people with disabilities become independent through community integration services)
- Reduction of $21.8 million in state grants for incarcerated youth offenders (program to encourage incarcerated youth to gain job and life skills)
- Reduction of $2.2 million in the Underground Railroad program (program that establishes tourism, leisure, and interpretative facilities related to the history of the underground railroad)

Understanding history is important because it can help people and professional organizations predict future consequences. Crompton's (1999) historical analysis of the tax revolts of the 1970s and 1980s provides a dismal picture of what the future may hold for leisure services if taxes are further reduced in the contemporary era. In regard to the tax revolts of the 1970s and 1980s Crompton noted:

> The financial challenges with which many park and recreation managers were faced in the past two decades constituted perhaps the most severe challenge in the field's history . . . the National Park Service Budget declined by $635 million from 1978 to 1996, which represented a budget decrease of almost 50%. At the same time, annual visits increased by almost 40 million, and Congress created 79 new park units . . . at the local level, the draconian plight of some agencies was illustrated by the parks department in New York. After experiencing waves of cuts throughout the 1980s, the department absorbed a 45% staff reduction between 1990 and 1994. This caused the executive director of the Parks Council, a support group, to charge, "The city has in effect announced that it is not going to take care of its parks" and the city park commissioner to observe that further budget cuts would amount to "giving liposuction to a skeleton" (1999, pp. 7–8).

Recent reports of how tax reductions have wiped out the Parks and Recreation Department in Cheney, Washington, (Chase and Shannahan, 2003) and caused the City of Salinas (California) to close down its 112-year old library system (which may make it the largest U.S. city to not have a library system) (Dolesh, 2005) further paints a dismal picture of the future of leisure service in the short term.

However, understanding history can also help professionals in leisure services in making future decisions and developing creative management strategies. For example, the case study of the demise of the Cheney Parks and Recreation Department (Chase and Shannahan, 2003) also highlights: 1) the lack of collaboration between leisure services and other human service organizations, and 2) the lack of marketing the benefits of leisure services based upon solid research and evaluation. In short, Cheney administrators learned that they should have been ". . . advertising and showing that all the benefits of keeping kids active will save on juvenile delinquency . . . [and that] The necessary act of self-promotion extends to the city government as well; all in the community must be aware of the value of parks and recreation departments" (Chase and Shannahan, 2003, pp. 51–52). In short, an important future direction for leisure services is to be proactive in highlighting the benefits of parks, recreation, and leisure services by developing solid evaluation (Edginton, Hudson, Dieser, and Edginton, 2004; Witt and Crompton, 2002) and being proactive in managing public perception (Panza and Cipriano, 2004). To this end, table 16.1, adapted from the academic work of Driver and Bruns (1999), summarizes the multiple benefits of recreation and leisure experiences. However, leisure service providers need to be aware that leisure can provide intentional and unintentional harm (see postmodern leisure theory or feminist leisure theory in Chapter 2) and need to be mature enough to accept negative outcomes and turn them toward beneficial outcomes (Edginton, Hudson, Dieser, and Edginton, 2004; More, 2002a, 2002b; More and Kuentzel, 1999). As More (2002a) reminds us, "and for every child who leaves the youth sports field victorious, at least one other goes home in defeat. If we are anxious to accept the credit for the benefits of recreation, shouldn't we also accept the blame for the hurt feelings, broken bones, and other negative consequences that occur so often during participation. . .?" (p. 68). Future leisure services need to be aware of both the negative and positive aspects of leisure and have an overriding objective to optimize net benefits of leisure services (Driver, 2002).

Is the future for leisure services all gloom and doom? Dolesh (2005) provides a convincing argument that, unlike the tax revolts era of the 1970s and 1980s, there are numerous local and state governments that are committed to developing leisure services and sites. Although Dolesh is fair-minded in highlighting local and state ballot measures that failed in 2004, he goes on to say that because more people understand the benefits of parks, recreation, and leisure services,

TABLE

16.1 BENEFITS OF RECREATION AND LEISURE EXPERIENCES

I. Personal Benefits

  1. Psychological

    a. Better mental health and health maintenance

      i. Wellness

      ii. Stress management

      iii. Catharsis

      iv. Prevention of or reduced depression, anxiety, and anger

      v. Positive change in moods and emotions

    b. Personal development and growth

      i. Self-confidence

      ii. Improved cognitive and academic performance

      iii. Sense of control

      iv. Autonomy and independence

      v. Leadership

    c. Personal appreciation and satisfaction

      i. Sense of freedom

      ii. Self-actualization

      iii. Creative expression

      iv. Spirituality

      v. Appreciation of nature

  2. Psychophysiological

    a. Cardiovascular benefits

    b. Reduce or prevent hypertension

    c. Decrease body fat and obesity

    d. Increase muscular strength

    e. Reduced consumption of alcohol and tobacco

    f. Reduced serum cholesterol and triglycerides

    g. Improved bone mass

    h. Improved functioning of immune system

    i. Respiratory benefits

    j. Increase life expectancy

II. Social and Cultural Benefits

  1. Community satisfaction

  2. Cultural and historical awareness

  3. Ethnic identity

  4. Family bonding

  5. Understanding and tolerance for others

  6. Reduced social alienation

  7. Pride in the community and nation

  8. Social support

  9. Enhanced worldview

  10. Prevention of social problems by at-risk youth

III. Economic Benefits

  1. Reduced health care costs

  2. Increased productivity at work

  3. Decreased job turnover

  4. Local and regional economic growth

  5. Contribution to national economic development

IV. Environmental Benefits

  1. Maintenance of physical facilities

  2. Husbandry and improved relationships with natural world

  3. Understanding human dependency on the natural world

  4. Development of an environmental ethic

  5. Environmental protection of biodiversity and ecosystems

Adapted from: Driver, B. L., and Bruns, D. H. 1999. Concepts and uses of the benefits approach to leisure. In E. L. Jackson and T. L. Burton, eds., *Leisure studies: Prospects for the twenty-first century* (pp. 349–369). State College, PA: Venture.

more people are willing to support them on local and state ballot measures. He reported: "In the 2004 elections, 111 of 147 local and state ballot measures that dedicated public funds for parks and open space protection passed in 25 states" (Dolesh, 2005, p. 8). For example, there was strong public support for two separate billion-dollar land acquisitions in Florida because people understand the benefits of parks, preservation, and leisure. Likewise, the outstanding example of the Special Recreation Associations throughout Illinois underscores how recreation organizations gain community support when leisure services are viewed as beneficial. For example, the 2003-2004 Annual Report of the Northeast DuPage Special Recreation Association (2004) sums revenue support as over a million dollars, which is primarily from community support (e.g., member partner contributions, program fees).

Furthermore, depending on one's interpretation, the tax cuts might be constructive because it will force leisure professionals to think differently and come up with creative leisure services. To this end, Kraus and Curtis (2000) remind us:

> ... In a governmental, social, or business environment that is undergoing rapid cultural and demographic change, organizations of all kinds need to be able to respond to new challenges rapidly and creatively ... Rather than be limited by past practices or by a conservative outlook that is afraid to risk failure, managers should be free to seek new and different solutions and to lead their organizations in potentially groundbreaking directions. An important element in such responses is the ability of managers to think and act in imaginative and innovative ways. (p. 353)

In fact, Florida (2002) has argued that approximately 30 percent of employed people in America are part of a growing "Creative Class," which he predicts will transform future work, leisure, and community endeavors. The "Creative Class" are people whose economic and social function is to create new ideas, new technology, and new creative contents. These people are transforming society because they engage in complex problem solving that involves independent judgment and requires high levels of education and human capital. In regard to the events of 9/11, Florida commented:

> It's now time for the Creative Class to grow up. We must evolve from an amorphous group of self-directed, albeit high-achieving, individuals into a more cohesive, more responsible group ... To be effective, the Creative Class may ultimately have to invent a new form of collective action. (2002, pp. 316–317)

In short, creativity is often developed through interdisciplinary and collaborative action (Csikszentmihalyi, 1996), and future leisure service professionals will need to be creative and innovative in their thinking and invent future services from collective and collaborative actions.

In this regard, leisure service professionals can become social entrepreneurs. According to Bornstein (2004), social entrepreneurs are transformative forces because they are "people with new ideas to address major [social] problems who are relentless in the pursuit of their visions, people who simply will not take no for an answer, who will not give up until they have spread their ideas as far as they possibly can" (p. 1). In fact, Bornstein suggests that the future success of nonprofit and human service organizations, which includes many leisure service organizations, will hinge on whether they become social entrepreneurs.

The multiple case studies presented in the book *Better Together: Restoring the American Community* (Putnam, Feldstein, and Cohen, 2003) exemplify social entrepreneurs and the creative spirit that involves making connections among people, establishing bonds of trusts and understanding, creating social capital, and developing networks of relationships that build community. Although these authors provide twelve case studies related to multiple sites and programs (e.g., interfaith and school community programs, neighborhood initiatives, cyber communities), two examples of leisure-oriented creative and community development bring clarity and hope regarding future endeavors of leisure services. First, the Near North Branch Library of Chicago was a collaborative project for two different neighborhoods to unlearn discriminatory and stereotypical beliefs and develop a sense of togetherness and community. The Near North Branch Library is located between the primarily White and wealthy Gold Coast neighborhood and the mainly African American and poor Cabrini Green neighborhood in Chicago. The library runs a number of reading, after-school, and leisure programs in which Gold Coast neighborhood residents help and mentor Cabrini youth toward developing life skills, such as reading and free time activity. Second, the Shipyard Project: Building Bridges with Dance in Portsmouth, New Hampshire, was a collective action that involved renovating a vacant World War II naval shipyard into a storytelling historical interpretative dance and performing arts programs. Stories regarding the sacrifice of women and families, naval soldiers, along with tragic events (e.g., the death of 129 sailors and civilian technicians due to an early atomic submarine accident) are shared through movement and dance. This performing arts project brought a community closer together through the creative and collective actions of people and leisure service leaders.

No Child Left Behind (NCLB)

NCLB, which President George W. Bush signed into law on January 8, 2002, is one of the federal government's most sweeping changes to education in a generation. NCLB has tremendous support by both Democratic and Republican lawmakers. According to the U.S. Department of Education (2005b), NCLB is based upon four pillars. First, there is stronger accountability for achievement results in reading, math, and science. Second, state and school districts have flexibility in how they use federal funds to increase achievement results in reading, math, and science. Third, there is strong emphasis on scientifically based educational methods. Fourth, parents will have more autonomy to have their child transfer to different schools if the school they are in does not demonstrate improved achievement performance.

Although on the surface the NCLB may not seem to affect leisure and leisure services, Noddings' (2003) critique of contemporary American education, including NCLB, suggests that modern education has reinforced the narrowness that education should be based solely on 1) developing a stronger U.S. economy, 2) teaching people work skills, and 3) giving every person an opportunity to do well financially. Noddings noted that important life variables such as homemaking, parenting, meaningfulness, community development, happiness, and recreation are not part of a formal contemporary education. As a consequence of economically-oriented education, leisure-oriented classes such as physical education, music, art, drama, and domestic science (along with play and leisure time during recess) are continuing to be viewed as secondary, less important, or totally irrelevant. As mentioned previously in this chapter, the Fiscal Year 2006 federal government budget already calls for the reduction of $35.6 million in the Arts in Education programs and a $2.5 million reduction in recreational programs specifically designed to help people with disabilities become independent through community integration services. Noddings suggests that a central aim for education should be to develop happiness and that the most important aspects of happiness come from developing:

- a rich social life
- friendship
- home
- parenting and interaction skills
- interpersonal growth
- spirituality
- community involvement
- being involved in nature

Noddings further suggests that recreation and leisure should be an important part of educational curriculum because it affects many of the variables that cause people to be healthy and happy.

Beyond Noddings' concerns, NCLB can influence leisure services in both positive and negative ways. On the positive side, NCLB allows state and school districts to experiment and have flexibility in how they use federal funds to increase achievement results in reading, math, and science. Potentially, schools can spend more time using leisure experiences to increase reading, math, and science during normal school hours or offer rich, leisure-oriented after school programs. Freysinger and Kelly (2004) suggest that 1) recreation during and after-school (e.g., recreation-based after-school programs) can make up for meaningless and damaging school experiences, and 2) leisure can make

Figure 16.1

The relationship among leisure, education, and human development.

Source: From: Ruskin, H. (1995). Conceptual approaches in policy development in leisure education. In H. Ruskin & A. Sivan (Eds.), Leisure education: Toward the 21st Century (pp. 137-156). Provo, UT: Brigham Young University Press.

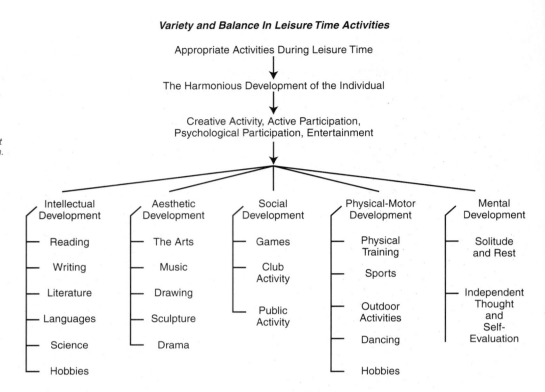

Variety and Balance In Leisure Time Activities

Appropriate Activities During Leisure Time

↓

The Harmonious Development of the Individual

↓

Creative Activity, Active Participation, Psychological Participation, Entertainment

Intellectual Development	Aesthetic Development	Social Development	Physical-Motor Development	Mental Development
Reading	The Arts	Games	Physical Training	Solitude and Rest
Writing	Music	Club Activity	Sports	
Literature	Drawing		Outdoor Activities	Independent Thought and Self-Evaluation
Languages	Sculpture	Public Activity	Dancing	
Science	Drama			
Hobbies			Hobbies	

learning more applied and enjoyable. For example, participating in sport or outdoor recreation programs can help a person learn and apply math skills and science skills. Figure 16.1 presents the relationship among leisure, education, and human development. In short, NCLB can be an opportunity for leisure services and leisure education programs to be recognized in public schools (regarding leisure education being part of the public school curriculum, see Shivers, 2000). On the negative side, curriculum planning might continue to socialize children and people to believe that work and success are more important than leisure and social life. Under NCLB, achievement is primarily focused on reading, math, and science (e.g., no achievement scores related to physical fitness), and many people may not see the relationship among leisure, education, and human development. Furthermore, because NCLB has a strong emphasis on scientifically based educational methods, it may cause a shift in recreation-oriented after-school programs being eliminated or replaced by academic-oriented after-school programs. The mindless belief that spending more and more time teaching an education subject will lead to greater learning (e.g., longer math classes, reduction in recess or physical education classes, academic-oriented after-school programs) is still a pervasive education curriculum held by most people (Noddings, 2003), which may prevent leisure services from being introduced into the school curriculum.

Social Trends and Leisure

A host of social influences will impact leisure in the future. Social conditions in society influence the lives of individuals—relationships with others, the use and perceptions of leisure, the relationship of leisure to work, spatial arrangements in living conditions, and the way people live and interact with each other and with the environment. A number of social trends influence leisure, including shifts in population patterns, changes in family composition, changing social

Random Events and Forecasting Leisure

We live in a fast-paced world where change is ever present. The Greek philosopher, Heraclitus (540 BC to 480 BC) notes that "nothing endures but change." As a result, we are told that to be successful we need to prepare for change, to look for opportunities in change, as well as manage change. In recent times, leisure service managers have applied such things as strategic planning principles to forecast and be ready for change. However, increasingly we are realizing that it is difficult, if not impossible, to account for all the random activity that shapes the global community.

In the last five years, we have been reminded that we live in a world punctuated by random, rapid, and discontinuous change. Consider the recent unrelated events of September 11, 2001, and the tsunami in Southeast Asia. Both these events have changed the world we live in. In the United States, we still suffer from the effects of September 11, 2001. America is far more vigilant today than it was at that time. We have changed dramatically, not only in terms of our sense of safety, but we also have been transformed in other ways, and we have been forced to respond to a host of unpredictable social, cultural, political, and economic events. We are not as free in our minds today as we were in the past. Leisure experiences have been dramatically compromised. International travel has been curtailed. Leisure in and around home environments has increased. Our safety at major events requires special arrangements limiting access by vehicles to stadiums, event centers, concert halls, etc. Individuals attending such events are closely monitored, in fact, often searched.

Organizations such as Hostelling International USA (HI-USA—described in a leisure line in Chapter 5) has struggled financially as travel has been curtailed. The Opening Doors/Opening Minds program (ODOM) was developed in part as a response to the tragic events of September 11, 2001. The bombing of the World Trade Center in New York and the continued 'mistrust' between countries and regions of the world indicate the relevance of this mission today (to help all, especially the young, gain a greater understanding of the world and its people through hostelling). The program is responsive to the deep fissures in understanding that exist among cultures and people. It is particularly responsive to young people's need to interact in a complex society filled with individuals from different ethnic, economic, and cultural backgrounds.

ODOM brings together the best of what HI-USA has to offer. Built on the foundation of the hostelling movement, this initiative combines mission-based programs and public awareness messages to reach today's young people and amplify their voices. It brings into sharp focus HI-USA's vision that hostellers can become caring world citizens who are catalysts in creating a more peaceful world. ODOM is an opportunity for today's youth to challenge their assumptions, increase their civic involvement, and expand the scope of their dreams.

In responding to this random, rapid, and discontinuous change, HI-USA moved away from typical strategic planning to what could be defined as tactical planning. Realizing that the only way to guide the way through such an unpredictable social, cultural, political, and economic event was to

Forecasting and planning in today's context is challenging. Our efforts at predicting the future of leisure is problematic at best. We can scan the horizon of the environment in an attempt to determine emerging fads and/or trends that influence the leisure behavior of individuals. However, the unpredictability of the world we live in today makes precise forecasting difficult, if not impossible. The best we can do is to monitor our environment closely and establish a set of values or principles that can guide our actions in times of crisis. These values or principles should be reflected in our vision and mission statements as well as being mission conscious in the programs we offer.

The recreation profession has a long tradition of responding to social concerns. Jane Addams, Joseph Lee, Frederick Law Olmsted, George Williams, Luther Gullick, and many others are remembered today for their innovation and ability to respond to the social ills of their generation. As Jane Addams herself wrote "the one thing to be

—continued

Random Events and Forecasting Leisure— continued

dreaded in the settlement (house movement) is that it loses its flexibility, its power of quick adaptation, its readiness to change its methods as its environment may demand." Today, recreation professionals need to be ready to adapt to a new world where change can happen in a blink of an eye.

Points to Ponder

- Consider the events of the December 2004 tsunami in Southeast Asia. What problems, issues, and concerns should this event raise for

recreation organizations? (Hint: Think in the broad sense of all elements of the profession: youth development, community development, health, and tourism.)
- How might the recreation profession respond to such traumatic events in the future?
- Research what the world community has done to respond to *quality of life issues* since this traumatic event? Can you find any information on how a specific recreation organization has responded to this event?

roles, greater equality for women, the blurring of public and private involvement in leisure, and increased diversity.

Population Shifts

The world population, continuing to expand rapidly, will dramatically impact society—including leisure patterns and opportunities—for decades to come. The world population was 6.1 billion in 2001 and is projected to grow to 7.8 billion by 2025. Further, projections suggest the world population will reach 9.0 billion by 2050. This can be compared with 1970, when the world population was 3.9 billion.

Middle-Aging of America   One prominent trend related to social structure is changes in population patterns. The rising median age of the population in the United States shows an increase in the proportion of Americans over the age of seventy-five, an increase in the proportion of middle-aged Americans, and a decline in the proportion of children and young adults (Law, 1995). Figure 16.2 illustrates the middle-aging of the United States. As the population bulge increases in age, leisure service professionals must respond to changing needs. People from the baby boom generation have entered middle age with expectations for leisure and life satisfaction that may differ from traditional models of leisure services (Kelly and Godbey, 1992). Traditional services focus on youth and have a social service perspective; baby boomers remain active, have different needs than youth, and demand greater accountability from service providers. Canada also shares many of these concerns.

Changing Leisure Needs   Enculturation is the impact of social and cultural influences—including parents, peers, religion, school, and other institutions—on the interests and desires of a people. Baby boomers have been enculturated to expect a variety of both work and leisure experiences. They expect experiences that involve risk, solitude, large groups, personal satisfaction, the out-of-doors, and technology (Godbey, 1989; Kelly and Godbey, 1992; Kraus, 2001). People continue to seek these diverse stimuli even as they age. Leisure services professionals face increasing challenges to provide for these interests. In addition, participants of all ages demand quality experiences customized to their individual needs; this expectation will grow for the baby boom generation, particularly in retirement years.

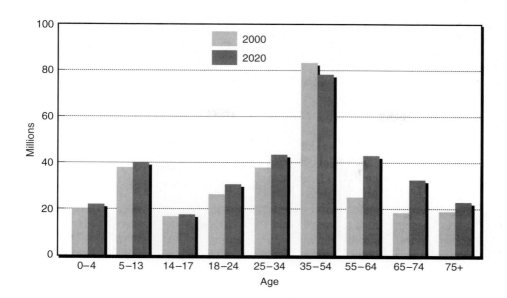

Figure 16.2

America Entering "Middle Age"—a surge in the number of people aged 35 to 54: 2000 to 2020.

Dramatic Increase of Older Population   Proportionately, older Americans will show the most dramatic population increases (see figure 16.3). Between 1960 and 1990 there was a tremendous shift in the population. This shift will continue as the "baby boom bulge" (that is, individuals born between 1946 and 1964) moves through their life span. Currently, these baby boomers represent one-third of America's population. In 2011, the baby boom generation will turn sixty-five. At that point, there will be a tremendous surge in the number of individuals, with growth for the population aged sixty-five to seventy growing by 74 percent between 1990 and 2020. This can be contrasted with the population under the age of sixty-five, which will increase only by 24 percent (U.S. Bureau of the Census, 1999). Overall, individuals are living longer, birthrates are declining, and people are waiting longer to have children. Those within the aging population generally experience better health than earlier counterparts, remain active longer, and have more discretionary income than ever before. These trends show a need for leisure practitioners to serve this growing population in a relevant manner. As most people age, participation in some activities declines while participation rates in other activities increase. However, active participation in leisure and aging is an interaction of biological, psychological, sociological, and historical factors (Freysinger, 2000).

In addition, as people age, they may lose physical strength and often live alone due to loss of spouse or partner. Therefore, older people tend to have greater concerns about safety, social interaction, and predictability in their lives, including their leisure, than younger consumers. This has implications for leisure providers in terms of staffing, programming, and facilities. For example, avoiding late evening programs, providing transportation to and from recreation facilities, providing well-planned programs, and involving participants in preparations will help to accommodate the growing older population.

Shifts in Population Distribution   Another population issue or trend involves the distribution of people across the United States. In the continuing flight from the effects of poverty, lack of health care, violence, and other social problems, the population continues to shift away from urban to suburban areas. More than 80 percent of U.S. citizens now live in urban areas; only 20 percent of Americans live in rural areas (U.S. Bureau of the Census,

Figure 16.3

Population age structure: 1960 to 2020.

Source: U.S. Bureau of the Census.

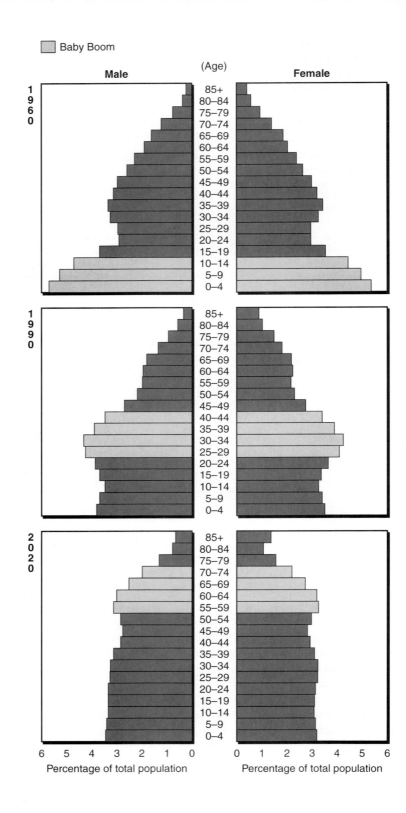

490

2003). The continuing influx of immigrants into the United States also results in changing cultural influences and impacts leisure, health concerns, and social needs. Language, employment, education, health, and other social issues must be addressed, as well as the provision of relevant, accessible leisure services to these individuals.

Overpopulation   Increased life expectancy, lower infant mortality rates, increases in immigration, and other factors underlie a continuing rise in population. This dilemma impacts the environment, the economy, education, and life satisfaction of people everywhere. The following excerpt from Davidson (1993) discusses world population trends:

> From the beginning of creation to 1850 A.D., world population grew to one billion. It grew to two billion by 1930, three billion by 1960, four billion by 1979 and five billion by 1987, with six billion en route. Every 33 months, the current population of America, 256 million people, is added to the planet.. . . The present is crowded and becoming more so.. . . When John Kennedy was elected president, domestic population was 180 million. It grew by 70 million in one generation. Our growing population has not dispersed over the nation's 5.4 million square miles. About 97 percent of the U.S. population resides on 3 percent of its land mass. Half of our population resides within 50 miles of the Atlantic or Pacific Ocean. (p.8)

Many countries are making excellent progress toward zero population growth, yet increased longevity and declining infant mortality rates offset some of these achievements. Many attribute contemporary social ills—rising health problems, increasing violence, poverty, and starvation—to overpopulation. Leisure professionals in urban and suburban areas are challenged to respond in new ways to the needs of people in these areas.

Changes in Family Composition/Family Concerns   Many issues affect life satisfaction, including economic status, personal health, and family status. The nature of the family has changed over the years and continues to evolve (Kraus, 2001). Once believed to consist of a homemaker (mother), breadwinner (father), 2.3 children, a pet, and ready access to an extended family, "family" is now recognized to mean different things to many different people. Families may consist of one parent, two parents, stepparents, older parents, grandparent heads of households, and adoptive and natural children. Single person households are on the rise, and families are getting smaller in size, with an increase in stepfamilies and blended families.

The book *Joined at the Heart: The Transformation of the American Family,* written by former vice President Al Gore and his wife, Tipper Gore, highlights how families have transformed in American society from 1960 to 2000. This includes:

- Americans are creating fewer married-with-children families: In 1960, married couples with children under the age eighteen represented over half of all families; in 2000, married couples with children under the age eighteen represented 35 percent of all families.
- The divorce rate has doubled: In 1960, for every four marriages there was one divorce; in 2000, there was a divorce for every two marriages.
- Single parents head more families: In 1960, only 5 percent of families were single-parent families; in 2000, single-parent families accounted for 13 percent of families.
- More children are being born to unmarried mothers: In 1960, only 5 percent of American children were born to unmarried families; in 2000, there had been a six-fold increase (33 percent).
- More mothers are working outside the home: In 1960, approximately 20 percent of married mothers with children under the age of six worked outside the family; in 2000, more than 60 percent of married mothers worked outside the home.

- Fewer people are married: In 1960, almost 70 percent of the marriageable population was married; in 2000, approximately 55 percent were married (cohabiting unmarried couples have increased fivefold from 1960 to 2000).
- Families are forming later: In 1960, women married at the age of twenty and men at twenty-three; in 2000, women married at the age of twenty-five and men at twenty-seven (first marriage).
- Families are having fewer children: In 1960, the average family had 2.3 children; in 2000, the average family had 1.9 children.
- Families are becoming more diverse: In 1960, less than half a percent of families were interracial; in 2000 almost 3 percent of families were interracial.
- More grandparents are playing an active role in raising children: Because the average life span has increased nearly ten years from 1960 to 2000, grandparents are living longer and participating more in the lives of their grandchildren. (Gore and Gore, 2002)

The family structure is going to continue to transform in the future. As the Gores remind us:

> For us, as for most Americans, family is our bedrock, and we believe the strength of the American family is the nation's bedrock. Now, because of the profound transformation of American families . . . it is time to boldly address the urgent need to provide every appropriate support to every kind of family—and so make it possible for all of us to discover the lasting joy and deep sense of connection experienced by those who are joined at the heart (2002, p. 341).

Al and Tipper Gore (2002) strongly advocate the importance of leisure and play in family development. Beyond sharing many personal and family stories regarding the importance of play and leisure, they reference many play and leisure experts and organizations (e.g., Boundless Playgrounds, Institute of Play, Mihaly Csikszentimihalyi, Robert Kubey, Brain Sutton-Smith) to underscore that the transformation of families in 2000 (from 1960) is also having a profound transformation on play and leisure. For example, they suggest that due to the lack of parental supervision (e.g., single families, both parents working) children no longer go outside and play—instead, children spend too much time indoors with electronic toys and watching television and computer screens. As explained in Chapter 6, the lack of physical activity among children and adults is a paramount factor in the obesity epidemic. The Gores also highlight the detrimental influence that the lack of play and leisure can have on children, adults, and families, such as contributing to stress-induced depression and different types of behavioral and family problems. They suggest that human service organizations need to be providing leisure and play opportunities to help struggling families (e.g., single parents).

The evolution of the family structure has tremendous implications for leisure services professionals. Children often are unattended during nonschool hours; the latch-key child has become the norm. The changes in family structure have altered the design and implementation of family programming. Child care has become a necessity for people from all walks of life.

Increased Numbers of Latch-Key Children   According to the National Institute on Out-of-School Time (NIOST) (2005) 44 percent of American families do not have any regular after-school care for their children. Grade demographic information suggests the following regarding children who are reportedly in self-care (latch-key children) from 3:00 P.M. to 5:00–6:00 P.M. (NIOST, 2005):

- Eleven percent are in first through fifth grade
- Thirty-four percent are in sixth through eighth grade
- Fifty-one percent are in ninth through twelfth grade

Drawing upon different studies, the NIOST also reports the following statistics regarding latch-key children:

- Nearly 36 percent of youth report that they spend time home alone after school once a week.
- Sixteen percent spend at least three to four days a week alone at home after school.
- Thirteen percent of youth spend five days a week alone at home after school.
- More than half of adolescents reported they would not watch so much TV or play video games if they had other things to do after school.
- Fifty-four percent of adolescents reported that they were bored after school and do not know what to do other than hang out, watch TV, or play video games.

According to a recent survey by Junior Achievement (2004) of youth between the ages of eight and eighteen only 14 percent said they participated in an after-school program and 16 percent said they are not interested in after-school programs because there is no variety in the programs (e.g., academic-oriented after school programs). However, there was strong support by youth to have after-school programs oriented toward sports, art, music, computer literacy, learning how to run a business, career counseling, and spending time with mentors. Duffett and Johnson (2004) reported that approximately 54 percent of parents feel that after-school programs should be recreation based so that children can have a break from academics, whereas approximately 38 percent of parents feel that after-school programs should be focused on academic skills.

Low-cost supervised after-school programs have become critical to the functioning of the family unit. Without such programs children are left unattended to watch television, play video games and Internet and perhaps engage in other less-than-healthy leisure-time alternatives. Leisure services organizations should carefully examine the escalating need for these programs as well as the provision of wholesome, safe, and supervised before- and after-school leisure services. Edginton, Kowalski, and Randall (2005) noted that nonschool hours present an excellent opportunity to provide leisure activities that provide positive and beneficial outcomes. There is also a need for programs for youth that teach them life skills to help them operate independently and make healthy decisions.

Changes in the Extended Family Twenty or thirty years ago one could count on the support and nurture of extended family members. Many family units lived in fairly close proximity to relatives, making child care and family leisure more broadly defined. In the nineties and beyond, the tremendous capacity for travel has moved many out of immediate reach of other family members. In earlier decades families often sought one another for support, love, and leisure; people now turn to themselves and their immediate family and community for such support. Often, grandparents, aunts, uncles, and cousins are no longer available for family-based leisure (Kelly and Godbey, 1992; Kraus, 2001). Provision of leisure programs that facilitate social interaction, including interaction among different generations, is increasingly important to the social health of individuals.

Changes in Social Roles

Social roles include behavior patterns defined by expectations, norms, customs, and rituals of society. Society in the United States continues to evolve as people and institutions come to new understandings of the world. Social roles, currently being rewritten across the globe, suggest that people will not necessarily embrace the social roles of the past.

Figure 16.4

Percentages of women and men in the workforce.

Source: Data from The Bureau of Labor Statistics, the U.S. Department of Labor.

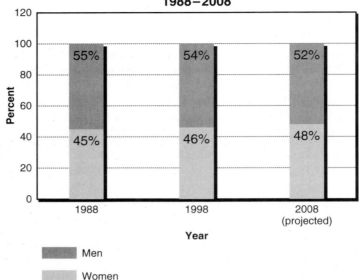

Most Workers Will Be Women
1988–2008

Percent (y-axis: 0, 20, 40, 60, 80, 100, 120)

1988: Men 55%, Women 45%
1998: Men 54%, Women 46%
2008 (projected): Men 52%, Women 48%

Year

- Men
- Women

A great example of changing social roles is the infusion of women into the political arena. President Clinton was one of the first American Presidents to offer women high-ranking government positions (e.g., Janet Reno was the first woman Attorney General of the United States of America), and President George W. Bush appointed the first African American woman as Secretary of State (Condoleezza Rice). While still low in overall numbers, the United States now has more women in the Senate and more female state governors and city mayors than ever before.

Shifts in Gender Roles Significant changes have taken place in the definitions of social roles for women and men. Women have entered the paid workforce in great numbers and will stay there. As depicted in figure 16.4, the workforce will be divided almost equally between men and women. In 1988, 45 percent of the workforce were women, and 55 percent were men. By 1998, the percentage of women had increased to 46 percent, and it is projected that by the year 2008, 48 percent of the workforce will be women and 52 percent will be men. Today, most women work out of economic necessity, although some work to retain a sense of self and individuation. The shift in gender roles also has resulted in increased leisure opportunities for women. Both women and men recognize the place of leisure in helping to define one's sense of self and adding richness to life.

Men also have new avenues for self-identification. Stay-at-home dads, "men of the 90s" who share in domestic life, and fathers who equally value work and family life are on the rise. Men and boys are finding it increasingly socially acceptable to engage in a variety of leisure experiences without the worry of gender-role appropriateness.

Elder Issues With the graying of the population and the loosening of gender role restrictions, the issue of family care becomes increasingly complex. Elder care now joins child care on the list of family needs. With two working parents, longer expected life spans, and decreased mortality of those with severe physical and mental impairments, care issues can become complicated (Henderson, Bialeschki, Shaw, and Freysinger, 1996). Rising health-care costs may make it commonplace for an elderly parent to receive care in the home of adult children. The leisure needs of the care-giver and the care-receiver will require consideration by leisure services professionals.

Linear Life Pattern   In the past most people lived a rather linear life pattern and experienced a similar sequence: childhood, part-time work, full-time work (at the same job for years), family, and retirement. In previous generations most people followed a specific, predictable pattern. One graduated from high school, went to college, took a job, got married, bought a house, had children, continued to work (often in the same work environment with the same company), and then retired (to Florida or Arizona). Today people tend to drop in and out of school, change careers three or four times, postpone childbearing until later in life, and retire into new jobs (Kelly and Godbey, 1992 Gore and Gore, 2002).

As job definitions change, family structures fluctuate, and as the economy necessitates, more people will enter and leave the workforce many times, change jobs in the search for self-fulfillment, and raise separate families. The entering and leaving of the workforce exposes individuals to a variety of experiences and people. Leisure interests and opportunities also change during the different stages of life (Kelly and Godbey, 1992; Freysinger and Kelly, 2004). The intensity with which a person pursues leisure interests varies, depending on the ebb and flow of life patterns.

Greater Equality in Sports and Athletics for Women

The general desire for equality for all continues to drive changes in the nature of leisure experiences. In the past decade, girls have grown up with relatively equitable opportunities in sports and athletics in public school. More women are demanding equal access to collegiate athletic teams than ever before. As women become involved and successful in sports, athletics, and other activities, the image of women as strong, capable individuals able to compete may help to open doors for women and girls in areas such as business, personal relationships, politics, and leisure.

Title IX   Aburdene and Naisbitt (1992) report that in the 1990s women made up the majority of new participants in weight training, cycling, and basketball. Nearly one-half of new golfers each year are women. Although Title IX, the law forbidding sex discrimination in schools that receive federal funding in the United States, was passed in 1972, only recently has its enforcement taken place. Women and girls will continue to reap the benefits of Title IX in coming years. The exposure to skill development and training in school years opens many leisure opportunities for girls and women.

College Athletics   Women now participate in college and high school athletics in record numbers (Aburdene and Naisbitt, 1992; Freysinger and Kelly, 2004). The number of high school females participating in competitive sports has increased 700 percent in the past twenty-five years (Freysinger and Kelly, 2004). The top ten sports for women in college include basketball, volleyball, tennis, cross-country, softball, track, swimming/diving, soccer, field hockey, and golf. Women also seek out nontraditional sports and activities. The first women's ice hockey tournament was held in 1990; weight lifting is becoming the choice of recreational activities for many women, as are rugby and boxing.

Adventure travel for women has positive repercussions in other areas of women's lives. Women now engage in coed and all-women trips. The support experienced on all-women trips may empower female adventurers to expand their leisure activities to new traditional and nontraditional leisure roles.

As women's leisure experiences impact and influence other aspects of their lives (e.g., career, family), society will experience further change. As women seek careers for experience, rather than jobs to fill time, they gain increased economic parity with men. More discretionary income can result in more spending for leisure activities (Aburdene and Naisbitt, 1992; Henderson et al., 1996).

Blurring of Public/Private Involvement in Leisure

The blurring of public and private sectors in the provision of many human services (Crompton, 1999) results from increased private involvement in social issues and increased state involvement in private issues. Currently, a shift from institutional responsibility to individual responsibility is taking place.

Cooperation between Public and Private Sectors Changes will occur in the roles of the public and private sectors in the provision of leisure services. More private agencies will become involved in what is now considered the responsibility of public agencies—services for those below the poverty line, at-risk youth, those with long-term health-care needs, and the like. For example, Schlatter (2004) highlighted how Central Park in New York City has recently used a public-private partnership to revive and upgrade the park. In short, a private group formed the Central Park Conservancy, which partners with city government and is able to get funding from corporate campaigns. Several examples of cooperative ventures in leisure services follow:

> The City of Portland (Oregon) Park Bureau entered into negotiations with Sea World to lease land in support of the development of a theme attraction—Sea World would build the amusement park on undeveloped public park land. A portion of the funds generated from the revenues would return to the city, which would, in turn, use these funds to develop and maintain the park land adjoining the Sea World facility. While this public-private venture did not come to fruition, it serves as an example of the potential opportunities that exist when government and business collaborate.
>
> The *Camp Adventure™ Youth Services* program provides an example of an entrepreneurial program operated within a public institution, the University of Northern Iowa. *Camp Adventure™ Youth Services* program, run much like a business, receives no tax subsidies and must generate its own revenues to sustain its operations. Its major partners include other public agencies, particularly the U.S. Armed Forces. This model of cooperation between two different types of government agencies has resulted in many mutually beneficial program services and relationships.
>
> AquaArena, a theme park located adjacent to Southwest Texas State University and purchased by the university with state funds, continues to be operated as a revenue-producing venture. In addition, it serves as a laboratory for the biology, archaeology, and recreation management departments. Similarly, the city of Santa Clara, California, in order to preserve open space from industrial development, purchased the Great America theme park when its sale to developers was imminent. These two examples show how private organizations and public bodies can work together to meet both the needs of the community and the natural environment. In both cases, the private organizations recouped their investment.

As these examples indicate, individuals and organizations now accept greater responsibility for social actions, becoming active where they once had little impact.

Increase in Diversity

The increasingly diverse populations in the United States carries over into the workplace, with more people of color, women, older persons, and persons with disabilities entering this arena. This phenomenon accentuates the need for culturally sensitive leisure organizations. Recent

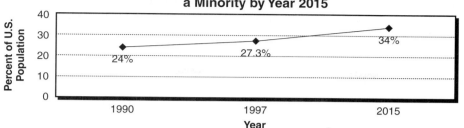

Nearly One-Third of Americans Will Be a Minority by Year 2015

Percent of U.S. Population

40
30
20
10
0

24% 27.3% 34%

1990 1997 2015

Year

Figure 16.5

Projected minority percentages.

Source: Population Reference Bureau. 1999. United States Population Data Sheet.

years have seen an increase in hate crimes and overt prejudice, while a resurgence in pride related to ethnic and racial identity has also taken place. Leisure services professionals must anticipate the needs and expectations of people from a variety of cultural backgrounds. Standard mechanisms for the provision of programs, customary games and activities, and underlying assumptions must change.

Increase in Number of People of Color   The race composition of the United States is changing dramatically. In 2000, 72.3 percent of the population was White. The Black population represented 12.7 percent and the Hispanic population, 10.2 percent. American Indians, Eskimos, and/or Aleuts made up 0.87 percent of the population. Asian or Pacific Islanders represented 3.8 percent of the population. It is estimated by year 2015 that one-third of Americans will be from a minority group (see figure 16.5). Sometime around the year 2050, all of the so-called minorities will together surpass in numbers the current Anglo majority. Indeed, the term *minority* will essentially lose its meaning. Our children or grandchildren will live in a society where, in today's terms, everyone will be a minority (Yzaguirre, 1998). Further, by 2050 it is projected that the proportion of the White population will decrease by 60 percent, the Black community will increase slightly, the number of Asians will increase tenfold, and Hispanics will almost triple their numbers (Nieto, 1992). Diversity has been significantly influenced by immigration; within the last decades of this century, immigration has played the largest role in the growth of our population since the beginning of the twentieth century (U.S. Bureau of the Census, 1999).

Leisure services organizations will have both a more diverse constituency and a more diverse staff. Obviously, leisure services delivery systems must prepare to respond to changing population patterns. The future calls for a responsive delivery system, with effective programming, personnel, administrative practices, and facility-usage policies.

Increase in Women in the Workplace   Currently women represent 59 percent of all *new* workers entering the workforce (Law, 1995). As indicated, it is projected that women will constitute 48 percent of the workforce by the year 2008. This influx of women will contribute to the projected increase of diversity within organizations. As more women enter the workplace, their leisure needs will change. Additional issues regarding child care, latch-key programs, and other support services will require action by leisure services organizations.

Increase in the Proportion of Older Individuals   In the next thirty years, the United States will experience a dramatic population shift. By 2030, it is projected that nearly 20 percent of the United States population will be sixty-five years of age or older (Hines,

2002). The dramatic increase in the proportion of older individuals has implications for leisure programs and services, as well as staffing. For example, there are many studies that document the postive effects related to leisure participation (e.g., Janssen, 2004; Richards, Hardy, and Wadsworth, 2003; Verghese, Lipton, Katz, Hall, Derby, and Kuslansky, 2003). It follows that future leisure services will provide an important component in the lives of older people.

Opportunities for Individuals with Physical Disabilities   As the Information Age shifts the national perspective from an industrial to a service economy, society places greater emphasis on knowledge than on physical ability. Computer-aided technologies allow individuals with physical disabilities to compete more effectively for employment within organizations, including leisure services organizations. In addition, the Americans with Disabilities Act will continue to have significant implications for this group, both in terms of work and leisure opportunities.

Health Trends and Issues

Health issues concern the continent as the gap between the haves and have-nots increases. Fewer people can afford health-care costs, and health-care reform has become the issue of the decade. People turn to leisure and physical activity as a way of maintaining personal health and fitness. Increasing numbers of insurance companies provide rate reductions to organizations that have a no-smoking policy, random drug testing, and employee-provided recreation and fitness programs.

With no cure nor successful long-term treatment yet found, HIV infection and AIDS continue to be at the forefront of health concerns, placing increased burdens on the public health-care system and stretching the imagination of leisure services providers. Leisure services providers may react to the increasing numbers of home-bound ill by providing services in homes. Despite concerns about substance abuse, addictions to drugs and alcohol will probably rise. Job stress, recognized as a detriment to health, will call for leisure in the management of stress. This section of the chapter discusses a number of health issues in relationship to leisure, particularly trends related to physical and social health. Many of these topics have an extensive impact on youth and society at large.

Changes in Physical Health

Both positive and negative changes have taken place in the physical health of American citizens. Issues related to physical health include a rising incidence of substance abuse and consequent costs to society, fitness concerns, the increasing problem of AIDS and HIV infection, a decline in youth fitness, health-care issues, and the rising stress level of all people.

Increase in Cardiovascular Fitness and Decrease in Obesity
Leisure services organizations can offer programs and services that improve people's health and physical quality of life. The development and availability of new treatment methods, along with a commitment to a healthier way of life, have cut the deaths of Americans from heart disease by more than a third, and from stroke by one-half (Wilkinson, 1989). Clearly, greater awareness and increased leisure values related to fitness and well-being have influenced this phenomenon.

As stated in Chapter 6 of this book, increasing cardiovascular fitness and decreasing obesity are going to be a major focus of health trends in the United States. According to the United States Surgeon General (2001), "Overweight and obesity have reached nationwide epidemic proportions" (p. v), and the entire population needs to become more active. Despite common knowledge that exercise is healthful, more than 60 percent of American adults are not regularly active, and 25 percent of adults are not active at all (Surgeon General, 1996). Since 1980, the percentage of children who are overweight has more than doubled (Wechsler, McKenna, Lee, and Dietz, 2004).

Continued Interest in Wellness Leisure services organizations serve as important vehicles for improving people's health and wellness through diet, information, and exercise. Studies indicate that most U.S. citizens are overweight, and show a clear link between poor diet and lack of exercise and heart disease and other ailments. As a result, Americans now recognize that proper diet and exercise contribute to better health. Many individuals eat healthier foods and participate in physical activities—often offered by leisure service organizations—that contribute to their fitness and well-being, including jogging, aerobics, water aerobics, fitness clubs, swimming, and various sports activities.

Increase in AIDS Increasingly, leisure professionals will be working and interacting with people who have AIDS or dispersing information about AIDS (e.g., youth centers and programs, therapeutic recreation programs). Statistics regarding AIDS and HIV already cause great concern and will become even more alarming in the decades to come. More than 20 million people around the world have died of AIDS-related diseases and in 2004, 3.1 million people died (AVERT, 2004). The following statistics from the Henry J. Kaiser Family Foundation (2004) provide a snapshot of the AIDS epidemic in the United States:

- In 2003, 405,926 people were estimated to be living with AIDS in the United States, and recent analysis suggests a potential increase of AIDS among the United States population.
- Almost 930,000 cases of AIDS were diagnosed in the United States through 2003, including 43,171 cases diagnosed in 2003 alone.
- The top five states with AIDS cases are: New York, California, Florida, Texas, and New Jersey.

Increased Stress/Increase in Employee Assistance Programs (EAPs) Increased stress, a symptom of the 1990s, will continue as an issue that requires attention in people's work and leisure experiences into the twenty-first century. Most of the nation's 500 largest companies had instituted some type of Employee Assistance Program (EAP) to assist employees with stress and other health-related matters (Wilkinson, 1989). Some attribute rising stress to the unstable economy, gender shifts in the workplace, the changing nature of work, and other factors. The changing nature of families, with more women juggling home and work responsibilities, also contributes to higher stress levels for both men and women.

Changes in Social Health

Both positive and negative changes have occurred in the social health of U.S. citizens. Issues related to quality of life, social health of youth and adolescents, materialism, and random violence stand at the forefront of discussion.

Increased Interest in Quality of Life/Balance Positive actions toward better social health increase along with concern for the quality of life. People will make decisions about work, family, and leisure based on quality of life issues—a balance of work, family, a healthy lifestyle, and time for self (Freysinger and Kelly, 2004). Many corporate workers now opt for more family or self-time instead of an increase in salary. As Robinson notes, ". . . quality time will become a status symbol and a luxury item" (1991, p. 23). In this study, Robinson (1991) also found that respondents take salary reductions in order to get more time off, and the findings cut across all segments of the workforce. Most individuals agreed that having free time is as important as making money.

Leveling Off or Continued Increase of Teen Pregnancy   Teen pregnancy rates go through cycles of leveling off and rising. Teen pregnancy rates increase as young people search for excitement, instant gratification, and something to fill the love-and-belonging void. In 1998, the birthrate was 48.0 for every 1,000 teenage girls in the fifteen- to nineteen-year-old age group. This is a decrease in the number of births per thousand for teens in this age grouping. In 1993, the figure stood at 56.5 for every 1,000 teenaged girls in the same category. For example, birthrates for White teenagers declined from 52.8 in 1991 to 46.8 in 1997 (U.S. Bureau of the Census, 1999) and for Black teenagers from 115.5 in 1991 to 89.5 in 1997. Children giving birth to children leads to increased needs for child care for young mothers, and adapted leisure opportunities. The leisure lives of young parents are severely disrupted. Leisure education and services that provide meaningful programs will help these youth. Leisure professionals must determine their view of leisure—as an instrument of social change or experience for its own sake.

Youth: A Dramatic Decline in Social Health   The social health of youth has deteriorated dramatically, and projections anticipate continued decline into the twenty-first century. Social health of youth includes such factors as success in school, being substance free, and other behaviors that are in accordance with social mores. According to Dryfoos (1990):

> *Youth at-risk* are those youth that exhibit behaviors that are associated with such factors as delinquency, substance abuse, adolescent pregnancy and dropping out of school/school failure. These types of *high-risk behaviors* are related to low achievement motivation, poor school performance, antisocial behaviors and conduct disorders, lack of parental supervision and support and living in areas of economic deprivation (p. 25).

Results from the 2003 Youth Risk Behavior Survey (Centers for Disease Control, 2004) suggest that numerous high school students are engaged in at-risk behavior. Statistics from this study include:

- 30.2 percent had ridden with a driver who had been drinking alcohol
- 17.1 percent had carried a weapon
- 44.9 percent had consumed alcohol
- 22.4 percent had used marijuana
- 33 percent of youth had been in physical fights
- 8.5 percent had attempted suicide

Moreover, at-risk behavior among youth also contributes to an increase in violent behaviors and more serious drug use (experimentation with marijuana leading to experimentation with cocain or heroin).

It is important that leisure services professionals be aware of the factors that put youth at risk, as well as strategies that can be used to help youth *build assets* and *reduce deficits* to increase the likelihood that they will engage in healthy, positive behaviors. There is a need for all agencies and organizations within each community to improve systems of service delivery, coordinate services, improve public policies, and enhance the climate of public support.

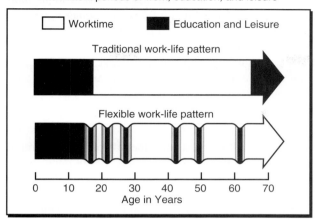

Work-Life Patterns Changing

Traditional work-life path evolving to
intermittent periods of work, education, and leisure

☐ Worktime   ■ Education and Leisure

Traditional work-life pattern

Flexible work-life pattern

0   10   20   30   40   50   60   70
Age in Years

Figure 16.6

The traditional
work-life pattern
has evolved into
a pattern of
flexibility,
reflecting current
lifestyles.

Increase of Materialism   Materialism and the visible display of it are achieving a new high in American culture (Schor, 1998) and occurs during leisure (Freysinger and Kelly, 2004). The organization indicates that "The 'good life' now requires 'a lot of money' (according to more than six in ten Americans, up from four in ten in 1975), as well as a job that pays more than the average" (p. 20). Whereas people preferred an interesting job over a high-paying one in the 1970s through the mid-1980s, both now rank as equally important, and things that money can buy now rank higher in importance than they did in 1981. As people recognize that the world has finite resources, however, the "good life" may be redefined to come from a balanced life rather than the accumulation of goods.

Return to a More Relaxed Lifestyle   According to a Time/CNN poll (1999), seven in ten people surveyed said that they would like to "slow down and live a more relaxed life." In addition a number of respondents, six in ten, indicated that "earning a living today requires so much effort that it is difficult to find time to enjoy life." Many individuals today want to focus less on work and more on time with their families (see figure 16.6).

Environmental Concerns

Environmental concerns and causes will continue to besiege the United States. Global warming, acid rain, losses related to biodiversity, and abandoned nuclear waste products will be health and environmental concerns of the decade. Individuals seeking a return to nature and their roots will place an increased load on the natural world. Designated recreation areas, in particular, may see this factor impact resource quality. Parks will continue to move toward closing their entrance gates once a preestablished visitor capacity has been met. User and entrance fees to outdoor areas will increase and the concern about the rights of all users will mount. Many environmental issues and concerns will continue to be linked to leisure. Political, social, and natural environments are inescapably intertwined. Governmental policies and regulations (or lack thereof) will heavily impact the availability of the out-of-doors for leisure pursuits. Continued logging and mining, particularly in the western states and provinces, may affect outdoor recreation areas.

The essence of the American ethos is subduing or conquering the frontier (Sax, 1980). When the United States was first settled by Europeans, conquering the wilderness drove people to points farther west. Cutting great forests, burning the prairies, and damming rivers and waterways were integral to survival of the culture. Even now, American citizens seem to buy into the philosophy of beating back nature and controlling the environment. It increasingly becomes apparent that this philosophy is no longer a viable belief structure. People now know, although they do not always act in conjunction with that knowledge, that subduing the environment results in the decimation of plant and animal species. Leisure services will continue to be severely impacted by human intervention within the natural environment.

Consider these facts that relate to issues of leisure and the environment both now and in the future:

- The United States is the world's largest consumer of energy, consuming 94.2 percent of the world's primary energy (U.S. Bureau of the Census, 1999). Interestingly, the United States only produces 23 percent of the natural gas, 10 percent of crude petroleum, and 21 percent of the coal of the world's production.
- The demand for energy is met primarily by fossil fuels—oil, natural gas, and coal. Fossil fuels will supply almost 90 percent of the world's energy by 2015.
- Twenty-four countries in the world rank above the United States in terms of the percentage of land area set aside as protected (World Resources Institute, 2000).
- There are forty-four biosphere reserves in the United States.
- The United States has twelve world heritage sites and operates seventeen wetlands of international importance.
- Almost 4 million children die each year of acute respiratory infections, linked with indoor air pollution (especially smoky cooking fuels) and outdoor air pollution (especially from industrialization) (World Resources Institute, 2001).
- In developing nations, there may be as many as 3.5 million to 5 million acute pesticide poisonings per year due to lack of protection during application, with millions more exposed to lower but still dangerous levels (World Resources Institute, 2001).
- More than 100 million people in Europe and North America are still exposed to unsafe air, and some air pollutants are proving more recalcitrant to control than expected (World Resources Institute, 2001).

Several environmental issues and trends will have an impact on the provision and nature of leisure service outdoor pursuits long into the future. This section of the chapter focuses on the ongoing battles between developers, the preservation of entire ecosystems, the depletion of resources, and the degradation of natural resources.

Development Versus Ecosystems

Ongoing battles will take place between environmentalists and developers who want to use the remaining virgin land and open space for different purposes. People will begin to realize that saving an ecosystem, not just a species, is the key to solving problems of overuse and destruction.

Recreational User Conflict   Recreational user conflict will continue to increase in leisure settings (Ewert, Dieser, and Voight, 1999). For example, Dustin (2003) underscored the ongoing and intense conflict in banning snowmoblies in Yellowstone National Parks, and Dustin, Schneider, McAvoy, and Frakt (2002) provided a case study regarding user conflict between American Indians and traditional rock climbers at Devils Tower National Monument in Wyoming. Recreational conflict is a condition that exists when one person or group of people experience or perceive an interference of goals, or the likelihood of incompatible goals, as the result of another person or group's action, threat of action, or person/group attributes (Ewert, Dieser, and Voight, 1999). Recreational user conflict is vast; it can occur between consumptive (e.g., hunters) and nonconsumptive (e.g., bird watchers) recreation users, between motorized (e.g., snowmobiles) and nonmotorized recreation users (e.g., cross-country skiers), between environmentalists (e.g., wanting to develop wetlands) and commercial recreationists (e.g., wanting to develop a private golf course), between ecotourists (e.g., learning about a culture) and large hospitality resorts (e.g., beach resorts). Moreover, some common examples of recreational conflict include: 1) the draining of wetlands for construction of highways, 2) the near extinction of populations of alligators and crocodiles in Florida to create safe water parks, 3) the destruction of an old-growth forest to develop a condominium complex with an ocean view, and 4) the damming of Hetch-Hetchy to develop a recreational water area and adjacent housing and rental units.

Recreational conflict is not just an outdoor recreation concern—it can occur in all types of leisure contexts (Ewert, Dieser, and Voight, 1999; Freysinger and Kelly, 2004). For example, Docheff and Conn (2004) explained how recreational conflict, poor sportsmanship, and violence are increasing in youth recreation and sport. They noted:

> The parents of millions of youth participating in organized sports today threaten coaches, assault referees and hurt kids . . . in May 2003, a little league secretary in Wakefield, Mass., faced criminal charges of assault and battery for allegedly kicking and swearing at an 11-year old boy who had been fighting with her son at the baseball field. In September 2003, a Toronto father was charged with assault for grabbing and shaking his 10-year-old daughter's face mask at a youth hockey game. (p. 63)

Recreational conflict due to poor sportsmanship is increasing, and leisure service professionals need to begin to take serious steps to address this concern (Ellis, Henderson, Paisley, Silverberg, and Wells, 2004). To deal with recreational user conflict, leisure service professionals can develop violence/conflict-reduction strategies, such as: 1) offering sportsmanship classes, 2) developing parental codes of conduct, (3) creating zero tolerance policies, 4) having silent games, 5) fining abusive spectators and players, 6) playing non-scoring games, (7) developing special programs focused on enjoying the recreational activity, and 8) developing program directives, monitoring strategies, and evaluation (Docheff and Conn, 2004). Leisure professionals also can deal with recreational conflict by developing pro-social behavior oriented toward the beneficial aspects of leisure involvement (e.g., pre- or post-sport game/event socials) (Ellis, Henderson, Paisley, Silverberg, and Wells, 2004), provide better communication regarding recreational rules and policies (Schneider, 2004) and develop an understanding of the recreational visitor, such as cultural backgrounds and inner perceptions/expectations of the recreational experience (Ewert, Dieser, and Voight, 1999).

Resource Depletion

The continuing patterns of resource depletion (such as the clear-cutting of the virgin old growth forests in the Pacific Northwest) pose a problem when humans continue to take from the environment, but do not put back. This will soon catch the attention of mainstream users—bird watchers, hikers, and picnickers. To preserve resources, people must realize that resources are finite and should be managed rather than collected and used. As trees are cut for timber and paper, new trees must be planted. Slowly, people will understand that using coal and petroleum-based energy sources will result in the eventual disappearance of those resources.

Continued Movement Toward Nonconsumptive Energy Sources

Nonconsumptive energy sources—those resources that do not get used up, such as wind and sun—will be increasingly studied and made available to the general public. People will consume energy and resource-based products but will look for "green" appeal. Use of postconsumer recycled goods will become increasingly mainstream (Zeiger and Caneday, 1991), and ecological harmony will become a major goal. Tourism will increase, by both national and international visitors, with genuine concern that the integrity of the resources be maintained.

Environmental Degradation

Continued attention will focus on the degradation of the natural world. For example, climbers used to climb the Himalayan Mountains in clear and pristine conditions. Climbers must now face huge mounds of trash left by other climbers, smell the odors of piles of human waste, and hike through barely recognizable mountain meadows. For several years to come people will continue to love the parks and natural areas to death; then there will be a resurgence in eco- and environmentally sound recreation and tour packages (Caneday, 1991).

New Perspective on Eco-Vacations   Eco-vacations, where people volunteer their labor to work in the out-of-doors (trail maintenance, research related to botany or animal life), will soon become "in" forms of leisure experience. Meeting multiple goals for service, socialization, and leisure, these opportunities will expand.

Continued Progress Toward Environmental Responsibility   As technology increases, so will the need for outdoor activity. People desire to relate to the natural environment on a personal level. Issues related to recycling, reusing, and reducing will become the norm in most communities across the United States and Canada. The cost of environmental cleanup will continue to be high, and environmental ethics will become an increasingly important topic of discussion (DeGraaf and DeGraaf, 1993). The National Audubon Society has developed travel ethics for the environmentally responsible traveler (World Resources Institute, 1993, p.151):

1. Wildlife and their habitats must not be disturbed.
2. Tourism to natural areas will be sustainable.
3. Waste disposal must have neither environmental nor aesthetic impacts.
4. The experience a tourist gains in traveling with Audubon must enrich his or her appreciation of nature, conservation, and the environment.
5. Audubon tours must strengthen the conservation effort and enhance the natural integrity of the place visited.
6. Traffic in products that threaten wildlife and plant populations must not occur.
7. The sensibilities of other cultures must be respected.

In addition to developing similar ethics, those in the leisure services profession must properly deal with the use and disposal of commodities and durable goods used in the provision of leisure services. The layout and design of new facilities, maintenance and refurbishing of existing structures, and the impact of programs and services on the environment will become integral to the provision of leisure services.

Ongoing Focus on Global Issues   The greenhouse effect and ozone depletion serve as two global examples of environmental degradation. Some scientists indicate that the greenhouse effect, an increase in the average temperature of the earth, comprises the most crucial environmental threat facing the world. The following lengthy quotation from Bell (2004) provides a realistic snapshot regarding how global warming may affect the world in the future:

> There is considerable evidence that the world is heating up. When averages are calculated for the entire globe, the 10 warmest years on record (through 2003) have all occurred since 1990. And the trend is upward: The 1970s were hotter than the 1960s, the 1980s were hotter than the 1970s, the 1990s were still hotter, and the 2000s are looking to be the hottest yet . . . If this warming trend continues over the next 100 years, say most climatologists and oceanographers, we will see some major environmental changes. Climatic zones will shift, rainfall patterns will change, and weather conditions will become more variable. In addition, the average sea level will rise 1–2 feet—and possibly higher—as glaciers and ice caps melt and as the ocean water heats up and expands . . . the predicted consequences would be dramatic . . . Warmer temperature and changes in rainfall patterns could increase the incidence of disease, as the new conditions would likely be more hospitable to mosquitoes, ticks, rodents, bacteria, and viruses. Extensive regions of low-lying coastal land (where much of the world's human population lives) would be in grave danger of flooding during storm surges—or even under water. It is not inconceivable that whole countries, such as low-lying Pacific Island nations or Tuvalu and Kiribati, could in time be washed away (pp. 5–6).

The primary reason for global warming (and ozone depletion) is due to consumption of natural resources and materialism (Bell, 2004). At the heart of consumption and materialism is Veblen's theory of the leisure class (see Chapter 2 in this book)—conspicuous consumption and conspicuous leisure are rooted in the visual display of wealth, such as expensive homes, cars, clothes, and recreation goods (Bell, 2004; Schor, 1998). The biggest cause of global warming is the carbon dioxide released when fossil fuels like oil and coal are burned for energy (e.g., needless travel in cars or airplanes). Godbey (1997), building upon research by the Natural Resources Defense Council, underscored that the United States population (which is 5 percent of the world's population) consumes 25 percent of the world's fossil fuels, 20 percent of the world's metals, and 33 percent of the world's paper (not to mention contributing to 72 percent of hazardous waste production).

In many ways, leisure professionals of the future may be the leaders in reducing global climate change through actions that will decrease the consumption of natural resources, especially carbon dioxide. Leisure professionals and services can be advocates and planners for developing cities and communities that embrace alternative methods of transportation, such as walking and bicycling trails. For example, Denver (Colorado) has a "bicycle expressway" that allows 1,000 bike commuters a day to get to and from work, and Palo Alto (California) has an extensive bikeway system in which city employees and some private corporations actually pay their workers if they bike to work (Alvord, 2000). By using the simple formula presented in figure 16.7, leisure professionals can help people estimate the cost of using a car and demonstrate how using different methods of transportation not only help a person be healthier (e.g., physical activity of biking), but can actually help a person save money. Likewise, the development of national, state, and local parks, along with trees and various shrubs, will help sequence carbon dioxide into oxygen.

Educational Issues

Changes occurring in educational systems across the continent include a rise in the raw numbers of people receiving postsecondary education. The more education people receive, the higher the likelihood of securing a good paying job and settling in with a career. This results in higher discretionary income to be spent on leisure. In addition, the higher one's level of education, the more exposed he or she may be to different forms of leisure; hence, the greater the potential for diversity in their leisure choices. In the future, people will stay in school longer and

Figure 16.7

Cost estimate for car use.

Source: From: Alvord, K. (2000). Divorce your car: Ending the love affair with the automobile. Gabriola Island, BC: New Society Publishers.

How much does your driving cost?

You can estimate your cost of driving with this worksheet. It helps you determine your out-of-pocket costs, then adds your non-monetary costs, and finally allows you to estimate and add external costs to get a grand total.

Distance (miles or km) you drive per year	_____
÷	
Mpg or km/l your car gets	_____
=	
Fuel (gallons or liters) used per year	_____
Yearly cost of car purchase (monthly payments × 12 OR purchase price divided by years owned)	_____
+	
Annual depreciation (ten percent of purchase price)	_____
+	
Yearly insurance premium	_____
+	
Annual license and registration fees	_____
+	
Yearly emissions test cost (where applicable)	_____
=	
Fixed cost of your car	_____ (A)
Fuel costs (fuel used per year above × cost per gallon or liter)	_____
+	
Cost of oil and oil changes	_____
+	
Tires (including snow tires if applicable)	_____
+	
Repairs and maintenance (other than oil and tires)	_____
+	
Out-of-pocket parking costs (meters, lots, etc.)	_____
+	
Bridge and road tolls	_____
+	
Tickets and fines	_____
+	
Car washes	_____
=	
Operating cost	_____ (B)
Other costs (e.g., misc. accessories, books-on-tape, car alarm, car stereo, lumbar support cushion, car phone, etc.) per year	_____ (C)
Your total yearly monetary driving cost [(A) + (B) + (C)]	_____
÷	
Distance you drive per year	_____
=	
Your money cost per mile or km to drive	_____

---

will tend to look to leisure as more than just a diversion (Godbey, 1989). An increased concern for ecologically safe leisure will correspond with a rise in education.

People will continue to seek leisure experiences for socialization, excitement, escape, and furthering educational and skill development. Some of the important educational issues to be presented in this portion of the chapter include desegregation and open enrollment, the reduction of school services and alternative uses for school facilities, lifelong education and development, and increased emphasis on higher education.

Desegregation and Open Enrollment

Continued efforts to ensure that public school systems are equitable between areas of high property tax bases and low tax bases will occur. Financial resources of school systems will change as parents and children decide which school to attend. Inner-city schools with diminished human and economic resources will be heavily impacted (Godbey, 1989; Kelly and Godbey, 1992). Shifting teachers and other resources may lead to an unstable educational system, which could affect the quality of education.

Decreased Support for Extracurricular Programs

A lack of adequate resources for schools often results in the elimination of extracurricular activities, many of which are leisure-based (Seefeldt, 1996). In school districts across the United States, battles over funding have led to the reduction or elimination of music programs, art classes, and after-school sport and athletic programs. Classroom activities may be affected as well. If this trend continues, some leisure experiences for young people will require funding through sources other than schools, creating a need for more private and public nonschool-based programs. Several examples that speak to the issue of support and lack of support for extracurricular programs and activities follow:

> In the Department of Defense Dependents Schools System (DoDDS), the school system no longer supports extracurricular sporting activities. For example, Seoul American High School, a secondary school providing educational services to family members of military personnel in Seoul, Korea, dropped its competitive sports program. The Morale, Welfare, and Recreation Services department, the community-based leisure service provider, now operates these programs. In the City of Chicago, the entire high school sports program was eliminated, only to be reinstated after massive fundraising brought in more than 1 million dollars.
>
> A counter example shows a school that has promoted and, in fact, internalized the importance and value of leisure and after-school activities and committed funds to that end. In the state of Indiana, any youth who tries out for any after-school program makes the team—cheerleading, band, football, and so on. This strategy toward participation and mass involvement promotes the idea that everyone can have a successful leisure experience.

The scaling back or dropping of after-school programs may also result in an increase in the number of at-risk youth—youth with little direction but with time on their hands.

According to Wilkinson (1989), the work-life patterns of individuals are changing. Individuals traditionally engaged in education and leisure early in life, work in midlife, and education and leisure again during old age. This pattern, however, is changing (Kelly and Godbey, 1992). Individuals will increasingly have within their life span recurring intermittent periods of education and leisure interspersed with their work life.

Increased Emphasis on Higher Education

Most new jobs will occur in the service sector, so people will need a higher level of education to compete effectively. Estimates project that 75 percent of all new jobs will require some college education.

Technological Influences

Technology will have a tremendous impact on the future of leisure services. New and improved equipment, the changing nature of job-related duties, and the creation of new leisure opportunities will result from continued technological development. Of the workforce, 2 percent are involved in agricultural jobs, 16 percent in manufacturing, and the remaining 82 percent in managerial and professional specialties, sales, administrative, and/or service occupations. This is a significant change from 1980 when 75 percent of the workforce was involved in nonagricultural or manufacturing-type positions.

Over the past fifteen years, leisure services professionals have seen the influences of technology on desires, needs, and expectations of leisure consumers. Computer, video, and electronic games have become readily available to the masses. Leisure activities made possible by improvements in technology include in-line skating, karaoke, and virtual reality games/software. Technological advances also have resulted in higher expectations of quality and the ability to respond quickly to changes, needs, and desires of leisure customers.

This section of the chapter discusses the impact of technology on the changing nature of time, systems and innovations/services and equipment, and transportation. As information systems continue to outdistance themselves, and the technological revolution results in increased information access for customers, leisure service providers will need to be responsive and on the cutting edge.

Changes in Time Use

People from western cultures believe that an increase in technology effectively releases additional time from the "time bank," which, in essence, becomes free time. This means that with technological advances, people expect more free time to engage in leisure experiences. Mere advances in technology and information systems, however, do not automatically free up additional time from work and subsistence needs (Kelly and Godbey, 1992). Contrary to popular belief, even with the invention of time-saving devices such as the microwave oven and the desktop computer, people actually have about the same or just slightly more free time than people had twenty years ago.

Changes in Amount of Leisure Time   Robinson and Godbey (1997) note that America's leisure (averaged for both men and women) has increased from thirty-five to forty hours per week. In 1989 America's leisure (averaged for both men and women) increased from thirty-five to thirty-eight and one-half hours per week and the work week for both men and women declined (Robinson, 1989). In further examination of these figures, however, Robinson (1989, p. 34) states, "Men ages eighteen to sixty-four report that they had forty hours of free time twenty years ago," and that they have the same amount today. Women in the same age bracket, however, report an increase in leisure from thirty-four to thirty-nine hours per week. Robinson also reports ". . . that Americans are facing a time famine and that an increasing proportion of Americans say they always feel rushed" (p. 35).

As indicated in Chapter 5, Schor suggests that less leisure is available to individuals. Many Americans are driven and unhappy despite the fact that they have achieved success in their work and perhaps even in gains in leisure (Schor, 1993). Further, Junin (2000, p. 71) suggests, "The pressure of today's life, reinforced by the workplace, economic, social, and political climate, has reduced our quality of life. We live to work and don't work to live." This author suggests that perhaps we need to downshift, simplify our lives, and create a slower pace of life in order to promote greater happiness.

From Baseball to Ballet?

Sometime in the millennial 1990s the arts will replace sports as society's dominant leisure activity. By one measure it already has.

A landmark 1988 report by the National Endowment for the Arts calculated Americans now spend $3.7 billion attending arts events, compared with $2.8 billion for sports events.. . . Just twenty years ago people spent twice as much on sports as on the arts. *In less than a generation Americans have reversed their leisure spending habits.*

. . .This dramatic change parallels the shift from an industrial to an informational society and has been accelerated by the coming of age of the baby boomers, a well-educated and . . . arts-loving generation.. . . In Boston, home of the Celtics, Red Sox, and Bruins, *twice* as many people went to the theater, museums, or art shows as attended sports events.. . . Sports still dominate the media, but with increased corporate support during the 1990s, consumers will be able to watch ballet as well as baseball.

A study of work hours conducted in five countries in 1990 by the Leisure Development Center (Japan), however, reports that the workweek in Japan, the United States, and Great Britain has increased since 1975 and the workweek has decreased in France and the Federal Republic of Germany (1991). Definitions of work, leisure, and other factors may impact on the interpretation of results of the two studies. Most Americans, however, feel a sense of time squeeze or time famine. Robinson (1989) notes that quality time will become a status symbol or luxury item as Americans continue to feel overworked and overwhelmed. Also, new standards or lack of resources often push people to do more in less actual clock time.

Fluctuations in Time Availability to Participate in Leisure   The time available to engage in leisure activities continues to change. Once leisure time occurred primarily during evenings after work, on weekends, and during holidays when people took vacations. Now leisure time tends to fall in less predictable time periods (Godbey, 1989; Kelly and Godbey, 1992; Robinson and Godbey, 1997). Work no longer connotes a 9:00 A.M. to 5:00 P.M. availability. People will continue to work varying hours. Weekends will no longer always be one unit of time. More people will have staggered days off from work, thus breaking up the forty-eight- to seventy-two-hour block of time often used for leisure.

The nature of vacations has also changed. In past years, an America worker typically started the first year of employment with one week of vacation and, with continued employment, worked up to three to four weeks off. People took these vacation days as integrated packages of time from one- to two-week periods. In the future, the trend for taking a day here and a day there will continue. People will have available more, but shorter periods of time in which to engage in leisure.

Systems and Innovations/Services and Equipment

New technology has resulted in the development of systems and innovations that make services and equipment extremely accessible and user-friendly. Almost anyone can set a DVD player, cook dinner, and teach a child grammar in the privacy of one's home. Children receive exposure to computers in preschool and elementary school and are often computer literate by the time they reach junior high school. The craving for increased sophistication in home toys and educational items is on the rise.

While advancements in technology have positive results, leisure service providers must also consider marginal impacts. These include more "couch potatoes" who sit in front of the television for hours, an increase in sedentary leisure activities, and a potential rise in thrill-seeking leisure. This section considers the increase in use of and access to home-based computers and electronics, improvements in leisure equipment, and improved safety in leisure experiences. It includes the following:

Lifestyle Coaching   There is a growing trend focused on lifestyle coaching. Much of the literature and information available is found in the popular press. An example of this is Martin Kimeldorf's work, *Serious Play: A Leisure Wellness Workbook* (1994). From a historical perspective, Chet McDowell's books, *Leisure Counseling: Selected Lifestyle Processes* (1976) and *Leisure Wellness: Concepts on Helping Strategies* (1983), provide a foundational basis for this type of work.

Home Electronics   Home electronic entertainment will become less costly and easier to use for the general population (Kelly and Godbey, 1992). The ease with which telecommunications enters the family home will impact leisure and leisure concepts. Many people will opt for the comfort of home-based versions of sporting events and computer simulations. Interactive television and movies will become standard in U.S. households. More passive leisure may result in increased needs to experience other sensory activities more fully or to achieve a balance between passive and physically active pursuits.

Improved High-Tech Leisure Equipment   An increase in technology has always had a corresponding increase in new and improved leisure equipment. This trend will continue and these changes will revolutionize the leisure industry. Jet-skis, fiberglass-bottom boats, in-line skates, high-definition television sets, and computer activities all provide new, high-tech, faster, more exciting forms of leisure activity.

New Roles for Commercial Enterprises   Stores have become skill teachers and leisure providers, as well as vendors of leisure equipment and toys. Oshmans Sporting Goods Company has several "super stores" in the west and southwest. Consumers entering the store not only receive assistance from store clerks but can try out a variety of equipment on true-to-size courts. Customers can try on a pair of basketball shoes and then play a pickup game of three-on-three on the in-store basketball court; potential racquetball or tennis players test new racquets in one of the in-store tennis or racquetball courts; a bow hunter can experiment with a new bow or hunting accessories in the target range; and those who want to purchase skis can try them out on the indoor ski slope. Shopping has become a leisure experience in and of itself.

Improved Safety   Increased technology also impacts safety and early skill development in some leisure activities. Alpine skiing, tennis, and golf can now be learned from the safety of an indoor facility with one-on-one instruction, indoor comfort, and cushioned slopes and courts. New materials receive constant experimentation in relation to favorite leisure pastimes. Fiberglass boats, tent poles that are impossible to break, the plastic composites used in lightweight bicycle helmets, and safety ropes and nets devised for safe gymnastics all serve as examples of the benefits of technology on the safety of leisure activities.

Simulated Outdoor Natural Phenomena With new inroads in commercial reproduction of activities usually found only in nature, some service providers can make them available in any desired location. Wave-tech swimming pools and life-size functional indoor and outdoor ski slopes with snow can now operate in areas and climates that were once incompatible with these activities. These commercially available leisure activities can bring opportunities for instruction and enjoyment to those who could not otherwise participate in them.

Virtual Reality: A New Medium for Leisure Virtual reality is a technological form that is interactive, visual, auditory, and kinetic. How would an individual like to meet with Susan B. Anthony and have her respond to questions? Or practice baseball pitching, watch the effort on the computer screen, and receive immediate feedback on style and accuracy? Virtual reality has great implications for leisure, entertainment, self-development, and education. In the future, youth centers may have virtual reality stations rather than video games.

On-Line with Networks An increasingly popular form of leisure activity involves participation in the expanding array of computer network services. Hobby clubs, special-interest groups, investment groups, correspondence between friends, and other types of network opportunities are available to individuals who have a modem, a computer, and who subscribe to one of the network systems. As more individuals purchase computers for personal use, this type of leisure activity will increase. Fiber optics allows for easy and convenient in-home setup.

Organizational Impacts of Technology New strategies and concepts for managing Technological/Information Era organizations are emerging. As we move from the Agricultural Era through the Industrial Era to the Technological/Learning Era, it is necessary to rethink the way that organizations and employees operate, basing systems on new assumptions and rapidly changing technology. A number of new concepts have emerged that relate specifically to the Technological/Learning Era of management.

Just as scientific management theory was formulated to systematize and offer structure to industrial technology, the "learning organization" concept has evolved to provide a foundation for organizations operating within the Technological/Information Era. "Forget your old, tired ideas about leadership. The most successful corporation of the future will be something called a learning organization" (*Fortune Magazine*). Within the Technological/Information Era, it is necessary to put into place organizational systems that facilitate a state of accelerated, independent, and collective learning on the part of individuals within the organization, that is, teaching individuals how to teach themselves.

Information from the sciences—*chaos theory, complexity theory,* and others—is increasingly being applied to management of individuals and complex organizations. A major theme of chaotic and complex systems is that components that may not look related may interact and influence each other (Gleick, 1987). It encourages managers to seek out and incorporate the complexity that exists in organizations. Chaos theory suggests that there are patterns of order that exist beneath the surface of chaos. Seeking the order that is found in these underlying structures and methods of interaction can assist in drawing energy from within any organization.

Transportation

Transportation has a tremendous impact on leisure and related factors; it offers access to leisure opportunities and serves as a leisure experience in itself. Transportation involves water-based transport (boats, jet-skis), ground-based transport (cars, buses, trains, bicycles), and airborne transportation (airplanes, gliders). New technologies will continue to transform transportation

(Naisbitt Trends Newsletter, April 30, 1992). In fact, in 1996 the Lockheed Corporation received a multibillion dollar government contract to develop a new space shuttle that will have the capacity to take tourists into space for a few orbits around the earth. The first space tourist travelled to the International Space Station in a Russian spacecraft in 2001. He paid millions of dollars for the adventure. Some transportation issues include the following.

Mass Transportation as a Future Necessity Mass transportation will become more affordable, convenient, and fast. More citizens will use mass transit as gasoline prices increase, commuting times get longer, and mass transportation becomes safer and more accessible. High-speed trains will enhance distant travel, and travel to major attractions will increase.

Transportation-Centered Destination Points Major transportation hubs (e.g., airports, bus terminals) will become leisure service centers in themselves. Entrepreneurs have designed unique destination points located at transportation hubs. Many larger airports already sport tanning booths, relaxation centers, and athletic courts (racquetball), as well as work stations complete with fax and Internet access. Shopping will continue as a high-tech leisure service activity for travelers. New and improved access to large shopping centers, discount shopping malls, and mall-amusement centers will occur.

The Mall of America (Minneapolis, Minnesota) and the West Edmonton Mall (Edmonton, Alberta) have become a new type of destination point, designed to be a vacation experience (complete with theme park) as well as a shopping destination. Amusement parks, leisure sports facilities, dining establishments, and other tourist activities have seen tremendous commercial success. The Mall of America, located near the Minneapolis airport, depends on this vehicle of transportation to provide a steady stream of shoppers and tourists.

Economic Trends

Economic changes will continue to influence the leisure habits of the general populace. Slow growth will continue, and it will be some time before the country will see the affluence of the 1990s again. People feel insecure about their jobs and may continue to have less trust in government; saving money may become increasingly difficult with greater government involvement in state finances; and people will spend cautiously. While leisure spending has varied little over the years, the demand for quality services and products, and people getting "their money's worth" has increased.

The economy tends to be cyclical. As we enter the twenty-first century the economy seems to be sliding backwards after the robust years of the 1990s. Due to the fact that the economy has shifted from a product-oriented economy to an information economy, changes in spending habits, consumer decision making, and other variables impacting on leisure practices may change quite rapidly. The half-life of knowledge and information continues to shorten, and leisure service providers must respond rapidly. The move from an industrialized to an information-based economy has resulted in a shift from valuing products to valuing ideas.

Changing Nature of Work

The nature of work has changed over the years; it will continue to evolve. Society has moved from being product-driven to information-based. People continue to work both out of necessity and in the search for self-identity. In the move toward an improved quality of life, people will find identity outside of work. Women in the workforce and jobs for teens will grow in importance.

Flexible work schedules, working during commuting hours, satellite offices, contingent workforce, telecommuting, and compressed workweeks will become more prevalent. "More than 93 percent of America's largest corporations offer a flexible workplace to accommodate workers for whom a daily 9-to-5 on-site work schedule causes difficulty" (Lynch, 1992, p. 58). People will continue to change jobs several times throughout their careers, entering and leaving the workforce as personal needs dictate. The work ethic will remain strong, yet will mesh with other aspects of people's lives. Time off for self and family will become increasingly important.

Flex Time Flex time provides an individual with blocks of time for work and leisure outside of a conventional 8:00 A.M. to 5:00 P.M. workday. Although flex time could mean going to work at 7:00 A.M. and leaving at 4:00 P.M., some workers have complete discretion to organize their work in blocks of time that meet personal as well as work goals. In many creative situations, work is accomplished around personal bursts of inspiration, insight, and effort. These highly personal bursts capture an individual's focus at peak times of energy and intellectual vigor. For example, higher education offers opportunities for flex time; professors can structure their schedules around class times, personal needs, and meetings. Any one of these activities might occur in the morning, afternoon, or evening.

Flex Place The physical location for people's work and play may become irrelevant in the future. People will work at home, in the car, on the train, in the air, or at a local coffee shop with multiple activities occurring at once. For instance, people now grocery shop, work, walk down the street, or drive cars while talking on a cellular phone. Laptop computers, fax machines, public access to the Internet, and other equipment enable work to occur in various locations. Many businesses such as coffee shops, hotels, and athletic clubs offer access to technology that will enable flex place activity.

Flex Schedule Rearranging the work schedule can facilitate larger or different blocks of time for work or leisure. A common form of this is the four-day workweek where people work ten hours a day and have three-day weekends. Such forms of organizing work time have not diminished worker productivity, and, in fact, have led to gains in employee morale and work functions. Selected occupations, such as airline pilots, flight attendants, fire fighters, oil riggers, and emergency-crew personnel, work a certain number of days on the job and have a similar number of days off. For example, an oil rigger might work twenty-eight days on the job away from home at an isolated off-shore oil platform and then have twenty-eight days to spend at home or on another job. Individuals in this type of situation often seek additional employment or serious leisure opportunities to fill those days.

Job Sharing Currently occurring in some work settings, job sharing will become an increasingly important vehicle to accomplish work tasks while accommodating the needs of individuals. Job sharing consists of two related people sharing one job (at home or at a separate worksite), or two unrelated people who work in environments that are conveniently organized to meet their current focuses in life. One worker might work mornings, another afternoons; one might work the first two days of the week, the other the next three. Job sharing greatly benefits a participating organization. Two different sets of skills and expertise become a part of the organization, employees tend to be highly committed, and benefits may be divided among the workers in a variety of configurations.

The portability of technology and the rise of telecommunications dramatically support flex time, flex place, flex scheduling, and job sharing. People from across the globe will continue to work together on tasks in two different time zones. For example, a person can interact, day or night, via computer, fax machine, telephone, and satellite dish. These forms of communication allow for instantaneous access to others; their computers or fax machines can receive and store the data or information until such time as they are ready to receive such communications.

Continued Growth of the Service Sector of Employment

The service sector of employment will experience continued growth. As the United States moved from agricultural and industrial societies to the information age, corresponding increases in jobs in the service area have resulted. As most leisure service organizations fall within the service category, projections anticipate growth in the number of future jobs, particularly in the commercial sector. As we look forward, many growth opportunities for employment in leisure services exist, especially dealing with child care, food service, lodging, and amusement and recreation (U.S. Bureau of the Census, 1999). These categories are projected as ones with the greatest number and/or percentage of change among occupations as we compare employment between 1996 and 2006.

Summary

Many changes face the leisure service profession in the next few decades. It has been said, "There are two rules about change: change is inevitable, and people hate change." To be responsive, to remain on the cutting edge and in the forefront of the leisure service profession, one must both accept and embrace change. These changes suggest several policy issues:

- Leisure opportunities will continue to evolve and be redefined by society (e.g. tax cuts and terroism)
- Family-based leisure services will be eclectic.
- People in their forties, fifties, and sixties will demand active leisure services.
- Cultural diversity and sensitivity will become hallmarks of quality leisure service programs.
- Accessibility for all people, and the delivery of services to all people, will continue to challenge the field.
- Parks, recreation, and leisure service programs will be in high demand due to the increased need for nonschool programs and the problem of unattended hours among youth.
- The ADA will alter access to facilities and programs and the way leisure services providers think about the delivery of services.
- The general population will demand a change in service provision, both in hours of operation and increased diversity in program offerings.
- The provision of services will meet an increased need for nonviolence education and an increased concern in dealing with violence.
- Service providers must address AIDS education and increased concern about issues related to AIDS.
- Environmental awareness will become integrated into all levels of leisure services organizations: administration, maintenance, program delivery, staffing, and facilities.
- The shifting work hours of users will require flexible programming hours.
- The increased interest in time off to spend with family will alter traditional ways of viewing family leisure.

Discussion Questions

1. How has 9/11 affected future trends in leisure services? Beyond what the authors have suggested, can you think of additional future trends in leisure services due to 9/11?
2. Do you think federal tax cuts will have a positive or negative aspect on the future of leisure services?
3. How might No Child Left Behind affect leisure services in the future?
4. How might the transformation of the family affect leisure services in the future?
5. How did you use out-of-school time when you were a child and adolescent?
6. Think of your future profession in leisure services, and predict some potential recreational user conflict scenarios and strategies you might use to reduce recreational conflict?
7. How might future leisure services address global warming?
8. Use the simply formula presented in figure 16.7 to estimate the cost of using a car. Did the estimated cost surprise you?
9. Identify five key population trends and their potential impact on leisure.
10. What do you think will be the role of leisure and leisure professionals in future society?

References

Aburdene, P., and J. Naisbitt. 1992. *Megatrends for Women.* New York: Random House.

Bureau of Justice Statistics. 1989. Edited by George W. Wilkinson, in *What Lies Ahead.* Alexandria, VA: United Way Strategic Planning Institute.

Caneday, L. 1991. Parks, recreation, and the environment: Allies or adversaries. *Parks and Recreation* (September), 88–93+.

Davidson, J. W. 1993. Overworked Americans or overwhelmed Americans. *Public Management* (May), 8.

DeGraaf, K., and D. DeGraaf. 1993. Environmentally hot or not. *Camping Magazine* (May–June), 24–27, 30.

Dryfoos, J. 1990. *Adolescents at Risk: Prevalence and Prevention.* New York: Oxford University Press.

Gleick, J. 1987. *Chaos making a new science.* New York: Penguin Books.

Godbey, G. 1989. *The Future of Leisure Services: Thriving on Change.* State College, PA: Venture.

Goodale, T. L., and P. A. Witt. 1985. *Recreation and Leisure Issues in an Era of Change.* State College, PA: Venture.

Henderson, K. A., M. D. Bialeschki, S. M. Shaw, and V. J. Freysinger. 1996. *Both Gains and Gaps: Feminist Perspectives on Women's Leisure.* State College, PA: Venture.

Jennings, L. 1989. Fordham Institute's index documents steep decline in children's and youth's social health since 1970. *Education Week 9*(9), 7.

Junin, S. 2000. Downshifting: Regaining the essence of leisure. *Journal of Leisure and Research 32*(1), 69–73.

Kelly, J., and G. Godbey. 1992. *The Sociology of Leisure.* State College, PA: Venture.

Kimeldorf, M. 1994. *Serious Play: A Leisure Wellness Workbook.* Berkeley, CA: Ten Speed Press.

Kraus, R. 2001. *Leisure in a Changing America.* (2nd ed.) New York: Macmillan.

The Leisure Development Center. 1991. *Leisure and Recreational Activities in Japan,* 7.

Lynch, A.F., ed. 1992. *What Lies Ahead: A Decade of Decision.* Alexandria, VA: United Way Strategic Institute.

McDowell, C. F. 1976. *Leisure Counseling: Selected Lifestyle Processes.* Eugene, OR: Center for Leisure Studies.

McDowell, C. F. 1983. *Leisure Wellness: Concepts on Helping Strategies.* Eugene, OR: Sun Moon Press.

Naisbitt Trends Newsletter. 1992. *11*(9): (April 30).

Nieto, S. 1992. *Affirming Diversity: The Sociopolitical Context of Multicultural Education.* New York: Longman.

Robinson, J. P. 1989. Time's up. *American Demographics* (July), 33.

Robinson, J. P. 1991. Your money or your time. *American Demographics* (November), 23.

Robinson, J. P., and G. Godbey. 1997. *Time for Life: The Surprising Ways Americans Use Their Time.* University Park, PA: The Pennsylvania State University Press.

Sax, J. 1980. *Mountains without Handrails, Reflections on the National Parks.* Ann Arbor, MI: University of Michigan Press.

Schor, J. B. 1993, February. *Overworked Americans: The Unexpected Decline of Leisure.* New York Basic Books.

Seefeldt, V. 1996. F. Smoll and R. Smith, eds. The future of youth sports in America. *Children and Youth in Sport: A Biopsychosocial Perspective.* Dubuque, IA: Brown & Benchmark.

Surgeon General. 1996. *Physical Activity and Health.*

Time/CNN, 1999. As appeared in *What Lies Ahead: A Decade of Decision,* from the United Way of America, 1992, United Way Strategic Institute, Alexandria, VA.

University of Maryland. 1989. Edited by George Wilkinson, in *What Lies Ahead.* Alexandria, VA: United Way Strategic Institute.

U.S. Bureau of the Census. 1999. *Statistical Abstract of the United States: 1999.* 119th ed. Washington, DC: U.S. Government Printing Office.

Wilkinson, G.W., ed. 1989. *What Lies Ahead.* Alexandria, VA: United Way Strategic Planning Institute.

World Resources Institute. 1993. *Environmental Almanac.* Boston: Houghton Mifflin.

World Resources Institute. 2000. *World Resources: A Guide to the Global Environment, 1998–99.* London: Oxford University Press.

World Resources Institute. 2001, February 21. *New Report on Global Health Warns Environmental Degradation is Contributing to Preventable Health Threats Worldwide.* www.wri.org/wri/press/wr98nr01.htm.

Yzaguirre, R. 1998. The new American identity. Edited by F. Hesselbein, M. Goldsmith, R. Beckhard, and R. Schubert, in *The Community of the Future.* San Francisco: Jossey-Bass.

Zeiger, J., and L. Caneday. 1991. Aldo Leopold's plea: A study of preservation. *Parks and Recreation* (September), 80–82.

REFERENCES

REFERENCES

Alvord, K. 2000. *Divorce your car: Ending the love affair with the automobile.* Gabriola Island, BC: New Society Publishers.

AVERT. 2004. *AIDS around the world.* Retrieved from www.AVERT.org.

Bell, M. M. 2004. *An invitation to environmental sociology.* 2nd ed. Thousand Oaks, CA: Pine Forge Press.

Board of the National Society for Park Resources. 2004. Sustenance for the American spirit: The role of parks and recreation in uncertain times. *Parks and Recreation 38*(4), 8.

Bornstein, D. 2004. *How to change the world: Social entrepreneurs and the power of new ideas.* New York: Oxford University Press.

Centers for Disease Control. 2004. *Youth risk behavior surveillance—United States, 2003.* Retrieved from www.cdc.gov/mmwr/pdf/ss/ss5302.pdf.

Chase, M., and Shannahan, R. 2003. Tax woes wipe out parks department: Lessons from the demise of the Cheney, Washington Park and Recreation Department. *Parks and Recreation 38*(12), 48–53.

Crompton, J. L. 1999. *Financing and acquiring park and recreation resources.* Champaign, IL: Human Kinetics.

Csikszentmihalyi, M. 1996. *Creativity: Flow and the psychology of discovery and invention.* New York: Harper Collins.

Dolesh, R. J. 2004. LWCF grants: Going, going . . . gone? A perfect storm of problems could result in decreasing funding. *Parks and Recreation 40*(1), 8–9.

Dolesh, R. J. 2005. Lessons from the 2004 state and local elections: Election results show both positive and negative trends for parks and recreation nationwide. *Parks and Recreation 39*(5), 16–17.

Docheff, D. M., and Conn, J. H. 2004. It's no longer a spectator sport. *Parks and Recreation 39*(2), 62–70.

Driver, B. L. 2002. Reality testing. *Journal of Leisure Research 34*(1), 79–88.

Driver, B. L., and Bruns, D. H. 1999. Concepts and uses of the benefits approach to leisure. In E. L. Jackson and T. L. Burton, eds., *Leisure studies: Prospects for the twenty-first century* (pp. 349–369). State College, PA: Venture.

Duffett, A., and Johnson, J. 2004. *All work and no play? Listening to what kids and parents really want from out-of-school time.* New York: Public Agenda.

Dustin, D. D. 2003. Ban snowmobiles in Yellowstone National Park: Why it's the right thing to do. *Parks and Recreation 38*(6), 444–471.

Dustin, D. L., Schneider, I. E., McAvoy, L. H., and Frakt, A. N. 2002. Cross-cultural claims on Devils Tower National Monument: A case study. *Leisure Science 24*(1), 79–88.

Edginton, C. R., Hudson, S. R., Dieser, R. B., and Edginton, S. R. 2004. *Leisure programming: A service-centered and benefits approach.* 4th ed. Boston: WCB McGraw-Hill.

Edginton, C. R., Kowalski, C. L., and Randall, S. W. 2005. *Youth work: Emerging perspectives in youth development.* Champaign, IL: Sagamore.

Ellis, G. D., Henderson, H. L., Paisley, K., Silverberg, K. E., and Wells, M. S. 2004. Bringing sportsmanship back to your youth sports leagues. *Parks and Recreation 39*(6), 46–51.

Ewert, A. W., Dieser, R. B., and Voight, A. 1999. Conflict and the Recreational Experience. In E. L. Jackson and T. L. Burton, eds., *Leisure studies: Prospects for the twenty-first century* (pp. 335–345). State College, PA: Venture.

Florida, R. 2002. *The rise of the creative class and how it's transforming work, leisure, community and everyday life.* New York: Basic Books.

Freysinger, V. J. 2000. Acting Our Age: The Relationship Between Age and Leisure. In M. T. Allison, and I.E. Schneider, eds., *Diversity and the Recreation Profession: Organizational Perspectives* (pp. 139–156) State College, PA: Venture.

Freysinger, V. J., and Kelly, J. R. 2004. *21st century leisure: Current issues.* 2nd ed. State College, PA: Venture.

Godbey, G. 1997. *Leisure and leisure services in the 21st century.* State college, PA: Venture.

Gore, A., and Gore, T. 2002. *Joined at the heart: The transformation of the American family.* New York: Henry Holt and Company.

Hines, C. H. 2002. Elderly Americans. *Population Bulletin 56*(4), 1–41.

Hamilton, E. S. 2002. One year later. *Parks and Recreation 37*(7), 44–50.

Henry J. Kaiser Family Foundation. 2004, December. *HIV/AIDS Policy fact sheet.* Retrieved from www.kff.org/hivaids/3029-04.cfm.

Janssen, M. 2004. The effects of leisure education on quality of life in older adults. *Therapeutic Recreation Journal 38*(3), 275–288.

Junior Achievement. 2004. *Nearly one-in-five kids want more variety in After-School programs, according to a new poll.* Colorado Springs, CO: Author. Retrieved from www.ja.org/about/about-newsitem.asp?StoryID=2224.

Kraus, R. G., and Curtis, J. E. 2000. *Creative management in recreation, parks, and leisure services.* 6th ed. Boston: McGraw-Hill.

Mannell, R. C., and Kleiber, D. A. 1997. *A social psychology of leisure.* State College, PA: Venture.

More, T. A. 2002a. The parks and being loved to death and other frauds and deceits in recreation management. *Journal of Leisure Research 34*(1), 52–78.

More, T. A. 2002b. A marginal user as the justification for public recreation: A rejoinder to Crompton, Driver, and Dustin. *Journal of Leisure Research 34*(1), 103–118.

More, T. A., and Kuentzel, W. 1999. Five reasons to have reservations about benefits-based management. In G. Kyle, ed., *Proceedings of the 1999 Northeastern Recreation Research Symposium* (pp. 295–302). Gen. Tech. Rep. NE-269. Newtown Square, PA: U.S. Department of Agriculture, Forest Service, Northeastern Research Station.

National Institute on Out-of-School Time. 2005. *Making the case: A fact sheet on children and youth in out-of-school time.* Retrieved from www.niost.org.

National Recreation and Park Association Division of Public Policy. 2003. Call to action: Bush cuts key spending. *Parks and Recreation 38*(3), 10.

National Recreation and Park Association Division of Public Policy. 2005, February. NRPA's Legislative update: President's FY 2006 Proposed Budget. *Dateline online.* Retrieved from www.public policy@nrpa.org.

Northeast DuPage Special Recreation Association. 2004. *2003-2004 Annual Report.* Addison, IL: Author.

Noddings, N. 2003. *Happiness and education.* New York: Cambridge University Press.

Panza, J. A., and Cipriano, R. E. 2004. People's perception of parks and recreation. *Parks and Recreation 39*(12), 22–27.

Putnam, R. D., Feldstein, L. M., and Cohen, D. 2003. *Better together: Restoring the American community.* New York: Simon & Schuster.

Richards, M., Hardy, R., and Wadsworth, M. E. 2003. Does active leisure participation protect cognition? Evidence from a national birth cohort. *Social Science and Medicine 56,* 785–792.

Ruskin, H. 1995. Conceptual approaches in policy development in leisure education. In H. Ruskin and A. Sivan, eds., *Leisure education: Toward the 21st century* (pp. 137–156). Provo, UT: Brigham Young University Press.

Schlatter, B. 2004. A tale of two city parks: How public-private partnerships have helped revive two Olmstead-designed parks. *Parks and Recreation 39*(1), 36–41.

Schneider, I. E. 2004. Less stress: How you can respond to and manage visitor conflict. *Parks and Recreation 39*(2), 68–73.

Schor, J. B. 1998. *The overspent American: Why we want what we don't need.* New York: Harper Collins.

U.S. Bureau of the Census. 2003. *Statistical Abstract of the United States: 2003.* 123rd ed. Washington, D.C.: U.S. Government Printing Office

U.S. Department of Education. 2005a. FY 2006 budget summary. Retrieved from http://preview.ed.gov/about/overview/budget/budget06/summary/edlite-section3.html

U.S. Department of Education. 2005b. No Child Left Behind. Retrieved from www.ed.gov/nclb.

United States Surgeon General. 2001. *The Surgeon General's call to action to prevent and decrease overweight and obesity.* Rockville, MD: Office of the Surgeon General, U.S. Department of Health and Human Services.

Verghese, J., Lipton, R. B., Katz, M. J., Hall, C. B., Derby, C. A., and Kuslansky, G. 2003. Leisure activities and the risk of dementia in the elderly. *The New England Journal of Medicine 348*(25), 2508–2516.

Wechsler, H., McKenna, M. L., Lee, S. M., and Dietz, W. H. 2004. The role of schools in preventing childhood obesity. *The State Education Standard: The Journal of the National Association of State Boards of Education 5*(2), 4–12.

Williams, R., Dustin, D., and McKenney, A. 2004. Leisure still has significance, even in this troubled world. *Parks and Recreation 39*(5), 12–14.

World Tourism Organizaiton. 2002. *A year after 9–11: Climbing toward recovery.* Madrid, Spain: Author.

Witt, P., and Crompton, J. 2002. Programming for the future: Parks, recreation and youth development. *Parks and Recreation 37*(12), 64–68.

CREDITS

CREDITS

Text and Line Art

Chapter 1

Excerpt, pp. 10–11: Seven Elements of Enjoyment from *Flow: The Psychology of Optimal Experience,* by Mihaly Csikszentmihalyi. Reprinted by permission of HarperCollins Publishers, Inc.

Chapter 3

Figures 3.12 and 3.13: Reprinted by permission of The Civilian Conservation Corps in Iowa, Iowa Department of Natural Resources, Dundee, Iowa.

Chapter 4

Leisure Line, p. 117: Excerpt as submitted from *Finding Joy: 101 Ways to Free Your Spirit and Dance with Life* by Charlotte Davis Kasl. Copyright © 1995 by Charlotte Davis Kasl. Reprinted by permission of HarperCollins Publishers, Inc.

Leisure Line, p. 121: From the *Kitchener-Waterloo Record,* June 19, 1976. Reprinted by permission.

Figure 4.7: From Willamalane Park and Recreation District, Springfield, OR. Reprinted by permission.

Chapter 6

Leisure Line, p. 174: From "Americans' Active Lifestyles Often an Illusion." April 8, 1996, as appeared in *Des Moines Register.* Copyright © 1996 by Associated Press. Reprinted by permission.

Chapter 6 (continued)

Figures 6.1 and 6.2: From Seppo E. Iso-Ahola, *The Social Psychology of Leisure and Recreation.* Copyright © 1980 McGraw-Hill Companies: Dubuque, Iowa. All Rights Reserved. Reprinted by permission.

Figure 6.4 text and excerpt, pp. 188–189: *From A Portrait of Young Adolescents in the 1990s: Implications for Promoting Healthy Growth and Development,* by Peter C. Scales, 1991. Center for Early Adolescence, University of North Carolina at Chapel Hill, Carrboro, NC.

Leisure Line, p. 200: From Paula Kephart, "Retiring Where the Mariachis Play" in *American Demographics,* 1994. Reprinted by permission of American Demographics, Inc., Ithaca, NY.

Chapter 7

Figure 7.5: City of San Diego Parks and Recreation Department, San Diego, CA. Reprinted by permission.

Figure 7.6: Reprinted by permission of Lane County Parks Division, Eugene, OR.

Figure 7.7: From Willamalane Park and Recreation District, Springfield, OR. Reprinted by permission.

Figure 7.8: Printed by permission of the National Program for Playground Safety, University of Northern Iowa, Cedar Falls, IA.

Chapter 10

Leisure Line, pp. 309–310: From *A Portrait of Young Adolescents in the 1990s: Implications for Promoting Healthy Growth and Development,* by Peter C. Scales, 1991. Center for Early Adolescence, University of North Carolina at Chapel Hill, Carrboro, NC.

Figure 10.2: From Black Hawk County YMCA, Waterloo, IA. Reprinted by permission.

Chapter 11

Figure 11.5: Used with permission of Play Station, Cedar Rapids, IA.

Chapter 13

Figures 13.1 and 13.2: © C. Edginton and S. Edginton, 1993.

Leisure Line, p. 418: Excerpted from "A Matter of Time: Risk and Opportunity in the Nonschool Hours," a report of the Carnegie Council on Adolescent Development. Copyright © December 1992 by Carnegie Corporation of New York.

Chapter 15

Leisure Lines, p. 453: From John Naisbitt and Patricia Aburdene, *Megatrends 2000.* Copyright © 1990 by Megatrends Ltd. By permission of Wm. Morrow & Company, Inc.

Figure 15.4: From Campus News Network (Newsletter), Office of Public Relations, University of Northern Iowa. Reprinted by permission.

Chapter 16

Leisure Line, p. 509: From John Naisbitt and Patricia Aburdene, *Megatrends 2000.* Copyright © 1990 by Megatrends Ltd. By permission of Wm. Morrow & Company, Inc.

AUTHOR INDEX

Thomsen, S. R., 184, 459
Tilove, J., 105–106
Tinsley, H., 24
Toalson, R., 218, 220–221
Toffler, Alvin, 71
Toman, P., 290
Trager, S., *181*, 183
Troiano, R., 185
Turner, V., 53
Turpin, T., 198

Unger, J., 191–192
Unger, L. S., 36–37
United States Citizenship And Immigration
 Service, 70
Uppal, S., 185

Van Andel, G., 379
Van Andel, G. E., 371, *372,* 373, 376,
 377, 381
Van Den Haag, E., 149
Vanderhoof, Mark, 95
Veblen, T. B., 49, 84

Verghese, 498
Vickers, P., 459
Voelkl, J., 29–30, 122
Voight, 502–503

Wadsworth, 498
Waelder, R., 60
Walters, W., 237
Watterson, Bill, 120
Wearing, B., 44, 52–53, 459
Wechsler, H., 180–181, 499
Weinmayer, V., 92–93
Weisse, C. S., 9
Weissinger, E., 27, 236
Wells, 503
Welton, G., 36, 53, 54, 82–83
Westendorf, B., 325
Westfall, R., 239, 266–267
Wheeler, 450
Wilensky, H., 44
Wilkinson, G. W., 498, 499, 507
Williams, A., 87, 88, 479
Wilson, J., 471
Wilson, M., 104

Wilson, W., 8
Wise, J., 41
Witt, P., 29, 61, 238, 482
Wolf, T., 305–306, 307, 339
Woodard, R., 14
World Tourism Organization, 164
Wright, M., 191

Xin, K., 458

Yi, Y. K., 12
Yoder, D., 51
Yzaguirre, R., 497

Zabel, D., 351
Zautra, A., 11
Zeiger, J., 504
Zeithaml, V., 397, 401
Zemke, R., 402, 405
Zigler, E., 128–129

SUBJECT INDEX

SUBJECT INDEX

B

Baden-Powell, Robert, 102
Balboa Park, 220
Barriers, 28, 29–30
Baucus, Max, 308
Bed-and-breakfast inns, 353
Beecher, Henry Ward, 239
Benefits, 239–240
Benefits-based management (BBM),
    208–209, 388
Benefit structure, of nonprofit organizations,
    308, 310
Big Brothers/Big Sisters of America, 311,
    312, 329–330
Black Hawk County (Iowa) Conservation
    Board, 230, *231*
Blakely, Marion, 399
Board of directors, 320
Boards, for leisure Services, 218
Body of knowledge, for leisure Services,
    425
Boredom, 47
Boston Sand Gardens, 70
Boyce, William D., 102–103
Boys Club of America, 102, 104, 112,
    184–185, 328–329
Boys Scouts of America, 102–103, 104,
    184–185, 324
Brain Reserve, 438
Braverman, Barry, 355
Broadcasted performances, 357
Bryant, William Cullen, 90
Bureau of Biological Survey, 287
Bureau of Commercial Fisheries, 287
Bureau of Fisheries, 286
Bureau of Indian Affairs, 277, 288–289
Bureau of Land Management (BLM), 271,
    277, 283–284, 469–470
Bureau of Outdoor Recreation, 107, 272
Bureau of Reclamation, 279, 292–293
Bureau of Sports Fisheries and
    Wildlife, 287
Busch Gardens Tampa Bay, 352, 357
Bush, George H. W., 274
Bush, George W., 479, 480, 481, 485, 494
Business ownership, types of, 346–348

C

California Park and Recreation Society
    (CPRS), 437
Calvin, John, 78
Camp Adventure™ Youth Services, 409
Campbell, Anne, 358
Camp Fires USA, 103, 104, 131, 316,
    326–327
Camping, 257

Canadian Outdoor Recreation Demands
    Study (CORDS), 108
Career development
    assessment and exploration, 439–441
    certifications, 443–445
    continuing education and professional
        development, 445
    education, 441
    ethics and, 426–427, *428*
    internships, 442, *443*
    introduction, 424
    networking, 442–443
    organizations and institutions for
        transmitting professional
        knowledge, 425–426
    organized body of knowledge, 425
    professional associations, 428–439
    professional experience, 441–442
    professional ideals, 427–428
    professional portfolios, 445–447
    public sanction, 426
    timeline, 444
Career opportunities, in public parks and
    recreation, 233–236
Carnival Cruise Line, 358, 364
Carnivals, 357
Carter, Jimmy, 108
Casino resorts, 353
Casual leisure, *45*, 50–51
Catharsis theory, 60
Catholic Youth Organization, 332
Catlin, George, 94
Cato the elder, 75
Center for the Study of Rural America, 256
Certifications, for professionals, 213,
    443–445
Certified commercial recreation
    professionals (CCRPs), 426
Certified Festival and Event Certificate, 434
Certified park and recreation professionals
    (CPRPs), 426
Certified pool operations (CPO), 426
Certified Recreational Sports Specialists
    (CRSS), 426, 434
Certified Therapeutic Recreation Specialists
    (CTRSs), 213, 375, 383, 426
Challenges, 10, 27, 47
Chaos theory, 511
Character formation, 21
Charges, 236, 246
Charles Bank Outdoor Gymnasium, 99
Cheney Parks and Recreation
    Department, 482
Chicago South Park District, 101
Chicago Sport and Social Club, 238
Chief executive officers/managers, 320
Child care, 237

Childhood, 178–186
Children, grandchild's play, 7
Christianity, 77–78
Church of Jesus Christ of the Latter Day
    Saints, 332
Circuses, 357
Circus maximus, 76–77
Citizen Board Member (CBM), 436
Citizenship, 117
Citizenship competencies, 192
City of Peoria Playground and Recreation
    Department, 225
City of San Diego (California) Park and
    Recreation Department,
    218–220
Civilian Conservation Corps (CCC), 88, 89,
    96–97, 253
Classic leisure, *45*, 53–54
Classism, 461
Cleanliness, 405
Clear Channel Communications, 364
Clients, clarifying relationships with, 124
Climbing walls, 228
Clinton, William (Bill), 494
Clubs, 417
Code of ethics, 427, *428*
Cognitive competence, 192
Collaborations, 318–319
Colonial America, 80–82
Comcast, 364
Commercial enterprises, 510
Commercial leisure services, 109
    characteristics of, 342–343
    corporations, 347–348
    entertainment services, 356–359
    entrepreneurial challenges, 366–367
    entrepreneurship, opportunities, and
        challenges, 362–363
    goals and functions of, 343
    hospitality and food services, 351–353
    introduction, 342
    leisure products (manufacturing),
        353–356
    in the natural environment, 360–362
    opportunities in, 363–366
    orientation to customers, 344–345
    partnerships, 347
    professional characteristics of, 344
    resource base, 343–344
    retail outlets, 359–360
    sole proprietorship, 346
    travel and tourism, 350–351
    types of, 348–350
    types of business ownership, 346–348
Commission on Americans Outdoors, 108
Commitment, 27
Committee for Smoke-Free Parks, 213

Empathy, 397
Employee assistance programs (EAP), 499
Employees, key behaviors of, 406–408
Employee Services Management
        Association (ESMA), 434
Enabling laws, 217
Enabling legislation, 244–245
Endangered Species Act, 287
Endowments, 246
Enjoyment, elements of, 10–11
Entertainment services, 356–359
Enthusiasm, 104
Enthusiasts, 173
Entrepreneurship, 362–363
Environment
        future concerns for, 501–505
        future degradation concerns, 504–505
        as mass leisure, 158–160
        mood and, 408
Environmental factors, program planning
        and, 413
Environmental mode, 48
Environmental services, 108
Epicureanism, 125
Equal Employment Opportunity (EEO)
        regulations, 465
Equity, 343
Essex County Park Commission, 221
Establishment, 176–177
Ethics
        leisure services profession and,
                426–427, *428*
        values and, 118–120
Ethnicity, diversity and, 458
Ethnic minorities, diversity and, 451
Evaluation, or programs, 417
Everson, Mark, 308
Existentialism, leisure and, 129–130
Expectations, exceeding, 406
Experimentalism, leisure and, 129
Expressive pleasures, 126
External barriers, 30
External/normative criteria, 9
Extracurricular programs, decreased support
        for, 508

F

Facilities, 410
        at local level, 228–229
        programs and, 239
Facility operators, 421
Fact finding, in professional
                associations, 431
Factory outlets, 359
Family First, 107
Features, 404
Federal Assistance Program, 287

Federal Aviation Administration, 399
Federal funds, 246
Federal government
        Bureau of Indian Affairs, 288–289
        Bureau of Land Management, 282–284
        Bureau of Reclamation, 292
        characteristics of federal leisure service
                agencies, 271
        characteristics of professionals, 275
        coordination with state and local
                governments, 245–246
        customer orientation, 275, *276*
        future challenges of, 298–299
        goals and functions of, 271–274
        introduction, 270
        National Endowment for the Arts,
                296–298
        National Endowment for the
                Humanities, 298
        National Park Service, 284–286
        resource base, 274–276
        tax cuts (Ownership society), 480–485
        Tennessee Valley Authority, 291–292
        types of agencies, 277
        U.S. Corps of Engineers, 289–291
        U.S. Fish and Wildlife Service, 287–288
        U.S. Forest Service, 278–281
        U.S. military's Morale, Welfare, and
                Recreation, 295–296
        Veterans Affairs, 293–295
Federal Job Information Center, 275
Federal Land Policy and Management Act
        (1976), 282
Federal Water Projects Recreation Act
        (1965), 292
Fees, 236, 246
Feminist theories, *45,* 52–53
Fern Ridge Reservoir, 290
Festivals, 357
Filmed performances, 357
Financial assistance, 209–210, 272
Fish and wildlife agencies, 256–258
Fishing, 257
Fitness centers, 228
Flea markets, 359
Flex time/place/schedule, 513
Florida Recreation and Park Association
        (FRPA), 437–438,
        442–443
Flow, 38
Flow experience, 61
Flow paradigm, 10
Flow theory, *45,* 46–48
FLYERS, 401
Food coaches, 107
Food services, 351–352
Forest Products Lab, 278
Forests, 255–256

Formative evaluations, 417
Fort Massac State Park, 251
Foundation grants, 316
Founders, 319–320
4-H, 104, 131, 323–324
Franklin, Benjamin, 37
Freedom, 25, 28–29, 37, 49–50
Freedom of choice, 117
Fresh Air movement, 104
Full-line discount stores, 359
Fun, 21
Fundraising, 316–318
Future orientation, 398
Future trends
        in diversity, 496–498
        the economy, 511–512
        education, 505–507
        the environment, 501–505
        extracurricular programs, 507
        federal tax cuts, 480–485
        in health, 498–501
        introduction, 478
        in leisure, 496
        No Child Left Behind, 485–486
        population shifts, 488–493
        post-September 11, 479–480
        social roles, 493–495
        social trends, 486–498
        technology, 508–511
        transportation, 511–512
        for women, 495–496
Futurist groups, 438

G

Gambling, 155
Games, 416
Gaming establishments, 356
Gannett, 364
Gay persons, diversity and, 451
Gender roles, shifts in, 494
Generalization theory, 61
Generational groupings, 6–7
Generations, program planning and,
        411–412
Geographically-based businesses, 362
Geographic location, diversity and, 461
Get R.E.A.L. (Recreation, Education,
                Activities, Leader) Program,
                238
Gifts, 313
Gila Box Riparian Natural Conservation
                Area, 283
Gila Wilderness Area, 280
Girl Guides, 103
Girls, Inc., 311, 327–328
Girls Club of America, 102, 104, 112,
                184–185, 328–329

Nature Conservancy, 338, 438
Needs
    anticipating, 406
    leisure and, 26–27
Needs assessment, for program
            planning, 415
Negativeness, elimination of, 400
Networking, 237, 442–443, 430
Neulinger's leisure paradigm, *45,* 46
New arts, 415
New York Times, 364
Niagara Falls, 94, 249–250
Nietzche, 129
Nightingale, Florence, 371, *372*
No Child Left Behind (NCLB), 485–486
No final end, 114
Nonconsumptive energy sources, 504
Noninvolvement, 475
Nonprofit organizations
    characteristics of, 305–308
    for conservation/preservation,
            338–339
    defined, 305–306, 307
    future challenges of, 339–340
    goals and functions of, 308–311
    introduction, 302–305
    job growth in, 305
    professional characteristics of, 319–320
    for relief, 336–337
    religious, 332–334
    resource base, 311–319
    service clubs, 339
    for special populations, 334–336
    types of, youth and voluntary, 321
    youth-serving, 321–332
Nonsectarian-sponsored organizations,
            322–330
Nordstrom, 409
No-relationship theory, 16
Northwest Special Recreation Association,
            223
Norwegian Cruise Lines, 358
Nostalgia, 25

O

Obesity
    in children, 180–184
    future decrease in, 498–499
O'Brien, Tim, 352
Occupation, diversity and, 461
Occupational Outlook Handbook, 233, 383
Officials, 420
Older adults
    diversity and, 451
    future increase in, 489, 497–498
    leisure and, 197–200
    program planning and, 411–412

Olmsted, Frederick Law, 90, 91, 92–93, 94,
            221, 487
Omnicom Group, 364
On-line with networks, 511
Opening Doors/Opening Minds (ODOM),
            162, 487
Open space, 239, 272
Optimal arousal theory, 61
Order, 405
Oregon Outdoor Conference, 267
Organizational philosophies, 133
Organizations, clarifying relationships
            within, 124
Other nonprofits, 321
Outdoor adventure pursuits, 159
Outdoor recreation, 416
Outdoor recreation and resources
    direct management of, 271
    state fish and wildlife agencies, 256–258
    state forests, 255–256
    state governments and, 249–251
    state parks, 251–254, *255*
    trail systems, 258–259
Outdoor Recreation Resources Review
            Commission (ORRRC), 108,
            245, 272, 481
Outdoors, simulated natural phenomena, 511
Outreach programs, 417
Outreach workers, 421
Overarching goals, 133
Overweight children, 180–184, 498–499
Owens, Pete, 352
Ownership society, 480–485

P

Parental status, diversity and, 461
Park and recreation boards, 218
Park and recreation departments, functions
            of, 218
Park and recreation laws, 216–217
Park development programs, 272
Park Ridge Senior Center, 412
Parks
    municipal, 90–93
    national, 93–94
    state, 94–98, 251–254, *255*
    state societies and associations, 435
Partnerships, 236–237, 318–319, 347
Perceived competence, 37–38
Perceived freedom, 37, 46, *47*
Perennialism, 128
Performance measurements, 399–400
Performing arts, 415
Personal competence, 191
Personal development, 25
Personal growth, 117
Personal responsibility, for quality, 400

Pets, leisure for, 150
Philosophical theories, *45,* 53–56
Philosophy (of leisure)
    attitude building, 113–116
    books and articles on, 132
    building, 125–126
    circumstances and, 113
    construction of, 130–131, 133
    defining, 113
    introduction, 112–113
    major philosophies, 126–130
    meaning of, in leisure service
            organizations, 133–134
    model for professional practice,
            135–137
    reasons for, 120–125
    values and, 116–118
Photography, 257
Physical capital, 152
Physical competence, 191
Physical disabilities. *See* Therapeutic
            recreation
Physical fitness/health
    future changes in, 498–499
    of youth, 180–185
Physical impairment, diversity and, 460
Physical resources, leisure and, 149
Physical well-being, 25
Pierce, Charles, 129
Pinchot, Gifford, 277, 280, 287
Pinel, Phillippe, *372*
Pizza Hut, 352
Planning, anticipatory, 399
Play
    childhood and, 178
    defining, 58–59
    movement of, 98–100
    theories of, 59–62
    work, love, worship, and, 114
Playground Association of America, 69, 104
Play It Again Sports, 359
Play Station Family Fun Center, 349
Pleasure Driveway and Park District Act, 91
Pleasure Driveway and Park District of
            Peoria, 225
Pleasures, 8, 126
Pluralism, 469–471. *See also* Diversity
Policies, diversity and, 466
Policy-making boards, 218
Political identity, leisure as, 44
Pomeroy, Janet, 334–335
Popcorn, Faith, 438
Population, future shifts in, 488–493
Pop Warner football, 184–185
Portfolios, professional, 445, 447
Positive affect, 38
Positive emotions, 9
Positive psychology, 8

San Diego Zoo, 263, 351
San Pedro Riparian Natural Conservation
    Area, 283
Satisfaction dimensions, 16
Scholarships, 316
School district, recreation services as part
    of, 226
Search Institute, 192–193
Sea Shepherd Conservation Society, 338
SeaWorld Orlando, 263, 351, 352, 357
Security, 24
Segregation, 475
Self-actualization, 114
Self-as-entertainment (S-A-E) theory, *45,* 48
Self-consciousness, loss of, 11, 48
Self-determination, 27, 38, 127, 379
Self-esteem, building, 474
Self-expression, 24
Self-improvement programs, 416
Self-mode, 48
Self-reliants, 174
Semi-independent boards, 218
Seminars, 417
Sensory pleasures, 126
Sensory stimulation/reduction, 21
Separatists, 81
September 11, 2001, 162, 260, 479, 487
Serious leisure, *45,* 46, 50–51
Servant leadership, 214–215, 403
Service(s)
    characteristics of, 402
    clubs, 339
    customer service, 408
    defining, 401–402
    ethic, 213–214, *278*
    to others, 24
    providing, 402–409
    value-added, 404–405
Seton, Ernest Thompson, 103
Settlement houses, 100–101
Sexual behavior, 156
Sexuality, diversity and, 459
Shriver, Eunice Kennedy, *372*
Sierra Club, 338, 438
Six Flags, 357
Skepticism, 125
Skills
    challenges and, 10, 47
    knowledge and, 21
Smith, Patti Grace, 399
Social activities, as mass leisure, 151–156
Social bonding, 25
Social capital, 152–154, 239
Social class, leisure as symbol of, 49
Social competence, 191
Social construction, leisure as, 44
Social health, future changes in, 499–500
Social instrument, leisure as, 41–42

Social leisure, 154–156
Social problems, therapeutic recreation and,
    389–391
Social psychological theories, 46–48
Social recreation, 416
Social roles, future changes in, 493–495
Social service organizations, 337–338
Social skills/interaction, promotion of,
    21–22
Societies, state park and recreation, 435
Society of Park and Recreation Educators
    (SPRE), 435–436
Sociological influences, of customers, 345
Sociological theories, *45,* 48–52
Sole proprietorship, 346
Solitude, 24
South Suburban Recreation Association, 123
Special districts, 222–226
Special events, 357, 417
Special-interest groups, 438
Special needs. *See* Therapeutic recreation
Special Olympics, 131
Special populations, 334–336
Special Recreation Management Areas
    (SMRAs), 283
Special recreation programs, 382
Specialty stores, 359
Spillover theory, 16, 44–46
Spiritual needs, 27
Sports
    as mass leisure, 156–157
    program planning and, 416
    programs for youths, 184–185
Sports Line, 359
Staff development, diversity and, 467–469
Standards, 274, 430
Starbucks, 364
Starr, Ellen Gates, 100, 103
Starwood Hotels & Resorts, 364
State and Private Forestry Northeastern
    Area, 278
State forests, 255–256
State government
    the arts, 261–263
    characteristics of state leisure
        services, 244
    coordination with federal and local
        governments, 245–246
    future challenges of, 266–267
    goals and functions of, 244–245
    introduction, 243
    other services, 263–266
    outdoor recreation and resources,
        249–259
    park and recreation societies and
        associations, 435
    resource base, 246–247
    tourism promotion, 259–261

    types of recreation resources and
        services provided by,
        247–248, *249*
State of mind, leisure as, 39–40
State of mind continuum, 46, *47*
State parks, 94–98, 251–254, *255*
State Preserve Act (Iowa), 266, 267
States rights amendment, 243
Statue of Liberty, 263, 351
Stimulation, 24, 25
Stoicism, 125
Structural constraints, 29
Strugglers, 173
Subjective variables, 12
Subway, 352
Summative evaluations, 417
Superordinate goals, 133
Supervisory roles, 232–233
Support staff, 320
Surgeon General, 183, 186
Surplus energy theory, 59
Surplus Property Act (1944), 253

T

Taco Bell, 352
Take Back Your Time, 146, *147*
Tangibility, 397
Taped performances, 357
Tax cuts, 480–485
Taxes, 246
Teaming, 400
Team leadership, 420
Technical assistance, 274
Technological era, 71–72, 105–109, 511
Technology
    future influences of, 508–511
    leisure and, 149–150
Telephone Pioneers of America, 229
Television viewing, as mass leisure,
    164–167
Tennessee Valley Authority (TVA), 271,
    277, 291–292
Tenth Amendment, 243
Texas Travel Information Center, 261
Theme parks, 109, 352, 357
Theory of Anti-Structure, *45,* 53
Therapeutic healing, 25
Therapeutic recreation
    assistive technology and, 389
    barriers to success, 377, *378*
    characteristics of, 375–377
    documenting outcomes, 388–389
    early reformers in, *372*
    emergence as profession, 370
    future challenges of, 387, *388*
    goals and functions of, 378–382
    introduction, 369